Memorial Book of the Molchad (Maytchet) Jewish Community

Translation of *Sefer zikaron le-kehilat Maytchet*

Edited by: Benzion H. Ayalon

Originally Published in Tel Aviv

By Meytshet Societies in Israel and Abroad, 1973

Published by JewishGen

**An Affiliate of the Museum of Jewish Heritage - A Living Memorial to the Holocaust
New York**

Memorial Book of the Molchad (Maytchet) Jewish Community
Translation of *Sefer zikaron le-kehilat Meytshet*

Copyright © 2015 by JewishGen, Inc.
All rights reserved.
First Printing: May 2015, Iyar 5775
Second Printing: August 2019, Av 5779

Translation Project Coordinator: Myrna Brodsky Siegel
Original Yizkor Book Editor: Benzion H. Ayalon
Layout: Alan Roth, Lynn Mercer
Cover Design: Nili Goldman
Indexing: Kathy Wallace

Published by JewishGen, Inc.
An Affiliate of the Museum of Jewish Heritage
A Living Memorial to the Holocaust
36 Battery Place, New York, NY 10280

The mission of the JewishGen organization is to produce a translation of the original work and we cannot verify the accuracy of statements or alter facts cited.

Printed in the United States of America by Lightning Source, Inc.

Library of Congress Control Number (LCCN): 2015936836
ISBN: 978-1-939561-31-2 (hard cover: 730 pages, alk. paper)

Cover photograph: Courtesy of Sergio Kowensky.

JewishGen and the Yizkor-Books-in-Print Project

This book has been published by the **Yizkor-Books-in-Print Project,** as part of the **Yizkor Book Project** of **JewishGen, Inc**.

JewishGen, Inc. is a non-profit organization founded in 1987 as a resource for Jewish genealogy. Its website [www.jewishgen.org] serves as an international clearinghouse and resource center to assist individuals who are researching the history of their Jewish families and the places where they lived. JewishGen provides databases, facilitates discussion groups, and coordinates projects relating to Jewish genealogy and the history of the Jewish people. In 2003, JewishGen became an affiliate of the **Museum of Jewish Heritage - A Living Memorial to the Holocaust** in New York.

The **JewishGen Yizkor Book Project** was organized to make more widely known the existence of Yizkor (Memorial) Books written by survivors and former residents of various Jewish communities throughout the world. Later, volunteers connected to the different destroyed communities began cooperating to have these books translated from the original language—usually Hebrew or Yiddish—into English, thus enabling a wider audience to have access to the valuable information contained within them. As each chapter of these books was translated, it was posted on the JewishGen website and made available to the general public.

The **Yizkor-Books-in-Print Project** began in 2011 as an initiative to print and publish Yizkor Books that had been fully translated, so that hard copies would be available for purchase by the descendants of these communities and also by scholars, universities, synagogues, libraries, and museums.

These Yizkor books have been produced almost entirely through the volunteer effort of researchers from around the world, assisted by donations from private individuals. The books are printed and sold at near cost, so as to make them as affordable as possible. Our goal is to make this important genre of Jewish literature and history available in English in book form, so that people can have the personal histories of their ancestral towns on their bookshelves for themselves and for their children and grandchildren.

A list of all published translated Yizkor Books in the project with prices and ordering information can be found at:
http://www.jewishgen.org/Yizkor/ybip.html

Lance Ackerfeld, Yizkor Book Project Manager

Joel Alpert, Yizkor-Book-in-Print Project Coordinator

JewishGen
Yizkor Book Project

This book is presented by the
Yizkor Books in Print Project
Project Coordinator: Joel Alpert

Part of the
Yizkor Books Project of JewishGen, Inc.
Project Manager: Lance Ackerfeld

These books have been produced solely through volunteer effort
of individuals from around the world. The books are printed and
sold at near cost, so as to make them as affordable as possible.

Our goal is to make this history and important genre of Jewish
literature available in English in book form so that people can have
the near-personal histories of their ancestral towns on their bookshelves for themselves and for their children and grandchildren.

Any donations to the Yizkor Books Project are appreciated.

Please send donations to:
Yizkor Book Project
JewishGen
36 Battery Place
New York, NY 10280

JewishGen, Inc. is an affiliate of the
Museum of Jewish Heritage
A Living Memorial to the Holocaust

Hebrew Title Page of Original Yizkor Book

ספר־זכרון

לקהילת

מ י ט ש ע ט

ערוך בידי

בן־ציון ח. אילון

Translation of the Hebrew Title Page of Original Yizkor Book

Memorial Book

To the Community

Maytchet

Edited by:

Benzion H. Ayalon

Cover of the Original Yizkor Book

מיינע שטעט

ספר זכרון

Foreword and Acknowledgements

for the Translation and Publication

The tragedy and horrors of the Shoah are beyond any measure, but something we cannot allow would be for the memories of the innocent Jews who perished - their names, the stories of their daily lives and the connections to the people they loved and the community they were a part of to vanish without any recorded trace.

A group of dedicated Maytchet survivors got together in 1973 to write memories of their beloved shtetl that is now void of Jews, and to honor family members who were hideously murdered by the Nazis and their local collaborators. Their hope was that through this Yizkor book the lives of the poor souls and the beloved shtetl they lived in would not be forgotten. We do not know where many of them were buried or where they were murdered so this Yizkor book is their only tangible commemoration.

To reach a broader audience, 15 years ago Jewishgen began the translation project of the Yizkor books from Hebrew/Yiddish to English. I volunteered to co-ordinate the translation of the Maytchet Yizkor book. In the years to come, each time someone with a bit of sensitivity comes to read the stories of the people who lived in Maytchet, perhaps there will be a small lessening of the overwhelming destruction and grief as their lives will be remembered. That is the least that we can do, as we know these dear people deserve to be honored, and their hopes and dreams of a better life will be remembered. And to some of us, like myself, we can be grateful to the shtetl and people of Maytchet that supported the start to the lives of our parents and grandparents who mean so much to us.

Throughout the past 30 years my life has been touched and enriched by the survivors and their family members that I have made contact with; some I met personally and others via e-mail and/or phone. I met Sarah Boretcky Biribis in Israel after discovering her story in the Yizkor book. On a trip to New York I met Martin Small who became my mentor. Other survivors I have been in contact with are: Rachmiel Bar, Channa Boretcky Mechtiger, Fanny Dunetz Brodsky and Mordechai Dunetz from the Bielski family, Mordechai and Tuvia Gorsky, Minna Gorsky Levin, Abrasha Hanelis, Littman Litow, Nachum Margolin, Tzira Rabets (Kaplan- Royak), Meir Novomiski, Nachum Rabinovitch, Charles and Morris Samuels.

Unfortunately during this period of time most of these survivors have passed away. I hope that now that the translation of the book is completed the victims of the Shoah and all subsequent survivors are looking down and "kvelling" – that through the translation of this book they and their beloved shtetl are being remembered now and for generations to come.

The translation of the book may not be perfect but I feel a great sense of pride with mission accomplished. There were multiple translators and the spelling of names and places may be inconsistent between various articles. The index itself in numerous cases was found to be incorrect and the transliteration did not fix such errors. Therefore, the index should not be considered complete. The Yizkor List of Holy Ones as well as names of victims in the Memorial Pages is incomplete. Since the book was printed in 1973 many victim's names have been found, and are listed on the Yad Vashem web site. Because this is an ongoing project I encourage you to go to: Yad Vashem and search the Database of Shoah Victims Names. If you know of someone who was murdered in the Shoah and is not listed, fill out a page of Testimony and register their name.

This project required the generous support of many people to make it a reality. I am grateful to all those who enabled me to do so.

The following people either translated stories, scanned photos or made a financial contribution to Jewishgen to hire the necessary translators. **Alyson Brodsky, Merwyn Brodsky, Sid Brodsky** *z"l*, **Ariel Dvorjetski, Tzivia Romanovsky Fishbane, Roz Greenberg, Merle Gross, Marcia Hirsch, Dina Litow Hirsh, Leon Litow, Nate Kolodny, Sharon Perlman Krefetz, Isaac Margolin, Elliott Miller, Esther Nayman Muller, Roni Rabinovitch, David Romanoff, Pedro Rubio** *z"l*, **Dov & Milton Schwartz, Sanford Sher, Madeline Shiffman, Amir Shomroni, Eric Siegel, Michael Siegel, Semadar Siegel, Shael Siegel, Martin Small** *z"l* **a/k/a Mordechai Leib Shmuelvitz, Roberta Strauchler and Chaya Turin.**

My appreciation also goes out to these dedicated volunteers and translators from JewishGen. A special thank you to Lance Ackerfeld, the manager of the JewishGen Yizkor Book Project who saw the project through from its early stages until its now completion. Joel Alpert, the coordinator of JewishGen Yizkor Books in Print Project, provided invaluable advice. Nili Goldman book cover design, Jerrold Landau, Sara Mages and Esther Mann Snyder translated various parts of the book. Jerrold also edited several parts of the book that were translated by others.

To everyone who wrote stories and sent in photos that make the appended pages so interesting and meaningful. Dena Hirsh and Leon Litow, Pedro Rubio *z"l*, **Leah Chanalas, Myrna and Shael Siegel, Tzivia Malka Fishbane, Sergio Kowensky and Joni, Bella Cantor, Julio and Jaime Epstein, Perla Ochman, Sheryl Prenzlau, Shlomo Polachek, Shoshana Ginzbursky, Alan Cohen, Ronnie Dunetz, Esther Mueller, Martin Dean of the U.S. Holocaust Museum. Russian translations by Rhada Eydelman and Regina Kushnir Brodsky. And a special thanks to my friend Marcia Hirsch for her photo expertise.**

I hope that you and your family treasure this book, which contains memories of our once vibrant ancestral shtetl Maytchet, and the beloved people who lived there.

Pedro Rubio made the initial and generous donation to start the Maytchet Yizkor book translation fund. Heroically battling cancer for 2 years he told me he hoped that he would live long enough to hold the completed book in his hands. Unfortunately that wish was not granted. It is ironic that he took his last breaths just moments after I sent a message approving the last edits. Pedro's efforts, joined with others, will live on in this Yizkor book.

Myrna Brodsky Siegel, Translation Project Coordinator

ESTONIA

RUSSIA

LATVIA

2012 Border
1940 Border

BELARUS

0 25 50   75   km
0   25   50   75 miles

LITHUANIA

RUSSIA

BELARUS

VILNIUS •

1940 Border

• MINSK

• MOLCHAD

POLAND

UKRAINE

Map of Molchad in Belarus

Geopolitical Information:

Molchad, Belarus is located at 53° 19' North Latitude, 25°42' East Longitude, 86 miles WSW of Minsk

Alternate names for the town are: Molchad [Rus], Maytshet [Yid], Mołczadź [Pol], Moŭčadź [Bel], Meytshet, Maytchet, Mitshat, Molchadz, Moltchad, Motsit, Motzid

Period	Town	District	Province	Country
Before WWI (c. 1900):	Molchad	Slonim	Grodno	Russian Empire
Between the wars (c. 1930):	Mołczadź	Baranowicze	Nowogródek	Poland
After WWII (c. 1950):	Molchad'			Soviet Union
Today (c. 2000):	Molchad'			Belarus

Nearby Jewish Communities:
Dvorets 8 miles NW
Novoyel'nya 11 miles NNW
Polonka 12 miles S
Haradzishcha 12 miles E
Novaya Mysh 15 miles SSE
Stolovichi 15 miles ESE
Dzyatlava 16 miles NW
Kozlovshchina 16 miles W
Baranavichy 19 miles SE
Tsirin 19 miles ENE
Navahrudak 20 miles NNE
Slonim 23 miles SW
Dolmatovshchina 23 miles ENE
Karelichy 25 miles NE
Negnevichi 28 miles NE
Belitsa 28 miles NW
Vselyub 28 miles N
Hałynka 28 miles WSW
Turets 29 miles ENE
Snov 30 miles ESE

Enhanced map from page 24 By Martin Small (Mordechai Shmulevicz)

Prepared for Myrna and Shael Siegel's Trip to Maytchet 2004

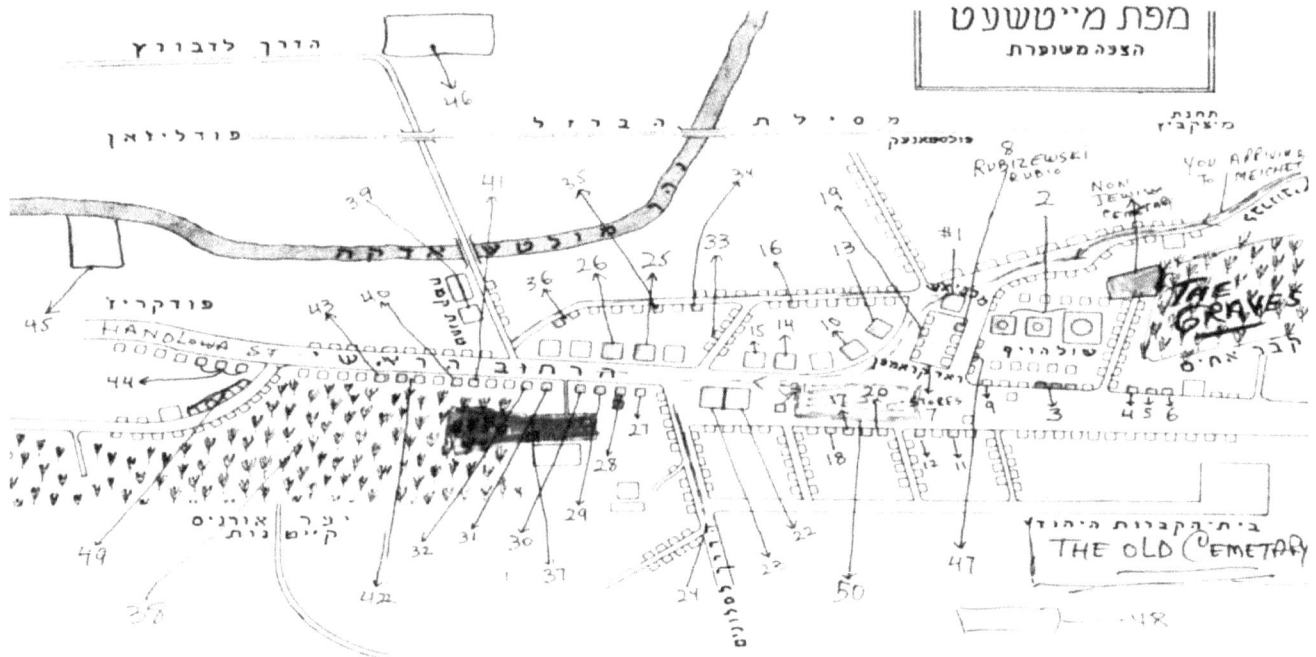

Legend

1. Fire Department - Head of Fire Dept. Martin's cousin Yossel Shmulewicz
2. Area of Three Synagogues (Shulhof) –
    2a. Bet Midrash,
    2b. Shteibl
    2c. Main Synagogue named "Kalte Schul" Large brick bldg., high ceiling painted biblical scenes, men's section 15-20 steps down and women sat in balcony, no heat and was used for holidays, Shtiebel for Chassidim and Beit Midrash smaller synagogue
3. Rabbi's House and Cantor's House
4. Novomiski Liquor business (Martin's Uncle)
5. Gilerowicz House
6. Korn's House
7. Line of Stores
8. Alter Rubiezewski (Rubio) House on top of Stores facing Bet Midrash
9. Lakhovitzki Pharmacy
10. House of Martin's Grandparents Abraham and Shifra Schmulewicz
11. Apteka---The Dvorjetski's Pharmacy
12. Chaim Meir Gorski's Shoe Store – they lived on street behind the store
13. House of Beryl Schmulewicz, the Mohel, brother of Martin's grandfather
14. Hardware Store of Michel Schmulewicz, Martin's Uncle
15. Rabinovitch Dry Goods Store (Uncle of Nachum Rabinovitch)
16. Israel Rabinovitch House (Nachum's father)

17. House of Vikna Belski
18. Bakery (Sora Henie was sales lady)
19. Freidl Margolin's store/cafe
20. Romanovski's House
21. The Water Pump
22. Volinski's Soda Factory and Store
23. Belitski Dry Good Store
24. Road to Slonim
25. Elke and Koppel Gorski's General Store on Street to Slonim and 2 doors from Church.
26. The White Church "Prowaslaw" (Greek Orthodox) Street behind was Catholic Church.
27. Martin's Uncle Michel Schmulewicz House Rented house and storage rented to Rabinovitch for storage of
        wheat and grains he sold in market
28. Martin's House parents Schlomo and Esther Schmulewicz, children Mordechai Leib (Martin Small),
        Pesha and Elka – behind house was Uncle Zimel's House – wife was Chaika Bilitski Address was 17
        Handlova
29. Uncle Michel Schmulewicz family residence wife Leah and sons Chonia & Moishe. Behind the house was
        a stable for cows.
30. Gilerowicz House
31. House of Priest from "Pravosiaw" White Church
32. Jewish Doctor's house, Dr. Shapiro---next to this was a small gentile cemetery
33. Chaim Meir Gorski the Shoe Maker's House; children Sachne, Yankel and Minya
34. Ozeransky (or possibly Orzechovsky House – son Bome lives in Russia and was in the Russian army
35. Gentile Doctor Feisher's house
36. Catholic Church and Living Quarters
37. Gentile Cemetery
38. The Health Forest (mostly Pine trees)
39. Water Mill
40. Mina Gorsky's House---the carpenter
41. Viloikhinski the shoemaker
42. Liberman's house and business – Wealthy man; had a telephone
43. House of Yosel Bielous (Brother of Martin's mother)
44. Houses of Moshe Aaron Boretcky and houses of sons and their families Shmuel, Noach and Ben Zion
        Boretcky
45. Moshe Aaron Boretcky's Flour Mill
46. Uncle Mikal Schmulewicz SMOLARNIA business (would bring roots from trees and burn for weeks to
        make tar to be used on roofs
47. Novomiski houses (on far right)
48. All Jewish houses
49. Martin's cousin Yudel Schmulewicz motel for guests who came for the summer to the health forest.
        Would tie hammocks between trees to use as beds
50. Weekly Market held on Wednesdays on right of map
Not numbered on map:
        Police Station across the street from Yudel Schmulewicz's motel
        Train Station built 1938 near the mass grave. The station used before that was in Mickiewicz 4 km.
        from Maytchet on the way to Baranovichi
        Slonimskaya Street was way to Slonim, Yurzdyka St.
        On road to Dvorets was another flour mill

Notes to the Reader:

Within the text the reader will note "{34}" standing ahead of a paragraph. This indicates that the material translated below was on page 34 of the original book. However, when a paragraph was split between two pages in the original book, the marker is placed in this book after the end of the paragraph for ease of reading.

Also please note that all references within the text of the book to page numbers refer to the page numbers of the original Yizkor Book.

This is a translation from: *Sefer zikaron le-kehilat Meytshet* (Molchadz (Maytchet), In Memory of the Jewish Community), editor: Benzion H. Ayalon. Tel Aviv, Meytshet Societies in Israel and Abroad, 1973

Note: The original book can be seen online at the NY Public Library site:

http://yizkor.nypl.org/index.php?id=1184

A Brief History of Molchad

The United States Holocaust Memorial Museum Encyclopedia of Camps and Ghettos 1933-1945, vol. 2 Ghettos in German-Occupied Eastern Europe, vol. ed. Martin Dean, series ed., Geoffrey Megargee (Bloomington: Indiana University Press in association with the United States Holocaust Memorial Museum, 2012), pp. 1241-1243.

Molczadz

Pre-1939: Molczadz (Yiddish: Meytshet), town, Nowogródek województwo, Poland; 1939-41: Molchad', Baranovichi oblast', Belorussian SSR; 1941-44: Molczadz, Rayon Goroditsche (Horodyszcze), Gebiet Baranowitsche, Generalkommissariat Weissruthenien; 1944: Molchad', Baranovichi oblast', Belorussian SSR; 1954: Baranovichi raion, Brest oblast'; 1991: Republic of Belarus.

Molczadz is located 139 kilometers (87 miles) southwest of Minsk. Jewish settlement here dates back at least to the sixteenth century. The first synagogue was built in 1648. In the mid-eighteenth century, the town's owners invited Jews to open two flour mills; others were then invited to open shops, a tavern, and workshops. In 1765, the Jewish population was 369. The town also attracted several Hasidic leaders and their followers. After the Third Partition of Poland in 1795, Mołczadż came under Russian rule. In the nineteenth century, Jews also worked as fur merchants, horse traders, shopkeepers, peddlers, and artisans. In 1897, the Jewish population was 1,188, out of a total population of 1,733 (68.5 percent). At this time Molczadz developed as a popular resort, and Jews provided services for vacationers. In World War I, the German army occupied the town between 1915 and 1918. There were severe shortages of food, but the Jews enjoyed some increased freedom in their personal and communal affairs

After World War I, the Jews of Molczadz received financial support from the American Jewish Joint Distribution Committee (AJDC) and other organizations. Subsequently a Jewish cooperative bank and a mutual aid society were established to assist small merchants and craftsmen. In 1922, the synagogue was refurbished and there were six Bet Midrash study centers. In the 1920s, most of the streets in Mołczadż were unpaved and unlit and most houses were built of wood. In the interwar years, the Jews were negatively impacted by Polish economic policies. Heavy taxes and unemployment led to increases in the numbers receiving communal assistance and in emigration. The Zionists ran a summer training camp for young Jews preparing to make Aliyah.

On September 17, 1939, the Red Army entered Molczadz and imposed a Soviet regime. The town was flooded with Jewish refugees from Nazi-occupied western Poland, some of whom subsequently fled to Wilno [Vilna, Vilnius], in the hopes of escaping to Palestine and the West. The Soviets closed down or nationalized most private businesses. Several Jewish owners were arrested and exiled to punishment camps in the interior of the USSR. Craftsmen were organized into an artisanal cooperative. The two Hebrew-language schools were closed and replaced by a Yiddish-language school with a Soviet curriculum. After the German invasion on June 22, 1941, Soviet forces withdrew and some Jews fled with them into the Soviet Union. The Germans captured Molczadz on June 29. On that day, they caught several Jewish youths that didn't make it across the former Polish-Soviet border. The Germans murdered them on the road to Slonim. Some sources indicate that soon after the occupation, Jews living with non-Jews were forced to move to separate houses together only with Jews (perhaps creating a de facto open ghetto). However, most surviving Jews recall that no formal ghetto was established in Molczadz.

Among other anti-Jewish restrictions imposed by the new German authorities, Jews were ordered to wear yellow patches, they were prohibited from having contacts with non-Jews, they were forbidden to use the sidewalks, and they were forced to surrender their horses.

The Germans set up a local auxiliary police under the command of a rabid anti-Semite. They ordered the Jews to select a five-man Judenrat headed by Ehrlich, a refugee from Czestochowa. They compelled the Judenrat to collect and pay special taxes. The Germans demanded money, gold, and jewelry, and subsequently clothing, shoes, furniture, and other items. Whenever a fine was levied, the Germans threatened to kill some Jews, if their demand was not met promptly. The Judenrat members did everything they could to meet these demands. The Judenrat also had to supply people for forced labor. Every day groups of men and women were sent on work assignments around the town, guarded by local overseers. On their way to and from work the guards beat and humiliated the laborers. Groups of Jews were sent to various labor camps. From one group of more than 20 people sent to the camp in Koldyczewo, several Jews managed to escape to join the partisans in the Naliboki Forest. [i]

On February 14, 1942, members of the local police, on their own initiative removed 20 Jewish men and women from their houses. They took them to a tar pit outside of town and murdered them. The Jews protested this Aktion to the German authorities in Baranowicze, which resulted in a death sentence being passed on the local police chief. However, his colleagues helped him to escape into the surrounding forests.

In January 1942, several members of prewar Jewish youth groups made contact with Soviet partisans operating in the area and also fled into the forests. In March they and their families then slipped into the Horodyszcze ghetto. In April 1942, several youths from Molczadz working at a farm in Dobrowszczyzna rose up and killed the anti-Semitic farm manager and his helpers. In early summer, a group of younger Jews, some of whom had experience in the Polish Army, formed an underground resistance group. They even approached the Judenrat to try to get some money to buy arms. From various sources, they obtained three rifles and several revolvers and began to train. There was also spiritual resistance in Molczadz, guided by the Stolowicze rabbi. Jews met in secret to teach the children and pray for deliverance.[ii]

As news spread about the liquidation of other ghettos, many in Mołczadż hoped that they would not share the same fate. In late May or early June 1942, the police ordered the Judenrat to mobilize 200 Jews to dig pits, allegedly for fuel storage tanks, in Burdykowszczyzna, next to the Russian Orthodox cemetery of Horodyszcze. On June 3, 1942, after they finished digging, the Germans shot the 200 Jews at the pits. Around this time, sensing an impending Aktion, the Jews of Molczadz began to dig bunkers and seek hiding places. Young members of the underground set up a guard to warn of the approach of hostile forces.[iii]

Before dawn on July 15, 1942, truckloads of German Gendarmes and local police from various posts in Gebiet Baranowitsche surrounded the town. At daybreak the Jews were ordered to assemble in the market square. Local police then combed the houses for stragglers. When the Stolowicze rabbi emerged in his prayer shawl, he was shot to death. The Jewish underground group sought to disrupt the encirclement by firing their weapons, hoping to create enough confusion for a mass escape. The Germans opened fire with machine guns and killed 20 Jewish fighters. Only nine made it to the forest. Another 60 Jews fled into the Horky Forest where, under the protection of partisans, they set up a family camp.

About 3,300 people assembled in the market square. They were lined up facing the wall, hands up, and searched for valuables. Then the Germans and local police took them in groups of 100 to the pits outside of Mołczadż. After ordering the victims to line up next to the pits and undress, they shot them. Over several days, from July 15-18, approximately 3,300 Jews were murdered. The operation was probably organized by the Security Police outpost in Baranowicze, assisted by German Gendarmes and police auxiliaries from the Baltic States as well as Belorussia, including some local police from Rayon Neswish (Nieswiez).[iv]

A number of Jewish specialist workers and their families were initially spared during the Aktion and put into a remnant ghetto. In August 1942, the Germans urged everyone still hiding in the forest or elsewhere to come back to Molczadz, guaranteeing their safety in the "new ghetto for the workers." About 200 people were gathered in Mołczadż altogether. After twenty days, on the pretext that they were heading for a new work site to dig peat they were taken to the pits and murdered.[v]

Young men in the forest joined various Soviet partisan brigades. Jewish partisans from Mołczadż settled accounts with several collaborators from their town and participated in other acts of sabotage along the railway lines. Some were caught, turned in by informants, or killed in action. A few sought refuge in the nearby Dworzec ghetto/forced labor camp. A number of Jews from Molczadz survived until the return of the Red Army in summer 1944. They included partisan fighters, people still in hiding, and refugees who had escaped into the Soviet Union in summer 1941.[vi]

Sources:

Information about the Jewish community of Mołczadż can be found in the following publications: "Molczadz," in Shmuel Spector and Bracha Freundlich, eds., *Pinkas Hakehillot. Encyclopaedia of Jewish Communities: Poland, Vol. 8 Vilna, Bialystok, Nowogrodek* (Jerusalem: Yad Vashem, 2005), pp. 404-408; Benzion H. Ayalon, ed., *Sefer-zikaron le-kehilat Meytshet* (Tel Aviv: Meytscher Societies in Israel and Abroad, 1973); and Leonid Smilovitskii, *Katastrofa evreev v Belorussii 1941-1944 gg.* (Tel Aviv: Biblioteka Matveia Chernogo, 2000), p. 187.

Documents regarding the destruction of the Jews of Molczadz can be found in the following archives: AUKGBRBMO (Arch. No. 3617, Case No. 35694); GARF (7021-81-102); NARB (845-1-6, p. 31); and YVA.

Samuel Fishman and Martin Dean

[1] "Molczadz," in Shmuel Spector and Bracha Freundlich, eds., *Pinkas Hakehillot. Encyclopaedia of Jewish Communities: Poland, Vol. 8 Vilna, Bialystok, Nowogrodek* (Jerusalem: Yad Vashem, 2005), pp. 404-405.

[1] Ibid., pp. 405-406.

[1] Ibid., p. 406; Benzion H. Ayalon, ed., *Sefer-zikaron le-kehilat Meytshet* (Tel Aviv: Meytscher Societies in Israel and Abroad, 1973), e.g., p. 304, "there was no ghetto in Molczadz." See also the comments of survivors posted (as of April 8, 2009) at http://www.jewishgen.org/Yizkor/belarus/bel178.html. Martin Gilbert, *The Holocaust: The Jewish Tragedy* (London: William Collins, 1986), p. 380 and *Rossiiskaia Evreiskaia Entsiklopediia* (Moscow: Russian Academy of Natural Sciences, Jewish Encyclopedia Research Center, "Epos," 2004), vol. 5, p. 442, however, both refer specifically to a ghetto in Mołczadż.

[1] *Pinkas Hakehillot: Poland, Vol. 8 Vilna, Bialystok, Nowogrodek*, pp. 406-407.

[1] Ibid., p. 407; and Shalom Cholawsky, *The Jews of Bielorussia during World War II* (Amsterdam: Harwood, 1998), p. 127.

[1] *Pinkas Hakehillot: Poland, Vol. 8 Vilna, Bialystok, Nowogrodek*, p. 407.

[1] Ibid., p. 407; and NARB, 845-1-6, p. 31. On the participation of police from Nieświeź

(now Nesvizh), see AUKGBRBMO, Arch. No. 3617, Case No. 35694, against Petr Sergeevich

Korolev, born 1915, 2 vols. On the nationalities of the perpetrators, see also

http://www.jewishgen.org/Yizkor/belarus/bel178.html.

[1] *Pinkas Hakehillot: Poland, Vol. 8 Vilna, Bialystok, Nowogrodek*, p. 407. According to
Marat Botvinnik, *Pamyatniki Genotsida Evreev Belarusi* (Minsk: Belaruskaia Navuka,
2000), p. 100, the 200 Jewish specialist workers and their families had been assigned to
dig peat and were moved into an enclosed ghetto

THE BRUTALITY OF THE BYELORUSSIANS

John Loftus in his book "Secret War Against The Jews", Chapter 21, "The Victors and the Victims", writes of the brutality of the Byelorussians against the local Jewish population of Maytchet and Baranovichi. If you can handle the descriptive brutality you will understand the extent of these heinous crimes against the unsuspecting local Jewish population.

THE FOLLOWING INFORMATION IS COURTESY OF DR. MARTIN DEAN, U.S. HOLOCAUST MUSEUM

Regarding the trial of war criminals in connection to Molchad, I have the following information about War Crimes trials in Poland:

Wladyslaw Filipowicz born October 8, 1920 and who served in the Belorussian Police in Molchad was sentenced to 5 years six months by a Polisjh court on February 27, 1974 for participation in "killing." He was released on June 7, 1974. The court case is held by the Polish Institute of National Remembrance (IPN), ref. SWZG sygn. 41-52.

At the same trial Jan Woroniec born October 2, 1922, was sentenced to 7 years on February 27, 1974, for taking part in killings of the Jewish population as an official of the Belorussian Police in Molchad. He was released conditionally on June 24, 1975. Both these men were of "Polish nationality" although they served in the Belorussian local police under the Nazis.

The entry in the USHMM *Encyclopedia of Camps and Ghettos* Vol. 2, pp. 1243-1244 (electronic version attached) mentions also a case from the Belorussian KGB archives, but this concerns the involvement of local policemen from Nieswisz in the murder of the Jews in Molczadz. There were almost certainly other trials of local Belorussiaan policemen from Molchad in Belorussia, but it is difficult to uncover these, unless they are also mentioned in the Polish trial record. The issue of whether there was actually a ghetto in Molczadz is debatable, as a formal ghettoization process did not take place there, although some Jews were forced to move in with other Jews.

The events in Molcahd are also mentioned in passing in German postwar investigations, for example into Gendarmerie chief Max Eibner in Baranowicze, conducted in Oldenburg, but a specific trial on the events in Molczadz did not take place.

———————————————

Family Notes

Table of Contents

CHAPTER ONE / OPENING

CHAPTER TWO / EARLY PERIOD

CHAPTER THREE / TORAH AND CHASSIDISM

CHAPTER FOUR / EDUCATION, SOCIETY, ECONOMICS

CHAPTER FIVE / PERSONALITIES, FAMILIES, FIGURES

Moshe Savitsky; Yisrael Belski; Yaakov Gilerovits; Naftali the Blacksmith;   Chana Shlomovitz

CHAPTER SIX / THE HOLOCAUST

Appendix - Not in Original Yizkor Book

Cover page from the Original Yizkor Book

Book of Memory

To the Community

Maytchet

Edited by

Ben Zion Haim Ayalon

The Synagogue Courtyard

**Published by the Organization of Maytchet Natives
in Israel and the Diaspora, Tel Aviv 5733 - 1973**

©

Printed in Israel – 5733 – 1973
Published by Mofet, Y. Reisman, Ein Hakoreh 6, Tel Aviv.
Telephone 32968
Zincography – Gershon Caspi, Tel Aviv

Preface

During the Great Holocaust in the tragic years 1941-3, in which the beastly Nazis annihilated 6 million Jewish martyrs, also the Jews of Maytchet met their bitter end, on the first to third days of Av 5702 (1942).

The first day of Av was proclaimed to be the annual "Yahrzeit" of our dear martyrs, when the few survivors together with earlier pioneers gather in Israel to honor the memory of our dear ones.

After a long period of preparation and organizational work, we are publishing this Yizkor Book to honour the memory of the Jewish community of Maytchet and environs and their dear martyrs. We did our best to collect all possible material in notes and pictures, in order to bring light in these holy pages on the Jewish life which flowed in our town for many generations. It is our aim that this Yizkor Book shall serve as a worthy memorial candle for the blessed souls of the dear Jews, people of Torah and Tradition, Zionist and public leaders, social fighters and many plain people, righteous and merciful.

It is a great privilege to use this book for writing down for the coming generations the names and deeds of our dear ones. In their honor we compiled material about geography, history, society and culture, family notes and lists of our martyrs. We hope Zionists and public leaders, social fighters and many plain people, that the coming generations will read these pages and learn about their forefathers, the martyrs who were tortured and died for being Jews, and who in their death granted us our lives.

On this occasion we express our sincere thanks to all those who assisted us in our holy task, and especially to the editor, Mr. Ben-Zion H. Ayalon, who had edited many memorial books before, and who gave his utmost dedication to prepare and publish this worthy book.

Tel-Aviv,   February

BOOK COMMITTEE

Chapter 1
Opening

Introduction

On the first day of the month of Av 5702 the beastly Nazis brought about the annihilation of the Jewish community of Maytchet and environment. This was the end of our dear ones, part of the Jewish population in Eastern Europe, who died as martyrs in the years 1941-2 during World War II. On the 30th "Yahrzeit", we humbly publish this Yizkor Book in memory of their blessed names.

It is a great responsibility to write such a book, since the authors have not put down their memories with regular calmness. Every sentence and every line in this book are bleeding with pain, whether written by old time pioneers or by recent survivors of the Holocaust. All the memories and writings were lovingly compiled, checked and edited, with the purpose of telling to our generation and the coming ones, to our children and grandchildren about the glory of the Jews of Maytchet and environment, who died as martyrs.

[Page 16]

The publication of this book was full of difficulties. Following the decision to publish a Yizkor Book, the book committee called upon all "landsleit" over the world to send in memories and pictures about the town. Some responded immediately, but most of the material was sent in during the very last time, when it was rewritten, and rechecked, while comparing notes with references in libraries and archives.

Blessed be all who contributed material and means. Special mention is due to the members of the book committee, who initiated the project and worked with dedication in the name of all Maytchet landsleit. There are not enough words in the human language to express the mourning over the Holocaust.

May all landsleit of Maytchet, from now and forever add on this first day of Av warm tears to the cup of tears which will never fill up.

Tel-Aviv, 1st day of Av

The Editor

[Page 17]

Foreword from the Book Committee

Six million Jews were killed by German murderers and their collaborators during the great Holocaust that befell the Jews of Europe in the years 1941-1945. Maytchet was annihilated in a tragic and cruel way, which we memorialize on July 15, 1942

This happened on the 1st to 3rd day of the month of Av in the year 5702 (1942). The terrible tragedy that stormed our little town was uncovered and every year this very bitter day of 1st of Av is the Memorial Day for the martyrs of Maytchet and the surrounding areas. The few remnants from the sword gathered together with their brothers and sisters who had previously come to Israel in order to memorialize and connect with the souls of our dear ones and to determine how to memorialize forever their memory and to make a permanent memorial. They decided to write this Memorial Book, which is the custom in Israel.

After a long period of preparation and organizational work, we published this book to memorialize the community of Maytchet, its vicinity, and the precious martyrs who lived there. We have tried our best to gather all possible material, memories, and pictures in order to bring to life in these pages the quality of the Jewish life and the different personalities who lived over the period of many generations in the community of Maytchet. This memorial book's purpose should be a fitting living memorial for the Jews, who were a people of tradition and Torah. They were Zionists and community activists, socialistic fighters, upstanding and righteous, and compassionate people who did many good deeds.

It was a very big responsibility to fulfill for our community, a charitable act to memorialize them through these pages in our hearts and the hearts of our children throughout the generations. For their sake and the sake of the perpetuity of Israel, it was our responsibility to recount the geographical, historical, communal, and cultural aspects of Maytchet; and also to list the family names and the names of the martyrs in order that the future generations shall dwell in the pages of this memorial book. We did this so that they may be able to envision the characters of their upstanding and righteous forefathers. The strong ones who died were holy martyrs and by their deaths they commanded us to live.

We express our thanks and appreciation to those who helped us with this holy work and particular to the editor, Alyon, who has published many of these memorial books. He spared no effort in order to publish this book and to be sure it was a fitting memorial.

1st day of Av 1972, the 30th Memorial Day of the martyrs of Maytchet and its surrounding area.

A Memorial book

Ever since we began to gather on the memorial day for our martyrs, we have been planning and hoping to see the day when we shall publish our Yizkor Book. This book which we have now before us is a product of a long and difficult operation.

On the eve of Rosh Hodesh Av 5742, we unveiled the little memorial plaque in the Cellar of the Holocaust in Jerusalem, and now this book is the second memorial project to remind us and our descendants of our birth town.

If not for this book everything would have been forgotten about life in Maytchet in earlier generations, all the suffering in our generation and all the struggle of the Jewish community until its annihilation.

Who but we can write it down for the coming generations. In reading this book we think about the home, the family, the town, the suffering and the tragic end. Blessed be the Landsleit Committee and the Book Committee who were active in publishing this book.

The Hebrew alphabet has been instrumental for many generations to preserve the events and memories of many communities, and we pray that it will also help preserve the memory of our perished little Maytchet.

On this occasion we extend thanks to all our active landsleit and especially to Mrs. Hana nee Borecki, for her important contribution of paper for the book.

Special appreciation is due to the writer and editor, Mr. Ben-Zion H. Ayalon, who although not born in our town, by compiling, reading, hearing and fixing the material, managed to feel with us the glory of Maytchet. With great symphaty and patience he helped the survivors to put down in writing all their sufferings in order to hand it down to the coming generations.

Please, dear G-d, that this book may unite all remnants of our town to remember our dear martyrs who perished on the Chvoinik Hill, on the road to the village Zahorna.

May this book find its worthy place in every home of our landsleit, so that it can serve as a family tree to all our descendants.

Nahum Margolin

People who worked on book:
Seated left to right: **Haya Lupchik, Hanna Mechtiger, Tova Shomroni, Esther Lozovsky**
Standing right to left: **Joseph Lozovsky, editor Benzion H. Ayalon, Nahum Margolin, and Moshe Korn**

[Page 19]

Foreward[1]
Translated by Jerrold Landau

In the bloody time of the greatest catastrophe in history, which took place to European Jewry during the years 5701-5703 (1941-1943), when six million dear Jewish souls were tortured and cruelly murdered with various kinds of deaths by the impure hands of the German murderers and their assistants, who looked upon Jewish blood and property like bloodthirsty beasts - the holy community of Maytchet was martyred in sanctification of the divine name on the bitter days of

> # First to the third of Menachem Av, 5702 - 1942

Since this was the gloomy climax of the terrible tragedy that swept through our town like a terrible storm, the survivors of Maytchet in Israel designated and sanctified the pious custom that on the sad day of Rosh Chodesh Av, which marks the *yahrzeit* of the dear martyrs of Maytchet and its region, the orphaned Maytchet Jews who were rescued in that time and made *aliya* to Israel, would gather together to connect with the pure souls of our dear ones. Year in and year out, at this gathering, they conferred about how to perpetuate their holy memory and make an appropriate "rectification" for their pure souls and their innocently spilled blood by publishing a Yizkor Book, as was done by all the Landsmanschaften in Israel.

[Page 20]

From that time, we did not rest with our intentions, and after a long time of preparation and organizational work, we finally succeeded in publishing the Yizkor Book to perpetuate the unfortunate, famous, historical Jewish community of Maytchet and the region, and its precious martyrs. We did all that we could to collect whatever material and pictures that were possible, so that we could bring to life in these holy pages the Jewish way of life of our ancestors who flowed for generations in the magnificent Jewish community of Maytchet. Our objective, and the strong desire of all the surviving Maytchet Jews throughout the entire world, is that this Yizkor Book should serve as a literary memorial candle for the dear Jews, people of Torah and tradition, Zionists and cultural activists, social strugglers and honest, common folk.

It is truly a great merit for us to fulfill a true charitable deed[2] toward our martyrs by perpetuating them in the Yizkor Book as well as in our hearts and the hearts of our descendents for generations. In their memory, we dedicate numerous chapters on geography, history, societal and cultural life, family memories, and a list of names of martyrs, so that the coming generations will be able to peruse and read the holy memorial pages with fascination and with holy trembling. In the eyes of their spirit, they will be able to see the bright personalities of their forbears, the pious, honest and heroic Jews who were tortured in sanctification of the Divine Name so that we would be able to survive and preside over the golden Jewish essence. We and the entire Jewish people will forever remain indebted to them. For them, the Yizkor Book is only a small repayment of a great, holy debt.

I also take the opportunity to express our sincere gratitude and appreciation to all those who have assisted us in our holy work, and especially the editor Mr. Ben-Zion Ch. Ayalon, who spared no effort to publish a superb book as is fitting and appropriate for such a literary monument

The Book Committee

Translator's footnote

1. This is equivalent with the Hebrew Foreword on page 17. Furthermore, the Hebrew section on page 18 is largely equivalent with the Yiddish section on page 21. The differences in the translation reflect the difference in style of the translators. The Hebrew translator opted to simplify the text so that it would flow better in English, without losing any critical meaning. The Yiddish translator opted to preserve the original style to the extent possible, along with the disjointed thoughts and run-on sentences, so as to preserve the emotional impact of the original. Both styles are legitimate, and the reader will benefit from reading both versions of the introductory material.

2. The term "*chesed shel emet*" (true benevolent deed) generally refers to a kind deed performed on behalf of the deceased, where there can be no expectation of reward.

[Page 21]

It Was Said With The Book[1]
by Nahum Margolin
Translated by Jerrold Landau

And I will give them in my home and within my walls a monument and a name[2]

An eternal name I will give him that will never be cut off.

(Isaiah 56, 5)

That which gave us no rest and is always bothered us - the setting up of a memorial and a name for our dear town - has now come to fruition. It has moved out of realm of hope and aspiration, and has been published as this monument in memory of our holy community, the community of Maytchet.

Every year on the memorial day to the destruction of our town that takes place on Rosh Chodesh Av, the issue of the book spurred plans, debates and hopes that the day would come when it would come to fruition. Behold, we are witnesses and our eyes see it. The dream has been realized.

This book that lies before us was not set before us on a silver platter. Many troubles and thoughts preceded its publication, for we were devoid of any experience, and did not know how to actualize our aspirations.

At a gathering of the natives of our town and its region in Israel on the eve of the Rosh Chodesh Av 5724 (July 9, 1964), the veil was removed from a the small marble plaque in the Holocaust Cellar on Mount Zion in the capital of Jerusalem, upon which are etched the words "In memory of the martyrs of Maytchet and it's area." This would have been the sole monument that in the future would remind us, our children and descendents about the rock that forged us, the root that nurtured us, the precious glory of our families and the frightfulness of our tragedy -- had the book that lies before us not been written.

The entire bundle of life in Maytchet throughout the previous generations, the entire episode of the atrocities and suffering that took place in our generation and that is folded in with the destruction of the community of Maytchet, the town in which we were born, in whose bosom we grew up, and from which we exited to redemption, and to our good fortune were saved and made *aliya* to the eternal Land of our fathers, the entire history of the struggles of this holy community of pure, upright Jews, the small community paved with the love of one's fellow Jew, thirsting for knowledge, filled with uprightness and the fear of Heaven, the community that did not lose its humanity and image even during the terrible tribulations of the Holocaust, the entire episode of these supreme struggles - would have been forgotten and buried along with those dearest to us in the pits of the "Chwojnik" that absorbed their pure blood - had this book that lies before us not been written.

For who would tell about the purity of the lives of our dear ones - if not for us who were designated for life?!

[Page 22]

For who would tell about the magnitude of their suffering, their desire for life and glory of their deaths - if not for us, the redeemed survivors in Israel?!

They are not forgotten from our hearts even in their deaths, for when we read what is written in this book, we unite with the home, the family, the town, their suffering, and their death agonies. This is a form of a great, powerful eulogy that had never been said over their graves - for there are no graves.

Would it be possible that the chapters of life of our family members would be erased from our memories and the memories of our descendents, just as they were erased from the consciousness of their murderers without shame and embarrassment?!

Would it be possible that the pure and holy actions of the martyrs, shining like the bright firmament, would never come to the consideration of the world?!

Therefore, the members of the organizing committee and the book committee who toiled to publish this book shall now receive the blessings.

For generation after generation, the Hebrew letter served the purposes of perpetuation and memorial. Whether it is engraved upon a gravestone or plaque in memory of the deceased holy martyrs, or whether it is printed upon parchment and books, these letters will be protected and will remain for many generations, just as they protected all of the spiritual property that was bequeathed to us by our forefathers in days of yore. Therefore, we primarily chose these letters for the publication of this Yizkor Book, so that it will serve as an eternal flame and monument to our town, its people, and it's past filled with awesome glory and suffering.

We hereby express heartfelt gratitude to all of the natives of our town living in Israel and the Diaspora who worked for and assisted in the publication of the book.

It is my pleasure to hereby thank the native of our city, Chana Mechtiger of the Boretcky family, for her generous donation toward the publishing of the book, which provided for the paper and etchings for the publication.

Special thanks are due to the author and editor Mr. Ben Zion Ayalon. Even though he is not a native of our town, through collecting, reading, listening, formulating, and arranging the pages of this book, he transported himself, his spirit and his soul to Maytchet, immersing his entire heart and soul in the depths of life, suffering and struggles of our dear ones there. He spared no effort, spoke to people, wrote down their stories and suffering, participated in the pain of the survivors who were forced to open wounds that seemed to have healed already, and toiled tirelessly to obtain the sources and find whatever material that was possible. He succeeded in publishing this complete book that lies before us.

[Page 23]

It is not only words of blessing and thanks that I have, but also stirrings of prayer in my heart. Let it be G-d's will that this book serve as the means of unifying all the survivors of our town who are scattered in all corners of the world into a mutual bond of brotherhood and friendship. Let these pages of memorial filled with the blood of the hearts of the writers serve as a permanent monument atop the desolate grave in the Chwojnik Valley along the way to the village of Cyrn (Tzirin) where the remains of our beloved ones, pleasant in their life and not separated in their death[3], are buried. Let the publication of this book be a fulfillment of the vow, "Remember, and do not forget that which the Amalek of our day, era and generation perpetrated."

It is fitting that this book be found in the home of every one of our townsfolk, for the town and the souls of its Jews are hidden preserved within it. Similarly, it should also serve as a book of genealogy for all future generations, and it shall be one chapter in the history of the eternal People of Israel.

Nachum Margolin

Members of the Organization Committee

**Standing from the right: Yosef Lozovski, Nachum Margolin, Moshe Korn, Moshe Ravitz
Sitting from the right: Miriam (nee Volinski) Kleinshtov, Sarah (nee Novomiski) Ahronovski**

Translator's footnotes
1. Esther 9:25 The literal Biblical reference means "She commanded through the book," or "It was said with letters."
2. Hebrew: Yad Vashem. This is the source of the name of the institution. Incidentally, this is from the prophetic portion [*haftarah*] read on all fast days other than Yom Kippur.
3. Samuel II, 1:23.

[Page 24]

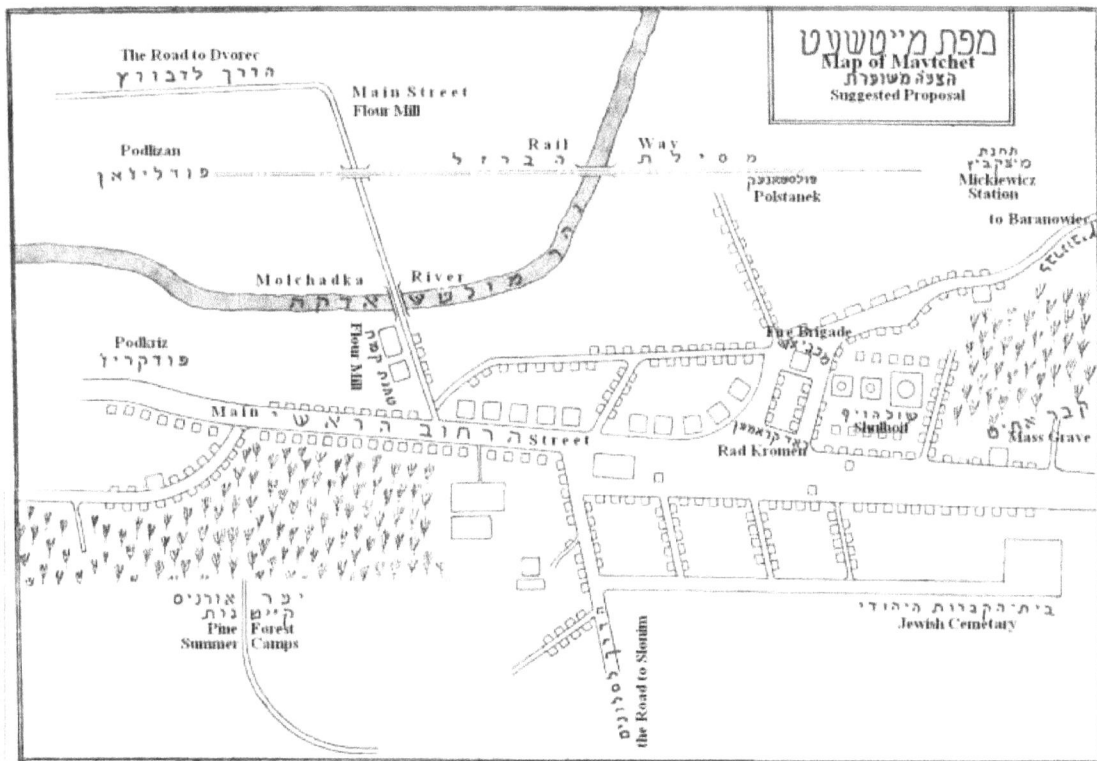

Map of Molchadz
see also Enhanced map

Map translated by Amir Shomroni

Enhanced map from page 24
By Martin Small A/K/A Mordechai Shmulevicz
Prepared for Myrna and Shael Siegel's Trip to Maytchet 2004

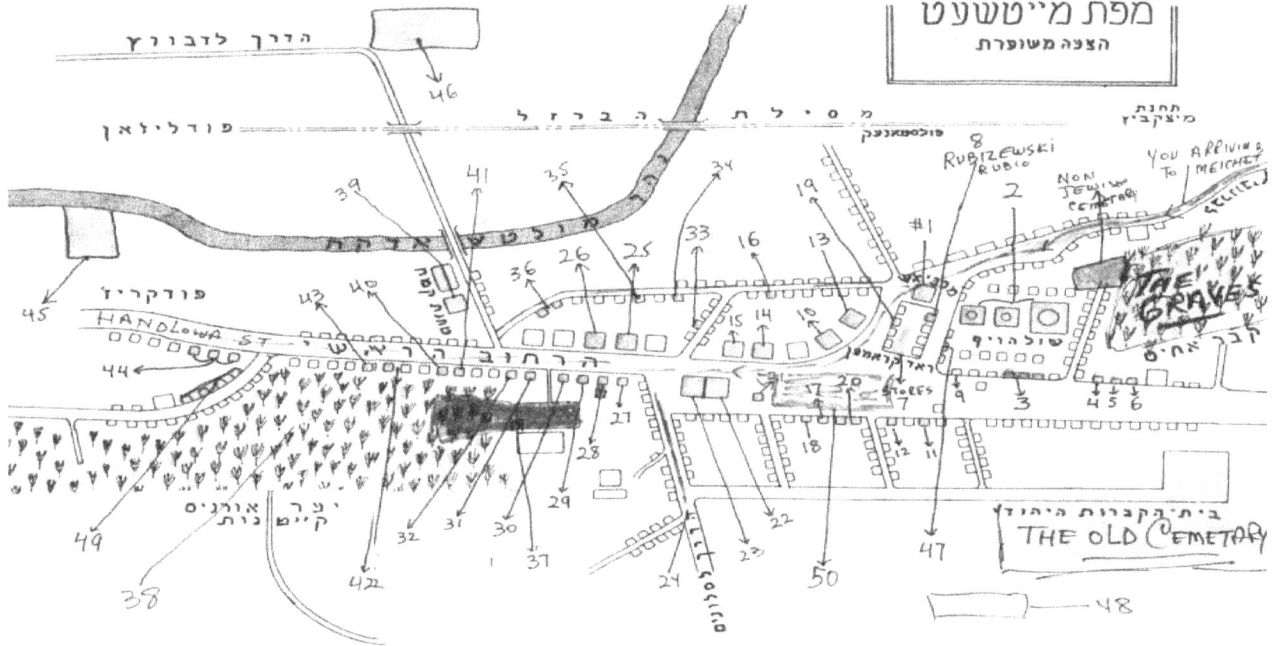

Legend

1. Fire Department - Head of Fire Dept. Martin's cousin Yossel Shmulewicz
2. Area of Three Synagogues (Shulhof) –
   2a. Bet Midrash,
   2b. Shteibl
   2c. Main Synagogue named "Kalte Schul" Large brick bldg., high ceiling painted biblical scenes, men's section 15-20 steps down and women sat in balcony, no heat and was used for holidays, Shtiebel for Chassidim and Beit Midrash smaller synagogue
3. Rabbi's House and Cantor's House
4. Novomiski Liquor business (Martin's Uncle)
5. Gilerowicz House
6. Korn's House
7. Line of Stores
8. Alter Rubiezewski (Rubio) House on top of Stores facing Bet Midrash
9. Lakhovitzki Pharmacy
10. House of Martin's Grandparents Abraham and Shifra Schmulewicz
11. Apteka---The Dvorjetski's Pharmacy
12. Chaim Meir Gorski's Shoe Store – they lived on street behind the store
13. House of Beryl Schmulewicz, the Mohel, brother of Martin's grandfather
14. Hardware Store of Michel Schmulewicz, Martin's Uncle
15. Rabinovitch Dry Goods Store (Uncle of Nachum Rabinovitch)
16. Israel Rabinovitch House (Nachum's father)
17. House of Vikna Belski

18. Bakery (Sora Henie was sales lady)
19. Freidl Margolin's store/cafe
20. Romanovski's House
21. The Water Pump
22. Volinski's Soda Factory and Store
23. Belitski Dry Good Store
24. Road to Slonim
25. Elke and Koppel Gorski's General Store on Street to Slonim and 2 doors from Church.
26. The White Church "Prowaslaw" (Greek Orthodox) Street behind was Catholic Church.
27. Martin's Uncle Michel Schmulewicz House Rented house and storage rented to Rabinovitch for storage of wheat and grains he sold in market
28. Martin's House parents Schlomo and Esther Schmulewicz, children Mordechai Leib (Martin Small), Pesha and Elka – behind house was Uncle Zimel's House – wife was Chaika Bilitski Address was 17 Handlova
29. Uncle Michel Schmulewicz family residence wife Leah and sons Chonia & Moishe. Behind the house was a stable for cows.
30. Gilerowicz House
31. House of Priest from "Pravosiaw" White Church
32. Jewish Doctor's house, Dr. Shapiro---next to this was a small gentile cemetery
33. Chaim Meir Gorski the Shoe Maker's House; children Sachne, Yankel and Minya
34. Ozeransky (or possibly Orzechovsky House – son Bome lives in Russia and was in the Russian army
35. Gentile Doctor Feisher's house
36. Catholic Church and Living Quarters
37. Gentile Cemetery
38. The Health Forest (mostly Pine trees)
39. Water Mill
40. Mina Gorsky's House---the carpenter
41. Viloikhinski the shoemaker
42. Liberman's house and business – Wealthy man; had a telephone
43. House of Yosel Bielous (Brother of Martin's mother)
44. Houses of Moshe Aaron Boretcky and houses of sons and their families Shmuel, Noach and Ben Zion Boretcky
45. Moshe Aaron Boretcky's Flour Mill
46. Uncle Mikal Schmulewicz SMOLARNIA business (would bring roots from trees and burn for weeks to make tar to be used on roofs
47. Novomiski houses (on far right)
48. All Jewish houses
49. Martin's cousin Yudel Schmulewicz motel for guests who came for the summer to the health forest. Would tie hammocks between trees to use as beds
50. Weekly Market held on Wednesdays on right of map

Not numbered on map:
    Police Station across the street from Yudel Schmulewicz's motel
    Train Station built 1938 near the mass grave. The station used before that was in Mickiewicz 4 km.
    from Maytchet on the way to Baranovichi
    Slonimskaya Street was way to Slonim, Yurzdyka St.
    On road to Dvorets was another flour mill

Chapter 2
Early Period

[Page 26]

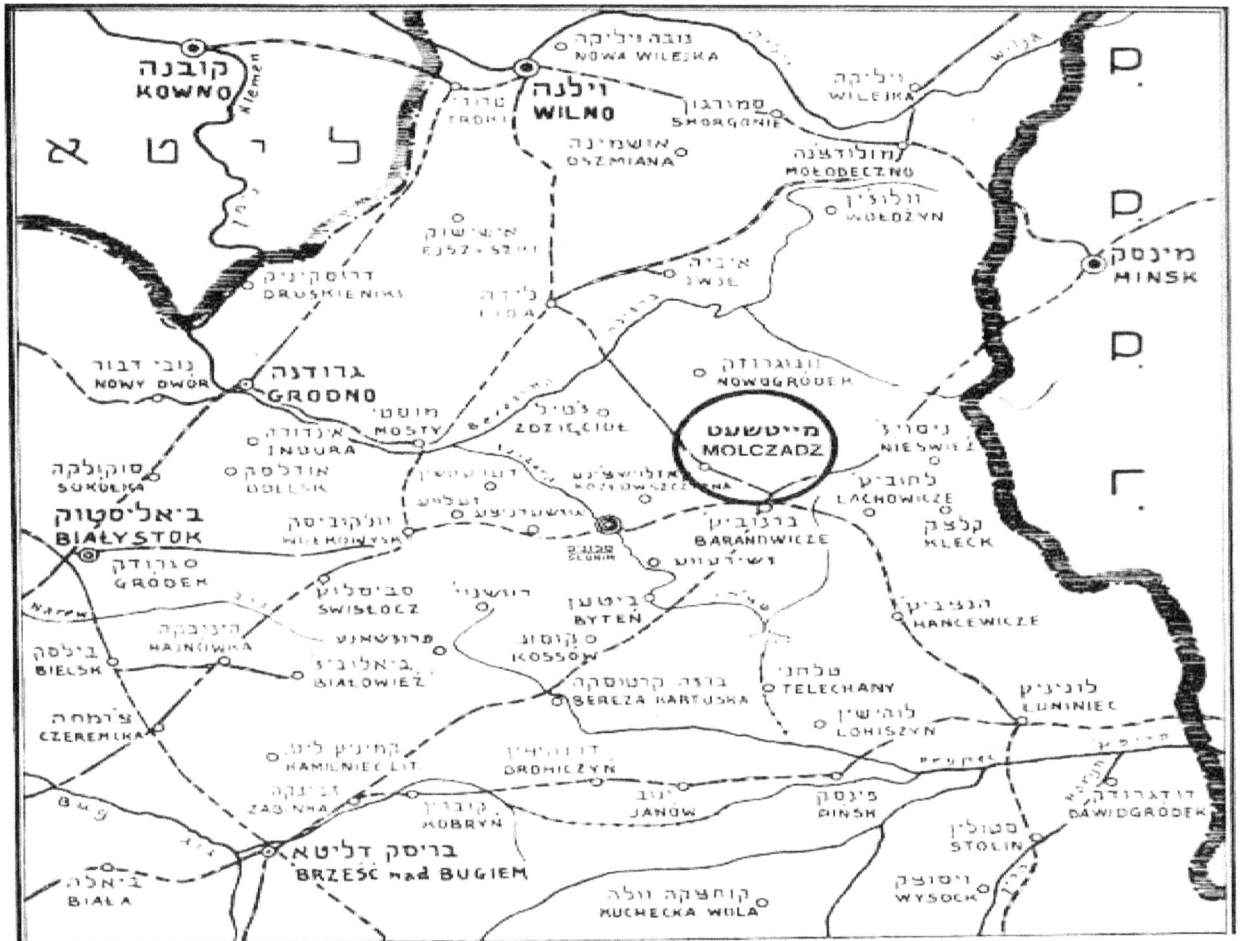

Map of the Region
Map of the region, with the community of Molchadz in the center

[Pages 27 - 41]

A general historical-geographic and Jewish socio-cultural survey

by Benzion H. Ayalon

Translated by Semadar Siegel and Esther Mann Snyder>

a. The name and its meaning

b. Sources regarding the early period of the town

c. Settlement of Jews in Lithuania

d. Area of many regimes

e. The disturbances of Tach veTat (the Chmielnitzky uprising) and other such disturbances

f. The region and its spiritual influence

g. Immediate surroundings and economic relationships

h. Maytchet in memorial books of the region

i. The Jewish town through the view of the newspapers

j. Summary of the first section

a. The name and its meaning

The name that is used by the residents of the city and surrounding vicinity is Maytchet. The name that appears on the official documents from the era of ancient Poland as well as the maps of modern Poland is Molczadz. This name came from the Molchad River, which passes through the region and flows into the Molchadaka River.

In general, cities and villages were named after geographical locations or historical people or events. This was not only for the purposes of identifying the area, but also to perpetuate it, such as the case with a historical event, a national hero, the name of institution. However, not every city merits a splendid family tree that denotes an important historic event. For the most part, a settlement is named for the river upon whose banks it was founded, such as Vilna for the Vylia River, Dvinsk for the Dvina River, and Maytchet for the Molchad River, which is a left tributary of the Neman. In a district with a long history, it would sometimes happen that various tribes and nations would live there in older times, and as their language is forgotten, so would be the meaning of the names of the rivers, mountains, and the like. Names of cities and towns that were called by their names have now completely lost their meaning, and are only decipherable by historians.

This was indeed the historical-geographic and demographic situation of the near and far area of Maytchet, from which it drew its livelihood and spiritual influence at the time of its founding and during its existence. During ancient times, this location was a meeting place of wandering peoples -- Russians, Byelorussians, Lithuanians, Tartars, and Poles. Even those who would travel from afar, wandering through the area at that time, would not pass over this region. These different tribes continually fought over who had the right to settle and govern this place. Everyone left behind a remnant of their presence in the cities and the settlements, such as fortresses or castles. And each thing, by their name, represents the times and places from whence they came.

[Page 28]

General view of Maytchet

[Page 29]

As has been stated, Maytchet is the name used by the Jewish residents, as they used to give such names in every place, and therefore does not serve as a source for research. However, the old original name Molchad has a definitive local ring, whose old meaning stems from the river that passes through the area.

We should note that besides our city and the river we mentioned, there are other settlements, including villages and farms, where the name Molchad is noticeable in the name. These include Molchanuff, Molchani, Molchanovka, Molchanovo, Molchnaska Huta and Molchanska Luka, and others. This is aside a string of names with the root Milchan. The article of Molchani in the Geographic Dictionary of the Kingdom of Poland theorizes that these names form a historical link with the ancient Slavic tribe called called Molchan or Milchan. which is mentioned by chronologists and historians.

The elders of the town tell the following joke that used to be widespread in the area: A high ranking Russian captain was passing through the area and did not know about the place and its name. He sent an assistant to ask the residents of the city about the name. When the aid came back the captain asked, "What is the name of the city'" He answered "Molchat," which in Russian means "be quiet." The captain slapped him on the cheek and shouted, "I asked, what is the name of the city!" The assistant responded once again, "Molchat"...

b. Sources regarding the Early Period of the Town

A major methodology utilized by researchers of Jewish history and communal life during the period of autonomy of the Jews of Poland and Lithuania is to peruse the ledger, which is the well-known "*Pinkas*" of the Council of Four Lands. This is known as a reliable source for information and details in this area. With regards to a Lithuanian city such as Maytchet, the most important Jewish source is the Ledger of the Council of the State of Lithuania, which is a book of minutes of the autonomous council of the Jews of Lithuania, which in the year 5383 (1623) separated from the Council of Five Lands, which then became known as the Council of Four Lands. This ledger is a reliable source of information on the Jews in the community of Lithuania, from the perspective of religious, economic activities, and family life, etc.

At the first meeting of the autonomous council in 1623, the Ledger of the Council of the State of Lithuania opens with a split into three regions -- Brisk [Brest], Horodna [Grodno], and Pinsk, as well as with the division of the regions into central communities and smaller communities that were depended on the central communities with regard to the imposition and collecting of taxes. According to this division, Maytchet is listed together with all the small towns around it, which were directly subordinate to the community of Slonim in the district of Brisk regarding to the payment of taxes and other matters. Furthermore, in the municipal and administrative edicts of Slonim, which was the regional city in that period, Maytchet is also mentioned as subordinate to it for administrative matters, intercession with the authorities, etc.

[Page 30]

Jewish encyclopedias are an additional source of information on the Jewish communities. They generally contain a number of lines on each settlement according to its size and importance. Nevertheless this information is sketchy and is very general. The information below appears in the Brokuaus-Efron Jewish Encyclopedia written in Russian:

Maytchet, early period

"Molczadz during the time of the Rzeczpospolita was a town in the district of Slonim. In 1765, 369 taxpayers lived in the community.

Today it is in the region of Grodno, which is in the district of Slonim. According to the census of 1847 the Jewish population of Maytchet was 340 people, and according to the census of 1897 the general population was 1,733, of which 1,188 were Jews."

It goes without saying that the general encyclopedias, rich in various entries, tend to dedicate their entries to central cities and places of historical and political importance, skipping completely over smaller communities. On the other hand, the various lexicons and geographical dictionaries, whose purpose is specific and whose scope is restricted to a specific country, pay equal attention to a city and a village, a railway and a roadway, and even the location of a small flourmill on the banks of an unknown river, without skipping over anything. This is what was written regarding Maytchet in the Dictionary of Geography of the Kingdom of Poland [*Slownik Geograficzny Krolestwa Polskiego*], which was published in 1889 in Warsaw (in Polish):

[Page 31]

 "Molczad is a town situation on the Saratowa River, where it flows into the Molchadka River, in the district of Slonim; which is SE of it alongside the Vilna-Romania railroad.

The total population is 1,128 (specifically 524 men and 604 women), of which 702 are Jews. In 1654 Maytchet was destroyed in a fire and the people in the town were released from paying taxes and civic duty for four years. In 1879 two thirds of the city burnt down.

The environs around the city were hilly with sandy soil and it was sparsely forested. It was a stop on the Vilna-Romania rail line (officially Molczad). There was a post office and a telegraph line between the railroad stations of Navolania (25 verst)[1] and Baranovichi (25 verst). It was 162 verst from Vilna, 63 verst from Lida, 189 verst from Pinsk and 301 verst from Kobrin."

c. Settlement of Jews in Lithuania

The Jews came from different areas of the Diaspora, and from different expulsions, and settled in Lithuania in the 14th century. The liberal Lithuanian ruler Gediminas (1336-41), who expanded the borders of his country to the Nieman and Bug rivers through his conquests and victories, was welcoming to settlers from outside, among whom were many Jews who were needed for the development of his large but still undeveloped country.

The liberal treatment of the Jews continued with full force with Gediminas' grandchild Witold (1430-86), who even granted the Jews special, far-reaching privileges in order to encourage them to build up and develop his country. Thanks to the humane treatment of these two princes and of the Lithuanian population, who were still pagans until the second half of the 14th century and had not yet been infected by the venom of Christian anti-Semitism, many Jewish settlements developed. The three largest Jewish communities were Brisk, Grodno, and Troki.

However, as was always the destiny of Jews of the Diaspora, after approximately 200 years of relative tranquility and after they put all their energy and blood into the building of a country that was not theirs, history repeated itself. "A New King Arose," "Let us deal craftily with them"[2] etc. Under the influence of the zealous Jesuits who gained influence in this country at that time, in the year 1495 the Orthodox Bishop Alexander Jagiellonczyk expelled all the Jews from his district confiscated their property, which they had obtained through great toil. When Maytchet was established along with other villages in the 16th century, there were only a few remote villages without Jews[3].

However, very soon the rulers of the country realized that the advice of the Jesuits was wrong and that their country sank very quickly into economic chaos without the hard-working Jews. The economic benefits that came to them from the diligent labor of the Jews disappeared as if had never been there, and the property that was confiscated went to the greedy church. Only after their eyes opened up to see the light, did they turn from their wicked thoughts and, in April 1505, the Jews were allowed to return to their homes, and with that return the Jews also went to new areas of our district with the idea that they would build up those areas as well.

[Page 32]

General view of Maytchet

[Page 33]

Here is the place to note specifically that after the cancellation of the expulsion decree, the pillaged property of the Jews was returned to them, but they never received the full rights back that they had before. Furthermore, they were burdened with a special tax, called the "Return Tax," (*powrotny*), which henceforth was a customary tax that every Jew had to pay to the Lithuanian State, together with the head tax, for the benefit of the national coffers.

We also find in the ledger of the Council of the State of Lithuanian from the middle of the 17th century, more than150 years after the return of Jews to the area, the concept of the "Return Tax" from the area towns of Dvorets, Zhetl, Maytchet, etc., which by that time had obtained the status of independent communities that paid taxes to the Council of the State of Lithuania.

Another transfusion to the Jewish body of Lithuania occurred after the unification or Lithuania and Poland from 1516 and onward, when the two sister nations unified into one kingdom. A new element was added to the Lithuanian Jewish corpus, the source of which cannot be fully defined, and that was the Polish Jews who streamed into and integrated themselves into that area that had become a part of Poland. That integration went very well. The scholarly Lithuanian Jews, who were so sharp that they received the name of "the brain" of Jewry, absorbed the religious fervor from the Chassidic Polish Jews, who were known as the "heart" of the Jewry. They complemented each other. From this one can understand the existence of the Chassidic courts in the big cities and the small villages in the area.

Lithuania's Jews experienced hard times, which were a normal part of Jewish life in the Diaspora, and about which we will talk in the next chapters. As our sages have said, "Be mindful of the children of poor people because from them comes Torah learning." Such it was with the Lithuanian Jews, including the area of Polish Lithuania, as they produced great names in all areas, with the entire Jewish people depending on their Torah and wisdom. Jewish natives of Lithuania became the pillars of the Zionist movement and the Hebrew culture in many of the countries of the Diaspora, such as South Africa, etc.

d. Area of Many Regimes

We cannot say how successful the post 1917 revolution regimes were in both abolishing the old world according to the revolutionary doctrine; and in building a new and better world. But when it comes to the Jews who had so much hope in the revolution and sacrificed so many people and much property-their world was literally darkened. Everything collapsed very quickly approaching World War II when Hitler, the firstborn of the Satan, may the name of the evil ones rot, destroyed almost all the Jews of Europe through his madness and cruelty. Few people survived this war of annihilation. Some of these survivors immigrated to Israel to build a new State and build up the country and build a new life for themselves.

The regime of Sodom and Gomorrah is only the end that testifies to the essence of other regimes that preceded it and greatly affected the character of the Jews in the Diaspora including our area. The Lithuanian Polish region, with Maytchet located at its center, was a battleground where Eastern and Western armies fought throughout the generations. It passed from one hand to another, but everyone had one deep-seated goal, to suppress the Jews, each in accordance to his way.

[Page 34]

The era until the end of the 13th century, was known as the era of settlement of that area with all the occurrences of incursions and retreats from both sides without any permanent regime, accompanied by the temporary invasions and attacks of external elements such as the Tatars, Cossacks, Swedes, etc. Only beginning in 1291, with the establishment of the Lithuanian archdiocese, did the Lithuanian rule became more permanent, lasting for 278 years until the merger of Poland and Lithuania in 1569. Lithuanian rule began with a liberal spirit toward the Jews, who were invited to inhabit the country and participate in the formation and building of the country. However, the attitude of the regime changed very quickly, and the Jews were commanded to leave the country after they devoted their lives and blood to the building of the country. However, the rulers of Lithuania very quickly regretted what they had done and the Jews were allowed to return, but the rend in the heart never healed. The real goal of the government was revealed in particular when it needed the Jewish money and it imposed a special "Return Tax" in return for their right of return; and which remained in force as a Jewish tax which they had to pay throughout the entire period of their rule.

With the "Lublin Unification" treaty between Poland and Lithuania, they became one country in all respects and the Polish government continued for 226 years. The attitude of the Polish government to the Jews was not as it seemed. On one hand there was a tradition of the respected Jews who excelled in the development of the country, and that allowed the Jews to have religious autonomy which was granted to them under the rubric of the Council of the Four Lands. On the other hand, the Polish people were very deeply rooted in anti-Semitism, and the liberal Polish government turned the vast Jewish center into a virtual ghetto. Every Polish landowner wanted with all his heart to see the Jews disappear except for his own private Jew, who was forced to sing and dance before him saying "How beautiful you are." These are the three typical symbols of the Polish Diaspora and its regime.

The third regime that left its mark upon the area in a very destructive way to the image of the Jew was the Russian regime, which established itself after the third partition and the complete destruction of Poland in 1795. It is proper to note that, whereas the preceding Polish regime was liberal to the Jews, albeit with a policy of degradation, the Russian regime acted with an iron fist and with a policy of oppression. Everywhere that the Russian regime reached, the Jews were limited in where they could live. The limitation was called *Krumi Yevreyeb*, which means everything is allowed to everyone except for the Jews. The civil rights of the Jews were gradually decreased until the Council was completely abolished. A law was enacted prohibiting Jews from living in villages, banning certain trades, etc. Pogroms also took place.

These were the three main regimes that lasted for several centuries and left their mark upon life in the area in general, and Jewish life in particular, throughout many generations. Nevertheless, we cannot ignore regimes that lasted for briefer periods, but whose influence lasted for a long time, such as the renewed Polish government that succeeded in quashing all the hopes and dreams of the Jews during its 19 years of existence. Of course, there was the Nazi regime that lasted for over three years, which was the most fatal and tragic to the local Jews who had already experienced so much pain and suffering, about which we will devote chapters later in this book.

[Page 35]

e. The Disturbances of Tach veTat (the Chmielnitzky uprising) and other such disturbances

In the wake of the Cossack Rebellion led by the enemy Chemil, the rebellious farmers swept through western Ukraine and the area of Podolia and Volhynia, drowning the Jewish residents in rivers of blood, until their bloody march reached Pinsk. Some sources say that they even reached the swamps of Polesia and arrived at the cities of Slonim, Grodno, and even Minsk, but there is no official confirmation of such. Nathan Nota Hanover listed in his book *Yaven-Metzula* all the names of the communities that were destroyed. He does not mention Slonim, and the nearby communities such as Maytchet, Zhetl, or others. Aside from the echoes of the terrible atrocities that overtook the Jews of Poland and the help that was given to the refugees, we find no mention of the atrocities in the Ledger of the Council of the State of Lithuania, that continued its activities during the years of Tach and Tat (1648-1649) and beyond without any interruption, until the end of its existence. We find that the 12th meeting of the Council took place in the month of *Shevat* in 1649 in the small town of Mistkevich. At the 13th meeting took place 1650 in Zabludova, large sums of money had to be paid by the Jewish communities of Dvorets, Zhetl, and Maytchet, and others who had to pay debts that were created in the winter of 1648.

The Cossacks attacked the Polish nobility and Catholic churches wherever they went. However, these incidents were not recorded in any municipal or district courthouse records in Slonim. There is also insufficient information in the history books of the area communities to reveal the tragic events that happened to the Jews. It is known; however, that many communities paid higher taxes during those years, which is a sign of their economic success.

In contrast it is clear that in the year 5416 (1655) the Cossacks arrived in the district of Slonim, destroyed the Catholic Monastery in Zyrowa, and viciously attacked the towns and villages in the area. Even though we do not have detailed information about killings of Jews, we still know that their economic life was almost paralyzed. The urban Christian and the Polish nobility with the help of the Catholic priesthood led by the Jesuits, who were growing strong in Lithuania at that time, spared no disgusting effort to attack the Jews and afflict their life.

With the great confusion, the Jews of Ruzhany were accused of a blood libel in the year 5418 (1658). This ended with the execution of two of the leaders of the community. This unfortunate event laid the groundwork for other libels and for the danger of general expulsion of the Lithuanian Jews. Feelings of fear overtook the Jews in the region and their communities, which were obligated by the state council to pay heavy fees to intercede in the libels, and were weakened to a low level. It was not only the communities of the area, but also the large community of Slonim that had to take out high interest loans from the priests of Zyrowa. They were unable to repay even the interest, and became completely dependent upon them.

[Page 36]

As if the load of troubles and tribulations of the Jews of the area was not full, from 1654 to 1655 the Russians and their Swedish partners that took part in the Thirty Year War of Poland attacked the Jews and killed many without mercy. The communities of Lithuania that miraculously survived the Cossacks during the tribulations of Tach VeTat, were now being murdered by the Russians and Swedes, and reached the point of poverty and desperation. Because of the terrible situation of the Jewish community, especially in the area of Novogrudok , the Council of the State of Lithuania could not deliver the correct head army to the state coffers. In 1712 a lawsuit was registered to the Supreme Court in Vilna for not paying the taxes of the sum of 25,000 gold coins.

The communities mentioned in the lawsuit included Slonim, Dvorets, Zhetl, Maytchet, Polonka, Stolovichi, Mysh Nova, and others. The verdict was a very harsh, and consisted of a death sentence for the community leaders if the money would not be paid within the time frame set in the verdict.

To sum up this difficult and bitter period that was the lot of the Lithuanian Jews, it must be stated that because of the continuous wars and poverty, there was a major plague spread through the area that killed many.

f. The Region and its Spiritual Influence

No historical period that is measured as a whole entity. Rather, it is part of a chain of generations and periods. Each period is part of a chain of epochs, and is a result of the preceding one and a base for events of future generations. Similarly, a geographical specific point is a sum of influences from external factors from other geographical centers, primary and secondary, that influence its existence physically, spiritually and culturally. It is clear that this little town in Lithuania is, first of all, Lithuanian in its essence.

The area of the influence of Maytchet, of which it is the center, developed between the Neiman River in the northwest and the Pripet River in the southeast and the large cities surrounding it: Vilna in the north, Grodno and Bialystok in the west, Brisk and Pinsk in the south, Minsk in the east, and Slonim in the center of the area. Before we describe the immediate region, i.e. the cities and nearby villages that conducted day to day commercial relations with Maytchet, we will describe more distant centers that had a significant spiritual and cultural effect on the area in general and on the city of Maytchet in particular.

[Page 37]

Vilna - It was an ancient and significant town with 235,000 people, with a Jewish population of 80,000 in 1941. It was formerly the capital of Lithuania, and then a district city in Poland, and finally the capital of Soviet Lithuania. It was a large center of European Jewry for Torah, Jewish wisdom, enlightenment, and arts. It was nicknamed the Jerusalem of Lithuania (Yerushalayim DeLita). Its educational and cultural institutions included: an ancient university, a science academy, a conservatorium, a rabbinical seminary, a teacher's seminary, secondary schools in Hebrew and Yiddish, an ORT Technion, a center for Yiddish culture called "Vilner Yiddish," YIVO, "Vilner Troupe", Bund, a printing press and newspapers. The printing press of the Romm widow and brothers published the Vilna edition of the Talmud. The periodicals included "Hakarmel", "Hazman", and "Haolam". Important scholars who lived there included: The Vilna Gaon, Rabbi Yehudah Halevi Horowitz, Adam Ha Kohen, [his son] Mikha"l, Yehuda Leib Gordon, Shmuel Yoseph Fine and others.

Grodno (Horodno) -- an ancient town on the River Nieman with 50,000 inhabitants; 20,000 of whom were Jews. It was one of the main towns in the Bialystok area during the era of Polish rule, and it is part of Soviet Byelorussia. It had commerce in wood, wool, and tobacco processing.

It already had a Jewish community in the 14th century. On account of its importance and great influence in the area, it was established as one of the three districts of the Council of the State of Lithuania. In 1789 the first Jewish press in Lithuania was set up by Baruch Romm. It moved from there to Vilna and became famous as the "Romm Press," and later, the "Widow and Brothers Romm." Rabbi Mordechai Jaffe, the author of "Halevushim", served in the rabbinate of that community.

Bialystok -- It was a district city during the era of Polish rule with more then 100,000 inhabitants, half of whom were Jewish (1939). The primary occupation of the local residents was with the textile and leather factories, most of which were in Jewish hands. Famous people included Rabbi Shmuel Mohilever, Zamenhof, and others.

Brisk of Lita (Brest Litovsk) -- it was the main city in the Polesia district, on the Bug River with 50,000 inhabitants and a large Jewish community. It was an important crossroad on the Moscow-Warsaw railroad.

In the 17th century, Brisk first became known as an important center of Lithuanian Jewry. The Council of the State of Lithuania designated it as a major district, and it became a location for conventions. Famous rabbis of Brisk included: the Maharsha"l, Rabbi Yoel Sirkes the author of the Ba"ch, Rabbi Chaim Solveitchik and others.

[Page 38]

Brisk was destroyed in 1648 by Chmielnitski's soldiers, but the line between Brisk and Pinsk served as the northern border of their bloody rampage.

Pinsk - It was a city in the region of Polesia with the Pinsk marshes at its center. In 1939 there were 37,000 inhabitants, of whom 24,000 were Jews. Most of the industry and commerce, mainly dealing with exporting wood to Danzig, was in Jewish hands.

There was a Jewish community from the 16th century, which was one of the three first districts of the Council of State of Lithuania. It played an active role in the dispute between the Misnagdim and Chassidim. The Jews suffered terribly from the Cossack pogroms of Chmielnitzki.

Minsk - The capital of Soviet Byelorussia on the Svisloch River, southeast of Vilna and on the Moscow-Vilna-Warsaw railway line. In the district of Lithuania, it is the twin city to Vilna in its population and Jewish cultural importance. Before the Holocaust there were 60,000 Jews out of a population of 238,000 individuals. In the 14th century Minsk was annexed to Lithuania and in the 16th century it became part of Poland during the 1569 unification.

From the 16th century, Minsk had an important Jewish community under the rubric of the Council of the Four Lands, and later in the Council of the State of Lithuania. In its time, Minsk was known as an important Torah center, with the following rabbis: Rabbi Yechiel Halperin the author of "Seder Hadorot", Rabbi Arieh Leib the author of "Shaagat Aryeh" and others. It was an important base of the *Mitnagdim*, had a great deal of *Haskalah* activities, and was an important Zionist center. It hosted the Russian Zionist council from 1902.

g. Immediate Surroundings and Economic Relationships

After we have described the broader district from which Maytchet absorbed its spiritual and cultural influences, directly and indirectly; it is now appropriate to turn our attention to the immediate area with its cities and villages, which set up their roots from the time of their establishment, and to look into the settlements with which it had day-to-day contact and which served as its base for livelihood and sustenance. First of all...

Slonim - An ancient, historic city dating from the middle ages on the banks of the Szczara River. Before the Second World War there were 14,000 inhabitants.

It is a very well-pedigreed city, whose elder generation was a pleasant mix of rabbis and scholars who were great in Torah, and Jews of renown who had a sharp Lithuanian "mind," and of Admorim and Hassidim who possessed a warm Jewish "heart'. The younger generation excelled in their sweet Jewish folksiness.

It was always a primary city and an example for other cities and towns whose residents came to Slonim to study in its Yeshivas, to spend time in the Hassidic courts, and to draw from its great spiritual treasuries in the realms of Haskalah, Zionism, revolution, etc.

[Page 39]

During the days of the autonomous Lithuanian Council, Maytchet and surrounding towns were affiliated with the large Slonim community.

Baranovichi - It was a relatively young city that was established after the construction of the Moscow-Brisk railroad in 1873. This place, which had formerly been a pine forest, became an important crossroads, and many inhabitants of the surrounding villages and even farther-away places were attracted to it.

Baranovichi developed mainly during the Polish regime, which established it as the district city instead of Slonim that served as such during the time of the earlier Russian regime. Administratively the councils of Mush, Maytchet, Polonka, Stolovich, and Horodishtch belonged to this community. Of the 28,000 inhabitants, less then half were Jewish. The diligent Jews were in control of most of the business and trades of the city, whereas the Christians were the government officials and the military people.

Baranovichi was the center for Torah and Hasidism. The two large Yeshivas attracted youths and young married men from the towns of the area. It also served as Jewish cultural center, with all its ramifications. Six weekly Jewish newspapers were published in Baranovichi, and the city exerted a strong influence on the towns of the area.

Stolovichi - It was a small town 7 parasangs[1] from Baranovichi, populated primarily by urban Christians (*misczans*) and a few hundred Jewish families. Stolovichi was situated on a main road, and served as a stopover from routes of many directions, for all routes led through Stolovichi. Its roads spread out in four directions, and were a stopover for horses and carriages.

Since it was an important crossroads, from early times Stolovichi had market days, which were known afar. The entire economy of the city, both of the Jews and the Christians, was based upon them. These market days indirectly affected the economy of other towns of the area, Maytchet included, for people would go there with their handiwork and various merchandise to sell.

Mush regarded itself as the mother town of Baranovichi. For a long time, people would call it New Mysh. It was an ancient city, as is shown by the old ledger that included historical facts. In the census of 1897, Mush had 2,995 people, including 1,764 Jews.

Mush is about four parasangs west of Baranovichi. In marriage documents and other certificates, Baranovichi is noted as "Baranovichi near Mush." Before Baranovichi was founded, Mush was a city blessed by G-d, whose Jewish residents earned their livelihood in a plentiful manner. However, once Baranovichi was founded around 1884 and became a railway stop, many of the residents of Mush moved there, to the point where it became emptied of its residents and sources of livelihood. From that time, it was a wealthy man who had become impoverished, but who retained his family tree in his hand.

[Page 40]

Zhetl[4] - It was a Jewish town on the road from Novogrudok to Slonim, about 12 kilometers from the Nowojelnia railway station. It had an old community with 3,000 Jews, who earned their livelihood throughout the generations in a meager fashion through their handiwork and by conducting small-scale commerce with the villages of the area. Despite being of modest means, the Jews of Zhetl were at a high level from a spiritual, cultural, and social perspective.

A large Yeshiva was established in Zhetl, in which Jews from all parts of Poland would come to study, and which was known for its geniuses. It also had Talmud study groups in which the scholars of the town and regular householders participated. It sent forth rabbis and scholars who of renown who were great in Torah. In the latter period, Zhetl was noted for its nationalist-Zionist activities and also as a center of the Jewish-Russian workers' movement.

Dvorets - It was situated close to Zhetl, and had a larger Jewish community than did Zhetl. The two communities shared a common lot throughout the generations, and appear for a long time as twin cities in the ledger of the Council of the State of Lithuania, that paid their tax quotas to the council in a joint fashion. However, with the passage of time, Zhetl developed to the point where it earned its status of an independent community, whereas Dvorets separated from Zhetl and was set up by the council as an affiliate of the community of Maytchet for that same purpose.

The Yeshivas of Volozhin and Mir - Without doubt, one of the wonderful traits, the fruit of the land with which Lithuanian Jewry was graced, was the voice of Torah that burst forth from the famous Yeshivas, which were the first and primary institutions in all the cities of Lithuania and the area. These included the Yeshivas of Slobodka, Radin, Ponovich, Novhorodok, and Slonim (in which the splendorous Maytchet Gaon Reb Hirsch served), Lida (in which the Maytchet genius KR"M served), Horodishets, and others.

However, we will discuss specifically the two large Yeshivas, which are Volozhin and Mir, which were like the Oxford and Cambridge of the Lithuanian region, whose good name spread throughout the Jewish Diaspora as centers of Torah and moralistic teaching (*mussar*), and whose sounds of Torah never stopped day and night. As is known, the Volozhin Yeshiva was founded by Rabbi Chaim the student of the GRA (Vilna Gaon) as a force of opposition against the Haskalah movement. Within it walls, there were Yeshiva heads, Gaonim and giants of Torah and fear of G-d; as well as 400 students who were diligent in their studies, including the national poet Ch. N. Bialik, the Maytchet Genius, and others. The Mir Yeshiva, which was closer to Minsk, had more students that Volozhin; but the crown of the first born remained with Volozhin.

[Page 41]

Maytchet youths in the Yeshivas of the area

Villages of the area - It is appropriate to point out an interesting fact, which was not a particularly widespread vision throughout the Jewish Diaspora but was quite typical in that district - that many Jews worked in agriculture. Jewish residents lived in almost all of the villages around Maytchet. Some of them worked in leasing, trades and commerce as did village Jews everywhere, whereas another portion worked in agriculture in the fields and gardens. Both groups regarded themselves as belonging to the community of Maytchet in all respects. As is known, even the Maytchet Gaon was born in the nearby village of Sennichenenta to his father who was the lessee of the post office and inn of the village.

The following is the list of the nearby villages whose Jewish residents added a significant percentage to the Jewish population of Maytchet:

> Ivankoviche, Byalolozy, Dokorva, Zahorny, Zverovshchina, Khoroshovchitsy, 41Yatra, Mitskevichi, Medbedzini, Serebrishche, Svortova, Kalisheniki, and Rohotna.

It should be noted that the Jewish residents of the villages succeeded in escaping the sword of the Holocaust more so than the residents of the town.

Editor's footnotes
1. Parasang and verst are old units of distance.
2. A reference to the first chapter of Exodus, when a new Pharaoh arose who did not know Joseph, and who enslaved the Jewish people.
3. This sentence is somewhat unclear, and I suspect it means that there were no Jews other than in a few remote villages.
4. Currently known as Dziatlava.

h. Maytchet in Memorial Books of the Region

Another source of information about the Jewish community in Maytchet can be found, without doubt, in the Yizkor books of the adjacent communities in the area, since they shared a common fate in terms of political and economic relations and also in the organization of the Jewish communities. It also should be noted, the problems concerning the general political matters and also the internal community life under the tyrannical government and the very difficult days including the poll tax levied on the Jews by the state, attempts to prevent blood libels and other vicious decrees, redemption of prisoners, aid to the families whose members were martyred, etc. The Jews of Lithuania suffered from another tax that was levied for the right to return to their former residence after the cancellation of deportations decrees.

[Page 42]

All these matters were daily occurrences of the Jews of Lithuania and brought for discussion to the Committee of the State of Lithuania, where each community tried to give as much as possible to the fund of the Committee which was directly responsible to the government for the payments. According to the amounts of payments and their changing details we can learn about the conditions that rose and declined of the community.

The early days of Maitshet

And this is what we read in the "*Shtetl Pinhas* (Ledger)", of the interesting work of Mordechai Vav. Bernshtein (Buenos Aires)
"In the meeting of the Committee from 1670, section 687, we read about the levy of "State amount": three gold coins, 46 large ones and 100 large Polish ones). From this we learn for the first time, that also Maitshet was part of the partnership." š Pinkas Zhetl (a/k/a Dyatlovo), edited by Baruch Kaplinski. Tel-Aviv, 1957.

[Page 43]

"In the meeting of the Committee in 1673, paragraph 706 we read: Dvorets (a/k/a Dzyatlava) with Maitshet eight large gold "*foil*"" to this Maitshet will give 6 "*gdo'f.*" From this budget we learn that Dvorets (which in the past was considered with Zhetl) became a partner with Maitshet, and we learn from this the portion of Maitshet in the general sum."

And in the meeting of 1679 - Dvorets and Maitshet 26 large ones and in 1684 they gave 18 large ones until from 1601 Maitshet separated from Dvorets and appeared as a separate community with 7 large ones.

In the Pinkas of Slonim, a book by Kalman Lichtenshtein, in chapter 4, we read the following excerpts about the town of Maitshet and its surroundings from its beginnings:

"Despite the terrible isolation of the Jews among the hostile non-Jews, the Jews of Slonim succeeded during the years 1550 - 1648 to enlarge its borders and to continue to found small settlements in the area, the way they had done in the first half of the 16th century. Thus we note the existence of Jewish settlements during this time such as Zhetl, Roviny, Dvorets, Maitshet, Polanka (a/k/a Stolevitch), Drohichin (a/k/a Drahichyn), Halynka (a/k/a Golynka), Kossovo, Byten, - small communities that were without a doubt founded by settlers from Slonim, who arrived there after the establishment and strengthening their central community."

In Chapter 6, of the above mentioned book, we read about the place of Maitshet among the family of Jewish communities in the area.

"Immediately upon the start of the Pinkas of the State of Lithuania, in the Committee of 1623, divided the state into three main regions: Brisk, Harodna, and Pinsk. Slonim was mentioned as belonging to the region of Brisk. In this section also are mentioned the communities of Roviny and Dvorets due to their growth in the beginning of the 17th century. From this we learn that many settlements in the area that had lesser Jewish populations than these two; and the fact of their existence was mentioned due to governmental and local acts - Slonimian, and they are: Ozernitsa, Kossovo, Drohichin, Zhetl, Byten, Seltz (a/k/a Syalyets) Polanka, Maitshet and a number of communities in the surrounding villages were directly subordinate to the community of Slonim."

In addition direct and indirect mention was made in the memorial books of other communities in the area, that indicate the beginning of the establishment of Maitshet and the difficulties encountered in its development.

i. The Jewish town in the view of the newspapers

How wretched and pitiful looked the lives of the Jews in the big cities, and especially in the small Jewish towns, in the view of the newspapers of those days.

[Page 44]

Whether in the Eastern part, the "valley of tears" as described by the author Mendele that is reflected in *The Melitz* by Tzederbaum in Peterburg and that of the Western side, in *Yavan Hametzula* by Hanover, reflected in the *Tzfira* by Slonimski in Warsaw, the area of Lithuania was a middle ground reflecting parts of both sides; two are better than one.

And we should know, that in those days the idea of Zionism had not yet evolved and there didn't appear among the Jewish communities any other solutions to resist the decrees as was done in the democratic countries. In addition, the older generation was still deep in its old ways, the swamp of exile, and were able to bequeath to their children only *tarbe* that has no end and all the long-standing Jewish way of life. Therefore even new generations physically strong but weak in spirit, plodded along in the same stagnant swamp.

The first houses in Maitshet

If life was so wretched and downtrodden and the writers whose opinions were so empty and superficial, as if there is nothing more in their world but only cursed poverty and meagerness, the community-shtibl, the disputes and rumors. And if the sky was so dark without any horizons, vision and hope ceased to exist in the closed heart without realizing the wretched situation. And if the town stood still for many years and no one arose to write in the newspaper anything more than a fire in the streets, or a murder or theft or until a bishop would arrive for a visit and a delegation of Jews with Torah scrolls went to greet him and other such "news." Therefore, it's not surprising that the image of the Jewish town in the view of the press was desperate and somewhat unpleasant, since that was the image and the character in sad reality.

[Page 45]

Here are a few excerpts from the reports of the correspondents of the towns and area around Maitshet, that "constantly ran news reports that would be published on the front pages for all to see" in the periodicals.

HaMalitz - a notice to tell Yaakov everything etc. that happened in Peterburg the capital, written by Alexander Halevi Tzederboim

Hatzefira - a periodical that reported news among the people of Yeshurun (Jews), published in Warsaw by Haim Zelig Slonimski.

MN- - - notifies: The number of Jews counted in our town is 280 families. There is one great synagogue that is standing since the year 5408 (1648), and another 6 *Batei midrashim* - Study Halls. Six organizations 1- Hevra Kadisha (for burials), 2- Bikur Holim (taking care of the sick), 3- Linat Zedek (hostel for the poor), 4- Hevrat Sha'ss (learning the Talmud) , 5- Hevrat Mishnayot (learning the Mishna), 6- Hevrat Tehillim (learning/reading the Psalms).

Rabbis 2, Rabbinical judges 2, shohet (ritual kosher slaughter) 3, cantors 2, beadles 8, teachers 13, writers of Torah scrolls, etc. 6, mikve caretakers 2, gravediggers 2, storekeepers 36, sellers of old clothes 6, horse traders 9, fruit salesmen 5, agents and intermediaries 7, bakers of bread and honey cakes 9, tailors and seamstresses 23, leather workers 21, waggoners 11, watch repairers 3, engravers 3, meat pullers 7, wood choppers and water carriers 7, chimney sweepers 2, manual laborers 9, musicians 4, makers of hand boxes 2, doctor 1, pharmacist, midwives 3, without any specific occupation 67, beggars 9.

These are the Jews who live in our town as counted.

Z --- (Grodno area). - On Monday night during the 10 days of repentance, a fire erupted and destroyed more than 100 houses and 3 Study Halls, also stores with their merchandise were burnt. The people of the city stand outside with their wives and children without a place to sleep. Therefore I ask of you in the name of the injured to quickly give them help whether in money or clothes and to send to ---.

MB ---We are told that on Shabbat Parshat Shmot there was a disturbance and confusion in the study hall during the prayers, between the leader of the prayers and the shohet - - - and there was such a great tumult that the neighboring Christians came to see what all the noise was about and they laughed that such foolishness about the leader of the prayers would cause the Jews to desecrate the House of the Lord.

H.P. - MM writes that from a nearby village three farmers came to a tavern run by a Jewish woman who poured them a drink, which they drank and became intoxicated. When she asked for payment they spilled out the liquor from the barrels onto the ground and they beat her badly almost to death. If only the police had arrived...

[Page 46]

MM. We are told that on Friday, before last Shabbat the prayer hall of the Hasidim became like a battlefield. They beat each other, threw dirt, insulted and cursed each other like fishwives at the market. About 60 pieces of glass were broken from the windows and even the wives of the Hasidim took part in the "holy" war. And the men even grabbed the head coverings off the women in front of all. Finally, they filed their complaints and petitions to the magistrate and the mayor of the city to our disgrace and shame.

M.A. writes MM. - Our town looks like a hut in the field, all the workers have stopped working and live from the air. Due to zero work they walk around the town all day and spend their time in idle talk. Formerly many urgently went to work in the "golden" countries, America and Africa, but even a change of place didn't improve their economic situation because those wandering from place to place didn't earn much. Only infrequently were they able to send money home to their families who were left penniless, and others had to return bitterly disappointed.

The education of the children was sluggish and poorly done. The people found no use for education and no one sought it. I am not exaggerating when I say that there was almost no one in the whole town who had any knowledge of our literature or any idea of our nationalism. No one here even read the newspapers because it didn't interest them in the least.

MB. writes. - Due to the lack of a Talmud-Torah (elementary school) the teachers sit in special rooms and each receives his salary of three to five rubles a week. Each must go around to the homes every Friday to receive this pittance. This money is insufficient to maintain the Talmud-Torah and the community stands apart and awaits the coming of the Messiah.

Recently the home of the local Rabbi was burned. Among his possessions that were destroyed were the documents of his birth and marriage. The rabbi attempted to acquire permission from the governor of the province, that the district council provide a copy of the documents that are kept in their offices. However, many fees are required, which he did not have; he asked the local council to help but they claimed they couldn't aid him since they had no money. Thus those requesting documents were sorely disappointed.

[Page 47]

j. Summary Table Part One

Dates and historic events - landmarks and other intermediate events in the Jewish settlement in the area of Lithuania and its regimes

Until the end of the 6th century	Prehistoric period/movement of primitive tribes, Slavs, Lithuanians, Teutonians
7th - 8th centuries	Beginning of small principalities, Slavic, in the East and Lithuanian in the West 200 yrs
9th - 10th centuries	Overthrow of Lithuanian princes and fortification of Slavic princes in the area 200 yrs
11th - 12th centuries	Constant clashes between Russians and Lithuanians and alternating control of each 200 yrs
1241	Invasion of the Tatars of Battu-Hen and their withdrawal in the same year 1 yr
1291 - 1569	Expulsion of the Russian princes to the East/Founding of the Lithuanian Archduchery/Consecutive Lithuanian government in the area for 278 yrs
1316 - 1341	The Lithuanian Prince Gadmin invites the Jews from various regions to settle in his land 25 yrs
1386 - 1430	Vitold the grandson of Gadmin grants special rights to the Jewish settlers who will develop his country 44 yrs
1495 - 1505	Jewish Deportation decree from Lithuanian by Alexander Yagilontzik/ in 1503 repeal of the decree and return of the Jews 8 yrs
1503	The approximate dare of the founding of the village of Maitshet

[Page 48]

1569 - 1795	Lublin Unified Covenant between Lithuania and Poland, autonomous Lithuania in the area and conseccutive Polish government for a period of 226 yrs
1623 - 1761	Rule of autonomous Committee of Jews of Lithuania 138 yrs
1655 - 1659	Russian invasion and war of the Swedes 5 yrs
1670	The Maitshet community is mentioned for the first time in the Pinkas (ledger) of Lithuania together with Dvorets and Zhetl
1795 - 1915	Final division of Poland and annexation of the area to Russia/Czarist Russian government for 120 yrs
1915 - 1919	German conquest in World War I 3 ½ yrs
1920 - 1939	After the interim Soviet rule - renewed Polish rule for 19 yrs
1939 - 1941	Soviet occupation according to the Ribbentrop - Molotov Agreement 2 yrs
1941 - 1944	Nazi occupation/annihilation of the Jews 3 yrs
1944	Annexation of the area to Soviet Byelorussia

Memories From My Birth Town

By Max Novomisky of Argentina
Translated by Madeline and Max Shiffman
Edited by Jerrold Landau

We hear this name very seldom now, and yet when we remind ourselves of this name, we get a pang in our heart. Maytchet is my birthplace and the place where all Maytcheters throughout the entire world were born. We were raised, and we breathed the good spirit from the old Jewish homes, the fresh air from the local river and the wide areas of cultivated soil. For hundreds of years, the small town of Maytchet was located in the midst of this G-d blessed natural setting. It hosted a traditional Jewish way of life with Torah observant, traditional Jews, as well as honorable, hard working people.

The town's river was called Molczadka. The river flows into the River Nieman, and forms a testimony to the very beginnings of the town. In the ledgers of the Council of the State of Lithuania, Maytchet is mentioned several times in connection with the tax rolls. From this, we can assume that, in the year 1765, there already existed a Jewish settlement. The question remains, who were the first Jewish inhabitants of Maytchet.

Besides the natural uses of the river, such as bathing in the summer and chopping ice in the winter, the Molczadka was used as a site for two mills, one at the very beginning of the river, and the other a few kilometers away. A bridge was built, with a small dam to hold the water in order to create energy to move the stones and rollers in order to grind the flour and press cloth. These two mills were built by a Jew whose name was Meyrim [Boretsky], who came to Maytchet and requested from the town nobleman, Mosziewski, to allow him to utilize the river. At that time, the very young nobleman allowed himself to be convinced, and the mills were constructed. In the one mill, Meyrim placed his older son, Moshe Aaron. Meyrim placed his younger son Itzele in the second mill, where as able to grind and sift flour, as well as to press cloth.

[Page 50]

Yaakov Dvorzecky's Pharmacy

[Page 51]

Thus, it was possible for Maytchet and the surrounding area to eat freshly milled and baked bread. The same nobleman, Mosziewski also allowed the construction of a row of stalls in the market place, from which they sold products of the mill and other goods, for which the Jews paid an annual fee. In addition, a large inn was also built nearby so that the farmers who came to the market could have food and drink.

From the last years I remember the only pharmacist in the village was Jacob Dvorzecky. And I also remember a dry good store owned by Iser Bilas and his family. There was a seltzer factory that sold cold drinks and juices during the hot summer months. One could also purchase ice that was prepared in the winter for the summer. All of the youth of Maytchet would come to the seltzer factory on Sabbaths to drink cold seltzer after eating their cholent. There was no money exchanged on the Sabbath, but notes were prepared in advance with names and charges, which were entered in a ledger. Many of the young people immediately went into the Chassidic shteibl (small synagogue), where they would peel seeds and then vandalize the prayer stands of the wealthy people. Many of the boys and girls would go to the woods, where everything around smelled magical. They would stroll back and forth, thinking of a better world. Unfortunately, very few of these youth had the opportunity to studying in a middle school or a high school, which was the road to intellectual professions. Very few were lucky enough to leave Maytchet and grasp something better. Many of those that did, eventually ended up in America, Argentina and Israel.

The Jewish population of Maytchet throughout that time remained middle class and provincial. They did nothing to conceal their Jewishness, and were hard workers -- they were tailors, shoemakers, tinsmiths, stuffers, furriers, and blacksmiths but most of them were involved in business. They worked hard all week at their meager livelihood, but on the Sabbath, each Jew became a king. Moshe Barishinski would stand in the middle of the market place and announce the advent of the Sabbath by shouting at the top of his voice, two or three times, "Women, it is candle lighting time!" Immediately the row of shops in the market would close, and the Sabbath candles would twinkle in each house. The Sabbath presence would glow over the Maytcheter women's faces. The Jews would enter the synagogue, some to the cold large main synagogue, and some into the Chassidic shteibl. The prominent Jews took their places at the front of the synagogue: Yichael Yitzchak, Yoseph the butcher, Rubichevsky, Leibe Yehoshua's and others. Yoseph Shimon stood in front of the ark and we would sing the "Lechu Naronona," beginning the service of the welcoming of the Sabbath. When they discussed the upcoming festivals, there was much joy with men as well as women. Even the little ones were happy because they did not have to go to cheder. The shtetl became still and they absorbed the heavenly happiness that one could only absorb during the festivals.

[Page 52]

Leibe, son of Yehoshua was a Torah scholar, and also knowledgeable in worldly literature. He could lead the prayer services and also read the Torah. He was an outstanding person with wonderful virtues. He used to frequent the Rabbi's house often and he helped him answer people's questions. He was able to straighten out disagreements people had. He would teach Gemara, Yoreh Deah [a section of the Code of Jewish Law], and Maimonides' Guide for the Perplexed twice a week. At the end of every year, he would celebrate the conclusion of the learning with a festive meal.

Leibe Yehoshua's was a Hassid of the Slonimer Rebbe and he would go to him and participate in the Shabbos meal together with many other Chassidim. Many non-Jews appreciated him and many learned Christians were happy to talk to him about important world questions, because he excelled with his sharp answers. In general he was an outstanding Jew with a very deep religious feeling to G-d as well as being warm and good natured. He passed away at an old age but he did suffer a great deal during the years of the First World War.

Moshe Aaron's Flour Mill

[Page 53]

Hirshke Leibe Yehoshua's was the bright personality of my father. In his early years he was a partner in the large mill. His father-in-law Itsele wanted him to continue to be a mohel. He was appreciated by all because of his swift technique and he was asked to go to the nearby small towns and villages. Understand, he did this for the sake of mitzvah and he did not take any money. Because of the work of the mill we lived a nice life. The house was open to everyone, whoever went to Dvorzec, Zhetl and further towns used to stop off in the mill where they would receive a place to sleep and eat. Just before the First World War the nobleman sold the land to my Uncle Moshe Aaron My father together with his brother-in-law Yitzchak Akivah built a windmill which was a wonder in Maytchet. But to our sorrow the mill did not last long. A very strong wind tore off the wings and the rudder and the windmill ceased to operate.

David Zvi Novimisky (Hershl the mohel)

[Page 54]

In those early years the town was immersed in their small problems of income and very seldom did they have an opportunity to enjoy social and cultural things. I remember one time a cantor came to Maytchet to daven (lead the prayer service). The whole town – men, women, and children -- came to the large, cold synagogue to hear this cantor. They sold tickets to the rich people and any tickets left they gave to those who could not afford to pay for a ticket. They did this at Chanukah, when there was a Purim play, and sometimes even for a theater performance.

The young people were always energetic and they would organize from time to time a speaker or a reading evening. After the Balfour Declaration there arose a national feeling when some of the studying youth would speak about Zionism. I remind myself that in my youth I had a friend by the name Wolf Rabinovitch who used to speak every Sabbath evening in the home of Abramovski about the return to Zion. Wolf and I studied together in the Minsk Technical School where we absorbed the national idea and when we came home for vacation we shared these ideas that we had learned in the big city with the youth of Maytchet.

Maytchet as well as the entire area suffered a great deal during the First World War and as soon as the Polish government took over, the majority of the young generation left Maytchet. Thanks to that they were saved from the horrible events of the Second World War. I left Maytchet in the year 1922. This was for me a colossal change in my life. Young and full of hope to establish a better home for myself, I went to the far-off Argentina. My warm letters describing my new land where people are not hungry and were content, encouraged other young people to leave Maytchet. Thereby a lot of Jewish people were saved, including my family.

[Page 55]

Descendants of Mohel from Maytchet in Argentina

[Page 56]

Right in the beginning when there were many Jews from Maytchet in Argentina, they organized a Maytcheter Landsleit group. From time to time there are meetings when families come together from near and far. Many young people of Maytchet met and married members from other cities and towns. The Lansdleit group organizes receptions for guests who come from America, Africa and Israel. At these receptions they reminisce about their old home -- the various experiences and episodes and mainly the hard life that they and their parents experienced because of the horrible regimes.

The Maytchet Landsleit holds an annual get together at the cemetery in the Tablada district of Buenos Aires, at the monument for the six million martyrs where we recite the Yizkor for our own families who perished at the impure hands of the accursed Nazis and their murderous assistants.

These lines written for the Maytchet Yizkor Book which will serve as a memorial in words for the martyrs, as well as for the future generations, who should read it with pride and learn where they came from.

[Page 57]

My Town Maytchet
(Memories of a Grieving Heart)
By Nahum Margolin
Translated by Esther Mann Snyder

A memorial candle in memory
Of my father R' Yehuda-Yitzhak
And my mother Badana née Yorzkovski,
May G-d avenge them

How grieving and bitter is the heart for all the Jews who were annihilated during the Holocaust that befell so many cities and towns, but much more so does the heart mourn over Maytchet, the town where I was born and grew up together with my brothers and sisters, the second and third generations in Maytchet. I lived the life of the community together with all the Jews in the town and collectively we yearned for the promised land of our forefathers, but they weren't privileged to see its comfort due to the terrible destruction that befell Bet Yisrael (the "House of Israel," the Jews). May these words, carved from a grieving heart, be a worthy remembrance to their pure souls, and a tribute to their holy memory.

The Jews of Maytchet weren't distinguished by great famous persons, or very wealthy men but, on the other hand, it was blessed with honest, good-hearted, hospitable and kindly persons and most importantly Jews loyal to the venerable tradition of our fathers and sages passed on from generation to generation. Who among us doesn't remember the great ideal of hospitality to the poor who would often stop in our town and ask for a place to sleep. For this purpose a committee was established, called The Committee for Hospitality, that was responsible for the hospitality of guests and fulfilled the holy Jewish tradition, "No one should have to sleep outside." Among the last members were, Yosef the teacher Shkolnikovitz, Heikl Izralvitz, and Eliezer Reznik, the butcher. An apartment was allocated for the guests and a special supervisor was appointed to oversee its administration. The last supervisor was R' Nachum Kovenski, who lived nearby. I remember how the members of the committee, with the help of the sextons of the synagogue, arranged meals for the guests in private homes of the Jews of Maytchet whether it was a weekday or Shabbat meal. It never happened that a Jewish guest didn't have a place to eat.

And who doesn't remember how the Jews of Maytchet kindly received the *magidim* (preachers) and *shda"rim* (fundraising emissaries from Eretz Yisrael) who would come to town to give sermons in the Bet Midrash between the prayers *minha* and *maariv*, and after *maariv* would put a *ke'ara* (bowl) near the door and each one that passed through placed a donation. On most of the Shabbats during the year these emissaries and famous preachers visited our town and stayed in private homes or in the hostel of R' Avraham Shmulovitz. On Shabbat afternoons, after the people had their Shabbat nap and the Tehillim group finished saying Psalms, the preacher gave his speech standing near the Holy Ark until it was time for *minha*, the afternoon prayer. The next day several householders went around to collect donations from among the residents for the preacher.

[Page 58]

I remember one interesting event. When I was 13 - 14 years old I studied in the Yeshiva Bet Yosef in Lechowitz and as was the custom in those days I ate at the home of one of the better off residents, R' Leib Rozovski, a bank manager and one of the important personages in town. The daughter of R' Leib married a yeshiva student from Klecak, and after his marriage the groom began to work in the bank. Before each holiday it was common that the former students remained faithful to their yeshivas and went to towns in the area to raise funds for their yeshivas. So it happened that this student came for Shabbat to Maytchet, to give a homily or speech for his yeshiva. He lodged at the hostel of R' Shmulovitz but had his meals in our home. On Shabbat afternoon he gave his sermon and the next day, Sunday, they went to collect donations. That night there was a train to Baranovichi and from there he had to continue to Lechowitz. Because there was no electricity in the streets, I accompanied him to the train station with a torchlight. On the way I asked him a number of questions, one of them asking how much his lodging cost him at R' Avraham's hostel. He answered that R' Avraham didn't charge him for the two nights he spent there and that asked that the cost should be considered his donation to the yeshiva.

The market place
On the right can be seen the hostel of Avraham Shmulovitz

[Page 59]

Also cantors and prayer leaders would come to Maytchet and they led the evening prayers in the Bet Midrash (study and prayer hall) and afterward put out a bowl for donations. Sometimes when a famous cantor or wonder child singer came to town they would charge an entrance fee.

The virtue of hospitality was even more prominent in our town during World War II, during the German invasion of Poland in 1939. As is known the war erupted on September 1, 1939. Immediately a stream of Jewish refugees began; many people who had been uprooted from their homes near the German border moved toward the East. Also many Jews from all the areas of the German invasion flooded to the part that was under Russian control. On their way East many refugees arrived in Maytchet where they found refuge and shelter among the local Jews. No Jew refused to help and all the refugees were welcomed with brotherly love; and there was one destiny for all, resident or stranger.

Yosef Shkolkikovitz (the teacher)

Yeshaya-Aharon Lazovski

Maytchet also excelled in the love of Jews in general and especially the love of Zion. All the Jews of Maytchet who kept the Jewish tradition and prayed three times a day "and our eyes will see the merciful return to Zion" and as upright and honest Jews they believed this with all their hearts but didn't know how to fulfill that wish. At that time the entry to Eretz Yisrael was closed and only very few were able to realize the dream of generations and come to the land of their forefathers to build it and be rebuilt by it. Especially notable were the elders of the town: R' Yeshaya-Aharon Lisovski, and R' Yisral-Zalman Shlovski, z"l. Both of them settled in Jerusalem and I was even privileged to meet with them in Jerusalem in 1941 shortly after I made *aliya* to Eretz Yisrael.

[Page 61]

Most of the Jews of the town were ardent believers in Zionism and *aliya* but lacked the means to fulfill this wish. However, all they could do was take part in activities for Eretz Yisrael by collecting funds for the Keren Kayemet, Keren Hayesod, Keren Eretz Yisrael of the Mizrahi and later for the Settlement Fund for Agudat Yisrael. Since the attitude of the Jews of Maytchet was purely nationalistic no one checked which factions or political parties stood behind these funds; everyone donated to all the funds. Due to this same attitude of pure nationalism all the youth, including religious and traditional, belonged to the local branch of the youth group, *"HaShomer HaZta'ir"* which began operating before the other parties. Later some of the youth joined training groups, to be able possibly to make aliya to Eretz Yisrael. Therefore, among the few from Maytchet who remained after the holocaust, were the members who went through the long track from "HeHalutz" through the training groups until they reached Eretz Yisrael.

[Page 60]

A row of stores

The Jews of Maytchet, who were distant from the large concentration of the Jews of Poland, didn't see the leaders of the Polish Jews except at the times of elections to the Polish parliament or the Zionist congresses, or when the leaders visited for fundraising, etc. Every visit of someone from the big cities was a great event that drew the town out of its daily routine and brought life and interest to Jewish public life; they exhibited a large measure of respect and admiration for the important guests, as is said, "and your eyes shall see your teachers." It was natural that Maytchet, as other small towns far from the large Jewish centers, itself became a center and maintained branches of all the large institutions and organizations.

About the way of life of the Jews in the town and especially the amicable relations between the people and the deep sense of responsibility for others, as in "All the Jews are responsible for each other." A number of interesting facts heard from trustworthy people should be noted. R' Azriel Korn z"l, the uncle of Moshe Korn, lived in America for sixty-three years. In old age, at 84, he made *aliya* in the spring of 1968, to settle there. Unfortunately he wasn't privileged to live long in Israel and on the following Rosh Hashana he passed away, may his memory be a blessing.

In his early days in Israel I sat with him in the home of Moshe Korn and heard many stories about life in Maytchet in the past; here is one story that characterizes all the good virtues of the Jews of Maytchet.

It happened about the year 1902. R' Azriel z"l who was then 17 - 18 returned to Maytchet for the vacation from the Slonim Yeshiva where he learned. A rumor reached the town that in the village of Mickiewicz, 4 kilometers away, some gentiles attacked the few Jews who lived there and their lives were in danger. Immediately, a group of Jews from Maytchet organized and went to the aid of their brethren in trouble. Among them were Azriel's father, R' Yitzhak Korn z"l. He hitched his horse to his wagon and together with a few others they urgently left on the road to the village. Azriel, who was strong and muscular, wanted to join the rescue convoy, but his father prevented him due to his young age. However, young Azriel didn't give up his right to defend Jews in danger, and so he ran all the way to Mickiewicz and arrived before the convoy. When he reached the town he started to fight with the gentile attackers, hitting and beating them until they fell. When his father arrived with the convoy, he came out to them and told them that he already had finished the job and the troublemakers were lying helpless on the ground. There was nothing left for the Jews of Maytchet to do but to put them on the wagons and bring them to the local police.

[Page 62]

Here is another example of feelings of responsibility and devotion on the part of the Jews of Maytchet in a later period. I happened to see a notice about a lecture by Dr. M. Dvorzetski on the subject "Self-defense in the History of the Jews." I went to hear the lecture both because the subject was important to me and because the lecturer was almost a native of our town. The lecture mentioned times, dates and places of Jewish self-defense among which he noted 1917. He said that before the end of the First World War, he happened to visit a small town named Maytchet and saw how the Jews practiced at night in cellars on how to use weapons, to defend the lives of the Jews from the dangers of rioters and murderers who were swarming the country in those days.

I heard from Yehezkel Ravitz another story, this one from recent times, that shows the exemplary devotion of the heads of Maytchet towards the public good. Although all those who lived in Maytchet know Yehezkel Ravitz, yet for the sake of future generations we should describe here some details of the life of this man and his family.

He lived with his extended family in a group of buildings around a courtyard at the edge of the road. In addition to the routine agricultural work, the family also owned a grain/grout mill and a straw and hay cutter. Despite his many private occupations, Ravitz was surely a clear public activist and his hands were full of work in every public institution in town. He was an officer in the fire department, was active in the drama society where his major function was as prompter, was a member of the administrations of relief and economic institutions. In addition, he was a member of the town council, and later he and Shlomo Shnitzki were representatives of the town in the regional community committee in Baranovichi. Therefore it was natural that when the Germans invaded the area and the Judenrat was organized in Maytchet, Hezkel Ravitz was a member.

Yehezkel Ravitz passed through many places on his travels from Maytchet until he reached the United States where he lives today. As all the other refugees he also went through much suffering and travails until he reached a safe haven. In 1964 he came to Israel for a few months to visit his nephew Moshe Ravitz and his family and other Maytchet natives living there. We met with him several times, and spoke with him personally when I asked him the real truth about the activities of the Judenrat in Maytchet after there were rumors and gossip about the integrity of the various Judenrats in various towns. Yehezkel told me that everything was done in complete sureness that all the members of the Judenrat which consisted of local Jews

[Page 63]

and refugees who lived in Maytchet, behaved in good faith and with devotion to every Jew. They didn't save any work or effort and sometimes even endangered themselves to help all the Jews. They all shared only one view and that was to get through as best as possible the time of the occupation and to hope for better times. Full of this awareness they didn't withhold any effort to save Jews and make somewhat easier their difficult life and help them to survive until the terrible time passed. The members of the Judenrat won the complete trust of the Jews of Maytchet who appreciated their devoted work and sacrifice.

Such was the town of Maytchet and such were her Jews, and the heart grieves over the merciless destruction and murder of men, women, old and young. Even during the worst time, the community heads volunteered to perform these activities with their heart and soul, although they were especially in danger. And to the bleeding heart, the head of a person joins in and asks, How did this happen? How were pure and innocent annihilated? How was this abomination done in under the sun, and the heavens didn't come down to earth, and the world wasn't outraged and didn't collapse?!

My heart, my heart goes out to you, Jewish Maytchet with the other holy communities that were lost and are gone. Is there a consolation? Is there any recompense for the pure blood that was spilled?!

R' Azriel Korn

[Page 64]

The Dead Maytchet Lives in Every Heart
By Haya Lubchik
Translated by Roslyn Sherman Greenberg
Edited by Jerrold Landau

Twenty-five years have already passed since our home was destroyed, mother, father, sister and brother were murdered, and still our beloved shtetl lives in our memory. As in a fantasy, we see floating before our eyes the large water mill in the neighborhood called "padlezan" – the green fields with the aromatic pine country-house forest and the rooming houses around the forest.

Thus we see our shtetl on a summery Friday afternoon. In the marketplace stand wagons. Gentiles from the neighboring small villages came to Maytchet. They brought things to sell, one a calf, another eggs and a little fruit, another some grain; and they came to buy what they needed, either goods from the dry goods store, or some shoes from Shinetsky's store, or a hat, a bottle of oil or kerosene. Merchants buy, and storekeepers sell – a small market day.

Market place on a week day

[Page 65]

Standing at the door of the business, waiting for a customer

The aroma of the Sabbath delicacies wafts through the air. Mothers bake challos for the Sabbath, and cook fish. Some cook pike and other cook small fish – the main thing is to prepare for the Sabbath. Children come from school in groups, happy, excited, and joyous, with schoolbags in their hand that had been sewed by their own mothers. Some were coming from cheder and others from the Tarbut School. Tomorrow is the Sabbath morning, where there is no school. The joy is great.

[Page 66]

The sun starts to set in the sky and travels further to the west. Soon comes the loud voice of Moshe, the Shamas, calling the people to synagogue. Business is over. The stores are closed. Shutters are closed and locked, either with two locks, one above and the other below, or with a long iron bar with a lock on the side. Jews go home to prepare for Shabbos (Sabbath). Gentiles travel away from the marketplace.

The sun has already set. Through the glistening windows, veiled with white curtains, twinkle the Shabbos candles in polished brass candlesticks, or in silver candlesticks, perhaps two to a table or three on a table, or perhaps even five. But in every window, through all the panes they twinkle and light the holy Sabbath. Tables are decked with white tablecloths and challahs are covered with various embroidered cloths. The Divine Presence is at rest.

There go the Jews dressed for Shabbos in traditional long coats or jackets. They go to the shul or to the Beit Midrash or the Hassidic shul, but they all go with the same holy spirit in their hearts to welcome the Sabbath.

In the marketplace it is quiet, empty and dark. In the dark, only the white goats roam around. They enjoy the leftovers – a bit of fresh hay, a bit of green grass or vegetables, which the horses left over. Satisfied, they lie down on the gangways or under the roof of the row of stores.

Friday night, after eating and after the songs, the young people of Maytchet go walking in the country-house forest. There one always meets new faces, people from the country houses, who just came to the shtetl. Whoever walks to the train station does this. Some of the youth are from the HaShomer HaTzair (a leftist/socialist Zionist organization). There on the small hill at the home of Sarah the Carpenter woman, the Maytchet youth enjoy themselves. There in a circle they danced a hora by the light of a kerosene lamp and they sang songs of Eretz Yisrael. The resounding voices spread far in the stillness of the night. These are sounds from young hearts that love, dream, and hope that tomorrow will be better and more beautiful than today.

This is the way a poor but beautiful Jewish life was lived for many generations. Mother and father bore the heavy yoke, bearing children and rearing them the same as everyone else, and the young searched in the dark the way to tomorrow. Many centuries the golden Jewish circle endured. And today, in the dead quiet in Maytchet, there is sad desolation in the hearts of the people of Maytchet in the whole world. There are no longer any Jews, burnt up, destroyed, empty and desolate. Our old beloved home is dead, but in our hearts still live the dear Jews of Maytchet. You are with us at all our happy occasions; we call our children by your names, which is a worthy remembrance of you.

[Page 67]

Jews in Great Svorotva and in Other Villages
By Yesha-ayahu Serebrovsky
Translated by Ron Rabinovitch

A small group of Jewish families lived and worked in some of the little villages that surrounded Maytchet. Even though their homes were in these nearby villages, these people were still considered citizens of Maytchet. They would go there for their civil affairs and for the religious activities.

Among these nearby villages were two with the same name, Svorotva. One was called Little Svorotva and the other was called Big Svorotva. What numbers were used to make this distinction is unknown. But there was a farm of a Polish "Paritz" near the village that was called Big Svorotva.

Among the residents of Big Svorotva was Rabbi Elchanan Gershovitch and his family. He was a teacher and a merchant. Shortly before the war he moved to Maytchet and it was here that he was murdered by the Nazis. Also living in the village was a family by the name of Serebrovsky and the head of this family was a wood merchant. At the beginning of the war the wife of Mr. Serebrovsky was murdered by the Nazis but he and his two daughters were able to flee. They were hidden by local Polish citizens, survived the Holocaust and immigrated to Israel after the war.

In the village of Novosyulki lived the family of Israel Yehuda Singalovsky, a successful merchant. The local Polish citizens were jealous of his thriving business and made the lives of him and his family very difficult. The family was forced to leave because of these hostile citizens and moved to the village of Dvorets. It was here they were murdered by the Nazis.

Living in another nearby village by the name of Druzdin was the family of Lifa Zochovitzki; they owned the local grocery store. Early in the war he fled to Maytchet and was murdered there. Only one of his sons survived the war and may have moved to the United States.

[Page 68]

Small Svorotva
by Haya Lubchik
Translated by Martin Small and Roslyn Sherman Greenberg

Small Svorotva—This is what my small village was called, in proximity to a second not much bigger village, which was called Big Svorotva. Small it was, since it numbered 70 houses in all, 5 of them Jewish. It lay a distance of 5 kilometers from Maytchet between some not so big hills and in not too deep a valley, surrounded by large forests and fields and an ebullient happy little stream that emptied into the Molchadka River.

The five Jewish families of the village were longtime inhabitants, that even the order that had driven the Jews out of all the villages, was not binding on the inhabitants whose land was handed down from generation to generation, maybe a lucky thing and maybe not. Who knows?

All five Jewish families diligently worked the land and fulfilled the verse: "With the sweat of your brow, you will eat bread." I remember how my father, may he rest in peace, used to sing this well-known song while he worked, "In the plow lies prosperity..." In regard to prosperity, the story is this: from the material standpoint there was indeed prosperity, while in our house nothing was ever missing and everything was good. But in the realm of spirituality very much was missing. There was not even a minyan of Jews to pray a public prayer. Of course, there was no synagogue. My father constantly complained that he was living a double exile. The whole week, as on the Sabbath, he prayed in the house, but on the holidays and the High Holidays he went to Maytchet to pray. His uppermost dream was to participate in public prayer or to learn a portion of Mishnios between Mincha and Maariv. The problem of teaching the children about their Jewish religion was made more difficult because they had to learn reading and writing as well. A teacher was brought to the village to teach the children.

In order to fill the void of studying Torah and prayer, my father engaged in doing good deeds toward others. When he had the opportunity to do someone a favor, he was extremely happy. A needy person never left his house with empty hands. He used to say, "Whatever I earn is not mine. It all belongs to G-d. I am just a temporary guardian, and with his permission, I give to anyone who is needy." My mother, may she rest in peace, was a real counterpart of his. She worked in the field and the garden, managed the household, and raised the children (we were four sisters). She had many worries and little "naches", but she was always happy with her lot and participated in the good deeds and charity of my father.

[Page 69]

Relations between us and the gentiles were good. They knew that my father Shlomo always had an open ear and an open hand that would help them in their time of need. "You are such a good person," they used to say, "not at all like a Jew." In their twisted outlook, a Jew was a bad person. Thus many, many years passed, and when the tragic day arrived, they showed themselves as real gentiles who returned a bad act for a good one. Without any human emotion, they dipped their murdering hands into the blood of their Jewish neighbors and helpers of many generations, and brought atrocities to the Jews of Svorotva.

That is the tragic way the few Jews from our little village got killed. Their holy names are:

1. Family Hershel-------Channa and her children; Tzippah and her children

2. Golda's Family

3. Channa and her husband and daughter; Sarah and her husband and three little boys.

4. David's Family------- his wife Alta, their daughter Vichne and her husband and little boy

5. Our Lubchik Family------my father Shlomo and mother Bracha; my sister Bluma and two children, my sister Sarahla and Davidel, my sister Minna and her husband Gershon and their three children: Sarahla, Shifrala and Yankela

[Page 70]

In the Village of Yatra
By Esther Malishansky (Lozovsky)
Translated by Ron Rabinovitch

Many Jewish families were living and earning their livelihoods in villages surrounding Maytchet, like a garland surrounding it. For many generations the Jews of the villages worked in agriculture alongside the local gentile farmers. Others were merchants, tradesmen, and agents for selling the agricultural crops and homemade products of the farmers, and bringing in merchandise and urban products to the village. During times of peace, their livelihoods were plentiful, and they maintained good neighborly relationships throughout the generations. During the holidays, they would come to Maytchet to celebrate together with the Jews who lived there. Therefore they viewed themselves as being residents of the city for all matters – as if it was Maytchet and its suburbs.

In the village of Yatra, just 12 kilometers from Maytchet, lived three Jewish families: Yankel and Batya Shmulovits, the Abramovitz family and the Malishansky family. There were also two women who escaped from Novogrudok during the wartime. The relationship between us and the local people was cordial, and we remained there until the first German *aktion* in the Novogrudok ghetto in the winter of 1941. When the policemen from Novogrudok came to look for us, they began making inquiries of our neighbors. One of our neighbors told them to go to another place and then came to warn us of the approaching troubles. After that, the policemen from the village of Potoshipobi came occasionally to bother us, so we were forced to flee, each one in a different direction.

My mother escaped to the forest. My cousins Lyuba and Noach Kowel and I fled to an estate in Yatra and hid in the barn. My father and my brother escaped to the home of a gentile acquaintance three kilometers away. Shmolovits and Abramovitz escaped to Maytchet. After the *aktion* in Novogrudok, we returned to the village and found empty houses that had been ransacked by our good neighbors. We all settled in one house. My mother returned from the forest but she was suffering of frostbitten legs. Dr. Yakobovitch, a refugee physician from Zapolia, came to our house everyday to help Mother's frozen feet, but he was not successful.

Survivors from Yatra told a shocking story of a desecration of holy objects and a strong injury to Jewish sensitivities. The few Jews of the village had a Torah Scroll which they used for reading during services with a *minyan* [prayer quorum]. When the Germans found out about it, they forced the Jews to throw it into a burning oven. When the Germans left the house after perpetrating their evil deed, the Jews put out the fire and were able to rescue several folios. When they asked the Rabbi in Maytchet what to do with them, he said that the rescued pages should be buried in the Maytchet cemetery.

This is what was done. They transferred the folios to Maytchet, conducted a funeral, and buried them in the local cemetery.

[Page 71]

After five months, the policemen came and took all the Jews from the surrounding villages to the Karelits Ghetto.

All of the villagers who were gathered from the nearby villages we were forced to remain in one house. They worked us very hard, filling sacks with potatoes and grain, which were sent to Germany. We were also forced to clean the houses occupied by the German soldiers and the local police. One day, an order was received to move some of the people, especially the villagers, to Novogrudok. We were a group of over one hundred people walking 25 kilometers. When we arrived in Novogrudok at night, they moved us to the prison rather than take us in to the ghetto. It was a night of nightmares. They made us remove all our clothing and then searched our clothes and bodies for gold. In the morning, they moved us to the ghetto and put us in the barn. We were sent to work at cleaning and other tasks in a military base. The Germans wanted to abuse us, so we were sent to the graves of the victims of the first *aktion* to cut some flowers to bring to the cook. After two weeks, they were short of workers in the Dvorzec Ghetto, so we were moved to work in the quarries there.

During this time, the Germans took some Russian prisoners to work in Germany. Some were able to escape to the forest, and this was when the local partisans became active. The Gendarme (police) tried to hunt them down, and they sent Jews in the front line to absorb the gunshots. That is how we became aware of the partisans. One day I went to Yatra to search for food with my mother and my brother Meir, and with the help of a gentile, we managed to bring some to the Dvorzec Ghetto. Before the massacre in Maytchet, the Jews there also supplied food to the Dvorzec Ghetto. About two months after the liquidation of the Jews of Maytchet, my family moved to the Jedon Forest — my father, mother, my brother Meir, and I; Pesha and Freda Abramovitz — his brother Michael Abramovitz had previously joined the partisans.

We were living outside under the sky, and at times worked at homes of nearby gentiles in order to get some food. When winter came, we moved to "Zemlianka". Sometimes the partisans came and killed German soldiers and the number of partisans grew day by day. We were joined by Jews who had escaped from the massacre in Dvorzec. After the exposure of the village in which we worked, all of the gentiles escaped with the Jews to the forest. They burnt down their village for collaborating with the partisans. After some time, the gentiles returned to their ruins, and the Jews remained in the forest.

Partisans of the Belski Otriad were active near Maytchet. When they spread out in the area to gather food, I joined them in active service. The Germans conducted a large search for partisans at the time of Purim, 1943. Out of the group of 27 partisans, only 7 survived. My father was captured, moved to the Novogrudok prison, and was murdered there. The survivors were my mother and my brother, Abraham Kaplan and his son, Tzim Kaplan and Sonia, Pesha Abramovitz.

The seven survivors went out to the Belski Otriad, and met a group of partisans who brought them there. At that time, I was on guard duty, and the commander did not inform me of the arrival of my mother and brother until the end of my shift. We remained in this Otriad until the liberation. From there we went to Novogrudek, where we were liberated in an official fashion and military style, with the granting partisan certificates.

[Page 72]

The Tragic End
By Haya Lubchik
Translated by Jerrold Landau

(A dirge)

It is deathly still in Maytchet, the townsfolk are happy[1],
The impetuous, stubborn Jews are no more,
Those who stumbled here
With their own Sabbath and their own festivals.
Although we lived in peace with the Jews,
We always thought about pogroms in our dreams,
And when the golden times came,
Why did you remain so indifferent from afar?!...

Come, townsfolk brethren with the German hordes,
Let us murder our former friends,
For what is there better in life
Than Jewish blood and Jewish pogroms?
Fruitlessly did the innocent, holy victims
Wait for a feeling of mercy from the world.
They lived to see the awaited hour -
First they murdered, then they also inherited!.,[2]

There they go, the multitude whom have been sentenced to death,
With pale faces and languid lips.
The fear of death peering forth from their eyes,
Hunched in pain, bowed in tribulations.
Mothers nestle their children in terror,
Fathers are wrapped in their *tallises*,

[Page 73]

Going on their final way, a multitude of the living dead.
They are escorting their own funeral procession!...

They are quiet, no sobbing is heard,
Only with "*Shema Yisrael...* and "*Echad...*[3] on their lips,
A shot... And they fall, some dead, some still moving -- Oh earth, do not
cover their blood!...
It is dark, even the stones are writhing,
"*Yisgadal...*[4] rustles the old, fluttering trees,
"*Kel Male Rachamim...*[5] drips down from the silent heavens,
From this funeral, nobody returns!...

Impoverished Jewish Maytchet, what has become of you,
You have been destroyed; your years have been cut off,

A deserted market, without shops, stalls,
The row of shops with their ripped open cargo,
The study hall, synagogue, and Hassidic *shtibel*,
Stand in shame, dazed with pain -
There is no longer any people to worship there, to supplicate,
No longer anybody to step over the doorstep.

The Tarbut School is enveloped in deep fury
Like a mother who has lost all her children.
With pain, it looks upon the large synagogue courtyard,
Where children used to dance and run merrily.
And upon the wide Maytchet fields
Let there be no more dew or rain,
Let only wild thorns and stones
Adorn your accursed paths!...

[Page 74]

However, a comfort glows in the hearts -
Only the bodies have been annihilated, not the soul...
The dear souls are eternally bound with us,
On joyous occasions, on festivals, they are with us,
We name our children with their names.

We, the surviving Jews of Maytchet

Will always be your burning eternal flame.
With pain, pride, and holy fire We will carry our beloved dear ones in our
hearts,
To go through the nights with the worries
And brighten the coming morning,
A memorial of words, and a well of comfort
For your holy, tormented souls!...

Translator's footnotes

1. The word '*miestshanes*' could mean townsfolk or estate owners. It is also likely a play on the name Maytchet, as the sound is similar. The meaning here is seemingly a derogatory term for Maytchet townsfolk.
2. See I Kings 21:19.
3. The first two words and final word of the verse "Hear Oh Israel, the L-rd is our G-d, the L-rd is one,... an integral part of the daily prayers, as well as the final words on the lips of a Jew at death.
4. The first word of the *Kaddish* prayer.
5. The first words of the Jewish prayer for the dead, recited at funerals, *Yizkor* services and other occasions.

[Page 75]

My Village and the Memories of my Birthplace
by Sara Biribis
Prepared by Myrna Siegel
Edited by Jerrold Landau

Maytchet, my village and the memories of my birthplace – the Jewish population was eradicated from the face of the earth by the hands of the sick inhumane nation, may their names and memory be erased *"Yemach Sheman"* from history. After being separated from it for 35 years, memories of my distant childhood come to my mind, awaking in my heart strong emotions and yearnings for the near as well as distant past – the warm house, the extended family and all that goes with it.

Maytchet was a famous city in Poland. It had mountaintops blessed with scenery and was a vacation city. A forest stretched out in a huge area near the city. Fresh air, the smell of pines and the forest, and fruit of all kinds attracted many thousands of summer visitors who came for their health from many Polish cities. Some came for pleasure and enjoyment, and others on doctor's orders for recuperation. Near the forest was the large inn of the Margolin family, which was booming with business from many people day and night. Not far from there flowed a wide river for whose clear water came thousands of people, including the local residents, to recuperate and relieve their fatigue.

Moshe-Aharon Boretsky the miller and his grandchildren

[Page 76]

The river had a close connection with the largest flourmill in the area, which belonged to our family, Boretsky. My grandfather of blessed memory, Moshe Aaron Boretsky, came from a very large and respectable family. The sons and daughters and their families lived together in close proximity in Maytchet. From there some immigrated to the States and many other branches were set up in cities and other small towns – most of them in Slonim. The closest ones were concentrated around the mill and frequently gathered. They even bought a large boat for the grandchildren to go boating together on the river.

On the right of the mill was a narrow street that ran between rows of high trees. This was wonderful expansive scenery that was enchanting to behold. On moon-filled nights the young people would gather and, accompanied by mandolins, would row on the water until the early hours of the morning. And they were in constant fear of the unexpected surprise from the gentile boys. Right next to the mill was a very large stone bench which, during the day, provided for a short rest and a breath of fresh air. And at night for undisturbed romance with the exception of a few cases when a Polish police officer on duty would approach them out of curiosity or more correctly jealousy to look and see who was there. But when you identified yourself by name, there was no unpleasantness.

I remember the train station from the days of the horse and buggy. And later, the bus line to Baronovichi that Yichael Shoptick managed. Afterwards it was renovated and turned into the famous train station which contributed greatly to the quality of life. At dusk despite the relatively far distance, many would walk out to accompany and to receive passengers and some just for an enjoyable walk.

On Shabbos, after resting from eating cholent [the Sabbath midday meal], when the weather was good the Jews went out en masse in the direction of the forest for a stroll. With the approach of *shalosh sudos* [the third Sabbath meal] the street emptied of its walkers with the exception of couples in love who found it difficult to part.

Our *Tarbut* school was one of the most important institutions in the city. It had in it most of the children in the town and it gave them knowledge and education. It produced many alumni groups, some of which continued on in Vilna. The respected memory of our teacher and principal, Abraham Shukhovitzsky, who was one of the school founders, was concerned about all of its needs, with whom he invested all of his energies. Among the graduates of the school were the best youth in town.

Maytchet was a Zionistic town. The blue box [*Keren Kyemet* collection boxes] was found in most homes. Achieving *aliyah* was one of the highest goals to the youth movements. A branch of *HaShomer Hamtzair* absorbed many of the youth and set up a teacher's club and had many activities. During summer vacations in the surrounding village areas they set up regional summer camps in which hundreds of *Shomrim* participated. This also contributed much to the enjoyment and way of life. The results were *Hachshara* and *Aliyah*. But only a few merited this and most died in the Holocaust. Discord, the Jewish disease, affected Maytchet where many political parties were set up. Independently they set up their own dramatic club that was worthy of praise, with a group of outstanding actors.

I lived a couple of kilometers away from the main part of town or more correctly to the entrance to it. All the Polish institutions were near our house and we lived house to house with our gentile neighbors. On the surface the relationship between the neighbors were good, but nevertheless you felt at times the anti-Semitism that oozed from them. From the days of my childhood I remember an unusual occurrence when one of the farmers married off his daughter and invited his Jewish neighbors to the party. He made available a large room, bought new dishes, brought in a Jewish cook and set up Kosher tables based on laws of Kashruth and Yiddishkite to the joy of the surrounding Jews and the host family.

[Page 77]

In the center of town all the stores were centralized on both sides of the road. That was the local center of trade. Dvorzecky's Pharmacy, Karawczok's Barbershop, Idel's grocery store, Sirshka's accessory and notions store, (*zawad*) of the Balinsky family, Romanovsky family grocery store, etc. etc. I remember them all by name and by sight; they all remain in front of my eyes. The large and fancy synagogue whose ground floor was designated for the men and the upper one for women. On Shabbot and holidays especially, they streamed there from the oldest to the youngest. I loved to stand next to my Aunt Dvorah and to quickly repeat seven times the prayer "*Lamenatzeach Livnei Korach*"[1]. It was a special experience to come and greet our parents after the fast and tell of the day's events on Yom Kippur. The "treifniks" were well known when, after following them into the forest, they were discovered with full plates of food.

A special memory was the Purim experience with *Shaluch manos* [Purim gifts]. We went from house to house with a frightened heart that someone would take an orange off the plate.

Pesach with all of its glories and its laws, remain indelibly etched in my memory. Turning the house inside out, the painting, making the dishes kosher for Passover, baking the matzo, the traditional beets in a wooden barrel. The wine, known as "Mead," then washing of the Pesach dishes.

The Jews rented land from the non-Jews for the purpose of planting potatoes, which they filled their cellars with a full year's stock. They also stored in their cellars barrels filled with pickles and sauerkraut. They made homemade wines (Vishniak) and different drugs that were prepared in case they would be needed in sickness and emergency. Every house had a cow, chickens for eggs and ducks for fat with *gribines* for Chanukah latkes, Pesach, etc. For the most part we existed on homegrown produce, baking of bread, meat, all milk and egg products, vegetables, fruits, etc. My mother, of blessed memory, with her own capable hands, planted the seeds for all the vegetables and took care of the house needs, and these were not small quantities for a family of eight people and also for the winter storage. In our garden the first tomato appeared, which many had never seen and did not know what to do with. The name of Maytchet also became famous for it's sour milk that you would cut with a knife, which acquired the nickname of "Maitchata Sour Milk."

Every Wednesday was market day. Farmers from near and far would come in mass, some on foot, some in vehicles, with baskets overflowing with agricultural produce. They had sour cream and cheese, vegetables and fruits of all kinds, eggs, chickens, cows and horses for sale. For these items they would barter or purchase what they needed – mostly vodka, which was poured into their stomachs like water. Towards evening, as the last farmers left the town, and the echo of their singing reached out to a distance, we knew that the time had come to gather the children into the house, to close the windows and the doors, and to be prepared for the results of their wild drinking. They would knock on the Jewish doors and scream, "Open the door – we are going to slay and massacre the Jews." When we didn't answer they would go back and fall drunk on the side of the road. The last night of the market was always a source of fear for us because we lived on the main road between the town and the villages.

Translator's footnote
1. Psalm 49, recited seven times in succession on the days of Rosh Hashanah prior to the shofar blowing.

[Page 78]

Jewry, Virtuous and with Difficulties
by Chaim Kravetz
Translated by Jerrold Landau

About the former life in Maytchet and the region.

I myself was born in Navahrudak, but I spent my childhood years in Maytchet. I arrived in Maytchet in 1917, and I remember a great deal about life in Maytchet. I had family there: Zelig Leizerovich the tailor was my father's brother; Chana, the wife of Mordechai Alperstein the tailor was my father's sister; and Michael Shlomovitz's wife Sonia was his cousin. Thus, our family was well represented in Maytchet. I therefore come to take part in the Yizkor Book and write about my early childhood years, which form a part of Maytchet Jewish life.

In our house, we heard word that the need in Maytchet was not as great as in Navahrudak. I therefore spoke to two neighboring children and set out with them by foot to Maytchet to seek help from our relatives there. We were ten children in the family, so when I set out, they would certainly not take notice, and that is indeed what happened. One of the children had a pair of old shoes, the other was wearing one shoe and one boot, and I was s barefoot. Thus did we set out on our way in the bitter cold.

Along the way, we stopped in the village houses to beg for food from the farmers. Some of them would give, and others threw us out, until we came to a village in which a Jew lived. The woman of the house took pity on us, gave us a supper of dairy soup, and put us to sleep on the ground with a bit of straw. Early the next morning, they woke us up and told us to go to a nearby village, Svorotva, where there were Jews who would give us something to eat. We set out on our way. My bare feet stuck to the frozen ground. I was going along and crying from the cold and hunger, until we arrived in Svorotva. There, we went into the house of a Jew named Reb Shlomo, who told us to sit by the table and gave us bread and butter, and an egg for each of us - a food that I had never seen before at home. After we ate, Reb Shlomo hitched up a horse and drove us to Maytchet. He left me off near Uncle Zelig's house, and my two friends went to their relatives. Reb Shlomo took me into my uncle's house, introduced me as his brother's son, and left. They treated me well with food and drink. In the meantime, Aunt Chana came, and when Uncle Zelig told her who I was, she took me to herself, for she did not have any children and wanted to have me as a child.

[Page 79]

Uncle *Mordecha*i was very stingy, and demanded that my aunt send me back home, but my aunt treated me as a mother would and delayed sending me back day by day, until a change took place. Uncle would go to worship with a rabbi who was paralyzed. He would help him get dressed, and he held him in great esteem. When he went there on the Sabbath, my uncle took me along to the rabbi, and I carried his *tallis* and *siddur*. The rabbi asked who I was, and my uncle explained everything to him. The rabbi then blessed him and wished him that this merit should help him have children of his own. The rabbi's blessing worked very well with my uncle, and when we came home from the services, he told my aunt that I can remain there, and that they would enroll me in a *cheder*.

On Sunday morning, my aunt took me to the *cheder* of Hirshe-Yudel the teacher, who lived in the synagogue courtyard, and I became a student among the other students. They made me an outfit and a pair of shoes, but they only let me wear them on the Sabbath. With regard to eating, the entire family participated. On Sunday and Monday I ate with Uncle Zelig, on Tuesday and Wednesday with cousin Sonia, and the other days with Aunt Chana, who used to also concern herself with me on the other days. She would go to Shmaya in the restaurant and get me pieces of herring, hard pieces of bread, and other leftovers, thanks to which I was sated with the participation of three families in providing food for one young child. Then, when I began to get accustomed to life and would eat to satiety, my parents came to take me home, but I strongly refused and remained in Maytchet.

[Page 80]

Maytchet youth enjoying a sleigh ride during the winter

I settled in well in Maytchet, and already had friends with whom I played *kneplech* [buttons]. And there was no shortage of buttons at my uncle the tailor, until he realized that I was carrying away all the buttons to play with. After that, when he threatened to send me home, I found another source for buttons. I would go to the *Beis Midrash* and when everyone was standing to recite *Shmone Esrei*, I took a small knife and cut the buttons off the coats - one day in the large *Beis Midrash*, the next day in the Hassidic *Shtibel*, etc. One Sabbath

[Page 81]

I won all the buttons from my friends. A big fight broke out during the time of joy, and I ripped my Sabbath pants. I was afraid to go home until my aunt got involved. The pants were fixed, but the era of playing *kneplech* was over. However, G-d does not let one down, and I found another game - taking loops of belts and running with them through Podkriszer Street to the hill, and going up the hill, or in the winter riding on the sleds that traveled in the town, as well as well as other pranks.

Mosheke the peddler was my uncle's brother-in-law. He had a weakness for serving as a cantor, and was always called to the prayer leader's podium. However, as usual, there was no shortage of pranksters. Someone would start rabblerousing, and another would stand by the podium. This caused great resentment, and after the services, there was a strong exchange of words. A celebration took place in the Beis Midrash on Sabbaths afternoons, where Yankel would be reciting Psalms. He would recite chapter after chapter by heart, and everyone would repeat after him with a sad but heavenly melody, that warmed the soul, especially in the winter. On the other hand, the youth would go to the "Zavad" to drink seltzer water and lemonade. I also went and saw that they drank, paid no money, but rather left some kind of little notes. I also wanted to take without money, but they did not give me, and my childish mind did not understand why.

There were also many other things that I did not understand at that time, and evoked great wonder. When my uncle would bring a hen from the village, he would not slaughter it during the day. Rather when everyone was already asleep they would wake me up and send me to David the *Shochet* to slaughter the hen. When my aunt went to the butcher shop to get meat for the Sabbath, she would purchase only half of what she needed, for she was afraid of an "evil eye." She would send me for the other half at a different butcher shop. It was the style in Maytchet that every Jew had a pair of goats, and Henoch would go to the hill with all the goats to graze them. It was a wonder to me how he became obligated to go with the entire town's goats. I recall with wonder the miller's daughter who had two long, thick braids, and when she went on the street, it seemed that there was more braid than girl. I am no longer a child and I have traveled the world, but I have never seen such beautiful braids as I had seen on the miller's daughter in Maytchet.

[Page 82]

Maytchet was a small town, but a true Jewish town which I will never forget. The Jews of Maytchet would go with their *tallis* bags to the synagogue to worship and study both on weekdays and on Sabbaths. Even in the evenings, there was never a shortage of a *minyan* [prayer quorum. Thanks to Maytchet, where I spent the years of my youth and was educated, I grew up as a Jew who could take the pen into the hand. Maytchet Jews did not live in wealth, but rather in great unity with each other both in joyous times and times of suffering. When there was a wedding in town, the joy could be felt everywhere. When they led the young couple to the *chupa* [wedding canopy], the musicians would go in front, and the entire town, young and old, would follow from behind. In my life, I have witnessed various weddings, but I only recall a true, joyous Jewish wedding from Maytchet.

The heart is full of sorrow and can find no comfort when one recalls that the virtuous and ideal Jews of Maytchet were so tragically murdered at the hands of the fake, murderous neighbors. They should be well recompensed for their worth, and the martyrs should be granted a true rectification.

Chapter 3
Torah and Chassidism
[Pages 85-92]

The *Gaon* [Genius] R' Shlomo Polachek
The *Ilui* [Prodigy] of Maytchet
by Benzion H. Ayalon
Translated by Esther Mann Snyder

The Gaon R' Shlomo Polachek, known by the honorable title, "The *Ilui* (prodigy) of Maytchet (now Molchadz)", was born on the fourth day of Hanukah 1877 in the small remote village of Sanitzinitsh near the town of Maytchet. His father, R' Yosef, was a religious person yet a simple country man who worked by leasing the post office and the public bath of the village. His mother was a modest, G-d fearing woman who died at a young age. When he reached school age, R' Yosef brought him to nearby Maytchet to study in a *heder* (Hebrew schoolroom) where after a while he was called the *Ilui* of Maytchet, and was praised throughout the world for his learning.

From his early years the child Shlomo'le was discovered to be a wonder child. Immediately after he entered the *heder* of the Maytchet teacher (*melamed*) to learn to read Hebrew, he was advanced to the class already studying *Humash* (Bible), and shortly after he was studying *Gemara* (Talmud) and he was only five years old! When he could learn no more from the teachers in town his father brought him to the Slonim Yeshiva. The Head of the Yeshiva was at that time R' Hersh from Maytchet, a great scholar, who insisted on accepting only talented youth. At first, he didn't accept Shlomo but after the child showed excellence in Talmud proficiency in an exam of several tractates, the Rabbi agreed to accept him and placed him in the highest class. Soon, even the level of studies in Slonim wasn't challenging enough for his talent, and he transferred to Novahrudak to his learned uncle, R' Mordechai Movshovitz. Shlomo'le learned everything very quickly and with amazing ease, grasped the Talmudic debates and the sharp-witted casuistry (*pilpul*). He knew how to answer cleverly every question and often expressed ideas similar to those of the great early commentators like the Tosfot, the Maharash"a and others, without having previously learned them. His brilliant mind was receptive to Torah learning and his prodigious memory helped him acquire an extraordinary expertise. It was sufficient for him to glance at a certain tractate in order to remember the issue by heart and to understand the depth of the question extremely quickly.

The next and most important station of the child prodigy was the *Etz Haim Yeshiva* in Volozhyn, which was famed as a place where one could learn with great rabbis and scholars, headed by the *Natzi"v* - Rabbi Naftali Tzvi Yehuda (R' Hersh Leib) Berlin. His acceptance at the Yeshiva at the age of twelve became known near and far. After he passed the interview with the head of the Yeshiva, where he answered all the questions and apparent difficulties with extraordinary sharpness, he was placed in a Torah knowledge "duel" against the Rabbi and Gaon R' Haim, the husband of the granddaughter of the *Natzi"v*. R' Haim who was later known as R' Haim from Brisk, the Genius of the generation, attacked the young Shlomo'le with all his strength and the youth returned the attack with greater vigor until R' Haim stopped and said with much wonder: The Prodigy from Maytchet!... and he carried this name and memory with much modesty until his last day...

[Page 86]

The Iluy studied in the Eitz Chaim Yeshiva for only three years (5649-5652 / 1889-1892), for it was closed by order of Count Balinow for failing to accede to the government edict to teach secular studies. Throughout these three years, Shlomo was the center of interest in the Yeshiva and outside of it. He especially won over the heart of Reb Chaim, whose soul was bound to his soul and who loved him and honored him as one of the great ones.

The Genius R' Shlomo Polachek
- the Prodigy from Maytchet

Shlomo's *bar-mitzva* was celebrated within the Yeshiva, and this was initiated by the *Natzi"v* himself. In his special relation to the young prodigy he saw special importance in the life of the Yeshiva and decided to diverge from the usual tradition at Volozhyn. The Natzi"v invited to his home the important people of the town and held a *Mitzva* dinner in the boy's honor.

[Page 87]

The Gaon R' Haim invited the *bar mitzvah* boy to give a *piplul* (casuistic discussion) before those assembled and even suggested to him which citations in the Talmud should be used as a basis for his speech. However, the great spirit and knowledge of Shlomo wouldn't be limited by this framework and he took off and as if floated through many, varied issues which came to his brilliant mind. It was like orchestra players obeying their conductor.

When he completed his first homiletic interpretation to the joy and cheers of the assembled, R' Haim said with fatherly affection: "My son, you didn't say what I thought, however, what you did say was better than what I thought." Shlomo's reaction was typical of his modest and humble character - he became very emotional that he had the courage to give a sermon before great Torah scholars until he began to cry out loud. R' Haim then said, "My son, don't be sad, also I cried at my *bar-mitzva*."

The Rabbanit Haya Rivka Polachek

In 1892, when the Volozhyn Yeshiva closed, the Maytchet Prodigy moved to the *Knesset Bet Yisrael* in Slobodka. The head of the Yeshiva, R' Natan Tzvi Finkel, who always praised his Yeshiva as one that was full of talented men and geniuses, was extremely happy with the arrival of the "Maytchetnik". However, the way of teaching ethics and morals (*musar*) in Slobodka wasn't to R' Shlomo's liking. In this Yeshiva they didn't espouse *musar* that derived from books of repentance but rather that which came from the heart and was expressed by good virtues and deeds, feeling of love for the other, etc. Since R' Shlomo's heart was drawn to his rabbi R' Haim, he left the Yeshiva and went to Brisk to live near his rabbi and to benefit from his inspiration. He set his place of learning in the *Bet Midrash Mishmar Kloiz* until the time came for him to take the military examination. After he finished his military obligation in Russia, he traveled to Vilna and joined the "kibbutz" of the Gaon R' Haim-Ozer Grodzinski.

[Page 88]

After Volozhyn, he made several stops along the way, however, Vilna was the most important stage in his life and in the formation of his character as the *Ilui* of Maytchet. Vilna, as is known, was a city where the *Haskala* (Enlightenment) movement built a base and greatly influenced its surroundings, and even the "wall" of the kibbutz of R' Haim-Ozer was breached by its influence. Most of the students of the kibbutz, who had already learned much Talmud and Rabbinic decisors (*poskim*) and wanted to start teaching, began secretly reading secular books, perhaps to become more prepared to lead their future students. However, the *Ilui* of Maytchet did this openly and set times both for Torah and secular reading, and was among those who looked but were not hurt by the secular knowledge. When the world of science was opened to him, he read many books in Hebrew and foreign languages. He read the Hebrew and foreign language newspapers and took a great interest in the sciences especially mathematics whose sharpness was appropriate to his brilliant mind. A famous professor in Vilna wrote about the Gaon of Maytchet that the world of science lost a great professor of mathematics. His interests were wide and he even played chess where he also displayed his genius and famous players invited him to play against them.

After he was released from military service and his brilliance became well-known, marriageable daughters of rich men and of acclaimed rabbis were suggested to him. However, in accord with his natural modesty, he found his future wife in the village of Ivanitz close to Minsk. He was twenty-three years old when he married Haya-Rivka Rubinchik, the daughter of a wealthy but simple and honest man and it was a good match. However, he hadn't yet found a place to settle down and still had some searching to do. After the wedding, he tried his hand in commerce, but he wasn't meant for it; after he lost his money in a short time, he returned to Vilna to study Torah in seclusion; after a time he was chosen to teach in the Yeshiva in Lida.

At that time the *Ilui* met with R' Aharon Rabinovitz, the son-in-law of R' Yitzchak-Yaakov Reines, the Rabbi of the town of Lida. Rav Reines, who was one of the founders of the *Mizrachi* movement, established a Yeshiva in Lida with a nationalist tendency and planned to merge Torah with general education, according to the method of "Torah with an occupation" which was widespread in Germany; the *Ilui* was comfortable with this orientation. R' Aharon was the one who had discovered the young Shlomo'le and brought him to Volozhyn and now he rediscovered him and brought him to Lida. R' Shlomo was twenty-eight when he was invited by Rav Reines to come and serve as the head teacher of the Yeshiva and supervisor of the Talmudic section.

The Lida Yeshiva was not just another stop along the way but opened a new period in his life. Until now he was known as a modest, quiet scholar, sitting alone in a corner and diligently studying on his own. From now on, his main attribute and quality as a teacher, educator and Torah lecturer took form. Even more so, he was "revealed," also to himself, to be an extraordinary Talmud lecturer who drew crowds of students from all the yeshivas in Russia to listen to his method of study, his explanations and new interpretations. For nine years he taught and lectured as thousands of students thirstily drank in his words, whose basis was in his brilliant logic.

[Page 89]

He never wrote down his new interpretations, however his students did so for many years covering 1500 lessons (*shiurim*), which they used to reread and study. They gave one copy of each lesson to their rabbi/teacher in the hopes that one day, perhaps when he was older, he would edit and publish them. However, due to his moving from one place to another and the travails incurred, which were caused by the difficult times during the first World War and the terrors of the revolution and the following pogroms, the precious treasure was lost. However, copies of some lectures were saved by his students and after he added his latest ideas which he innovated in the Yitzhak-Elchanan Yeshiva in America, the book was published in 1947 in New York; it was entitled "New Interpretations of the *Ilui* from Maytchet." The project was initiated and edited by his son-in-law, R' Yehuda-Leib Goldberg.

Rabbi Reines, the founder of the Yeshiva in Lida, passed away on 14 Elul 1915, as if the heavens darkened so he wouldn't see the destruction. With the dangers of war and its terrors threatening to break down the Yeshiva walls, five days after his passing, the heads of the Yeshiva and about 110 students decided to leave, besides many students who dispersed each to his own destination. Among them were the *Ilui*, Rabbi R' Avraham the son of Rabbi Reines, R' Eliyahu-Ber the supervisor (*mashgiah*) and others together with their families. After the many travails they suffered on the roads disrupted by corps of soldiers, the Lida Yeshiva was invited to settle in Yelisbetgrad in southern Russia. Charitable persons from near and far promised to donate to the material sustenance of the Yeshiva.

The Yeshiva was active for six years in Yelisbetgrad, and the *Ilui* from Maytchet was the moving spirit. He had administered the Yeshiva in Lida for 9 years in comfort and with sufficient means. But here, the Yeshiva was in a situation of poverty and distress, while outside there was fighting and at home fear of hunger and need. Thus hundreds of students sat and learned Torah and wisdom in an isolated island in the midst of a sea of blood, fire and smoke. They hoped that the situation would soon pass and they would be able to return to the good old days. But, the war was over in the rest of the world and only in Russia was there fighting between the revolutionaries and anti-revolutionaries, who killed many and especially took out their anger on innocent, helpless Jews. And they reached Yelisbetgrad. There were bloody battles between the "red" and the "white" camps that fought each other for control of the government. They erupted into the town and did much damage; there were terrible rumors of gangs of rioters that destroyed many communities across Russia and slaughtered thousands of Jews in strange and cruel ways. The robber Grigori and his gang outdid other gangs and were thirsty for Jewish blood; they attacked Yelisbetgrad and carried out a great slaughter. For three days the murderers rampaged like wild animals and cruelly killed men, women and children. About four thousand Jews were murdered. With great courage the *Ilui* withstood the tumult of the war and even spread a spirit of calm and safety in the Yeshiva, but the cries of his tortured and dying brothers wounded his heart so deeply that he never fully recuperated until his last day on earth.

Due to the terrible conditions, the Yeshiva had to shut its doors and the students dispersed. Soon after the signing of a peace treaty between Russia and Poland, R' Shlomo acquired a visa to leave the horrible country, and after many weeks of difficult travel and illnesses the family crossed the border to Poland and arrived in Bialystok, where he taught in the *Tachkimoni* Yeshiva for a year. Then he received a telegram from America inviting him to teach at Yeshiva Yitzhak-Elchanan in New York. He delayed his answer for a while due to personal doubts as to whether he should continue his travels and go overseas or to stay where he was, since he was tired of moving around.

[Page 90]

On the advice of his friends and admirers he decided to travel to America alone to observe the situation and conditions of Jewish life there and whether they would be appropriate for him and his family. After just a short stay he made the fateful decision to accept the position of head of the Yeshiva [Rosh Yeshiva] at Yeshiva Yitzhak Elchanan to the joy of all his friends and those who had heard of him. He immediately sent documents to bring his family to America. They experienced difficulties in travel at that time of troubles and dangers to the Jews and finally reached the safe shores. New York was a large Jewish center where R' Shlomo would be able to administer the

Yeshiva and the students in a calm atmosphere and would be surrounded by a respectful attitude and boundless admiration.

Street sign in Jerusalem. *Ha'lluy* **Street, named after R' Shlomo Polachek from Maytchet**

The *Ilui* became involved in local activities. He was an active member of *Mizrachi* and devoted to the idea of a renaissance of the Jewish people in its holy land. He was also a member of the Rabbinical Union of the United States and Canada and learned thoroughly the state of affairs of American Judaism and its complexities. He worked devotedly for the *Ezrat Torah* fund that gave financial support to rabbis and heads of yeshivas in Europe. He had two more grand plans that he wished to accomplish. One was to visit Eretz Yisrael and see with his own eyes the holy land that was being rebuilt from its desolation. The second was to arrange and publish the Torah interpretations of his admired rabbi, the Gaon R' Haim of Brisk. Unfortunately he became very weak and wasn't able to complete these plans. He served six more years teaching Torah at the Yeshiva, but the terrors and horrors he witnessed in Europe seemed to have entered his blood and filled his mind with suffering thus leading to his early death after a short illness of two weeks. He was only 50 years old.

[Page 91]

He passed away on 21 *Tamuz* 1928 while still murmuring his last words of Torah on his death bed. His wife passed away in New York on 5 Elul 1950.

If the *Ilui* of Maytchet wasn't privileged to go physically to Eretz Yisrael, his heart's desire, then he went spiritually. The City of Jerusalem, with the initiative of Rabbi Shaar Yashuv Cohen, Deputy Mayor, decided to memorialize his amazing person by naming a street after him, "*Hallui* Street, R' Shlomo Polachek", in the Kiryat Moshe neighborhood, near streets named after Rabbi Reines and other great Torah scholars. In an impressive ceremony that was held on 21 Tamuz 1968 on the 40th anniversary of his passing many participated including his family, city dignitaries, government ministers, past students, many rabbis and yeshiva students and the Chief Rabbi, all of whom had heard of the *Ilui* of Maytchet as an incredible legend from past days.

Even with the passing of the delicate soul, his story didn't end. His great spirit didn't die. His spiritual legacy that he gave to the people of Israel, his profound Torah interpretations - were held deep in the hearts of his students and his many admirers across the world. The memorial sign granted him in Jerusalem the holy city, was a monument to his blessed memory that will remain in our spirits forever.

Finally, it should be mentioned that the two sons of the *Ilui*, both graduates of Yeshiva Isaac Elchanan, are prominent men of science in the areas that the *Ilui* was drawn to in his youth. One is Dr. Aharon Polachek[1] - a famous mathematician, expert in the field of electronics and associated with the Atomic energy Commission of the government of the United States. The second one is Dr. Abraham Polachek - Head of the Faculty of Medical Studies in the Veterans Hospital in Brooklyn[2].

The *Ilui*'s daughters are: Risha[3] who is married to Jacob Pines and lives in New York. Libby is married to Rabbi Israel Mowshowitz who serves as the rabbi in the Hillcrest Jewish Center in New York and is the Chairman of the Trustees of the synagogue at Kennedy Airport. Sarah and her husband Rabbi Yehuda-Leib Goldberg live in Israel. Rabbi Goldberg is associated with the Chief Rabbinate in Haifa. Two grandsons of the *Ilui*, the brothers Shlomo and Moshe Goldberg are engineers who also live in Israel.

Jerrold Landau's footnotes
1. The grandson of the Iluy, Shlomo Polachek, indicates that Aharon was known in English as Harry Polachek
2. Abraham's son, Shlomo Polachek, indicates that the original is slightly incorrect, and his father's position should be noted as: Chief of Medicine at the Veterans Administration Hospital in Brooklyn. Abraham made *aliya* after retiring. Two of his children made *aliya* as well
3. Shlomo Polachek notes that Risha was known as Rose in the United States

[Pages 92-96]

The Rabbis of Maytchet and its Scholars A

1. Rabbi R' Yosef Mordkovski, ztz"l - RY"M
by Rabbi Aharon Surasky
Translated by Esther Mann Snyder

The Gaon [genius] and Hasid Rebbe Yosef-Mordechai Mordkovski ztz"l, or as he was called, "R' Yashe the Maytcheter", a native of the town of Maytchet was among the finest Hasidim in Slonim, and served as the first head of the Yeshiva *Torat Hesed* of the Slonim Hasidim in the city of Baranovich; he taught very many students. His wonderful personality and character, a figure carved totally from dignity and wells of spiritual purity filled his whole body.

Rebbe Yashe was a great genius in Torah, pure hearted and devout. His brilliance shone brightly from his face. He was rich in knowledge and ideas, open hearted and great minded, reaching heights as one of the ancient Hasidim - and everything was marked with nobility. In the small Slonim synagogue (*shtibel*) in Baranovichi the Hasidim used to tell stories about his radiance. From every movement and simple word of R' Yashe, even from every blink of his eye, people would be influenced and felt that here stands a man of wonders who encompasses in his soul all the world and he walks slowly all his life as someone who is walking in the highest sphere called "nobility" [in Kabbala]. Superior genius emanated from his sharp casuistry (*pilpul*) on a difficult passage, and he reached the level of nobility when he fervently prayed the *Nishmat kol hai* prayer. His nobility was adorned with a certain grace, a quality of holiness, natural modesty and all other virtues that noted spiritual refinement.

A Noble Soul

This is how he looked: short stature and slim, bent over and withdrawn, his face adorned with a short yellowish beard and his eyes always shining and sparkling. R' Yashe carried all through his life burdens of torments and suffering. He suffered for many years with incurable tuberculosis of the bones. When they poured iodine on his open wounds for disinfection and cure, his screams made one's hair stand on end. He never had any respite from his tribulations, not calm, nor peace, yet despite this, joy and happiness was always on his face.

[Page 93]

R' Yashe was also dignified in his clothes, his walk and his eating. His character was the living embodiment of the *Shulhan Aruch* (Code of Jewish Law). He was always calm, moderate and never ran nor skipped. If this was the case on weekdays, on Shabbat he walked as is written, "He walked with small steps" as is appropriate for the "escort" of the Shabbat Queen. Even on a winter Shabbat, when the road was full of deep puddles and the rain came down in torrents, he didn't, G-d forbid, walk any faster. The dignity of the Shabbat engulfed him with a glow not of this world. Also in his ways of eating he behaved with dignity. Once it happened that he hadn't eaten for a long while and the hunger bothered him, yet when they brought him a loaf of bread, he didn't have a knife with which to cut a slice. R' Yashe relinquished the bread and continued to be hungry. The dignity won out over his hunger...

His originality was enchanting. His attitude to every matter was according to his own criteria, with concepts he created himself, the deed of a one of a kind genius. He distanced himself from this world and all its useless materialism; he was much higher than such crassness. He couldn't understand, literally, why a person would need furniture in his home. Once, R' Shmuel'ke sent him from Slonim to Minsk, to live there for a time, so he could influence the Hasidim in the local *shtibel* and arouse them and reawaken their faith. The community gave him a spacious apartment to live in, furnished beautifully and adorned with expensive drapes. R' Yashe was not used to such things. The wealth, exaggerated comfort and all the material accessories troubled his soul. How could he consent to live in such a place? He invited several of the important Hasidim to sit with him and they sang melodies of devoutness for a few hours and spoke words of faith until R' Yashe felt that air in the apartment was somewhat purified.

R' Yashe was always full of devotion, without being distracted, full of restrained fire. His young students viewed him as an ancient Jew, a *Zadik*, a righteous person who grew up in the cave of R' Shimon Bar-Yohai. Since the time he went out into the world and saw people busy with the routine tasks of life, his heart became full of wonder, "They receive the life of the world, yet they deal with life of the hour!"

R' Yashe was a good model also in giving charity. He never had a personal income and all his life he was supported "straight from the hands of the Holy One." When someone slipped a loaf of bread into his home, he would, first, estimate its value and put aside *maaser ksafim* (giving a tenth of income to charity). Once, his friends collected 200 zloty to enable him to travel to the summer resort of Otbotzk for a cure for his pneumonia. As soon as he received the money he put aside *maaser* (10%), 20 zloty for charity.

[Page 94]

He had all the virtues of the Rabbis; all the specialness of a noble soul, those called by the Sages "Princes of men," adorned him. His great Rabbi, the *Admor*, author of the *Divrei Shmuel*, spoke of him thus, "R' Yashe is a gaon in Hasidism as he is a gaon in Torah!" Also the great Rabbi Rebbe Mordechai-Haim of Slonim, when he returned to Eretz Yisrael after visiting the author of the *Divrei Shmuel*, about 70 years ago, spoke about his special meeting with R' Yashe from Maytchet, saying with emphasis," I never imagined that in Lithuania there are such good Jews..."

A Masterly Pedagogue

Rebbe Yashe excelled in teaching Torah and was a superior educator. He was considered the molder of the character of the new generation of Baranovichi Hasidim, who grew to glory after the First World War.

The days then were chaotic. The Slonim community that had developed there for generations had now reached a condition nearing disintegration. The violence of the war that depressed everything, caused a number of precious and enthusiastic Jews to forget that they were Hasidim, that it was incumbent on them to be connected to the Rebbe. The time was that of the changeover of *Admor*im due to the passing of the *Admor* Rebbe Shmuel'ke, ztz"l, and they should be behaving as Hasidim. Against the backdrop of spiritual neglect in Baranovichi, R' Yashe appeared as the savior from Maytchet, who moved there with his family. He returned the crown to its former glory as he spoke to each person, with strong faith and kindness, his whole intention was to restore the destroyed altar of G-d. R' Yashe instilled a new spirit in the Hasidim. And they, enthusiastically hastened to the *sofer* (scribe) to buy new *tefillin* (phylacteries), to get a new *talit katan* (four-cornered, fringed ritual garment); the more devoted among them bought extra, new large *talitot* (prayer shawls) in order to have made from them larger *talits* according to the *mehadrin* (meticulous observance) size. Those concerned with cleanliness started again to dip in the *mikve* (ritual bath) for extra purity for the morning prayer. Old and young, they all were influenced by R' Yashe, and began to travel to Rebbe Avraham, who lived at that time in Bialystok, until he finally agreed to their wish and moved his court and Bet Midrash to Slonim.

(* About this splendid generation see a wonderful description in the collection, *Siyum HaTkufah* (End of a Period), appendix to the book *Zichron Kadosh* (Holy Memory), in memory of the *Admor* Rebbe Shlomo from Baranovichi, published by Yeshiva *Bet Avraham*, Jerusalem. At the end of the booklet there is a list of the Slonim Hasidim in Maytchet who perished in the Holocaust).

At the request of his rabbi, the Admor of Slonim, R' Yashe founded in Baranovichi the Yeshiva *Torat Hesed*, a place of Torah and education for the young Hasidim. There was a previous attempt to establish this Yeshiva before the World War, by the *Admor* Rebbe Shmuel'ke and the Gaon Rebbe Zev-Meir Sheinberg, the rabbi of Baranovichi. However, the troubles and pogroms erupted and both these great rabbis died. Now, it was decided to implement this holy idea. R' Yashe was appointed head of the Yeshiva and taught Torah to many. He shared with his students the treasures of his rich spirit with generosity and an open heart. According to his best students, listening to his lectures was a real spiritual joy. R' Yashe would share with them the pangs of learning, bringing the hard work of his new innovations, learn with them the Talmud with great thoroughness, as if this was the first time he tried to understand and learn the Talmud. After he covered a section with them in a simple fashion, he started to look for the hidden complex issue. When it was found, he attempted together with his students to find a reasonable explanation for the difficulties that had arisen. At the end of the class, that lasted 5 - 6 hours every day, the issue studied became very clear and illuminating.

[Page 95]

R' Yashe meant everything to his students: a genius, a righteous man, a hasid, modest and the highest virtue - the noblest character. Every step he took, every breath expressed dignity and refinement. The worst reprimand he was able to give to a student who was talking with his friend about matters not related to the Torah, demonstrates his character: "Why aren't you afraid of committing such a serious sin as 'And you spoke about them and not worthless words! '"

The Virtue of Trust

Two "findings" happened to R' Yashe without his looking for them, and he told about these things himself. One - on the day that he was to perform the commandment of *Pidyon HaBen* (redeeming the firstborn) of his son R' Noah, he didn't have any money but his trust was great. He went out to the street and by chance saw a shiny coin sparkling in the light; it was worth five *sela*.

The second, happened before a holiday; he wanted to visit the Admor but he didn't have the money for a train ticket. R' Yashe wasn't worried because he always said, "Jerusalem is surrounded by mountains." If a man must travel to his Rebbe, which is almost like making a pilgrimage to Jerusalem, the mountains will block his way, that is there are obstacles and he must overcome them. He didn't even consider cancelling his plans which were in his eyes an unbreakable rule. He would say, "What do I care about the roar of lions, first I must take a bag of bones (from the Yiddish), and pointed to his body and bring it to the court of the Rebbe. All the rest doesn't matter."

Then he sat and thought - What shall I do? I can't travel by train because I have no money, but in order to go by train my legs have to take me to the station and to the platform and that I can do by myself. Immediately, he packed his bag and left the house. On his way to the platform, he found a silver coin on the street that was enough to pay for the train ticket and he traveled to the Rebbe...

[Page 96]

R' Yashe passed away at a young age after much suffering and torments. This was at the end of the month of Tishrei, 1931. Two wallets were found in his room. One - where he would put "money for Eretz Yisrael"; and the second - contained 12 zloty that he had been saving up for almost a year to buy a beautiful *etrog* for *Succot*.

No descendants of R' Yashe survived; all his family perished in the Holocaust. He didn't leave after him any written studies in Torah. But a few of his best students from Yeshiva *Torat Hesed* remained alive and his spiritual legacy lived on in their hearts. One of them was the Rav R' Nahum-Zev Barzovski z"l who came to Eretz Yisrael in 1935 and later served as the Rabbi of Slonim Hasidim in Bnai Brak until he passed away in 1969. R' Yashe had a wonderful dynamic personality, he was a symbol of nobility - his students reflected the image of their Rav. Another one was his younger brother, the rabbi R' Shalom-Noah Barzovski, the founder and head of the famous Yeshiva of the Slonim Hasidim in Jerusalem, *Bet Avraham*. He is today one of the geniuses of the generation, a wonderfully talented educator, one of the recognized leaders of Torah Judaism and a prominent personality in the Rabbical Council of *Agudat Yisrael*. Additional students of R' Yashe live in various places in Israel and abroad, almost all of them excelling in lofty idealism and occupy important educational positions. These include Rabbi Moshe Chichik, the principal of the *Ohel Yaakov* school in Tel Aviv and others, many who actively fulfill the Torah of life they learned from their much admired rabbi and teacher.

May his memory be a blessing.

[Page 97]

2. Rabbi R' Noah Mordkovski z"l - A Man of Maytchet

Translated by Esther Mann Snyder

Rabbi R' Noah Mordkovski z"l, born in Maytchet (Molchadz), was the son of R' Yashe from Maytchet, who served as the head of the yeshiva *Torat Hesed* (see more about it above) and who lived for many years in a lonely hut near the train station *Mitzkovitz* - which was 4 kilometers from the city. Those who knew the father and the son used to declare the truth of the saying "As was the father so was the son. " R' Noah was a calm and patient person and a noble soul, excelling in good qualities, and as if a scarf of gentleness was wrapped around his character. He also was an excellent scholar, among the elite of the students in Yeshiva *Torat Hesed* and also a diligent Hasid who worked hard until he could be considered a high level student. He was liked and loved by his teachers, was friendly with his peers and later on - by his own students.

After his marriage he moved to the city of Lodz, the Manchester of Poland without the noise and commotion of a large industrial city. Here he was appointed a head teacher in a yeshiva for youth that was established by the *Habad* Hasidim in that city. He succeeded very well in education and won the affection of his pupils, being considered an exemplary figure. Also in the *shtibel* (small synagogue) of the Slonim Hasidim he was an admired and accepted person. The young Hasidim followed him as if captivated.

The Nazi Holocaust destroyed what was dearest to him, his home and his children. On the day of the *bar-mitzva* of his eldest child the murderers, may their names be erased, took him and his three younger brothers and slaughtered them. R' Noah himself experienced the horrors of the Holocaust and remained alive but his wounded soul never recuperated, the cries of his lost children constantly pierced his heart and kidneys. At war's end he found his way to Czekia to a displaced persons camp, where he taught Torah out of real devotion. He became ill with fatal tuberculosis and from day to day his condition worsened but he didn't cease teaching the surviving youngsters. He received an invitation from Jerusalem, Yeshiva *Bet Avraham* of the Slonim Hasidim, to come and teach the youth and have a positive spiritual influence but before he managed to respond he passed away.

His younger brother, R' Aharon Isser Mordkovski, z"l, a dear, modest and pleasant Jew was among a group of Jews who were taken out of Maytchet by the Germans after the general killings and led to a forced work camp in Kadelichova, near Baranovichi. He died there in G-d's name after a short time.

May G-d avenge his blood.

[Page 98]

3. HRH"H R' Yisrael Zalman Shlovski ztz"l
Translated by Esther Mann Snyder

A magnificent figure of a devout Hasid, a superior Hasid, such was the patriarchic personality of R' Yisrael-Zalman son of R' Avraham Halevi ztz"l Shlovski, from Maytchet (Molchadz). When I was a young child I met him, when he lived in Jerusalem, after he had lived a long time and passed the age of eighty (*gil hagvurot*). I was always drawn to him. I liked to look at his radiant face, his long beard white as snow and his goodly eyes like windows of his soul that shown through. I coveted his fervent prayer that was full of yearning and soulful pleading when he led the prayers like a sinning son before his father in heaven. I had a special pleasure when I sat next to him in the Bet Midrash (study hall) and listened to his pleasant voice as he learned Torah so deeply that he forgot about everything else. He would sit studying for many hours without a break, without moving his eyes from the volume before him, not even for a moment. I also stood next to his bed during the last minutes of his life, on the Sabbath evening, *Parshat " P'kudei"* of the year 1948, in his simple home in the neighborhood of *Bet Yisrael*. His eyes were glazed and on his face was spread an expression not of this world.

The Hasidim in the *shtibel* used to call him "one of the remnants of the Great Knesset". My curiosity led to investigate his history. In my naivete I though that the old R' Yisrael Zalman was from that time … as if that's the way he looked when he was born. After a time I realized that like all people he went through many stages in his life, from the crib to the grave, but he had what the Hasidim and others said on the festival of *Simhat Bet Hashoeva*, "Happy we are if our youth didn't shame our old age." From his early days his eyes were full of good heartedness, simplicity, innocence and compassion. Even as a child he had a natural tendency to pour out his soul during his prayers, even then he was especially G-d fearing, and even during his lively adolescence he gave all his devotion to learning Torah. The Torah was his delight. R' Yisrael-Zalman loved the Torah with a limitless love. He also loved every Jewish soul as he considered every Jew as a "living Torah."

Childhood learning

R' Yisrael-Zalman Shlovski was born in Maytchet (Molchadz) in about the year 1863. His father, R' Avraham Halevi, instilled in him the essential seeds of a pure Jewish education and cultivated in him the desire to ponder and study the Torah. But his father died at a young age, before his son Yisrael-Zalman reached the age of ten. He followed the funeral to the cemetery while crying bitterly and saying loudly, "Who will teach me Torah, who will hire for me a rabbi and teacher."

[Page 99]

His mother, now widowed, had almost no means. Good neighbors, merciful Jews began to take care of their needs. The diligent orphan was sent to school. When he turned thirteen and became a *bar mitzvah* he went to study in a Yeshiva in a nearby town and did very well. In addition to his diligence, the boy Yisrael-Zalman excelled in virtues and good manners, was punctilious in performing all the *mitzvot* (commandments) and fervently said his prayers from memory.

Rabbanit Zlata   **R' Yisrael-Zalman Shlovski**

The Gates of Hasidism

Despite his young age the neighbors spoke very highly of him, as was done in those days and also from the goodwill of friends who viewed themselves obligated to care for the orphan and in this way to help him recuperate over the great loss to the family. They suggested to him as a bride one of the girls of Maytchet, Zlata... whose parents lived in the same lane as his mother who was a widow. He accepted the suggestion and they became engaged to be married. However, the bride to be noted that maybe it was too early since the future groom was only fifteen years old. He hadn't yet studied enough Talmud and Rabbinic decisors (*poskim*), "there was great doubt whether conditions of life would allow him to continue his studies," she said. It was then decided that he would go to learn for another period in the famous Yeshiva in Slonim and rise in his levels of Torah.

Here in Slonim, occurred the biggest turning point in his life. He grew closer to Hasidism. His father wasn't connected to Hasidism and its rabbis. Even he himself wasn't acquainted with and didn't know their way of life. In Slonim there lived a (*Zadik*) righteous man, Rebbe Avrahamele Veinberg, a Torah genius (author of the books, *Hesed leAvraham, Yesod HaAvoda, Be'er Avraham,* and others). He had been the head of the local Yeshiva and after the death of his rabbi the *Admor* (Head Rabbi and Teacher) Rebbe Moshe from Kobrin, the Hasidim appointed him in his place. This righteous man established a new dynasty, which is the dynasty of the *Admor*s in Slonim for generations to come. His *Bet Midrash* (study hall) became the center and magnet for hundreds of Hasidim from near and far; the Slonim group grew and spread from year to year and the city became a metropolis of Hasidism in Lithuania. For some time, the young Yisrael-Zalman had a secret ambition to get to know the *Zadik* and his ways. One day, while he was sitting and learning in the study hall together with his study partner of the same age, Yisrael-Zalman suggested that they both get up and go together to see the "Table" (*tish*, in Yiddish) as the Rebbe would hold such "Tables" also during the week and give Torah lectures to all those in attendance. He had to work hard to persuade his friend to join him. The boys were captivated by the Rebbe's study hall, where the Rebbe sat at the head of a table and gave a flowery, fiery speech about the Torah and musar (ethics and morals). They were extremely excited and moved from the first moment they became Hasidim and stayed with the Rebbe.

[Page 100]

When R' Yisrael-Zalman returned to Maytchet for his wedding, everyone noticed that he had become a different man, and pointed to him and whispered in amazement, "a new person has arrived in our town! " He joined the Hasidim in Maytchet who prayed in a special *shtibel* (small synagogue) and would travel often to the Rebbe who lived in Slonim. He became integrated into the life of the Hasidim and became like one of them, a born Hasid. However, R' Yisrael-Zalman didn't go too far. He stood with his feet on the ground, taking part in this world, finding work and livelihood from producing candles. The man was great because of his natural simplicity, his innocence, openness, and his graceful speech. The great *Admor* displayed much affection to this fine young Torah student and this was noticed by the sharp eyes of the veteran Hasidim.

Serves in Sanctity

When the *Admor* Rebbe Avraham ztz"l went to the heavenly Yeshiva, on 11 Heshvan 1884, his grandson Rebbe Shmuel, son of Rebbe Michel-Aharon ztz"l, followed him as the head of the community, which he led for 32 consecutive years. The name and fame of the new Rebbe grew and grew from day to day as one of the heads of the Diaspora. He was prominent as an extraordinary personality, a holy man and apart from this world, roaming in higher worlds and yet well integrated into the lives of his followers and trying to improve the general conditions of the people, as a "ladder standing on the ground and his head reaching the heavens." The new Rebbe viewed R' Yisrael-Zalman as someone who was worthy to fulfill the role of "serving in sanctity" [attending the Rebbe's needs]. The Hasidim who asked about this found many hints, and some mentioned the story of the *Zadik* Rebbe Mendele from Riminov, among the heads of Hasidism in Galicia, who chose as an attendant for himself Rebbe Tzvi Hirsh. When asked what did the *Zadik* see in this man, he answered, "Isn't it written in the Bible, 'He who walks in the path of innocence and in awe of G-d, he shall serve me'"...

[Page 101]

The purity of the soul of Yisrael-Zalman was now revealed in all its glory. When he heard of the Rebbe's intention, he went to him and apologized submissively, "I am very worried, I fear that from such closeness to the Rebbe my mind won't be clear and my Hasidism will be impaired, like the gabbaim (men who stand on either side of pulpit where Torah is read)... " However, R' Shmuel, who knew very well his character and understood his worry, calmed him and said, "I guarantee you, Yisrael-Zalman, you will not be hurt by this. "

And indeed, Yisrael-Zalman was not harmed by his new role. For many years he served the Rebbe with awe and reverence, as a servant towards his master. He became a member of the household and very close to him, he decided who and when someone could meet with the Rebbe and he managed the "court. " Nevertheless, whenever he had to stand before the Rebbe face to face, his heart beat strongly - he was considered one of those who can enter without asking permission. He prepared himself with reverence whenever he entered the holy room, inspected his clothes with care, straightened his beard and sidelocks (payot in Yiddish), retied his sash and knocked with awe on the door.

From now on, he divided his time between Maytchet and Slonim. He spent months with the Rebbe or traveling with him. He knew how to manage all things with wisdom, faithfulness and devotion.

On Sabbaths and Holydays he conducted the activities at the Rebbe's "table" when the Hasidic community was invited. He served him the foods and at the same time also took care of the guests who had come from other places, read out the names of the people who had contributed and also mentioned the names of the sick and oppressed who needed help. In addition, he listened attentively to the words of the *Admor*. The day after Sabbath or a holyday, R' Yisrael-Zalman wrote down the Rebbe's words, and the Rebbe checked everything that was written. Once he wasn't accurate enough due to all his tasks and the Rebbe called him and said, "You deserve a flogging. " R' Yisrael-Zalman was very shocked until one Friday when going to the mikvah (ritual bath) the rebbe took a small branch and pretended to whip him on his shoulders. R' Yisrael-Zalman was relieved as if he had been spared a terrible punishment.

The notes of R' Yisrael-Zalman later on served as the main basis for the collection of teachings of the *Admor* Rebbe Shmuel ztz"l, which were published in a book by *Yeshivat Bet Avraham* (Jerusalem, 1969) more than fifty years after his death (*Divrei*

Shmuel). In the preface to the book (p.29) it is written that "most of the book was based on the notes from the words of the Rebbe, by the holy attendant R' Yisrael-Zalman Halevi Shlovski, z"l. Many thanks to R' Eliyahu-Benyamin Tanenhoiz (Kuziel), the grandson of R' Yisrael-Zalman, who while in Europe after the terrible Holocaust, as a remnant of the annihilation, went to Maytchet where his grandfather had lived and searched for and found the notes on the roof of the house where they were well preserved, and gave them to us." The episode of finding the notes was publicized in more detail in the newspaper *HaModia* (Issue 3063, 14 Elul, 1960).

[Page 102]

R' Yisrael-Zalman's belief in the sages has no equivalent in this world. Until his last day he used to tell wonderful things about the great *Admor*, deeds that have witnesses. Here is one story: Once a fire broke out in the home of R' Yisrael-Zalman in Maytchet; the room where he made candles was totally destroyed. All the machines and devices went up in flames - his livelihood was gone. He traveled to the Rebbe to tell of his woe. The *Admor* asked for details about how the candles were made and he told him the particulars. The Rebbe told him, "Listen, G-d gives his blessing that your workshop will produce twice as much. Don't give up, go and build a new room and you will do very well. " R' Yisrael-Zalman said at the end of the story that there is nothing to add, what the Rebbe said came true. The righteous man decrees and G-d fulfills.

Lover of All Jews and Judaism

The highest of his noble virtues was his love of Israel - Jews and Judaism. R' Yisrael-Zalman fulfilled the saying, "Love your fellow man as yourself" in its simple and deep meaning, in a manner so natural and so touching, that a simple pen cannot describe the place that each and every Jew found in his heart.

We remember the words of the Head of the Yeshiva *Bet Avraham* in Jerusalem, the Gaon Rebbe Shalom Noah Brazovski, in the introduction to his book, *Divrei Shmuel*, mentioned above (page 25).

"...And it's worthy to mention here the faithful escort who accompanied the *Admor* in all his travels, this is, of course, the servant of holiness the famous teacher and rabbi R' Yisrael-Zalman Halevi Shlovski z"l". Our Rebbe spoke about him thus: R' Yisrael-Zalman was the best of attendants, of whom it can be said, that if he was great in the position of a faithful shepherd as he was - in his virtues of nobility and goodness - then he was the most appropriate one to be the attendant to the faithful shepherd [the Rebbe himself]. The RY"Z loved every Jew even a small child, as if it was his son and brother, and thus became among the Hasidim of Slonim a symbol of loving his fellow man. He was happy in the happiness of others and sad in the sadness of another as if it was his own sorrow. Here is a small detail, but very enlightening, that tells much about the position of attendant to the faithful shepherd. At the funeral of our Rabbi which was held in Warsaw in the midst of the First World war, when no one could enter or leave and the Jews were forbidden to take part in the funeral, what did R' Yisrael-Zalman do? He walked after the coffin the whole long way from the house of the Hasidim of Warsaw to the cemetery. The whole way he said out loud before him all the names of the Jews from tens of *shtibels* all of whom he knew from memory, the men, women and children. Such was the faithfulness and devotion of the attendant of the faithful shepherd.

Hasidism - the cluster of his life

After the war, R' Yisrael-Zalman was devoted to the young son of the Rebbe, the *Admor* Rebbe Avraham from Bialystok-Baranovichi (author of the book *Bet Avraham* on the Torah) who followed his father in the holy service. He was considered, of course, very distinguished by the Hasidic community, young and old alike surrounded him with waves of admiration. The new Rabbi felt respect and honor for R' Yisrael-Zalman but he himself didn't change and remained a devout Hasid, submissive and self-deprecating before the great *Admor*. When the Rabbi passed away suddenly, on 1 Iyar 1933, R' Yisrael-Zalman courageously held the community together unified around the young successor, the *Admor*, Rebbe Shlomo-David-Yehoshua, the only son of the author of the *Bet Avraham*, whom he cared for very much.

[Page 103]

R' Yisrael-Zalman rose to spiritual heights in his relationship with the young *Admor*. When the young Rebbe, only twenty years old, was "crowned," the Hasid who had known his grandfather (author of *Yesod HaAvoda*) treated the young *Admor* as his respected rabbi in every way. But not only that: in 1936 R' Yisrael-Zalman and his wife Zlata moved to Eretz Yisrael. After only a few years, the terrible Nazi violence occurred. In this Holocaust more than 50 of his descendants perished - sons and daughters, sons-in-law and daughters-in-law, grandchildren and great grandchildren. Only one of them survived, R' Eliyahu Tanenhoiz, today in Jerusalem. And yet when the news arrived R' Yisrael-Zalman accepted it as the will of heaven and didn't complain or cry until... his grandson told him that the *Admor* Rebbe Shlomo-David-Yehoshua was killed by the Nazis. At that moment his heart was torn and he moaned bitterly, "Oy to me, also the Rebbe is gone! Also in the following days he couldn't be consoled, saying that the murder of the holy Rebbe wounded his heart even more that the personal tragedy of the murder of so many of his descendants!"

The rest of his life he spent in the apartment in Jerusalem that was given for his use by the generous R' Yosef Weinberg, a Slonim hasid, near the home of the Rabbi, the

Righteous one, Rebbe Mordechai-Haim Slonim, ztz"l, head of his community in Eretz Yisrael. Close to his home stood the *shtibel* of the Slonim Hasidim in Jerusalem and R' Yisrael-Zalman became the moving spirit among them. It is interesting to note for several reasons the following letter that R' Yisrael-Zalman sent to the Slonim Hasidim in Eretz Yisrael and abroad about two years before his death.

"To my dear beloved brothers who are in my heart wherever they may live, may they be blessed and enjoy goodness forever."

"I thank G-d for his great benevolence, who let me live and reach old age to live with my people and brothers in Jerusalem, the holy city that should be rebuilt, and enjoy the sight of the excellent young men learning Torah, full of faith and Hasidism, blessed by G-d while we sit in our Yeshiva *Bet Avraham* in Jerusalem. And our rabbi RY"A who worked hard to establish here the cornerstone to Torah and prayer and love of our fellow men in the city of Zion."

"In this bitter time, when my heart is broken and torn to pieces from all that happened to our people, that was taken from us all the holy and dear to us in the diaspora and only a few remained, I don't have anything to console me and revive my painful and wounded soul but only the sound of learning Torah that emerges and rises to me from the wonderful young men of our holy Yeshiva. Dear men who are full of the awe of G-d, who were able to be a model in the time of our Rabbi *Yesod HaAvoda* that I was privileged to be in his protection."

[Page 104]

"The sound of the Torah rises to me in my home day and night from the wonderful young men in the Yeshiva and that is my only comfort since I was hurt by the hand of G-d. I remained one of a few from all my precious family and my brothers and friends, may G-d have mercy on us to save us and take us soon to a great light."

"I turn to you my dear ones to maintain with all your strength this holy Yeshiva that guards the holiness that will not be extinguished and watch over the holy community of precious youth who shall continue in the path of faith that was passed on to us generation by generation."

"By this virtue, the living G-d commanded us to save our remnant and to give blessings of life and peace and good to all the helpers of our Yeshiva. And our eyes should see that G-d will return to his people, Yaakov will be joyful and Israel will be glad."

Your friend and one who loves you from his heart and soul
Yisrael-Zalman Halevi Shlovski

In due course

One night at the end of the month of Adar I, 1948, R' Yisrael-Zalman saw in a dream the *Admor* Rebbe Shmuel ztz"l from Slonim who called out to him, "Yisrael-Zalman, come to me!" With very much worry he told his friends about the dream. Indeed, after only a few days R' Yisrael-Zalman was called to the heavens. Old and "full of days" R' Yisrael-Zalman was gathered to his Rebbe in the heavenly Yeshiva, and "there serves him". His soul left in purity at midnight on Sabbath eve, 2 Adar II, 1948, at the age of 85.

The days were days of war after the declaration of the establishment of the State of Israel. The road to the Mt. of Olives, which was the traditional burial place, was totally closed. Therefore, they buried him, after the Sabbath, in a temporary cemetery of Agudat Yisrael on Shmuel HaNavi Street, in northern Jerusalem. A large crowd followed him despite the heavy rains and regardless of the sound of gunshots heard during the funeral. They buried him on condition that when the road to Mt. Olives opened they would bring him to a permanent burial there. After 21 years passed, and following the liberation of the Old City of Jerusalem in the Six Day War, it was accomplished by his only grandson R' Eliyahu Tanenhoiz. In the month of Adar 1968, the Slonim Hasidim in Jerusalem assembled - including young men who had never met R' Yisrael-Zalman and had only heard about him - to accompany the pride of the group to his last resting place. He was buried in the Prophets Section at the heights of Mt. of Olives which overlooks the place where the holy Temple stood, on Mt. Moriah.

His beloved wife, Zlata, may she rest in peace, passed in Jerusalem on 27 Nissan 1954 at the age of 82 and was buried in the cemetery of Har Hamenuhot.

[Page 105]

4. Rabbi R' Shalom z"l - Head of the Rabbinical Court in Maytchet
Translated by Esther Mann Snyder

He was one of the great Hasidism, who visited frequently the elder Hasid Rebbe Mordechai Malkovitz ztz"l (died in 1810), an early *Admor* (Head Rabbi and teacher) in Lithuania. In the pamphlet Ma'ase Avot, appendix to the book *Tovat Avot* (a collection of Biblical discourses of the *Admor*s from Lakhovitz-Kobrin-Slonim, third edition, Jerusalem, 1970) appears this story:

Our Teacher (*Maran*) S"K from Slonim heard from Our Holy Rabbi and Teacher Rebbe Nahum Shub z"l this story from the early days when Rebbe Shalom z"l still was a rabbi in Maytchet and Rebbe Nahum z"l was a *shohet and bodek* (ritual slaughter and inspector) and both were very poor. One day one of the Hasidim went to Lakhovitz before Shabbat and when he bade farewell to R' Shalom he asked him to please mention him to the Rabbi S"K and say in his name, "What is the purpose of his leaving me such a poor man that I don't even have a piece of bread to eat?" The hasid did as he was asked and when he returned to Maytchet he told R"S the words of the Our Teacher (Maran), "Tell R' Shalom, that I thought that when he became old he would request from me high levels and illuminations in the Torah and prayers, and yet at the end he asks for food."

Later, after the second Shabbat, R"S visited Our Rabbi and the whole time he was with him he didn't mention anything. When he was about to leave, the S"K said to him, R' Shalom, Do you believe that a real Jew is able to know the root of the soul of a man of Israel in all his reincarnations?; one who already passed to the root of the soul of the first man, Adam, and in all the reincarnations that he will still have to experience until the coming of the Messiah. And R"S answered, I believe. Again he asked, do you have anything else to ask? And R"S answered, I have nothing more to ask. And then his heart was calm. Later, Our Rabbi z"l arranged for him to be appointed to the Rabbinate in Vilyeyka, and told the people of the town that they must supply all his needs. That is that he should have chicken or meat for lunch every day and there should be people at his holy table every day of the week, and he should be comfortable.

[Page 106]

5. Rabbi R' Yaakov-Sender Grinberg (May G-d revenge his blood), The Last Rabbi of Maytchet
Translated by Esther Mann Snyder

Rabbi R' Yaakov-Sender Grinberg was the last of the rabbis in Maytchet, and he perished in the Nazi Holocaust, dying a hero's death (as will be told), and was one of the best young rabbis among the Lithuanian (Lita) Jews in Poland. He was a great scholar, brilliantly talented, with a broad vision and horizons, a wonderful speaker and active in public matters. From his youth he stood out as a perfect personality and he was known in the world of rabbis and Yeshivas.

Rabbi R' Yaakov-Sender Grinberg

He was a scion of a family of geniuses and Hasidim. His father, R' Avraham Grinberg z"l from Slonim was the son of the Our Teacher (Maran) from Drobin, one of the respected members of the *Gur* Hasidim in Poland, who was a devout follower of the great *Admor* Rebbe Yehuda-Leib Alter z"l, author of the book *Sfat Emet*. The rabbi from Drobin decided at one point to leave his community and move to Slonim. This was after he received the approval of his Rabbi who conditioned the move that his child would study with the same teacher with whom studied the sons of the *Admor* Rebbe Shmuel'ke from Slonim. Thus R' Avraham Grinberg studied with the same teacher as the young son of the Rebbe, who was later known as R' Avraham'le, the *Admor* (Head Rabbi) of future Hasidim, known also by the name of his book, *Bet Avraham*. When R' Avraham grew up he married Miriam-Gittel, the highly intelligent daughter of the Hasid R' Moshe Mintz z"l, who was associated with the father of the Slonim dynasty, the *Admor* author of *Yesod Ha'avoda*. He was one of the important personages, a wonderful man who served G-d all his life; he was both intelligent and clever and didn't seek honors. All their descendants followed the path of Torah, the boys in Yeshivas and the girls in the school *Bet Yaakov of Agudat Yisrael*. Rabbi Yaakov-Sender was the eldest of the sons and he had two brothers. One was Rabbi and Gaon Rebbe Haim-Haikl who wrote a few books of *Halacha* (Jewish law) and served as a rabbi in the town of Keneh (today named Kamajai and is north of Vilna) and served also as a member of the Committee of Publishers of Vilna. He fled during the Holocaust traveling through Japan and China to Eretz Yisrael. He was a neighborhood rabbi in Tel Aviv and a publisher of rabbinic journals from time to time until he passed away on 15 Heshvan 1970. The second brother was the Rabbi and Gaon Rebbe Shmuel, who studied in the Mir Yeshivas in Poland and America and now lives in Brooklyn.

[Page 107]

Rabbi Yaakov-Sender excelled in his studies even as a youth. He was gifted with a sharp comprehension and a great desire to know and understand, was blessed with personal charm and many youth of his age befriended him. He had a fiery personality and was always looking for new spiritual ideas and seeking wider horizons. At a very young age he began learning Torah in the local Yeshiva in Slonim from the Head of the Yeshiva the Gaon Rebbe Shabtai Yogel ztz"l (who, at the end of his life, was living in Ramat Gan and started a Yeshiva there in place of the one that was destroyed in the Holocaust). He also studied with the staff of teachers until his Torah knowledge became so scholarly that he was able to make new interpretations of the texts. He was in the highest class of young Hasidim who were studying in this " *mitnaged*" (against Hasidism) Yeshiva, as the leader of the group. He spent a short time in the Radin Yeshiva, the Yeshiva of the *Hofetz Haim*, and in other yeshivas until he was ordained as a rabbi. Due to his good reputation he was invited by the *Admor* from Stolin-Karlin to be the Head of the Yeshiva that was built by him and called *Bet Yisrael*. Here, was spread before him a wide field to teach Torah. He had an excellent manner of speaking, with interesting and illuminating explanations, with pedagogic exegesis and therefore his students thirstily drank in his words. While he was still at the beginning of his career, people foresaw a shining future for him like a rising star. Thanks to the efforts of the *Admor* of Slonim, who was close to him, he was exempted from military service in the Polish army (this episode is told fully in the collection *Ahimeir* that was published by his brother Rabbi Haim-Haikl, in Tel Aviv, Summer, 1968). The small community in Brosh (near Volkovisk) invited him to become their Rabbi.

From there he came to Maytchet. Theoretically, he was appointed to the position of local rabbi but in practice he was part of the public Jewish life in all Poland-Lithuania whether in his energetic work for Torah education or in his integration into the organization of Agudat Yisrael. His lively personality didn't allow him to rest on his laurels. He corresponded about halachic questions with the great rabbis including the Gaon Rebbe Haim-Ozer Grodzinski from Vilna. These letters were the basis of his important book on the laws of divorce, Kochav MeYaakov, which was printed close to the beginning of the Nazi Holocaust.

[Page 108]

When the days of wrath arrived Rabbi Grinberg stayed with his community and didn't leave them. Together with them he shared the cruel fate. He proved his courage on the threshold of death, when the Germans came to his home in the summer of 1942 to seize him together with all the Jews of Maytchet who were being taken to execution. He stood up against the murderers, grabbed an axe and courageously attacked the German officer who stood before him and severely beat him. This action made an inerasable impression on the people. However, a few hours later he was caught again by an armed corps that led him to the road from which no one ever returns.

May his memory be blessed.

6. Rebbe Nahum Shu"b z"l
- from the Lechover Hasidim in Maytchet
Translated by Esther Mann Snyder

When Rebbe Nahum Shu"b was young he lived in Maytchet and his prayers shone brightly. He was very poor and lacked even a piece of dry bread, all his livelihood came from the Holy One... He quieted his hunger with Torah and sated his thirst with prayers reaching the heavens as was done in Lachovitch, and all his bones would sing and pray. And yet when the *Admor* Rebbe Mordechai Malkovitz ordered him to move to Slonim to work as a shohet and bodek (ritual slaughter and inspector) and his meals would be given to him, he complained to his rebbe:

-- What did you want from my life, what was I lacking in Maytchet? In Slonim I don't have the lofty Sabbaths that I had there. And the prayers also aren't as they were there, not shining enough... when I was hungry and wore one shirt for seven weeks, then I prayed in a completely different manner...

Aharon Sorski (The Hasidic Greats, in *HaModia HaTzair*, Jerusalem, issue 185, p. 8)

[Page 109]

7. R' Yitzhak Gratzikovitz (G-d should avenge his blood) (Itshe Kozlovicher)
Translated by Esther Mann Snyder

R' Yitzhak Gratzikovitz z"l was one of the notables in the Maytchet community. He was the son of Moshe Aharon Gratzikovitz, a well known figure among the Slonim Hasidim in Baranovichi, and married one of the young woman in Koslovich, a village near Maytchet. He made his home there, managed a flourmill that was driven by the power of the stream of water from the river and was blessed with 8 lovely children. He lived for while in the town and shared the fate of the Jews of Maytchet during the Holocaust, when he moved with his family into the town and lived there until the bitter end.

R' Yitzhak had a dear, fine soul, all the good virtues and was loved by all; he was a charming person. He was known as a real Hasid that "all his bones will say. " In the winter days he would sometimes use an axe to break the ice, which was half a meter thick, in the river in order to perform a ritual immersion before he prayed in order to add sanctity and purity to his prayers. His rabbi the *Admor* Rebbe Avraham'le ztz"l from Slonim loved him very much and showed special attention to him before all the Hasidim, something done rarely, and was also pleased when R' Yitzhak would assist him - which was considered special honor. Everyone who knew R' Yitzhak well was ready to swear that the man was totally without an evil inclination, was without any tendency to sin and see ugliness in the world - he was by nature good and did good deeds. It was as if all his being was merged with the root of goodness under the sun.

Even his exterior appearance was charming. He was tall and stood erect, a strong build and courageous. Because he lived alone in the desolation near the flourmill, he always had a gun (licensed from the Polish government) and the wicked feared to annoy him.

He perished on *Kiddush HaShem* (martyrdom) together with his family, murdered on *Rosh Hodesh* Av 1942, and was buried in a mass grave together with the rest of the martyrs from Maytchet.

May G-d take avenge on his blood.

[Page 110]

8. The Rabbi, the Gaon Rebbe Meir Meirim z"l, Head of the Rabbinical Court in Maytchet
Translated by Esther Mann Snyder

A handsome young man, clever and sharp - so was Rebbe Meir-Meirim in his youth. His great diligence in studying the Torah and his wonderful purity were greater than his natural qualities. While still quite young he found his place among the great scholars in Kobrin, and was considered a gaon (genius) and very devout.

When he reached the age of 15 the Maytchet community appointed the amazing young *Ilui* (brilliant one) as its rabbi, (as described in his book *Nir*, Volume I). He was perhaps the youngest rabbi in history. He quickly became admired by the residents who immediately saw his brilliance and greatness. He was gifted with a quick and sharp grasp of matters. It is told that on his first Shabbat as rabbi in Maytchet, all the Jews thronged to his home to welcome him. When the people came to his home again during the week they were surprised to find him sitting and learning Torah with his face to the wall, not turning his head to see who had come. When he was asked about it he answered that he recognized the sound of each one's footsteps from the first time they came to visit. Through the years RM"M (Meir Meirim) went from Maytchet through the glorious communities of Vishnova and Shvintzion, to carry on the crown of the rabbinate in Yakovshtat, the great city. His reputation preceded him. In a short time he became known as one of the geniuses of the generation, people from all places sent him Jewish law questions, great gaonim of the generation read his answers and quoted his innovations in their books, using them to glorify their own ideas.

One halachic discussion with the RM"M out of many we find, for example, is in the book of responsa (answers to questions posed) of the Posek (decisor) of the generation, the Gaon Rabbi Yitzhak-Elchanan Spector, head of the Rabbinical Tribunal in Kovno, *Shu"t Eyn Yitzhak* (8 *Even Haezer*, para. 34) who quoted him. And also in the collection *Tvuna* edited by Rebbe Yisrael Salanter, the founder of the Musar (ethics and morals) movement, there is an important Torah article by the RM"M.

Word of his innovations on the Jerusalem Talmud spread and amazed rabbis and scholars with their originality, their depth and honesty. During his work going through a version with defects in the text, he would re-arrange some passages and make corrections or study an especially difficult wording, the gaon was able to solve many questions and complications and refute casuistry that was given about a problem that actually did not exist. It is told of the famous gaon of Slonim, Rebbe Eizl Harif, known as having amazing expertise in the Jerusalem Talmud and was called "a Tanna" [one of the rabbis of the time] of the Jerusalem Talmud. He once sat at a party with some of the great ones of the generation including Rebbe Meir Meirim, and spoke about his innovations while the others tried to refute them and who attempted with all their intelligence to contradict his words. Rebbe Meir Meirim who sat to the right of Rebbe Eizl didn't take part in the discussion and was silent. Sometimes when R' Eizl read a passage, Rebbe Meirim quietly hummed a different melodic reading, as if meaning to say: the simple interpretation is totally different, instead of the melody of a difficult issue the passage should be read with the melody of a pause, of a Tanna helping to understand the passage. The Gaon of Slonim was surprised, he silenced the debaters and yelled out: why do you need these *pilpulim* (casuistry) and refuting my words, here is Rebbe Meir Meirim who in his melodic reading refuted my whole case...

[Page 111]

Parts of his writings on the tractates of the Talmud (*Zeraim* - Warsaw, 1875; *Moed* - Vilna, 1890; *Nashim*) were published after death, by his children and grandchildren who later became the foundation stones of the scholarly writing on the Jerusalem Talmud. In addition, he wrote a book entitled, *Luloaot* (Vilna, 1876).

His character and personality were preserved in the tradition of wonderful stories. He was very modest and full of virtues. Once he traveled in a train car full of Jews, as a regular man. One of the travelers, somewhat capricious, noticed the gaon because he was wearing a small talit (four-cornered, fringed ritual garment) under his clothes next to his skin and another one on top of his clothes, in order to fulfill both opinions on how one must wear it. The man started to mock him, annoy him and even to humiliate him. When they reached the city a large group awaited at the station to welcome the Rebbe. The man quickly realized his mistake and went to the Rebbe's home to apologize saying that he didn't know whom he was insulting. He added a request, that he was about to receive employment from a rich person in town, and please would the Rebbe not spoil his chances and not mention the occurrence to anyone. But the Rebbe responded, "I will do even more than that, I will go with you to the rich man and recommend you because if I do not repay you with a good deed in place of a bad deed, then I worry that I won't fulfill the instruction, 'not to hold a grudge'".

Another time, a simple person humiliated him before the members of the community. Rebbe Meir-Meirim remained silent, forgave the insult and even behaved nicely to him. The members of the community came to him with an argument: "Rebbe, isn't it true that a Torah scholar who doesn't take revenge like a snake is not really a scholar? " The Rebbe answered: Listen. If I had taken revenge and after a long life I arrived at the court of heaven and they would ask me, why I took revenge. I would answer: What do you mean "why", every scholar who doesn't take revenge... Nu, imagine the laughter there. Now that I haven't taken revenge, when I will be asked why didn't I take revenge, since a scholar must take revenge on the insult to the honor of the Torah. I would answer them: I didn't know that I was a Torah scholar, how would I know?

His great wisdom that was demonstrated in his judgments became known. Even non-Jews who were involved in a dispute came to him for a resolution of their argument. He was asked why he refuses to take payment from the non-Jews yet he agrees to take from the Jews. He answered, my Jews know that it is only payment for time taken away from learning Torah, but the gentiles will think it is payment for the judgment and that is forbidden.

One case that came before the Rebbe involved a father and his son. The father claimed that his son was obligated to pay for his clothes and to support him. The son claimed, on his side, that he was very poor and had no money to pay for such things. The Rebbe delayed the decision until the next day and told them he would deal with the matter publicly. However, they should reverse their claims: the son should claim that he wants to clothe and support his father but the father will argue that he would not take a penny from his poor son. And so it occurred that this strange case was argued before a crowd and the Rebbe Meir Meirim gave a true decision saying that the rich people in the community should see to it that the son will have enough money to support his father and thus the father and son became reconciled.

[Page 112]

Later he was appointed the Rabbi of the city of Kobrin, where lived the *Admor* Rebbe Moshe ztz"l, and where RM"M lived until his last day. When The *Admor* of Kobrin passed away, the RM"M followed the new *Admor*, the Gaon and Righteous One Rebbe Avramele from Slonim, who authored the books *Hesed L'Avraham* and *Yesod HaAvoda*. Both of them also became connected through marriage when the daughter of Meir-Meirim married the grandson of the Rebbe, the Rebbe Yitzhak Matityahu Sandberg. The young couple moved to Eretz Yisrael, 100 years ago and made their home in Teveriya (Tiberias) and built a large family. (One of their granddaughters, daughter of Rabbi Pinhas Mintzberg, son-in-law of the Rebbe Sandberg, married R' Eliyahu Tananhoiz (now in Jerusalem) the grandson of the Hasid R' Yisrael Zalman Shlovski z"l of Maytchet, about whom we wrote in a previous chapter.

It is told about Rebbe Meir Meirim that he never spoke a false word. Once he was asked to give false testimony in order to save the life of a Jew being taken to his hanging. To save a life (pikuah nefesh). He was very upset and prayed to G-d to save him from telling a lie. And on that very day, he passed away. It was on 6 Heshvan 1874.

A Call for Help

By the Rabbi, R' Yisrael-David son of Yehuda, Head of the Rabbinical Court in Maytchet. Appeared in the newspaper, Hatzfira, 20 Iyar (20 May)1879.

The people of our town had not yet forgotten the anger of G-d three years ago, when many homes were set on fire and burned down to the ground. And now, G-d's hand touched us again on the Sabbath eve; when everyone was asleep, a loud scream awakened them from their sleep. The fire came from G-d and burned all the houses and stores in town with all their possessions, and no one escaped the damage. And despite the prayer houses in town, G-d spilled his anger and the great synagogue built beautifully, that was just completed and the Bet Midrash (study hall) with the Torah scrolls all were destroyed in the conflagration in the city of Maytchet.

It was a dark and tragic Sabbath day that was lit with flames. Oh! Whose heart will not be bereaved over the calamity that turned the city into a desert and many people were starving. Therefore, I will tell all the faithful tribes of Israel about the terrible disaster which happened to us. And you, the readers of *Hatzfira*, with the G-d of Abraham who always has mercy, please have pity and mercy on the wretched people of our town and bring them help from afar as was done by the cities near us, and especially the Rabbi R' Yosef Rozen, Head of the Rabbinical Court of Slonim.

This will be a wonderful charitable deed.

One distressed by the distress of his people, Yisrael-David son of R' Yehuda.

[Page 113]

Rabbis and Scholars B
The Gaon and Tzadik Rabbi Meir Marim
- head of the rabbinical court of Maytchet
by Moshe Zinovitz
Translated by Jerrold Landau

Rabbi Meir Marim came from the town of Novaya Mysh near Baranovichi, where he was born to his father Rabbi Moshe Shafit. He was the grandson of Rabbi Moshe the rabbinical judge of the town, at the time when the head of the rabbinical court there as the rabbi and Gaon Rabbi Yechiel. Rabbi Yechiel tended toward the Hassidic movement. He was one of those who frequented the father and son, Rabbi Mordechai and Rabbi Noach of Lachowicze. Thanks to him, the Hassidism of the Baal Shem Tov became rooted in the region of Slonim and the surrounding towns, including the town of Maytchet. Thanks to Rabbi Yechiel, who had great influence upon the Talmudic and religious image of Rabbi Meir Marim, this young man became one of the frequenters of the *Beis Midrash* of the Hassidic movement. Even after this young man became known as a rabbi and *Gaon* [rabbinical genius] in the region of Slonim-Navahrudak and beyond, he remained faithful to that movement and later forged a connection with the Admor Rabbi Moshe of Kobrin. After Rabbi Moshe's death, he would travel, along with most of the Hassidim of Kobrin, to the Admor Rabbi Avraham of Slonim, who was a veteran Slonimer Hassid. Later, he would travel to the in-law of this famous *Admor* and was numbered among his very few confidantes and close advisers. The connection of Rabbi Meir Marim to Slonim Hassidism added weight to the *Admor* style of Hassidism, which held a respectable place amongst Polish Lithuanian Jewry until the era of the Holocaust.

As far as we know from the sources, Rabbi Meir Marim served as the head of the rabbinical court of Maytchet during his youth, and later moved to serve as the rabbi and head of the rabbinical court in Wiszniew, Jakobstadt (Jekabpils), and Swięciany (Svenčionys - a district city in the Vilna region). From there he moved to Kobrin, where he passed away.

In the book "Or Yesharim" by Moshe-Chaim Kleinman of Brest-Litovsk (that includes the history of Rabbi Mordechai and Rabbi Noach of Lachowicze, Rabbi Moshe of Kobrin, and Rabbi Avraham of Slonim), several stories of the great righteousness of Rabbi Meir Marim are included. The author of that book states that the descendents of the Hassidic movement in those districts would stream to him as the "Great *Gaon*; the splendid, mighty tower; sharp and expert; the light of lightning; the Sinai and uprooter of mountains[1]; who lights up the land and its inhabitants. He has ten measures of traits and secrets; he is crowned with good traits; he is the celestial abode of Hassidism the wellspring of modesty, very righteous, sublime and wonderful in his deeds and his holy mannerisms, perfected with sublime, high character traits. He received every person pleasantly, related properly to the poor people, and assisted every distressed person to the best of his ability, as is told about him by the people of the city of Kobrin. He walked in the ways of G-d very discreetly."

[Page 114]

The aforementioned book brings down the following story of Rabbi Meir Marim: He married off his young son to the daughter of a certain householder who was a relative of the famous Admor Rabbi Yitzchak of Nieschiz (a town near the city of Kowel in Volhynia region in Ukraine). The writing of the marriage agreement (*Tenaim*) took place in the home of the Admor of Nieschiz, and in the agreement, the father of the groom Rabbi Meir Marim was described as " *Hagaon Hatzadik*". The Admor of Nieschiz himself read the *Tenaim* before those present, and when he came to the word " *Hatzadik*" he paused for a moment, looked at the face of Rabbi Meir Marim for a few moments, said "Yes, Yes!" and continued on with the reading of the *Tenaim*.

The elder householders in Kobrin (where the writer of these lines lived in the summer of 5684 - 1924, and the time that the Yeshiva Gedola was founded there by the *Gaon* and head of the rabbinical court, Rabbi Pesach Pruskin), could give additional details that typify the holy mannerisms of this rabbi, *Gaon* and *Tzadik*. One of these is as follows: Rabbi Meir Marim was known as a person who hated monetary gain and satisfied himself with little. When he was accepted as the head of the rabbinical court of the four aforementioned communities, he advised the householders therein that all the householders, rich and poor alike, should join together in paying his salary at the rate of one kopeck a week, so that he would not come to a challenge and so that he would not stumble by showing favoritism to some of the residents of the town.

Rabbi Meir Marim was also renowned as a *Gaon* of the generation. Even the extreme *Misnagdim* [opponents of Hassidism] from among the *Gaonim* of Lithuania considered him as such. He was wonderfully proficient in the *Bavli*, *Yerushalmi*, *Tosefta*, *Mechilta*, and the entire body of Talmudic literature. He excelled in his orderly style of learning, as is demonstrated in his splendid composition "Nir" on the *Yerushalmi* [Jerusalem Talmud][2], that earned great acclaim in the rabbinical world throughout the Diaspora. This book served as a general useful guide for all people who study the Jerusalem Talmud. In the introduction to his book "Commentaries and Novellae on the Jerusalem Talmud" (New York, 5701, 1941), the renowned, scholarly Talmudic researcher Rabbi Levi Ginzberg[3], who was an expert on the Jerusalem Talmud, deliberates on the important essays on the Jerusalem Talmud written by the scholars of Lithuania during the last century, stating that , "They returned the forgotten Torah of Israel to its original place, and without them, we would not have found our hands and feet within the Talmud of the Land of Israel." Among these, he includes the book "Nir" on the Jerusalem Talmud by Rabbi Meir Marim, whose value was considered great even from an academic perspective. The aforementioned scholar wrote on this subject, "The book 'Nir' by Rabbi Meir Marim on the three first orders (*Zeraim*, *Moed*, *Nashim*)[4], is a fine example of healthy research, and the skepticism of the author testifies not only to his modesty, but also to his clear intellect that does not minimize the great difficulty that a true researcher encounters when he comes to emend the text by means of logic."

In his introduction to his book "The Jerusalem Talmud in its Straightforward Meaning," the renowned scholar and Talmudic researcher, the rabbi and professor Saul Lieberman[5] writes the following about the book "Nir": "The commentaries of the Gaon Rabbi Meir Marim of blessed memory, currently published only on the first three Orders, are deep and to the point. However, whereas the style of this *Gaon* in his composition is to bring to the fore various possibilities of differing explanations; he does not decide which explanation is correct, which is close and which is far off. From his concise style and innuendoes, one must ponder the meaning of his words no less than one must ponder the Jerusalem Talmud itself."

[Page 115]

When the aforementioned composition of Rabbi Meir Marim was brought before the Gaon Rabbi Yehoshua Izak Shapira ("Eizel Charif") of Slonim, the Slonimer looked into the book and said, "I too can compose a book like Rabbi Meir Marim (The Gaon Rabbi Yehoshua Izak Shapira wrote an important work "Noam Yehoshua" on the Jerusalem Talmud), but to be as righteous as he is already beyond my ability."

In the eulogy booklet on the passing of Torah personalities of his generation written by the rabbi and Gaon Rabbi Moshe Nechemia Kahana, a principal Yeshiva Head of Yeshivat Eitz Chaim of Jerusalem, he also notes the passing of "The rabbi and Gaon Rabbi Marim of holy blessed memory, the head of the rabbinical court of Kobrin, who was known and famous for his Torah, righteousness, integrity, and wisdom."

With regard to the emphasis on the word "and his wisdom" in the above words of appreciation, we should specially note that despite all of his piety and righteousness, Rabbi Meir Marim was known for his proficiency in the Russian, Polish and German languages, even though he did not flaunt this internally or externally. His fluency in Germany helped him to be accepted by all segments of the community of Jakobstadt (in Kurland, Latvia) where German was the spoken language of the local intelligentsia. Given his knowledge in religious research and general subjects, he always had the upper hand in debates with various *Maskilim*, and thereby sanctified the name of Heaven[6]. Many of the statements of Rabbi Meir Marim in this regard circulated among the elders of the aforementioned towns in which he served in honor, and it unfortunate that they were not written in the pages of a book so that they following generation would know about them.

In this article, we should also note the two sons of Rabbi Meir Marim that we know about, who were raised and educated in Maytchet, the town of his first rabbinical seat. The first was Rabbi Betzalel Chaim, the head of the rabbinical court of Viezin[Z] of the Vilna district, who prepared the aforementioned "Nir" book for print, and the second was Rabbi Aharon Yehoshua Shafit. In order to pacify the family of Rabbi Meir Marim, his second son was appointed as the government rabbi of Kobrin. He knew how to speak Russian, and represented the community of Kobrin to the government with propriety and wisdom. Rabbi Aharon Yehoshua tended toward the Slonimer Hassidim, and he always helped them with respect to influence in communal institutions. When official matters became complex with the Russian government, he made *aliya* to the Land of Israel, settled in Tiberias, and was active in affairs of the Kollel Reisen-Slonim.

The son of Rabbi Meir Marim's sister , Rabbi Avraham Aharon Yudelovich, also had a connection to Maytchet. He was the author of important works in Jewish law and teaching. Rabbi Avraham Aharon, a native of Novahrudak, studied Torah with his uncle in Maytchet during his youth. He served in the rabbinate in the towns of Selvovij, Kuznetsovi, Konstantinov, Turov, Kepaliai, Manchester England, and then in several communities in the United States of America. Rabbi Avraham-Aharon wrote a book of response called "The House of my Father" on the four sections of the Code of Jewish Law; "Darash Av" on matters of exegesis, "Tapuchei Zahava, and several other works on Torah topics. Rabbi Avraham Aharon noted several times in these books the greatness of his uncle the author of "Nir" on the Jerusalem Talmud.

[Page 116]

We find information in various sources regarding the connection of the Gaon Rabbi Meir Marim to the community of Maytchet as the head of the rabbinical court. In this regard, we will note the book "Nachalat Avot" by Rabbi Levi Savchinsky, in which it is written, among other things, that he was accepted as the head of the rabbinical court in Święciany, a regional city in the district of Vilna, in the year 5609 (1849), after he had already served as the head of the rabbinical court of Wisniewo in that same district, where he served in the rabbinate after his tenure in Maytchet. From this, we can determine that the time of Rabbi Meir Marim's rabbinical tenure in Maytchet was prior to the year 5600 (1840). Rabbi Meir Marim is described as follows in that book, "This excellent *Gaon* was great in his time, pious and modest, righteous and sublime." According to the author of that book, that *Gaon* was only 15 years old when he received the rabbinate of Maytchet as has been noted above.

Apparently, Rabbi Meir Marim served as the rabbi and head of the rabbinical court of Maytchet after the head of the rabbinical court of that place, Rabbi Yehuda HaKohen, left for medical treatment in Vilna. He died there in the year 5683 (1823) and was buried in the old cemetery of that community where they buried famous *Gaonic* rabbis.

Rabbi Meir Marim died on the 18th of *Cheshvan* in Kobrin, and is buried there. His grave was next to the grave of his close friend Rabbi Moshe the Admor of Kobrin. The name and memory of Rabbi Meir Marim remain etched and guarded in the hearts of all the members of the communities in which he served honorably as the rabbi and head of the rabbinical court. On account of his open affiliation with Hassidism, this movement became deeply rooted in Maytchet, Święciany, and Jakobstadt just as in Kobrin. The Hassidim were a significant spiritual and communal factor in those towns.

On *Tisha Be'Av* and during *Elul* and the Ten Days of Penitence, when the Jews of Kobrin would visit the local cemetery (on the other side of the Zamukhavetz River), they would also supplicate over the graves of its famous rabbis and *Admorim*, and especially at the grave of Rabbi Meir Marim, whose name was guarded with them as a miracle worker who could bring salvation. They would even leave notes of supplication at his grave.

Translator's footnote

1. A Talmudic expression for a person who has acquired both the breadth (Sinai) and depth (uprooter of mountains) of Torah.
2. There are two versions of the Talmud: the Jerusalem Talmud, and the Babylonian Talmud. The Babylonian Talmud, given its later date, is the version most commonly studied. However, there are certain tractates, particularly regarding the agricultural laws, that are only found in the Jerusalem Talmud.
3. See Louis Ginzberg, http://en.wikipedia.org/wiki/Louis_Ginzberg
4. The *Mishna*, and consequently the Talmud, is divided into six "Orders": *Zeraim* (seeds or agricultural laws, *Moed* (Sabbath and festivals), *Nashim* (women, marital laws), *Nezikim* (damages, tortes, civil law), *Kodshim* (Temple sacrificies), *Taharot* (Ritual purity).
5. See http://en.wikipedia.org/wiki/Saul_Lieberman
6. I.e. brought honor to religious Judaism by being able to hold his own in the debates with freethinkers.
7. Viciulnai or Vyzuonos.

[Page 117]

The Rabbi and Gaon Rabbi Yehuda Leib HaKohen
by Moshe Zinovitz
Translated by Jerrold Landau

The rabbi and Gaon Rabbi Yehuda Leib HaKohen was known as one of those who was close to the Gaon of Vilna[1] and who later was attracted to the Hassidic movement and became a student of the great Magid of Mezeritch, the Gaon Rabbi Dovber of holy blessed memory. The Gaon Rabbi Yehuda Leib first served as a preacher of righteousness [*Magid Meisharim*] in Maytchet. At the end of this days, he fulfilled this role in Antopoli in the Kobrin district, Grodno region, where he was buried in the year 5567 (1807).

The book "Divrei Negidim" serves as an authoritative source on the personality of the Maytchet rabbi. This book is a novel commentary on difficult issues on Rashi's commentary on the Pentateuch, the five *Megillot*, and the *Haftaras* of the entire year, published by Rabbi Meir the son of Yaakov Krolowiecki, the *Magid Meisharim* of Lomza. This book is divided into two editions: a) "Shevet Yehuda" with the sharp didactics of Rabbi Yehuda Leib HaKohen of blessed memory, who was called by everyone, "The diligent one of the city of Metzad."; B) "Irme Kedem" focusing on straightforward methodology of the author, who states that he is the fifth generation of the *Magid Meisharim* of Maytchet.

In the preface to the book, the aforementioned author writes that Rabbi Yehuda Leib HaKohen was one of those close to the Gaon of Vilna and his *Beis Midrash*, while simultaneously being a student of the great Magid Rabbi Dovber of Mezeritch[2], and the son-in-law of the righteous Rabbi Moshe Elyakim the author of "Beer Moshe", the son of the righteous Rabbi Yisrael the Magid of Koznitz. In the approbation[3] to the book "Divrei Negidim" by the rabbi and Gaon Rabbi Eliezer Simcha Rabinovitz, the head of the rabbinical court of Lomza, he notes that the author of this book is known to him as a virtuous rabbi, who preaches well and fulfills well that which he preaches. In this approbation, he notes especially that the great, diligent rabbi and Gaon, Rabbi Yehuda Leib HaKohen was one of those who frequented the *Beis Midrash* of the Gaon of Vilna.

Many famous rabbis, *Gaonim* and *Admorim* of Poland who adorn the book "Divrei Negidim" with their warm approbations note the connection of the aforementioned Rabbi Yehuda Leib with the Magid of Mezeritch of holy blessed memory. These include the Admor of Gur who is the author of "Sfat Emet", who received this book graciously and especially noted that the author is one of the students of the holy rabbi, the Magid of Mezeritch. The name and memory of Rabbi Yehuda Leib HaKohen is also included in the book "Shem HaGedolim Hechadash" in the following words: "There is a large canopy over his grave in Antopoli. In his will, he stated that anyone who supports the publication of his manuscripts can place his name atop his grave, and will merit living offspring and sustenance for all the days of his life."

Translator's footnotes

1. See http://en.wikipedia.org/wiki/Vilna_Gaon
2. This point of his connection to the Gaon of Vilna and the Magid of Mezeritch is stressed numerous times, as it shows that he had roots in the *Misnagdic* [anti-Hassidic] style, but moved toward Hassidism.
3. In rabbinical literature, an author will solicit notes of approval from well-known rabbis and include them in as part of the preface to the book. These are known as approbations (*Haskamot*).

[Page 118]

Rabbi Shmuel, Head of the Rabbinical court of Maytchet

by Moshe Zinovitz
Translated by Ron Rabinovitch

The venerable Rabbi, the head of the Jewish Community, was a descendant of the famous Shochor family from Mir. His father, Rabbi Chaim Leib, was known there as "Rabbi Chaim Leib Nagid" to distinguish him from the famous Rabbi Chaim Leib Tiktinski, the head of the Mir Yeshiva. Rabbi Chaim Leib Nagid was the grandson of the honorable Rabbi Josef David Eisenshtadt, who was the head of the Bet Din and the Mir Yeshiva.

Rabbi Chaim Leib Nagid was a learned man who did many good deeds. He was a textile merchant who sold his merchandise in Minsk, Moscow, Warsaw, and Lodz. All the people in the area came to buy from him in his factory in Mir. Although he had a flourishing business, he spent most of his time during the day learning in the Beit Medrish. His wife Lifsha and his daughters operated the business.

Lifsha was the sister of Rabbi Naphtali Zvi Judah Berlin (known also as the Netziv), born in Mir and the head of justice and Volozhin Yeshiva. Her father was the great Rabbi Jacob Berlin, who emigrated to Israel in 1850, where he became an honorary officer in the "Eitz Chaim" Yeshiva in Jerusalem. He died in 1870, and is buried on the Mount of Olives in Jerusalem.

The second son in law of Rabbi Jacob Berlin was the genius Rabbi Yechiel Michel Epstein, who was the head of justice in Navahrudak and the author of the famous book "Aroch Hashulchan", which deals with all the volumes of the "Shulchan Aruch" (the Jewish religion code of laws).

Rabbi Shmuel was the son of Rabbi Michael, the older son of Rabbi Chaim Leib Nagid. He was a student in the Volozhin Yeshiva, succeeded in his studies and got an honor from his uncle, Hanatzviv. Due to his uncle's words, he got the job as the head of justice in Maytchet, which he was in charge of for many years. He was very popular in the Chasidic circles, both in the town and surrounding areas, and when the Admorin of Slonim (the masters and teachers) Rabbi Abraham and Rabbi Shemuel of blessed memory made their annual visit to Maytchet, he would reciprocate with a visit to Slonim.

[Page 119]

The Gaon Rabbi Zvi Hirsh of Maytchet
by Moshe Zinovitz
Translated by Jerrold Landau

Rabbi Zvi Hirsh lived and functioned in the area of Slonim more than a century ago. Apparently, he is to be identified as Rabbi Zvi Hirsh of Maytchet, who served as a Yeshiva head in the Yeshiva of Slonim, which examined and accepted the Genius [*Iluy*] of Maytchet to the Yeshiva. The rabbi and Gaon Rabbi Avraham Aharon Yudelovich, the nephew of Rabbi Meir Marim the head of the rabbinical court of Maytchet, mentions Rabbi Zvi Hirsh in one of his compositions in the book "Darash Av". This Maytchet *Gaon* is also mentioned by the Slonim writer Mr. Zavlocki in his article "The Congregation of Jacob in Slonim" that was published in the Hebrew annual "Kneset Hagedola" in Warsaw in the year 5651 (1891) (fourth book). The aforementioned article, dealing with issues of the community of Slonim, also surveys the Slonim Yeshiva with its Yeshiva heads, classes and teachers. Among others, it mentions Rabbi Tzvi HaKohen Rizikof of Moychad[1] in a positive light, as teaching the eighth grade, and describes him as an "effective educator, sharp and honorable. His style of learning finds favor with the people of our city. He forges a path through the Sea of Talmud and the thick waters of the commentators. A new light will be shed over this expert style of study."

In the book "Divrei Menachem" (Jerusalem 5685 - 1925) by Rabbi Menachem HaKohen Rizikof, the son of Rabbi Zvi Hirsh, the following words of eulogy and appreciation for his prominent father are included, as we read there:

"On the 11th of Nissan, 5672 (1902), the holy ark[2] expired and was buried in the 71st year of his life. He was eulogized by great rabbis. The great Gaon Rabbi Moshe Betzalel Luria, the head of the rabbinical court of Suwalki stated in his eulogy that were the Holy Temple to exist, he would be the High Priest. He was buried in the old cemetery next to the great Gaon Rabbi Yehuda Bachrach and the Gaon and Kabbalist Rabbi Yitzchak Izak Chaver. May his soul be bound in the bonds of eternal life."

Rabbi Menachem adds the following about this father:

"The little learning that I gleaned from my father of blessed memory was like a drop in the ocean in comparison to the great Torah of my holy father. He was very diligent, and his mouth never desisted from learning day and night. He would count each letter just as the one counts money, and he was expert, by heart, in the entire Talmud with *Rashi* and *Tosafot*. He was also a person of fine character traits, modest, hating reward and content with his lot. His entire mannerism and demeanor was one of holiness. Torah was his vocation from his youth until the final moment of his life. He hated honor definitively, and did not want to accept the position of rabbi, even though several important towns wished to honorably appoint him as rabbi. When he served as a Yeshiva head in the Yeshiva of Slonim, flocks of fine youth and important students gathered around him to draw from the wellsprings of his Torah. He was an expert pedagogue with his fine, pleasant explanations. The students loved him with their heart and soul, and honored him greatly. Many of his students occupy rabbinical seats in large and important cities, and many became important laymen who are expert in Torah. He did not leave behind his Torah novella in writing, even though every lesson that he delivered in the Yeshiva was full of new ideas of Torah that the students enjoyed."

[Page 120]

In the year 5684 (1894), 18 years prior to his death, he became a Yeshiva head in the large Yeshiva of Suwalki, from where he disseminated Torah. The Yeshiva grew there during those years, and many benches were added to his class. Even some people of Slonim who moved from there to hear would come to listen to his classes. He studied in this Yeshiva with wonderful diligence until his final day, 11 Nissan 5672 (1902). He died and was buried in the 71st year of his life.

We should also note that the son of the Maytcheter, Rabbi Menachem HaKohen, was great in Torah, and was greatly imbued with expertise and sharpness. Two of the *Gaonim* of Jerusalem, the rabbi and Gaon Avraham Yitzchak HaKohen Kook the Chief Rabbi of Israel[3], and Rabbi Tzvi Pesach Frank[4] the head of the rabbinical court of Jerusalem, describe him in their approbation to the aforementioned book as a renowned rabbi and *Gaon*, a treasury of Torah and teaching, who already earned a name from his important book on the laws of *treifot*[5]. Indeed, the son was like the father.

Translator's footnotes
1. Sic. (As it is written)
2. A literary reference to a person suffused with Torah knowledge.
3. See http://en.wikipedia.org/wiki/Abraham_Isaac_Kook
4. See http://en.wikipedia.org/wiki/Tzvi_Pesach_Frank
5. Improper slaughtering and various diseases and imperfections that would render an otherwise kosher animal not kosher.

[Page 121]

Rabbi Isaac-Naftali Belski and His Family
by Dov Shlomovitz
Translated by Ron Rabinovitch

One of the great Rabbis of our generation who formed Maytchet's Jewish life with culture and Torah before the Holocaust was Rabbi Isaac Naftali Belski. Although he was paralyzed for many years and could not leave his house, he contributed a great deal. His sons-in-law were scholarly, highly educated and helped him. Rabbi Belski was the spiritual leader of the town. The inhabitants revered their Rabbi who suffered with physical problems; they helped and admired him very much. There was a permanent minyan in his house and many Jews came to be there; some came to pray and others to visit and give him honor.

Rabbi Belski had one son and three daughters. The oldest daughter, Golda, married Rabbi Elchanan Goldstein from Maytchet, who was scholarly and well-educated. His commitment to G-d and his devotion to the people were to be admired; the inhabitants of the town and the local government officials admired him as well. The government appointed him as the "Rabbi Mit-Am (Rabbi of them) and he was also a religious teacher for the Jewish pupils in the Polish school, "Pobshachna".

The second daughter, Rosa, married a Yeshiva student from Mir, Rabbi Dov Abbel, during the time when the elderly Rabbi was still the head of the Jewish community. The Jews liked Rabbi Abbel and saw him to be the successor to the elderly Rabbi Belski.

The third daughter, Liba, was engaged to Rabbi Shlomo Podoleski from the Navaradok Yeshiva. Unfortunately, she died when she was still young and before he came to Maytchet. Rabbi Podelski was a wonderful preacher and everybody went to the synagogue to hear him. He was the candidate to be the Rabbi from the Mitnagdim movement (this is the opposite of Hassidim).

This became a complicated situation. Both sides did not want to recognize the other's candidate. They even stopped buying candles and yeast at the Rabbi's house as they had been doing for quite some time in the past. This was the situation until Rabbi Jacob Grinberg came from Slonim. The Mitnagdim accepted him because he was a Slonim Hassid and some of the other Hassidim accepted him as well. The government wanted the Baranovici Rabbinate to make the decision. The war started and of course this problem was never resolved.

At the time of the Aktion, Rabbi Belski went out to the street wearing his prayer shawl and teffilin. That is where the Nazis shot and killed him.

[Page 122]

The Spiritual Center in Maytchet
by Nachum Margolin
Translated by Ron Rabinovitch
Paragraph on Malke Romanovsky on page 130–131
translated by Tzivia Malke Romanovski Fishbane

1. The Shul–Heif

From the commercial center location in the areas of the Rad–Kramen [the row of shops], there was a small narrow alley that led to the wide "Shul–Heif" [synagogue courtyard], where the synagogues, Chadarim, the bathhouse with the ritual bath (*Mikve*) and other buildings stood. This was the Jewish spiritual center of Maytchet.

There were three permanent houses of worship: The Synagogue, the house of study (*Beit Hamidrash*) and the "Shtibel" of the Hasidim. The Synagogue was a large, splendid building with a fine dome over it with paintings of Jewish works of art. Some of the veterans of Maytchet said that Italian builders built the original synagogue approximately 300 years ago. In 1922 it was renovated and returned to its old glory.

People worshipped in this synagogue on Saturdays and Holidays, therefore, the Jews who worshipped there were nicknamed "Sabbath Jews." On the weekdays they all worshipped in the "Beit Hamidrash".

[Page 123]

Immediately prior to World War II the Cantor was Reb Shaulke –a very talented and fine chazzan. The trustees were Josef Shkolnikovitch, Hazel Motchkovski who was the chairman of the charitable fund (*Gemilut Chasadim*) and Moshe Belski. The Shammes was Nachum Kowenski.

The Beit Hamidrash (house of study) was the main house of worship where most of the people prayed and studied the Torah during the day and at night. On the weekdays there were several Minyans, one after the other, and on Sabbath, there were two. Between afternoon and evening prayers there was a lesson of Chapters of the Mishna. The Talmud study group also conducted study sessions, and regular Jews maintained a group for the recitation of Psalms. The two trustees of the Beit Midrash led the study sessions, but on Sabbath afternoons they brought preachers from other places to deliver lectures.

The row of shops opposite the Shul–Heif

The prayer leaders in the Beit Midrash were Reb Leib Chaim Wolinski, Reb Yeshaia Aharon Lozowski (they were also trustees) and Moshe "The Melamed" (*teacher*). Rabbi Yeshaya Aharon always cared for the heating in the Beit Hamidrash and prepared wood for the oven. There were other trustees: David Rabinovitch (Dudzie the researcher), David "The Hoicher" (The *tall* man) and Chaikel Izralevitz "Der Baker" (The Baker). The shammes was Moshe Breshenski.

The Shtibel was the third prayer place where the Hasidim of various Admorim (Hasidic masters) prayed. From time to time the Admorim came to the Shtibel, each on his assigned Sabbath, to be with their community. Their appearance brought joy to the inhabitants. The Shtibel's worshippers brought the "Cholent" (Sabbath stew) and drinks. The ordinary people would come to see the Rabbi and to hear his words of Torah – and the city of Maytchet was happy and glad. The Admorim who came to visit were, the Slonimer Rebbe the Stoliner (*from Stolin*), the "Koidanover"(*from Koidan*), the "Galicianer"(*from Galicia*) and others.

The trustees of the Shtibel were: Reb Yosef Shimon Girshovitch, Reb Leib Winograd and Reb Isser Bilwas. The prayer leaders were: Israel Zalman Shlovski, Reb Yosef Shimon Girshovitch and Reb Yaakov who was the son–in–law of Rabbi Kopel Gorski.

Over and above the regular houses of worship, there were various minyans in private houses on Sabbaths and holidays, such as in Rabbi Belski's house who remained at home because of his paralysis, at Yudel "Der Shuster"'s house (*The shoemaker*) and at the Simchat Torah minyan of the Zionists, who arranged this minyan annually, the income of which was dedicated to the Jewish National Fund.

Prior to the 1930s, Rabbi Belski served as the Rabbi of Maytchet. He suffered from paralysis at the end of his days, and his son–in–law Rabbi Dov, the husband of his daughter Rosa, filled his place and subsequently inherited his rabbinical position. His second son–in–law Elchanan Goldstein served as the Rabbi Mitaam (government appointed rabbi). In 1935 there was a quarrel between the two sides, and an additional rabbi was brought in. The dispute continued until the outbreak of the war. The Polish authorities intervened in the dispute and demanded a verdict from the rabbinate of Baranovici. They did not succeed in instilling order into the question of the rabbinate when the terrible war broke out, and put an end to all of the problems of Judaism along with the Jews themselves.

[Page 124]

2. In the Congregation of Hasidim and Admorim
The history of Hasidim in the area and its place in Maytchet

The Hasidic movement started in Lithuania the middle of the 18th century. It had its earliest beginnings in the town of Slonim, which was the origin of most new movements and social streams in the Lithuanian area. From there it spread to the nearby and far–off cities and towns. The Hasidic movement penetrated into the area of Lithuania during the middle of the 18th century, and gained many adherents from among the circles of rabbis and students. However, most of its followers came from the common people and the tradesmen, who regarded that new movement as a counterbalance to the rigid circle of students who were ruled in an absolute fashion during the long period of the Council of the State of Lithuania, as well as after that period.

Furthermore, even though the general background of the growth of Hasidism in the region of Lithuania is not different from that of the region of Volhyn–Podolia, which was the cradle of the movement – that is the searching for a means of salvation for the downtrodden masses of Jews, who were wearing away from economic and spiritual tribulations at home and outside, we cannot neglect the prominent line of difference. This was that the region of Lithuania was the natural stronghold of the staunch Mitnagdim [opponents of Hasidism], who fought a holy war against the Hasidic sect. Therefore, the establishment of the movement in this region was more difficult than in any other place, and ended up with a compromise, whereby at first the Chabad Hasidic movement of Rabbi Shneur Zalman of Liadi was accepted. This was because of the dedication of Chabad Hasidim to learning. Only much later did general Hasidism become established in the area. Finally, a local Hasidic movement rose in the area.

The differences and typical traits that Lithuanian Hasidim were noted for were nothing in comparison to the complex and perplexing factors of the fierce battle that affected all of Reisen – waged by the Lithuanian Mitnagdim against the "sect" of Hasidim. In the years 5532 / 1772 and 5541 / 1781 the weapon of ex–communication was used by the community of Vilna when the GRA (Vilna Gaon) was placed at the helm of the camp of Mitnagdim. This led to a flood of letters of accusation and poisonous declarations. The situation degenerated the point of a distressing act of slander in the year 5556 / 1796, that led to Rabbi Shneur Zalman of Liadi being bound in chains and imprisoned in St. Petersburg. This bitter fight against the Hasidim cast its heavy shadow over the region and its impressions could be felt throughout the entire world with the division of the Jewish people into two disputing camps. This miserable fight became an integral part of the history of Lithuanian Hasidim. The victory of the Lithuanian Hasidism that was openly expressed by the miraculous liberation of the Rabbi of Liadi became a Hasidic heritage throughout the entire world, where the 19th of Kislev, which is the day of liberation, is celebrated as a day of joy every year until this day.

[Page 125]

While Chabad Hasidism was still celebrating its victory, and before the wrath of the two disputing sides had calmed, a new branch of an independent Lithuanian Hasidic movement from Lachowice and Slonim arose. In the year 5552 / 1792 Rabbi Mordechai from Lachowice (and his son and successor Rabbi Noach) established the Lachowice branch of Hasidim, and served as its first Admor. Lachowice Hasidism, which absorbed the influence of Karlin Hasidism, first struck roots in the nearby area and gained adherents not only from the general populace, but also from the circles of scholars. It did not take long for Lachowice Hasidism to spread throughout the area, and gain a strong following in Slonim, Mush, Stolevitch, Maytchet, Polonka, Mir, and even in towns of Pulisia towns: Kobrin, Pruzhany, Malachy, Shereshov, and others.

After the death in 5593 / 1832 of Rabbi Noach of blessed memory, the second Admor (Great Hasidic Rabbi) of Lachowice, his student Rabbi Moshe of Kobrin became his successor. The name of the branch changed to "Kobrin Hasidim" branch, or "Lachowice–Kobrin". The Kobrin methodology crystallized – which obligated the continuation of study, but made sure to attract the masses of people, for whose benefit and to raise their level they developed a populist, simple tendency toward Divine service, without demanding the intellectual sophistication and didactics of the Mitnagdim.

The success of the Lachowice–Kobrin Hasidic branch that was adopted by so many people in the area for more than 70 years spawned new local dynasties in Koidanovo, Slonim, etc. In 5618 / 1858, Rabbi Avraham Weinberg was "exiled" to Slonim, where he founded the Slonim dynasty and became its first Admor. He was the student and Hasid of Rabbi Noach of Lachowice, and some say, even of Rabbi Moshe of Kobrin. He was an excellent Torah student, and served as the head of the famous Slonim Yeshiva. Because of the difficulties at this time, and because of the resistance of the Mitnagdim who were the chief spokesman in the community and the Yeshiva, Rabbi Avraham was forced to continue as a private teacher to the children in his own Cheder. Later on, he became the Admor, and regarded himself and others regarded him as the leader of a large group of Hasidim throughout Lithuania.

Thus, the branches and dynasties of Hasidism fortified themselves against the wall of Lithuanian Mitnagdim, and the unique methodology of Lithuanian Hasidism crystallized in contrast to the general Hasidism of Volhynia–Podolia. Fortunately, the area did not break up into exclusionary and inimical spheres of influence. Especially in small towns like Maytchet, the Hasidim affiliated with different Admorim who visited on set occasion, and conducted their table celebrations in a shtibel or another location, to the joy of all the Hasidim.

It is so typical that this Gaon and Tzadik at such a high level, who stood out among the other Hasidic leaders of his generation, left a spiritual inheritance with two fundamental books: "Honor to Abraham" (*Chessed le–Avraham*) and "The Basis of Divine Service" (*Yesodei Ha–avoda*), where he outlined the unique style of the Lithuanian Hasidic branch and its relationship to Divine service. On account of his first book, he became known as "The Author of Chessed le–Avraham." He marked the connection to the Land of Israel in his books, and highly praised the value of the commandment of the settlement of Israel. This marked a change of the point of view in the Hasidic world of his time. He also assisted his Hassidim in the holy cities in a practical fashion. During this time, the Hasidim, including his grandson Rabbi Noach, started to immigrate to Tiberias. Until his last days, Reb Avraham did not desist from this holy work.

[Page 126]

He served as the Admor more than 26 years in splendor, replete with activity. After his death in 5644 / 1884, his grandson Rabbi Shmuel Weinberg became the Admor. He preserved the fame that emanated from his renowned grandfather, and continued to attract Hasidim to the Slonim court in his own merit. He continued to fulfill the deeds of his father by establishing Hasidim in the Land of Israel, and he even collected money for this holy purpose with his own hands.

After many years had passed, the Lithuanian Hasidim saw that the Maytchet Hasidim had followed the teachings of their Rebbes, even to the extent of adopting the mitzvah of immigrating to the Land of Israel. Once they arrived in the holy land, they became ordinary citizens and put aside their old country traditions.

In summary, it is worthy to note that in the multi–colored tapestry of the Hassidic courts of Lithuania, the Hasidim of Maytchet and many other towns wove golden threads. They followed after their Rebbes in the paths of Hasidism and also took part in the aliya of Hasidim to the Land of Israel, but they were not referred to by the names of their towns. In the year 5664 / 1904, a mysterious man was revealed in Maytchet in the garb of a farmer, who refused to reveal his name, for he was an adjured kabbalist. He was known as a "Master of the Divine Name" [*Baal Shem*] and a miracle worker, who distributed talismans and charms for various types of problems, and he cured ill people who the expert doctors gave up any hope for recovery. His roo was crowded with ill people, handicapped people, barren women, etc. — both Jews and gentiles who came from near and far to ask his advice

A detailed list of the acts of the "Master of the Divine Name" of Maytchet was published in the "Hayehdi" newspaper, issue 27, from 1904.

[Page 127]

3. Melamdim, religious and public figures

Many years have passed since I have been in my birthplace, Maytchet. I saw my town in good times, and also saw it in the start of its dying days. Now after so many years I want to write my memories. Of course I will start with my childhood days, which I remember so well, and begin with the Cheder (religious elementary school).

We laughed when we heared the expression "infants at school", but this is true because we were very young when we started to learn the "Alef-Bet" in cheder. I remember when I began at the chedder of Rabbi Moshe Chaya Rachels in the spring, just after Passover. His house was in the "Shul-Heif" (area of synagogues) between the Beit Hamidrash and the Shtibel. That place instilled a feeling of holiness in the children's hearts. When my parents brought me the first day, Rabbi Moshe was sitting near the table with his "title" (little stick) in his hand. I was sitting near him and began to learn the letters, while my grandmother Shaina (of blessed memory) was standing behind me. She threw candies on my sidur and said, "This is the gift that the angels send you like they send each boy who starts to learn in the cheder".

My first teacher, Rabbi Moshe, was a simple man who was devoted to his young students. His wife, Chaya Rachel, had a bakery, and he took the bread to the market, especially on Wednesday, which was the market day in town. After a while, when I learned to read in the Sidur (prayer book), I moved with other boys to the Cheder of Rabbi Koppel Gorski, where we studied the Chumash and Rashi. Every Sunday, we began to learn the weekly portion of the Law, and if we could not finish before the week-end, Rabbi Gorski would recite us a short version so we could start the new portion on the subsequent Sunday. This way, we quickly heard all the stories of the creation of the world, our ancestors stories, and of the Jews leaving Egypt and surviving in the desert.

[Page 128]

I can remember one winter, there was heavy snow and I was the only student that came to school, while the others stayed at home. On this day there was a medical check by a representative of the government. I remember they checked to see if my head was clean and if I had any wounds on my body; they did not find any marks on me.

Rabbi Koppel Gorski of blessed memory was a very learned man in the Torah, and like my first teacher Rabbi Moshe Chaya Rachels, was also very old. Rabbi Gorski's wife Elka-Perl had a grocery store, and was helped by her daughter Kroshe, and son Yechiel. Every Wednesday was market day, and Rabbi Gorski finished the lessons at noon and went to help his wife in her store.

I learned for a few years at the Cheder of Rabbi Koppel, and then I went to a more advanced Cheder, that of Rabbi Shimon Shack of blessed memory. This school was a little different from the others, as the pupils were older, so they were divided up into two classes. Here we studied until very late at night, with a break at noon when we had our lunch. I remember at night we went back home after dark, being guided by lamps and candles. In the winter, each pupil took a turn to bring a bottle with gasoline to fill the lamps in class. It was in this Cheder that I learned to write in Hebrew and Yiddish, and later wrote Hebrew grammar from the Bible. The higher class started to learn Polish after arrangements were made with the "Tarbut" (Public) school. The pupils went to classes there twice a week to learn Polish.

In this Cheder the teacher tested the pupils every Thursday. All the children were sitting around the long table and each one took his turn and read a sentence from the "chumash" (Bible). I felt sorry for the child that did not know how to continue to read the sentence when it was his turn. The same happened on Friday when the pupils had to read the verse from the weekly portion of the Torah and then chant the weekly Haftorah with the correct melody. The Rabbi led the teaching, and every child was obligated to come to one of the three prayer sessions held in the Beit Hamidrash in the morning. The Rabbi himself came to the second minyan, and this way he knew who came to the first, second and third minyans. Rabbi Shimon was very clever and very strict. Unfortunately he died prematurely.

I have to say that I even studied one year in the Polish government school called "Powszechna". Among all the gentile children we were just four Jewish children. Besides me there was my friend Michael Rabets and the Guttman sisters(grandchildren of Elta Pintzenski). We studied there just one year, and then they opened up a new Hebrew School "Chorev", which consolidated all the Cheders of the town. All the Jewish pupils then went to the "Chorev" school. Some of the teachers were Rabbi Joseph Shim Gershovitch, and Rabbi Shimon Cherberovitzki. There were also teachers who came from Vilna to teach at the school--Rabinovitch who taught

Judaism and history, Shimonivtch who taught Mathematics, and another one who taught the Polish language.

[Page 129]

I also moved to the "Chorev" school. After a while I moved to study in the Yeshiva out of town, and came back home just at the end of the semesters. I ended my Yeshiva studies when I went to an agricultural school to prepare for emigration to Eretz Israel.

Maytchet was a town like all the others in the area, and life was normal. There was one market day each week, some fairs every year, and also some manufacturing, etc. But basically Maytchet was a rest and vacation town. Every year many Jews from the surrounding area came there to rest. There was a forest and rivers for people to swim. There were some pensions and guesthouses for the vacationers to stay. During the later years, just before the war, some buildings were built in the forest, and during the summer the town was full with people; they loved to walk on Pedkriz and Pedlejan Streets. The people of the town had their differences, but they did not quarrel with each other. Only a couple of years before the war, when Rabbi Belsky died, the people could not agree on his successor. It was then that they had a serious disagreement.

I would be remiss if I did not remember some of the people who were dear to me, and part of my life. Reb David the shochet (slaughterer) was a religious and wise man, and worked in his butcher shop until he was very old. His house stood behind the great synagogue. Reb David used to pray in the "Shtibel". My grandfather, Reb Asher Orzechovsky, prayed in this Shtibel on Saturdays and Holidays, and his chair was near Reb David, the shochet. We, the grandchildren, always sat around him and I would pray with him. I remember we gave him honor because he was old and had a long white beard.

Reb Shemaryahu Sapir, the son-in-law of Reb David, the "Shochet", was a watchmaker and the agent of the Polish newspapers. He had a modern beard and was a little different then the other people. He was very active in the "Mizrachi" movement, and participated in every circle and institute in town. He found a common language with all the people, and was very active in the Zionist foundations and conferences.

[Page 130]

Shmerl Sapir

Asher Orechovsky

Malke Romanovsky and family

Concerning Malke Romanovsky, "Those who run from honor, honor chases them." She was a woman with a very good heart. There was a big grocery store in her house. She always found time to do good deeds for unfortunate people. She had two beautiful customs. She used to prepare the strings on the tzises with her own hands and give them to anyone who came to her for them. Another beautiful thing she did was, on every Passover eve, she would give out charoses that she made herself to the children of the city.

[Page 131]

They would come to her house after the Mariv services and before the seder to receive charoses.

Reb Yehuda Rabinovitch (known as "Yudel Der Shuster") was a dignified and charitable man with excellent character. Until he was old, he was very involved in the community and headed the "Tehilim Society" in the town. When he became old, he got the honor of being an honorary member in many institutes in town, and had a minyan in his house on Saturdays and holidays. His son Jacob was a member of the fire department orchestra, and another son, Moshe-Tzvi, was a member of the cantor's choir, and an officer in the fire department.

When the Shochet Reb Raphael Gelman became the town's cantor, he organized a choir of children and adults. The tryouts were in Reb Yudel Rabinovitch's house. The cantor sang a sentence and the candidate would repeat it after him. After Reb Raphael Gelman immigrated to the U.S.A. his successor as cantor and shochet was Reb Shaul-ke. He also had a choir, and Moshe Tzvi Rabinovitch was a member of it.

Rabbi Abraham David Zuchovitsky, the head of the "Tarbut" school, was very educated and very involved in Zionist organizations. I remember he always spoke in Hebrew. His wife Malka and her sister Chana taught in the "Tarbut" school.

Abram-David Zuchovitsky

Isaac Liberman

Reb Isaac Liberman sold old clothes and was an honored person in town. He was the main speaker at the great demonstrations in 1929, speaking out against the 1929 Arab riots in Eretz Israel. He was the speaker in other demonstrations after Hitler's rise to power, and also after the Pogrom in the town of Pashitic. Whenever there was a demonstration in the town, all the Jews closed their stores and gathered at the great synagogue to hear Reb Isaac Liberman.

[Page 132]

Reb Catriel Lichter was a simple man. He worked as a shoemaker, was a member of the "Acts of Charity Union", a member of the local bank management, and was the representative of all the manufacturers.

Catriel Lichter

Reb Nachum Abramovsky was a religious student and a dignified man. He had a linen store, but was very involved in the education of the children. He was concerned with their welfare, and helped the children and the teachers. The children loved him, and when he died, they all accompanied his body and prayed for his soul.

Nahum and Sara-Rivka Abramovsky

[Page 133]

Reb Isar Blaus was a good man and worked in his linen store with his son Zeidel. Reb Isar had a speech impediment, which made it difficult for him to deal with his customers. But when he taught lessons in the Shtibel, his stuttering was greatly improved.

Shimeon Lahovitsky had a medicine warehouse. His home was the place where the public figures would meet. At times he was a member of the town council, and would help the people in the community.

Zvi Volochvinsky was a very hard working and humble man. He was the representative of the manufacturers of the town.

Zvi Lahovitsky   **Shimeon Volochvinsky**

I have described some of the Maytchet Jews, but you have to know that everyone was like these people. Every man lived with his faith, his conscience, and his way of life. They were all a part of their town and their nation; they all have a glorious past and wanted a better future for the children of the town.

[Page 134]

Rabbi Yisrael Elchanan the "Maytcheter"
by Rabbi Yosef-Eliahu Peniel (Piklani)
Translated by Jerrold Landau

Rabbi Yisrael Elchanan was known by this nickname because Maytchet was the rock that forged him and the cradle of his birth. There, he received his education in the home of his parents, and there he absorbed the Torah and fear of Heaven that forged his noble personality. He was graced with wonderful diligence, and spent his nights as days in his dedication to Torah, worship, commandments, and good deeds, to the point where both the spirit of his fellowman and the spirit of G-d derived pleasure from him. Hearing his praises that went before him, the expert scholar, rabbi and Tzadik Rabbi Yosef Eliahu Feinsilber of nearby Zhetl chose him as a husband for his righteous daughter Chaya Hadassah.

There, he found a broad arena for his activities, taking interest in everything that was taking place with respect to religion and society in the town. There, he displayed his dedication by offering help and assistance to anyone in need. I recall that on Sabbath eves, we would always be late in sitting down to our meal, for Father of blessed memory would pass by all the synagogues in order to ensure that arrangements were made so that the poor guests would have a place to eat and sleep. Of course, he would bring a guest home as well. Throughout the week, he would collect for the society of charity and benevolence. He was especially active in supporting the Yeshiva of the city, and he concerned himself with all the needs of the students as a dedicated father. He was a member of the Committee of the Yeshivas; he disseminated Torah in public, and had many students. Mother also assisted him, and for some time, she maintained a home kitchen for the Yeshiva students.

A short time after their wedding, when the worries of livelihood afflicted him, he wandered afar to teach young children so that he could earn sustenance for his home. However, after a brief time, he returned home with the faith that G-d would provide for his livelihood locally. He always satisfied himself with little, so as not to benefit from this world more than necessary. Mother of blessed memory was a faithful partner who accepted everything with love, and never complained. She accompanied him and his activities with endless dedication, and due to her, a festive atmosphere always pervaded in the house, especially on Sabbaths and festivals.

When father decided to found a *cheder* in the house, people came to him from the most important households, for they knew of his boundless dedication, righteousness and ability to study. From their perspective, the students revered him greatly. Even when they grew up, they would call him Rebbe, and come to visit with him, to chat and consult with him. He was graced with an exceptional sense of responsibility. No obstacle, problem or weather situation would keep him from his activities at the institutions that he took care of. He also never missed a class in the *Mishna* and *Talmud* study groups morning and evenings.

He had refined emotions, and was alert to everything taking place in all arenas. He especially excelled with the love of the people of Israel and the Land of Israel. He was filled with joy at any good news that arrived from the Land of Israel; and, on the other hand, he felt great anguish at the opposite. The children also absorbed these good traits. At the first opportunity, he sent his daughter to the Land of Israel. A few years later, she brought her parents to her, and their joy was boundless. When they made *aliya*, all the people of the city accompanied them on their way, and parted from them with feelings of reverence and great longing. Even when he lived in our Holy Land, he continued with his activities to the extent possible, particularly with Torah and prayer, as was his custom. However, in the latter years, when the world war broke out, he became very weak from worry about the second daughter and her family who did not succeed in being saved from the vale of killing. First his faithful wife died from great anguish. This broke his spirit completely. However, even as he lay on his sickbed, he did not desist from occupying himself with words of Torah. His soul departed in purity. They repose in honor in Raanana.

May their memories be a blessing.

Rabbi Yosef-Eliahu Peniel (Piklani)
Alta Borechki and her two children Herzl and Marim

[Page 137]

Chapter 4
Education, Society, Economics
Maytchet General Survey
By Benzion H. Ayalon
Translated by Martin Small a/k/a Mordechai Leib Schmulewicz
II. Between Two World Wars

a. General background
b. In Retrospect
c. Town Panorama
d. Government and administration
e. Public and national activity
f. Educational organizations
g. Trade and handicraft
h. Agriculture
i. Transportation
j. Jews of Maytchet.

a. General Background

The traditional Polish Anti-Semitism that ran in the blood of the Polish leaders between the two world-wars (1919-1939) inflamed the darkest urges of the Polish people, who lost all humane and moral restraints in their relationships with the neighboring Jews, who had played an important part in the development of their land. The evil Polish behavior at this time of dire straits not only allowed the Nazis to perform their satanic scheme, but also assisted the criminals who willingly participated in the mass destructions of Jews on their land.

In spite of that, the short period between the two world wars was lively and encouraging for the Jews of Poland and Maytchet, for three reasons:

1. In the initial recovery of the renewed Poland, which was revived after a long era of enslavement under the iron hand of the Russian Czar, was a different spirit, and the leaders of the time allowed the Jews to assist in the construction and rebuilding of their country.

2. The border erected between Russia and Poland led Russian Jewry to degeneration and destruction, religiously and nationally, thus the fate of Polish Jews was the lesser of two evils.

3. The Jews knew persecution and oppression for many generations under the Russian Lithuanian and Polish regimes, and they were, at this point, not selective, accepting every peace and cooperation effort with happiness and honest loyalty. They had no choice but to believe that a new era awaited them– A time of labor and positive actions as citizens of the country and Jews.

[Page 138]

Indeed, in spite of the difficult financial straits and the heavy taxation, which were not bereft of Anti-Semitism and discrimination, they endured this time with happiness in view of the possibility that they would live and strive for better days. The gloomy days of the Polish minister Graevsky expressed the situation in a nutshell. Responding to the radical Anti-Semites he said: "thrashing the Jews with the financial whip and squeezing taxes out of this till they go bankrupt, Why not, that is a good idea! But physically hurting them? No!"

This was the atmosphere in which Jewish life was led, and although the conditions were difficult and fluctuating, and perhaps for that reason, a wide network of public and national-Zionist activity had developed in order to fill the gap by adding toil and energy. The short sighted Jews accepted their decree, and their life force dictated their actions: do everything and live. Jews who were more far-sighted realized there was not room to live wholesome Jewish lives in any place but the Land of Israel, and gave all their lives and energy to work towards the ideal of a Jewish state. But neither realized that they were living on the tip of a smoking volcano, and whoever did not escape was doomed.

And still these years will remain engraved in our memories more than any other era. Specifically because it was close to us and in honor of our dear ones who lived during those years fighting for our existence and were killed for the sake of G-d and the People of Israel.

b. In Retrospect

After the many changes that took place on account of the shift in borders and the changes in government and regiment, one thing at least, which is the natural condition of the place, which no one had any control over, stayed unchanged, as engraved in our memories.

Near the confluence of the Svorta into the Molchadka river is this small place named Molchadz, or Maytchet by the Jews. Anyone who nears the place on the way from the village Mitskevitz, the train station of Maytchet and the train line of Vilna-Rovno, will see from a distance the Polish Catholic church buildings and the Belarusian Eastern-Orthodox church, and upon reaching the town, the "Shul-Hof" (street of the synagogues) with the big synagogue belonging to the Jewish community. The three holy places will attest to the fact that from the beginning of times, this place was intended for the three religions, but the Catholics and the Eastern-Orthodox, the eternal arch rivals, cooperated as did Midyan and Moab, assisting in the destruction of the Maytchet Jews.

For more than 400 years, over 400 Jewish families lived and worked in Maytchet and in adjacent villages. In the vast sea of hostile population they knew high and low tides of persecution and peace, of building and destruction. But with all the conditions and circumstances, they continued to share the burden of the difficult Jewish life, fulfilling the commandments, studying the Torah, placing efforts on education, culture, charity and benevolence, public and national activities, days of happiness and sorrow.

[Page 139]

The only thing the Jews of Maytchet lacked in this fateful time was a prolonged peaceful period, in order to prepare themselves for what was yet to come. The Jewish youth especially regarded it as a desperate need to prepare cadres of pioneers and send them to Israel to build their new homeland. Also to raise consciousness with members of the Jewish nation who did not yet realize the danger they were in. But the peaceful times were not long; there was too much work and their life work was stopped in its prime.

c. Town Panorama

Physically, the town did not undergo many changes in the years before the Second World War. Its old streets remained unpaved and unlit just as they had always been, and the mud and puddles on rainy days were a common sight. Aside from the paved main road which led to the train station, all other paths leading to district towns were dirt roads in which transportation was mainly conducted by horses and carriages, except for one car, which was the only modern innovation of the time.

A few new public buildings like the slaughterhouse and the bath-house were built during this time at the demand of the authorities. Only few small stone houses and two story houses were built. The old wood houses stood erect, covered with wooden shingles, and some of straw. Only the stores were covered with tin roofs and clay shingles. Water supply to the houses was provided by water drawers (which was a device with two rectangular containers and a pole that was placed across the shoulders to carry water to the houses). The Jews of Maytchet remember Shalom the Water Carrier, who would charge less money when required to carry water to a more distant location, explaining that he got a chance to rest on the way. There were also some self-service wells and springs with fresh water from which to drink.

All these imparted Maytchet with a unique identity of a typical Jewish village, where the wealthy were scant, and the poor supported themselves off each other sparingly but with love and justice. It was distant from the din of civilization and all that goes with it, but "its poverty was becoming to the Jews." There was so much Jewish grace to every small and poor home, especially on the Sabbath and on holidays, when the presence of peace and love prevailed over them. At these divine moments, every heart was filled with happiness, and every mouth cried in admiration "How goodly are your tents, Yaakov, your dwelling places, Israel..."

d. Government and Administration

As Maytchet was a small town, there were only minor changes in its administration. The Polish government gave it the status of Gemina (local council). The head of the Gemina was a Russian Voyat (head of council), who was usually easy on the Jews and fulfilled his obligations towards the residents without discrimination. Among the members of council were always 2-3 Jews who were in charge of protecting Jewish interests. The Gemina controlled the jail house, the police house, the post office and the magistrates' court.

[Page 140]

According to the civil administration rule which was set by Polish authority, the city of Baranovichi was stated as the county town and Maytchet was subordinate to it in all issues pertaining to the duties and rights of the citizens as well as the communal issues within the Jewish community. The city of Novogrudok served as the District town,

The Jews of Maytchet were famous for their affinity to centers of Torah and merchandise in the area, but because of government rules in small towns, they were forced to wander to the district and regional towns in order to take care of their personal day-to-day matters, big and small, from an appeal at the district court to reporting to military service and issuing a birth or death certificate. This phenomenon was part of the Jewish folklore in the villages, that one person belonged to several places, to the point that he could not give one answer to the question "Where are you from, brother Jew?" A Jew was born in Maytchet, registered in Baranovichi, reported at Slonim, married in Zhetl and a resident of Dvorets.

After many generations in which Maytchet was subordinate to Slonim and Grodno, the hegemony was passed to Baranovichi as the county town and Novogrudok as district town, and the confusion grew.

e. Public and National Activities

Among the social-cultural values that the Russian government passed on to the area after its long regime was a total lack of public organizations. The Russian government viewed any organization as an underground nightmare aiming to defeat the regime. And since the Jews of the area had not experienced any organizations over the generations, they did not realize they were lacking and stuck to the conventional miserable community institutions of the time: Chevra Kadisha, visiting the sickly, night's lodging, management of synagogue affairs, charity etc. The Zionist movement did not fare better at the time since the Russian officials did not differentiate between a socialist and a Zionist (purposely or inadvertently) and they were all liable for severe penalty.

A new leaf was turned in the social and culture life of the Maytchet Jews when the Polish regime took over and more freedom of action was granted. It influenced specifically the younger members, a fertile ground for every blessed seed that blew in with the new spiritual winds which appeared in the free Jewish world. Local public institutions changed only a little. The Jews of Maytchet fulfilled the renowned rule: "hold on to this, but do not relieve your grip on that," and did not neglect the old institutions in light of the new ones.

[Page 141]

The Fire Brigade – During this time a fire brigade and orchestra was established, constituted of volunteers. This was the only orchestra in town, and all members of it were Jews. Profits were used to maintain the brigade and renew its equipment as well as for support and help of its needy members. The orchestra played polkas and krakoviaks to the "usadinks" (Polish settlers) at New Years parties, etc. For weddings they would bring in special klezmer from Baranovichi. The head of the fire dept. was Yosel Schmulewicz who also played the clarinet in the band.

The Public Library – A public library was established, which held many books in Yiddish, Hebrew, and the native tongues. David Volinski was the librarian, and the library was at his home. This library did not have a name or affiliation, and it only had one aim – to provide spiritual food for the seekers of knowledge in the town, from all classes and schools. At some point, the library moved to reside in the "Tarbut" school, and the new librarian was Noach Kosterovitzki.

Tending To The Sick – at the initiation of Zelig Volinski, brother to Shifra and Miriam and with the participation of Yosef Skidelekovitz, Katriel Lichter and others, an "Ezrat Cholim" (tending to the sickly) organization was established to provide assistance with medicine and tools for the sickly and needy, as well as couples who made rounds sleeping besides the sickly.

A Charity Fund – In accordance with Jewish tradition in every town and village, Maytchet too established a charity fund headed by Katriel Lichter. This fund was used as support to needy families, offering short term loans without interest to petty merchants and craftsmen to buy merchandise they needed for their business, or just to Jews in distress.

In the national arena there were Zionist institutions and organizations divided by parties and schools: The Shomer Hatzair movement, Ha-Halutz, the general Zionists, The Mizrachi, the National Fund (Keren Kayemet), the Keren Halysod Foundation Fund, the Hachshara Kibbutz etc. The wealthier Jews of Maytchet did not display any opposition or envy, but responded with much affection to all the Zionist movements and contributed generously to every national aim.

Maytchet was not lacking in small organizational cells, Zionists and non-Zionists: Dror, Tiferet Bachurim, Bunds etc.

f. Educational Institutions

As the custom of the Jews was in all villages at the time, the traditional Cheder served for many generations as the utmost source of education for every Jewish child, a "workshop" where the soul of the nation was created, though lately, in light of the modern educational methods, the Cheder lost some of it glory, but if we discuss unforgettable knowledge acquired in childhood, everyone admits that this can only happen at the Jewish cheder.

Thus, the pain and fury at the cruel and harsh hand of the killers who violated this last fort of Judaism and destroyed it along with the innocent children who did not sin, and silenced the voice – the voice of Jacob and the hands of Esau.

[Page 142]

Zionist Library

[Page 143]

These were the last cheders in Maytchet: (Cheder is a room or school where Jewish boys started learning Hebrew at the age of three and would study six to ten hours a day six days a week.)

Moshe "Der Toiver" (Moshe the Deaf One) – The cheder of Moshe 'Der Toiver" served the children who needed help from the big synagogue in the Shul-Hof (street of the synagogues" Moshe was also the cantor for the morning prayers in the Bet Midrash (House of Study). Students who once studied in that cheder are full of longing for those days, with the good and bad. They relate the story of one winter day when the students of this cheder got together and declared war on students of a different cheder, holding heated battles until a truce was declared and they all went back to study.

Shimon Shak – The cheder of Shimon Shak's was known as "Der Lechevitsher" (From Lechoviche, a shtetl about 30 miles from Maytchet) for advanced students of "chumash" and so on. This cheder was not located in the Shul-Hof but rather in the center of the village. He also had another innovation; he contacted with the "Tarbut" school, and his students received lessons in Polish.

Koppel Gorsky – The cheder of Koppel Gorsky' was considered an advanced one, for it was aimed for children who studied the "chumash." These students viewed themselves as full fledged adults, and they did not deem the students of the children's cheder worth playing with.

Talmud Torah – In actuality, there was not such an institution in Maytchet, as in other villages and towns. Really, this was just a cheder, but the teacher who ran his cheder in the synagogue gave it the name "Talmud Torah" in order to make it seem more important.

The Polish School "Povshachna" – This was an elementary Polish school that provided free education to all nationalities in accordance with the compulsory education law. Only a few Jewish students attended, as most of the Jewish parents willingly waived free education and sent their children to a private and expensive Hebrew school. Rabbi Belski's son-in-law, Rabbi Elchanon Goldstein, taught religion to the Jewish students in that school.

At the time the Russian ruled, till 1914, there was a Russian high school in the place.

Hebrew Kindergarten – As part of the Hebrew educational system that included most of the Jewish students in Jewish and Zionistic Maytchet, kindergarten teacher Gonik ran a Hebrew kindergarten which also served as intermediate classroom and a gateway to the "Tarbut" elementary school.

Tarbut Hebrew School – This was the main school in Maytchet and greatly appreciated by the Jews; so much so that it replaced the traditional cheder. This school was established approximately in 1925, when the Hebrew educational chain "Tarbut" was only beginning to grow. The Zionistic activists in the area put much effort, affection and devotion into this place, till it grew and flourished in its efficient organization and comprehensive curriculum, and with a talented cadre of teachers, the school won recognition of the government. Indeed, it was a lighthouse for the children of Israel in the darkness of exile, growing and being educated in the light of Torah and its values, to the love of Israel and the recovery of the nation of Israel to ritual Jewish law and action. The school went through various stages in development until it stabilized and ensured its honorable and glorious existence. To our terrible agony and sorrow, the enemy got to it and its fame was extinguished. The school was destroyed with its students, parents, teachers and activists in the catastrophe of the big Holocaust.

[Page 144]

Tarbut School building on Yorzika Street

[Page 145]

The school began under the directorship of Abraham David Zukovitski, who married into Maytchet and organized the school on Yorzika Street. Very soon it had seven full classes with 200 students, both male and female. With time, it moved to "Beit Olam" (Jewish Cemetery) Street in a building with a big yard and all the necessities required was rented from a Gentile (whose last name was Moshey). The great Chanuka and Purim bazaars were held there, as well as plays put on by the children and theatre clubs; theatrical productions which left an educational impression on the students and spectators. All revenues were directed, of course, towards the school maintenance.

In the drama club of the Tarbut School the actors and organizers were: Chezkel Rabets Yankel Gilerovitz, Leibel Gilerovitz, Gela Skolnikovitz or Skidelekovitz, Alta Boretcky, Feigle Boretcky, Esther Shmulewicz and others.

When the school expanded it moved to a third location in suburbian Pedlejan, in the house of Michael Shmulewicz. Among the teachers were: the principles' wife Malka Zukovitzki, Channa Boyarsky, Katz, Bossie Shepsenholtz, Keizer, Mrs. Bloch and others.

Religious School "Chorev" A religious school was established at the initiative of the orthodox parent committee, local teachers and several external teachers. The school principle was Mr. Teller. In the beginning, the school had four classrooms, but over time it grew and expanded and reached 120 students. In fact, this was a natural process of moving from the cheder method to that of the school and modern education in general.

The staff included: Reb Meir Teller, Reb Yossef-Shimon Gershovitz, Reb Shimon Harbrovitski, Reb Yakov Ginsburg, Reb Reuben Lamshevsky, the daughter of Yitzchak-Herschel Kaplan, Mr. Rabinovitz (from another place), a teacher of the Torah portion of the week on Friday night whose beautiful interpretations drew a large audience, Teacher Shimonovitz (from another place) for math and one student teaching the Polish language. In its last years, "Chorev" hosted six classes. chain "Tarbut" was only beginning to grow. The Zionistic activists in the area put much effort, affection and devotion into this place, till it grew and flourished in its efficient organization and comprehensive curriculum, To create income, the Parents Committee would initiate a play: "The Selling of Joseph." The following participated in the play: Yechiel-Leib Rozansky, the synagogues' caretaker, Yehuda Leib Lamshevsky and Moshe Shmulewicz. The productions were held at the beit midrash in the beginning, and later, in the school's kindergarten.

[Page 146]

Laying a corner stone for the Chorev School

In 1933, the "Chorev" youth established a drama club, members of which were: Shmuel Noah Belsky (chairman), Meir Lazovsky, Yossef, son of Rabbi Velvel and the female teachers.

There was a small yeshiva for graduates of the Chorev in the Shul-Hof held in the Bet Midrash.

Advanced Studies – Upon termination of elementary school, many of the Maytchet children went to work. Those who had capability and initiative went to high schools in Vilna, Bialystok, Brisk, etc. The ultra-orthodox continued at yeshivas in Kletzk, Baranovichi, Slonim, Lyakhavichi, and Mir. A few of the Maytchet youth went to colleges in other countries and overseas. A list of the students can be found in a separate chapter of this book.

An important note in conclusion: there were no Yiddish educational institutions in Maytchet.

[Page 147]

g. Commerce and Business

The fact that commerce and business were always in the hands of Jews, wherever they resided, is an undisputed reality. The reason for this was the unique social conditions the Jews had in the Diaspora. The question is only the extent of commerce and the types of business which were suitable for the needs of the Jewish community in Maytchet, and who took part in what business. Despite a small number of wholesale traders, most of the Jews in the town took part in petty commerce and craft. Aside from the daily proceeds, their trade depended on sales on market days and fairs. Also, there were a large number of straggler peddlers who went around the local villages offering haberdashery of sorts to the wives of the farmers in return for cash or agriculture. In Maytchet itself there was a market every Wednesday, and the tradesmen would wander to the various markets in the area and outskirts.

Besides trading in textile, leather, food necessities etc., for the daily consumption of the residents, the wholesalers of Maytchet traded in rags and linen which were exported overseas, while the retailers resided in "Red Kremen" (Shop Street), where there were a variety of shops that sold confectionaries, leather, grains, many food stores, clothing, butchers and others. The small shopkeepers bought their merchandise from local wholesalers, while the prominent merchants traveled to other towns; specifically Baranovichi but also to Slonim, Vilna, Warsaw, and others.

Construction – There was little building done in the town itself. Most of the structures were wooden homes with wooden or straw shingles, built by simple craftsmen or farmers. Fires in town were common, and from time to time the wooden houses would burn down. Naturally the citizens of Maytchet, as in other Jewish towns, would count their dates in relation to the big fire, until a bigger fire would come along and cause the previous to be forgotten. In 1924 a whole street caught on fire on a market day when most of the residents of the village were out of their homes. When the local fire brigade ran to get horses that would carry water to put out the fire, the farmers ran away from the market with their merchandise.

Only a few houses were made of stone, and even fewer were two-stories high. Construction was mostly done by Joshua Aharon Lozovsky and his sons. They built many public structures, i.e., the slaughterhouse, the fire brigade house etc, but mostly they built out of town in estates, etc. Another construction worker Mikal Shmulewicz, and among the wood merchants Moshe Shmulewicz was popular.

Other Professions – Tar factories, a profession relative to the wood trade, also belonged to the Lazovsky family in Maytchet and just outside the shtetl to Mikal and Zimel Shmulewicz. They built with their wood in the summer and burned tar in the winter. Tar and tar products like turpentine and such were exported to Slonim and then overseas, coal to factories, etc. There were two windmills in the village, powered by the local river water. The big one belonged to the Boretcky family while the small one belonged to David Belsky. There was also a grits mill and a straw chopper, both of which served local residents and the farmers in the vicinity. Boarding houses were among the occupations of the Jews of Maytchet. There was an inn which served as a boarding house to the agents and merchants from out of town, as well as some food houses. A list of all the commerce and business can be found henceforth.

[Page 148]

h. Agriculture

This uncommon occupation should be mentioned as well. It was scarce among the Diaspora Jews, but naturally in this area there were a recognizable number of Jews in Maytchet who dealt in agriculture and other jobs in farming and gardening. Some of them lived in the many villages adjacent to Maytchet and cultivated farms and raised produce. Some of them worked in estates as lessees or hired workers. Within the town itself almost all of the Jewish residents had pieces of land flanking their homes where they grew vegetables and fruits for their personal consumption and sale.

In 1919, as part of the efforts of the Jewish help organization "HIAS" to help rehabilitate the Jews who became impoverished after W.W. I, loans were given to the Jewish residents in Maytchet to cultivate their farms, gardens, housekeeping, etc.

i. Transportation

Complex transportation routes and elaborate roads are one of the hallmarks of states which have an advanced western-European culture. Czarist Russia was way behind in this area. The legacy of the Russian government for over 120 years was a total lack of paths and roads, and therefore there were not as many motorized vehicles. The streets of the town itself were only partly paved with coarse and sharp rocks, except for the train station, to which a paved road led. During the German occupation in WWI roads were paved out of wooden logs.

The main form of transportation between the villages was horse and carriage. The Jewish carters were therefore a prominent professional cadre. They drove the merchants to nearby towns and local passengers to Slonim, Baranovichi, the train station, etc. for their personal arrangements. Until 1930 the only stop the train made was in the village of Mitskiewicze, four km. from Maytchet on the Vilna to Rovno train line. From that point on, the station for boarding and getting off for travelers (Palstanak) was next to the town.

[Page 149]

After the previous generation of carters rode horses, one of their sons breached the gate and brought in the first Maytchet bus. The craters still used the dirt path to Slonim, but took the train or bus to Baranovichi.

j. Jews Of Maytchet

So thus the dear Molchad Jews pass before our eyes, their families and peers, their business and Jewish lifestyle, weaved in golden thread for centuries. Some of them were people of Torah and good deeds, public activists and loyal Zionists, people of trade and industry who negotiated in faith, righteous craftsmen who enjoyed the fruits of their labor - a whole community of men and women, old people and youth, whose homes turned into graves on account of the sins of their generation. And when we long for them, we leaf through the memorial volume of the Maytchet book, saturated in the blood of our hearts, and the dear community arises from the dead. Our thoughts rush through the pages which are read of their own accord, years and eras fly by like a dream. The lively folklore of the town passes before our eyes like a play, happiness and agony, spectacular visions and horrifying ones chase each other, till we can hardly keep up with them and absorb their content.

Here is a beautiful picture of Friday nights, flooded with light and happiness, Sabbath tables full of holiness and soulfulness; of Passover Seders and holiday meals, filled with a yearning of the soul and endless longing. In every house in Maytchet a Jewish family sits around a glorious laid table. The father sits majestically at the head of the table, next to his wife, the mother, dressed up for the Sabbath and holiday and like olive trees around the table, are the happy and glowing children and grandchildren who receive with happiness and good manners the abundance of love pouring out of the hearts of their joyful parents. And those late afternoons on the Sabbath and holidays, who will ever comprehend them? When satisfaction and the blessings of God wear them out, and they fulfill the tradition of "sleeping on the Sabbath is pure pleasure," while the youth fill the town's streets with youthful din and the gaiety of life. Some of them are out taking walks, others visiting, some go to their organizations or clubs or to social-cultural meetings. They fill the town with fresh and bubbly life like a mighty stream of water which flows way beyond its borders, in the gardens and bushes, in the fields, in the mountains and valleys.

The pages are turning fast and the visions appear and vanish alternately. Here they are, the tormented righteous people of Maytchet, grim death on their pale faces ... trees are bending in terror and fear, bowing with deep sighs to mother earth, their howl escorting a whole congregation of Jews, big and small, on their last path of torment and death. The souls of their forefathers descend to earth, floating above the heads of those condemned to death, lamenting in a silent unearthly cry the untimely end to the lives of their sons.

[Page 150]

Breathless from evil and agony, we stand before the great common grave on blood hill, "Chwoinik", where fathers and mothers, brothers and sisters and young children who haven't yet lived or sinned are buried. How terrible it is to meet the deathly terrorized gaze of babies who are being held to the cold bosom of their dead mothers. The pure eyes of Moshe'lech and Shiomo'lech, Chaya'iech, and Sara'iech are penetrating us with question, fear, and supplication!

The memorial volume for the righteous people of Maytchet, who have blood, fire and pillars of smoke inscribed on their bodies and souls, is not a conventional book but an alter on which we will sacrifice our afflicted hearts in memory of the righteous people of Maytchet. It is not a book but a memorial tombstone, in which we will lay to rest our holy community, and where we will come, and our children and grandchildren after us, to be alone with their holy memory, and our cry of despair will merge with the sound of our brothers' blood as it cries to us from the earth!

Alte Boretcky and her two sons Herzyl and Meyerim

[Pages 151-153]

The Students – The Golden Youth
by Nachum Naor (Orzechovsky)

The most frequently accepted meaning of the concept "Golden Youth" refers to children who come from privileged and affluent homes, whose needs are provided by their wealthy fathers while they themselves live for the most part without any ideal or important purpose, and spend their time indulging in entertainment and a hedonistic lifestyle. The Jewish youth in the cities and towns, including Maytchet, did not act this way. Aside from carrying on the traditions of their ancestors, meaning spending their time studying Torah and engaged in Divine service, they also found a way for their vibrant hearts, and felt the ideas of the Haskalah, progressiveness, social justice and national revival. On the one hand, they filled the schools and famous Yeshivot locally and in the nearby cities in order to enrich their spirit in the crucible of the souls of the nation. On the other hand, they founded youth groups, went to places of Zionist training [hachsharah] in order to forge the image of the Jew of the future, and to actualize the dreams of their youth, unparalleled by any other nation.

Golden Youth of Maytchet

[Page 152]

It is regarded as a wonder that despite the concerns of their own daily existence, and at times, even that of their parents, they took upon their young shoulders the great task of preparing the Jewish generation for a better future.

This is how the Maytchet youth acquired the honorable name of "Golden Youth." Not because of *yichus* [family status] but rather because of what they themselves did. They dedicated their best energy to their holy task, and filled the town with the sounds of Torah and light, and bustling, vibrant life. Their young hearts tasted the content of a life worthwhile living. However, their life was abruptly cut off, and many of them did not live to fulfill their dreams of arriving in the desired Land of Israel and building it up and being built up by it. Many of these youths, who were beloved and pleasant during their lives and were not separated in death, fell under the hand of the destroyer who cut of their heads during the terrible Holocaust. For them, our hearts ache, and we weep in the recesses of our souls.

These are the names of the studying youth of Maytchet, each in his own place and calling, to the extent that we can remember:

Yeshiva bochars (boys) of Maytchet

In Yeshiva Baranovichi – Gershon Romanovski (who is a Rabbi in New York) Shmerl Abramovski, Yehuda Shvstik, Eliezer Volinsky

In Yeshiva Novogrudok – The brothers Shilem and Daniel Rabinowitz, Reuven and Ben Zion Lomshavsky, Mordechai Yoselevitz, David Brishinsky

Yeshiva Lechowitz: Dov and Chaikel Shlomovits, Mishael Ravitz, Nachum Margolin

[Page 153]

Yeshiva Radin: Brothers Sholom and Zev Romanovski, and Eliezer

Yeshiva Mir: Yakov Boretcky, David Wilensky

Yeshiva Ruzhany: Gavriel and Meir Lazovsky, Chaikel Shlomovitz

Yeshiva Kletsk: The brothers Mordechai and Yosef Koton

Yeshiva Pinsk: Son of Chainka Zusman

Yeshiva HaMaalot: Yoseph Hassid

Yeshiva Slonim: Eliezar Orzechovsky

The following youth studied in the public high schools and higher vocational institutions: Chaya Sarah Boretcky and Mayer Ginsburg — in the Epstein Gymnasium of Baranovichi. Tova Polonsky (today in Israel, her name is Shomroni) — in the teachers' seminary of Vilna. Joseph Zusman — in the Technion of Vilna. Moshe Margolin — in the commercial school of Baranovichi. Nachum Naor — in the ORT School in Brisk. Adi Dvorjetski, the son of the pharmacist Yakov Dvorjetski, in the University of Lemberg.

It is important to note the names of the doctors and pharmacists who belonged to the intellectual sphere of the Jews in the shtetl, and they are: Doctors/medics — Dr. Kramer and Dr. Kaplan. Pharmacists — Yacov Dvorjetski, Leib Romanovski and Shimon Lachovitsky These are the names of the rabbis and the faithful scholars who followed the Torah and traditions, as well as teachers and intellectuals who are mentioned in separate chapters in this book.

[Page 153]

Trade and Labor
By Dov Shlomovitz
Translated by Ron Rabinovitch

Molchad Jews began their commercial careers when they settled in the town many years ago. They were permitted to settle here in order to promote the commercial atmosphere of the area which was primarily agricultural. As time went on the business atmosphere improved. They exported agricultural and trade material from this area and imported basic goods and articles for the citizens. The area grew and prospered and the local population was well provided for.

When the Russians ruled this area, the Jews were not permitted to conduct business beyond the parameters of their immediate area. They were allowed to continue trade within the community and thus remained a resource for the citizens of Molchad. With the return of the Polish rule, the freedom to expand the trading area (especially in their early years) when the governing power was more tolerant of Jewish commercial expertise.

But these tolerant years did not last long. After World War I some of the commercial institutions were able to recover. The blackmail machine of the Polish finance authorities, like the Gravskis, started to operate cruelly. This was the beginning of the bitter struggle between the Jewish tradesmen and the local authorities who wanted to destroy the Jewish businessman and replace him with a local Pole or a local Russian. The struggle between the independent Polish authority and the Jews expanded and this led to the erosion of the Jewish commercial well-being.

[Page 154]

To the best of my memory, the following is a list of names of the Jews of Molchad that worked in the main commercial branches of the shtetl.

Clothing branches

Manufacture – Iser Bilas, Alter Abramovitz, Nechama Bardo, Nachum Abramovski, Yona Orzechovsky, Leibel Vinograd, Shalom Rabinovitch, Moshe Belski, Laser Biltzki, Beryl Shmulovitz.

Tailor and clothing – Moshe Mendelevitch, Zelig Laserovitch, Moshe Savitzki, Chaim Leib Zimerman, Freidel Belski, Sara Korostovski, Chaya Rachel Kravchok, Hinda Gorski, Tzira Rabinovitch, Rakovitzki, Moshe-Leib, Chaim-Yona, Zimel, Channa.

Fancy goods – Mary Volfovski, Michel Stolovitzki, Entzel Belski, Isaac Katan.

Hat makers – Monni Rabinovitch, Yaekel.

Leather and shoes – Reuven Braski, Noach Goldstein, Eliezer Polonski, Shlomo Shnitzki, Nachum Ravitz, David Mirski, Josef Luski, Moshe Korostovski, Shmuel Korostovski, Tzvi Volochvienski, Chaim-Meir Gorski, Zenbel Der Shuster, Yudel Rabinovitch, Herschel BronitzkiMoshe Brashanski, Hetzel Brashanski, Isaac Shamshilovitch and sons, Moshe Lemshovski and son, Catriel Likter, Hazel Mordukovski, Herschel Novomisky, Baruch-Joshua Shkolnikovitz, Yehuda-Leib.

Food branches

Food – Beryl Romanovski, Shlomo-Herschel Shlomovitz, Josef and Shimon Gershovitch, Alke-Pearl Gorski, Pearl Rozanski, Chaynke Zisman, Sima Boyarski, Shimon Charborovitzki and son Yudel, Tzira Rabets (Kaplan), Deiche Korostovski, Chaya-Sara Shlomovitz, Esther Rabinovitch.

Restaurants and drink places – Leib Chaim Wolinsky, Shemaya Rabets, Leib Margolin, Israel Belski, Herschel Shlovski.

[Page 155]

Bakeries – Isar Isralvitz, Ytze-Yaekel Shebtzik, Moshe-Yehuda Belski, Chaya-Rachel, Chaya-Cherna.

Grains and flour – Isar Epstein, Israel Rabinovitch, Dudze Rabinovitch, Zelig Rabets, Moshe Rabets, Shlomo Bitanski, Leibel Gilerovits, Abraham Serebrovsky.

Home appliances and iron – Joseph-Chaim Shapira, Laser Gordon, Hertzel Korlitzki, Michel Shmulovits, Rabbi Asher Orzechovsky, Gedalia Yatvicy.

Eggs – Simcha-David.

Industrial branches

Mills – Moshe-Aharon Boretsky and sons, David Belski.

Grinding mills and oil press – Abraham and Yechiel Gorski, Yehuda Rabets and sons.

Tar burning – Lozovsky family.

Seltzer – Lieb Chaim Wolinsky.

Building branches

Building – Yehushua-Aharon Lozovsky and sons, Michael Shmulovits.

Woods – Moshe Shmulovits, Shlomo-Laser Rabets, Robijevski, Leib and his son Yehuda Kravchok.

Services

Doctors – Dr. Kremer, Dr. Kaplan.

Pharmacists – Jacob Dvorzecky, Shimon Lachovitzki, Leib Romanovski.

Banks – Yehushua Novomisky, Mordechai Rabets, daughter of Chaikel Isralvitz.

Agents – Chatzkel Rabets, Shmerel Safir.

Transportation – Joseph-Eliyahu Plavski, Moshe Shebtzik and sons.

Inns – Abraham Shmulovitz

Photographs – Tzira Mordkovski

Glazier – Mordechai and son Abramovski.

Resort houses – Shaina Margolin, Shlomo-Laser Rabets.

[Page 156]

Youth In Maytchet
By Haya Lubchik
Translated by Roslyn Sherman Greenberg

Who of us doesn't remember the "Tarbut" School that was headed by Abraham-David Tshuchavitsky and Malka the teacher. This was truly the cradle of our Molchad youth. With great love and devotion the teachers sowed and nourished in our young hearts and minds the love of Eretz Yisrael. They established from the children of Molchad the members of the large Jewish circle, which was never torn apart completely, and with great patience they fulfilled the holy bidding "And tell it to your children."

The blue Keren Kayemit LiYisrael box was inserted, through the children, into every house. Every wedding and every gathering was accompanied by a "bliml" (ceremonial planting) dedicated to the Keren Kayemit LiYisrael fund.

I remember how in the Tarbut School a Chanukah evening was arranged with a big bazaar. Every homeowner had to tax himself with something for the bazaar. The money was dedicated to the Keren Kayemit LiYisrael. Naturally, my father, may he rest in peace, ordered that a beautiful big goose be chosen to be donated to the bazaar. We were village Jews. The honor of giving the goose to the bazaar committee fell to my lot. Indeed, I must say, since geese existed in this world, a goose never had such an honor as did that white goose.

She was put into a big beautiful basket dressed up with a blue ribbon, and she had the foremost place. She also participated with her hoarse goose's voice, calling everyone to participate in the bazaar. Thus, many such events were arranged often. This united the youth in one undertaking, living with a goal and an idea.

Remembering the "HaShomer HaTsair" (a leftist/socialist Zionist organization) from our shtetl. On a hill on Podkritsh Street, this group would meet at the home of Sarah Krovchik (Sarah the Carpenter woman). There in the small house with a total of two rooms, the boys and girls used to gather, singing and dancing, sweet and carefree children by nature, with a deep belief in a better, lighter future. They danced hand to shoulder drawing out the circle.

[Page 157]

Commissioner of J.N.F. and assistants

[Page 158]

Life, although it was a poor one, and stringent, was still lived with dreams and hopes. The hope gave us a goal and sweetened the lives of our young people. The Molchad youth always felt the merit of enriching their cultural life.

In the shtetl, a drama circle was also founded. It would give performances. The stars of the drama circle were Alte Boretsky, Leibl Gilrovits, and others. The room was in the firemen's building, and when there was a large attendance and there weren't enough places on the benches, we used to sit on the water barrels of the firemen. But this was very pleasant, and it really brought great happiness and enjoyment.

The shtetl lived differently in the summer. Molchad had a reputation as a place for country homes. The dry pine forests attracted the dwellers from the larger cities where the air was dusty. The big-city people used to come to Molchad to heal themselves and revive themselves with the clean pine air. This brought a good income to the shtetl, whether in material or in business connections. Shopkeepers used to take in receipts, the dairy and the meat. The people from the country houses were big eaters. They didn't deprive themselves of the best that Molchad had to offer—milk, butter, meat, and eggs, everything was offered to them. And we, the youth, were happy to meet new faces, new people, new songs and new hits, enriching our repertoire with new material. And in the beautiful summer nights, friends would enjoy being with each other.

I would like to write more and more about you, my small shtetl, how much beauty, naturalness, humility and warmth there was in you, but I open my eyes and I see the big mass grave by the green bridge. The earth still wakes fresh from the murdered dead, holy sacrifices. .

[Page 159]

Maytchet in the press
by Moshe Zinovitz
Translated by Jerrold Landau

In the recent Jewish press

"Bafreiung," April 18, 1921 -- On Monday April 4, a meeting took place here with the participation of Mr. Nachimowski from Baranovichi. He spoke about the Zionist Movement and the need for "Young Zionism" amongst the Jewish working population. He urged activity toward the "Keren HaAvoda" [Workers's Fund] in the coming work month.

After the meeting, 38 members registered for "Tzeirei Zion" [Young Zion] and set up a committee to begin the work.

"Dos Vort,' Vilna, 19 Shvat 5688 (1928) - The largest contributors[1] to the Committee of the Yeshivas, of 3 zloty and higher, in Maytchet. Yitzchak Novomiski - 8.85 zl; Sara-Rivka Abramovski - 9.60 zl; Moshe-Tzvi Rabinovitch - 5.77 zl.; Leib Novomiski - 5.55 zl.; Yisrael Belski - 35 zl.; Zelik Liubavich - 4.25 zl.; Chaikel Izralvitz - 3.75 zl.; Yehoshua Aharon Lozovski - 4 zl.; Yisrael Chaim (Shinovski) - 3.65 zl.; Refael Stein - 3.70 zl.; Reuven Shevchik - 3.50 zl.; Moshe-Pinchas Shmulevicz - 3 zl.; Shalom Leib Rabinovitch - 3 zl.; Chaya-Eidel Damenichev - 3 zl.; the prayer leader and *shochet Gelman* - 3 zl.; Naftali Zawolochki - 3 zloty.

"Dos Vort," Vilna June 12, 1929 - From Maytchet, the sum of 35 zloty for the saving of the Yeshiva of Hebron has come in to our editor from Rabbi Yitzchak-Naftali Belski

"Dos Vort," Vilna, Torah portion of Beshalach, 5698 (1938) -Thanks to the reorganization of the local Chorev committee, the local Chorev School reached a significant height. A first-class teaching personality was engaged, and the religious situation of the school was rectified appropriately.

[Page 160]

At the request of the Chorev Committee, a special examination commission consisting of the local rabbi and Gaon Rabbi Yaakov Grinburg, the *shochet* Reb Avraham Garbarz, and Reb Yisrael Budowla visited the school. The fundamental examinations that were conducted produced gleaming results.

Recently, the ten year anniversary of the local Charitable Fund was celebrated. A special delegate from the Vilna "Yekopo"[2] was sent to the celebration. Various speeches were delivered. Rabbi Yosef Chasid brought greetings from Agudas Yisroel. The presentation of Rabbi Grinburg, whose speech made a significant impression, was especially impressive.

On Tuesday of the Torah Portion of *Vaera*, a conclusion celebration [*siyum*] of the local Chevra Shas [Talmud Study Group] took place in the large *Beis Midrash*. The teacher of the class, the local rabbi and Gaon Rabbi Yaakov Grinburg, delivered a profound *Hadran*[3] on Jewish law and lore. Then, the crowd rejoiced at the celebratory meal. Special congratulations are to be given to the local *Gabbai*, Mr. Shmuel David Rabinovitfch, the initiator and master of ceremonies of the festive meal.

(A Maytcheter)

Wednesday, Torah portion of Tzav - A concluding celebration [*siyum*] of the Order of *Nashim* was celebrated by the local Chevra Shas. Rabbi Yaakov-Sender Grinburg, may he live long, delivered a content-filled *Hadran* in front of a packed *Beis Midrash*. After the *Hadran*, the gathering made their way to the rabbi's house, where a festive meal was held. In a dignified spirit, the rabbi once again spoke words of lore on the issues of the day. After that, Rabbi Yosef Chasid, a student of the Beis Yosef Yeshiva of Nowogrudek, delivered an emotional speech. Following this, the city's cantor Reb Shmuel Sokolovski performed some cantoral numbers. The gathering celebrated and rejoiced throughout the entire night. That impressive joyous occasion will remain in our memories for a long time.

(A resident of the city)

Translator's footnotes
1. Literally, "charity boxes."
2. See http://www.encyclopedia.com/article-1G2-2587521236/yekopo.html
3. The prayer at the conclusion of study of a Talmudic tractate - here referring to the accompanying speech.

[Page 161]

The Coming of Passover
By Haya Lubchik
Translated by Roslyn Sherman Greenberg

The strong gray winter goes away little by little. A warm breeze forecasts the beginning of spring. Winter shows its last strength and sends down a white snow that covers our shtetl. The rays of the sun, with its warm breezes, change the newly fallen snow into a brownish thin mud. The mud fills all the streets, lanes, courtyards, and doesn't forget to push into the holes in the houses and shoes. The snow on the roofs is also melting, and the roofs look like a patched garment or a half-shaved face.

It's already after Purim. In the shtetl, we prepare already to bake matzos. In Molchad, as usual, we used to bake matzos in two locations. It was a combined effort; i.e. two or three householders used to gather in one of the designated houses to help each other with their own hands. This, you can understand, was less expensive, just the flour and other ingredients were needed. There were also rented houses that were converted into matzo factories, such as Henya-Basha's, Sheine-Malke's and also one on Shaseiner Street. In Henya-Basha's house the rest of the year there was a tailor shop. After Purim the house was changed into a matzo factory. First we would spread out smooth, white boards from wall to wall, creating a big table for the group. Afterward we used to put aside special places for those who spilled out the flour, the water pourers, the kneaders and rollers, etc. We paid only for the baking. Last of all we used to kosher the oven, carry in "Our water", and all who were needy could come, bring his bit of flour and bake. The one who made the holes in the matzo was her son Chaim. (A tool called a "reddler" was used to make the holes and this job was usually given to a youngster.) Then would come householders with their own water pourers, flourers, kneaders, and rollers, and they paid only for the baking. Those who didn't have all the necessary people would hire helpers.

In a brave, happy mood we would bake the matzos. The spring breeze, which brings with it the smell of the earth freed from snow, would mix with the smell of the matzo baking, which made the senses drunk. It awoke in people feelings of hope and longing for a better and more beautiful life. When the matzo was baked, each person brought his package of matzos home and put it in a clean corner. In every house in a certain corner, a wooden keg covered with a white tablecloth tied around it stood on a little hay. There, beets were marinated for Passover borsht. Spring and Passover, like indivisible twins, came even closer to our shtetl.

[Page 162]

Two weeks to Passover. We carry everything out of the house into the courtyard. We wash benches from the table, cabinets, and shelves. All are scrubbed, polished, rinsed and buffed once again, scoured and washed. The copper pans, basins, mortars, and pots we polish and we scrub up to three times, and they shine as if they were bleached by the sun, saying, "Well, tell me which of us shines the most?" The spring breeze blows the clothing and other articles in the courtyard. They appear once each year. We have a little happiness together, and both have great pleasure.

One week to Passover. Winter has vanished. Passover and spring in its whole splendor are already on the edge of the shtetl. The houses are ready, like citizens, for a great parade. The white curtains are bright through the clean panes. The scoured yellow-gold tables, benches, etc. are back in their places, covered with white tablecloths. The copper utensils fill the house with reflections from the rays of the sun. Whitewashed walls, polished door hardware, even new sticks for the forks, and brooms from fresh birch twigs, which bring the scent of the woods. The beds are decorated with clean linens. Plumped-up cushions, which were sewn during the long winter evenings, dress up the beds. Every house is ready to welcome the dear, great guest—Passover.

A harder question was the clothing for the children. There was a solution. For the bigger children, new clothes were bought. For the smaller ones, the clothes that had become too small for the big ones were taken apart and remade so that each child should wear something new and be complimented. New shoes were bought for each child.

And now it's already the last day before Passover. In the evening, the father searches for chometz. The last bit of chometz gets put into a corner so it should not be seen. In the morning the chometz gets burned, and we bring in the important guest's packages—the Passover utensils. What magical charm and flavor these Passover utensils possessed. How much joy and enchantment they brought into the hearts of the children. The tiredness and the sadness of the soul from the hard life all vanished.

[Page 163]

The Zionist Movement in Maytchet
Translated by Jerrold Landau

"Hashomer Hatsair" – after the events of the war and the horrors that followed, the news of the Balfour Declaration was received with very great enthusiasm by the Jewish communities of Poland. However, at a time when the Zionist organizations throughout the country were emerging from the underground and were forced to progress in the face of the great historical event, only weak echoes of the footsteps of redemption reached us from the cities of the interior of the country and broke through the imaginations of the Jews of Maytchet, especially the youth. The area in which they were able to give expression to the feelings of their hearts was through the first Jewish youth movement, Hashomer Hatsair, which was tolerated by the government in the same manner as similar Russian and Polish Boy Scout movements.

The following were among those who stood at the helm of the chapter of Maytchet as founders and counselors: Shakna Gorski, Moshe Epshtein, Sara Boretcky, Chemda Margolin, and others.

With the founding of this youth organization, the foundations of physical and spiritual education, the development of orienteering talent, the nurturing of the traits of helping and benevolence, faithfulness to the state, and love for the national values of the nation were all laid down. Almost all the Jewish youth of the area were attracted to the chapter. Some of them formed groups and brigades. Heads of the groups and brigades were appointed. They occupied themselves with training protocols accompanied by Hebrew marching songs; physical training; listening to lectures and instructional classes on general scouting and the foundations of Judaism and nationalism; song; games; etc. They especially found their place with their impressive parades on *Lag Baomer* and all other appropriate occasions, when they marched with the permission of the authorities through the streets of the town with their scouting uniforms, waving their flags to the tempo of the Hebrew commands and Hebrew marching songs, on their way to their activities in the nearby forest.

The good name of the new movement spread in a positive fashion through the local community of parents and educators, who encouraged the members and received them politely when they came on "Flower Days" or on the campaign days for the Jewish National Fund and other Jewish institutions. It should be noted with satisfaction that the Hashomer Hatsair movement, which was the first of the Jewish national movements, implanted feelings of national pride in the heats of the adults, and even provided the impetus to the founding of the Zionist organization of Maytchet.

Summer camps for Hashomer members of the entire region were set up around Maytchet.

General Zionists – The Zionist movement of Maytchet arose on the foundations of complete unity and harmony. There was never any divisiveness and fragmentations, as there was in larger cities.

[Page 164]

Summer Camp of Hashomer Hatsair

[Page 165]

Virtually all the Jews of Maytchet were inculcated with the Zionist idea. Whatever the outlook of each individual was, they would all sit together at one table with a single objective before their eyes, namely: national revival and *aliya* to the Land of Israel, to build it and be built by it. The name "General Zionists" had no implication of doctrinal factionalism. It would be more accurate to say that the "General" Zionist organization included Jewish Zionists from all strata and outlooks.

Shmaryahu Sapir a watchmaker and newspaper contractor, served as the chairman of the Zionist organization of Maytchet. The Jews of Maytchet remember well his enthusiastic speech delivered in the Great Synagogue in the year 5689 (1929 or 1930), in which he expressed the mass protest against the bloody events that were perpetrated in the land of Israel at that time. The active, veteran members of the Zionist organization were Chatzkel Ravits, Yankl Gilerovitz, Leibl Gilerovitz, and others.

Leibl Gilerovitz

[Page 166]

Hehaluts Organization
1. Alter Rabets, 2. Leibel Gilrovitz, 3. Mordechai Krufchuck, 4. Shmuel Lozovsky,
5. Yosef Lozovsky, 6. Lazar Epstein, 7. Rabets, 8. Moshe (son of the comedian),
9. Moshe Rabets, 10. Shmuel Korisofsky

[Page 167]

Their major activity was the registration of as many members as possible into this organization, which was indeed noted as the largest organization in town. They were very active in the national institutions such as the Jewish National Fund (*Keren Kayemet), Keren Hayesod*, and others. They made sure to send out members to *hachsharah*[1] to prepare them for *aliya* to the Land of Israel. The General Zionists were the main source of *aliya* of the middle class. We must only express sorrow that their successful activities in this realm were interrupted by the Second World War, and only few of them succeeded in their goal. Therefore, the number of survivors of Maytchet is small.

Evening course for workers. Maytchet, 1930

Hechalutz – The Hechalutz organization first arose through the efforts of the Zionist organization, and with its support as the executive arm with respect to the politics of *aliya* to the Land of Israel. With the passage of time, and with the work of actualization that they took upon themselves, Hechalutz developed and became a unique entity that stood on its own and was ideologically affiliated with the central Hechalutz organization. From that time, it received its directives and guidance directly from the national headquarters, and was assisted with support from the local Zionist Organization in exchange for recommending its members for *hachsharah* and obtaining permits for *aliya* (certificates).

The local Hechalutz sent its members to local *hachsharah* locations as well as those in the region, and even made sure to support the travel expenses of its needy members from its own funds.

The heads of Hechalutz in Maytchet included Leibl Shmulovitz, Noach Mordukovski, Yosef Lisovski, Alter Ravitz and others Mizrachi – The Mizrachi chapter of Maytchet, which included the Orthodox Zionists who made efforts to actualize the motto of "Torah and Work" in the building of the nation and the Land, was also prominent, if not in numbers then in quality. It is fitting to note that their organization did not stand in opposition to the spirit of unity that pervaded in the general Zionist organization. On the contrary, it complemented that spirit, for it made it possible to include additional strata of Jewry and join them to the general Zionist efforts.

[Page 168]

Hechalutz Hamizrachi (Mizrachi Pioneers), which served as an additional destination for *hachsharah* and *aliya* to the Land of Israel, arose through their efforts and their supports.

Mizrachi members included: Reb Yosef Shkolnikovitz, Yisrael Belski, Reuven Borski, Shmaryahu Safir, and others.

Small organizational cells of Zionist and non-Zionists, that arose in Maytchet during a later era included Freiheit (Dror), Tiferet Bachurim, and Bund.

Translator's footnote
  1. Programs for preparation for *aliya*

[Page 169]

Maytchet in Pictures A

First meeting with survivors who arrived to the Land after the Holocaust
The names on the photo, from the reverse side
**1. Reuven Berski. 2. Shmaryahu Sapir. 3. Rafael Gelman - the cantor and
shochet. 4. Yitzchak Gilerovitz. 5. Avraham Gilerovitz. 6. Moshe Savitzki. 7.
Yitzchak Liberman. 8. Yehuda Rabinovitch. 9. Yosef Shkolnikovitz. 10. Shimon
Mirski. 11. Yisrael Rabinovitch. 12. Moshe Tzvi Rabinovitch. 13. Yisrael Belski.
14. Shimon Lakhovitzki. 15. Chaim Mendlovich. 16. Moshe Belski. 17. Eliezer
Bilitzki. 18. Yechezkel Ravitz. 19. Yitzchak Berkovitz (teacher). 20. Leibel
Gilerovitz. 21. Yaakov Gilerovitz. 22. Noach Goldshtein. 23. Katriel Likter. 24.
Tzvi Vlochinski**

[Page 170]

Farewell party for Cantor Rafael Gelman on the occasion of his immigration to the United States
[Page 171]

Family farewell party on the occasion of the *aliya* of Yosef Lozovski

[Page 172]

An outing of the Tarbut School of Maytchet, *Lag BaOmer*, 5691 (1931)

[Page 173]

A show at the "Tarbut" School

Some of the descendents of Moshe Aharon Boretcky

[Page 174]

A show at the "Tarbut" School

Names on the photo from the reverse side:
1. A teacher from outside. 2. Avraham David Zukovitzki. 3. A teacher from outside. 4. A teacher from outside. 5. Malka Zukovitzki. 6. Gunik (kindergarten teacher). 7. Chana Boyarski. 8. Chaya Esther Kaplan. 9. Reuven Berski. 10. Shmaryahu Sapir. 11. Moshe Tzvi Rabinovitch. 12. Yechezkel Ravitz. 13. Yaakov Gilerovitz. 14. Leibel Gilerovitz.

[Page 175]

The Keren Kayemet [Jewish National Fund] committee

[Page 176]

A performance of "Shulamith" by a group of amateurs to raise money for charity
Maytchet, July 9, 1921

[Page 177]

A reception for a government personality

[Page 178]

Members of the Keren Kayemet [Jewish National Fund]

[Page 179]

Classes in the Tarbut School

[Page 180]

A class in handiwork

[Page 181]

 Mordechai Belski. 2. Mina Ravitz. 3. Shimon Gilerovitz. 4. Ethel Romanovski. 5. Pulchik (a teacher from outside). 6. Mina (the daughter of the rabbi of Sinyavka) . 7. Chaim Epshtein. 8. Libaka Izraelovitz. 10. Yehoshua Novomishiski. 11. Tzila Biteknski. 12. Nachum Gilerovitz.

1. Malka Zukovitzki. 2. A teacher from outside. 3. A teacher from outside. 4. Tronski (a teacher from outside). 5. Yechezkel Ravitz. 6. Avraham David Zukovitzki. 7. Chana Boyarski. 8. A teacher from outside. 9. Tzila Bitenski. 10. Libaka Izraelovitz

[Page 182]

Row 1 - right to left: **1. Manya Novomisky 2. Etel Rubizewski 3. Teacher not from Maytchet 4. Teacher not from Maytchet 5. Gunik, a teacher**
Row 2 – right to left: **6. Katz, teacher at Tarbut School 7. Malke Zukovitzki 8.Chaim Novomiski 9. Nachum Gilerovitz 10. Rivke Novogrudsky 11.Teacher not from Maytchet**
Row 3 – right to left: **12. Teacher not from Maytchet 13. Alte Boretcky 14.Yehoshua Novomisky 15.Hana Boretcky Avraham 16. David Zukovitzki**

[Page 183]

Sixth grade. 1937

[Pag 184]

From left: **David Milchovski, Bracha Mlinikovski and Alter Ravitz, Tzerna Strolovitzki and Mordechai Motzkovski, Zelda Epshtein**

Standing from right: **the teacher Aharon Kravtzik, Alta Dvorzecky (mother of Chana Boretcky)**
From left: **Yitzchak Liberman, Tzila Dvorzecky**

[Page 185]

A. *Hehalutz* in Maytchet
Translated by Esther Mann Snyder

The founding of a branch of *Hehalutz* in Maytchet happened later than in other places. In 1932 the following active young Zionists assembled and prepared the foundation for the *Hehalutz* movement in town - Yehuda Ben-Moshe (Shevchik), Noah Mordkovski, Pesach Melenikovski, Label Pitzanski, Fruma Belski, Label Shmulovitz, Bracha Mlinikovski, Shilem Rabinovitz, Yosef Lozovski, Alter Ravitz and others.

They rented an apartment in the home of Sarah Kravtzik (The stalerke) on Podkrizh Hill, together with the youth movement *Hashomer Hatzair*, which had already formed a club in this house. Since they shared the space and in general believed in the same goals, they often held joint activities, such as bazaars on Chanukah and Purim, parties and fundraisers, and assembling on Simchat Torah. Actually the branch of *Hehalutz* was established by the initiative of the Zionist movement in Maytchet and its active support, so that it would encourage the policy of making aliya to Eretz Yisrael. However, after a time, *Hehalutz* became a distinct independent organization and as such was in contact with the district center of *Hehalutz* in Baranovichi and the main center in Warsaw from whom it received instructions for activities.

The local branch of *Hehalutz* took upon itself the fulfillment of Zionist aspirations (*hagshama*) sending its members to training centers in towns and locations near and far and even subsidized from its funds travel expenses to Eretz Yisrael for those without means. In order to raise funds and for the training of the members for manual labor, they worked at various jobs in town including cutting trees, cleaning, etc. Other members were sent to work on the roads, etc. and half of their income was given to the movement and the other half left for their personal living expenses.

Because the organization began late, it didn't manage to get very much done. Before it succeeded in developing fully and reaching "fulfillment" which was it's main purpose - training and aliya, the pre-war emergency conditions began and later the violence of the war itself disrupted all regular work. That is why there was just a small number of pioneers from Maytchet who succeeded in going to Eretz Yisrael and the small number of survivors of the holocaust from Maytchet. Nevertheless, the movement succeeded in sending members to far-off training camps from where they were somehow able to reach Eretz Yisrael in a legal way or an "illegal" manner.

[Page 186]

***Hehalutz* members**

[

Page 187]

B. The Story of the Travails of *Hehalutz* in Maytchet

By Yehuda Ben-Moshe (Shevchik)
Translated by Esther Mann Snyder

In 1934 I was sent for training to a training group (*kibbutz*) in the bloc *Tel Hai* founded by the center of *Hehalutz* in Bialystok. From there I was transferred to Milaytchitz, which was a small group of 12 members where we worked in a ceramic factory and were also sent from there to other places to organize more training groups. After a time the group in Milaytchitz dismantled and the members were transferred to Bielsk-Podlaski, a large group of 120 members, who worked in every possible job. Due to the large debts that had accumulated the members of the center in Bialystok came to dismantle it and to send the members to the various groups in *Tel Hai*. I was sent to the Shaharia group in Vilna. I remained there and worked during the two critical years, 1937 - 39. People already spoke openly that a war would soon begin and since there weren't enough certificates [to go on aliya] and time was running out, I decided to go on Aliya B (illegal immigration). In July 1939 I received a telegram to urgently prepare my affairs and to travel to Warsaw. Eight hundred people from all over the country were concentrated in a large hotel and we were told that they could not promise the success of the plan and anyone who was fearful or hesitant should return home.

During the night we climbed onto trucks that brought us to the train station where a train was waiting to take us to take us to Romania, posing as tourists. When we reached Constanta, Romanian police entered the train, arrested all of us and placed two guards by each coach for a whole week. One night a few members secretly left the train and set fire to nearby warehouses. Consequently, they moved the train to another location where we stayed another three days until a directive arrived to allow us to board a Greek freight ship that was carrying cattle. We had to make do with terrible crowding, but most importantly, we had finally departed towards our goal.

After the first week all our food was used up. We had thought that in this amount of time we would already have reached Eretz Yisrael and therefore brought food to last one week. In our distress we went down to the store rooms of the ship and took potatoes which we cut into small slices and divided among the members. As a result many became ill with dysentery and others died so we had to put the bodies into the sea. After that we suffered from a lack of water, which was spoiled, diluted with chlorine and distributed with a cup. In these terrible conditions we were worried about keeping up morale and chose a culture committee whose members went from bed to bed, sang songs, told jokes and encouraged the members as much as possible.

After a month of travel filled with suffering and travails, we were notified that passengers from a burning boat of *ma'apilim* (illegal immigrants) would be added to our boat and they had a large store of food. We made a bridge of ropes and helped 600 of them to leave their burning boat and come on to ours, which of course added to the unbelievable crowding but they brought much food with them. Our boat continued to "wander" around the sea for another month, travelling at night and hiding during the day because no port allowed us to anchor. When we reached the area of the port in Beirut we asked for fuel for the boat. They didn't allow us to come close to the port, but for payment that came from Eretz Yisrael, a petrol boat came out to us and refueled the boat.

[Page 188]

Standing from right: **Malka Kostrovitzki, Shilem Rabinowitz, Shashke Strolovitzki, Pesach Mlinikovski, Tcharne Strolovitzki, Alter Ravitz, Chaya Rabinowitz, Leizer Volinski**
Sitting: **Noach Kostrovitzki, Nachum Gilerovitz, Bracha Melnikovski, Sara Margolin, Leibel Shmulovitz, Noach Dobkovski**
Below: **Noach Mordkovski, Mordechai Ravitz**

[Page 189]

From there we sailed to the area of Netanya that was known as a place for (illegally) entering Eretz Yisrael and signaled the shore that we wanted to debark. The English discovered the signal and shot their guns at the boat killing a few of us. This happened on a Thursday night and on Friday morning we assembled for a general meeting and in our great anguish we decided that we would reach the shore no matter what or we would sink the ship. We also swore an oath before the dead that were lying near us that we would not leave until we could bury them in the holy earth of Eretz Yisrael. At 12 noon, fifty persons were chosen from among those who knew how to swim and were told to notify the people on the shore that when the boat came close they should immediately come out to receive us.

On Sabbath eve, at 10 o'clock, the people started leaving the boat and some even carried others on their shoulders. About 250 people managed to leave until the

English noticed what was happening and signaled us to stop or they would shoot at the boat. Eventually they boarded the ship and arrested everyone. Nevertheless, we received encouragement from the personnel of the Jewish Agency not to panic or be afraid. After they managed somehow to come to an agreement with the English, we climbed onto vehicles of the bus company *Egged* and were transferred to Sarafand. We stayed there for a whole week under the rule of a military camp until members from the *kibbutzim* came and brought us to the Borochov school in Givatayim where they divided us into groups to be sent to various *kibbutzim*.

I was sent to Ramat-Rahel where I worked for two years. After that I worked in a potash company in the northern part of the Dead Sea and other work in building the country and in its defense. Thus I earned for myself and my family the right to settle as citizens in the yearned for Eretz Yisrael.

C. About *Hehalutz* and the Training Groups (How I came on Aliya Twice)
By Nahum Margolin
Translated by Esther Mann Snyder

In the middle of the night between the ninth and tenth of October 1939, I got off at the train station in Baranovichi from the freight train that arrived as usual. I had to wait for a few hours until early morning to get on the train that leaves Baranovichi to Vilna so that I could reach home - to Maytchet. At night Yakov Okun, May G-d revenge his blood, met me at the train station and asked in surprise, "Nachum, what are you doing here, they said in Maytchet that you went to Eretz Yisrael?! " These words were emphasized due to the unordinary atmosphere after 40 days of Soviet occupation. He told me that my young brother Moshe, May G-d revenge his blood, was also waiting for the train that would return him home from Baranovichi. I didn't find him at the train station because he had already boarded the train and was waiting for it to start.

[Page 190]

The rumor that I was in Eretz Yisrael was only a successful ruse that I had planned a few weeks before the start of the war when no one even imagined that our town would be conquered by the Soviets. In order to understand this I must return to an earlier period. In 1935 I was studying in the Yeshiva *Bet Yosef* in Lahovitz. At that time a few friends got together and we founded the branch of *Hehalutz HaMizrahi* in town with the intention of joining training groups so we would be able to go to Eretz Yisrael, after a while. In general, during the 1930's, the youth from all the movements thronged to the training groups due to their enthusiasm for the idea of *shivat Zion* (returning to

Zion) among the youth of Poland. Also the youth of Maytchet dreamed of going to Eretz Yisrael and a number of young people left the town and joined training groups.

I remember the youth, who during those years went to the groups sponsored by *Poalei Zion* and *Hehalutz* - Laibel Shmulovitz and Chaya Rabinovitz - both of whom succeeded in going to Eretz Yisrael and whom I met there; unfortunately both of them are no longer alive. Shilem Rabinovitz, Leibl Pintzinski and another few members did not make it to Eretz Yisrael and perished in the holocaust. In addition, Pesach Melnikovski and Yehuda Shevchik, may they live long lives, live today in Israel. Also the youth from *Hashomer Hatzair* joined the training groups and went to Eretz Yisrael, some before the holocaust and others after it. They include Hemda Lubrani nee Margolin, Sarah Biribis nee Boretcky, Hannah Mechtiger nee Boretcky, and Yachna Ezrahi nee Belski, Reuven Rabinovitz and Yitzhak Movshovitz - all of them in Israel today. Some youth from *Poalei Agudat Yisrael* went to the training groups: Dov Shlomovitz who managed to reach Eretz Yisrael and Shalom Romanovski z"l, who didn't go to Eretz Yisrael, survived the holocaust, emigrated to the Unied States , raised a famly and passed away in 1968. Some of the youth of Maytchet also joined *Hehalutz Hamizrahi* and two of them succeeded in reaching Eretz Yisrael - Yitzhak Lublinski and the writer of this article.

In our town of Maytchet, despite it being a small town, the youth organized in various movements as was the case in other towns in the area. There was even a group from the *Bund*, however, most of the youth belonged to Zionist pioneer movements, and the intention was always to reach Eretz Yisrael. However, unfortunately, the process was very lengthy, the "gates" to Israel were locked, the Mandate government limited the immigration and did not allocate enough certificates for all the pioneers and thus many of them remained for many years in the training groups until they finally reached Eretz Yisrael. This was also my fate. In May of 1935, immediately after Pesach, I left the group in Brisk which is near the River Bug. I stayed at the *kibbutz* for six months and then moved to another *kibbutz* that was in Antopol near Kobrin. Again, I stayed for half a year and I then requested to transfer to a different *kibbutz* where there were young pioneers of my age. The situation of aliya to Eretz Yisrael worsened and I didn't see any chance of leaving for Eretz Yisrael soon. Therefore, I preferred - at least from a social aspect - to join a *kibbutz* more appropriate for my age and to live there and wait patiently until my turn would come to make aliya. Indeed, right after Pesach 1936 I transferred to a kibbutz named *Ovadia*, which was in the town of Slavkov, which was located between the cities of Olkush and Dombrova-Gornicha, in the area of Zaglembia. This *kibbutz* was the first *kibbutz* of *Hehalutz Hamizrahi* in Poland where the pioneers were organized in groups and cycles on a cooperative basis to go to Eretz Yisrael and continue *kibbutz* life there. The people were of a high standard and I found my place and full satisfaction there.

Activists of the Keren Kayemet

Standing, right to left: **Etel Rubizewski, a teacher from out of town; Moshe-Tzvi Rabinovitz, Esther Epstein, Hannah Boretcky, Yehoshua Novomiski, Kayla-Rakhel Rabinovitz**.
Sitting, right to left: **Veiskind (a teacher from out of town), Malka Zukovitzki, Alta Safir, Shmaryahu Safir, Yehezkel Ravitz, Haya Dubkovski.**
Bottom row: **Alta Savitzki, Leibl Gilerovitz**

During the years I spent in kibbutz Slavkov, a number of cycles of members made aliya but due to the limited aliya and the scarcity of certificates, it was decided to make aliya in any way possible. And indeed, a number of members made aliya through "Aliya B" (illegal immigration) and thus my turn came in the summer of 1939. That summer I went to the district capital in order to undergo medical examinations before military service. When it was determined that I was capable of serving in the army, the kibbutz began to hasten the process of making aliya. Then it was decided that I would go to Eretz Yisrael at the end

[Page 192]

Pesach Mlinikovski and Leibl Shmulovitz - the first pioneers from Maytchet

[Page 193]

of August that summer. Thus, at the beginning of the month I traveled home to Maytchet to bid farewell to the family. At home, I didn't tell them and didn't reveal to anyone that I was about to go on Aliya B. I completed all the final preparations, they dressed me from head to toe, packed new clothes in a large new suitcase, and in mid–month I said goodbye to my family and went on my way to Warsaw. Since my wife Tzipora, who was then my girlfriend from the kibbutz, was also traveling to her home in Kowel to prepare for her aliya to the Land of Israel in a legal fashion, we decided that on the way from Maytchet to Warsaw I would go to Kowel for a few days to meet her family. Then, in mid–August 1939 I reached Kowel; and there I awaited additional instructions from the center in Warsaw.

During those days that I waited for the notice to arrive that I could start my journey, I sat down and wrote a few letters. I sent them to my friend Baruch M. who was already in Tirat–Zvi, including letters to my parents in Maytchet. and I asked my friend to send these letters according to the dates I had written on them so that the family wouldn't know that I was going on Aliya B and thus would save them from undue worry regarding my path of aliya. Indeed, my friend did as requested. Immediately after he received the letters, he sent the first one to my parents, in which I informed them that I boarded the boat which was sailing to the Land of Israel, and I would write them again shortly on the journey or when I arrived at the coast. He did not succeed in sending out the rest of the letters, for the war had already broken out. However, the first letter that my friend sent to my parents in my name arrived in Maytchet in a miraculous fashion after the outbreak of the war. In this way, my parents receive the "good news," that I was apparently in the Land of Israel.

**Aryeh–Leib Margolin and his wife Badana nee Yorzkovski,
May G–d Avenge their Blood**

[Page 194]

On Tuesday, October 10, 1939, early in the morning, I left the train in the station of Maytchet, while my brother Moshe got off from another coach, while returning in the same train from Baranovichi home to Maytchet, this was because I hadn't been able to find him in Baranovichi. While we walked together from the station he told me that he had had a feeling that the letter he received from me from Eretz Yisrael was just a ruse, and that in reality it was written by me but not sent by me because he recognized that the handwriting on the envelope wasn't mine. He said that it was good that it was sent because his parents were very worried about their eldest son, Yaakov, who had been drafted into the reserves of the Polish army and they hadn't heard from him for six weeks after the defeat of that army. When my letter arrived it removed one worry from their hearts.

When we, my brother and I, entered our home and my parents saw me they couldn't believe their eyes. My brother's guess that I sent the letter in order to relieve some of the family's worries was correct and the plan succeeded.

The Perpetual Wanderer

[Page 195]

The Organization of Maytchet Natives in Israel
and the World, and its Activities
by N.M.
Translated by Jerrold Landau

As we come to present an overview of the Organization of Natives of Maytchet and its Region in Israel, and its activities, it is appropriate to first describe the makeup of our organization in Israel, the people who belong to it, and how those people came to it. We can assume that in what was called the "Old settlement" [*Yishuv Hayashan*] in the Land, which included almost exclusively people whose prime goal was to fulfill the commandment of the settlement of the Land of Israel, there were some individuals during various periods who stemmed from the town of Maytchet. I can base this assumption on personal testimony from the elders of my family, who stated that one of the fathers of the family made *aliya* to the Land, died there, and is buried in the Mount of Olives Cemetery in Jerusalem.

To the extent that we all recall, and as is related in this book, the final two people who made *aliya* with the aims of the "Old Settlement," that is for the purposes of fulfilling the commandment of the settlement of the Land of Israel [1], were Reb Yehoshua Aharon Lisovski of blessed memory, and Reb Yisrael Zalman Shlovski of blessed memory. The rest of the residents of Maytchet and its region who made *aliya* to the Land of Israel during the last fifty years came here for different reasons. Their main motivation for *aliya* to the Land was the idea of Chibat Zion [2]. Others made *aliya* under the rubric of the various Zionist pioneering movements, and still others came as tourists or students and remained in the Land. Holocaust refugees, who had gone through the various Zionist movements and preferred to set up their households in the Land of Israel rather than the Diaspora, arrived after the war.

The first founding meetings of natives of Maytchet and its region in Israel began in 1946, when the Holocaust survivors began to make *aliya* to the Land of Israel. I especially recall the first meeting that took place in the home of Shifra and Yosef Lozovski in Rishon Lezion, at which the first Holocaust survivors who began to arrive in the Land of Israel were present. Later, after the details of the Holocaust and the date of the final annihilation of our townsfolk became known, annual memorials for the Holocaust victim began to take place on Rosh Chodesh Av of every year. At first, various local memorials took place, for the most part in private houses of Maytchet natives, including Moshe Kleinshtov of blessed memory and his wife Miriam may she live, Shifra and Yosef Lozovski, Binyamin Stolovitzki, Nachum Rabinovitch and others. The members Miriam Kleinshtov and Chaya Chaikin were dedicated to the annual memorial. These two members also made sure to set up meetings between natives of Maytchet and its region in Israel with guests from the Diaspora. The first meeting of this nature took place at the beginning of the 1950s in the home of Miriam Kleinshtov in Tel Aviv. Mr. Ben-Zion Kobinski of Argentina was present.

[Page 196]

The expanded organizing committee with the guest Yechezkel Ravitz from the United States

Sitting from the right: **Reuven Rabinovitch, Esther Lozovski, Tov Shomroni, Yechezkel Ravitz, Miriam Kleinshtov, Yosef Lozovski, Chaya Chaikin, Chaya Lubtzik**
Standing from the right: **Nachum Margolin, Moshe Korn**

Maytchet natives hosting Yechezkel Ravitz

[Page 197]

Maytchet natives at the ceremony of the unveiling of the memorial tablet of the community of Maytchet in the Holocaust cellar

[Page 198]

On Rosh Chodesh Av 5722 (August 1, 1962), after the annual memorial that took place in the home of Miriam Kleinshtov, a general meeting of the natives of the town was held, at which it was decided to work toward publishing this book. In the wake of this decision, an expanded organizing committee was chosen, consisting of nine members: Chaya Chaikin, Chaya Lubtzik, Yosef Lozovski, Esther Lozovski, Nachum Margolin, Moshe Korn, Miriam Kleinshtov, Reuven Rabinovitch, and Tova Shomroni. This committee acted in all areas: it maintained communication with all the natives of Maytchet and its region, initiated meetings for various events, disseminated the idea for the publication of the book also among the natives of Maytchet and its region in the Diaspora, organized and conducted various welcome parties for all Maytchet natives in the Diaspora who visited Israel, and worked toward strengthening the social connections among the natives of the town in the land. The crowning achievement of the activities of this committee was the setting up of a memorial plaque for the martyrs of Maytchet and its region who perished in the Holocaust. This monument is engraved upon a marble tablet located in the Holocaust Cellar on Mount Zion in Jerusalem. The veil was removed from the memorial plaque on the eve of Rosh Chodesh Av 5722 (July 9, 1964). At that time, the annual memorial event took place in the presence of most of the natives of Maytchet and its region in Israel. The memorial took place at the memorial monument in Jerusalem the following year as well. Starting from Rosh Chodesh Av 5626 (1966), the annual memorial ceremony for the martyrs of our town took place in a special hall in Tel Aviv or its area.

Among the Maytchet natives of the Diaspora who visited Israel were Mr. and Mrs. Marim Spencer (Pintzinski) of blessed memory and Mr. and Mrs. Alter Albert Kodovich, who visited Israel in 1963. As on all similar occasions, a warm, enthusiastic reception was arranged for them in the home of Esther and Meir Lozovski, with the participation of members of the organization. On that occasion, the guests gave over a sum of money to the organization, as a gift from the Committee of Maytchet Natives of New York and several private individuals, for use toward the charitable fund for the needy from among the natives of Maytchet and its region in Israel.

After the annual memorial ceremony on Rosh Chodesh Av 5726 (July 18, 1966), a general meeting of all the participants was conducted. Given that the activities for advancing the publication of the book had become more urgent, it was decided to spread the committee out further by setting up four smaller committees in order to involve a larger number of members in the communal efforts. The following people were chosen to the organizational committee: Sara Ahronovski, Yosef Lozovski, Nachum Margolin, Moshe Korn, Miriam Kleinshtov, and Moshe Ravitz. The following people were chosen for the charitable fund committee: Chaya Chaikin, Yitzchak Lubelinski, Mina Levin, Yosef Lozovski, and Pesach Mlinikovski. The following perople were chosen for the book committee: Chaya Lubtzik, Esther Lozovski, Yosef Lozovski, Chana Machtiger, Nachum Margolin, Moshe Korn, and Tova Shomroni. The following three members were chosen for the audit committee: Yerachmiel Brunitzki, Binyamin Stolovitzki, and Reuven Rabinovitch. Indeed, most of the members of the committees acted in accordance with their tasks.

The Organization of Natives of Maytchet and its Region in Israel is not different from other similar organizations, and its activities do not deviate from those of other similar organizations. Throughout no small number of years, the organization acted to perpetuate the town and the Holocaust that fell upon its

[Page 199]

Jews during the Second World War. This objective reached its fulfillment with The Book of Maytchet in which these words are inscribed for memorial throughout the generations.

Nachum Margolin eulogizing the martyrs of Maytchet

Cantor Yaakov Semak reciting Yizkor

[Page 200]

Maytchet natives in Israel connect with the memory of their martyrs

Finally, we should note the organizations of Maytchet natives throughout the world. They have a single purpose before their eyes: to form a common framework so that the natives of the city can meet together, to bring to the fore memories of the town and its dear ones, and to provide assistance and support for Maytchet natives throughout the world. The main point is to support any plan whose aim is to perpetuate the martyrs of our community with the honor due to them, and to conduct an annual memorial day for the martyrs.

In the first place, we must note the long-time Society in New York, which was founded at the beginning of the 20th century and maintains its own cemetery as is the custom with Landsmanschaften. The organization in Israel is in constant contact with them. A similar organization exists in Argentina, which also goes back a long time. We also maintain a constant connection with them. Aside from these, there are individuals and non-organized groups in Canada, Mexico and other countries. Maytchet natives in the Diaspora who visit Israel, or vice versa, enjoy an enthusiastic welcome party, which engenders mutual joy.

N. M.

Translator's footnotes
1. I.e. for religious reasons.
2. See http://en.wikipedia.org/wiki/Hovevei_Zion

[Page 201]

Maytcheter Jews in New York

Taken from an American Jewish Newspaper - no date given

Translated by Milton Schwartz and Martin Small (Mordechai Leib Shmulewicz)
Edited by Jerrold Landau

"The Maytcheter Jews in New York recite *kaddish* in public for their martyrs. They created a help organization for the State of Israel."

This is a copy of an article that appeared in an American Jewish newspaper, mentioning, among other things:

**A photocopy of the title page of the 1938
calendar of the Maytchet Gemilut Chessed fund**

This past Sunday, the Maytchet natives who live in New York and the surrounding area held a memorial gathering in memory of the Jews who were killed in sanctification of the Divine name. Maytchet is a small town near Baranovici where about 800 Jews lived.

[Page 202]

The town is known for its geniuses, scholars, rabbis, and teachers.

The Maytchet native Rabbi Gershon Romanoff spoke with much enthusiasm about the town and called upon everyone present to observe the *Yahrzeit* (annual memorial). They lit six candles and recited *Kaddish*. The Maytchet natives in America do good work in memory of the town and those who were murdered there. Each year they purchase over $3,000 of Israel bonds through their society. They help the United Appeal, HIAS (Hebrew Immigrant Aid Society), and ORT, and they do not forget their fellow townsfolk in Israel.

The Maytcheters also created a fund in Israel in memory of the Gemilut Chassadim Fund that existed in Maytchet. Recently, when one of the survivors of Maytchet became a bride in Israel, the society sent her $300 as a wedding present.

The longtime president of the Maytchet group in New York is Isaac Kurtin. The Financial Secretary was B. Lokoff and is now B. Goldberg. Together with Al Rubio, Al Kudivitz, M. Spencer and Yechezkel Roberts, a full series of projects were planned in memory in memory of the Jewish town of Maytchet and its Jewish citizens who once were and are no more…

(Additional notes to article in the Maytchet Yizkor Book added by Milton Schwartz and Martin Small: After Isaac Kurtin passed away, Charles Samuels became the President and B. Goldberg was the secretary. After B. Goldberg died, Martin Small became the secretary. In 2000 there were too few people attending the meetings and the group dissolved. All the money from their treasury was sent to the Maytchet Gemilus Chesed fund in Israel.

The Maytcheter Fraternal Aid Society has two cemetery plots in the New York City area. One is at the Mt. Lebanon Cemetery in the Queens, New York and the other is at Beth Moses Cemetery in Huntington, Long Island, New York.)

[Pages 202 - 204]

Maytcheters in Argentina
A Letter from Ben-Zion Sack
Translated by Milton Schwartz and Martin Small (Mordechai Leib Shmulewicz)
Edited by Jerrold Landau

Dear Friends and Landsliet,

Esteemed Friends and Fellow Natives!

First of all, I would like to greet you for your initiative to perpetuate the town with a book certain aspects of our common native town. You are to be congratulated for your massive undertaking. I know this will not be easy for you; however, unfortunately I cannot help you very much financially, as I am simply a worker with limited means, and I cannot collect from others for I do not come in contact with our fellow natives. The only thing I can do is to write a few words to accompany the picture that I am hereby sending you. I believe that it is a historical picture that will illuminate a story from our town in the latter years of its existence. You will certainly find some familiar faces, which will remind you of a period of the history of Maytchet to which I have strong feeling - that is: the years 1928 until 1930 when I left for Argentina. Here is the story.

[Page 203]

Workers Evening Courses, April 15, 1930 Maytchet

In 1928 there were, among others, Maytchet youths studying in various schools in Vilna. Three friends -- Joseph Sussman, Molia Kravchik and I -- became acquainted there with left wing student movement, which we joined. We decided that we would form a workers' organization in Maytchet when we came home for Passover. We did not know what type of organization this would be, for there were issues with legalization. When we found out that the left leaning Poale Zion founded a society to offer evening courses for workers, so that they could continue on with their activities which were forbidden in feudal Poland, we grabbed on to the idea with both hands even though we did not share the same political ideas as theirs. We got in contact with them in Warsaw, obtained a copy of their mission statement, and obtained a permit to found a branch in Maytchet.

We worked with all of our youthful enthusiasm for two years. Our objective was to raise the cultural level of the young workers of Maytchet. The numbers were not large, since Maytchet did not have any industry. There were only young boys and girls, tailors, shoemakers, and furriers. Even a wagon welder joined. We conducted the work with sincerity. We arranged evening classes in which Molia Kravchick taught reading and writing, Yosef Sussman taught arithmetic, and I taught history and political economy. These were our winter programs. In the summer we would go out every Saturday for a walk in the forest, or conduct a discussion about current events.

[Page 204]

In addition, we set up a library and reading room. Every evening after work we would get together to read newspapers, take out a book, or just socialize with acquaintances. We also organized a drama group, and performed several plays. One play that I remember was the Jewish King Lear by Jacob Gordon. Those who remember the plight of the young workers in Maytchet in those times will understand what a wonderful undertaking it was. True in Maytchet there was cultural activity earlier on, but only amongst the wealthier children. The children of the workers could not participate in that group. On the other hand, the most impoverished people, including those who never went to *cheder* or school, came to our group. With this cultural center we literally raised them to the level of human beings. They were thankful to us and gave their last pennies to keep up the club.

Where they all today? Some probably survived and live in America, Argentina and Israel. The rest have perished with all the Maytcheters. Amongst them were my mother and brother Lazer. Let these words serve as a memorial for the survivors of their near and dear ones.

[Page 207]

Chapter 5
Personalities, Families, Figures
My Parents' House - The Orzechovsky family
By Nahum Naor Orzechovsky
Translated by Nate Kolodny
Edited by Sara Mages

I will always remember the town of Maytchet. I was born there and there my childhood passed, and there is where I left the dearest to me – my parents.

Yonah and his wife Kriena Orzechovsky and their daughter Hanna-Mara

My father Yonah, blessed be his memory, was born in Maytchet to his parents, Osher and Shaina Orzechovsky. My father was an educated man and a scholar. In his youth he studied in the Novogrudok Yeshiva and later completed his studies in Russian Schools. My mother Kriena, may she rest in peace, was born in the town of Novaya Mysh (Mush) to her parents Leib and Tovah Vilbensky.

[Page 208]

After their marriage, my parents settled in Maytchet together with my father's parents. They had three children--my older sister Hanna-Mara, myself, and my younger sister Chasha. The family earned a living from the iron trade and that was the reason that my grandfather Asher was called "Reb Asher, iron shop owner" (*Der Aizenkrammer*). Later on my parents became fabric merchants and while my grandparents still dealt in iron, my parents sold fabric in the shop.

Both my parents came from large families. My father's parents had two sons and four daughters. My father lived in Maytchet all his life, but his brother Nathan immigrated to the U.S. shortly before W.W. I. He had a large family and lived to see many grandchildren before passing away in 1964.

Mrs. Feiga-Rachel Weisbord née Orzechovsky

Three of my father's sisters also immigrated to the U.S. They are Fanny, who lives near Chicago, Chasha Freyda who lives with her husband Julius Kolodny in Los Angeles, and Chaya Sarah, may she rest in peace, who married Baruch Ross (Razvetzky) from Zhetl in Novaya Mysh (Mush) before immigrating to the U.S. My father's fourth sister was Bedna Margolin who built her house with Reb Aryel Leib in Maytchet.

My mother's parents came from Novaya Mysh (Mush). Her parents Leib and Tova Villenky had seven sons and one daughter. My mother's brothers were Mordechai, Yoel, Herschel, Yitzhak, Dov and Yosef.

[Page 209]

With the exception of Ashe and Yosef who stayed in Mush, the rest of them moved to Baranovichi. All of them were in the meat business. My mother had an aunt in Maytchet, Etta, the sister of grandmother Tova and the wife of Yitzchak Gilrovitch. They (Etta and Tova) were the daughters of Nachum Mordechovsky, who was also called Tseshler because he owned land in the village of Telsia near Slonim. I was named after him.

I did not know all of them very well because I was still young when the Nazis came. I cannot but mention them here, hoping that these few lines will serve as a kind of a memorial to honest and innocent soul that were special in their own way and that in their death left to me and my family a great spiritual heritage.

I was the only survivor from all of my family, except those who immigrated to the U.S. The rest of the family, who are still alive in Israel, are my cousins Nachum Margolin and his sister Freidel Makarensky and Ethel Villensky, daughter of my Uncle Mordechai Villensky. My two other cousins, Rachel and Brania, daughters of Dov Villensky, live in the U.S.

Yoel [Julius] Kolodny and his first wife from the Orzechovsky family

We are the only ones amongst many youngsters in our family who survived the Holocaust. Each one of us went through a long journey of suffering until we reached a safe place.

My own youth in Maytchet was very much like that of any other child. I studied with a Melamed (Jewish teacher) Gorsky and then continued my education in Horeb School.

[Page 210]

For a short time I was a Yeshiva student in a small yeshiva that was founded in Maytchet in 1935, and later I graduated from the ORT School (vocational institute). I continued my studies in the ORT school in the town of Brest nearby.

W.W. II broke out during that time and, following the Ribenthrop-Molotov Pact, Brest became a Russian territory. The Russians converted the Ort Institute into a government technical institute and I stayed there until June 1941.

On June 7, 1941 some of the students, including myself, went to participate in advanced courses that were given in Vitebsk, Russia. Two weeks later war was declared between Russia and Germany. On that same day I tried to return to Maytchet. I failed, as did all my attempts to go back.

I shall not describe in full detail the path of suffering and blood I've experienced, like other survivors of the Holocaust, until the victory of the allies over Nazi Germany. At the end of the war I joined the Bricha (Escape) organization that took care of refugees.

I arrived in Israel in 1947. The memory of my last farewell from my parents and family in 1941 is still fresh. The days before the war were mentally and economically difficult and so was our farewell before I had left for Vitebsk. None of us knew that this would be our final farewell.

These words are published in the memorial volume for Maytchet community thirty years after the events occurred. Today, in the 1970's and in the State of Israel, I believe that our children should be given the opportunity to learn more about the struggle of the past generations of the Jewish people--especially the terrible period that had so much to do with the formation of the new State of Israel. I am pleased to know that my grandfather's presence in this book will contribute to this educational effort.

Nahum Naor Orzechovsky

[Page 211]

The Dvorzecky Family
By Dr. Meir (Mark) Dvorzecky
Translated by Ron Rabinovitch
Edited by Sara Mages

My father, Dov-Ber Dvorzecky, was born in Maytchet. His father, Rabbi Yechiel Isaac Dvorzecky, was also born in Maytchet and lived there until he immigrated to Israel. His grandfather, Rabbi Shemaryahu Yehuda Dvorzecky, lived and died in Maytchet.

The following is the Dvorzecky Family:

Rabbi Shemaryahu Yehuda Dvorzecky was a wood merchant in Maytchet. His wife's name was Sima but some people called her Liba.

Their son Rabbi Yechiel Isaac Dvorzecky was a wood merchant also. He was one of the Zionist activist in Russia who was a delegate to the second Zionist Conference in Basel, Switzerland. You can read about this in the Zionist newspaper - "Di Walt", by Dr. Theodore Herzl. On the delegate's list he is listed as one of the representatives of the Basel second Zionist Conference. He immigrated to Eretz-Israel and lived in Rehovot from 1926 until his death in 1932.

He married Chana Gele Landoy, daughter of Eliyahu Landoy from Lida. I remember some of her brother's names: Michael Landoy who died in Vilna, Nathan (Natte) Landoy who died in Lida, and Joseph Landoy who died in Rehovot. My grandmother, Chana Gele Dvorzecky, came to Eretz-Israel with my grandfather, Rabbi Yechiel Isaac, and she died in Rehovot in 1928. They had 3 sons and 5 daughters: Dov, Jacob, Isaac, Mechle, Malka, Sonia, Hadassa, and Sima.

I. My father Dov-Ber received his ordination as a Rabbi at the Slonim Yeshiva. He married my mother Tzivia. She was well educated, knew several languages and worked as a draftsman. She was the daughter of the Rabbi and architect, Rabbi Eliyahu Rumanov from Vilna, who dedicated his life to preparing an accurate map of the Temple. He drew sketches of the Temple and its sacred objects, which was published in Vilna. My late father was actively involved in the Zionist movement during his entire life as well as the Jewish community of Vilna. I heard stories that he was imprisoned when the Czar's police saw him holding a blue and white flag in a demonstration which was held 1905. He was an educated and proud Jew and had large library of religious books.

[Page 212]

His first occupation was a wood merchant in Maytchet and the nearby area. Later on he audited the accounts at the Jewish community in Vilna. He became ill while in the Vilna Ghetto and died on the last candle of Chanukah,1941. My mother was transferred at the time of the German Aktion, September 23rd – 26th 1943, to an unknown place (possibly Ponary or Majdanek).

R' Dov-Ber Dvorzecky z"l and his wife Tzivia hy"d (née Rumanov)

a. Lisa graduated high school in Vilna and the Pharmacology department at Vilna University. She married Zev Lifshitz from Baranavichy and moved to Baranavichy. During the war her husband was transferred to Krasnoye Camp near Maladzechna (Molodeczno) and he died there. Lisa and her daughter Madzia moved to Maytchet and they were killed there with their Uncle Jacob Dvorzecky at the time of the mass killing, July 15, 1942.

b. Sima graduated from the Klutz high school in Vilna. She married Aharon Ginzburg from Vilna. During the Soviet regime she was transferred to Siberia. She came back with the "Riphariation" movement and immigrated to Israel in 1948. She died Tamuz 23rd 5728, July 19, 1968. Her son Isaac married Yaffa of the Kleingrob family and they have 3 children: Vardit, Sima and Uri. They are now living in Tel Aviv.

c. Meir (Mark) Yehuda Shemarahu (the author). I was one of the survivors of the Ghetto Vilna and of concentration camps in Astonia, Stutthof and Dautmergen (near Natzviller).

[Page 213]

I received a medical doctor degree from Vilna and a PHD of History from Paris. Presently I lecture about the Holocaust at Bar Ilan University in Tel Aviv. During the war I was an officer and fought in the Lvov Defense Battle. Later on I was captured by the Nazis near Krakow but managed to run away to Vilna. I was a member of the underground in the Vilna Ghetto as well as in the camps. I managed to run away from the camps to the Salagav Forest in Germany. I married Chasia Geffen. We have a son Dov who is an assistant Physicist at Ber Sheva University and is married to Esther Artman from Haifa. We also have a daughter Tzivia who has a master's degree in history from Tel Aviv University.

II. Jacob graduated from the High School of Pharmacology and he owned a pharmacy in Maytchet. He was highly educated in the fields of history and literature. He was loved by everyone, both Jews and Gentiles. He married Helena Starlatzki and they both went to their death at the time of the German Aktion in Maytchet July, 1942. I understand that some Christians wanted to save him but he didn't want to leave his family and fellow Jews. They had 3 children:

> Edie graduated from the Polytechnic in Warsaw. He was an engineer and his wife's name was Ella and their daughter was named Miriam.

> Vita graduated the high school pharmacology department in Warsaw. Witnesses say she was able to escape from Maytchet and joined the Partisans. Unfortunately she did not survive the war but I am not sure how or when she met her death. Perhaps she was killed in a battle or possibly died from typhus while hiding in the forest with the partisans.

> Eliyahu was transferred to Bedzonys near Vilna. (We received one letter sent from Bedzonys to the Vilna Ghetto). He was murdered there during the mass killing in July 9, 1943.

III. Isaac (Isadore) graduated the higher school of pharmacology. He immigrated to Eretz-Israel before the war and there he married Miriam Olkin. They had one daughter, Shoshana and she married Abraham Melnikov. Isaac died and was buried in Rehovot on Tevet 12th 5726 April 1, 1966.

IV. Mechle lived her entire life in Maytchet. She was married to Tzvi Hirsh Barashinsky. They were both killed by the Nazis in Maytchet. Their children:

> Shemaryahu – Possibly killed in Maytchet.

> Elkana – He finished high school and lives in USSR.

[Page 214]

Eliyahu – He was a student in Vilna University and later in the University in Paris. He was killed in Paris by the Nazis.

V. Malka was married to Shmuel Rabinovitch, an ardent Zionist who immigrated to Eretz-Israel before the First World War. They settled in Rehovot. Shmuel Rabinovitch died in Rehovot in 1939; Malka died in Rehovot on the eve of Hanukah in 1971 at the age of 92 or possibly 97. Their son Joshua (Chalamish) graduated Hertzelia High School; he lived in Rehovot and was one of the guards in the "Hashomer" and the "Hagana" movements.

VI. Sonia married Zev Liberman. She died in Romania and her husband died in Rehovot. Their children are:

Arie (Yakir) – he graduated high school in Belgium. At the present time he lives in Rehovot and is the head secretary of the municipality and was a member of the Hagannah. He married Rina Finger and their daughter Gila married Dr. A. Yochtman from Tel Aviv University. They have a daughter Iris and three sons named Ofer, Jacob and Doron.

Leyuba was in France during the war. After the war she immigrated to Israel and married an engineer by the name of Eliyahu Solel Soloveitzik. They live in Tel Aviv.

VII. Hadassah (Dashe) married Nachum Rabinovitch from Warsaw. She was killed in the Warsaw Ghetto. Their children were Leyuba and Eliyahu. Hadassa, her husband Nachum and daughter Leyuba were killed in the Warsaw Ghetto. Also Eliyahu moved as a refugee to Maytchet and he was killed there by the Nazis.

VIII. Sima graduated high school in Russia, married Shaul Luria and died in the USA in 1970.

I have been told that Moshe, brother of Rabbi Yechiel Isaac Dvorzecky, lived in Drohichin and had two daughters: Sima and Rivka.

The following tale of the immigration of Rabbi Yechiel Isaac Dvorzecki was told in Maytchet:

[Page 215]

On the day after Yom Kippur, Rabbi Dvorzecky's house was burnt down. He didn't allow anyone to stop the fire and said "It is God's way and we have to leave the Diaspora immediately and immigrate to Eretz-Israel." The next day he packed his possessions and immigrated to Eretz-Israel with his wife.

The people in Maytchet said that he was an ardent Zionist and had planned for many years to immigrate. But he could not afford to do so because of the difficult economic conditions. The long delays disappointed him and many people suspected that he himself burnt the house to enable him to leave the Diaspora.

Sara Rivka, the sister of Rabbi Yechiel Isaac Dvorzecky, married Nachum Abramovski. Their children:

1. Tehila was a dentist in Russia.
2. Shemaryahu was killed in Maytchet.
3. Shalom was killed in Maytchet.
4. Dov –Berel was a dentist. He was killed in Maytchet.
5. Musya married Baruch Reiter. They immigrated to the USA and had two sons. She died in New York in 1972.
6. Sima immigrated to Eretz-Israel where she married Elkana Ben-Chur Yentis. They had three sons: Nachum- a surgeon, Betzalel – a publisher with his father and Amos – an engineer. Sima died in Tel Aviv July 24, 1965.

Michael Landoy, the brother of Chana Gele Dvorzecky from Maytchet, had three sons and two daughters: The sons were Isadore, Salomon and Joseph. Joseph settled in Rehovot and had two sons, Eliyahu and Shmuel; both of them became farmers. Michael Landoy's daughter Chasia died in 1962. The daughter of his other daughter (name not given) married Moshe Kaganovitch who came from the Vilna Ghetto. Today he works as a scientist at the Weitzman Institute located in Rehovot.

As recorded in the tales, the Dvorzecky family lived at first in Drohichin and their name was Shlovski. At the time of the Drohichin riots, one relative of the family (Shemaryahu-Yehuda or his father) killed one of the rioters in self defense after he was attacked by them. He had to escape from Drohichin and changed his surname to Dvorzecky. From this tradition all the Dvorzecky family saw themselves as part of the Shlovski family from Drohichin.

After the war I heard about four heroic partisans from the Shlovski family in Drohichin: Avigdor was killed in a battle near Dravnaya road, Sima was a Partisan-nurse and was killed by the Vlasov army, Feige was killed in the forest and Shlomo was killed in a battle in the forest.

The Russian name of "Maytchet" is Molchadz, and the following is the explanation I heard, when I was young boy, of how the town got its name: One day the Russian Tzar, together with a convoy of his army, were in the area. The inhabitants went to greet them with water and salt. They complained about their poor life under the squires and about the heavy taxes they had to pay. The Tzar became very upset with the greeting he was given and shouted at them: "Maytchet!" (Be Quiet!) And from that time on the town was called "Maytchet".

[Page 216]

At the time of the First World War my parents, Dov and Tzivia Dvorzecky, moved from Vilna to Maytchet.

Town elders

Sitting from Right: **Yechiel Yitzchak Dvorzecki, Tzvi Boriszanski A. Rabinovitz**
Standing from right: **Sh. Boriszanski, unknown**

I began my education with Rabbi Jacob Ginzburg, who taught me grammar, Bible and Rashi. He wanted us to know all the words in Hebrew, so he forced us to memorize the words that appeared in the book "Gulat Hakoteret". That book had a lot of letters and in each one there were single words. He told us that the pupil who knows all the letters by heart, would know perfect Hebrew.

[Page 217]

Every morning we came to his house with lights and every evening we came back with the same lights. I can still remember the running lights in the streets of the town when there was snow.

Later I learned Bible (Eyov, Mishley, and Kohelet) with Rabbi Jacob Liberman who was a serious student of the Torah. He was the father of Zev Liberman who married Sonia Dvorzecky; they are the parents of Arie Yakir (Liberman) from Rehovot. One relative of Jacob Liberman is the famous Rabbi and Professor, Shaul Liberman.

At the time of the First World War there was a Zionist movement in Maytchet and I had the honor of being a member of this group. Its name was "Flowers of Zion" (Pirchei Zion). Some of my friends who were also members of the group were: Leibel Gilrovitz, Eliyahu Borishansky and Arie Yakir Liberman. We decided to establish a Hebrew theater in Maytchet. We performed a Hebrew play "One" (Echad) and we even established a small choir. (I remember one of the songs written by Isaac Katzenelson).

At the end of World War I, some of the men organized a self-defense organization in Maytchet. Among the members were Shemaryahu Borishansky, Shemaryahu Abramovsky and Berl Abramovsky. The secret meetings took place at the home of the pharmacist Jacob Dvorzecky. They bought weapons and were trained to shoot while riding galloping horses. My mother Tzvia transported the weapons from place to place in baskets.

To this day I really do not know where I was born. Some of my documents say Vilna as my birthplace but most of the others say Maytchet was my place of birth.

[Page 218]

Reb Nathan the son of
Reb Asher Orzechovsky of blessed memory
By Yisrael Neiten
Translated by Jerrold Landau
A Maytchet personality

Nathan Naten, and his wife Chana Lea Naten

Reb Nathan Orzechovsky (Naten), a native of Maytchet, was a typical Lithuanian Jew[1] - one of the remnants of the previous generation. He had the splendid countenance of a scholar with excellent character traits. He was pleasant in his mannerisms, and very discreet and modest. With him, the words of our sages were fulfilled, "Everyone who meets the approval of his fellow man also meets the approval of G-d"[2]. He was loved by all who knew him, -- old and young, men and women.

Reb Nathan was born in Maytchet around the year 5655 (1884) to his mother Sheina and his father Reb Asher Orzechovsky, one of the town notables, who earned his livelihood in his time by running a shop for iron implements. Reb Asher provided his children with a proper Jewish education. He sent both of his sons to study in the famous Yeshiva of Nowogrodek. Aside from Reb Nathan, Reb Asher Orzechovsky had one other son and four daughters. His son Reb Yonah, may G-d avenge his blood, also studied like his brother in his youth in the Yeshiva of Nowogrodek, and excelled as a great scholar. He married Kraina of the Volinski family of Nowa Mysz, and established his family in Maytchet. They had one son and two daughters. All of them perished in Maytchet in sanctification of the Divine Name during the Nazi Holocaust, except for their son who succeeded in escaping from the Holocaust. The daughters were as follows[3]: 1) Mrs. Badana Margolin may G-d avenge her blood, who established her family in Maytchet with her husband Yehuda Yitzchak, who was called Liba Asher's[4]. They had five sons and two daughters, all of whom perished in Maytchet in sanctification of the Divine name, except for one son and one daughter who succeeded in escaping from the Holocaust: 2) Mrs. Feiga Rachel Weisbord who established her family in the United States and has one son and grandchildren; 3) Mrs. Chaya Sara of blessed memory (died on 17 Cheshvan 5724 / 1963) who also immigrated to the United States along with her husband Reb Baruch Ross (Rozovski), a native of Zhetl who lived for some time in Maytchet until they went to the United States. They settled in Chicago where he serves as a *shochet*, prayer leader and teacher to this day. She left behind three sons, one daughter, and grandchildren 4) Mrs. Chasha Kolodny, the wife of Mr. Yoel Kolodny, who also lives in America and has a son, a daughter, and grandchildren. As noted, all established wide-branched family of righteous people who proudly bear the crown of their pedigree from Reb Asher of Maytchet.

[Page 219]

As has been mentioned, Reb Asher sent his son Nathan to study Torah in Nowogrodek with the Gaon and Tzadik Yosef-Yozel Horowitz of holy blessed memory (5608-5680 1848-1920), where he amassed a comprehensive knowledge of Talmud and its commentaries and reached the level of an eminent scholar, to the point where he was numbered among the excellent students of the Yeshiva. In Nowogrodek, he befriended the man who later became famous as a great Gaon and Orthodox leader, Rabbi Elchonon Wasserman, may G-d avenge his death, who later served as head of the Ohel Torah Yeshiva of Baranovichi, and served on the world Council of Torah Sages of Agudas Yisroel[5]. Rabbi Elchonon was his contemporary, and resided together with him in a room that they rented together. They would sharpen each other with *Halachic* discussions and became very close friends.

As has been mentioned, Reb Nathan was immersed in Torah studies during his youth, and even obtained rabbinical ordination. However, when it became his turn to enlist in the Russian Army (known as *Prizev* in the vernacular) he was worried about the difficult challenges that would await him with regard to observing religion in the army.

Therefore, he quickly left Russia and immigrated to the United States in the year 5671 (1911).

There, he married Chana Lea Ginzberg, the daughter of Reb Moshe Baruch of Riga, who served as a *shochet* in the community of Chicago. Due to the circumstances of the place, he was forced to seek his livelihood in business. However, first and foremost, Reb Nathan concerned himself with his ability to observe Torah and the commandments appropriately. Therefore, he occupied himself with private business that would not have the issue of Sabbath violation, despite the many difficulties in America at that time. This was considered as a great challenge at that time, and he withstood it with fortitude.

His wonderful family grew with the passage of time. He had six sons and one daughter: Yaakov Yosef, Yisrael, Yehuda, Nachum, Isser, David, and Liba. All of them were well educated and successful, in a way that any Jew could be proud. His acquaintances and relatives appreciated his talents. Even though he was very modest and taciturn, pearls, fine words, fundamental ideas, wonderful explanations on the Torah portion, and the like, came forth whenever he opened his mouth. His Torah and commitment to truth were beloved by everybody, for they were blended together. To his children he was not only a good and dedicated father, but also a friend and a true comrade who tried with all his soul to imbue them from his rich spiritual treasury. They returned his love in a boundless fashion.

[Page 220]

Like his father Reb Asher, Reb Nathan also attempted to impart to his children Torah and the ways of the world. Despite his difficult material situation, he encouraged all of his children to be diligent in their studies. He would constantly tell them and remind them that as long as they study, he would do everything to ensure that they would not be forced to interrupt their studies. Indeed, all of his children studied, and Reb Nathan could take pride that the adage "The ways of the fathers are a sign for the children" was fulfilled. In 1964, when he had reached the age of 80, the song of his life was silenced, and his soul departed in purity and joy, in accordance with the verse, "she laughs at the last day"[6]. This took place on the holiday of Purim. That morning, he prepared to go to the synagogue to hear the reading of the *Megillah*. He walked slowly through his house, and as he passed by his son Rabbi Yaakov Yosef, he suddenly slinked into his arms lifeless, in supernatural peace, as someone who dies through the kiss of Heaven. May his memory be a blessing.

Baruch and Chaya-Sarah of blessed memory (nee Orzechovsky) Ross

Yisrael Neiten

Translator's footnotes
1. Lithuanian here being used in the broad sense of the term.
2. Pirke Avot 3:13.
3. Now referring back to Reb Asher's four daughters.
4. The possessive case nickname was frequent among the Jews of Eastern Europe. This name means that he was the son of Liba and Asher.
5. See http://en.wikipedia.org/wiki/Elchonon_Wasserman
6. Proverbs 31:25.

[Page 221]

Sima Ben-Hur (Abramovsky)
by Dr. Nachum Ben-Hur
Translated by Ron Rabinovitch
Edited by Sara Mages

My mother, Sima Ben-Hur, was born in the Lithuanian/Polish town of Maytchet, which is near the town of Baranavichy. Her parents were Rabbi Nachum and Sara Rivka Abramovsky. She had a pleasant childhood growing up in a home that was filled with a warm Jewish atmosphere. The town was located at the edge of a forest, which was a resort area for tourists throughout the year. In this pastoral area, people found an escape from their problems. The teenagers especially found the forest a quiet place to gather their thoughts and think about making plans to immigrate to Eretz Israel; for redemption and the revival of the nation of Israel.

My mother's father Rabbi Nachum Abramovsky was a dignified and well educated man, who was a lecturer at the synagogue. He was very bright and knowledgeable in the contents of the Bible. He tested the Torah students in town and arranged for all their needs. Because he was so wise, he was in charge of many important public affairs. My mother, Sara Rivka, was known for her beauty and wisdom. Their house was where the intellectuals and the Zionists gathered to discuss and implement their ideas.

My mother was born into a well to do home filled with a love of Torah; her parents taught her high moral standards. From the early days of her youth she absorbed the importance of education as a path for her life. Her parents made sure she had a good secular education as well. Despite the difficulties for Jews in those days, she was able to complete the Russian high school, culminating her education with a pharmacy course. When she immigrated to Eretz Israel in 1924, she worked in a pharmacy in Jaffa and also in Tel-Aviv, which at that time was a small town.

In Israel she met Elkana Ben-Hur, a descendant of Rabbi Betzalel and Rabbi Dov Yentis from Lodmer (Volodymr-Volynskyy). Elkana also came from a home filled with love of Jewish tradition. An active member of the "Hachaluz", (Pioneer movement) he was the first in his family to implement the Zionist idea, immigrating to Eretz Israel in 1923. He came with his mother Frieda, who was the daughter of Rabbi Elkana and Chaya-Rachel (Weitzman). In 1927 Elkana and Sima married in Tel-Aviv where they established their home.

[Page 222]

They encountered many difficulties during their forty years of marriage. These years were a period of struggle between the few Jewish people in the settlements seeking to find a way to be a nation and a free country. The few Jews in the land faced Arab riots during the 1920's and 1930's, the German threats during World War II, the invading

Arab armies during the War of Independence; and the terrorist attacks during the Sinai campaign. But Sima and Elkana stood together striving to establish a generation that absorbed their thinking and feelings. My mother always gave her children a strong education that emphasized the need of knowledge of the world that surrounded them. Sima, who was born into a wealthy home, always told her children that money is not the unique thing in the world–the real wealth that brings a person happiness is knowledge and education. This is how she directed the path of her three sons: Nachum who is a surgeon, Betzalel who runs the family printing company and Amos who is an engineer.

R' Nachum and his wife Sara-Rivka Abramovsky z"l

She was known for her wisdom, her good advice, and her charity. She loved to talk with educated people; especially about the Russian poems and songs she learned in her childhood. She always conceded and gave way to other people and everyone admired and loved her.

She died on 27 Tamuz 5725 (July 24, 1965). A large crowd escorted her body to the cemetery. She left behind a loving husband, three sons, grandchildren and many relatives who would remember her forever.

May her soul be bound up in the bond of life

[Page 223]

More information about the Sima Ben-Hur family

My grandfather, Rabbi Nachum Abromovsky, was a religious and kind man with a good Soul who was very hospitable.

My grandmother, Sara Rivka, was the sister of Rabbi Yechiel Isaac Hacohen Dvorzecky. She was a very active and temperamental woman who was smart and sharp and made all the decisions in the house.

My mother's oldest sister, Tehila became a dentist, and at an early age moved to the middle of Russia, leading a difficult life.

My mother's brothers that were killed in the Holocaust and left no one behind:

> Shemaryahyhu (Shmerel)---he was a very religious man.

> Shalom---he was very handsome, tall and kind and was loved
> by everyone.

> Dov-Berel--- the youngest brother was a dentist and a beloved
> man.

Her younger sister, Musya, remained in Maytchet and was a "carbon copy" of her mother. She married Baruch Reiter who immigrated to the U.S.A. She joined him there later. They had two sons; one of them is a Zionist and lived in a kibbutz for 10 years before going to the U.S. to complete his studies. With the publication of this book we were informed that Musya and Baruch Reiter had both passed away.

On Tuesday, 10 of Sivan 5732 (May 23,1972) Elkana Ben-Hur died. He was buried on Thursday, 12 of Sivan 5732. Accompanying his body were his 3 sons, their families and many relatives, including the "The Star" Freemasons of which he was a founding member.

[Pages 224-227]

Reb Moshe Aaron Boretsky and family
by Hana Boretsky Mechtiger
Prepared by Myrna Siegel

In the west entry of our shtetl Maytchet on the road that leads to the villages Dvoretz and Zhetl my grandfather Reb Moshe Aaron Boretcky's mill stood which he got from his father Reb Meyerim of blessed memory. This area was a small empire because in that area lived the extended family of Reb Moshe Aaron, and the distance between the houses and the villages were one to two kilometers. Between the houses and the post office building there were only a few houses and the Boretcky family home was located in that area.

My grandfather Moshe Aaron and my grandmother Hana Freidl, his wife had had five sons and four daughters. They all lived close to their parents. Only two sons, Jacob and Yizachara, emigrated to the United States. My grandfather Moshe Aaron had a very noble look. He was very handsome with a long white beard. He was very charitable. The elders of the town told how when they would meet him shabbat evening walking to the synagogue a very long distance, they asked him: "It does not matter, on Saturdays and holidays every Jew and even Jews from other villages would come to the synagogue. But on Friday night this is a very long distance. Is it not beyond your strength?" and he would answer: "For distance I will receive a bigger mitzvah. As concern for my age, I receive my rewards during the days of the week. And I am obliged to fulfill my duty and to thank whoever gave me my rewards." And beyond that he would continue and say, "Try to imagine the pleasure I had when I returned from the synagogue to my home Friday night and they all came towards me, the sons, the daughters, the grandchildren, and would receive me and welcome me with shabbat shalom blessing."

Farmers came to the mill with wagons and they would bring with their grain. They would pay for flour with money or barter. Moshe Aaron gave part of his earnings to the poor people of the city.

As has been noted, my grandfather Reb Moshe Aharon was blessed with many descendents. His son, my father Reb Noach, married my mother Alte, daughter of Naftali Hertz and Sima Dvoretsky, who at first lived around Maytchet and later moved to Baranovich. My father set up his household in Maytchet near his parents' home and helped his father with the mill, and my mother Alte was one of the first teachers in the first Hebrew School of the town. My parents had two daughters and two sons. I [Chana Mechtiger] was the oldest daughter. I went out to a hachsharah kibbutz near the time of the outbreak of the Second World War, and I arrived in the Land of Israel after many tribulations. I live there today. Their second daughter, Feigle finished studies in the "Tarbut" seminary for kindergarten teachers in Vilna, even though she was orphaned from our father Reb Noach, who died at a young age in 1930. She began to work as a teacher in Maytchet. I still have Feigele's letters that she sent to her relatives abroad, written in the Hebrew Language. From them, it seems that she dreamed of coming to Israel and continuing her studies at the Hebrew University in Jerusalem. From the content and style of her letters, it is apparent that were she to have been able to realize her desire, she would have become an expert in the field of education, the field that she had always been interested in. To our sorrow, she perished in the Holocaust with our mother and two brothers, Meyerim and Herzl.

[Page 225]

Noach Boretsky
(Died 1930)

[Page 226]

A second son of my grandparents Reb Moshe Aaron and Hana Friedl Boretsky was my uncle Reb Shmuel. he married Ethel Block and they had two daughters and four sons. Like his brother, Reb Noach, Shmuel also worked with his father in the mill. Reb Shmuel served in the czar's army as an officer and his wife was a very devoted homemaker and also an actress in the local drama club. The entire family of Reb Shmuel was liquidated in the Holocaust apart from one daughter who made aliyah to Israel in one of the earlier Zionist movements "Hashomer Hazier" in 1936.

The third son was my Uncle Benzion who was married to Chasha Sharshovsky. They perished in the Holocaust and their only daughter survived. She was extremely beautiful and the lead actress in the drama group of the city. After many hardships and a miracle, she survived and went to Eretz Israel after the war. There she established her family.

Alte Boretcky and her two sons Herzyl and Meyerim

The daughters of Moshe Aaron married and established their own families. My Aunt Miriam lived in Horodishtch, Poland and she was killed there with members of the family.

My Aunt Dvorah who was married to Moshe and my Aunt Henya who was married to Label Lozovsky. Both of them established their families in Maytchet. The son-in-laws worked in the mill and they all lived in the neighborhood until they were exterminated in the Holocaust.

My Aunt Nachama, who was a widow, continued to live with her parents Moshe Aaron and Hana Friedl. She was also killed in Holocaust.

[Page 227]

The Boretsky family was large and everyone knew them there were many branches. The children supplied bread to all the farmers and supported the poor people in town. Their good deeds did not save them in the Holocaust. Their end was like all the Jews of that town. May their names be remembered.

Two Letters from Feigl Borecky
Prepared by Myrna Siegel

Here are two letters that were brought to the editor which were written by Feigele from Maytchet before the Holocaust. The letters written in a wonderful Hebrew and lots of warmth, express endless love to Eretz Yisrael and strong desire to make aliyah after finishing her study in the Hebrew seminar in Vilna. But the enemy arrived too soon andended her life dream.

Those letters are being published as they were written and let it be as a memory for her pure soul.

1st Letter:

Greetings to my dear Uncles and Aunts,

After a long silence I take my pen in hand and will tell you what is happening with me and ask to hear news from you. First of all I would like to know how you are doing and how are my Uncle and Aunt, *The Americans*? How are little Batya, and infant Zvi? I send greetings to all my family who are very dear to me. My Uncle and Aunt in America, I want you to always be aware of our fondness. I wish to G-d the time will come for our meeting. "*Shevat Achim Gam Yached*" (Brethren will sit together).

My beloved Uncles and Aunts, I am thinking that you would like to know who is the one who is writing to you. I am Zippora (Feigl) who studies in the Tarbut seminary in Vilna for kindergarten teachers. I'm in my second year and in another year and a half I will finish. Then I will get a job. But to my sorrow I find it difficult for me to fulfill my aspirations. In my long journey I have encountered many obstacles that are not making it possible for me to arrive at my destination. But despite everything, I move forward with an elevated head, and I will not allow my head to bend and surrender to those obstacles. And I am thinking that you would give me a helping hand.

[Page 228]

I am writing this letter from home. I came here for the winter holidays for 18 days. I have leave to stay home until January 9th. I think I, the unfortunate one, will have to stay longer because my mother cannot afford to send me further. I found the house in a very bad state. The pale face of my mother and her white hair frightened me. Every corner of the house is full of sorrow. It is not the same house that was joyful and fun. My mother gave all her strength for me and she cannot do any more. My little brothers can only add another tear to the cup of misfortune and weeping. So my dear ones, I have decided to turn to you. If you are indeed concerned for me, please add another brick, another hand, and the building will be completed.

Feigl (Zipora) Boretsky

I am confident that you will take my letter seriously and you will extend a helping hand to me. For, "If not now, when?" If not you my loved ones, who will be interested in me? I have no one to turn to. The gates of heaven are closing in front of me.

Once more I am turning to you with a request that you should really understand me and my thoughts. This letter should not remain with you as a piece of paper that is turning over in the wastebasket. I shouldn't have to stay in the house and be a joke and laughing stock in everybody's eyes.

My dear uncles and aunts -- I would like very much to know what impression Eretz Yisrael made on you. Also I, the young one, am longing and hoping for the land of our forefathers. The day of redemption will come for all the Jewish people, and we will be as all the other peoples. We will plant, we will plow, and we will harvest. We have suffered enough carrying the heavy load and the hard yoke on our shoulders that the Diaspora imposed on us. There will come the day when we will be free people. For you will hear the voice from afar: "Peace, peace will be in the Land," and "A wolf will live with a lamb and a tiger will sleep with a little goat..."

[Page 229]

I ask you once more that you reply to us and also you should send a photo. Batyale and little Zvi should also write to us about how the Chanukah Holiday passed in Eretz Israel. I extend my greeting to all of you. Greetings to Shifra and her husband. I am inviting you to Poland -- please come! Zippora, who is fighting for a brighter future.

2nd letter:

Greetings to you my dear ones:

My eyes were lightened from happiness, drops of tears dripped, the happiness is big. You my dears answered my request. Thank you very much my dear uncles and aunts, really you were the only ones who understood and know how short the time is and it is important to deliver the help. The day I received your postcard I didn't know what to do, I was confused, I ran to the seminar to let them know that I also may be able to attend the exam, that I am a student as all the others. I was jubilant.

The exams passed by very quickly and the day arrived which I matriculated. Dear uncles and aunts, it is hard for me to express my happiness and feelings. My poor little pen is not able to deliver everything on the paper. My heart beats with excitement. I am excited. For three years I was fighting however I won the battle and I worked hard until I arrived to the day of light. I am at home now for a week, and again my happiness is not full, my mother's pale face and her hair that was whitened from problems frightened me and expressed the big change in the house. I felt that I am the guilty in it all, true. I am the one who caused the bad situation in the home. But I did it not out of badness. I wanted to study. And I was forced to run and leave the little isolated village, in my heart two forces are fighting. My heart shrinks from pain as I am looking at my mom. Oh dearest. The human always fight and will never be content with he has. However I will try to be different. My first ambitions I fulfill and I will try to fulfill further. I will stand again to the battle with life and I am forced to step forward. To study further, not to delay. However first I have to be grateful for all of those who knew to appreciate my studying in Vilna and who try to help me in the needed moment. Now I will get a job and I will work, in order to earn a bit, and afterward I would like to make aliyah and to study in the University, if only it will work out for me. My ambitions to make aliyah, because this is the only place for me.

With lots of love,

Ziporra

[Page 230]

My Parents - The Boretcky family
by Sarah Boretcky Biribis
Translated by Jerrold Landau

A.

My mother Ethel of blessed memory was orphaned at an early age. Her father passed away at the age of 33 years. Her mother remarried and was forced to leave her children and move to her second husband. While she was still very young, she bore the burden of tending to the household and caring for her three brothers, two of whom were even older then her. Later, she was accepted at a large hide enterprise. Thanks to her golden hands, she was assigned as the chief cutter and allocated work to many other stitchers. In this way, she earned an honorable livelihood.

My mother was a very wise woman with many talents. She had an unusually sweet voice and was always happy and full of life, with a constant smile on her face. She was also a lead actress in the amateur acting group. She had the lead role in every performance. She played "The Witch" (*Mechashefa*), "Mirele Efrat" and many other roles of this genre. She read many books. Before I immigrated to Israel she would sit on long winter nights with a book on the table, as she was knitting beneath.

She had a good place in the community, for everyone admired her. Her origins were from a fine, honorable, family. I did not know her parents, and do not know anything about them. However, her mother's brother was a well-known rabbi in Lida. All of his sons were teachers, whereas other cousins were Torah scholars, pharmacists, etc. Mother spent years in the home of this uncle in Lida, where they loved her as a daughter and a sister in every way, and there were sufficient reasons for this.

I remember her from the age of three, when we fled as refugees at the end of the war and lived in one room - mother, Nathan and I. We lived a life of poverty, with simple, unsalted food, and wearing a work dress, albeit nicely decorated in red. I wore shoes that were too large for my feet. I recall that there was only one bed for the three of us, and one day, an additional one appeared, made of two poles covered with burlap. Of course, we took turns sleeping in it at night. Once at midnight, I realized that mother was not beside me in the bed. I searched around in the dark and found mother sitting next to a soldier in uniform, talking to him. I got up with a scream. I chased the soldier away, as I was afraid of him. This soldier was my father whom I did not yet know.

[Page 231]

My mother suffered a great deal in her life, but she sustained us with great wisdom and maintained herself until Father returned from the war. My friends were always jealous of me that I had such a mother, progressive and wise, young in spirit, and a good friend. I loved my mother very much.

Our home was always open to everyone. It was always filled with male and female friends of all ages. All of them felt good there, for Mother also joined us, and my friends included her and took advice from her. Six children grew up in difficult conditions in our home, but they received a good education. They were trained to work with their hands, to perform good deeds, and to be involved with Zionism. Five of us were in the Hashomer Hatzair movement. One left, and our parents were also aligned with us. Despite the age difference between my parents, with Mother being 12 years younger, they always had exemplary good relations, without any disputes at all or raised voices. The children sometimes argued amongst themselves, as do all children.

The image and memory of Mother will remain in my heart until my last day.

B.

My father of blessed memory

I do not know very much about the history of my father Shmuel. I did not know him at all until the end of the war, and even for some time after. I knew that there were nine children, and I thought that there were another one or two who died. The entire family lived together with our grandfather Moshe Aaron Boretcky. I do not recall Grandmother at all.

I got to know my father for the first time at the age of five or six. He served as a captain in the Russian Army throughout the entire wartime period. I had no sense of a father, and I always asked, "What is 'father'? What does he look like?" and other such questions. The family was reunited when he returned. I was six years old. From then, I remember him well. He was a handsome, tall, strong man, with a full head of hair. He was intelligent and good hearted. Wartime stories never stopped, especially on Sabbaths, festivals, and long winter nights when the family would sit around the table.

Our parents told us a great deal about their tribulations, and everything connected with the wars.

My father had visited many countries and his stories sprang out as from an overflowing fountain.

Before I made *aliya* to Israel I hoped that my brothers would follow together with my parents. However, destiny was cruel, and everybody was annihilated without a memorial. They were not even buried like humans.

Their memory will always be blessed and preserved forever.

[Page 232]

My parents - Wolinsky family
By Miriam (Wolinsky) Kleinshtub
Translated by Jerrold Landau

A Jew of Maytchet fell ill with smallpox, was hospitalized, and died. This was during the First World War. In order to prevent the spread of the disease, the Germans ordered that he be buried in the closest cemetery, which happened to be a Christian cemetery. My father of blessed memory did not make peace with this. At night, he snuck into the cemetery along with two other Jews, disinterred the body, and transferred it to a Jewish burial.

When he returned home toward morning, Mother said to him, "You endangered your life!"

Father responded, "So what? Is it possible to leave a Jew buried in a Christian cemetery?"

The good of the community always stood at the center of Father's concerns. Even though he was not a native of Maytchet, he was completely involved with the life of the town. He would serve as a prayer leader on the High Holidays. For a certain time, he served as the *gabbai* [trustee] of the *Beis Midrash*, and was a member of the *Chevra Kadisha* [burial society], charitable fund, and other communal bodies.

My father, Reb Chaim Leib Volinski of blessed memory was born around 1870 to his parents Moshe Naftali and Lea Freidel near the town of Drohiczyn in the Pulsia district of Poland. They maintained an agricultural farm there, which they had leased from a certain landowner. My father had 11 brothers and sisters. The entire family would gather together at every holiday, and they would not be short a tenth man for a *minyan* [prayer quorum].

My mother Kunia-Rivka of blessed memory was born in Slonim to her parents Reb David and Dvora Shochetowicz, who earned their livelihood from the liquor trade. They had one son and three daughters.

My parents lived in Maytchet from the time of their marriage in 1899. Our family had the nickname "Zawadczyk," and everyone in the region knew who was meant by this nickname. This nickname was on account of the soda and carbonated water factory that my parents' owned. They also opened a tavern for soft drinks ("Pywiarna") next to the factory. These two businesses were housed in the wooden building in which we lived, located in the center of town, part of which was purchased by my parents from the landowner of Kleshnyaki. Isser Bilas of blessed memory and Yakov Dvorzecky of blessed memory also lived in this house. Yaakov Dvorzecky ran his pharmacy out of his house.

The building in which we lived underwent many incarnations. During the First World War when Maytchet was conquered by the Germans, the building was expropriated by the conquerors and served as a hospital. Part

[Page 233]

of the family went to live with Hershel Shlovski and another part went to live with Moshe Shevchik until the hospital was transferred to a different location.

My father extinguished several fires that broke out in the building. One of the fires that he put out was when the house served as a hospital. From the house that we were living in at the time, he noticed smoke coming from he building. He hurried to the place and succeeded in controlling the fire. My father also saved the home of Isser Bilas from being consumed by fire. My father was accompanying the Kosterovitzki brothers, the sons of Yehoshua of the village of Sycewicze, who were studying in Maytchet, back home after they had supper with us. One the way, Father noticed fire bursting forth from the house of Isser Bilas. He hurried over and gained control over the fire, which had been caused by a maid who hung up the laundry over a kerosene lamp that had overturned.

As I had already noted, Father was very much occupied in communal affairs and in assisting those in need. In cases of attacks on Jewish girls, my father concerned himself with the daughters of two families who lived next to us. He entered their house, dressed the girls in boy's clothes, and hid them in our house.

We were eight children in the home: five sisters and three brothers: David, Golda, Zelig, Roza, Shifra, me, Leizer, and Lea Freidel.

We all studied - the boys in various *Yeshivas* and the girls in school. Our studies did not prevent us from helping our parents in their business. I recall that we would not take money from the residents of the town on the Sabbath. Every customer had a page in a ledger. We would put a note prepared from the outset in the appropriate page, listing the amount of the purchase.

Father's death in 1923 was a great blow to all of us. We slowly organized ourselves to continue with life, and we helped even more in running the business. As time went on, the children began to leave the house and establish their own families. My brother David married Teiba Rivka of the Avilev family of the town of Lubcz, and he set up his family there. My brother Zelig got married in Maytchet and helped Mother run the business. My sister Golda got married to Eliezer Polonski and lived near us. They had a sewing workshop and a leather store. My sister Roza married Yitzchak Meir Topoli and set up her home in Maytchet. Her husband served as a *shochet*, and would also perform *shechita* for the Jews of neighboring villages. Only my brother Eliezer and my sister Leah Freidel did not get married before the outbreak of the Second World War.

The world war sealed the fate of the Jews of Maytchet, including my family members who remained in Poland. Most of the family members perished in Maytchet. My brother David and his family perished in Lubcz, and my brother Eliezer perished in the Kozlochowa Camp.

Of the entire family, only my sister Shifra and I survived. I made *aliya* to the Land in 1932 as a tourist with the first exhibition of the Orient Fair[1] that took place in Tel Aviv in those days. I married Moshe Kleinshtov, and we have three sons and a daughter, as well as grandsons and granddaughters. My sister Shifra married Yosef Lozovski while still in Maytchet. They made *aliya* to the Land in 1933 with their baby girl. Their *aliya* was possible because her husband was a well-to-do tradesman, and the British were only issuing *aliya* permits at that time to those who had means. They settled in Rishon Letzion, and have two daughters and a son, grandsons and granddaughters.

[Page 234]

Our hearts ache over the loss of our most dear ones. May their memories be a blessing.

Translator's footnote
    1. See http://en.wikipedia.org/wiki/Orient_Fair

Standing from left: **Moshe Kleinshtov, his wife Miriam, Yosef Lozovski**
Sitting: **Shifra Lozovski and the children**

[Page 235]

Memories from Maytchet
By Mordechai (Munia) Hassid of Buenos Aires
Translated by Jerrold Landau

The son of Shimon Yitzchak "the Magid" who would travel through various towns received his nickname Munia Zushke's on account of his mother Zushke who travel through villages for her fowl business in order to feed her nine children. The father was a native of Zhetl and the mother a native of Maytchet, where they established their home on the Street of the Cemetery, and where Munia and the other children were born.

In 1928, he escaped from the Polish "*Priziv*" (draft) and moved to Argentina with his future wife, Feigel of the Boshlovitz family of Slonim. They got married in Argentina and established a family. He manufactures mattresses and is successful in his business. He has a married son and daughter.

The Landsmanschaft of Maytcheters in Argentina consists of 65 families, 35 of whom are in Buenos Aires. They gather together annually to memorialize the martyrs of Maytchet, as well as whenever a Maytcheter comes from Israel to visit his family. Almost all of the Maytcheters in Argentina are Zionists with their hearts in Israel, and saddened by the tribulations of Israel. There was a great awakening during the Six day War. They voluntarily donated large sums of money. They will certainly rejoice with the joy of Israel once peace is established.

On the other hand, the youth, that is the Maytcheters who were born here, are somewhat distant from Judaism, and the parents relate to the situation with great worry and doubts about their future with respect to Israel, and with respect to the preserving the memory of Maytchet in their hearts. However, what the mind does not do perhaps time will do, and one must not despair of a miracle during this period when so many miracles took place in Israel.

Maytchet natives in Argentina greatly appreciate the holy task of perpetuating the town and its martyrs though publishing a Memorial Book, in order to thwart the aims of the enemy who wished to wipe out the name and memory of the Jewish towns from beneath the heavens. Now it will be proven before the entire world that "The eternity of Israel will not deceive"[1]!

Translator's footnote
   1. I Samuel 15:29

[Page 236]

Gedalya and Nehama Yatvicky
By Yitzchak Binyamin (Yatvicky)
Translated by Jerrold Landau

I myself was a resident of Dworzec (Dvorets), but I have memories of my youth from Maytchet, where I studied a trade and got to know many dear Jewish families. I especially see a duty to express true gratitude to my aunt and uncle Gedalia and Nechama Yatvicky. This was during the 1920s, and I was about 14 years old at the time, when I came to Maytchet to study the sewing trade with Leizer Polonski (the son-in-law of Zawadcki). I stayed at the home of my Uncle Gedalia.

Incidentally, it is worthwhile to mention the work conditions that pervaded during those days, when no professional organization existed in the town, and every person did what was right in his eyes. During the first year, I worked as an apprentice without pay. During the second year, I began to receive a salary of 250 zloty (50 dollars) a year. The workday extended from early morning until after the *Maariv* service, and even later[1] in the winter. Others who worked in this trade aside from

Polonski included Noach Goldshtein the brother of Rabbi Elchanan Goldshtein, Nachum the Shteper [stitcher] and others.

Uncle Gedalia was a Torah oriented, observant Jew who earned his livelihood honestly. After a hard day of work in his household implements store, he would run to the *Beis Midrash* to teach a class in *Mishna* between *Mincha* and *Maariv* to the congregation of worshippers. Aside from the commandments between man and G-d that he fulfilled with his entire soul and means, he was also diligent with the interpersonal commandments, and was therefore beloved and accepted in the eyes of G-d and man. In 1935, he was taken hurriedly to Warsaw for an urgent operation by the well-known physician Dr. Soloveiczyk, but he died there and is buried in the cemetery of Praga.

I will now note some incidents that typify those fateful days. When the Germans invaded Poland in September 1939, I was serving as a Polish soldier in Warsaw. As part of the war effort, we took up defense positions behind the monuments of the Praga Cemetery. When dawn broke after the nighttime activities, to my great surprise, I noticed that I was standing next to the gravestone of my uncle. I showed this to my platoon commander, and he found this astonishing. As is known, the defense operations did not last long, and I was taken prisoner by the Germans. I was freed from prison two months later, after the Polish-German agreement[2].

Aunt Nechama was a woman of valor who helped in the business and performed acts of charity and kindness in the life of her husband. She continued with the household implements store after she was widowed. Her home stood on a hill in the town next to the home of her brother Yisrael Belski (Sara's) the baker. When the Germans entered Maytchet in 1941, the family of Liba Margolin was forced to leave their house and live with Nechama Yatvicky.

[Page 237]

During the *aktion* in Maytchet, they all hid in the cellar of the house, the entrance to which was well hidden for a long time. However, the residents of the cellar were eventually exposed by one of the gentiles. They were taken to the communal grave in Chwojnik to be murdered.

Maytcheters who were partisans

Sitting fro the right: **Moshe Ravitz, Mina Levin (Gorski), Dvora Mlishinski, Esther Lozovski, Chaim Kravitz**

Standing from the right: **Chanan Peleg, Abrasha Chanale's, Baruch Lewin, Meir Lozovski, Freidel Mkronski (Margolin), Moshe Korn**

Translator's footnotes

1. The time of the Evening Service (*Maariv*) varies during the year in accordance with the time of nightfall.
2. The term used here is "agreement," but "surrender" might be more appropriate.

[Page 238]

Reb Joshua Aharon Lozovsky of blessed memory

By Yosef Lozovski
Translated by Jerrold Landau

First of all, I recall my paternal grandparents very well. My grandfather Dov Ber Lozovsky of blessed memory was an educated, honorable Hassidic Jew. He worked as a potter and earned his livelihood from the work of his hands, as was the custom of Maytchet Jews for generations. He also had the generous character traits with which the Jews of the towns excelled in those days. I recall the day of his death, which took place during the time of the First World War. He returned from the synagogue in a merry mood on Purim after hearing the reading of the *Megilla*. On his way back, he went to his son's house, drank a *LeChaim* in honor of the holiday, and returned home healthy and hale. A few hours later, they came to Father to inform him of his death. I also recall Grandmother who was very old at the time of her death.

My father Reb Joshua Aharon of blessed memory studied at *Yeshiva* until 25. Only after filling himself with Talmud and decisors of Jewish law, to the point where he became known as an expert scholar, did he marry 14-year-old Chana of the Skolnikovitz family. They had ten children, of whom they raised four brothers and three sisters[1]. Aside from me, one brother, Meir Lizovski, made *aliya* to the Land after the war. The rest of the brothers and sisters perished in the Holocaust, may G-d avenge their blood.

My father of blessed memory had a splendid countenance with a flowing beard. He got along well with people, and walked uprightly with G-d and man. He sent his sons to *Yeshivas* and raised them with Torah and tradition, in accordance with the custom of his fathers. He was a building contractor and a manufacturer of tar, charcoal and bricks. His sons also took part in the business and helped him develop it, even though they were working in their own right.

Due to his flourishing business, he was well off, so he merited two tables - Torah and business. He built a large house, as was fitting for his status. He also knew how to benefit his fellowman from his fortune, his strength, and his voice. As a contractor, he helped build the Chorev School, he fixed up and renovated the synagogue, and performed other such important activities in the realm of religion. He acted benevolently with his fellow by offering assistance to anyone in need. It goes without saying that he made sure to never sit down for a Sabbath meal unless there was a guest eating at the table. Finally, he excelled as a fine prayer leader with a sweet voice that was enjoyed by the congregation.

His wife Chana, that is my mother of blessed memory, died at the end of the first World War. He remained a widower as long as he still had daughters at home. He married a second wife after the daughters got married.

[Page 239]

The writer of these lines was his primary assistant in his many business endeavors. He also built himself a large home and planned to dwell in peace, as is the custom of Jewish men. However, the relative quiet before the great storm that was about to shake the foundations of Diaspora Jewry awakened him to thought and action. One day in 1933, I decided that I could no longer sit upon a quaking mountain. I arose, liquidated my house and business, and made *aliya* to the Land of Israel where I built my permanent house in Rishon Letzion.

After a short time, my father and his wife came to me, and lived in my house for two years. In 1937, Father desired to live in the holy city of Jerusalem, where he earned his livelihood from delivering Torah classes to the congregation of worshippers and those who studied in the *Beis Midrash*. He died in Jerusalem at the old age of 89, and is buried on the Mount of Olives. His wife lived a long time after him.

May his soul be bound in the bonds of eternal life.

Management of Ezrat Cholim"

1) Chanan Kostininski (chairman) 2) Moshe Belski (vice chairman) 3) Manya Novomiski (treasurer) 4) Yitzchak Gilerovitz 5) Yaakov Novogrodski 6) Yosef Shkolnikovitz 7) Shmaryahu Safir 8) Zelig Volinski 9) Reuven Breski 10) Yosef Lozovski

Translator's footnote
    1. I assume that this means that three of the children died young.

Page 240]

Family Lubetcky
By David Leib Lubetcky, United States
Prepared by Myrna Siegel
Edited by Jerrold Landau

I left Maytchet as a young child, but I had a large family who remained in Maytchet. My parents were born in Maytchet, and also my two grandfathers and two grandmothers lived in Maytchet. A large part of the rest of our family was also born in Maytchet. They are buried in the Maytchet Cemetery.

My grandfather Meyerim Lubetcky was born in the town of Turcz. He married a Maytchet girl named Doba. They remained in Maytchet and there they lived out their years. They had six daughters and two sons. One of his sons was my father Yitzchack Akivah Lubetcky, may his memory be for a blessing.

My grandfather Meyrim Lubetcky's occupation was leasing land from landowners of the area. Later in his life he abandoned this. Since my grandfather was a great scholar and very wise Jew, he served as an emissary for collecting money for Yeshivas. At the same time he became interested in medicine. He studied medical passages from the Talmud and Maimonides. He wrote prescriptions in Latin and also Yiddish. Everything in the name of Heaven. He considered this to be a great mitzvah to write prescriptions for healing the people, mainly for poor people. Both Jews and gentiles would come to my grandfather to ask advice. They even turned to him as an arbitrator for a variety of disputes. When he was out of the country as a fundraiser, people would wait until he returned so he could arbitrate for them.

My grandfather Meyrim was an uncle of the renowned Yeshiva Master [Rosh-Yeshiva] in Grodno, Shimon Shkop.

My other grandfather was Itzchak Boretcky and my grandmother was Sarah Rachel. They were born in Maytchet. They were the parents of my mother Yachne Rivka. My grandfather Itzchak was a brother of Moshe Aaron Boretcky and they each had a mill.

[Page 241]

The two mills were built by their father Meyrim Boretcky and he gave them to his two sons.

My parents Yitzchak Akivah and Yachne Rivke immigrated to America. We were three children -- me, my brother Eliezer Shmuel and our sister Sarah Rachel (Sylvia). Unfortunately, my parents and sister died in America.

I left behind a large family in Maytchet. From my mother's side there was the Boretcky family and the family of Hershl Novomiski the mohel. His wife Nechama Devorah, peace be upon her, was a sister to my mother. On my father's side were his sisters Sivia and Chianke. Sivia was the wife of Chackel Israelvitz and the other sister Chianke was married to Isser Zusman. All had a large extended families.

Yitzchak Akivah and Yachne Rivke Lubetcky

I am writing what I remember about my family in Maytchet for the Yizkor book; the physical beauty of the area and the good people that lived there. It is important that future generations know their origins and who their ancestors were.

[Page 242]

My Family - the Margolin Family
By Chemda Lubrani (Margolin)
Translated by Jerrold Landau

As I come to describe my family in Maytchet, I must start out by describing the earlier period of my family. In truth, I was not born in Maytchet. My family only began living there in 1923, after the death of my father Reb Mordechai Margolin of blessed memory.

My grandfather Reb Yaakov Yosef Margolin was a native of the town of Zamiechow in Russia, where he served as the town *shochet*. He and his wife Chasia, may she rest in peace, established their household in that town, where three sons and two daughters were born.

Reb Mordechai Margolin

The eldest son, Moshe of blessed memory, set up his home in Russia like his father. He had three sons and three daughters. One son and one daughter, Yaakov Margolin may G-d avenge his blood and Dvosha Shinovski may G-d avenge her blood moved to Poland during the Bolshevik Revolution. Their final place of residence was Baranovichi. They perished in the Holocaust without leaving any survivors. The rest of the sons and daughters of Moshe of blessed memory live in Russia today, and have large families.

[Page 243]

The second son was my father Reb Mordechai of blessed memory. During his youth, he served in the Russian Army during the Russo-Japan War (1905). Then he moved to the town of Starobin near Slutsk, where he married my mother Sheina, the daughter of the *shochet* of Starobin, Reb Gedalyahu Kadoshin of blessed memory.

Eventually, my grandfather Reb Yaakov Yosef Margolin of blessed memory died, and my grandmother Chasia remained a widow. To my great sorrow, my second grandmother, the wife of my grandfather Reb Gedlayhau also died after some time. After that, my grandfather Reb Gedalyahu married my grandmother Chasia, and they both continued to live in Starobin.

After the death of my grandfather Reb Gedalyahu of blessed memory, my father Reb Mordechai continued on as the *shochet* of the town until the year 5681 (1921). My parents gave birth to three sons and three daughters: Yaakov, Avraham, Abba, Dvosha, Sara, and me.

In 1921, the gentiles perpetrated a pogrom against the Jews of Starobin, killing many victims. Some of the Jews of the town succeeded in escaping the town and saving themselves from the pogrom. My family was among then. Then, we moved to Poland and first settled in the town of Horodziej, where my father of blessed memory also served as a *shochet*.

The third son of my grandfather Reb Yaakov Yosef of blessed memory was Aryeh Leib Margolin. He set up his family in Maytchet, and married Badana, the daughter of Reb Asher Orzechovski of blessed memory. They had five sons and two daughters. Most of them perished in the Holocaust, with the exception of a son and a daughter who survived the Holocaust and live today in Israel.

The first daughter of my grandfather was Rivka, who married Reb Yaakov Sadovski of blessed memory. They lived in Baranovichi and had three sons and two daughters. My uncle Reb Yaakov Sadovski died in 1941, whereas his daughter Chasha died in her childhood in 1920 due to an accident that took place in their house. Two of his sons live today in the Land. The first one, Moredechai, made *aliya* in 1936, and the second one, Kalman, survived the Holocaust. The rest of the family perished in the Holocaust, except for one of the grandchildren, the son of the second daughter Chiene, who succeeded in surviving and lives today in the Soviet Union.

The second daughter of my grandfather Reb Yaakov Yosef was Sara. She set up her family in Jekaterynoslaw, Russia. To our great sorrow, we do not know any further information about her.

As has been mentioned, our family moved to Horodziej after the pogrom in Starobin. Two years later, my father became sick with a malignant illness, and was taken to Warsaw where he died on 17 Av, 5683 (1923). After the death of my father of blessed memory, our family decided to move from Horodziej to Maytchet, where my uncle Aryeh Leib Margolin, the brother of my father of blessed memory, lived.

[Page 244]

In Maytchet, we opened an inn for vacationers. At first, we lived in the home of Yaakov Zlotnick, which was next to the house of Yitzchak Liberman. We ran the inn in that house. Later, we moved to a larger home in Podelzan. The inn was run primarily by my mother and my sisters Dvosha and Sara. I only helped them, because I was still studying in Baranovichi at that time. After a few years, I went to a *Hachshara Kibbutz*, and I made *aliya* in 1936. My brothers Avraham and Abba worked in leasing dairy enterprises from the landowners of the area, and they manufactured Swiss cheese. My eldest brother Yaakov remained in Baranovichi, married there, and opened a store that sold paints and chemicals. He was killed during the first bombardment of Baranovichi in 1939, and his family perished in the Holocaust.

Sheina Margolin

Slowly but surely, our home in Maytchet emptied. My brother Avraham got married. He first lived in Baranovichi and moved to Horodziej after a few years, where he perished along with his family. My brother Abba died in Maytchet in 1939 after contracting pneumonia due to the cheese manufacturing that he was engaged in. My sister Dvosha got married in lived in Baranovichi. During the Holocaust, she moved with her entire family to Maytchet, where they perished along with the rest of the family. My sister Sara married Yehoshua Rabinovitch in Maytchet. She continued to run the inn together with Mother until the murderers got the upper hand, and killed them along with the rest of the Jews of Maytchet.

May their memories be a blessing.

[Page 245]

Reb Zvi-Hirsh Aharonovitz
Translated by Chaya Horwitz Turin

Reb Tzvi Ahronovitz

From my memory as a child I can envision a visit with my grandfather Reb Tzvi Ahronovitz of blessed memory and my grandmother Shaina Cheisaha of blessed memory. We traveled from the city of Baranovichi to the village of Sirotva next to Maytchet. We were welcomed at the railroad station in Maytchet with a horse and wagon. While my mother and her five children were in the wagon we could not wait to see the faces of our grandmother and grandfather.

We came for the holidays. It was late in the afternoon and we came to the place where they were excitedly waiting for us. Here they were, our grandfather with his beard and strong body like a farm worker. He joyfully welcomed us and took us into his house. And right in the entrance of my grandfather 's house we see a few Jews eating and drinking. We ask, "who is in the next room." Our grandfather explained to us that it is a mitzvah to help the poor and we have to do it all year round, not only on Purim. And he did this mitzvah not only in theory but also in practice. And this is what the rabbi in the cheder in the city taught the students in addition to learning the Torah. And here we see our grandfather performing the mitzvah in the full meaning of the word, as our forefather Abraham did. In his house he provides two rooms, one is for prayer. I remember how happy my grandfather was to have prayer in his house. We grandchildren always remember how joyful it was in the house of our grandfather at holiday time.

[Page 246]

Grandfather was a misnagid. He likes to learn the Torah and it was deep in his heart. And the love of Eretz Yisrael, our nation of Israel, the Torah of Israel was embedded in his blood. He would always tell us that Eretz Yisrael was a very far place. Every child from childhood should wish that one of his days he will be able to live there. And we saw in his fact the sadness that he could not fulfill this. But he merited at least to see his daughter, my dear mother, with her children emigrate to Eretz Yisrael and this made him very happy. To watch her pack all her belongings and accompany her to the train to make aliyah to the Holy Land, I don't ever remember seeing a happier face. His love for Jews was unbounded. I think he fulfilled the saying of Rabbi Akivah that you should love your neighbor as yourself. Whenever he could help someone, it would make him very happy to do that. His love and learning of the Torah was unbounded.

His sons were sent to the Yeshiva to study Torah and the daughters married learned men. And my grandmother, she should rest in peace, she went to yeshivas to find for her daughters the best husbands. And nothing was spared to accomplish this task. This was the only house that all the daughters were married to scholars. Their daughter Michlah married one of the greatest scholars known as "The grandfather of Novogrudok." When he died she married again to the Rabbi from Dabrowice. The daughter Channa married Aaron Pinchuck and he was the head of the Yeshiva in Kletsk.

The daughter, Zipora, married a Rosh Yeshiva from Novogrudok. And the youngest son remained in the house to help all of them with their families. They all perished in the Holocaust. Another son, Rabbi Pesach Aronovitch was able to go to South Africa before the war. There he started a family and studied Torah. He passed away a number of years ago in Johannesburg from a heart attack.

Our mother Fruma Bracha, may she long live, she married our father Yitzchak Aaron Ha Levi Horowitz and he was a descendant of the Shiloh Kadosh. He was an important Chassid from Slonim. In Eretz Yisrael he whole-heartedly engaged in public works until the day of his death. He was an overseer of giving poor people loans interest free and he died the 4th day of Av 5729 in Kfar Saba, Israel.

[Page 247]

Some relatives of our dear mother also emigrated before the Holocaust. We children, who emigrated to Eretz Yisrael in the year 5694, were raised in the secular environment that permeated Kfar Saba. Nevertheless through the influence of our parents, we and our parent's grandchildren remained religious and followed the laws of the Torah. We had love for Eretz Yisrael and some of us served in the underground and the army. For the

Love of the land for our fellow Jews we served in the army and the underground. There is no doubt in my mind that through the influence of my parents and with G-d's help that the Torah should never cease from the lips of our children and descendants.

Yakov Horowitz
One of the grandchildren

[Page 248]

Reb David-Hershel Novomiski and his family
by Sara Aharonovsky
Translated by Jerrold Landau

Reb David-Hershel the son of Reb Leib, a splendid branch on the Novomiski family tree, was a scholarly Jew, a Hassid, and well educated. He would get up every night for *chatzot*[1], immerse in a *mikva* [ritual bath] prior to the prayers, etc. Since he excelled with his exceptional intelligence and his expertise in worldly affairs, the rabbi would include him in rabbinical judgments among disputing merchants. He would come himself before the rabbi with great modesty in order to avert a summons from the beadle, which would have an element of presumptuous.

He was a third generation, famous *mohel* [ritual circumcisor]. This was a holy tradition of service that he had received from his father and grandfather. He ran a leather goods store, from which he sustained his large family with comfort. As a *maskil*, he took an interest in modern sciences, especially physics. It was said that when he was lying on his sickbed, he debated a physical law regarding when ice would float on water. He managed to prove his point on the basis of words of Torah.

His wife Nechama-Dvora was known in town as a righteous woman, who was the helpmate of her husband in acts of charity and benevolence, in running a Jewish home immersed in Torah and tradition, and in educating her children to Torah and commandments in the best tradition of the Novomiski family, whose name was known in a praiseworthy fashion in Maytchet and other places. She died in 1918 of the typhus epidemic, which spread after the First World War.

Reb-David Hershel and Nechama-Dvora had many children. They raised a righteous generation of seven children - five sons, and two daughters. They are as follows:

Avraham-Yosef was the eldest son, who was ordained as a rabbi at the age of 18. He studied *shechita* [ritual slaughter] and immigrated to Argentina. He raised a family there and works as a *shochet*. He visited Israel in 1965.

Meirim-Max is a journalist who also immigrated to Argentina. He visited his sister in Kfar Azor, Israel in 1966.

Yehoshua is a confectionary merchant who immigrated to Argentina, where he established his household and family.

Meir received a national Hebrew education in the Tarbut School. He lives in Argentina.

[Page 249]

Pua (Poya) studied in the Tarbut School and married a refugee from Germany. She perished in the Holocaust with her husband and their two children Chana and Feitel, along with our father and his second wife Esther-Rachel.

Pua (Poya) Novomiski

Sara is the writer of these lines in memory of her family. She married Aryeh Aharonovsky who came from Eretz Yisrael to visit his family in Mir. There, they met, got married in father's house, and traveled to Eretz Yisrael in 1935. They are among the first who settled the land in Kfar Azar. They established a home and ran a farm. They have a son and a daughter.

Sara Aharonovsky (nee Novomiski).

Translator's footnote
1. *Tikkun Chatzot* is an optional, private prayer service recited at midnight by especially pious people, in commemoration of the destruction of the Temple.

[Page 250]

Sheine Rachel Simkof-Bader
by Moshe Zinovits
Translated by Roslyn Sherman Greenberg
A Maytchet-American Jewish Writer

Sheine Rachel was born on September 18, 1899 in the town of Maytchet which is in the Province of Grodno in Russia/Poland. Her father was a teacher and her mother ran a cheder for small children. Until the age of nine she learned from her mother and after her mother's death, she studied to be a seamstress and was raised by relatives.

At the age of 17 she joined her brothers and sisters in America, where she worked days in a shop and at night she studied further in school. In her early years she wrote songs and short stories, but her works were not published until 1925 in the "Free Workers Voice," New York. She authored a succession of pieces that were staged in Yiddish theaters in various countries since 1916.

Through the years she published songs, childrens' stories, in America in the following publications: "Free Workers Voice", "Yiddish Day Page", "The Day", "Morning Journal", "Forward", "The Future", "The American", "Childrens' Newspaper", "Childrens' Journal", "New Yorker Weekly", and others in New York; "The Yiddish World", Philadelphia; "The Yiddish Courier", Chicago; " Canadian Eagle," Montreal; "The Yiddish Journal" Toronto, as well as in the Yiddish newspapers in South America.

In book form were printed: "In the Struggle of Life", two volumes of stories with a prologue by Gershon Bader. Volume I, New York, 1943, 253 pp.; Volume 2, 1949, 287 pp. With reviews by S. Niger, Z. Shniourk M Vities, A. L. Baron, A Almi and Abraham Reisen. Of her 25 plays the following were performed on the stage: "Victims of Love" (1916); "A Name after my Mother" (1918); "Open Your Eyes" (1920); "Before the Wedding" (1924); "Secrets from Every House" (1926); "For Parents' Mind" (1927); "Girl of my Heart" (1930); "Why Girls Run Away" (staged by Ludwig Zatz in 1932); "Hello, Molly" (staged by Molly Picon in Argentina in 1932); "The Lucky Widower" (1964) performed in Israel. Ready to be published now are two volumes of prose, titled "My Life in the Theater."

[Page 251]

Until 1930 she worked in a dress shop. Later she supported herself through her plays that had been performed. She lived in New York. Her husband was Gershon Bader. Her descriptions of her childhood are fraught with idealism and with drama. (S. Niger) "She portrays her old poor home faithfully and honestly." (Abraham Reisen). For a rich bibliography, see : Lexicon of the New Yiddish Literature, sixth volume, New York, 1965.

Maytchet Zionist Association

From top right: **Wolf Rabinovitz, Chana Berman, Golda (Rabbi Belski's daughter), Moshe Leberman**
Second row: **Yaakov Ginzburg, David the son-in-law of the shochet, Baruch Roses (Razovski)**
Sitting: **David Volinski, Noach Goldstein**

[Page 252]

The Polonsky-Edlin Family

By Tova Polonsky Shomroni

Translated by Amir Shomroni

My family has deep roots in Maytchet for many generations. My paternal grandmother Libe is the oldest member of my family that I can recall. She was blessed with many children and unfortunately became a widow at a comparatively young age. Only two of her many children remained in Maytchet; my father Avraham Polonsky and his sister Sara Melnikovsky; the remainder of the children emigrated to the New World. Their descendants have integrated themselves into the new life in America and in the summer of 1966 I visited them in their homes.

My father Avraham Polonsky was attracted to Mushe Edlin and not long after their meeting, they married. My mother Mushe was the daughter of Hinde and David Edlin, my maternal grandparents. My grandfather was a committed Jew and and a Torah scholar. From my birth both my maternal grandparents sheltered me and were intimately involved in my early upbringing offering wise consul. In my early years we lived together with them and although I do not remember exactly how long, I do remember I was attending school. My younger brother Pesach had difficulties distinguishing between an Aleph and a Bet when he started school and my grandfather would belittle him as he watched me trying to help him learn. Comments from my grandfather such as "Er hot a farshtopte kop, zi haut a kop" (he is thick headed and she has a good head). My memories of my maternal grandparents are vague because they unfortunately passed away when I was a child. My paternal grandmother Libe Polonsky lived a longer life and I was a married woman when she passed away.

The relationship between my immediate family and my aunts and uncles on both sides were strong. My maternal grandparents, Hinde and David Edlin, had seven children; four girls and three boys. Haya Perl, Sara Malke,, Hana Ida, my mother Mushe, Haim Yehoshua, Avraham Yitzhak and Yehuda (Yudil). My aunt Haya Perl emigrated to the U.S.A. and married Margolis. My aunt Hana Ida married Yehoshua (Yoshe) Polonsky who was my paternal uncle. They prospered in the U.S.A. and I am in close contact with their descendants. My aunt Sara Malka got married in Tiktin. Their son Yehezkel and daughter Shoshana live with their families in Israel near us; their other daughter live in the U.S.A. My uncle Haim Yehoshua settled in a shtetl near Warsaw. My uncle Yehuda (Yudel) emigrated to the U.S.A.

My uncle Avraham Yitzhak's journey from Maytchet was more twisted and he ended up living in Glasgow, Scotland where he became actively involved in the Jewish community.

[Page 253]

When I was a student at the Teacher's Seminary I lost contact with him and he died in 1930. 40 years later, with much research, my youngest son Amir succeeded in locating all of my uncle's six descendants, their children and grandchildren. They were living in the British Isles in various cities, including Glasgow, Edinburgh, and Manchester. I only had vague knowledge about them and they knew nothing about me. I was thrilled to discover first cousins and they were no less excited to find me, a cousin living in Israel!

Avraham-Abba and his wife Mushe Polonsky

My father and mother were the loving parents of seven boys and girls. Their first born was my elder sister Freidl. While she was still in diapers, my brother Moshe Haim was born. Not too long after his birth, the cries of my brother Yehezkel filled their home. It did not take long for my parents to be blessed once again with my birth and they named me Tova. Along came another brother, Pesach followed by my youngest sister Peshe and then David who was the last child to be born. In our house on Beit Olam Gass (the Cemetery Road) all seven of the children, mom, dad, grandma and grandpa Edlin and later on my grandma Libe.

In 1928 I was studying in Vilnius where I had completed my first year of studies in the Dr. Tcherno Hebrew Teacher's Seminary. I received the news of my father's death and returned to Maytchet. My mother was left a widow with four children who were still living at home. My older sister Freidl had already married and my brother Moshe Haim was living in Argentina. Because of difficult circumstances at home it was agreed that my brother Pesach would emigrate to Argentina to join Moshe Haim. I would return to

Vilnius to complete my studies and Peshe and David would remain at home with our mother. For some unknown reason Pesach's departure to Argentina was delayed and the ship he was supposed to be on sunk in the Atlantic Ocean. He eventually made his way to Argentina, married and raised a family. In 1965, after many years of separation, we had a reunion in Israel; two years later I visited the family in Argentina.

[Page 254]

After my father's death life was very difficult for my mother. I completed my studies in Vilnius and in 1936 I made aliyah to British Mandate Palestine with my late husband Yehoshua Shomroni (of blessed memory). Our son Shmulik was born in 1939 and when he was 6 months old, at the request of my mother, I mailed her some of his curls and tiny cut fingernails. After the war our neighbor in Maytchet, Freidl Margolin, who now lives in Kibbutz Negba in Israel, told me that my mother died from a disease and was buried in the Jewish Cemetery in Maytchet. I never will know if my mother received the package I sent her.

Yehezkel and his wife Menuha (nee Mordokovich), and their daughters, Esther, Sarah., Dvora, Freidel and her husband Israel Moshe Izralevich, Reizelle and Asnale, their daughters and their son Issar, Peshe and her husband and my brother David who was still a young boy, were all murdered, holy and pure. May the Lord revenge their blood.

Oh Maytchet, a little piece of land, forgotten by G-d, on the highway between Baranovichy and Lida, in between the windings of the Molchadka River and the Blotes (Swamps). A shtetl bustling with Jewish life and activities; what has remained of you? A foaming grave in the "Chaboynik" or perhaps only a holy memory that urges us to praise you on the leaves of the Memorial Book.

Tova Shomroni (Polonsky)

[Page 255]

My Family in Maytchet
By Moshe Korn
Translated by Jerrold Landau

As I remember my parents' home, depressing memories fly up, and feelings of pain and anguish fill my heart. All of my dear ones, benevolent people of good deeds, people of toil and labor, were murdered in cold blood by the conscienceless Nazis. Those goodhearted people, whose good deeds benefited all those around them, are no more. All of them were uprooted from the earth.

In Maytchet, my father was known by the long name Avraham-Berl-Itza-Ahrake's. This name includes three generations: my father Avraham Dov Korn of blessed memory[1], my grandfather Reb Yitzchak Korn of blessed memory, and my grandfather's father Reb Aharon Korn of blessed memory.

These three generations were all born in Maytchet. To my dismay, I have few details about them, for I was unable to glean a great deal of family information due to the fact that I was quite young at the time of the outbreak of the Second World War. I was young when I began to go through the era of the Nazi bloodbath in Poland, which did not pass over our town.

My father's grandfather Reb Aharon Korn served as the *feldscher*[2] of the town, and he was nicknamed "Aharake the Doctor." Apparently, in that far-off era, there were not enough physicians to enable small towns such as Maytchet to benefit from certified medical services, therefore, those people knows as *feldschers* occupied themselves with medicine. A *feldscher* was more than a nurse and less than a doctor, but in Eastern Europe, he had the status of a doctor. To the best of my memory, they used to say at home that my father's grandfather Aharake the doctor accepted and took care of both Jewish and gentile patients. The farmers of the area would also come to him for treatment, or to take them to their homes in the nearby villages by wagon so that he could treat the sick.

Now that I have mentioned my great-grandfather the *feldscher*, it is fitting to mention the final *feldscher* who served in Maytchet, Reb Moshe Urul (Reb Moshe the *feldscher*). He was the father of Zilpa Bas and Esther Urul. His daughter Esther was known in town as an excellent actress in the dramatic club. The era of *feldschers* in Maytchet ended with the death of Reb Moshe Urul of blessed memory, for after his death, Dr. Korman, who served as the physician of the area, settled in the town. After a long period, Dr. Korman left Maytchet and moved to Slonim. He was replaced by Dr. Kaplan, who served as the physician of the town and the area until the Holocaust.

My *father*'s grandfather Reb Aharon Korn had two children - a son and a daughter. The son was my grandfather Reb Yitzchak Korn. The daughter, Sara Rivka, married Leizer Kadish Stolobitzki, also a native of Maytchet, and established her family in the town. They had three children - a son and two daughters. The son Tzvi also married in Maytchet and lived there together with his parents. The daughter Kreina married in Baranovichi, and the second daughter Yehudit married Abba Shmulovitz

Like his father, my grandfather Reb Yitzchak Korn continued to live in Maytchet, where he established his family together with Grandmother Kreina. They had three children - two sons and a daughter. My grandfather was a brave Jew who was among those who organized a self defense organization in town in his time. He was also a member of the *Chevra Kadisha* [burial society]. A tragedy took place in 1935. My grandfather went to bathe in the Molchada River near the town, and unfortunately drowned.

[Page 256]

Avraham Dov Korn of blessed memory

**The *feldscher* Reb Aharon Korn
of blessed memory**

My grandfather's oldest son was my uncle Reb Ezriel Korn of blessed memory. He immigrated to the United States during his youth, and made *aliya* to Israel in 1968 after living in the United States for 65 years. To our sorrow, he did not live for long in Israel, for he died after several months.

[Page 257]

My grandfather's daughter Dvora Michla also immigrated to the United States. She established her family there, and lives there to this day.

My grandfather's second son was my father Avraham Dov Korn. He married my mother Liba, and they established their family in Maytchet. We were five children in the family: Ezriel, Shabtai, Mordechai, Feivel Leib, and I, the eldest. My father also continued in the family tradition, and was a member of the *Chevra Kadisha* of the town, like his father. I recall how he took me with him during my childhood to participate in the festive celebration following the 7th of Adar, the fast day followed by the feast for all of the *Chevra Kadishas* in the world. My parents lived in the same building as Grandfather and Grandmother, and they worked together in the family plot of land that they owned, that extended from their home until the bog (the *blettes*).

My father of blessed memory was among the first 22 Jews who were taken by the local gendarmes on 27 Shvat 5702 (1942) and brought to the coal making area (*smolarnia*) behind the flour mill, where they were murdered. This group included Avraham David Zukovitzki, Alter Charlap, Shalom Rabinovitch, Eliezer Blitzki, Sonia Cherbanski, Esther Chrolnik (sister of Mordechai Kravtzik who married Berel Chrolnik), and others. I recall how I ran to the members of the Judenrat and begged their assistance in order to free my father and the other Jews. Indeed, Leibel Gilerovitz took advantage of his travel permit and traveled to Horodshits and Baranovichi. I accompanied him as a wagon driver in the Judenrat's wagon. Leibel Gilerovitz attempted to stop them, and succeeded in receiving an order from the German office to free them, but it was already too late: the gendarmes had already murdered the members of the group.

We - my mother, brother Leibel and I - succeeded in surviving the vale of murder in Maytchet through great miracles and unusual means. We arrived in the Dvoretz Ghetto, where we thought we might stay and survive, but the decree was already issued, and I lost my last relatives during the siege and hunt in the Dvoretz Ghetto. Of all the family, only I survived. After difficulties and tribulations, I arrived in Israel in 1946. Now that I am able to perpetuate the memory of my family members in the Book of Maytchet, I feel that I have fulfilled a holy duty to the pure and innocent martyrs who were murdered for no fault of their own by the children of Satan and their accursed assistants during the years of the Holocaust.

May their memories be a blessing.

Translator's footnotes
1. The Hebrew name Dov and the Yiddish equivalent Berl are frequently used interchangeably.
2. An old-style barber-medic.

[Page 258]

The Family of Moshe Aharon Shevchik
By Yehuda Ben-Moshe (Shevchik)
Translated by Jerrold Landau

These lines are written in the Memorial Book of Maytchet so that the coming generations will remember and not forget our fathers who lived in Maytchet and were murdered by the enemy and foe during the era of the Holocaust. Only my brother Yechiel who now lives in the United States and I remain as the last survivors of our family in Maytchet. Therefore, I wish to form a bridge between the past and the future, between our large family in Maytchet and our descendents who never knew our family from close. Let this book serve as a family genealogy book, and if one of our descendents wishes to find out about the roots of the family, let them find it in this book.

**Reb Moshe Aharon Shevchik of blessed memory,
and his wife Velka Shevchik may G-d avenge her blood**

My father Reb Moshe Aharon Shevchik was a native of Maytchet, as were my grandfather Reb Aharon Shevchik and his wife, my grandmother. We can assume that the preceding generations of our family were also natives of Maytchet, except for my mother Elka of the Cigelnik family, who was a native of the town of Polonka. She married my father in Maytchet, where they established their family.

[Page 259]

My grandfather Reb Aharon was a merchant in the villages ("*korobelnik*"). He sold all types of merchandise to the farmers and bought their produce. My father also was involved in this business, as was my uncle -- my father's brother Reb Yitzchak Yaakov Shevchik. My uncle's wife Zelda also ran a bakery, where she sold various baked good in the town, especially to the farmers on market days.

My father also had a sister in Maytchet who was married to Simcha David. Uncle Simcha David worked in the egg trade. He would buy eggs from all of the peddlers in the town and from all the merchants who would buy eggs on market days, and export them to Baranovichi and other large cities.

As time went on, my father left his peddling business, since my mother was not content with Father being absent from the home throughout the week. He obtained the right to transport travelers in town. Maytchet was a vacation town, and many travelers passed through. The railway station was in the village of Mickiewicz, a distance of about four kilometers from town. They would travel by wagon until 1930. I recall how Father set up a large hut in the shape of a bus atop a flat surface, decorated it nicely with images of peaceful settlements, and attached it to horses to provide transportation.

When the children at home grew up, my brother Yechiel studied to be a driver. We first obtained a taxi in 1931, and immediately thereafter, two buses. The taxi provided special services. One bus traveled the Maytchet - Baranovichi line through the town of Mush, and the second bus traveled the Maytchet - Nowogradek line through the towns of Dvorets and Nowjelnia.

In modern times, transportation by taxi or bus is considered commonplace, but in Maytchet of the 1930s, this was novel, literally a new discovery. I recall how the bus set out for the first time from Maytchet to Baranovichi. As it passed the villages along the way, there were cases where the farmers were frightened of the bus and ran away. They did not understand how something of this nature could travel without horses...

I recall a sad event with the bus that traveled the Maytchet Baranovichi line. The bus station in Baranovichi was on Sentorski Street, in the courtyard of Eli Shevchik, who had a large grocery warehouse. That day, one of the drivers placed a bicycle on the roof of the bus. That day, one of the non-Jewish hired drivers was driving the bus. My brother Yechiel warned him that he would not be able to pass under the electric wire in the yard, but the driver did not listen to my brother, began to drive, and got stuck in the wires. He got of the bus and wanted to go up to the roof to enable passage. My brother warned him again to not do this, because it was fraught with mortal danger. However, the driver insisted, went up to the roof, and got electrocuted. Since the city council of Baranovichi had some responsibility in this situation because the wires in the yard were not at the right height, and these were not isolated wires, the matter was not clarified fully and was somehow obfuscated...

[Page 260]

Our father Reb Moshe Aharon died in 1933. My brother Yechiel got married with a girl from the city of Ruzhany, where he set up his family. He obtained one bus and set up a bus line in his new city of residence. My brother Aharon and I also studied driving, and we continued the business together with our brother Zeev (Velvel). In 1934, I went out to a Hachshara Kibbutz in order to prepare to make *aliya* to the Land of Israel. My brother Aharon got married in Maytchet and continued in this work along with our brother Zeev until the outbreak of the Second World War, when destruction overtook the entire family in the same manner as the rest of the Jews of Maytchet. Only my brother Yechiel and I survived.

My brother Yechiel was exiled to Russia, and his family perished immediately with the entry of the Germans. He passed through seven levels of hell, and ended up in Austria after the war, where he worked as a nurse and a hospital director. There, he met Mirl Lemkin, the daughter of the sister of Rabbi Elchanan and Noach Goldstein. They got married and moved to the United States, where their only daughter was born. I survived the war because I succeeded in escaping Maytchet before the bloodbath - literally a few months before the outbreak of the war, when I made *aliya* to the land of Israel as part of the Aliya Bet[1].

My father of blessed memory was an upright, straightforward man with a good heart, who loved to do good deeds to his fellow, whether by giving charitable gifts to all who asked, or by giving charity in private. He always assisted the charitable emissaries by collecting donations, and he was the trustee of the Chevrat Tehillim [Society for Recitation of Psalms] in town. During the First World War, when our town was captured by the Germans, the conquerors emptied out all the residents from the large building across from us in which the Blass, Volinski and other families lived, and converted it into a temporary hospital.

There was a firefighter's brigade in Maytchet, which consisted solely of Jews until 1935. There was also a firefighter's band, conducted by Eli Busel of Zhetl. The chairman was Shimon Lahhovitski, and my brother Yechiel was among the organizers of the band. I was also a member of the band. All the members of the band worked on a voluntary basis, and a portion of the income of the band, which came from playing at weddings and celebrations, was designated to common expenses as well as the Jewish National Fund.

Translator's footnote
1. See http://en.wikipedia.org/wiki/Aliyah_Bet

[Page 261]

My Ties with Maytchet
By Zeev Rimon (Romanovski)
Translated by Jerrold Landau

My ties to Maytchet were roundabout but significant. I was born in the village Gorki, located 14 kilometers from Maytchet and 24 kilometers from Slonim. My parents - Avraham Romanovski (Avremel Harker) and my mother Sara Mesha, also of the Romanovski family (they were cousins) sent me to study in Maytchet when I was 4 ½ years old. My memories of that early period are of course very vague. I only remember that I was given over to the care of a certain elderly woman, and that my first teacher who taught me the alphabet was prone to anger, and often demonstrated the strength of his arm to me. Despite my childish strength, I apparently tried to protect myself and perhaps even attacked back. For this reason, the relations between us were so damaged that after one semester (about a half a year), I concluded my academic career in Maytchet and continued my studies in Slonim. However, I continued to visit Maytchet on occasion because most of the family was there.

As I have stated, my parents lived in a village. Like all the villages in the Pale of Settlement, Maytchet was surrounded by village Jews, "*Yishuvniks*" as they were called. This term was considered equivalent with boorishness and ignorance, and also served as prime material for all types of jokes within Jewish folklore for many generations. As one who saw this life from up close, I can state that among them there were Torah scholars and people who were very far from ignorance. However, in general, it can be stated that nine measures of the exile fell upon these Jews, the majority of whom were very poor. They settled amongst the gentiles, at times in very remote corners, due to the vicissitudes of earning a livelihood. These *Yishuvniks* were always prone to various types of persecution and degradation from their neighbors - much more so than the Jews of the cities and towns. Life was difficult to bear. If this was the case for the adults, it was even more the case for the young people. However I will not discuss this topic at length in this article. And I will be forgiven for having "stolen" a few lines to mention this. The Holocaust and destruction leveled the experience of all type of Jews - in the city, the town, and the village. All met with a common fate.

*

At the beginning of the 1930s while I was in Warsaw, I received news that my oldest brother died of blood poisoning and was buried in Maytchet. I was later told that my brother refused to be taken to a doctor in the city, lest the "neighbors" rejoice at seeing him in such a situation... During the 1930s, I was informed through a telegram that my father was very sick, and that I must come immediately to Maytchet. I arrived in Slonim after traveling on a train all night, and from there, I went to Baranovichi. I arrived in Maytchet toward the evening, as there was no earlier train. Apparently,

Father was suffering death throes all day, but he held on to his last strength so he could see me before he died. Indeed, when I arrived and leaned over his bed, a smile appeared on his pale face, he kissed me, uttered a few incomprehensible words, and died. My son Avraham, who bore the name of his grandfather - my father - fell during the conquest of the Golan Heights during the Six Day War[1]. My mother suffered a stroke a few years later. I visited her in Maytchet during the summer of 1939. When I parted from her, I did not know that I would never see her again.

[Page 262]

When I visited Maytchet, for the most part I would stay with my mother's sister Aunt Nechamcha. Her husband Yaakov Ginzbrug, Uncle Yankel as we called him, was a teacher of Bible, and, if I am not mistaken, also grammar. He was a strict man, but it was said that anyone who studied with him knew Bible very well. A great tragedy afflicted them during the latter part of the First World War. Their three daughters died one after another within a short period from one of the diseases that spread during that period[2]. They were left with an only son, Meirka. After that tragedy, my aunt became more pious. This was expressed in various ways, primarily through good deeds. As is said, she was a good soul, and many people admired her. Aunt Roza was a midwife in Maytchet and the area for many years. Incidentally, after the Holocaust I was told that Aunt Nechamcha and Aunt Roza remained alive for many months, and were the last members of the family to be alive. They ran from one hiding place to another until the hand of the enemy caught up with them. Aunt Zlata and her husband Eliahu moved from Maytchet to Baranovichi where they perished.

However, the unofficial head of the large family was Uncle Leib Romanovski. He was a pharmacist who worked for many years in the pharmacy of the Dvorjetski family in Maytchet. Later, he purchased his own pharmacy in the town of Baksht near Lida. The two orphaned sons of my brother Meirka and Leibele, were educated by him. The joined the partisans and fell in one of the battles with the Germans. Uncle Leib lived in the interior of Russia until the 1920s. The Bolshevik Revolution caused him to leave, and he returned to Maytchet. I loved him and he was very close to me. He looked upon my Zionist activities in a forgiving manner. Even though he did not oppose it, Zionism did not speak to his heart. A friend of mine who moved to the town of Baksht in extremely cold weather and succeeded in surviving, told me that he met my uncle there, talked with him a great deal, and that Uncle Leib was a pleasant conversationalist. Among other things, he told my friend that if he succeeded in surviving, he would come to me in the Land. He did not merit such, and I also did not merit to see his dream come true.

[Page 263]

Let us now return to Maytchet. Sometimes, I enjoyed visiting Father's brother, Uncle Berl Romanovski (not to be mixed up with Berl Romanovski, the owner of the grocery business). Uncle Berl was involved in manufacturing Dutch cheese. Aunt Elka was the mainstay of the house. Their only daughter married Noach Godlshtein, who was active in the firefighters and the dramatic club. There was a pleasant calm in their house, and I felt good with them.

Earlier, I mentioned the other Berl Romanovski, who was in the first class in town in terms of his position and status. The fathers of Berl and my father were brothers. Whenever I was with him, heartwarming characters of "the Village" or of "Reb Shlomo Hanagid" of Sholem Asch[3] fluttered before me. Berl was a G-d fearing Jew, but what I particularly appreciated about him was his patience toward the ideas and behavior of his fellow. It was good to chat with him. He was very intelligent, with a good temperament. I recall that during one of our discussions, we talked about somebody who was somehow able to reconcile his conscience. He said to me with a smile, "How surprising, you know that by law one is permitted to shorten the mustache or beard a bit if it interferes with eating..." His wife Malka was a righteous woman in the full sense of the word. She was always involved in charitable deeds and helping the needy, in most cases by giving discreetly. Their home in the middle of the market square was always open wide to anyone in need.

I was especially friendly with their eldest son Shalom Romanovski. He was saved miraculously during the Holocaust, and was the only survivor of the entire family. At the end of 1946, I was sent by the kibbutz to visit the survivors in Poland and the refugee camps in Germany and Austria. I met him in Linz, Austria, and our joy was boundless. He went to the United States and served as a kashruth supervisor at one of the abattoirs near Chicago. We remained in constant contact by mail. He suffered a stroke about two years ago, and died the same day. He left behind a wife and three daughters. His eldest daughter wrote to me that during those sad days, even before the end of the *Shloshim*[4], she gave birth to a son and named him Shalom. His coffin was brought to Israel at the beginning of 1971, and he was buried in Jerusalem.

*

This is a summary of my connection to Maytchet. As in every place, there was certainly no shortage of shadows, but the shadows have been have become blurred in the "light" of the great conflagration, to the point that that they disappeared completely. Maytchet with its youth, with whom I often met, remains etched in my mind. I also recall its well-known pine forest, which attracted many convalescents from near and far, where I also spent a month. I recall Maytchet with all of its institutions and organizations, even though they were of modest scope. Maytchet was a typical Jewish town, and was cut off from the land of the living. I recall it with sorrow, honor and awe.

Translator's footnotes

1. This was in 1967. The sentence is apparently parenthetical, as the following sentence goes back to the 1930s.
2. Quite possibly the influenza pandemic.
3. See http://en.wikipedia.org/wiki/Sholem_Asch
4. The thirty day mourning period after a death.

http://www.jewishgen.org/Yizkor/Molchadz/mol255.html - f261_4r

[Page 264]

My Connection With Maytchet
By Zelda Rozovski (Likter)
Translated by Jerrold Landau

Even though I am not a native of Maytchet, I was connected to it from several perspectives. First of all, I had a double family connection with it - my mother Rivka of blessed memory was a native of Maytchet, and she lived there with her family until her marriage to my father Mordechai Leib Likter of blessed memory of Zhetl. My second family connection with Maytchet was through my uncle, my father's brother, Kasriel Likter of blessed memory, who lived in Maytchet. In addition to this double family connection, I was also personally connected to the town. I loved it, was attracted to it, and spend a great deal of time there. I would come to Maytchet every summer before the Festival of *Shavuot*, and remain there until after *Simchat Torah*. I had many friends in Maytchet, and I was a frequent visitor in many houses in the town.

I recall that our central meeting place was in the house of one of the daughters of Shlomo Hershel Shlomovitz and in the house of Zawadchik. Since the daughters of Reb Shlomo Ahronovitz of the village of Svorotova were also one of the group, we would often go to that village and spend a great deal of time with Dvora Ahronovitz and her sisters.

Thus, I would often visit Maytchet. Today, after so many years, when I recall this town, I feel a pleasant duty to recall the "grace of my youth" of the town. I was attracted to it and its residence because they all received me so well and pleasantly, to the point of true soulful connections. During those days, the youth had from whom to learn, for in most cases the Jews of Maytchet were goodhearted, of pleasant character, welcoming of guests and doers of charitable deeds. It is possible that all this stems from the fact that Maytchet was a small town surrounded by many villages, with each village having only a few isolated Jews. As a central town among the villages, Maytchet naturally was the Jewish center of the region, with all that such entails. On account of this, strong connections were forged between all the Jews of Maytchet and the region. They lived together as if one family.

As has been said, I had many relatives in Maytchet. My grandfather Reb Isser Lisagorski of blessed memory was born in the village of Plekhovo near Maytchet. He moved to Maytchet along with his parents at the end of the 19th century. He married my grandmother Yenta, may peace be upon her, established his household, and had sons and daughters. After a few years, my grandfather Reb Isser died, and Grandmother Yenta was left as a young widow with small children. She remarried to a relative named Zlomonovski, who was also a widower with young children. This marriage was very successful. All the children bonded to the parents and were dedicated to each other in an unusual fashion.

[Page 265]

As time went on the children grew up, and each of them established their own family. It even happened that my aunt Sara Leah Lisagorski, my mother's sister, married her stepbrother Sender Zlomonovski. Of all the relatives of my grandfather Reb Isser of blessed memory, my uncle Reb Mordechai Izak Lisagorski was the only one who remained in Maytchet. All the rest left the town. Some of them got married and lived in the area, and some, including Grandmother Yenta immigrated to the United States.

My mother's brother, my uncle Reb Mordechai Izak Lisagorski, was a soldier during the First World War. He was injured during one of the battles and remained handicapped with partial paralysis. Despite this, he served as the Torah reader in the *Beis Midrash* for many years. He had five children, a daughter named Gruna and four sons. All of the sons had the names of angels: Michael, Gavriel, Azriel, and Refael. I recall how he attempted for many years to have the Polish government recognize his handicap, so that he would be able to receive monthly stipends. However, the Polish government ignored his requests and he was forced to find his livelihood by support from his brothers who had immigrated to the United States. I recall how my uncles, the brothers of Uncle Mordechai Izak, would send 100 dollars every month. When I visited Maytchet, I would accompany Uncle Mordechai Izak and his wife Aunt Alta to the post office, where he received the money from the United States.

As I mentioned, several of the brothers of my mother and of Uncle Mordechai Izak immigrated to the United States. Uncle Chaim David Zeler and Uncle Moshe Lisagorski acclimatized well to the new country, raised large families, and remained dedicated to their brothers and families. Just as they supported their brother Mordechai Izak, they did not turn away from the rest of their family. Uncle Moshe Lisagorski served in the American Army during his youth, and passed away at an old age in 1967. The second uncle, Chaim David Zeler, lives in the United States to this day. He is active in the Maytchet organization of that country, and has visited Israel a number of times.

As I have already mentioned at the beginning of my article, my mother Rivka of blessed memory was born in Maytchet. She married my father Mordechai Leib Likter in Zhetl, and they had seven children - four sons and three daughters: Isser, Zalman, David, Yerachmiel, Beila, Liba, and me. They all perished in the Holocaust except for my sister Liba and me, who succeeded in being saved from the vale of murder. My sister lives in the United States today, and my husband and I have established our family in Israel.

My father had a brother, Kasriel Likter, who married Chaya Sara in Maytchet. They had one son, Yaakov. Uncle Kasriel and Aunt Chaya Sara perished during the Holocaust in Maytchet, but their son apparently survived. However, to my great sorrow, I have not been able to track him down to this day.

Today, after decades have passed since the most terrible period in the annals of our family and of the Jewish people, I can only bless those people who have found it fitting to perpetuate the memory of all the martyrs who perished in the Holocaust. Let his Memorial Book of the community of Matychet serve as an eternal light to the souls and a perpetual monument to the memories of all the martyrs of Matychet and the region, those near and dear to me among them.

May their memories be a blessing.

[Page 266]

My Parents' - Stolovitsky Family
By Benjamin Stolovitsky
Translated by Avi J. Levin

The home I grew up in was a traditional Hassidic Jewish home, as were most Jewish households in Maytchet. We lived in a tranquil atmosphere until the 'battle of annihilation'. My father, Zemel Stolovitsky, was a renowned grain merchant. My mother, Chaya-Tcherna, was a woman of valor, who managed her house with dignity and worked alongside my father in their business. Together they raised their children and gave them a foundation of Jewish education in accordance with the best traditions.

In order to sustain his family with dignity, my father worked long hours. Nevertheless he managed to find time to go to the *Bet Medrash* for daily prayers and listen to a lesson in Torah as well as be available to assist those in need. My mother also was concerned in the well being of others and availed herself to assist them in their time of need as much as possible. In this wholesome atmosphere we grew up with strong Jewish identification as was customary in our town.

I lived in this loving house together with my parents, my two brothers Laibel and Moshe, and my sister Shaina. We had many family members and close friends living nearby.

Chaya-Tcherna Stolovitsky nee Shlovsky and her son Benjamin

[Page 267]

They were an integral part of our household in times of joy as well as sorrow.

As a member of a pioneer youth movement in Maytchet, I yearned to emigrate someday to the Land of Israel. However, World War II broke out with all of its great atrocities, putting aside my hopes and of many other youths. Nevertheless, there were also those amongst us who did not say that we should despair in such a difficult situation. We traveled to Vilna, where many pioneers gathered, and from there we took different paths to emigrate to the Land of Israel. I consulted with a number of friends about joining with them on their paths; and how we would resist the difficulties and the many dangers that we would encounter. We crossed borders, encountering many difficulties, hunger and much poverty. Full details of my travels are recorded elsewhere in this book.

Shortly after I arrived in Eretz Yisrael I was drafted into the British army. During my army travels to other lands, I heard from refugees who were fleeing from the valley of slaughter about what was happening in our general area, and specifically in Maytchet. In my heart I prayed that my father, who had close business relationships with important people in the region, perhaps had been saved with their help. But when I returned to The Land of Israel from my army service, my last hope was shattered to bits. From the tales of survivors of Maytchet, the bitter fate of my family members became known to me, as they had been included amongst the human sacrifices of the Holocaust.

I was somewhat comforted when I was told that my father fought valiantly until his last day. He, together with other family members, became part of a large partisan division which was organized in the nearby forests. They inflicted heavy blows on the enemy, causing them many casualties. He fell in the line of duty with strength and honor.

[Page 268]

Shlomo-Hirshl Shlomovitch and His Family
by Dov Shlomovitch
Translated by Ron Rabinovitch

My grandfather Chaikel Shlomovitch, of blessed memory, was one of the "Hatufim" (the boys that were kidnapped to serve in the Russian army). He was well past 30 years of age when he returned from an extended time spent in the military. He was assigned to be a servant to an army doctor, during which time he was able to observe and learn much about medicine. Upon his return to Maytchet he was able to obtain a license to be a medical assistant and he served as the Community Medical Assistant.

He married in Maytchet and had six boys and one girl; four of them emigrated to Canada and three remained in Maytchet where they established their homes. Those who remained were my father Shlomo-Hirshl who was a merchant; a second son my Uncle Yaekel who was a cowherd merchant; and his daughter, my Aunt Gute who married Azriel Shkolonikovitch.

My father Shlomo-Hirshl of blessed memory had three sons and four daughters. One son, Chaikel, is living in Canada. The second son, Eliezer, was killed during World War II while serving in the Polish army. I am the third son, Dov, and I live in Israel with my family. All four of my sisters were murdered along with my parents during the Holocaust.

Our house was observant and all the children received a strong religious education. I studied in the Baranovici Yeshiva and was a member of the "Tiferet Bahurim" committee, during which time I attempted to get to Eretz-Israel. After training for a period of time in a Kibbutz like atmosphere located in Vilna, I was able to come to Israel (Palestine) in 1938. I married a woman in Haifa and established my home there. Unfortunately the situation in Eretz-Israel was very difficult during this period and I was unable to bring the other members of my family to be here with me. Consequently they were all murdered.

This story serves as a memorial to their innocent and clean souls.

[Pages 269-270]

Members of My Family at Maytchet
by Haya Rivka Dissin
Translated by Isaac Margolin

I myself was not born in Maytchet, but my late father Rabbi Jona-Joseph Tchertuk and his father the late Rabbi Jacob Tchertuk were born there. Also the parents of my grandfather lived there, and they also were born in Maytchet.

My grandfather Rabbi Jacob was married to my late grandmother Hasha-Freidel the daughter of Rabbi Ze'ev and Badena Pikelni and they lived in Maytchet. They had two sons and one daughter. One son---Jona-Joseph, who was my father, married my mother Henia-Feiga Reznik from Ishishok. In 1900 they immigrated to the US, were they had two daughters, me and my sister Rachel-Lea. In the US I married my husband the late Rabbi Peretz Dissin, and I have two sons and a daughter, Israel-Jacob, Jona-Joseph and Mina. My younger son, Rabbi Jona-Joseph, made aliya to Israel with his family and live in the sacred city of Jerusalem.

After the marriage of my grandfather Rabbi Jacob Tchertuk to my grandmother Hasha-Freidel, her parents Rabbi Ze'ev and Badena Pikelni returned to live in Maytchet with their children, Israel-Elchanan, Eli-Chayim, Arie, Joseph, and Shaina-Chana. Three of their sons immigrated, Eli-Chayim, Arie and Joseph, and the son Israel-Elchanan married a girl born in Zhetl, were they built their family. The daughter was married to Joshua Kostribizki and they stayed in Maytchet were they had three sons and three daughters, Jacob, Noah, Berel, Hasha, Beila and Malka. Besides the son Berel who lives now in Argentina, the rest were killed at the Holocaust with their families.

The other son of my grandfather, David, married a girl from the village of Biten, and in 1905 they immigrated to the US, were they had sons and daughters.

The only daughter of my grandfather, my aunt Shaina, stayed in Maytchet and married Rabbi Asher Orzechovsky, and they had two sons and four daughters Nathan, Jona, Badena, Haya-Sarah, Feige-Rachel, and Hasha. Most of their descendants immigrated to the US where they made their families, except the son Jona and the daughter Badena, who had many children in Maytchet. Unfortunately, along with the other Jews of Maytchet, they were killed in the Holocaust, except thee of them -- Nohum Orzechovsky, Freidel, and Nachum Margolin, the only survivors from the whole family at Maytchet and now live in Israel.

My uncle Rabbi Asher was from Zhetl, where he was born to his parents Rabbi Nachum Eli and Hana Rozensky. He changed his name from Rozensky to Orzechivsky to avoid the fate of the "kidnapers" of the Czar's army. He had three other brothers in Zhetl – Berel, Yakir, and Samuel-Shalom, and three sisters, Lea, Mera, and Sheindel.

[Page 270]

When I remember my relatives in Maytchet, I am sad for the youngsters and the persons who were killed. They were murdered in cold blood by the Nazis who have no shame.

My grandfather, the late Rabbi Jacob Tchertuk, was old fashion and his ambition was to make Aliya to Eretz Israel. In 1903 he made his long way from Maytchet to Eretz-Israel. He wanted to bring his family also to the Holy Land, but due to the difficulties of the time he was not able to fulfill it, and was never to see them again. On Yom Kippur (1910) he died and was buried in the Mount of Olives cemetery in Jerusalem.

God bless his soul.

Haya-Rivka Dissin

Rabbi Asher Orzechovsky

[Page 271]

People and Personalities
by Nachum Margolin
Translated by Jerrold Landau

Reb Shlomo Shnitzki - Reb Shlomo Shnitzki, may G-d avenge his blood, had a store in the row of stores in the marketplace to sell shoes and hides. He lived with his family in a dwelling above the store. Shlomo was a quiet, even-tempered man. He served as the representative of the community on the district communal council of Baranovichi, and was a member of several local institutions.

Reb Avraham Garbash and Reb Leib Winograd, may G-d avenge their blood, were both sons-in-law of Reb Yisrael Zalman Szlowski of holy blessed memory. The former was the husband of his daughter Chana and the latter was married to her sister Dvosha. Neither were natives of Maytchet. Rather, they came from Congress Poland. Therefore, their mode of dress was different than that of other residents of the town. They both used to wear Hassidic hats and *kapotes*, as was the custom of the Hassidim in Congress Poland. However, they both acclimatized well to our Lithuanian town [1]. The two families were blessed with many children. Reb Avraham Garbash was one of the *shochtim* [ritual slaughterers] of the town, and Reb Leib Winograd was a merchant. He had a textile store, and was one of the *gabbaim* [trustees] of the *shtibel*.

Leibel Gilerovits, may G-d avenge his blood, was the son of one of the honorable families in the town. All of the Gilerovits families in the town owned lands in the area, and the family members were occupied with agriculture. When Reb Shlomo Bitenski of blessed memory died, his wife Sonia, may G-d avenge her blood (Besky) continued with the wholesale trade of grains. When the business became large-scale, Leibel Gilerovits joined her as a partner, and both together ran the business. With the passage of time, Leibel married one of the Bitenski daughters. Leibel Gilerovits was a communal activist, primarily in the Zionist institutions. He was a captain of the firefighters, and was even an actor in the dramatic circle of the town. When the Germans invaded, he was appointed to the Judenrat of the town. According to the testimony of the Holocaust survivors, he acted faithfully and with dedication to ensure that no harm would befall the Jews of the town. According to the same sources, Leibel Gilerovits was influenced by Rabbi Dastolovitz, who was a great *tzadik*. This influence was so great that Leibel turned into a believer and observer of the commandments. Leibel Gilerovits made use of the "Pasir Schein," the permit of movement that he possessed as a member of the Judenrat, to frequently travel to Stolevitch in order to meet the rabbi and receive his advice on all matters. Leibel shared the same fate as the rabbi and the Jews of Maytchet who perished in the Holocaust.

Reb Alter Abramovitz, may G-d avenge his blood, was a modest, wholesome Jew who occupied himself with business. He had a textile shop in the row of shops. He was a great scholar. He disseminated Torah in public, and gave a Talmud class in the *Beis*

Midrash. He and his wife Menucha had two sons and two daughters. The eldest son Noach, may G-d avenge his blood, studied the laws of *shechita* [ritual slaughter] in town and became a *shochet*. The second son Berl, may G-d avenge his blood, also studied in *Yeshivas*, and succeeded in moving to Lithuania in 1939; however, he apparently perished in the Holocaust.

[Page 272]

Aside from the Pikalni family, we had other relatives in the town of Zhetl, the family of Moshe Aharon Leibovitz of blessed memory, whose wife Leah of blessed memory was the sister of my grandfather Reb Asher; and the family of Moshe Razbaski, the father of my uncle Reb Baruch Roses who lives today in the United States. He had a double family connection with Uncle Reb Yisrael Elchanan - Reb Yisrael Elchanan was the brother of Chasha Freidel - the mother of my grandmother Sheina Orzhochovski, may peace be upon her, whereas his wife, Aunt Hadassa, was the cousin of my grandfather Reb Asher.

Rabbi Yisrael Elchanan Pikalni and his wife Hadassa

Reb Yisrael-Elchanan Pikalni had always been connected to Maytchet throughout the years. He remembered its kindness during his youth, and would often visit. In addition to the fact that he was a native of Maytchet, he had many relatives in the town. Aside from our family, he was also related to the Kosterovski family. Similar to him, the children of that family would also visit the town, and during the visits, there would always be the problem of where to stay - with one family or another.

Reb Yisrael Elchanan had two sons and two daughters. One son, Reb Yosef Eliahu Peniel (Pikalni) is in Israel and served in the holy task of *shochet* in Kfar Haroeh. The other son Chaim-Zeev perished in a tragedy in 1920, when he drowned in a river when he was only 18 years old. One daughter Henia also lives in Israel, and was married to Reb Yechezkel Rosenblum of blessed memory of Raanana. The other daughter Bodna Breina perished during the Holocaust in Baranovichi along with her husband Moshe Chaim Nebeski and their seven children.

Uncle Reb Yisrael-Elchanan and Aunt Hadassa succeeded in making *aliya* to the Land of Israel in 1934. They lived with their daughter Henia Rosenblum and her family in Raanana. Aunt Hadassa passed away on the 7th of Av 5700 (1940), and Uncle Rabbi Yisrael-Elchanan passed away on the 4th of Elul 5702 (1942) at the age of 72.

May their memories be blessed.

[Page 273]

Reb Moshe Savitski - was an educated, intelligent Jew, with a warm Jewish heart, and who would often host guests. His house was open to everybody, and Jews from the villages of the vicinity ("Yishuvniks") would stay in his house when they would come to Maytchet for business or other affairs. He was also a Zionist with a consciousness. He had two sons: Avraham Zeev and Yisrael; and one daughter: Alta. To our great sorrow, his daughter died in her prime, whereas the sons were influenced by the atmosphere that they absorbed in their father's home and made aliya to the Land of Israel -- one in the 1920s, and the other in the 1930s.

Yaakov Gilerovits   **Yisrael Belski**   **Moshe Savitsky**

Reb Yisrael Belski was a scholarly Jew who earned his livelihood from the bakery he owned in Maytchet. He occupied himself faithfully with communal affairs, and was active in most of the institutions of the town. He was a member of the Jewish National Fund committee, as well as a faithful member of the *Chevrat Shas* [Talmud Study Group] of Maytchet.

Reb Naftali the Blacksmith was a short Jew, with a beard and *peyos* [side curls], who earned his living from the toil of his hands. He had a Blacksmith shop on Jurzika Street. Despite his age, he was agile, and easily took control of the animals that were brought to them to make iron shoes for their feet [2]. Regarding him it is possible to quote the verse, "Naftali is a hind let loose who gives forth pleasant words" [3]. He was an upright, straightforward man with fear of Heaven. I recall that during the 1920s the leader of the Generation, the author of the Chofetz Chaim of holy blessed memory, who was a descendent of Aaron the priest, turned to all of the *Kohanim* in Poland asking them to commence the study of the priestly service. Since Reb Naftali was a *kohen*, he responded to the call of the Chofetz Chaim, organized the *Kohanim* in Maytchet, and began to study with them that which they were commanded.

[Page 274]

Chana Shlomovitz - Chana the wife of Reb Shlomo Tzvi Shlomovitz would always greet the people of the town warmly, with a smile on her lips. She was imbued with the traits of modesty and diligence, and concerned herself with her fine, large family. In her life and her death, she served as a symbol of the typical Jewish mother of all generations. Due to these sublime traits, she succeeded in helping sustain many needy families in Maytchet in a discreet and quiet fashion.

When she went from door to door with a kerchief in her hands to collect donations, the Jews of Maytchet received her pleasantly. The Jews of the region (Yishuvniks) also knew her, and many Jews of the surrounding villages would come to her house to stay over or to take care of purchases and selling in the town. They did not leave her house without leaving a donation - whether of money or the produce of their farms.

She was a righteous woman in the full sense of the term. She was involved in acts of charity and assistance to the needy. In all cases, she was strict on ensuring that the gifts be made in a discreet fashion. Every Thursday, she would transfer to the needy of the town whatever she succeeded in collecting on their behalf.

About such people, the wisest of all man wrote in the final chapter of his book: "A woman of valor who can find ... and she will be praised in the gates for her deeds. [4]"

Reb Shlomo Tzvi Shlomovitz and his wife Chana

Translator's Footnotes

1. Lithuania is used here in the broader sense of the term.
2. Horseshoes.
3. From the blessings of Jacob to his sons. Genesis 49:21.
4. Referring to King Solomon, the traditional author of the Book of Proverbs. The quote is from Proverbs 31:10-31.

[Page 275]

Maytchet in Pictures B
Translated by Jerrold Landau

Naftali Hertz and his wife Sema Dvorzecky, the grandparents of Chana Machtiger

Maytchet natives at a family gathering

[Page 276]

Sarah Rabinovitz of the Margolin Family   Dvosha Jukovitsky of the Margolin Family

[Page 277]

Avraham Margolin, his wife and children

Chana Losovsky from the house of Boretsky

Moshe and his wife Dvorah from the house of Boretsky

Uncaptioned. A family photo

[Page 278]

Bluma Bosel (nee Aharonovich)   Mina Berman and Dvorah Melinkovsky

A gathering of Maytchet natives in Israel with Yechezkel Ravitz

[Page 279]

**Yitzchak-Meir and his wife Golda Tapoli
(nee Volinski) and their children**

Yechiel Shebchuk and his wife Mira (nee Lamkin)

David and his wife Teiba Rivka Volinski

[Page 280]

David and Hinda Eidlin, grandparents of Tova Shomroni

Yechezkel and his wife Menucha Polonski   Moshe Chaim and his sister Freidel Polonski

[Page 281]

Seated from left: **Yechiel-Yitzchak Dvorecki, Chaya-Gela Dvorecki, Yehoshua Chelmish (Rabinovitz)**
Standing from left; **Elkana Ben-Hur, Sima Ben-Hur, Malka Rabinovitz, Shmuel Rabinovitz**

The descendents of Reb Yechiel-Yitzchak Dvorecki
Sitting from left: **Sima Ginzburg (Dvorecki), her son Yitzchak Ginzburg and his wife Yaffa, Rina Yakir, Sima Ben-Hur (Abramovski), Malka Rabinovitz-Chelmish, Elkana Ben-Hur, Dr. M. Dvorecky**
Standing from left: **Aryeh Dvorecky, Tzvia Dvorecki, Aharon Ginzburg, Lyuba Solel, Dov Dvorecki, Aryeh Yakir, Eliahu Solel, Yehoshua Chelmish (Rabinovitz)**

[Page 282]

Rabbi Yisrael-Elchanan Pikalni and his family

Banner reads "Farewell on the occasion of the departure of our members to America."

Top row from right: **Yaakov Gilerovits, Esther Arul, Chaya Berman, Baranovichi, Sima Abramovski (Ben-Hur), Nechama Shmaryahu Barishinski**

Second row: **Noach Goldstein, Chana Berman, Yechezkel Ravitz, Zlata (Nechama Ginzburg's sister), Munia Rabinovitz**

Third row: **Wolfa Rabinovitz, Liba Gilerovits-Rabinovitz, Moshe Liberman, Sonia Goldberg-Rabinovitz, Zeev Liberman**

Bottom: **Musia Abramovski (Reiter), Nechama Boretcky**

[Page 283]

Script on photo reads: "Leadership of Gemilat Chesed" [Charitable Fund]
1) Iser Bilas, 2) Hezl Machkowski, 3) Chana Kostilinski, 4) Chaim Mendlovitz, 5) Kasriel
Lichter, 6) Moshe-Tzvi Rabinovitz, 7) Tzvi Vilokhinski, 8) Yaakov Novogrodski

**Maytchet natives in Israel at a gathering with visitors from the United States:
Mr. R. Goldberg and his wife Sonia (nee Rabinovitz)**

[Page 284]

**The leadership of the Folks Bank 1) Shimon Lakhovitzki (director), 2) Yitzchak
Gilerovits, 3) Shlomo Shnitzki**

The leadership of the tradesmen
1) Chaim Mendlovitz, 2) Mere Belski, 3) Moshe-Tzvi Rabinovitz, 4) Yehuda Rabinovitz, 5) Moshe Savitzki, 6) Yisrael Belski, 7) Kasriel Likter, 8) Noach Goldstein, 9) Yechiel Ravitz, 10) Tzvi Vilokhinski

[Page 285]

Maytchet Natives as Soldiers in Foreign Armies
Translated by Jerrold Landau

Yosef Lozovski as a Polish soldier

Mordechai Ravitz as a Polish soldier

Avraham-Dov Korn as a Russian soldier

[Page 286]

Abba Margolin as a Polish soldier

Moshe Lisagorski as an American soldier

Yaakov Margolin as a Polish soldier

Noach Dubkovski as a Polish soldier

[Page 288]

The Holocaust

[Pages 288]

Remember the Holocaust of Maytchet
by Dr. M. Dvorzecky
Translated by Amir Shomroni

Remember the Shoah of Israel; remember the destruction and the uprising. Thou shall have them for token and for lesson for years of many generations:

And joined shall be this memory unto thee alway - when thou sittest in thine house, and when thou walkest by the way, and when thou liest down, and when thou risest up:

And thou shall betroth unto thee for ever the memory of the brethren who do not exist any more:

And shall be the memory in your flesh, in your blood and in your bones:

Gnash thy teeth and remember; when thou eatest thy bread – remember; When thou drinkest thy water – remember; When thou shall hear a song – remember; When the sun rises – remember; When the night comes – remember; And in the day of feast and solemnity - well remember:

And a house that thou shall build, thou shall leave a breach, that the destruction of the house of Israel shall be alway before thee.

And a field that thou shall plough, thou shall raise a heap of stones - a monument for the brethren who were not brought to an Israel-grave.

And when to the Huppah thou induct your children, thou shall prefer above thy chief joy the memory of the children whom to Huppah shall never be inducted:

And shall be one flesh: The living and the dead, the slain and the remnant, those who are gone and they are not - and the remnants that are escaped;

Hear O, man of Israel, the voice that crieth unto thee out of the depths: Keep not thou silence, keep not silence.

Remember the Shoah of Maytchet-annotated

[Page 289]

The Soft Whisper of the *Haboinik* – The Hill of Blood
(For the Memorial Day of the Maytchet Community)
by Ben-Zion H. Ayalon
Translated by Esther Mann Snyder

A hushed whisper passes from one treetop to the next and the only answer is the sound of a low wail that gets stronger by the hour, until a great sound of courage and fear fills the whole grove and a stormy wind come up.

In speechless silence, as mourners and the chastened, the trees of the *Haboinik* that are on the Hill of Blood stand all year long. Since the last groan of a tortured infant from the grave reaching to the sky became silent, there hasn't been another gust of wind to rustle their branches and cause the treetops to whisper. A bird hasn't chirped while flying and a bee hasn't hummed on her honey. When death spread its black wings on those in the grave pit, nothing moved until its desire will be returned to the grove, until the innocent blood is atoned for, the blood that screams from the earth of the "*Haboinik.*"

But what is one day from two? What is the noise and tumult that passes today in the grove that is different from the past? Have the trees breached their vow and desecrated the oath of silence? Or perhaps the death cries of the murdered lying in the forest erupted in a storm to the heavens, came and didn't move from there until they received a promise of revenge for their blood spilled by animal-men, consolation and repair for the victims who died in the name of G-d (*Kiddush Hashem*) and the Jewish people.

Indeed, many acts of violence were committed in the pleasant shadow of the trees by cruel, inhumane murderers. Divine commandments and holy human obligations were trampled with a rough foot and desecrations were performed before the eyes of the whole world and no one helped and the day of revenge hasn't arrived although the time has passed. –

Today is Tuesday, 3 Menahem Av, the memorial day for the dead of the community, when the survivors of Maytchet convene to commune with the memory of their holy dearly departed. On this day, when the remainders of the families assemble in the land of Israel for a memorial assembly, those lying in the grave pit will awaken from their long sleep of death and even the trees which accompany them and eulogize them will stop the deathly silence of the forest in order to participate in their memorial. It has become a rule.

Every year, at the set time, there is activity in the forest. From the early morning the holy souls rise from their grave, each soul with its hand on its wound and or its bruise, sitting on the edge of the pit waiting for evening when they will be remembered well, for raising of its soul and for correction (tikun). And when each one's name is mentioned, it immediately rises on high and with one swoop reaches the hall of assembly, where it will listen with much satisfaction to the memorial. Every word of praise for its activities in the valley of tears, when still alive, will bring cure to the wound, and each expression of sorrow and every tear will come as relief and comfort to its pain. One by one, group by group, when their names are mentioned, the souls will rise up above the grave pit and fly to the memorial hall – they see but are not seen, floating above and filling the space. When the lights are dimmed and the sound of the Kadish (memorial prayer) said by the people for the widower or for the anonymous child, will be heard in the hall, the boundaries will be blurred. The moans and tears of the living will be mixed with the return of the organs of the holy souls and joined together for a full communing, for the rising of the soul and its correction.

[Page 290]

With a shout of endless joy the holy souls return in flight from the memorial to the forest *Haboinik*, having risen and been corrected, ready to return to the pit where they will rest peacefully in their grave. However, no living soul can achieve the intensity of the pain that is not of this world of those souls that remained sitting on the edge of their pit and their names forgotten by the hearts of the living. Embarrassed and anguished they return after midnight with a quiet wailing to their graves with hope for the next year. And, the trees of the forest, witnesses and guardians of their welfare during the days of the year, take part in the happiness of the "corrected" ones and express their joy with a quiet whisper of their treetops; however they also moan a deep moan from the depths of their trunks for the sorrow of the forgotten ones.

And a secret whisper passes from one treetop to another and receives in response a thin wail all through the night. A humble sound of courage and fear that seized the whole forest and caused a stormy wind, getting weaker and slighter until it stops. The next day the deathly silence returns to the forest *Haboinik* until the next year and until the great day will come of revenge and repayment.

[Page 291]

Self-defense in Maytchet
Translated by Esther Mann Snyder

In normal times, when fear of the authorities existed and stable order prevailed in the land, the relations between the Jews of Maytchet and the gentiles were good and decent. However, sometimes the good order deteriorated because of war, changes in government and other times of unquiet and the gentiles felt that the leash was loosened and then their neighbors and friends organized into gangs to rampage among the Jews.

However, the Jews of Maytchet didn't act the same way as Jews in other places who generally feared the non-Jews and dogs. In the hearts of the Jews of Maytchet, which were made without fear, was found a deep feeling of Jewish honor that they were prepared to defend with courage and even with weapons. In order to take precautions and with the aid of released Jewish soldiers, the Jewish youth organized and established a strong self defense force that knew how to fight back against any attackers. There were occurrences when some gentile friends who respected the honorable stand of the Jews, gave advance warning of the intention of the terrorists to attack. The members of the self-defense group went out early towards them outside of the town and secretly waited and when the terrorists approached they shot at them and drove them away.

And here are descriptions of some acts of courage, in which the Jews of Maytchet used force to prove to the terrorists that Jewish blood will not be shed easily.

Once there was a rumor that in the village of Mitzkovitz the gentiles attacked the Jews living there. Itzye Aharkis, the son of the medic Korn, immediately took action and together with Yekel Haikis went out in a wagon to aid the Jews who were being held and whose lives were in danger, a few against many. Itzye's son, Ezrial Korn, who due to his young age was not allowed by his father to join the expedition, secretly went out by foot and reached the place by running before the wagon. When the two courageous Jews arrived in Mitzkovitz, Azriel went out to meet them and announced briefly, "I already finished the job, all the violent gentiles are lying beaten and tied up on the ground. There is nothing left for you to do but to put them on the wagon, bring them to town and give them over to the authorities."

Another action of Itzye Aharkis concerned the wheat merchant Bitenski with whom Itzye was travelling to Slonim to buy wheat. While on their way, far from any town, they encountered an armed bandit, who awaited passers-by in order to rob them. While the bandit threatened them with weapons, the Jews attacked him and demanded their money or they would kill him. But Itzye didn't lose control, gave the reins to Bitenski, climbed down from the wagon and quickly took hold of the armed bandit, put him in the wagon and brought him to the police who had been searching for him a long time.

[Page 292]

Also during the terrible war of annihilation by the German Nazis and their murderous gentile helpers, there were acts of heroism by the Jews of Maytchet. In cases where it was clear that they couldn't prevail they preferred to choose the way of Samson from the Bible, that is, to kill the murderers even if it meant they themselves would die. In a few other times the Jews managed to escape. Many found a way through the forests joining the Partisans and fought together with them a war of revenge against the Germans and the local murderers who tirelessly searched for Jews until they found, killed and spilled the innocent blood of the Jews.

Oy to us, that the cruel enemy's iron hand reached the proud heroes of Maytchet and slaughtered them. May G-d revenge their blood.

The directors and council of the "Folks Bank"
1-Shimon Lahovitsky 2-Yitzhak Gilrovitz 3-Shlomo Shnitzki 4-Dov Romanovski 5- Moshe Belski 6- Chaim Mendelvitz 7- Eliezer Gordon 8- Katriel Likter 9- Leib Gilrovitz 10- Herzl Karolitzki

[Page 293]

My Travails in the Holocaust
by Moshe Korn
Translated by Esther Mann Snyder

Due to the fact that the Jewish and gentile populations of Maytchet were mixed, the authorities couldn't find a permanent place for a ghetto. Therefore, the Jews didn't really live in a ghetto but they did suffer from the usual limitations, such as, wearing the yellow badge, prohibition against walking on the sidewalks, etc. and generally attempting as much as possible not to be seen outside.

The Germans didn't stay over in Maytchet; they would come from Baranavichy and Gorodische to institute rules and decrees against the Jews. These included collection of "contributions," taking of valuables and gold, horses, boots, leather, material – anything the Jews owned, recruitment of people for work, etc. However, they themselves did not go to the homes of the Jews, but rather everything was done by the Judenrat.

The chairman of the Judenrat in Maytchet was a refugee named Erlich from Czestochowa. His deputy also was a refugee, from Soblek, named Apelboim. Local residents were Leib Gilrovitz (a grain merchant), Chaim Shlovski (a butcher) and Yehezkel Ravitz.

It should be noted that Leib Gilrovitz was not religious, but when the Germans arrived he became G-d fearing and followed the commandments. Here is a story about him. He had a brother who was a doctor named Moshel Gilrovitz who escaped to Stolovichi near Gorodishche. And in Stolovichi there was a rabbi who was great scholar. When Leib happened to visit his brother in that town, the Rabbi influenced him and convinced him that only by doing repentance and only by becoming religious would the evil decrees be cancelled.

Immediately after this, the Germans entered the town and wanted to frighten the Jews, as they did in every town, by killing the first victims. They seized a few Jews and told them to take the Germans' bicycles and ride them to Slonim. On their way the Germans shot and killed them. When the Jews had not returned after a few weeks, the Jews in town started to investigate the matter and learned of their terrible fate from the gentiles who came to market. One woman, who went out alone to search for her husband, never returned. Then, R' Avraham-Beryl Korn went to look for them in order to give them a Jewish burial. He found the hat-maker Monya Rabinovitz and buried him in the Jewish cemetery in Maytchet.

After a few days, a regime of forced Jewish labor began. They demanded one person from each household to work – in the estates, in "gamina," in the police, etc. The rule was very strict and after a hard day's work they forced the Jews to lick the hoes with their tongues, as if to clean them, but mainly to abuse and beat them. To avoid the mischief of the Germans, the Jews themselves searched for ways to find work so they could fulfill their work obligation and receive a meager portion of food. The craftsmen were sent to Kadelitzbo – a camp from which no one returned.

[Page 294]

After the forced labor rule, a series of decrees were initiated which were accompanied by cruel abuse and ended in murders. On one Friday the Germans came to the town to find horses. They also came to our home and when they didn't find our horse, which was then in Baranavichy, they took a girl and some other people from among the Jewish refugees who were in our home. They took them to Stolovichi and on the way they killed the girl. While on the road they saw the wanted horse that had returned from Baranavichy and seized it. The mother of the girl went to Stolovichi to ask help from the rebbe, but it was hopeless.

On 27 Shvat 5702, Sabbath, 14 February 1942, the local police, headed by Commander Falulihkh, assembled 20 men and 2 women, took them on their own authority and shot them near the tar factory on the road to the village of Horaishvitzitz. Among them were my father, Avraham-Berl Korn, Avraham-David Jokhovitzki – a teacher in the Tarbut school, Alter Harlap, Shalom Rabinovitz, Sonia Tzrulnik, Krabchuk and others. I ran to the Judenrat and turned for help to Gilrovitz and he advised me to saddle up the horse belonging to the Judenrat and travel at night to Baranavichy to the deputy Komissar. Yisrael-Haim Shinovski, who had hidden near the cemetery, joined us and we reached the ghetto in Baranavichy in the morning. The vitza-Komissar contacted Maytchet but it was too late. After this, Falolikh escaped and joined the Partisans and his place as commander of the police was given to Sashka Mashai, the past deputy. The day after his appointment my brother Azriel approached Mashai and asked him if he knew what happened to our father, then took out his gun and drove him out.

Things continued with suffering for a relatively long period; each day had its edicts, its operations and its victims. Bad news reached us from near and far about the slaughter and liquidation of the ghettos, but the tired souls hovering between life and death refused to believe. As long that their souls existed they deluded themselves with a vain hope and carried the burden of the decrees with superior courage - maybe there would be mercy and a miracle would occur and salvation would come soon. But the miracle didn't happen and about May 1942 the police came and took the Jews to dig pits, as if they were needed to store fuel tanks. Digging of the ditches lasted for a few weeks and their hidden purpose penetrated the consciousness of the workers. They even joked among themselves, "this will be my place and there will be yours..."

When the pits were ready, and after the news reached us of the slaughter in Baranavichy and in Gorodishche, the Jews of Maytchet sat and waited with dulled emotions for their day of calamity. Whoever still had any strength dug a hiding place in his home or yard hoping that perhaps he might be able to hide from death. Young men who were ex-soldiers organized and equipped themselves with weapons. They stood guard outside the town in order to notify the people of the town about any suspicious activity so they could hide or escape.

[Page 295]

On the night before (Rosh Hodesh) the beginning of the Hebrew month of Av, 5702, Wednesday, 15 July 1942, the Germans arrived from Gorodische and Baranavichy and surrounded the town including the Jewish guards and caused panic and frenzy. My mother and two brothers and also the refugees who were in our home went into hiding. My younger brother, Shabta'l, and I started to run but everything around the city was closed – no one leaves and no one enters. During the panic there was a rumor that Chaim Sheine-Malka's (Shlovski) had a number of rifles. We ran toward his house and there they gave 3 rifles to the ex-soldiers: Noah Mordkovski, Yaakov Margolin and Chaim Shlovski himself. From there we advanced towards Dvorzecky's pharmacy and through the yard to the nearby fields. There a crossfire awaited us and only a few of us succeeded in breaking through the siege. They were myself, Noah Mordukovski, Eli Shmulovitz, Chaim Barishinski, Alter Korlitzki and the grandson of Hanna-Sima - a total of 9 got through and all the rest were killed including my brother whom I wasn't able to help.

We ran 6 -7 kilometers until we reached the forest, tired and frightened. When we sat down to rest we realized that the grandson's hand was wounded and Eli Shmulovitz removed his shirt and bandaged the hand.

It should be mentioned that very little was done with the rifles we had and even if we had had more rifles there was no one who could use them. Noah Mordukovski managed to shoot only once and had no more bullets and because of our fear we started to run. The other two were later killed while holding the rifles. When we realized that there was no purpose in carrying an empty rifle, we hid it in the hyssop bushes, and made our flight.

We heard echoes from gunshots all the time and even when we distanced ourselves deep in the forest we heard the sounds of explosives. We stayed in the forest until evening but we feared to remain there lest the wandering hoodlums would find us and hand us over to the Germans. Therefore, we went in the opposite direction and met other Jews from Maytchet who succeeded in escaping. They weren't interested in joining us because each one thought he might be able to hide with a gentile acquaintance. In this way we wandered around for a few days without food until we reached the Dvorets ghetto. We sneaked in among the laborers who worked in loading rocks and in this way we entered the ghetto at the end of the day, to live with them and to plan together a possible escape.

In Dvorets we found the boy, Moshe Daikes who was wounded and full of burns. Others from Maytchet were: Zimel Stolovitzki with his family and his brother Mikal with his wife, Mikal Shmulovitz, Avraham Garbarz (the ritual butcher), David Shtein and others. There we also discovered what had happened to the Jews of Maytchet, who were taken out of their homes and from their hiding places and brought to the pits in the "*Haboinik*" which was near the village of Zahorany and not far from the "Fashistank". There they were very cruelly murdered and thrown into a mass grave, some still half alive.

[Page 296]

The "aktzia" (round up of Jews) lasted for three days, however, most were killed on Wednesday, Rosh Hodesh (beginning of the month) Av, 5702, 15 July 1942. The enemy used the other two days to search for Jews hiding in homes and secret places.

One day David Shtein notified me that my mother and little brother had survived and had just arrived in the Dvorets ghetto. I ran to them and saw a terrible sight. My mother was wearing only a sack and my brother was wounded and they both were in a terrible, horrible state. After they recovered a bit from the trauma, my mother told me the brutal story of what transpired in Maytchet. She and my two young brothers, one was 4 years old and the other was 6, and the refugees who were in our home hid in a hiding place under the floor. The parents of Mashai the chief of police told him that no one from our home had been taken in the "aktzia"

and they should quickly send the police to find them. The police discovered the hiding place and took them all out with threats that they would be thrown into a burning pile of hay and would burn to death. After they left, the police ordered them to remove their shoes and then led them through the town where they had to lie on the ground with their arms outspread. Meanwhile they brought the rabbi from his hiding place and also other Jews and led them all barefoot to the pits. There they were ordered to take off their clothes and jump into the pits on top of the bodies that were already lying there. Mother took the two children in her arms and found a corner to lie down in, covering the terrified children with her body.

The gentiles who were serving the Germans started to shoot at the victims. The older boy was wounded but my mother and the smaller child were not; however, the younger boy's arm was broken from the fall into the pit. After a while they recovered somewhat and crawled to another side of the pit; since the enemy was busy killing Jews on the other side they didn't notice the movement. With superhuman effort they managed to climb out of the pit and started to walk toward the village of Zahoranay in the hopes of finding some clothes to wear. However, they found the young gentile men and women there having a party and quickly ran away to the village of Kalishniki. There, a gentile woman gave mother a potato sack to cover her nakedness and asked her to leave quickly lest the woman be punished for her deed. On the way, a gentile man attacked her, grabbed her by the hair and started to pull her back to the pit. She and the child started to cry for mercy but the evil gentile didn't care about her screams. Luckily another gentile came by and started to argue with first one, saying that once they escaped from the pit they shouldn't be forced to return, and they were released. And so they continued on their way until they reached the forest where mother roamed for a few days with the unclothed child and without food. Finally, one gentile took mercy on her and brought her to the outskirts of Dvorets and let her go. Thus she came here in a state of complete and utter exhaustion.

The supervisor of the Dvorets ghetto was a liberal German, about whom it was said that he had a tendency to ignore the presence of Jews from the surrounding area who had escaped from the slaughter in their villages.

[Page 297]

He also turned a blind eye to the regular rules of discipline in the ghetto and didn't prevent the residents of the ghetto from going out to search for food, etc.

Moshe Daiches, who was apparently sent by the Judenrat in Maytchet to acquire weapons in the villages and therefore was absent from the ghetto on the days of the "aktzia", also came to Dvorets. And then he learned that in addition to the rifles that his brother-in-law Chaim Shlovski distributed, there were 2 pistols hidden in the home of his mother-in-law, Tcharna Di Bekeren, and despite the danger involved he traveled to Maytchet after the massacre to bring the guns. Also David Shtein, who already had managed once to escape from the slaughter, left Dvorets before the liquidation of the ghetto and joined the Partisans of Bielski and was killed by the Germans who had set an ambush killing them when they went out looking for food. Despite the crowded conditions of the ghetto we were able to find a small attic at one butcher for mother and the boy where they stayed for four months. We received a meager portion of food in the ghetto (watery soup) and other than that we would go out to the villages to work in threshing for the gentiles and brought home a little extra food.

At that time, we organized groups of youth to go out into the forests and join the Partisans. I took my mother and brother and we all went to the forest. There we met: Lipman Litaborski and his sisters, Zelda Gilrovitz, the Shoshan brothers from the village of Dokrovi, Vita the daughter of Yaakov Dvorzrcky. the owner of the pharmacy. Meanwhile mother became ill and couldn't fulfill her duty as a Partisan and I had to return with her and my little brother to the Dvorets ghetto and remained there until the destruction of the ghetto on 18 Tevet 5702, 28-12-1942. On the day of the round-up in Dvorets there was a terrible frenzy in town and the youth who had weapons started to escape over the fence. I also was able to escape from this ghetto for the second time. I took my little brother Leibel and we started running toward the cemetery, but the Germans didn't let people approach the fence. So, we went back and ran in a different direction where I came upon my mother who was crawling with all her strength. In answer to my question, she said that they wouldn't let her into the hiding place because it was too crowded. I stopped running, took her and forcefully pushed her into the hiding place. Then I continued running with my brother. The youth began shooting to try to break through the fence and the Germans returned the shooting; during the frenzy my little brother's hand let go of mine and he disappeared.

I succeeded in climbing into the attic in the Kapelovitz home not far from the fence and hid on the edge near the roof (stricha) where I covered myself with straw and old things that were lying there. From there I heard the sound of gunshots and terrible shouts, and I decided that I would lie there until night and then escape under cover of darkness. At night, I came down from the attic and found a few Jews who were looking for a refuge for themselves. We slowly came close to the nearby fence but the Germans noticed us and opened fire. I returned to my hiding place in the attic until I might be able to escape the next day. In the morning, a German came up to the roof and did a careful search until he found me. He shouted at me to come down and when I didn't he took a stick and poked me until I had to get up and follow him. Outside I saw many Jews facing the wall with their hands raised. We were made to hand over any and every valuable we had with us and then we were transferred to the Judenrat building.

[Page 298]

There, many Jews who were removed from their hiding places were assembled, among them those wounded by the grenades thrown at them, lone children who had roamed around searching for food, one of them was the daughter of Yonah Mordukovski. The Gestapo entered the Judenrat and demanded that Jews hand over all their possessions before they would be transferred to Crimea on closed trucks that were parked near the building. It wasn't difficult to guess that they intended to bring us to the pits and we talked with each other about preparing scissors, knives and any other tool to cut the canvas of the covered trucks and jump out. Meanwhile, I noticed the cover over the opening to the basement of the building. I lifted it and went inside and others followed. But I understood that the place was not safe, that the Germans would probably search there and take everyone out. I looked around and saw that the beams were made of metal bands; I quickly removed two bricks from the wall and held on to the metal beams and leaned my feet on the opening in the wall. Indeed, the Germans came in and forcefully took all the Jews to the waiting trucks. I remained holding on between the roof and the ground hoping to last until night and then escape.

In the meantime, all the possessions that were removed from the victims were brought there and guarded by the Germans and therefore I couldn't risk going out. The next day police guards took their place and stood there all day. However, I took advantage of the short break when they stole the valuables and went to take them home and then I ran away. Before I left I managed to grab a loaf of bread and a blanket and I quickly ran towards the train tracks. When I reached the nearby forest, I was so thirsty I licked the snow, covered myself with the blanket and lay down to rest. When I recovered somewhat I wanted to continue on my way, but I didn't know the right direction and worried lest I return to Dvorets or the village of Biliadka most of whose residents were policemen. At any rate, I started walking and according to the sound of dogs barking, I knew I had arrived at Biliadka. I hastened to leave the area and travel in a different direction, reaching one farm where I sneaked into the granary and hid among the clover. I lay there all day even when the gentiles came to work there, but they didn't notice me. Toward evening I left and reached a village where I met 2 -3 Jews from the Dvorets ghetto. We entered an empty house, lit the stove and stayed there for a few days but we left the place lest we be revealed.

They went their own way and I continued toward the village of Yatra. On the road I heard that there were Jews in the area so I turned to the forest. Following the footprints there, I reached a hiding place and found there: Avraham Kaplan, Freidl Margolin, the Melishinski family, Noah Mordkovski, Yakel Shmulovitz. The hideout was very small and after a short stay I joined a Jewish refugee from Poland, who during the time of the Russians worked in a flour mill and knew about the Partisans who were in the area. We both went looking to join the Partisans. At first, they viewed us with suspicion and open hostility and plotted to kill us and only due to the intervention of the landlady were we saved from death. Yet when we reached the village of Zafaliye and with the help of an acquaintance were we finally accepted by the partisans and even into the "Otriad Grozni" which had previously tried to kill us.

[Page 299]

I took part in the activities of the Partisans until the liberation and was lucky enough to fight next to Barukh Levin, the highly praised Russian hero. I actively participated in the operative campaigns, such as: blowing up bridges, derailing trains and attacks on the Germans, etc. When the Russians approached our area and entered the forests of Nalivok, they asked the commander of the Partisans for two fighters to join them in their patrols in order to cross the Neiman river and to bring information back from there. One gentile and I were chosen and in very dangerous conditions we succeeded in bringing information from the other side and were credited with excellence.

After the Russian conquest I was sent by the Partisans to Minsk and from there I returned to Horodishetz, where I was part of a battalion whose role was to clear the area of "pockets" of the enemy. As part of my duty I came to Maytchet and found Mashai, the head of the police during the German occupation, who was guilty of the death of innocent Jews. I arrested him in order to take him to Gorodische but because it was night I transferred him to the building of Yaakov Gilrovitz who would guard him until morning. In the evening the priest came to speak on his behalf and asked for a straw mat for Mashai to lie on. In the morning Mashai's father came and offered to help bring his son to Gorodische I agreed and rode on my horse accompanying the wagon. I handed him over to the authorities with a written accusation; they transferred him to Baranavichy for a court-martial, where I testified as the main witness. He was sentenced to death by shooting.

[Page 300]

A War of Life and Death
(Memories of a Jewish Partisan)
by Avraham Chaneles
Translated by Esther Mann Snyder

In January 1941, in the midst of World War II and the Holocaust, the Ribbentrop-Molotov Agreement was still in force and in our area the quiet before the storm existed. I was still of elementary school age and I studied in the Soborov military school in Baranavichy. However, after a short while we suddenly received the information that the Agreement was abrogated by the Germans who had attacked Russia on July 2, 1941. All the students together with the administration personnel of the school were transferred and moved from Baranavichy to Minsk, from Minsk to Smolensk and from there to Byerazino. We attempted to cross the Byerazino River, but due to violent acts by the Germans who had been advancing after us, we didn't succeed – the commander-principal was wounded and the pupils were left on their own.

My cousin, Meir Chaneles, myself and another few gentile pupils decided to return home. When we arrived in Minsk, the Germans were already in control with all their evil and criminal activities as usual for them. We tried to find our uncle but he had managed to escape beforehand to the Ural Mountains. From Minsk we went to Stowbtsy, where our aunt gave us food and provisions for the journey and told us to run away from the danger awaiting the Jews. We came in during the night and left at night, traveled to Baranavichy and from there to Maytchet. We arrived home during the Succot holidays. We found our parents, a brother and two sisters, our grandmother and cousins, all in one large house in Polvark, four and a half kilometers from Maytchet. The situation was very tense and quite tragic; Jews were being kidnapped for work and never returned. We all waited in fear for what would happen next. We were given provisions and clothes and quickly left since the local police had already learned of our return and were searching for us.

In about January 1942 we connected with the Partisan underground that referred us to a certain "hotor" (farm) where the commanders stayed. We received orders from them: not to travel in large groups and not to stand out, and especially to carry out acts of damage, to blow up bridges, burn grains, etc. Under pressure from the family we tried to stay close to home. During our breaks we buried our weapons and kept our connection with the Partisans a deep secret. In March 1942, they moved our family including us to the ghetto in Gorodische, because there was no ghetto in Maytchet.

[Page 301]

In February, the authorities were informed that Meir and I had weapons and that we were in contact with the underground; they came to inspect us and do a search. The chief of police in Gorodische, Olasik Valla, his secretary Ravinski and a few officers arrived at our home, which was in "Polvark"; when they didn't find us they caught my cousin Abrasza Chaneles and wounded him mortally in the abdomen. They didn't allow us to bring a doctor and he died of his injuries. Another member of the underground, Yitzhak Lakhovitzki son of Shimon from Maytchet, was caught. They arrested him and transferred him to Gorodische in order to execute him but he escaped with the help of the underground and disappeared.

We lived in the ghetto of Gorodische outwardly like the others there, but secretly we continued to maintain our contact with the underground. Our family members who worried about us, and maybe about the whole ghetto, didn't allow us to go about as we wanted. Nonetheless, we would go to Stolovichi, by an underground cave, to carry out destructive actions. Among these activities were also punitive actions against the Germans and their collaborators for their cruelty and inhumane conduct. In April 1942, a group of young Jews from Maytchet worked in the Bordokovshtzina farm between Maytchet and Gorodische. The manager of the farm was Grinvetzki, the brother-in-law of Olasik Valla, the chief of police. After these Jews complained to us about the treatment of the manager, we came at night, caught him and his helper and killed them. In this group were: Moshe Margolin, Feiga Boretcky, Hannah Belski and others. The two girls had cooperated with us previously and brought us weapons and ammunition that they took from the Germans. The group continued to work at the farm.

After the Shavuot holiday, June 1942, the last "aktzia" (round up of Jews) occurred in Gorodishche. At 2 p.m. they took all the Jews out of the ghetto and directed them towards the marketplace to await instructions. My brother Yitzhak, my cousin Meir and I had been working in the horse stables of the Germans. Then, Olasik – the police chief of Gorodische, and Sasha Masai, the commandant of Maytchet, arrived and told us that they had come to take us, supposedly, to bring ethyl alcohol from the factory in Vilna. When we neared the marketplace and saw the crowd of Jews lying on the ground facing down, we understood what was about to happen and we started struggling with our captors. My brother was killed and Meir and I fled. The next day we reached the area of our family's farm, where we wanted to collect the buried weapons, and vigorously continue the underground activities. We enlisted Jews from among the refugees we met along the way and gave them guns. To my joy, my little sister, Hanna'ke, aged 9, came and told us that she had run into Germans who asked her if she was Jewish but she answered no and that she was just out gathering herbs to make medicine for the Germans. They liked her answer and let her go.

Our group grew stronger with more people and weapons and during the war and also during the retreat of the Germans and until the liberation we worked in various "otriadim" and participated in daring and dangerous operations like: attacks on the police, destruction of bridges, derailment of trains, battles and ambushes.

[Page 302]

Germans and collaborators were driven away and wiped out and we took weapons, supplies and other equipment. Among the courageous fighters here is a list of active Partisans from Maytchet and the vicinity who excelled in amazing courage and were awarded military decorations or who were killed in action. Among them were: Konia Shlovski, Hanan Shmulovitz, Mordechai-Leib Shmulovitz, Yehoshua Zlotnik, Itzak Lakhovitzki, Laizer Zukovitzki. Yitzhak and Laizer who took part in "Otriad Grozni" were killed near Maytchet by an anti-semitic unit named after Stralkov. Meir Chaneles was outstanding and received a military medal as a senior Partisan but was killed by Polish collaborators. David Ravitz, Yaakov Margolin, Chaim Epshtein and others were active. Among the Partisans, girls also took part: Liza (Leah) Ephstein, (now Kovensky living in Argentina) who served as a machine-gunner near Yavorskaya Road and caused heavy losses to the enemy, Esther Mlishinski participated in "Otriad Belski" (now Lizovski in Eretz Yisrael), Freidl Margolin in "Otriad Grozni" (now Mckranski, Kibbutz Negba), Vita Dvorzecky was a nurse in the Grishka company and died of typhoid.

The workers of the Folks-Bank

1-Shimon Lakhovitzki (manager) 2- Yehoshua Novomiski (bookkeeper) 3-Livka Izralvitz (treasurer) 4-Mordechai Ravitz (clerk)

[Pages 303 - 306]

The Rise and Fall of Maytchet
by Freidl Margolin Mckranski
Translated by Isaac Margolin

I received a request from the memorial committee to contribute memories of my hometown, Maytchet. I was lucky to survive the slaughter and to arrive on a safe shore in my beloved land. But I will never forget those who didn't survive, and even if it opens wounds, I will return and relive the most horrible period that I lived. I must tell what the Nazis and their local allies had done to us. After generations of peaceful coexistence, in difficult times they betrayed us and helped our enemy destroy us.

In Maytchet, a small village, as like the other villages in the region, the Jewish inhabitants worked in various occupations, and so did our family. I remember from my childhood our grocery store. Most of the clients were rural farmers, and we especially looked forward to the sale days of Wednesday and Thursday. On Wednesday the weekly market day took place, in it the local farmers came to sell their products and buy their needs. On Thursdays it was the local Jews who bought things for the Sabbath.

I still remember the brick-kiln (*zigalne* in Yiddish) that my father was partners with Rabbi Joshua-Aharon Lozovsky, Rabbi Hiekel Israelevitz, and a local gentile named Tashuma, who managed a grocery in the village. Farmers of the neighborhood worked in the brick-kiln in a very primitive way. They took the bitumen and worked the material they put into molds and put it into an oven that was fueled by wood. This oven had a wooden roof, and because of negligent care of the vents, there was a great fire in 1927. The roof and the entire structure was burnt in the fire.

In our house, as in every Jewish house in the village, there was a cow that provided milk and other milk products for our needs. We also had a horse and wagon. Every summer we would rent a piece of land to sow crops such as potatoes. After Passover we cleaned the manure from the cowshed and stable and brought it to the land we rented to use as fertilizer. My father ploughed the land and all the children and neighbors helped to sow the potatoes. Before Rosh Hashana the local farmwomen came to dig the potatoes. The children sorted them and filled the bags to carry home. While we were working, we would roast potatoes in the field to eat and have fun.

[Page 304]

During the time, when my elder brother Jacob had grown up, he helped our father sell the crops, which they bought mainly from the crop traders in our village, and took it to sell at Baranovichi. On their way back they brought different merchandise for the village grocers. In the early thirties we closed the grocery store and built a fast food cafeteria mainly for the neighboring farmers. The whole family worked at the restaurant, at crop trade, and to supply merchandise for the grocers. We were all busy with work.

As time passed and I grew up, we became partners in the textile store with Berel Shmulovits, and I was appointed to run this store. Our family consisted of dad, mom, five brothers and two sisters, and each had their share of different work to support the family. But when the children were grown, each went their own way. The business became slow; only the restaurant and the textile store remained. My brother Jacob was drafted into the Polish army, my brother Nachum went to train to live in a Kibbutz and be prepared for Aliya (immigration to Israel), my brother Moshe studied in high school at Baranovichi, and the rest of the children remained at home. And so we arrive at September 1, 1939 – the day WW II began.

According to the Ribenthrop-Molotov Pact, Maytchet fell under Russian occupation. Immediately when the Red army entered the village, it brought in the Soviet regime and the whole economic life that prevailed until it was abolished. The stores were empty of goods, some of it sold with no possibilty to renew it, and part of it was hidden not knowing what the future would bring. We were forced to trade with material to buy food. Life became hard, but slowly we managed by taking new jobs in the larger city of Baranovichi and started to adjust to our new life until the German and Russia war broke out in June of 1941.

The treacherous German attack on its former ally developed into a blitzkrieg and before anyone could pull them selves together from this situation, the Nazis entered the village and the troubles began. A police force was established from the local gentiles and also a "Yudenrat" (Jewish committee similar to a town council) was established, and the infamous German order before elimination was in place in the village with all it's might. Before long the Germans gathered two hundred boys and girls and sent on the pretext to work in the village of Burdykovschina. When they arrived there they all were shot down and killed, among them my brother Moshe and my cousin Chana Mare Orzechovsky. A few months later another few hundred youngsters were selected to be sent to a labor camp in Baranovichi – among them my brother Abba and my husband David Rabets whom I had recently married. My young sister Chasha and I were left to live in my flat at the Rabets's house, and my parents with my brothers Jacob and Mordechai lived at their apartment, which was located in the house of Nechama Yatvicky.

So the days went on, the weeks and the months. From the neighborhood we heard rumors about ghettos, tortures and murders. But since there was no ghetto in Maytchet, the dreary life went on some how, and we prepared ourselves for any trouble that might come. With bribes the people succeeded in postponing the end and meanwhile they established a self-defense that included army veterans who organized it.

[Page 305]

For their disposal were several old guns, that were hidden with Hayim Shelubsky, and they also dug a "Sichron" (hideout), to hide in due time. We also built a big "sichron" in our house, which was hard to find, and we waited to see what would happen.

One day an order arrived to the "Yudenrat" to recruit the Jews to dig holes for big fuel containers, that had to be placed at the "Havoinik" (hidden place in the woods) close to the Provoslav cemetary. Among the village Jews the opinions were divided at the meaning of the order. Some said, that these holes were not to be used for petrol tanks, but for burial of the Jews of Maytchet. But in any case they were obliged to dig the holes. A few days before July 1942, we received word that the Germans with the participation of the local farmers, had surrounded the village. The members of the self-defense arose immediately to action. They tried to break through the siege near the pharmacy of Dvorzecky toward the mountains on the way to Slonim, but the Germans opened fire and all the youngsters, twenty in number, were killed in this action, and among them my brother Jacob. One of them survived, Noah Mordkovsky who managed to escape and now lives in the U.S. On Rosh Chodesh Ab (June 1942) many troops surrounded the village and started to lead the Jews to the "Havoinik". They moved from house to house, search and found hidden places and pulled out their victims to be killed, and so it lasted three days. My parents managed at first to hide in their hiding place, until one gentile, a pig trader, continued to search until he found them and brought them to the holes. My sister Chasha and I and the family of my husband David stayed in our hiding place, as did several others. At night we left the hiding place, crossed the swamp and the railway and ran away to the forests.

After the butchery in Maytchet a few Jews returned from the forests according to a false promise that nothing will happen to them, and of course all of them were caught and killed. Everyone who stayed in their hiding places went to the forest and decided that they will run away and hide separately. And so it was, my sister and I ran to the village of Midzbidzina and arrived at an acquaintance, a gentile named Bezerovski, who let us to hide in his attic. So we lived a few weeks, the gentile brought us food and at nights we even entered his house. To this place we heard the disaster that happened to the Jews of the village and among them all our family: Dad, Mom, brothers Jacob, Moshe, Mordechai, granddad (Asher) my uncles and aunts and their families were all dead. The only ones who survived were my husband David and his nephew Abba, who were in the Baranovichi ghetto. We thought about our situation and, with the consent of our host, we decide to be united. One day Bezerovski took his wagon and drove to Baranovichi to bring back David and Abba to us. They arrived at the Baranovichi ghetto and came to my aunt Rivka Sadovski's house and met David and Abba who were willing to join us. But since it was a day or two before Yom Kippur they decided to stay in Baranovichi until after Yom Kippur, for then the farmer will return to fetch them to his house. At the first day after Yom Kippur, which was on the Sabbath day the gentile came with his wagon as agreed, but he didn't find any one there, for at Yom Kippur all the Jews of Baranovichi were killed, among them the rest of our family.

[Page 306]

So I stayed alone in the farmer's house until one day he said, that the fact that I'm staying there was known and the police and the gentiles are looking for me. That night I ran away to the nearest forest and after that I arrived to a farmer named Slavoi and was hidden at his house. One day I met Moshe Rabets and he told me, that in the Sbrotba forests there are around twenty Jews of our village. I started to wonder and search for them, for I was not able to bear the loneliness, and so I arrived finally to their hiding place and met Joshua Rabets, and the family of Moshe Rabets and others. I joined them and lived the hard life. At night we went out to the nearby villages to search food and the farmers gave it willingly. But this uncovered our existence, and one day in the hiding place they attacked us and they killed everybody. Miraculously Sarah Rabets (Kaplan) survived, she was wounded while running away but survived and now lives in the US.

When we heard about the butchery of the people in this hidden place, we felt no security in our hidden place and decided to leave it. At the same night we went away and without knowledge arrived in the Dvorets ghetto. We stayed there only one day and at night we went out very quietly from the ghetto and I continued to wander until I arrived at the village of Zapolia. There I found one farmer that knew our family and he agreed to hide me in his house. I stayed at this gentile's house in Zapolia for one month until I found out about a partisan organization in the area. I went out to the nearest forest to look for the partisans, and I met them and was accepted at the "Otriad" [partisan group] named after Ivan Grozni. I lived in this place and was active with the group for six months until the liberation in the summer of 1944.

[Pages 307-308]

The Bravery of Zimel Stolovitsky
By Abrasha Hanelis
Translated by Ron Rabinovitch

These are some of my memories of Maytchet during the Holocaust period. In this town lived a grain merchant named Zimel Stolovitzky, a man with a long beard. At the last "Aktion" he survived with part of his family and they went to hide in the Horki Forest, about seven kilometers west of the town. The forest's area was approximately 200 hectares; two kilometers wide and in the interior were water and swamps. Among the agriculture villages that surrounded the forest were Beluzi, Flochva, and Horki. Zimel Stolovitzky had many acquaintances in these villages.

At the time of the mass murderers, he organized a group of the Maytchet "Action" survivors. There were about 60 people, including women and children, and they built a camp in the forest. They managed to buy weapons consisting of eight guns, twelve pistols, one machine gun and some hand grenades. Zimel Stolovitzky and his group also were able to buy food in the nearby villages.

At the end of August, 1942 I moved with my group near this area. We approached the camp quietly and about twenty meters from it we heard voices speaking in Yiddish. I told my friends that we found a group of Jews and we should approach carefully so as not to frighten them. When we came upon their place, the camp guards stopped us and asked for our identities. We told them that we were Jewish Partisans and we want to visit them. The chief of the camp, Zimel Stolovitzky, came out with a gun and a pistol and asked what we wanted and who we were. We repeated that we were Jewish Partisans and he then invited us into his camp. There we found acquaintances from Maytchet and we were very happy to see them. We remained in this camp for about two days.

At this time there was a conference of Jewish and Christians Partisans in the Horki Forest, in the area where Zimel's camp was. Zimel told us about the Nazis spies and murderers that took part in the "Aktion" in Maytchet and said he wanted to attend this conference. We went to speak with the head of the conference, who was the head commander of all the partisans in this area; he agreed to invite Zimel Stolovitzky and was eager to meet with him.

At their meeting, Zimel told the commander that there are groups of Nazis spies who claim to be partisans. Zimel asked the commander to investigate to see if they are really partisans fighting against the Nazis. At the same time that Zimel spoke with the commander, two spies came to the camp. One of Zimel's group announced that they arrived and were harassing the women and shooting their guns into the air. Zimel asked the commander to help him take the weapons from the spies. The commander agreed and went to the camp with his staff and along with Zimel, they killed the two spies. Searching their pockets, they found certificates identifying them as Nazis policemen.

[Page 308]

Two days later all the partisans left the area. Zimel Stolovitzky asked us to help supply his group with weapons. We managed to give him two guns and fifty bullets. In October, 1942 the Nazis attacked Zimel's camp in Horki forest. The Nazi regiment had tanks and hundreds of soldiers and they surrounded the forest, closing all the entrances and exists to the forest. They attacked the base where the sixty Jewish survivors from the Maytchet area were staying. The base was surrounded with bunkers and other defensive positions and the fighters of Zimel's camp fought valiantly for three hours. Unfortunately the group lost twelve people. Zimel Stolovitzky sent for help from other partisan groups, but when the Nazis realized that the partisans were coming, they ran away. The survivors moved to the Dvorets Ghetto.

When the partisans, including myself, came to help we found a burnt camp. Because this camp was at a centrally strategic junction for the partisan movement, we decided that we would remain here. The partisan commander said that there should be a memorial to the heroes that succeeded to push back the Nazis. He announced that Zimel Stolovitzky and others will be registered as heroes in the history of the partisans.

[Page 309]

Three Who Set Out on a Journey
by Binyamin Stolovitsky of Petach Tikva
Translated by Jerrold Landau

On September 17, 1939, the Russians entered the town and imposed their order, or more accurately, disrupted all of our protocols and plans. I was 15 ½ at the time when I was cut off from the nurturing source of nationalist Judaism, and I joined the Pioneer youth group. Of course, this was not for reasons of conscience, but rather to protect the peace of the home and the family before the authorities. I should point out that there was no direct pressure to do so, for the attitude of the authorities was reasonably liberal at first. Indeed, many of the youth did not join, and nobody protested.

It was not long before the first refugees began to arrive from German occupied western Poland, and were hosted in the Jewish houses of the city. A refugee was also hosted in our house. He told us of the decrees and the tribulations that hovered over the heads of Polish Jewry under the yoke of occupation. With the influence of his stories that shook the heart and soul, and with the news of the daring deeds of the youth of the *kibbutzim* who escaped to Vilna and prepared to go from there to the Land of Israel, the desire to be among them was aroused in me.

One evening, I met with my two friends, Nachum Rabinovitch and Moshe Kroshinski, in order to discuss practicalities. My female cousin came along with me. To my sorrow, this before the news of the impending Holocaust had penetrated the hearts of the parents, and we were forced to keep our actions secret. We decided to embark on the journey while there was still time, and we even set a time for our departure without informing the household of our plans.

Due to our strong connections with the gentiles of the region from the former times, I knew personally the director of the railway stationmaster in Mickiewicz, and I relied upon his help, that he would not ask superfluous questions. We furnished ourselves with food for several days and appropriate clothing for the journey, and we set out, attempting to the extent possible to appear as young students in order to avoid suspicion. I turned to the stationmaster and purchased three tickets to Lida, where there was a concentration of pioneering youth who were ready to steal across the border to free Lithuania.

When we got off the train in Lida, we fell right into a snare for the *chalutzim*[1], who had aroused the suspicion and ire of the authorities. We fled for our lives in order to hide until the wrath would pass. The three of us reached the house of a Jew at the edge of the city. When we saw a bearded Jew through the window, we dared to knock at the door and ask permission to enter. The family members were afraid of our appearance. After we told them the purpose of our arrival, they had mercy on us and took us up to the oven to spend the night. When we got up in the morning, the Jew asked us to recite the Traveler's Prayer [*tefillat haderech*]. Even though they were poor, they provided us with food for the journey. We set out to search for the "connection."

[Page 310]

When we saw lads in leather jackets - which was one of the signs of recognition - exiting and entering one house exchanging secrets with each other, we knew that we had arrived at the right place. While we were still amazed at what was taking place, someone whom I immediately recognized as Berile, the director of the Shomer Hatzair youth camp in Mir, came out of the house. I approached him and asked him to help us with our affairs. He brought us into the house and turned us to Sheika Wiener, a member of the main defense and the central smuggling organization. However, instead of encouraging us, he spoke to us seriously about pushing off our plans to another time, because of the large number of *chalutzim* older than us who were knocking on the doors of *aliya*.

After we suffered this disappointment, we left the house, and I spoke seriously to my two friends about making the journey on our own, since my father's family had acquaintances in the border town of Turgal, and I hoped for their assistance. From Lida, we continued on to the Gavya station on the Lida-Vilna railway line, with the intention of continuing by foot along the railway tracks. When we got off the train in the town on the eve of the Sabbath, it was already dark, and we looked for a synagogue in which we could spend the night. In the darkness of the synagogue, we noticed a pile of wood that was prepared for lighting the oven. We lit the oven to warm up and fell asleep of exhaustion. Early in the morning, when the gentile came to light the oven, he saw us, became quite startled, and asked who we were. We told him something, left the place, and continued along our journey following the telephone lines, with a breathtaking snowstorm hammering at our faces.

After walking for several hours, someone passed by us. When he approached us, we recognized Berile. I was very glad to see him and attempted to turn to him, but, out of fear, he made as if he did not know me, and continued along his way. We also continued along our tortuous way until Turgal. There, I looked for and found one of the acquaintances of my father's household. He recognized immediately, and his first question was whether Father knows. When I responded in the affirmative, he took us in and fed us, and we spent the night.

The next day we surmised that there would not be a strict guard on Sunday, and we set out for the border. A kilometer away from the town, the telephone lines led into a forest, and we continued along until night fell. Suddenly we heard a whistle from the forest. We immediately lay down in the snow and waited for what would happen. A group of about 20 people who were speaking Yiddish amongst themselves came near us. We realized that these were the *chalutzim* who were headed for the border. We joined them without them realizing this in the darkness of the night. As we approached the border, a gentile came from the other side to receive us at the agreed place. He counted the people in order to receive his fee per head, and he found three additional people. To our good fortune, Sheika Wiener was in the group. He rescued us from our predicament and we crossed the border to Eisiskes in peace. From here, we were taken by bus to Vilna, to the *chalutz* gathering center on Subacz Street. There we met the brothers of my two fellow travelers, Berl Kroshinski and Reuven Rabinovitch. There were other Maytcheters, including: Chana Boretcky, Vichna Belski, Moshe Vilkomirski, Itche Movshovitz, and others.

[Page 311]

After several days, the people divided up by party stream, and we were transferred to the Hashomer Hatzair Kibbutz on Jagilonska Street. The three of us joined the youth of our age. We were about 20 people in total. There, groups to study Hebrew were organized for us, and in the spring, they set up for us a vegetable garden on leased land, that served as a source of livelihood and of training. I recall a general meeting that took place one evening in which about 600 people participated, in order to bid farewell to some members before they set out for the area of occupied Poland in order to organize the movement anew. Among those who set out were Anielewicz[2], Yosef Kaplan, Chaika Grossman, and a Polish girl named Irina from among the command of the Polish scouts in Warsaw. She had lived in Vilna as a refugee and collaborated with Hashomer Hatzair.

Thus, we lived and worked there for two months in preparation for making *aliya*. During that time, the Lithuanian authorities moved from a position of sympathizing to a position of direct cooperation with the Communist guard, and they began to track our steps. That was the time of the war with Finland. The British government sent clothes to Finland, but somehow, those clothes reached us, and we dressed up in blue uniforms as students. After the final annexation of Lithuania, we dispersed to smaller groups in private rented houses. Due to the expected and unexpected dangers, the time came to work urgently toward *aliya*.

It was preferred that all of the youths born after 1923 would travel as part of the Youth Aliya[3], including the students who were of age, we three among them. Indeed, we received a directive from the Land of Israel Center in Kovno to prepare for the journey. We went to the Interior Ministry in Kovno to obtain our travel certificates. Once the exit date was set, we returned to Vilna. On the designated day, we went to the train station and joined the caravan of those making *aliya*, setting out for Moscow in order to obtain student visas for Turkey. There, we stayed at the Moskovski Hotel. Immediately after obtaining our Turkish visas, we set out via Kiev to Odessa, in order to board the Sapantia ship.

Our plan finally was realized, and we arrived safely in the Land of Israel. There, we were divided up to various Kibbutzim, and I ended up in Kibbutz Ein-Hashofet. From there I joined Kibbutz Lehavot. At first I enlisted in the Palmach[4], but when news of the Holocaust reached us, I enlisted in the Jewish Brigade and arrived in Europe, where I found two female cousins in the camps who had arrived from Russia. During the time I served in the brigade, I was involved in saving and smuggling efforts. When I returned from the army, I entered into the period of the disturbances prior to the establishment of the State. I served in the Hanegev unit of the Palmach.

Translator's footnotes
1. Zionist pioneers who were intending to go to Israel.
2. Seemingly the Mordechai Anielewicz of Warsaw Ghetto fame. See http://en.wikipedia.org/wiki/Mordechai_Anielewicz .
3. See http://en.wikipedia.org/wiki/Youth_Aliyah
4. See http://en.wikipedia.org/wiki/Palmach

[Page 312]

With the Nomad's Staff
Reuven Ravinovitch
Translated by Ron Rabinovitch

In 1929, when I was a 3rd grade student in our *Tarbut* school, I became involved with the *Hashomer Hatzair* movement along with Moshe Vilkomirski and Chanan Zukovitzki. We were all nine years old. The commander of the youth movement in our area was Nachum Gilrovitz and the head of our group was David Bass. As school vacation was over, our first public activity with the school and the movement was to stage a protest at the big synagogue against the bloody riots in Israel in 1929. Our second activity, which remained engraved in my memory, took place during the 18th Zionist Congress when we were included in the distribution of *Shkalim* and general activities to support *Eretz Yisrael*. Also, at home, there was a Zionist atmosphere such as contributing to the National Funds, which was enough to charm a young boy whose goal was to realize the Zionist dream.

In 1933, I completed the 7th grade of school and was still involved with every program and activity to promote "The Redemption." During the Passover of 1939, I went to Rovno to prepare with Channa Boretsky. There were other Maytchet folks, including Moshe Vilkomirski, Isaac Movshovitz, Vichne Belski, Beryl Kroshinski, Channan Zukovitzki and Reuven Bitenski. At Rovno we lived in the Kibbutz-house and worked in factories, mills, sawmills, etc. The women did housework. The war found us there.

I had a piece of luck and at that time I became sick and could not recuperate under the conditions at the Kibbutz, so I had to return home after few days when the roads were difficult, just five days before the Russian occupation. Of course nobody knew about the Russian-German agreement and they were only worried about the Germans coming closer and talked about escaping into Russia. Meanwhile, on Sep 17th 1939, the Russians unexpectedly entered the area and all our plans changed. At that time our friend Moshe Vilkomirski returned from Rovno and told us that the kibbutz was going to disperse because of the situation. After we received messages that Vilna was going to be a part of independent Lithuania, I went to Vilna with Vilkomirski to check on the possibilities there. The situation was not so clear and there was turmoil, especially in our people's grousps. So Moshe Vilkomirski stayed there and I returned to the Kibbutz in Rovno to tell them about the situation and to advise them to move to Vilna as quickly as possible.

On the way from Vilna to Rovno I stopped at my home in Maytchet for a few days. Vichna Belski came with me and when we returned to Rovno, we were divided into small groups in order to move to Vilna. On the way back from Rovno I stopped again in Maytchet to take the supplies necessary for the long journey. As the teenagers heard about my coming and that I was going to Vilna, they came to talk to me, but most of them didn't accept our plans. Their opinions didn't turn me from my decision and I went to Lithuania, to a transit center. As one of a group of 20 people we went through Eshishuk on the night of Yom Kippur and crossed the border where group leaders from both sides helped us. It is worth mentioning that during the first weeks the Russians and the Lithuanians chose to ignore what we were doing and gave us the chance to do what we had to do. The Lithuanians even helped us, but they wanted to do it without publicity. At night we arrived at Eshishuk and the first thing in the morning we transferred to Vilna by trucks and went to the Kibbutz's absorption center on Sobatac Street.

[Page 313]

After a few days all the Kibbutz's movements began to organized on their own and our movement, *Hashomer Hatzair*, was established on Tartaki Street. We stayed in Vilna for three months in readiness and, at the beginning of March, 1940, we moved to Vilkomir (currently Ukmerge) inside Lithuania, were the local Jewish community accepted us with much warmth and extended a brotherly helping hand. There we organized as an independent kibbutz and worked, even though the Lithuanian law forbid refugees from working.

In June and July 1940, the Russians feared the Germans would enter the area, so they joined the Baltic states to the Soviet Union. Our kibbutz remained until the end of the year, but then, after some friendly hints from the local citizens, we divided into small groups and lived in private houses for more then six months. After complete annexation of the area to Russia, it was possible to reconnect with our home after being cut off for more then a year. But our activities stopped because we had to be very careful. No one could travel abroad and certificates were only available to a few people. Only the Youth Aliyah organization (*Aliyat Hano'ar*) was permitted as a special program. In this program there were just three younger men from Maytchet – my brother Nachum Rabinowicz, Benjamin Stolovitzki, and Moshe Kroshinski who traveled via Moscow to Odessa on the ship "Svetlana".

As the connection with home was created again, my family came to meet us and to see our departure. We sometimes went home, but in secret ways. We were afraid of the consequences, so we met them in Baranovichi. The last visit of my father to see me in Lithuania was a few days before the onset of the German-Russian war. When the war started we again took up the nomad's staff and fled with nothing on us to Dvinsk, the only route into Russia. We walked a hundred kilometers to the Lithuanian/Russian border. The Germans bombed all the roads in front of us so we went through the forests until we arrived at the Russian border. There we took the train to Saratov, Russia on the way to the Persian border, in central Asia.

Near Samarkan we organized again into groups. There we learned the fate of our friends who disappeared and we met with some of them. In this place we were together and worked for the next four years. At the end of the war we returned to Poland where we kept busy with *Aliya Bet* activities till 1950 when we finally arrived in Israel.

[Page 314]

My Personal Experiences
Tsira Royak (Rabets)
Translated by Ginny Gilbert

This happened on a Wednesday morning—Rosh Chodesh Av. Tuesday at 1:00 a.m., we already saw that we were encircled by the murderers. We understood that bad fortune had arrived, so we went into the hiding place that we had earlier prepared—myself with my three children, Zlate with her three children. My husband, Velvel, shut us in and went into Yeshihe's unfinished house where my mother and another woman, a "bazshenke," were also hidden. (This term refers to a Jew who ran from their home in Western Poland or Germany eastward to flee from the Germans. Many were in Maytchet and surrounding towns being sheltered by the people there when the Germans ultimately caught up with them.) In the morning they found my mother and the woman and they led them to the graves.

[Page 315]

But they did not find *Velvel* and as soon as it got dark he went to the home of a Christian acquaintance and hid there.

We sat in our hiding place until 4 o'clock in the afternoon on Friday, when the gentiles found us. They came looking for our belongings under the floor and when they saw us they got scared. They were Sergevitcher and Palenker, gentiles who dealt with my father and bought from me in the store, so they let us run. We went over the line and the lake. We were afraid of fleeing together so we separated. Zlate took her children, and I took mine, and we went into the woods. It didn't take a half hour before we heard them shooting in the woods. I gathered the children and ordered them to lie still and not move. When the shooting ended, a boy, a "bazshenets" who used to know Chatzkel, approached us. He gave the children bread and a green onion which made them happy.

The boy and I separated. He went to Medredzhine (a small town near Maytchet), and the children and I went to the home of our Christian acquaintance where we found Velvel and Chenia Shmulovits. Our joy was indescribable, because he thought they had finished us off, and I thought he was no longer alive. We spent 6 weeks in a dog house, but all of a sudden it became very risky because the murderers started searching every house. The Christian woman could not keep us in hiding any longer, and at midnight in a heavy rain we went into the "Swarotwa" forest.

We wandered around for 2 weeks under the open sky, and when it got cold we gathered together in a dugout ringed with pieces of wood. When more people arrived, we made another dugout, in which were my brother Selig and his little daughter (his wife and two sons had perished), my brother Hirshel with his wife and three children, Yudie the carpenter and his family, Bunya Gilerovits and my nephew Chaim, and Minnie and two children. We stayed for several months until there arrived from Baranovichi Chaim Novomisky and another couple of Jews, who didn't notice the forest was encircled. The murderers let them go and followed them, and as soon as they went into a shelter, they shot them. I went out a while to see where they were, and immediately a shot hit me and I fell. They thought I was dead, so they threw me off the hill, and I felt nothing and heard nothing. The surrounding gentiles offered their help, and together they murdered all the hidden Jews. Yulek came to me, and seeing that I was still alive, he and his son took me and put me in a potato hole.

[Page 316]

At night they took me into the house, washed my wounds and bandaged them. I begged them to take me to the woods, but Yulek thought that maybe Velvel and the children fled and found themselves with the same Christian. At night he took me there, but I found no one there. Since I was left alone and could not stand on my feet,

I wanted to go to Dvorets but they were afraid. For thirteen weeks I stayed with the Christian, who kept me in a cold corridor. When I realized I could not remain there because they were hunting in the vicinity, I pleaded for them to cut my foot and take out the bullet that was embedded there so that I would be able to leave. She asked a person who was a "feldsher" (a field surgeon), who performed the operation, and my feet started to heal.

One night when I was lying in the corridor, some partisans came in and found me. They ordered me to stand with my face to the wall and put a gun against me to shoot me. The Christian stood up for me, arguing that the Jewish partisans would take vengeance for me and it would be better that they should leave me alone. Another night I again heard knocks on the door. I thought the partisans had returned to finish me off, but it was Chenia Shmulovits who came to get a salve that the Christian made for various sores and boils. My meeting with Chenia was very heart rending. We cried ourselves out about the great misfortune that we lost our loved ones. I told her that Chatskel was not far from here and we begged our Christian to bring him.

When Chatskel came, we discussed our lot and decided to dig a shelter in the ground not far from the house. But at night when they went out to dig the hole they realized that it would not be secure and we decided we would go where Chenia was.

[Page 317]

That was a crawlspace under a floor in the house of a gentile Polish farmer by the name of "Glatki", where there were seven men and one girl. After spending the night, we went to the owner and begged him to let us stay a couple of days until my wounds could heal. He agreed and treated us as a father would. We stayed 9-1/2 months. Then we had to leave, because in the village there was already some gossip that there were Jews at Glatki's house. We left the crawlspace and went into the woods where there were partisans.

The men were accepted by the partisans, and the "bezhenke"girl and I were left in the woods with more women and a few men. I went with Cheykel into a bunker where we saw a girl sick with typhus. She lay in a plank cot and could not move. Her mother had died a few days earlier, and there was no one to help her. Cheykel and I took her down, washed her, and put a clean shirt that I had on her. Day by day she got better. But as a result of this, I became ill with typhus and lay for three weeks on the cot with no help. But from trouble one does not die. I lived through this, my fever left, but I could not stand on my feet due to weakness.

In the meantime we were informed that the murderers knew where we were, and they were going to encircle the woods. As soon as it became light we heard shots being fired. All who could walk left the woods, but I could not and I remained. This went on for 5 days—in the morning they would leave and in the evening they returned. One morning we learned the murderers were planning to enter the woods. Everyone ran from the woods. They saw a group of riders whom they took for partisans who were also running to hide. But these were the murdering policemen who killed everyone except a very few who managed to be saved. I went out of the mud hut and leaning on a stick, I went a little further and at night I returned to the mud hut. I began to search for a way out of the woods because I was afraid that when they found me, they would torture me so I would tell where they might find more Jews.

When I went out of the woods, I met Abraham Kaplan and his daughter and son, but they ran very fast and I could not keep up. As I was slowly walking alone, not knowing where, I heard shots from all sides. I lay with my face down so I would not see the murderers. I don't know how it happened, but the murderers passed and did not see me. I lay there until dark and noticed a house in the distance, so with all my strength I managed to get there and go in. Standing there was a young woman cooking food. I begged her to give me something to eat and let me warm up. She said her husband would soon arrive. A gentile with an axe showed up almost immediately, and I thought that this was my end. He took pity on me, however, and ordered that I be given food. Then he told me to get up on the warm stove and piled wood all around me.

[Page 318]

In the morning the gentile went into the woods looking for Jews or Partisans. When he returned, I pleaded with him to return me to the woods. He took an axe as though he was going into the woods. He went ahead and I followed him from afar. En route he warned me not to look into the ravine because there were all the murdered Jews. And truthfully, when I went by I was horrified, seeing the unfortunate murdered people. On the other hand, I envied them that they were no longer there and I have still to suffer. On arriving at the bunkers I found no one, and the gentile with the axe immediately turned back home.

When it became dark, about 30 people slowly appeared. During the day we went and hid in lime holes and at night we returned to the mud huts. This lasted for 3 weeks, until we got exhausted and decided not to return to the lime holes. We gathered a little flour and went to the second bunker to bake a loaf of bread. When we returned with the bread we saw a sled with people go by. We became frightened and ran to the side. When we finally came into the bunker, I was told that Sholom Romanovsky came with several partisans to take me with him into the woods where his detachment was. I went with them, and in a few days the murderers arrived in the woods, encircled the bunker in which I previously stayed, and murdered everyone there.

After 5 days and 5 nights, we came to the detachment where I found Freidel Margolin. Several days later they took me to Bielski's detachment, where I found many Jews; among them some acquaintances—Zelda (Gilerovitz) and Litman (Litaworsky), Yosef Shmulovits, Chaya-Esther Kaplan, and her father and brother. Several days later

Maier Lozovsky, Sholom Zhuchovitch, and Chenia arrived from Kozlitsheve. They made a mud hut and took me in. We were there for some time together. After that, Litman and Zelda made a mud hut for themselves and took me in.

[Page 319]

It became a little easier for me to carry on with my unfortunate life when I found myself among friends. After being with Litman and Zelda for three months, we learned that the murderers retreated and ran into the woods. Each day we were ready for important happenings. In a short time we went out of the woods, but to tell the truth, we didn't want to go out to see the destruction, and not to have anyone to come to on this cursed earth into which the innocent blood of our loved and dearest ones was soaked.

[Page 320]

Maytchet Partisans
by Moshe Rabets
Translated by Sara Mages

At the beginning of 1942, a Jewish resistance group was organized in the village of Mednevich near Molchadz [Maytshet], the place of residence of the Chaneles family. Among the members were: Abrasza Chaneles (son of Yakov), Abrasza Chaneles (son of Baruch), Meir Chaneles, and their friends Yitzchak Lachowicki and David Rabets. Two months later, the group was discovered and the police inspector Walya Aolasik and the police secretary arrived unexpectedly from Haradzets to arrest them. A battle developed between them, Yitzchak Lachowicki was captured by the police, and Abrasza Chaneles (son of Baruch) was seriously injured and later died from his wounds because the Nazis didn't allow the Jews to receive medical help. Yitzchak was imprisoned in Maytchet's jail, and sentenced him to death. Feigale Boretcky and Chanale Belski, two young women from Maytchet who were connected to the resistance, worked at the Nazi police station. One day they learned that Yitzchak Lachowicki will be transferred to Haradzets where his sentence will be carried out, and they informed the resistance members. Abrasza Chaneles, who was friendly with Volodya Yortchek the head of the village of Stantsiya, came to Yitzchak's aid. On the day that Yitzchak was transferred under heavy guard through the village of Stantsiya, Volodya welcomed them and invited them for drinks and refreshments. He served them alcoholic beverages until they got drunk and fell asleep. Then, Meir and Abrasza entered and removed parts from the guns to disable them. At the same time other members, who were equipped with pistols and hand-grenades, stood on guard. When the policemen awoke from their drunkenness they didn't notice the missing parts, and continued on their way to Haradzets. However, on the way Lachowicki managed to slip from the guards and escaped.

He returned to the resistance group which continued its operations with greater vigor. After the "*aktzia*" in Maytchet we organized a partisan group in the Svorotva forest, and inducted Moshe Ravetz, Freidel Margolin, Konya Shlovski, Hanya Shmulovits, Mordechai-Leib Shmulovits, Abrasza Lublinski and Yehusua Zlotnick to our ranks. We established a relation with Russian partisans and they issued an order to increase our squad to 25 members. We reached this number very quickly, and started to take care of the weapons that we received from the residents of the villages, voluntarily or by force. When we became a considerable striking force, we received orders to sabotage railroad tracks, roads, police stations etc. We also carried out orders to obtain medical drugs that were greatly needed for the healing of wounds. Yitzchak Lachovitsky revealed a special expertise in this field because his father had a pharmacy and he knew where to look.

[Page 321]

After the *"aktzia"* in Maytchet about 45 of Maytchet's survivors gathered in the Svorotva forest. They established two bunkers and settled there. It was at the beginning of the winter of 1943. At the same time, partisans came from Yavorskaya Ruda to collect food in the villages around Svorotva. One of the Gentiles informed the police, and when they chased the partisans through the forest they discovered one of the survivors' bunkers. It contained about thirty survivors including six who escaped from Baranowicze Ghetto. A bloody battle developed, and when it ended all the residents of the bunker were killed. Only one woman, who was outside, was saved from death. She managed to escape and hid with a Christian acquaintance who kept her until the Germans began to withdraw. Later, she moved with the help of Jewish partisans to the Bielski partisan detachment, and she continued to operate there until liberation. She was Tsira Rabets who now lives in the USA.

Abrasza Chaneles was one of the most active members of our group. He, Yitzchak Lachovitsky and Konya Shlovski were responsible for the supplies. They went to the villages near the forest and brought food and weapons that were necessary for our existence. Abrasza knew the environment and the residents well. He even knew which one of them had a weapon, and took it willingly or by force. Thanks to this small group of courageous men we were able to endure and continue our struggle for life until the search and the discovery of one of the bunkers. The members of the second bunker moved to Dvorets and joined a labor camp under the command of a German engineer, who allowed them freedom of movement to find food and the like. Among those who moved to the labor camp were Freidel Margolin, my sister Zlata Kaplan with her children, and others. A short time later the labor camp was liquidated and they were killed. Only a few of them managed to escape.

I and another young man by the name of Efraim Dobkowski were among those who were in the second bunker that wasn't discovered by the Germans. We didn't go with the other members of this bunker go the labor camp in Dvorets. We stayed and waited for the partisans who caused the search in the forest that ended with the discovery and the liquidation of the first bunker. They traveled with two food carts to their camp.

When we joined them they gave us a gun with bullets, and told us to walk half a kilometer ahead of them and report on any German movement. We arrived safely to their camp, but immediately afterwards a large German force, which was especially taken from the front, arrived to fight against the large number of partisans in Yavorskaya Ruda. A great battle ensued and all the partisans in the area participated in it. The commander of one of the detachments was a Jew by the name of Dr. Atlas who was wounded in this battle and died. The battle lasted three days and ended in a stalemate.

Since the partisans weren't prepared yet for combat operations, only for "sabotage and escape," the headquarters decided to divide the forces into groups of twenty, who operated according to central orders, but received the maximum freedom to initiate and carry out their operations. Abrasza Chaneles and another refugee from Maytchet returned to the vicinity of Maytchet. We joined a local partisan detachment and operated with them. We performed all sorts of acts of sabotage on railway tracks, roads and bridges. We initiated attacks on German camps and police stations that were located in the villages, destroyed them and took their weapons.

[Page 322]

We, especially Abrasza who excelled in fulfilling the orders assigned to him, received the appreciation of our commanders for our successful operations.

We parted soon after, Abrasza remained in the "Grozny" detachment, and I was transferred to the headquarters of the "Pervomaiskaya brigade" and served as quartermaster. After liberation I arrived to Baranowicze and from there I visited Maytchet, which was occupied by the Gentiles, and walked to Minsk. In 1946 I learned that I could immigrate to Israel. I moved to £ódŸ and from there to Szczecin and then to Berlin. I arrived to Marseille from the American sector [of Berlin], and immigrated in the illegal immigrant ship "Latrun[1] to Cyprus. After a year stay in Cyprus I arrived to Israel. Also Abrasza Chaneles wandered some distance and arrived to Israel "to built and be built in it."

Translator's footnote
  1. The story of the illegal immigrant ship "Latrun"
     http://www.palmach.org.il/show_item.asp?levelId=42858&itemId=8650&itemType=0

[Page 323]

Survivor's Tales
Minna Gurski Levin
Translated by Semadar Siegel

We lived in the village of Ivashkovtsy (Ivankovitz), 10 km. from Molchad, which, for us, was the community, economic and Jewish cultural center. When the war broke out in 1939, the Russians occupied the area. Our parents stayed in the village and the children moved to Baranovichi because there was no future for Jews in the village.

On June 22, 1941, when the Nazis launched their invasion into Russia, we returned to the village to get our parents and escape with the Russians. But the Nazis advanced so fast that we had no time to escape. So we stayed in the village until 1942. Amongst us was the family of Mordechai Lev, his single brother Yehuda and his sister Masha. The family of Alter and Miriam Gorski, two sons and a daughter, and a few other refugees from Poland joined us.

In February, 1942 the Nazis gathered all the Jews from the surrounding villages into the village of Novaya Mysh (Mush), which was near Baranovichi. On Saturday – 19 Tamuz 5702 (July 7, 1942) they took all the Jews, including the 1200 inhabitants, out of the town. They shot them and buried all of them in one mass grave, which had been prepared in advance. Very few escaped this action and for five months they continued to live in Novaya Mysh (Mush).

The Gorskis--my father, my brother Tuvia and I were sent in a group of 10 people to a work camp. We were sent to Peskovtsy, 10 km. from Molchad in order to work in the fields. We worked for six months on the farm and conditions were not too bad. We had food and good relations with the gentiles.

When rumors came about the action in Molchad, the gentiles urged us to escape from the area because our end was close. Only July 16, 1942 we escaped to the forest in Lyushnevo, in the area of Slonim. There were 20 workers from Molchad on the farm near Lyushnevo. The day after our escape from Peskovtsy they gathered all the Jews from Lyushnevo and took them to Baranovichi. On the way, a few escaped from the truck and survived. Ten of the people who escaped from Peskovtsy stayed in the forest for a whole week and later everyone went on their own way. That is how my father, my brother and I survived.

We wandered in the forest until winter. We never stayed at night where we were during the day so we would not get caught. Just before winter we built two underground shelters. But father was very weak and depressed because of his wife and sister-in-law's death. He did not have the strength to go out of the shelter. The children were the ones to go out and beg for food from the gentiles.

[Page 324]

Yan Rutzki from Peskovtsy was a wonderful Polish person who treated us with respect and acted humanely towards us. There was one gentile who informed on him to the Nazis. The Nazis beat him 29 times and warned him that if Tuvia Gorski comes again he has to bring him to them. In the beginning we did not go to his house although he asked us the come and also offered to dig us an underground shelter in his house so that we should not endanger ourselves by walking to him. In the meantime my father died on February 26, 1943 and the Polish person continued helping us like a righteous gentile.

The day we went into the underground shelter and also just before he died, our father requested that we bury him on his land. Then if Mordechai (Mottle) Gorski, who was drafted in the Russian army, returns, he would know where to find his father's grave. He also asked us to prepare shrouds from his clothing by removing the buttons, take one tzitzei from his tallis, wrap him in his tallis, and put him in the grave with his feet first according to Jewish Law.

After my father died we met with some partisans but they refused to take us in because we had no ammunition. So we continued wandering in the forest until the liberation. We heard shooting of the war nearby and we saw the Nazis retreating. On July 9, 1944 we went out of the forest to Ivashkovtsy (Ivankovitz) to see our house, which was occupied by refugees, and we then walked to Yank. Tuvia was drafted into the army and I stayed in Baranovichi. After the liberation, Yank Rutzki continued helping us and brought us food. When I left for Israel I separated from him in a very warm way.

Tuvia Gorski was wounded in a battle near Kaliningrad (Koenigsberg). After he came out of the hospital he was released from the army because of his injuries and he went to Gorki to his brother. From there he went to Baranovichi and on to Israel via Poland and Germany in 1949. Mordechai Gorski went on a leave and never returned to the army and arrived in Israel at the end of 1948.

[Page 325]

The Raid...and the Meeting
A. Ben-Shalom
Translated by Sara Mages

These lines were written on the 22nd Independence Day of the State of Israel, and more than half a century after the event (one of many) that fell in my lot. The beginning of the story is in the fall of 1942. Our group, which included about twenty young Jewish men and women, were among those who fled on the day of the mass killings in Maytchet (1 Menachem Av 5702 - 15 July 1942) from two workplaces in the nearby villages. The group settled in one of the remote forests, about 30 kilometers from the town.

At that time, we were already armed and some of us even had Russian "automatic" weapons. We obtained them from the local farmers who collected them after the Red Army retreated from the Germans. Moreover, within a few months (since mid-July 1942) we successfully completed the process of organization and became a fighting unit with a recognized standing in the area. Since the unit commander and his deputy, and especially their families, were known in the area for a many years, a sympathetic atmosphere was created around them (and around the group) among the local population. It enabled us to establish an intelligence network, which served as a fertile ground for creating "legends" about our great strength. Needless to say, that we haven't done anything on our part to deny them, on the contrary, we contributed quite a lot with special operations to nourish them.

I deliberately skip over the group's history until then, and about its actions in rescuing Jews (from Dvorets Ghetto and other locations), and mention, that our group's name reached one of the illustrious Russian partisan regiments in the area (named after "Zolotov"). The commander of this regiment, who was in the rank of a major, invited us to participate in an extensive raid on Maytchet. He had an impressive appearance and a memorable beauty. He was a legendary figure of a commander and friend. To this day I believe, that he was a descendant of the glorious Jewry of Russia (later he fell in one of the partisans battles). One way or another, may his memory be blessed.

With enthusiasm and tremendous elation we accepted the long awaited invitation on the spot. Although we had hoped for it, we didn't believe that the time for revenge really arrived. We moved swiftly and "swallowed" kilometers towards the goal. At twilight, and before the sun went down, the city was surrounded, almost unnoticed, by the entire invading force. We were stationed on the road leading from the train station, about a bowshot from the mass graves.

[Page 326]

We were given the task to eliminate any opposition to the invasion of the town and capture the head of the council (Voight), who stole the property and the souls of Maytchet's Jews. My good inclination force me to mention in this place, that before the battle began, the battalion commander galloped alone on his horse near the police outpost, which in addition to the local police was also manned by the Germans. He stunned the enemy with his courage to such extent, that the soldiers forgot to activate their weapons, and when they did, fortunately for us, it was too late for them. The action of a single man constituted, from lack of choice, the "softening" which was customary before an assault. I'm convinced, then as now, that this conscious risk was the deciding factor in breaking the moral of the soldiers in the outpost, who fled for their life when the battle intensified.

When the signal for the assault and the cleansing operation was given, our group was divided into two teams. One, under the command of the group's commander continued into the town, while the second team located the house of the head of the council. We surrounded it and called its inhabitants to get out. The residents of the house, who locked themselves behind lock and key, refused to get out. Even our warning, that we'll burn the house with its occupants, was in vain. After the farm's buildings (the cowshed and the barns) were set on fire and the house also caught on fire, its inhabitants started to shower fire at us with the few rifles that they had. Of course, the residents of the house risked their lives in this action, and we decided to carry out the verdict. However, we made sure that the animals and the chickens were able to escape from the fire. When the fire intensified, a few figures started to crawl out of the house. They, as we found out later, were hiding until then in the cellar. We shot those who came out to the light of the flames.

Surprisingly, the head of the council wasn't among those who came out, but it wasn't the only surprise. A shocked girl, about 4-5 years old, stood next to the bodies. She stared at us with eyes wide with fear and with a mute plea begged for her life. In a flash stood before my eyes hundreds of Jewish children that the hand of the reaper had no mercy on them, and their mute pleas and heartbreaking cries didn't help them. I haven't forgotten the knowledge that I acquired in my childhood, and "Remember what Amalek did to you" was still one of the verses that I've used. Nevertheless, I knew that I wasn't going to kill the girl. While wondering about the matter, my ear caught the sound of a gun being cocked behind me, and before I heard the thunder of a shot I held the gun barrel with my hand and raised it. When I turned my face to the girl, my eyes caught her look which inadvertently was engraved in my memory. A short time later we left the area leaving only smoking embers behind us.

Two years have passed. New operations have caused the heart to forget the previous ones, including the raid on the town of Maytchet. Far away, in the Naliboki forest, the partisan brigade, in which I served, merged with the advancing Red Army that defeated the Nazi beast. Under the recommendation of the brigade commander I remained in the rear to help with the renewal of the civil structure in the Baranowicze region. I decided to visit Maytchet, and for the first time I headed to my ancestors' graves and to the hill of death where those, who were more precious to me than my life, were buried together with all of the town's Jews. The ground sank and the depression clearly marked the killing pits. I kissed the blood-soaked soil, and parted from those who dwelled in it while making an oath that I would leave, as soon as possible, the bloody country and the murderers who reside in it. On my way back I went to the town center that its appearance was totally different. Except for me there wasn't a single Jewish soul. Since I never had ties with the local Gentiles or with the Russian refugees that were brought by the Germans, I decided to leave the town without a delay.

[Page 327]

My feet stood next to the cantor's house (one of the houses that remained intact), and without intending to do so I found myself stepping on its threshold. A Gentile, with an accent from central Russia, greeted me. I sat on a chair totally exhausted from all that my eyes have seen in the last few hours. The occupant of the house told me that he was a refugee from Smolensk, and that he lived in the house since his house was destroyed in the war. He asked me if it was my family's home. I said no, and for no reason I told him who were the previous occupants of the house. Before I finished my words my eyes caught the face of a girl about seven years old. She stared wide-eyed at my face and at my weapon. From oblivion suddenly emerged and stood before me the image of the girl from the burnt house of the head of the council. Something in the girl's strange look reminded me the other girl and the whole incident. A few moments later I asked the homeowner if she was his daughter. Much to my surprise, I was answered negatively. This and more, he declared that she wasn't even related to him. When his words aroused my curiosity (because for a moment I thought that she was a Jewish girl) and probably also his fears, he told me the following story:

"It was so - as I've been told, two years ago a Jewish partisan group raided the house of her father who served as the head of the council during the German occupation, and killed her entire family. By unexplainable miracle only the girl survived. Her mother, brothers, uncle and aunt were shot to death, and her father suffocated in the cellar where he hid from the partisans who besieged his house and set it on fire. At dawn, the girl, who was feverish and shocked from the events of the previous night, was taken in by the neighbors. The townspeople fed the girl and alternately took care of her until I arrived to the place. Being childless I expressed my will to adopt her - a matter that was made possible to me. Since I know her, this girl is staring with penetrating eyes at every man who carries a weapon, as if she was looking for someone of something."

Even before the refugee finished his words, I, without saying a word, got to my feet that carried me far away from this house. I never returned to Maytchet, the town that so many of the fibers of my being are connected to.

[Page 328]

Partisans, Fighters and Avengers
by Hanan Shmulovitz (Brooklyn, New-York)
Translated by Sara Mages

The story begins with the Pololich's affair. At first, he had the reputation of a liberal who sympathized with the Jews, but eventually he changed his mind, became a persecutor of the Jews and killed many of them, and the story was as follows, -

Volodya Pololich, from the small town of Svorotva, studied tailoring in Maytchet with Moshe Savitzki. He was considered to be a liberal and was involved with the Jews and the Christians. Later on he moved to Slonim to study cutting. When he returned to Maytchet he opened a workshop at the home of Michel Shmulovitz. He was welcomed in this home because of his liberal views and felt as a family member. After a while, he married a local Christian woman, moved elsewhere, opened a larger workshop and wrote on the sign: "A Christian Enterprise," according to the spirit of the times in Poland. This went on until 1939. When the Red Army entered, he became active in the Communist Party and hoped to get one of the party's positions. The party activists gathered at a meeting and submitted his candidacy for election. And here, one of the Jewish communists stood up and testified that he wrote on his sign: "For Christians only," and consequently he wasn't elected. Pololich withdrew from a political career for a short time, returned to Svorotva and kept the matter in his heart.

Reuven Bitenski

[Page 329]

When the Germans entered to the region they planned a geopolitical plan, according to which, the area of Belarus will be disconnected from Poland and would receive political independence. By doing so the Germans hoped to draw the citizens to their side. An Urban Initiative Committee was also founded in Maytchet, and its members were: the local priest, Donik Kutzko, Pololich and others. Here, the debt owner was given the opportunity to collect his debt, and he started to conspire against the Jews of Maytchet. He prepared a list of 18 Jews, noted next to their names: communist, anarchist, crazy, etc., and all of them were executed in Horodetz. He immediately prepared a second list of 22 Jews, and went from house to house demanding ransom, but at the end all of them were executed. Only one of them, Moshe Belski, escaped from his hands, but he later perished among the partisans. When the "Judenrat" [Jewish council] was established in Maytchet, its chairmen, Erlich and Leibel Gilrovitz, reported Pololich's communist deeds to the German commissioner in Baranovichi. The Germans gave him the death penalty and also prepared the gallows in Maytchet, but his Christian friends smuggled him at night. He hid in the woods until the partisans organized themselves, and he joined them. And now we'll return to the story about the partisans, fighters and avengers, -

At the outbreak of the war, and after the Russians arrival to the area, I was sent to work in Volozhin. When the war was renewed in June 1941, I fled to Russia with the Soviet Army, but the Germans cut our way and I remained near the Berezina River. Given no choice, I headed back to Maytchet and it took me two weeks to get there. At that time, the ghetto was already in existence with a "Judenrat" and forced labor. The best youth was sent to work in Baranovichi, Koldichevo, Lesnaya, etc. After I worked for a short time in Lesnaya I returned with the whole group to Maytchet.

Here [in Maytchet], we were engaged in digging pits that the Germans claimed that they were designed for storing gasoline. We understood that it was not the case and looked for ways to escape from the town, but those who left didn't returned. We started to collect weapons. My friend, Vitya Kozobei, brought me a gun with fifty bullets. We felt that the massacre was approaching but there was nowhere to go. On the night before the liquidation, I, Reuven Bitenski, Noah Mordkovski and Meir Rabets lay in the field with the gun together with many others. At 4 o'clock in the morning we heard dogs barking and saw that the Germans encircled the town. Several of those who lay in the field tried to break the circle with gun shots, but most of them fell on the spot and only a few (10-12) escaped. I hid in a "small dam" in my uncle's house. Forty people hid there, but the Gentiles discovered us and handed us to the Germans. I left the cellar and jumped to the river. They shot after me, but I managed to escape to my friend Kozobei. There was another Jewish family there - Tzira Kaplan, her husband and their children.

We hid there for about two months. From time to time we left for the forest to search for Jews, and they told me that Pololich wanted to see me. I, Elkana Szelowski, Avraham Medlinski and others went to see him, and he brought us to the Zolotov detachment. They didn't accept us, but helped us to get organized and even gave us a commander by the name of Petke.

[Page 330]

Elkana Szelowski, whose father was murdered by Pololich, couldn't restrain himself and told Zolotov about Pololich's past, but the commander told him that they need him during the war, and he will be brought to justice only after the war ended.

We got organized in a short period of time, and the following members joined us: Abrasza Chaneles, Meir Chaneles,Yitzchak Lachowicki, Zuchowitzky, David Stein, Melech Tzokrkaf, Meirim Borecky and others. We decided to carry out our first mission on Yom Kippur eve, but we were warned not to do any act of revenge in the town during our mission. On the next day we attacked the German post that guarded the railroad tracks, and destroyed it. Until now we were in the Svorotva forest. From there we moved to the Horki forest where we found a large group of armed Jews who were organized by Asher Shoshan. We also found several Jews from Maytchet who escaped from Dvorets Ghetto. Meanwhile, two partisans, who moved from another detachment, joined Petke and started to conspire against the Jewish survivors. In a secret council we decided to eliminate them, and Meir Chaneles and Lachowicki carried out the decision.

During my stay in the forest I learned the details about the fate of the bunker's occupants. After most of the people were discovered and murdered, my mother and the rest of my family survived. When they heard about Asher Shoshan and his group, they went to the village of Dokrovha to look for him. They knocked on a farmer's window and asked him about Shoshan. The Gentile captured them, handed them to the authorities, and they were executed. To scare the Gentiles, so they wouldn't continue to do such things, we decided to kill this farmer. We searched and found him, took him out of his house, and shot him. Abrasza Chaneles, Asher Shoshan, Litman, Litvavarski and others participated in this operation. We also burnt the granaries and houses of those who worked for the Germans until they were forced to flee to other locations. It was sort of an action against those who helped the Germans to punish the Gentiles who hid Jews.

In the course of time we moved to "Natasha Pushcha" [Natasha wild forest] to join the partisans who were located there. At that time the forest was surrounded by small tanks. We defended ourselves, to the best of our ability, to prevent the Germans from entering the forest, but it was in vain. They attacked us and killed ten men and women from the families that were in the forest. Under the cover of the night we retreated to the Svorotva forest. On the way, I met with my cousin Yosef Shmulovitz who was hiding in a Gentile's house. I knocked at the door and was offered to stay there. At first I refused and continued to the forest, but at the end I agreed and went back to him. A short time later I found my brother Moshe. Others also joined us, and again, we were a group of ten (winter of 1942). When spring arrived, I informed Abrasza Chaneles, who was able to join the "Grozny detachment," to come and get me. He came, took me and Mordechai Leib Shmulovitz and we arrived to the "Grozny detachment," that because of its size was divided into brigades.

I fought in the "Pervomaiskaya brigade" and participated in many operations. Our position was in the area between Maytchet, Horodysche and Karlitz. One day, the Germans decided to push us into the forest and destroy us. For two days we fought valiantly on the banks of the Niemen River to prevent the Germans from entering the forest, but they broke in by the Polish partisans' position. We were forced to retreat to lake "Kormen" and separated into small groups. We entered the waist deep water, crossed the water barrier under the direction of Boris Grozny, and fled.

[Page 331]

We were liberated on July 1944. Most of us were sent to the regular Red Army which continued with the war. I was sent to a Sovkhoz [Soviet farm] in Karlitz to work as an accountant. At the first opportunity I got to Maytchet and discovered that Pololich served as chairman of the local Soviet Council. Maytchet's survivors informed the persecutor about his real face, but his local friends threw the complaint to the trash. When Yosef Shmulovitz realized that Pololich wouldn't be brought to justice, he contacted the military prosecutor (a Jew), who promised to investigate the matter. An order was sent to arrest him and prosecute him, but his friends warned him, and he escaped to the forest where he organized a partisan unit against the Red Army. At that time he killed Yosef when he met him in the forest.

But the thief will come to a bad end. A Red Army detachment tracked him down and destroyed him and his men.

[Page 332]

My Memories from Mournful Maytchet
by Yaacov Lachovitsky (Baranovichi - Bnei Brak, Israel)
Translated by Sara Mages

In the month of Tamuz 5700 (1940), on the eve of the establishment of the ghetto by the Nazis, may their names and memory be erased, I moved with my family from the city of Baranovichi to the town of Maytchet, where I was hoping to find shelter and salvation. Here, I joined my brother, R' Yitzchak Grtezikovitz, may the Lord avenge his blood, who managed the flour mill in the nearby village of Kozlovitz (7 km), and stayed at his home until the end of the holiday period. During that time, I looked for employment and worked in various jobs for the Christian population in the villages and the surrounding area. At the beginning of the winter, an order was issued by the occupation authorities that all the Jews who live in small villages, must move to cities and towns in which there was a concentrated Jewish community. A Jew wasn't allowed to live alone in his current place of residence - and I was forced to enter with my family into Maytchet's town limits. Like me, many refugees arrived and gathered in the town from various locations. The Jews of Maytchet, who excelled in their kindness, did everything they could to satisfy the refugees' needs. Teachers took the trouble to organize a "heder" [religious elementary school] for the tender children of the displaced, so they can continue their studies even in a period of rage and terror. From among the many kind figures I especially remember R' Berel Romanovski, a precious Jew with high intelligence who did good deeds. He gave his private home to the community council, to the public officials who acted on behalf of others. In this home I found a hiding place in middle of the winter, during the days when the Germans hunted men and took them out of their homes to "work in the forest" (in the last period, before the final liquidation). The occupants of the house hid me in the attic and took care of all my needs, and the women brought me food several times a day - and saved me from death.

It is amazing to note, that unlike other Jewish communities in occupied Poland, the Germans haven't established the public prison cell known as the "ghetto," and for a long period of time the town's Jews didn't suffer from their abuse despite the establishment of a local police etc. In this respect, Maytchet was like a "ship in the middle of the ocean." At that time, we, as religious Jews, attributed it to the young "Rabbi of Stolevitch." A "Tzadik Nistar,"[1] who later proved to be an exemplary person who protected the Jews of Maytchet during the days of the Holocaust. At that time, nothing, big or small, was done in Maytchet without his knowledge and guidance. Even Mr. Erlich, the chairman of the Judenrat who was appointed as "Elder of the Jews" by the occupiers, was constantly in contact with the Rabbi of Stolevitch. He always consulted him on how to behave and what to do (on the occasion of the publication of a new command by the Nazis, the imposing of ransom, etc.).

[Page 333]

The rabbi of the village of "Stolevitch" was related to the *Tzadik*, Rabbi Yisrael-Meir from Radun, who was known all over the world as the author of "*Chofetz Chaim*" ["Desirer of Life"]. He was the rabbi of all of the Jews of Poland and Lita in the last generation. This rabbi was a *Tzadik* and a son of a *Tzadik*. His father, the former Rabbi of Stolevitch, was a great Torah scholar who also served, for a certain period of time, as the dean of "*Yeshivat Torat Chesed*." The *Yeshiva* [Rabbinical College], which belonged to the Slonim Hassidic dynasty, was located in the nearby city of Baranovichi. He had the reputation of a miracle-maker, and many Jews were saved by him from trouble and distress. Later, when his son grew up and took his place, he also became famous as a miracle-maker, and many flocked to him from the surrounding towns to seek his advice and be blessed by him. His admirers believed in his power to perform miracles, knew for sure that the future lies open before him and the Holy Spirit excites his soul, as the Hassidim say: "The Divine Presence speaks through his throat." And here's an episode that was preserved in my memory: Mr. Shevtzik, a man from Maytchet who ran a wholesale grocery store in Baranovichi, was among those who sought his advice. And here, six months before the outbreak of the world war, he came across a good deal. He planned to sell his grocery store and invest the money in the new business, but when he asked the Rabbi of Stolevitch for his consent, the rabbi rejected it and said: "Should you eliminate a business and undermine the foundation of your income for only six months?" Vague words. The torrent of bloodshed started exactly six months after that...

After the Holocaust started he decided to save and protect all the Jews who lived in his area. He was especially concerned about the Jewish community in the nearby town of Maytchet. In his hometown Stolevitch - as in Maytchet - the Germans haven't established a ghetto and didn't bother the local Jews for a considerable period of time. The matter was a wonder in people's eyes because the town was located right by the main road, the highway leading to Baranovichi, and from the day the war started it was constantly bustling with the movement of military vehicles and the forces of the German occupying army. The *Tzadik* prayed non-stop for the wellbeing of his brothers. At night, he didn't turn on the light in his house and engaged in hidden matters. How can I turn on a light when the world is wrapped in terrible darkness," he said. More than once he expressed his amazement," how the sun can shine in days so bleak for humanity, how the heavenly bodies can illuminate the earth when beasts of prey, in the form of people, are running wild on it?" When I was forced to leave the village and move to Maytchet, I saw the *Tzadik* in my dream and asked him what I should do. He encouraged me and said, "The wicked don't have control on you," and so it was.

During the war, by the order of this *Tzadik*, the Jews of Maytchet organized shifts who read Psalms day and night. A *Minyan* prayed relentlessly in every street and every alleyway for salvation from the murderers. One day, when Mr. Erlich visited him, the *Tzadik* told him that he feels a hidden interference in his prayers for the wellbeing of Maytchet's Jews, and asked him to investigate the reason for this. When Mr. Erlich returned to the town, he talked with the community activists who dealt with *mitzvoth*. They started to search and explore until they found that one of the children of the refugees who came here wasn't circumcised, and his father refuses to enter him into the covenant of Abraham *Avinu*. They immediately returned to the *Tzadik*, and he confirmed, that he meant it when he told to his people how to act under the current danger.

[Page 334]

As long as the Rabbi of Stolevitch was alive, Maytchet and her Jews didn't fall into the hands of the oppressor. In the winter of 5702, he appeared in the dream of one of Maytchet's Jews and poured his bitter words: "The defiled Gentiles plot against me, how can I leave you like sheep without a shepherd." A few days later, a large group of officers, dressed in SS uniform and armed with machine guns, arrived to Stolevitch. At first, they surrounded the house of the *Tzadik* and he was caught in their trap. They killed him a martyr's death. Immediately after, they annihilated all the Jews of Stolevitch to the last one.

And indeed, the written word took place: "The righteous is taken away from before the evil" [Isaiah 57:1]. The bitter and impetuous day of the glorious community of Maytchet arrived immediately after the assassination of the Holy Rabbi of Stolevitch. On a gloomy day, the murderers attacked the town, gathered all the Jewish residents, and selected from among them about 300 healthy young men who were expelled to the vicinity of Baranovichi. There, they were recruited together with the deportees from the city of Lida for the building of the forced labor camp in Koldichevo. They remained in the camp until they were liquidated. The remaining Jews, including the elderly, women and children, were taken to the nearby fields and were ordered to dig large pits that eventually served as their graves. On *Rosh Hodesh* Av, in the year 5702, the extinction knife was raised on them and the sound of their blood - the blood of brothers and sisters, boys and girls - emerges and shouts at us from the earth to this day.

We, the survivors, will remember our loved ones with trembling and awesome respect. We will remember what the Amalek of our generation did to us - "Don't forget!"...

Translator's footnote

1. *Tzadik Nistar* - is a hidden *tzadik* (righteous one) whose righteousness remains unknown to his community. In every generation there are 36 *tzadikim nistarim*, who are also called the *Lamed-Vav Tzaddikim* .In folk tales, they emerge from their self-imposed concealment and, by the mystic powers, which they possess, they succeed in averting the threatened disasters of people persecuted by the enemies that surround them. http://en.wikipedia.org/wiki/Tzadikim_Nistarim

[Pages 335-336]

My Memories of Maytchet
by L. Ozersky
Translated by Jerrold Landau

A letter from Winnipeg, Canada

Many greetings to Mr. Nachum Margolin.

I am writing to you, the oldest son of the Ozersky family, the son of Shlomo the Sofer [the scribe's son]. I doubt that you remember me, for I studied in the Slonim Yeshiva and used to come home only on Passover and the festivals. However we were neighbors. We lived in the circle of stores, and your father had a store in the same circle. I was good friends with your Aunt Kroina and Uncle Yona, and especially with their older daughter, who was murdered at Passover time in Majentek[1], where the murderers killed everybody.

That tragic case remains well in my memory, for the next day I made an escape. I went out to the Zarecer forest, and from that time, I never came back to Maytchet. I went to Baranovichi, spent two months in the ghetto there, obtained a gun with 40 bullets, and organized a group of 24 girls and boys. At night, we left the ghetto with 15 guns and eight grenades, cut through the wire, and went out to the forest. Thus, I became the only survivor of our entire family.

I very much want to obtain some information about my family in Maytchet, and when they were killed. If any of you know any details about them, I would be very grateful to know. I observe the *yahrzeit* of the entire Maytchet community of *Shabbat Chazon*[2]. I recite *Kaddish*, read the *Haftorah*, and give a *kiddush* for the entire synagogue. I know that my younger brother Chona was murdered in the slaughter before *Tisha Be'Av*. I know nothing about my father and mother, my sister Malka and my middle brother Berl.

Now, regarding the Yizkor Book, I can state with certainty that you are doing a very important and holy task by perpetuating our dear and beloved martyrs, who were so tragically and cruelly murdered in sanctification of the Divine Name in our native town of Maytchet. The traitorous earth of Maytchet should be accursed forever, and accursed shall be the gentile neighbors who helped murder the Jews in order to inherit – Did you kill and also inherit[3]?!... No Jew should return to Maytchet again – this Yizkor Book will be the only memory of our native home and of our dear Maytchet Jews, our parents, brothers, sisters, children, and friends. It will tell about the synagogues and houses of study in which the Jews of Maytchet worshipped and studied for many generations, and about the societal institutions and activists which exemplified the finest Jewish traits of charity and benevolence; about the youth organizations that dreamed and worked to build up a Jewish nation in a Jewish Land, and thanks to which we have indeed attained a strong, independent Israel in the land of our fathers. All, everything, will be perpetuated in the Yizkor Book that will even be a place for the ancestral graves, so that every Maytchet Jew throughout the entire world will be able to remember and weep on the day of the memorial and *yahrzeit...*

[Page 336]

A value cannot be placed on the words of the book, and blessed shall be the hands that have carried out this holy work, that is a worthy rectification and elevation for the souls of the holy victims of the unforgettable common grave, as well as for those who survive throughout the world, who will peruse through the pages of the Yizkor Book with holy trembling and remember their fine Jewish origins. Every Maytchet Jew should support this endeavor with writings and money, just as our forbears would write a letter at the celebration of the conclusion of writing a Torah scroll, in order to take advantage of the holy merit.

I hereby submit my writing and my support, and wish you and all of your collaborators a great blessing of "More power to you!"...

Translator's footnotes
1. Quite possibly the Majdanek Death Camp, although not completely obvious from the spelling of the original.
2. The Sabbath prior to the *Tisha Be'Av fast*, known as the most somber Sabbath of the year.
3. The accusation of Elijah the prophet to King Ahab after Ahab arranged the death of his neighbor Naboth in order to take over his field. See Kings I 21:19.

[Pages 337-342]

Maytchet Natives in Lithuania
During the Period of the Second World War
by Nachum Ben-Arie
Translated by Jerrold Landau

Before I begin to write a few things about the Jews of Maytchet who lived in the independent State of Lithuania and then in the Soviet Republic of Lithuania that was annexed to the Soviet Union, I will preface and describe in a few words the general era that served as an era of salvation for the Jews. During this era, many thousands of Jews were saved and reached safe shores at a time when the Second World War engulfed the world in its full fury. This saving of Jews was done with quiet and wisdom, in a similar manner to the era of the salvation of the Jews of Hungary during the period of the war (1944)[1], which had no small number of similarities.

When Poland was trampled at the beginning of the war, a stream of Jewish refugees began to move to Lithuania, which was an independent republic in those days. Among the refugees were many pioneers and Zionist youth group members who were organized in various party frameworks and many of whom lived in various *hachshara* [*aliya* preparation] *kibbutzim* throughout Poland. The passage from occupied Poland to independent Lithuania was carried out through a variety of means, both legal and illegal.

After the defeat of Poland in September 1939 and its partition between Germany and the Soviet Union that was arranged by the foreign minister of Germany (Von Ribbentrop) and the foreign minister of the Soviet Union (Molotov) eight days before the outbreak of the war, and which specified that Germany would receive the western portions of Poland while the Soviet Union would obtain the eastern portions; Vilna and its environs, among other places, fell into the hands of the Soviet Union. In October 1939, rumors spread through Poland that the Soviets were preparing to transfer the district of Vilna and adjacent regions to the government of Lithuania. Therefore, many Jewish refugees began to move to Vilna with the hope and belief that a neutral country such as Lithuania would serve as their gateway to the wide world. These rumors came to reality on October 27, 1939, when the Soviets transferred all the areas around Vilna to Lithuania and established a closed border between the area of Soviet occupation and Lithuania. The border line ran through the town of Radun[2] on the Soviet side and the town of Eishyshok (Eišiškės) on the Lithuania side. Thus, many Jewish refugees found themselves in independent Lithuania; some whom had arrived prior to the closing of the border, and others who had crossed the border illegally after the closing of the border.

[Page 338]

On Friday, September 1, 1939, when the Second World War began with the German invasion of Poland, I was in the town of Sławków in the district of Zagłębie in western Poland. There, I was a member of the Hamizrachi *Hachshara Kibbutz*, preparing for my *aliya* to the Land of Israel. A few days after the outbreak of the war, I, along with several other youths, joined the stream of refugees moving eastward. My aim was to reach my parents' home in Maytchet, and at the end of September, after many tribulations and after I stumbled into the German Army and later the Soviet Army along the way, I reached home.

Maytchet was then under Russian occupation, and, as a Zionist *chalutz*, I felt myself as a bird in a cage. Then, the rumors that were spreading through Poland about the transfer of the Vilna area and district to Lithuania reached me; and my father, may G-d avenge his blood, advised me to get in touch with my girlfriend – today my wife – who was then at her home in Kovel, and to go to Vilna together with her. Since I did not yet know about the organization of the *chalutzim* over the border, I hesitated. I considered the situation and came to the conclusion that in the end the Soviets would conquer the entire state of Lithuania, and our situation would then be even more difficult, since aside from being Zionists, we would be considered to be deserters. In the meantime, I worked to solidify the economic situation of our family, and I was accepted at a government courses to prepare workers for co-ops. However, in the latter half of December 1939, after completing the course, which had included no small number of segments on the doctrine of Stalin, concluded, I felt that my place is not with the Soviets, and I decided to do everything I could to leave Maytchet. At that time, rumors spread about sneaking across the border between Russia and independent Romania. Therefore, I decided to set out immediately for Kovel, and to decide together with my girlfriend how to proceed. Indeed, at the end of December I reached Kovel where a surprise was awaiting me: messengers came and informed us that my comrades from the *kibbutz* were gathering in Vilna, and there was a great deal of activity by the active members of the movement to sneak across the border to Vilna. These messengers gave my girlfriend an address in the city of Bialystok where, as had been said, we would be able to join with the organized members to cross the border to Vilna.

I remained in Kovel for one day as I deliberated and thought about the matter with my girlfriend. Leaving the city had to be done in secrecy. The separation from the family and leaving our parents during such a difficult time was a very heavy factor – and my girlfriend, despite that she had spent more than two years in a *hachshara kibbutz*, was still connected to her parents and her family. In addition, would we even reach our destination during such a disorderly time? After much deliberation, we received the blessings of her parents and set out. We waited all night at the Kovel railway station for the train to Bialystok. As we were waiting in the railway station we met a friend, also a native of Kovel, who had been with us in the *kibbutz* and with whom we had made the journey from the *kibbutz* to Kovel, primarily by foot, after the outbreak of the war. We told this friend about our plans and gave him the address in Bialystok. Indeed, he also arrived in that city a few days later, on his way to Vilna. My girlfriend's parents waited with us at the railway station, and when the train arrived toward morning, we pushed ourselves with difficulty onto the train and set out for Bialystok.

[Page 339]

In the afternoon of that day, we arrived in Bialystok and went to the address that we had. It became clear to us that this was the address of a female member of our movement. In her house, we met other members who had been together with us on the *hachshara kibbutz*, as well as members of other *kibbutzim*. They were happy to greet us when we arrived, and our arrival encouraged them and increased the hope that we would all succeed in crossing the border to Lithuania. The members were near despair after we waited a long time for the emissaries who were supposed to come from across the border to transfer additional groups, but were delayed in coming. After a few hours, a member arrived who also had been with us on the *kibbutz* and was also active in the smuggling operation. He told us of the many difficulties that had taken place in the last few days. It was hard to maintain contact, the emissaries did not return again from across the border, and it seems like crossing the border became impossible – in short, we were out of options. After we dissected the situation, we came to the decision to leave Bialystok immediately and set out for Lida, the closest city to the border. We immediately sent someone to the railway station to purchase tickets, and after we gathered all the members together, we went to the railway station in Bialystok. After a few hours of waiting, the train came and we travelled to Lida.

We reached that town in the morning hours, and went to a synagogue where most of the refugees had gathered. On the way to the synagogue, I saw from afar two girls from Maytchet, and it seems that they were in Lida for the same purpose that I had come to that city. However, since I did not want it to be known in town that I was close to the border, I evaded them so that they would not recognize me. In the synagogue, we again met a few members who had been with us in the *kibbutz*, and they were also happy about our arrival. All of them remained in the synagogue, whereas I along with an active member of the smuggling operation set out to determine the possibilities of crossing the border. Since we did not succeed in finding such possibilities, we decided to set out toward the border by foot to go to a town or village adjacent to the border, from where we would determine the possibilities of crossing the border. When we set out from Lida we met a farmer who was on the way from Lida to his home. In conversation with him, it became clear to us that his brother-in-law who lives with him smuggled people across the border. We joined up with the farmer and went by wagon to his house, which was 12 kilometers from Lida. His brother-in-law was not at home, for he had not yet returned from his nighttime "activities". We slept over at the farmer's house and the next morning we decided to return to Lida to bring the people, and we would all wait in the farmer's house until his brother-in-law returned.

Thus it was. We returned to Lida by foot, and took the rest of the members. We were a group of six males and two females. Another friend went with us to familiarize himself with the route so he would be able to utilize it a few days later, since he was waiting for his relatives who were supposed to arrive in Lida. That day was a wintery day – a typical end of December day. A thick snow fell, and we walked in single file with a distance between each person so that we would not be noticed. We reached the farmer's house and waited until nightfall, but his brother-in-law had not returned yet. Since the farmer was concerned about housing so many people in his house, he advised us to go to the house of another nearby farmer. A group of Jews were housed there, together with a Jewish border smuggler, who was a resident of the town of Eišiškes on the Lithuanian side of the border.

[Page 340]

This group had attempted to cross the border the previous night, but they did not succeed, due to a comb-out by the Red Army. We got in touch with the border smuggler, whose name was Shevach, and he agreed that we should accompany him – of course in return for a specified payment. I immediately gave him a sum of money up front, and we agreed that he would receive the remainder after we would cross the border.

That night, Shevach hired two sleds and we set out on the way. We passed through a forest and reached a certain place where he sent the wagon drivers and sleds back, and we continued on foot in single file. Along the way, we had to pass through the main road leading to the town of Radun, however we suddenly noticed horsemen of the Red Army going through the road. Therefore, we lay down in the snow and waited until the road was cleared of the horsemen. Then, we crossed the street and continued along our way until we arrived in the town of Eišiškes toward morning, tired and broken. We were brought to Shevach's house. He informed the people whom he had to inform, and the entire group of about 20 people dispersed to various houses. Two girls of our group were transferred that very day, which was a Friday, by public bus to Vilna. Of course, this transfer was made possible by the use of names and certificates of local girls. The men, I among them, were brought to Vilna on Saturday night by wagons.

Of course, we were not the only ones who arrived in Vilna. Hundreds of male and female *chalutzim* and other religious youths from chapters of Hechalutz, the Mizrachi movement, Hashomer Hadati, and Bnei Akiva in Poland gathered in that city, as well as religious youth from Germany who had been deported to Poland prior to the war due to their Polish origins. At that time, I remained in the *kibbutz* absorption center on Kiovska Street. After some time, institutions were activated, houses were rented, and all of the *chalutz* refugees were distributed according to their former group affiliations. Committees were chosen, and we attempted to enter into an orderly life. Additional members came as refugees also in January 1940, and all of them were absorbed into the *kibbutzim*. Of course, all of us were registered in the offices of the civic registry, as if we had arrived in Vilna before the day that it was transferred by the Soviets to the Lithuanians.

After we were divided up into various *kibbutzim* in Vilna, our common livelihood was made possible by various temporary jobs and by assistance from the American JOINT[3]. All of the refugees, without differentiation, received the same assistance. The JOINT organized communal kitchens for the solitary refugees, and distributed various provisions to the families and the *kibbutzim*. After four or five months, the government of Lithuania issued a directive, according to which some of the refuges had to leave Vilna and move to outlying cities. This fate befell me and other members, and we left Vilna. I joined a Jewish farm 12 kilometers from Kovno, where a *kibbutz* of our movement existed and we were employed in agricultural work and packing provisions that we received from Jewish suppliers in Kovno.

After a short time, in June 1940, Lithuania was annexed to the Soviet Union as a Soviet Republic. The regime changed and we succeeded in leaving the agricultural farm while there was still time. The group was separated, and we dispersed in small groups in the nearby town of Godlawo, (Garliava) a distance of seven kilometers from Kovno.

[Page 341]

Our group consisted of four males and one female. The males worked in Kovno. Every day, we walked or drove with saws and axes to Kovno, where we worked at cutting trees, whereas the female worked as a homemaker. Despite the breakup of the *kibbutzim* and the dispersal of their members to smaller groups, a constant communication was maintained between the groups and the central institutions. We, the members of the *kibbutzim*, prepared ourselves even for the possibility of persecution due to Zionism, as well as for oppression and imprisonment. The members of the headquarters prepared plans for the eventuality that we might have to go underground. Group heads were appointed, and means of communication were prepared, including a secret writing code for the case of need.

We remained in Lithuania for one year. The first half was in independent Lithuania, and the second half was in the Lithuanian Soviet Republic. During the year, the activities of the Offices of the Land of Israel in Kovno increased. Various central personalities rose to the leadership of the office, including Dr. Zerach Warhaftig[4]. People worked through all means available in order to obtain *aliya* permits to the land of Israel, entry visas to various countries throughout the world, and other transit visas. I recall that I went to the Japanese consulate in Kovno and left with an entry permit (or transit permit – I do not recall exactly which) to Japan. Hundreds and thousands of refugees did as I did. The Dutch consulate also placed its stamp on passports, permitting the passage to various islands[5]. At a time of need, we had our own "consul" who issued passports, visas and permits of various sorts. All this was done in haste until the set date when all of the foreign embassies and consulates in Kovno were ordered to close their offices and move to Moscow. I was sent to the British consol and received a passport with a permit for *aliya* to the Land of Israel on virtually the final day.

After the period of the issuance of passports, visas, entry permits and transit permits ended, the principal period of obtaining transit permits through the Soviet Union began. This period was a very difficult and demanding period. We did not act as individuals, for there was no possibility of us working as isolated individuals. To our happiness and good fortune, Dr. Warhaftig stood at the helm of the movement that acted with exceptional dedication, and whose levelheadedness was businesslike and logical. I will mention the following story as an example: We had to bring the list of candidates for *aliya*, whose names had been certified by the British consulate of Kovno, to the central office of the Soviet underground guard in Moscow in order to receive the permit. There were leaders who were concerned about bringing lists of names to such a dangerous place, but Dr. Warhaftig acted in a levelheaded manner and understood that daringness and bravery were both required, and that if the list of candidates were not presented, it was clear that we would not be able to leave. Even if we were to give in the list, there was a possibility that we would not receive the exit permit or transit permits through the Soviet Union. Finally, we decided to take the risk and present the list of candidates who had been approved for *aliya*, and to request the transit permits and exit permits. We also added an incidental note that explained that no benefit would accrue to the Soviet Union from people such as ourselves if we would remain and not be permitted to leave.

At the end of December 1940, I received a summons, along with other refugee members, to appear at the Soviet secret police station in Kovno. I remained in the station all night, since many people were summoned there. My turn came toward morning, and I received the awaited transit permit and exit permit. We immediately carried out all the necessary actions, and we set out to Moscow under the auspices of the government Intourist Soviet tourist agency. We spent two nights at the splendid Hotel Moskovski in Moscow. In that city, we obtained a transit pass through Turkey from the Turkish consulate, and we then set out by train to Odessa via Kiev.

[Page 342]

The train trip from Kovno to Odessa via Moscow and Kiev took four or five days, of which we remained in Moscow for two days. Throughout this brief time we were able to see and get to know a bit the "Garden of Eden" in which we lived, and to our dismay, in which our Jewish brethren still live. This brought us to many tears, of sadness and joy together, in the isolated cases where we had the possibility of revealing to them that we were on our way toward the Land of our Fathers. We were witness to several confessions and expressions of true longing for the Land, which welled up from the depths of the hearts. I recall that at one railway station between Kiev and Odessa, an older woman boarded the train with a basket in her hand containing cheese cookies that she sold the passengers. I was convinced that this woman, whose head was covered in a thick winter kerchief, was not Jewish, and therefore we consulted among ourselves in Yiddish whether we would be able to purchase cookies from her lest they not be Kosher. To our great surprise, the woman understood our language, and when she found out that there were Jews in front of her, she burst into tears and told us that she was also a fellow Jew who kept Kosher, and that her husband was a *shochet* [ritual slaughterer]. She added, "I wish that I could also join you with my family." In a parenthetical statement I feel the duty to add and note that her words are accurate even today, thirty years after that meeting, and that the truth of these words applies to the vast majority if not all of the Jews of the Soviet Union

When we arrived at the Odessa railway station, representatives of the Intourist company were waiting for us. They transferred us directly to the port. After the usual inspection, we boarded a Russian ship called Svantia, and set sail for Koshta[6]. This board sailed in a direct line to Odessa-Koshta and we learned later that other members were also transported on the same ship. We spent a week in Koshta, and then set out by train for Syria and Lebanon, and arrived in Beirut. From there, we continued by bus, and arrived in Haifa on January 6, 1941. There, the head of the Aliya Department of the Jewish Agency of that time, Mr. Moshe Shapira, greeted us, blessed us heartily, and wished us success in our new life in our old-new Land.

This episode of *aliya* to the Land from Lithuania was one of the most splendid chapters in the book of torments that our present generation endured. It was enabled through the faithfulness and uprightness of people dedicated to the public, and was carried out without noise and fanfare – but rather the opposite – quietly and discreetly. Therefore, this episode was not followed by bitter outcomes. It is fitting that the people who worked at organizing this *aliya* be given appropriate publicity in this episode of salvation – publicity that was not given to them to this day.

Translator's footnotes
1. Referring to the saving of Hungarian Jews by Swedish diplomat Raoul Wallenberg.
2. There is a footnote in the text here, as follows: This town is known as the residence of Rabbi Yisrael Meir HaKohen of holy blessed memory (1838-1933), the author of the book Chofetz Chaim.
3. The Joint Distribution Committee.
4. Later a Knesset member in Israel. See http://en.wikipedia.org/wiki/Zerach_Warhaftig
5. Dutch colonies such as Indonesia, Curacao, etc.
6. Seemingly Constanta, Romania.

[Pages 343-345]

Maytchet Refugees from Maytchet in Vilna
by Isaac Movshovits (Nir David)
Translated by Jerrold Landau

In 1938, I set out for *hachshara* in the Rovno *Kibbutz* under the auspices of Hashomer Hatzair, and I remained there from that time and following the outbreak of the war. The following people of Maytchet were together with me in the *Kibbutz*: Yitzchak Movshovits, Reuben Rabinovitz, Reuben Bitenski, Moshe Vilkormirski, Berl Kroshinski, Vikna Belski, Chana Boretcky, and Chanan Zukovitzki. At the outbreak of the war, the Soviets occupied the district of Rovno, and the Germans occupied the western district of Poland. The *Hachshara Kibbutzim* in the west escaped to the Soviet district, and the local *Kibbutzim* absorbed them and even concerned themselves with providing them with work and food.

Thus was the situation for about three months, until December 1939. Throughout this time, we searched for ways to leave the Soviet occupation area in order to go to the Land. A few went to the Romanian border, and a few even succeeded in crossing and continuing on to the Land, but many were caught and sent to prison. As is known, the Russians annexed Vilna to Lithuania, which was still considered to be an independent country. We saw this as a viable possibility for leaving the country, and groups of *chalutzim* began to stream in the direction of Vilna. With this we should say that the Lithuanian border was open until October 27, 1939, and anyone who arrived before that date crossed in complete freedom; but after that date, we were already forced to "steal" across the border, with all the dangers involved in that.

In Vilna, the refugees were organized by Zionist party, and the *kibbutz* members organized by their units. These organizations suffered from difficult birth pangs due to the growing number of refugees who gathered there, and whom the city could not absorb and sustain. However, the JOINT filled the void, and offered them great support. If this was not sufficient, the Lithuanian government did not at all regard the large concentration of refugees in Vilna in a positive light, and made plans to disperse them throughout the entire country of Lithuania under the auspices of population dispersal. As a means of coercion to carry out the plan, they utilized the law that forbade refugees from working, so they forced us to suffice ourselves with chopping trees and sanitation work. On the other hand, Vilna was a major Jewish city with many cultural institutions, and during our free time, we found a warm corner to read. We were also happy to use the Jewish bathhouse for free, for the purposes of cleanliness and to warm up.

In March 1940, all of the former members of the Rovno *Kibbutz* moved to the outlying city of Wilkomir. There, we rented a large building and began to organize. We founded a carpentry shop for men, a sewing shop for women, and we also cultivated a vegetable garden. Chanan Zukovitzki who had completed a degree in agriculture in Ludomir, was responsible for overseeing the vegetable garden, and we were almost able to sustain ourselves from independent work. A tragedy occurred in the month of June – Moshe Vilkormirski jumped into the river and broke his elbow. We took him to the hospital in Vilna where he died after a month. This sad event had a strong influence on the *Kibbutz*.

[Page 344]

At that time, Lithuania was annexed to the body of the Soviet Union, but it retained a certain degree of economic independence. The Russians would send their soldiers there from the front to recover, and they confiscated one of our two houses for that purpose. In that manner, we lived next to them for several months. There were many Jews among them. We often held stormy debates with them on the topic of the situation of Jews in the Soviet Union versus the Russian goal of liquidating Jewish schools and other institutions.

The Russians slowly got organized in the area and began to confiscate the large businesses. The belt around our activities began to tighten more and more, and we were finally advised by the local Communist committee to join them as an organized group. As a reaction to this, the center decided to disband the small groups, so that each could exist in an independent fashion.

In the spring of 1941, the border between Lithuania and Russian Poland became friendly and free, and it was possible to move between the two countries, so I decided to arrange a visit home. I arrived in Mickiewicze without any difficulty, and visited with my parents and my family. I remained there for three or four days, and returned to Wilkomir out of fear of difficulties with the law. When I returned, the eve of the outbreak of the Great War was already felt in the air, and the Russian armies began to move in the direction of the German border. In a lightning quick consultation, we decided to liquidate our organization and return home via Vilna, but the war advanced in a sudden fashion, and there was no longer way of return.

We left Wilkomir in the direction of Russia. Two Russian autos took us up along the way, and we continued to the Russian border via Latvia. There we had a bad accident when one of our cars turned over. We lost our path as a result. Some were wounded and taken to the hospital. My wife and I returned to the border town of Shebezh, where they transferred us to trains and transported us to the depths of Russia. The Germans pursued us, bombed the roads, and make the escape difficult, until we stopped in a *kolkhoz*[1] and somehow managed to maintain ourselves. After we recovered a bit from the difficulties of the journey, we began to search for a different place close to the border, and the lot fell upon Toshkent.

I reached Toshkent in August 1941, and from there, we were transferred to a *kolkhoz* in the region of Namangan. Since we were the first refugees, they received as guests. At first, we worked with them in a sewing workshop, and then I set myself up as electrician in a dam building business. After some time, we were drafted into a work group in Tscheliabinsk. There I got sick and was returned to Namangan to recover. After I recovered from my illness, I was transferred to Samarkand where I met Reuben Rabinovitz. We also received letters from Chanan Zukovitzki, who was in the Lithuanian Army and worked as a watchman on a medical train. We eventually stopped receiving letters, and found out that he had died in an attack on the train. We also received information that Berl Kroshinski, who had served in the Red Army, was wounded and freed in Ashchabad on the Iranian border.

[Page 345]

I was still in Samarkand at the end of the war. When Poland was liberated, it was possible to enlist in the Polish Army and thereby reach Poland. However, in the interim, we received letters from Nieśwież, and we discovered that my wife's brothers and sisters had survived there. We set out for Nieśwież, and then moved the entire family to Lódz, Poland. There, a movement of "smuggling" was taking place, and the end of the transports seemed to be on the horizon. We were transferred to Germany, where I met Vikna Belski. From there, we made *aliya* to the Land with a certificate in the year 1947.

With all the difficulties and tribulations that overtook the members of our *kibbutz*, each on his own path, hidden strands remained between the members, who returned and reorganized themselves in Nir David.

Translator's footnote

1. A Soviet collective farm. See http://en.wikipedia.org/wiki/Kolkhoz

[Page 346]

Partisans and the Jews in the Forests of Maytchet
by Mark Dvorjetski
Translated by Ariel Dvorjetski and Jerrold Landau

(Meitshet, Meichet, Moichet, Molchadz) was one of the "Jewish towns" of western Byelorussia, that is to say in the eastern district of Poland prior to the Second World War.

The stories of the destruction of the community of Maytchet, the underground movement, the escape to the forests and the participation in the partisans - are very similar to all the neighboring towns near forests in this area of Byelorussia. The town was located next to the Lida-Baranovichi railway line, and was therefore one of the small stops where refugees from Poland settled during their escape from the German armies who had conquered the western sector of Poland.

When this town was conquered by the German armies, it was surrounded by concentrations of Jews and ghettoes: Navahrudak, Navajelnia and Dvorets from the north, Haradzets and the Koldichevo Camp[i] from the east, Baranovichiand Slonim from the south, and Kozlovshchina and Zhetl from the west. All of these centers of Jewish concentration were in a 30-50 kilometer radius of the area. It was also surrounded by various partisan units: Tzorani on the east, Grozny on the north, Soborov, the unit of Dr. Yechiel Atlas, The Povaida (Victory) brigade of Bulek, the Orlianski (Burba-Mavek) brigade, and Kaplinski's brigade on the west.

Maytchet was surrounded by the Maytchet Forests that were known for their beauty, the Horki and Svrotova forests, the Thick Forest (Pushcha Lipichan). The Thick forest (Pushcha Lipichan), Ruda-Jaworska and Dobrobchina forests were about 40 kilometers away, and the Puscha Naliboki was about 70-80 kilometers northeast. There were many partisan units as well as a Jewish family camp headed by Tuvia Bielski.

As a result, the town found itself on a crossroads of the partisan groups. With time, the fact of the existence of the partisan units became known to the Jews of Maytchet thanks to the militant acts of the partisans that had a loud echo throughout the entire population of the area. However, the severe isolation of the Jewish population at all points of concentration prevented the possibility of maintaining contact with the Jewish populations in the areas of settlement, and of course with the partisan units in the forests. However, at a time of straits, when an aktion was impending - that is to say, a partial or complete destruction of the Jewish population of Maytchet, as well as during the period when the murderous deeds were being carried out (as they were being transported to the pits, or during the shooting at the pits), a definitive possibility existed for those willing to risk their lives, to escape to the forests of the region. We should also realize that a certain number of village Jews (Yishuvniks) who knew their way around the forests lived in the areas around the town.

[Page 347]

The escape to the forests brought with it several difficulties. The Jews with families would go out to the forests to search for refuge, along with their wives, parents and children. In general, they did not have weapons. They would set up hiding places (bunkers) in the forests, and would sustain themselves from what they found in the fields, or what they obtained from going out to the neighboring villages to request food or to engage in barter in exchange for clothing, vessels, valuable, and money. These Jews were known as the "Bunker People", however, they are also called "People of the Family Camps" in Holocaust literature. By going out to the villages of the district to obtain food, they "exposed" themselves, and caused slander among the farmers of the region and German attacks in order to liquidate the "Bunker Jews" (for example, the liquidation of the Jewish bunkers in the Svortova Forest). The youth would begin to form clandestine groups in Maytchet itself as well as in the settlements of the area (such as in Meidvidzina) in order to forge contact with the partisans of the area and to obtain weapons. With time, this would cause them to be noticed by the independent partisan groups, and later, they would be able to join the fighting groups as partisans.

These two forms of life in the forests were at best unstable, and at worst vagrant. Everyone who went out to the forest would at the beginning live a life of secrecy in the forest without contact with a partisan group (that is, they would be a "Bunker Person"). They would only turn into a partisan after joining a partisan unit. They were "temporary bunker people," but there were adult Jews with wives and younger and older children, who were never accepted into a partisan unit. They remained in the forests in a permanent fashion until the end of the war or until they fell into the hands of the Germans or a neighboring enemy population. These were the "permanent bunker people." There were also cases where a Jewish partisan would leave his unit due to the anti-Semitic atmosphere and go out to the forests to search for a more comfortable unit. In the meantime, he would turn into a "bunker person."

Most of the bunker people perished at the hands oaf the Germans and their accomplices. Sporadic news from these bunkers in the forests reached us from those still left in the town. We can surmise that the number of bunkers in the forest was larger than what is known to us.

The Jewish refugees who reached Maytchet, both from Greater Poland and the Jewish centers in the region, played a significant role in Jewish life of Maytchet during the time when the eastern sector of Poland was occupied by the Soviets following the Ribbentrop-Molotov agreement, as well as during the Nazi occupation. Also, a number of Jews moved from Baranovichi to Maytchet, for life was relatively easier there for some time. At the beginning of the winter of 1941, a command was issued by the German army that all Jews in the small towns must move to larger Jewish communities. At that time, many Jews from the villages of the area arrived in Maytchet.

[Page 348]

As heard from Moshe Korn, the Jewish Council (Judenrat) of Maytchet was composed of five people, including two refugees: Erlich of Czestochowa who was appointed by the Germans as the chairman of the Judenrat, and Apelbaum of Suwalki. The rest of the members of the Judenrat were Jews from Maytchet: Yechezkel Ravitz, Leibel Gilerovitz (the wheat merchant), Chaim Shlovski (butcher), (according to Trunk, Yosef Korn was a member of the Judenrat). We also find the name of a refugee who came to Maytchet from Suwalki, Misha Medlinski, among the list of Jewish partisans of Maytchet. He later organized a fighting unit in the Svarotova Forests. On the other hand, a significant number of Jews of Maytchet were hauled to work or fled to Baranovichi, Dvorets, Koldychevo, Lesnaya,, and went on to the partisans in the forests from those places.

The Jewish community of Maytchet endured two partial actions, and then a final aktion that decisively liquidated the community.

The first aktion took place on the 27th of Shvat, 5702 (February 14, 1942). Eighteen Jews of Maytchet (according to others, 22 Jews) were chosen by the local gendarmes and hauled to the other side of the flour mill, at the place of the coal making plant (smoliarnia), and were murdered there.

The second aktion took place on the 18th of Sivan 5702 (June 3, 1942). The approximately 200 people who were chosen to die were taken out to Bordokovshchina via the village of Horodishtch and murdered there

The third aktion, which was the liquidation aktion, took place from the 1st to the 3rd of Av 5702 (July 15-17, 1942). The Germans concentrated all the Jews and chose approximately 300 healthy people, who were hauled to the area around Baranovichi. They were put to work together with the Jews who had been deported from the city of Lida, to build a forced labor camp in Koldychevo. The rest were taken out to be murdered in Chwojnik near Maytchet - men, women, elders, and children. Before that, they were ordered to dig large pits that served as their graves.

Regarding the Forest Jews (partisans and bunker people) from Maytchet, the underground cells, the participation of the people of Maytchet in the partisan units and partisan battles, the acts of treason of the anti-Semitic neighbors, the acts of revenge against the murderers of Jews, and of the partisan heroes in Maytchet who fell in battle activities - there are numerous echoes from several articles in the Book of Maytchet, in the "Lexicon of Bravery," in the story of Moshe Kahanovitz, in various other books, and in various testimonies relating to that period. Often, these testimonies are missing dates and places, and there are even names of people who are called by their local nickname (for example Moshe Diechs instead of Moshe the son of Deicha Korostovski, Konia Shlovski instead of Elkana Shlovski).

I wish to bring here a summary of the Jewish problems in the forests of Maytchet as describe in all the various testimonies and publications:

Several of the survivors describe the attempts at defense on the night of the liquidation aktion (July 15, 1942).

[Page 349]

At a time when the Germans surrounded the town, the members of the independent defense organization attempted to break through the siege. However, they ran into heavy fire from the Germans, and about ten youths fell. The only survivor was NoachMordkovski (today in the United States)[1].

M. Korn also writes about that night: The underground people had three guns that were distributed to the former soldiers Noach Mordukovski, Yaakov Margolin, and Chaim Shlovski. A group of Maytcheters wished to break through the forces, but they encountered cross-fire. Noach Mordukovski was only able to shoot one shot with his gun, because he had no bullets. The other guns did not have bullets, and their bearers fell with useless guns in their hands.

Most of these that fled from that group were killed. Only nine people survived[2].

Khonan Shmulevicz tells about the armed group that was organized in Maytchet in the summer of 1942 before the great slaughter. Ruben Bitenski, Noach Mordukovski, Meir Ravitz, and he himself, Khonan Shmulevicz belonged to that group. They had a gun with 50 bullets that they received from a gentile friend, Vitia Kozovei. They lay down with the gun in a field next to the town on the night before the liquidation. Many other people from the town lay down with them that night. When they sensed that they were surrounded by the Germans, they wished to break through the siege with gunshots. However, most of them fell on the spot, and only a few (ten or twelve) escaped. Khonan Shmulevicz succeeded in jumping into the river and hiding with his friend Kozovei. Another Jewish family was there - Tzira Kaplan (Ravitz), her husband and their children[3]). Kaplan eventually joined the "Grozni "Otriad."

(Apparently the three preceding testimonies relate to the same event.)

They hid there for about two months, and went out to the forests from time to time to search for Jews. He, (Khonan Shmulevicz), Avraham Medlinski, and Elkhona Shlovski made contact with the Zolotov Otriad. The members of the Otriad did not accept them as members of the Otriad, but did help them get organized, and also gave them a commander named Petke[4].

At the time of the aktion of the liquidation of the Maytchet Ghetto, Ziml Stolovitzki went out to the Horki Forest and organized a partisan unit of 60 Jews of Maytchet. They killed two anti-Semitic Nazi spies, in whose pockets were found certificates stating that they served in the Nazi police[5]. The Nazis attacked Ziml's camp in October 1942. Twelve people, including Ziml Stolovitzki, were killed after a stubborn battle.

[Page 350]

Two testimonies, one from Khonan Shmulevicz, and the second from Moshe Ravitz, tell of a group of Jewish partisans who were organized in the Svorotova Forests.

Moshe Ravitz tells that the organizer of the group was Yitzchak Lochovitzki. Among others, the following people were members of the group: Yehoshua Zlotnik, Avraham Lublinski, Freidel Margolin, Chania (Khonan) Shmulevicz, Mordechai-Leib Shmulevicz, Moshe Ravitz, and Elkhona (Konia) Shlovsky. Those active in the group included Abrasha Hanelis (the son of Yaakov), Yitzchak Lakhovitzki, and Elkhona Shlovsky. They would go out to the villages of the area and obtain food and weapons, either "willingly or by force"[6].

Khonan Shmulevicz tells of a group that was organized in the Svorotova Forests, and gives the names of its participants as Abrasha Hanelis, Yitzchak Lakhovitzki, and he himself, Khonan Shmulevicz. He also gives the names of other members of that group: Meirim Boretcky, Meir Hanelis, Zukovitzki, Melech Zukerfop, and David Stein[7].

Apparently, both of the above were describing the same group, but separate activities that were carried out by that group, such as the liquidation of the police station, the removal of the railway tracks, etc.

From Svorotova, the group moved to the Horki Forest where there was a large group of Jews with weapons, organized by Asher Shushan. Other Jews of Maytchet who had escaped from the Dvorets Ghetto were also located there. In the meantime, two partisans who had left a different Otriad joined Petka, and began to plot against the Jews. After taking secret council, they decided to remove them from the path. Meir Hanelis and Yitzchak Lakhovitzki carried this out[8].

A Jewish underground group was set up in the village of Medvinotsya near Maytchet. Among its members were Avraham (Abrasha) Hanelis (Ben Yaakov), Avraham (Abrasha) Hanelis (Ben Baruch), Meir Hanelis, Itzchak Lakhovitzki, and David Ravitz. After about two months, this group was exposed, and policemen appeared suddenly. During the battle between them, Abrasha Hanelis (Ben Baruch) was injured severely and he died of his wounds. Itzchak Lakhovitzki was also captured. He was imprisoned in the Maytchet jail and sentenced to death. When he was being hauled to be put to death in Horodistch via the village of Shnicheshnitz, Lakhovitzki succeeded in escaping from the police[9].

[Page 351]

This was an underground movement which apparently didn't have time to connect with other partisans from the region. According to M. Ravitz, some connections with this underground movement were with two ladies from Maytchet that worked at the Nazi police office, Feigala Boretsky and Chana Belski.

After the Aktion in Maytchet (July 1942), refugee fighters were gathered at the Svortva Forests. They were about 45 people. They established two bunkers. In one bunker roughly 30 people hid, including six who escaped from the Baranovich Ghetto. In the second bunker about 15 people hid, (it should be understood that among these people were Issac Lakhovitski , Moshe Ravitz and others who were mentioned before[10]).

A partisan group from Ruda-Jaworska came to the villages of Svorotva to pick up food, while being chased by the police, who found the first bunker (which had about 30 people). After a bloody fight all the bunker people were killed. Only one woman survived, Tsira Ravitz, who was hidden by a Christian acquaintance, and afterwards moved with the help of Jewish Partisans to the Otriad (Partisan Group) of Tuvia Bieslki[10].

After the murder of the members of the first bunker, the people of the second bunker were separated. Several people moved to Dvorets and joined a work camp (among them Freidel Margolin, Zlata Kaplan with her children and others). Some time after that, the camp was liquidated and all the people of the camp perished. Only a small number of people were able to escape. Moshe Ravitz and Efrim Dubkovski stayed in order to wait for the Partisans from Ruda-Jaworska, who came to pick up food and because of them the police searched the forest and demolished the first bunker. The partisans let them join their group and gave them rifles with bullets. When they reached the location of the Otriad, they were attacked by a large German force. A big battle developed and all the partisans from the surrounding area participated, including the unit that was led by Dr. Yechezkel Atlas. He was critically wounded in this battle and died[10].

According to Moshe Ravitz' account, after this battle, the command decided to separate the forces into groups of 20 people who operated through a central command but were granted freedom of action and planning.[11]

[Page 352]

We will devote here some words to the unit of Dr. Atlas, which operated near the Szczara River, about 40 kilometers from Maytchet, and in which some of the Maytchet people who participated in the critical battle in which Dr. Atlas died.

Dr. Yechezkel (Heniek, known by others as Yechiel) Atlas was a legendary name within the Jewish partisan movements in the Byelorussian forests, and he is mentioned in many testimonies and articles. Dr. Altas was born in Rawa-Mazowiecka (Warsaw

Region), in 1913. In 1938 he graduated from the University of Milan as a physician (M.D.) and returned to Poland. After the war began, he escaped with his parents and sister to Lvov (which was occupied by the Soviets), from there to Slonim, and finally settled down at the town of Kozlovschina (about 13 kilometers from Maytchet). In the beginning of Spring 1942 the German perpetrated a massacre in the town and he was transferred as a physician to the village of Wielka Wola, on the River Szczara. After the massacre at the nearby town of Drohichin (26 July 1942), he went to the forests with a young Jewish group and organized them into a Jewish Fighter Group, who was led by Boris Bulat[ii], a Commander of a Soviet partisan battalion. Dr. Atlas and his group participated in many battles and revenge actions, and his name was a symbol of the Jewish fighter throughout all the Byelorussian forests. He fell down in a battle on 5 of December 1942. The unit continued to bear his name even after his death[12].

Moshe Korn tells about groups of youths that were organized in Maytchet, to go out to the forests and join the partisans. He took his mother and brother and went out to the forest. There he met with Litman Litowarski and his sisters[iii], Zelda Gilerowicz, the Shoshan brothers from the village of Dokrowa, and Vita, the daughter of the pharmacist Jacob Dvorjetski[13].

In one of the forests he found Avraham Kaplan, Fraydel Margolin, of the Mlishinski family, Noah Mordukovski and Jacob Shmulevicz[13].

He finally joined the Grozni Battalion, and was destined to fight alongside Baruch Lewin. He succeeded to cross the Neiman River under conditions of mortal danger, and bring back reports from the other side. He was rewarded for excellence for this.[13].

[Page 353]

Mina Levin (Gorski) tells about another group of the Forests Jews from Maytchet. She lived in the village of Ivankovichi (10 kilometers from Maytchet). They remained in the village until 1942. In February the Germans concentrated all the Jews from all the villages in the town Mush, near Baranovich. On Saturday, 19 of Tamuz (July 4, 1942), all the people were deported along with the local Jews, about 1,200 in number, and murdered[14].

Ten of them were sent as farmers to the Paszkowcze farm to work in its fields. They worked in the farm for about half a year. On July 16, 1942 they escaped to the Balushni Forests near Slonim. The ten people (including the Gorski family) remained in the forest for about a week and then separated. The Gorski family (the father, the son Tuvia, and the daughter Mina) wandered around the forests, went out at nights to search for food at other farmers, and lived in a bunker. That was the way they lived for that period till July 9, 1944, the liberation day of that area from the German[15].

Revenge Action on a Farmer from Dukrowo

The Maytchet partisans carried out some acts of revenge upon non-Jews that harassed Jews, robbed them, murdered them, or transferred them to the Germans. There was a goal in those actions to frighten anti-Semites, in order to stop them from perpetrating the acts of murder and hatred.

We already described earlier the revenge upon two partisans who joined the "Paetke."

Khonan Shmulevicz tells that his mother and other family members went to the village of Dukrowo to seek a shelter with the Shoshan group (see above). One of the farmers captured them and transferred them to the German authorities who murdered them. Abrasha Hanelis, Asher Shoshan, Litman Litowarski and others decided to kill the farmer as a punishment. They took him from his house and shot him. Later they burnt the houses and granaries of all those in Dukrowo who worked for the Germans[16].

Act of Revenge on a Murderer from Maytchet

The secretary of the "Gemeine" (The Town council) and the mayor ("Woyot") and his son were capturing the Jews who escaped the slaughter in Maytchet, robbing them and transferring them to the German gendarme. The Jewish partisans in the surrounding area (survivors of the town of Maytchet and Dvorets, who were gathered in the Horki Forests) decided to carry out a revenge action, to kill the secretary and his family members, in order to show the farmers in the area there is a Jewish presence that takes revenge on the murderers of Jews.

The operation was carried out at night on July 25, 1942. A group of Jewish partisans approached the home of the secretary, set the home on fire and began to shoot through the windows of the burning house. As a result of this revenge action, the secretary of the town as well his family members were killed. Only a 5 year old girl survived by jumping out a window.

[Page 354]

One of the main activists in operation was Moshe Daychs, one of those who escaped the slaughter in Maytchet, (as I was told by Mr. Margolin from Maytchet, his name was Moshe Korostovski, and was called Daychs, in memory of his mother, Daycha[17].)

Act of Revenge on the family members of Police commander

Olasik Wola was the police commander in Horodishtch near Maytchet. He transferred Jews for death to the Germans. On April 1942 a group a young Jewish people from Maytchet worked in farm in Wrodokowszyna between Maytchet and Horodishtch. The farm manager was Grynwecki (cousin of Olasik Wola). In the night, young Jews from Maytchet captured him and killed him and his assistant. Among the assassins were: Moshe Margolin, Feigala Boretsky, and Chana Belski[18].

Olasik the police commander in Horodishtch, and Sasha Masaj the Maytchet Commander were known for their ruthless actions against the Jews.

Masaj was arrested after the war, brought to trial before a military court in Baranovich, and sentenced to the death penalty by shooting.

The Judenrat in Maytchet and the Underground Movement

We don't have credible testimonies about the Judenrat approach to the underground movement in the Maytchet Ghetto. What did he know about that? Did he oppose the movement or bless it? We found only a few words that the Holocaust researcher, Y. Trunk says that he read a testimony about the fact that the Judenrat member Yosef Korn came during the night before the massacre to the witness (who didn't spend the night at his home as he was afraid of being jailed), and alerted him about the forthcoming danger. He advised the young people not to sleep that night and be prepared for any action "if something begins"[19].

[Page 355]

In the testimony it was described that Moshe Daychs was apparently sent by the Judenrat in Maytchet to buy weapons in the villages (Moshe Korn).

Sabotage Attempts on the Railway Lines near Maytchet

Attempts to perpetrate acts of sabotage on the railway lines in the area of Maytchet in order to derail trains were not infrequent.

Sh. Borenstein, Munia Rubalski, Asher Bigdosh, Berek, Yisrael Karpavski, and Avraham Lebkovitz attempted an act of sabotage on the Maytchet-Novojelnja railway line on October 24, 1942. However they arrived there during a time when no trains were passing by (according to the people of the area, this was for two weeks). They waited two more days for a train, then left those railway lines and transferred to an action on the Baranovich-Lida railway line[20].

On the other hand, we are aware of a successful sabotage action on the Maytchet railway line carried out by ten partisans, including Yaakov Granchok, on August 1943. The objective succeeded. The train was derailed, and those who carried out the act were later decorated with the "Warrior of the Homeland" (See what is written about Y. Granchok later on).

A Partisan Child from Maytchet

Shmuel Borenstein, who was a partisan in the unit of Dr. Yechezkel Atlas, tells in his story about a ten-year-old child from Maytchet who became a partisan. From the article we can determine that the meeting with the child took place between October 20 and November 7 1942:

Late one night, we passed through some village, and suddenly a small voice of a child called after us, "Partisans, wait!" We stopped. A small child of about ten years old stood on the road. Even though a heavy autumn rain was falling and the cold was very harsh, the child was barefoot and almost naked. He was shivering.

"What do you want, child," I asked.

"I want to go with you," answered the child.

The child that we took with us stood frightened next to the door. I called him to the table. The child studied us with great interest. An expression of surprise could be seen in his large, black eyes.

"You are Jews?" asked the child. "I am also a Jew!" He approached the table with unsure steps. These words from the child frightened us. Only now as we looked at his face with the light of the oil lamp could we see that his face was that of a Jewish child.

David was the name of the child who was a candidate to be a partisan. He was from the town of Maytchet. He was miraculously saved from the slaughter perpetrated by the Germans in that town a few months previously. David fled at that time to one of the villages in the area that he knew. The farmers fed him for some time, and he tended to their cows in return. All of his relatives perished. David suddenly became an adult who was forced to concern himself with his livelihood. At first he found some sort of sustenance, but his situation worsened from day to day. The Germans threatened anyone who hid Jews with the death penalty, and David began to wander from town to town. The farmers chased him away, and the shepherd lads threw stones at him.

[Page 356]

One day, David realized by chance that there were people fighting against the Germans, and they were called partisans. From that time, he attempted to make contact with those people in order to join them. He would wander between the villages during the day, getting a morsel of bread from here or there, after pleading. At night he would stalk the roadways waiting for the partisans to pass by. The child did not imagine at all that any Jews were still alive. How great was his surprise when he realized that those partisans were Jews.

We fed the child. He was very hungry, and it had been some time since he had eaten a satisfying meal.

We continued along our way. I covered the child with my coat and held him on my laps. He grabbed on to me strongly and fell asleep. After a short time, we arrived in our district. We met some of our friends. We told them about everything that happened to us and gave them our treasure, Davidka.

We finally succeeded in somehow escaping the trap... We finally arrived at our place. Before the camp, the person standing on guard was - our Davidka. The child held the gun, double his size, with great importance. Next to him stood Yekutiel Chmelnitzki, who treated him like his own child...[21].

* * *

From what is brought down above, we see the era of revolt and attempts of Jewish uprising in one of the Jewish towns of Byelorussia.

Revolutionary groups arose in Maytchet itself and the nearby villages. It was very difficult to obtain weapons, and the partisan units did not want to take on new members without weapons.

Many people from Maytchet escaped to the forests, especially before, during and after the *aktions*. The escapees scattered in all the forests of the area. The armed youths would finally succeed in joining partisan units. The old people and those who had to care for wives, parents and children would be left without a partisan framework, and would seek refuge in the forests. They would build "bunkers" there and go out to the farmers of the area to beg for food as a gift or as a barter exchange.

The acts of revenge carried out against the murderers of the area instilled fear upon the farmers and prevented additional acts of murder of Jews.

[Page 357]

Many of the partisans, both natives of Maytchet and those who were in Maytchet during the wartime, were singled out for praise by partisan decorations for acts of bravery. Many of them fell as heroes in battle.

Maytchet Jews who Fell in Partisan Battles

I will now include several brief biographies of partisans from Maytchet or who were active in Maytchet who fell during the course of carrying out their partisan duties. The material was culled from the "Lexicon of Bravery," by looking through the sources mentioned in the bibliographic list at the end of the article:

Meirim Boretcky

He was born in the town of Matychet in 1914. He went out to the forest on April 15, 1942. He joined a partisan unit which later became the Grozny Unit under the leadership of Boris Grozny, a Red Army man who escaped from German captivity. Since he knew the area very well, he assisted greatly in gathering weapons from the population. He and two other Jews were guides for three units, Grozny, Zolotov, and Soborov, which attacked the army stationed in Maytchet (August 1942).

He participated in acts of ambush and derailing trains. He would assist Jews who were not yet organized in units with food, clothing, and weapons. He fell in battle on June 17, 1943 during the large search in the forest of Naliboki, when he attempted to break through the enemy encirclement and cross the Brozka River. His friends found his body on the Neiman River, and he was buried in the Partisan Cemetery[22].

Reuven Bitenski

He was born in a village near Maytchet.

In February 1942, he left Maytchet with a group of youths. A farmer named Kolias who befriended him introduced him to a group of Russian partisans who wandered through the forests of the area. They agreed to accept approximately 50 Jewish youth into their ranks, he among them.

Bitenski often went to the Maytchet Ghetto, where he conducted a collection for weapons, and took out small groups of Jewish youth to set them up temporarily with farmers of the area.

Once, during a visit to the ghetto, he was suddenly surrounded by the police and the German Army. The group that he had put together made efforts to break through the siege. During the confrontation, the Jewish fighters killed two Germans, but at the end most members of the group fell, Bitenski among them[23].

[Page 358]

Vita Dvorjetski

She was born in Maytchet, the daughter of the Maytchet pharmacist Yaakov Dvorjetski She graduated from the high school of pharmacy in Warsaw. She went out to the forests during the liquidation of the ghetto. Some say that she fell in battle; and others say that she died of a serious bout of typhus in the forests, without medical aid. She served as a nurse in the Grishka Unit[24].

Moshe Zilberman

He was a native of Maytchet. He escaped to the forests of the area and joined a group of escapees from the Baranovich Ghetto who were affiliated with the Pogachov Brigade. He and his friend from Baranovich, Izia Osharovski once went to Baranovich to obtain German weapons. There, they encountered a German sleeping in his bed. Zilberman killed the German. They took the weapons that were in the corner, and began to dress up in a German uniform as camouflage. One of the Germans who entered the house opened fire and wounded Osharovski severely. He was taken to the hospital where he died after great suffering. Zilberman succeeded in escaping during the confusion that arose, and he reached the partisan base in the forest in safety.

After some time he was killed by Russian partisans from the Chigankov Unit. The commander of the murderers, Chigankov, punished them by transferring them to a different unit in a far off area[25].

Moshe Medlinski

He was a native of Suwalki. He moved to Maytchet when the Germans invaded. When Maytchet was conquered by the Germans, he escaped to the Svorotova Forests and organized a group of fighters consisting of young Jews who came to the forest from the nearby towns (Maytchet, Dvorets etc.). He helped organize the Grozny Unit, and was appointed as the commander of a brigade in that unit.

His talents were displayed in acts of sabotage. He stumbled into a German ambush as he was crossing the Lida-Baranovich railway line next to the Wygoda station. He defended himself and when there was only one bullet left in his cartridge, he shot himself so as not to fall into the hands of the Germans[26].

David Kantarovitz

He was born in Maytchet. During the war, he escaped from the Zhetl Ghetto on July 15, 1942 along with a group of young people. They went to the Horky and Rohatyn forests.

On July 25, 1942, he participated in a revenge operation carried out by the group against the secretary of the Maytchet council, who turned in Jews who had succeeded in escaping from the slaughter in Maytchet.

He returned to the Zhetl Ghetto with three of his friends in order to remove weapons from the hidden storehouse and transfer additional youths to the forest. That day, August 6, 1942, the ghetto was surrounded, the partisans attempted to break through the chain of guards who were holding wooden rods and stones. Kantarovitz fell at the hands of the Germans that night[27].

[Page 359]

Eliahu Kubinski

He was from Maytchet. He was one of the organizers of resistance in the town. He fell while attempting to break through the German siege on the day of the liquidation of the ghetto[28].

Reuven Kozlovitz

He was one of the organizers of the rebellion in Maytchet. He fell while attempting to break through the German siege on the day of the liquidation of the ghetto[29].

Meir Rozanski

He was born in 1925 in Maytchet. He escaped from the Dvorets Ghetto to the forests of Naliboki in December 1942, and joined the Kalinin Unit (under the command of Bielski). He participated in all the actions of the unit. He participated in many acts of train derailments along with his friend Yaakov Zingermeister. He enlisted in the Red Army along with him at the end of the war. They passed through the village of Byalolozy in the Kazlouscyna district before going out to the front. Members of a murderous anti-Semitic gang attacked them and murdered them[30].

Meir Romanovski

He was born in 1921 in Maytchet. He worked in the pharmacy of his adoptive uncle Romanovski in the town of Bakshty.

He was transferred to the Iwye ghetto along with the Jews of Bakshty in February 1943. He hid on the day of slaughter in the ghetto (May 12, 1942). Later on December 31, 1942, he was among the 29 members of the underground organization who broke through the barbed wire fence and escaped under a volley of shots to the village of Chrapinevo, and from there to the Moyan Forest, where they set up a bunker.

After four of the activists of the group were murdered by fighters of the Chapayev Unit on February 6, 1942, and their hiding place was discovered by shepherds, he fled with his friends to the Naliboki Forests where they joined the Aleksander Nayevski Unit.

He fell with three Jewish partisans as they returned from laying mines on a railway line around Juraciszki, a few days before May 1, 1943[31].

[Page 360]

David Stein

He was from the city of Maytchet. He escaped from the labor camp in Dvorets and joined the Kalinin Unit. He went out to supply missions when the Germans began the hunt. The group that he joined ran into a German force, and he fell in battle along with four of his friends[32].

***

I will bring down here several details about Jewish partisans who participated in battles near Maytchet and fell in these battles or after them in partisan actions.

Yaakov Granchok

He was born in Derechin[iv] in 1925. He fled to the forests on June 22, 1942, when the ghetto was liquidated. He was accepted into the Abramov brigade of the Bulak Unit in the forest of Lopacin. He joined in all the battles of the unit as a machine gunner.

In August 1943, he went out with a group of ten partisans to derail a train on the Maytchet line. After he shot dead the German who was standing on guard, the partisans derailed the train. After this act, he was decorated as a "Warrior of the Homeland".

In November 1943, he stood on guard along with his friend Berl Beker in one of the areas of the Roda-Jaworska forests, wearing the uniforms of German soldiers that they had taken as booty from their actions. The commander of the Shubin Unit and his men were situated in the area where the two of them stood guard. The uniforms of those two mislead them. They thought that they were Germans and shot them.

Granchok fell dead and was buried in a military ceremony. His friend was injured[33].

Avraham Lobovski

("Levaderik")

He was born in 1924 in Derechin. He served as a machine gunner in the Podeida (Victory) Unit under the command of Bulak. He especially excelled in the battle of Ostrov on July 3, 1942, where they took two Germans prisoner.

He ambushed Maytchet along with nine of his friends on May 22, 1942. He covered for his friends, and they all succeeded to escape. He was captured by the Germans who entered the house of a farmer in which he stayed after he had an operation. He died after a brief battle.

[Page 361]

He was cited for praise three times in the daily roll call of the unit. He received the award of Warrior of the Homeland, First Class[34].

Pinchas Pinus

He was born in 1917 in Suwalki. He was a shoemaker. When the war broke out, he moved to Derechin where the Soviets were in authority.

He escaped from the Derechin Ghetto on June 22, 1942 to the forests of Lipiczan. He joined the unit of Dr. Atlas and was wounded in a battle against the police of Derechin. He participated in many battles and excelled in setting the bridges over the Shchara River at the end of 1942. He was appointed as a commander of a division.

During the period of the hunt, he went to the region of Maytchet with his division to gather food for the brigade. On his way from Maytchet to the base on July 5, 1943, he was attacked by 150 men of the Stralkovchi gang. They pushed back the Russians as they were carrying the bodies of two of their victims, Boyarski and Perlman, and succeeded in exiting the battlefield.

After he derailed four German trains, he was granted the award of Warrior of the Homeland, First Class. After the liberation, he enlisted in the Red Army and fell on the front[35].

Shabtai (Shepsl) Alinburg (Also Nachmanovich)

He was born in Warsaw in 1917. He was a baker by profession. He was one of those active in the anti-Nazi underground in Zhetl and Navahrudak.

He escaped from the Navahrudak Ghetto in 1942 with a group of nine armed youths who had gone out to the Borki Forests (around Stowbtsy) under the command of Yechiel Yoselovitz.

On July 25, 1942, he participated in the liquidation of the secretary of the local authority of Maytchet.

When the news reached the forest that the Zhetl Ghetto was about to be liquidated, he and his three friends David Kantorovitz (a native of Maytchet who is mentioned earlier on page 358), Shlomo Lipmanovitz and Frankel were told to break into the ghetto to take the women out to the forest and bring the weapons stashes to the underground organizations.

He entered the ghetto with his friends on August 6, 1942. However, toward morning, the ghetto was surrounded by the Germans, and Alinberg fell during the battle with the Germans[36].

[Page 362]

***

Aside from the partisans mentioned in this article or whose biographies are included here, A. Chaneles includes another list of partisans who were active in Maytchet, who excelled with their exemplary bravery, and who were honored with military decorations or who fell in bravery:

> Kunai (Elkin) Shlovski, Chanan Shmulovitz, Mordechai Leib Shmulovitz, Yehoshua Zlotnik, Yitzchak Lochovitzky, and Leizer Zukovitzki were active in

the Grozni unit and some[v] were killed in the area of Maytchet by the anti-Semitic Stralkov (Stralkovitzki) unit. Meir Chaneles received a military decoration as a veteran partisan and was killed by Polish collaborators. Yaakov Margolin, Chaim Epstein and Liza (Leah) Epstein served as machine gunners around Ruda-Jaworska (today the latter is Kovensky in Argentina). Freidel Margolin (today Mckranski in Kibbutz Negba) served in the Grozni unit. Ester Mlishinski (today Lozovski in Israel) was active in the Bielski unit[37].

Text footnotes

1. P. Mkronski, Book of Maytchet, page 305.
2. M. Korn, Book of Maytchet, page 295.
3. Ch. Shmulevicz, Book of Maytchet page 329.
4. Ch. Shmulovicz, Book of Maytchet, page 329.
5. From the Letter of A. Hanelis in the Book of Maytchet page 308. This story is similar to the preceding story.
6. Ch. Shmulevicz, Book of Maytchet, page 330.
7. M. Ravitz, Book of Maytchet, page 320.
8. M. Shmulevicz, Book of Maytchet, page 330.
9. Moshe Ravitz, On Maytcheters in the Partisans, Book of Maytchet page 320.
10. Moshe Ravitz, Book of Maytchet, page 321.
11. Moshe Ravitz relates that he and another Maytchet refugee returned to the Maytchet area and joined a local partisan group and worked together. They participated in some attacks on railways, roads and bridges, attacking German camps and police stations at the villages. After a brief time they left the partisan group. Moshe Ravitz moved to the command headquarters as the logistician of "Pervomaiskia Brigade" and Avraham Chaneles stayed at Grozni Otriad (M. Ravitz, Book of Maytchet, page 321).

    It is worth mentioning some inaccuracies in M. Ravitz story. According to him all the activities and the battle in which Dr. Atlas died was in the beginning of the winter 1943. However it is well known that Atlas died in December 6th 1942. That means that this story took place at the end of the winter of 1942.

12. Lots of details are told about Dr. Atlas and his Activities as a forests fighter in the book of S. Burstein on Dr. Atlas (two editions); in his article : "Dr. Yechezkel Atlas", in "Yediot Lochmei Hagetaot" [Information of Ghetto Fighters] number 9-10, pp. 23-28, in the paper of Y. Granatstein and M. Kahanovitz "Yehezkel Atlas", in Yad Vashem information ("Yediot") Number 25-26, pp. 35-37, in the book of M. Kahanovitz "Milchemet Hapartizanim Hayehudim Bemizrach Europa" [The War of the Jewish Partisans in eastern Europe] (Hebrew and Yiddish), and "Sefer Hapartizanim Hayehudim' [Book of Jewish Partisans] (mentioned often), in the "Sefer Milchemet Hagetaot" [Book of the Ghetto War] (mentioned often) , in "Lexicon Hagevura" [Lexicon of Bravery] Parts 1 and 2 (mentioned often) , in many testimonies in the archives of that period, and the booklet "Niv Harofe" ("Talk of the Physician").

13.   Moshe Korn, Book of Maytchet, page 297. Vita Dvorjetski, the daughter of Jacob Dvorjetski didn't from the forest. One of the rumors said that she fell in battle. Other rumors said that she passed away due to severe typhus fever.

14.   Regarding the Mush story, read the paper of Dr. Z. Levinbook on the Baranovich Memorial book, p. 511.

15.   Mina Lewin (Gorski), Book of Maytchet, page 323.

16.   Ch. Shmulevicz, Book of Maytchet, page 330.

17.   See a detailed description of this revenge act in the article of Yechiel Yoselvich (In Pinkas Zhetl, p. 404). According that description it could be understood that the following people participated in the operation: Shalom Ogolnick, Bejamin Yorosh, Shefsel Namanovich, Chaim Slomka, Frankel, David Kantarovich, Shaul Sachnovich, Shlomo Shipmanovich, Moshe Daychs (Korostowski), two more lads from Vilna and himself, Yechiel Yosalevich (now living in New York); also, "Lexicon Hagevura", part 1, p. 61 tells that Shabtai Elenberg was one of the participants at that Revenge act. (Shabtai Elenberg = Shefsel Namanovich?)

A detailed description of this act is also written in A. Ben Shalom Article "The Meeting and the Attack", Book of Maytchet, p. 326. He was also participated at that operation.

Also see a description in: M. Kahanovitz, p. 376, M. Kaganavich, part 2, p. 341.

18.   Avraham Chaneles, Book of Maytchet, page 301.

19.   Trunk, p. 169. Testimony is located at the YIVO Archive in New York.

20.   Borenstein, page 97.

21.   Sh. Borenstein. "Plugat HaDoctor Atlas" [The Unit of Dr. Atlas]. Published by Hakibutz Hameuchad. Second edition. Pp. 110-112.

22.   The testimony of Mordechai Leib Shmulovicz. P"ChCh [Partisans, Pioneers, and Soldiers], collection 24; "Lexicon Hagevura" Section I, page 85. "Sefer Hapartizanim" page 679.

23.   Kahanavitz, pp 342-343, Kaganavitch Section II, 242-243.

24.   A. Chanales, Book of Maytchet, page 302.

25.   The testimony of Leib Trauba, "P'ChCh" [Partisans, Pioneers, and Soldiers] collection 37; L. Lidovski, Yad Vashem, Manuscript, page 120; "Sefer Hapartizanim", Section I, page 613; "Lexicon Hagevura", Section I, pp. 162-163.

26.   Testimony of the lawyer Wlintski, "P'ChCh" collection; Kahanavich, pp. 127-290. "Lexicon Hagevura", Section II, p. 54.

27.   "Pinkas Zhetl", page 404; "Lexicon Hagevura", page 139.

28.   "Sefer Hapartizanim", Volume II, page 756; "Lexicon Hagevura", Section II, page 148.

29.   "Sefer Hapartizanim", Volume II, page 753; "Lexicon Hagevura", Section II, page 148.

30.   Leizer Savitzki, "P'ChCh" [Partisans, Pioneers, and Soldiers], collection 7; "Lexicon Hagevura", Section II, page 117. "Sefer Hapartizanim", Section II, page 766.

31.   Testimony of Goldschmid and Hirsch, "P'ChCh" [Partisans, Pioneers, and Soldiers], collection 70; Testimony of Tania Imber, Yad Vashem Archives, Jerusalem; "Lexicon Hagevura", Section II, page 128; "Sefer Hapartizanim", Section II, page 769.

32.   Yafa: "Partizanim", pp. 66-67; "Lexicon Hagevura" Section II, page 159; Apparently this is the David Stein who was mentioned in the article by Ch. Shmulovitz on page 330 of the Book of Maytchet.

33.   Masha Kolkovski-Gornitzky. Questionnaire. Yad Vashem Archives. "Lexicon Hagevura" Section I, page 129; "Sefer Hapartizanim", Section II, page 129 (where the year of his birth is given as 1927).

34.   Seminar Lipiczan: "Lexicon Hagevura", Section II, page 24; "Sefer Hapartizanim", Section II, page 718.

35.   Seminar Lipiczan: "Lexicon Hagevura", Section II, page 108; "Sefer Hapartizanim", Section II, page 744.

36.   Mentioned in the questionnaires of B. Jaros: Dr. A. Alptert, A. Magid, Sh. Griling, A. Grachovski, A. Rozovski, A. Savitzki, Sh. Obsievich, Tz. Yoselovski, Kahanavich. pp 340-341. Kantaravich, Section II, 248. "Sefer Hapartizanim", Section I, pp 671-828. Pinkas Zhetl, pp 404, 418-419.

37.   Avraham Chaneles: Book of Maytchet, page 302.

Translator's footnotes

i. See http://en.wikipedia.org/wiki/Koldichevo

ii. See   http://jewishpartisans.blogspot.co.uk/search?updated-max=2011-10-05T14:49:00-07:00&max-results=7 which includes story of Atlas, as well as confirmation of Boris Bulat.

iii. The names of the sisters were Grunia and Shifra (as confirmed by Ariel Dvorjetski).

iv. There are several locales in Belarus which could fit this name. I am not sure which is meant, and I chose the one closest to Maytchet.

v. The original text did not have the word 'some'. I added the word in, as it is known that both Chanan Shmulevicz and Mordechai Leib Shmulevicz survived the war and lived long and productive lives in the United States changing their names to Charles Samuels and Martin Small. Myrna Siegel, the translation coordinator of this Yizkor Book, had met them both.

[Page 363]

Literature of the Community of Maytchet[1]

Shmuel Borenstein, "The Unit of Dr. Atlas," The story of a Jewish partisan, published by Hakibbutz Hameuchad, 5708 (1948). Two editions (Short form: Bornstein).

Yechel Yoselovich, Revenge on a Maytchet Murder. In Pinkas Zhetl, page 404 (short form: Yoselovich).

Yehoshua Yaffa. Partisans, Tel Aviv, 1951 (Short form: Yaffa)

Yeshayahu Trunk, The Relationship of the Judenrats to the problems related to weapons to be used against the Nazis. From Jewish Resistance During the Holocaust Era. Proceedings of a convention of Holocaust educators, Jerusalem, 1968. Page 169. (Short form: Trunk).

Moshe Kahanovich. The War of the Jewish Partisans in Eastern Europe. Tel Aviv, 5714 (1954). (Short Kahanovich).

Dr. Z. Lewinbok. From the Baranovich Yizkor Book.

Lexicon of Bravery. The partisans and underground fighters in the western districts of the Soviet Union. By Y. Granatstein and M. Kahanovich, Jerusalem, volume I – 5628 (1968). Volume II 5629 (1969).

The Book of Jewish Partisans. The Workers' Library. Volume I — 1957. Volume 2 — 1958.

The Book of Ghetto Fighters. The House of Ghetto Fighters and Hakibbutz Hameuchad. 1954.

Pinkas Zhetl. Edited by B. Kaplinski. Published by the Organization of Zhetl Natives, Tel Aviv, 1954. (Short form: Pinkas Zhetl).

Moshe Kaganovich. The War of the Jewish Partisans in Eastern Europe. Buenos Aires, volume I and II, 1952. (Short form: Kaganovich).

N. Kantarovich. The Jewish Resistance Movement in Poland. "Sharon," New York, 1967. (Short form: Kantaravich).

Testimonies, questionnaires, and manuscripts from the Yad Vashem archives in Jerusalem:

Seminar Lipiczan – Collective memories of the partisans who were active in the forests of Lipiczan.

A dossier of testimonies from: A. Alpert, B Jarush, A. Magid, Sh. Groling, A. Grochovski, L. Savitzki, Shl. Osiovich, Y. Yoselovski, L. Trauba, the lawyer Wilenski, H. Goldschmidt.

Questionnaires: Masha Kolkowski–Groznicki.

Testimonies: Tanya Imber.

Lizer Lidowski: A manuscript in Yad Vashem.

Memorial Articles in the Book of Maytchet: by A. Chanales, P. Mkronski, M. Lewin, M. Koren, Shlomovich, and M. Ravich.

Translator's footnotes

1. This bibliography (entitled literature), does not have an entry in the Table of Contents, and is apparently a bibliography of the previous chapter.

[Page 364]

Death Chronicles of Maytchet
(The Days of Bloodshed of Maytchet)
Translated by Amir Shomroni

September 1st 1939 - Outbreak of World War II
September 17th 1939 - Russian conquest of the area
June 22nd 1941- German invasion into Russia

* * *

First Action

Saturday, 27th of Shvat 5702, February 14th 1942 –
Murdering of 18 (22) people at the Tar Furnaces on the road to
Horoszwicicz (Horoshvitzich)

* * *

Second Action

Wednesday, 18th of Sivan 5712
- Murdering some 200 people in Burdykowszczina (Burdykovshtchina)
on the road to Horodiszcze (Horodishtche)

* * *

Third Action

On Wednesday, Thursday and Friday 1st – 3rd of Av 5702, July 15th -
17th 1942
– Destruction of the Ghetto of Maytchet

*

On July 17th 1942 – 20 Jews of Maytchet were transported to
Baranovichi for extermination.
These Jews worked in the farm "Loszniwa" (Loshniva) at the Loszny
(Loshny) forest. Some of them escaped.

Remembrance and Perpetuation

[Page 367]

These I Remember and I Moan...
Translated by Jerrold Landau
Words of eulogy and lamentation delivered annually at the memorial evening of the Organization of Natives of Maytchet and its Region in Israel

We have gathered this evening, as is our custom every year, in order to reunite ourselves with the holy memory of those dearest to us - fathers and mothers, brothers and sisters, sons and daughters, good friends and neighbors, along with the memory of all the martyrs of Maytchet and its region, who perished in the Holocaust in the sanctification of the Divine Name and the Nation of Israel during the bitters days of

1 to 3 of Av, 5702 - July 15-17, 1942

The memory and spirit of the dear martyrs flutter in the air of this hall, among us and over our heads, since they were not brought to a Jewish burial. The situation of the Jewish people,, who have suffered tribulations in the blood-soaked exile, that after every attack and disaster in which victims fell from amongst our Jewish brethren, was that it has been possible to bring the victims to a Jewish burial, to supplicate over their graves and to unite with their memory. This is not the case with this terrible, tragic Holocaust, which deprived the victims of the merit of being buried in a Jewish grave, and deprived us of the possibility of visiting our ancestral graves, to pray and to unite ourselves, to eulogize and weep over the victims in accordance with Jewish custom. Therefore, they hover amongst us, demanding restitution, rectification, and the elevation of their souls.

***

We are talking about one third of the Jewish people, two thirds of European Jewry, who perished in the Holocaust. You, the survivors of the destruction of Maytchet and its region who witnessed the great tragedy, are living witnessed that in Maytchet, not one third and not two thirds were murdered, but to our sorrow and agony, the entire community of Maytchet was destroyed. Not even one person of the city and two from a family[1] survived to tell the coming generations about what the enemy has perpetrated. As long as we are alive - and we are alive in the merit of the martyrs for in their deaths, they commanded life to us - we have the duty to carry out the will that they charged us next to the pits: "Remember that which Amalek has done to you!"[2]... This is a charge that is not written in ink, but rather in the blood that is screaming to us from the earth and calling upon us to make a name and a memorial to their souls, and perpetuate them in a memorial book for generations.

***

As is known, *Sefer Hachinuch* enumerates all 613 commandments in the order of the Torah portions. At the end of *Ki Teitzei*, we find two commandments among the others. One is the positive commandment, "Remember that which Amalek did to you" - a commandment to remember and to bring to memory, to tell and to repeat over in all generations that which Amalek did to us. The second is a negative commandment, namely, "Do not forget!" - to not forget and not to cause to forget. It is said in the sources, "Remember" is with the mouth, and "Do not forget" is in the heart. What can we do to avoid forgetting? How can we ensure that not only ourselves, upon whom the hand of Amalek came to destroy us, but also the future generations will not forget, for they too are obligated in this commandment? The answer to this is found in the Torah portion of *Beshalach* (Exodus 17:14), also regarding Amalek, "Write this as a memorial in a book!"

[Page 368]

***

Is there a man that is a poet, and are their words that can describe that magnitude of the tragedy?! Maytchet is in mourning, having lost all of its Jews, men, women and children, in one day. Were it not that a small remnant remained, we would have been likened to Sodom and compared to Gomorrah[3]. This event occurred thirty years prior to today. The last of the Jews of Maytchet and the region were taken by force from their homes and hiding places. The arm of the murderers even reached them in the depths of the earth[4], and hauled them to pits that were dug in deceit upon the Chwojnik Hill by the victims themselves. There, they were all slaughtered in cold blood and great cruelty. The martyrs - mothers and fathers, brothers and sisters, sons and daughters -- stood next to the pits in silence as they accepted the judgment. No cry of wrongdoing or plea for salvation emanated from their throats, for the victims knew very well that nobody would save them. With great spiritual might that is unparalleled among the nations, they went silently to their own funerals, as they recited *Kaddish* for themselves, as they sanctified the Divine Name and the name of the Jewish people, as they gave up their souls reciting "*Echad*"[5].

***

Not too long ago, we were all witnesses to the great event that was, Heaven forbid, liable to inflict a Holocaust upon the State of Israel[6]. With the assistance of the Rock and Redeemer of Israel, and thanks to the great will to live and the supreme might of the fighters of Israel, a miracle took place for us and we won the war. However, the price of victory was paid in very many houses in Israel, where they are mourning for their loved ones who fell victim on the altar of the native land. Just as in the era of the Holocaust, victims were demanded of the House of Israel to establish the state, and now victims were demanded in the battles to preserve it. Our comfort is that these victims did not die in vain. Both categories of victims[7] are holy and pure as the brightly shining firmament. In their deaths, they charged us with life. May their memories be blessed.

***

For many years, we, the few who remained alive, could not fulfill the charge of the martyrs written with the blood of their hearts, "Remember and do not forget!..." Not only this, but we never rent our garments, we never recited *Kaddish*, and we did not carry out any of the customs of mourning in accordance with tradition and law, for we were unable to do so. Over the years, we did not even set up a monument in memorial of their holy and pure souls. However, from now on, we need no longer torture ourselves over this omission, for we are now able to carry it out. G-d willing, this very year, an appropriate memorial will be established in the form of a book that will describe Jewish life throughout the generations, the story of the tragic deaths in Sanctification of the Divine Name, as well as the story of the might and greatness of the brave natives of Maytchet who protected the honor of Israel with their blood and brought us to this point.

[Page 369]

Every Maytchet native in Israel and throughout the world should spend some time in solitude with this book, uniting themselves with the memories, and shedding a tear over this monument. Next to the eternal flame that burns in each of our homes as we bring this memorial book into our homes, we can say with a light sigh, "Today, we have pushed aside the disgrace of the years from our hearts."

***

The Blessings of Rabbi Mordechai Kaplan. Rabbi Mordechai Kaplan was a native of Maytchet, who studied in Maytchet in his youth, then in Baranovichi and Minsk, and finally studied in Jerusalem for two years. From here, he immigrated to the United States in 1909, where he served in the rabbinate for many years. After he retired in the United States, he returned to live in Israel amongst his people in general, and amongst the Maytchet natives in Israel in particular. He lives in Tiferet Banim.

He takes interest in the affairs of the Maytcheters in Israel, and especially in the activities of the organizing committee. He is a faithful member of the Maytchet community in Israel, for he remembers the town from his young days. He participates regularly in the annual memorials, where he discussed memories of the town and its Jewish life. He blessed the book committee for its successful efforts to perpetuate the memory of the martyrs of Maytchet and its region in the memorial book.

From the time he was in Maytchet, he recalls a rare event that was a topic of conversation for everybody. At that time, when he was nine years old, the mother of the "Maytchet Genius" died. They placed the Maytchet Genius on a chair and he eulogized his mother.

Translator's footnotes

1. A Biblical term for a near total destruction. Here, it is referring to their being no survivors in the final *action*.
2. Deuteronomy 25:17.
3. Isaiah 1:9.
4. Seemingly referring to underground bunkers.
5. The final word of the first verse of the *Shema*.
6. Seemingly referring to the Yom Kippur War.
7. Those who died in the Holocaust, and those who fell in the battles of Israel.

Memorial for the People Who Have Gone
Translated by Jerrold Landau

With regard to the holy ones who are in the earth, they are mighty, and they are my desire! (Psalms 16:3)

From days of yore, even before there was a Chibbat Zion movement[1] to inherit the land in general, it was the dream and strong desire of Jews throughout the Diaspora who were faithful to their people, Torah and the holiness of their land to desire the earth of the Land of Israel, and to wish to be buried in its holy soil, and thereby to obtain the great merit of "its land shall expiate its people…"[2].

It was the pleasant lot of the dear residents of Maytchet, who were beloved and pleasant during their lives, and not separated in their deaths[3], who made *aliya* to the Land either before or after the Holocaust, to live in the Land amongst their people and together with their families. They merited to fulfill the commandment of the settlement of the Land of Israel, to built it up and protect it, in order to bestow it to their children after them as an eternal legacy. When their time came to go the way of all the earth, for they completed their mission, after their eyes witnessed the wonderful vision of the generations of "When G-d returns the captivity of Zion"[4], they passed on to their eternal world full of honor and reverence from their family members and faithful friends and acquaintances.

Let the clods of their earth be sweet for them, and let their souls be bound in the bonds of life.

Translator's footnotes
1. An early Zionist movement, predating the formal Zionist movement. See http://en.wikipedia.org/wiki/Hovevei_Zion .
2. Deuteronomy 32:43.
3. I Samuel 1:23.
4. Psalms 126:1.

[Page 370]

Memorial Candle for Yehoshua Shomroni z"l
by Shmuel and Amir Shomroni
Translated by Amir Shomroni

Among the names of the holy martyrs of Maytchet carved in this Memorial Book, and among chapters of Memorial stories of the Shoah, we wish to light a candle in memory of our late father – R' Yehoshua Shomroni (Shike Shmerkovitch) z"l.

Our father was born in Voronovo – miles away from Maytchet – a shtetl like the other shtetls in Poland – in the district of Lida. The fate encountered our father z"l with Tova (Doba) nee Polonsky – may she live long – in Voronovo, where she began her life saga and her evolution to becoming a Hebrew teacher.

When they immigrated to Eretz Israel they built – ex nihilo - their home, a source of pride; which imbibed it's culture and spirit from the beautiful and pure life of their two shtetls.

Eventually, when the collection and editing of the two memorial books for the holy martyrs of the two shtetls was commenced (not incidentally the editing of the two books did commence simultaneously,) the home of our father and mother, our home, turned into kind of a holy center for meetings, discussions, taking notes, organizing, correspondence, et cetera; enthusiastic actions of meticulous work of editing the two books – the Book of Voronovo and the Book of Maytchet. Not once, did it seem to us, that our father's enthusiasm in the preparation of the books, as well as the erection of the monuments for both, his shtetl's martyrs and our mother's, had rendered him elixir of life to continue, and to live to see them published.

But before its completion, on a wintry morning, his heart betrayed him. It is difficult for us –as well as his associates, who turned their nights into days in compiling this magnificent collection – to exactly define what his contribution or influence was in this book. But nevertheless it is clear to us that his spirit, enthusiasm, energy, his profound humor, and his personality in general, left his mark on these holy pages.

We are privileged that this memorial book will be an honorable memorial candle to our father, R' Yehoshua Shomroni z"l.

His sons – Shmuel and Amir

Avraham Rimon of blessed memory
by Aleksander Novitz
Translated by Jerrold Landau

He was born to Zev and Genia Rimon (Romanovski) on Kibbutz Yagur on 27 Shvat 5706 (January 29, 1945). Already at a young age, he excelled in his variegated talents, his good heart, his willingness to help, and his positive influence on his surroundings. Among other things, his classmates said the following in their discussions of him: "We grew up together for many years, but the time was indeed too short to understand a small amount of that large, complete world - which was Rimon. He was 'the spiritual father' to all of us. It is impossible to live up to him; it is too complex and cannot be done. He helped us all in extricating us from personal crises. Rimon lives as long as we all live."

[Page 371]

The soldier Avraham Rimon

Yehoshua Shomroni

The young girl, Esther Biribis

Moshe Kleinshtov

[Page 372]

Avraham was drafted into the army at the end of 1965 as a reconnaissance officer. During the Six Day War, he was sent with his unit to the Golan Heights to capture the Tel Faher outpost[1]. He was hit by the shooting of a Syrian sniper. His final words were: "I am going to die - continue on."

Among other things, the members of the reconnaissance unit said the following about Avraham: "He had every good thing in bountiful proportions. But the entire good and the entire truth is that everything that is said of him now - was said of him also when he was alive with us. This is the personal greatness that is very rare."

Rimon was the best youth in the reconnaissance unit. Everyone said so. In general, when one eulogizes a deceased person, traits that he did not possess are attributed to him. Rimon, however, had all the good traits that are possible to find in a person. I asked myself more than once: How is it possible that he was a person without a taint - perfect in the full sense of the term?

Avraham was praised by the commander of the Northern Command for sticking to the mark and for his self-sacrifice. He was 21 when he fell.

Translator's footnote

    1. See http://en.wikipedia.org/wiki/Tel_Faher

Moshe Kleinshtov of blessed memory
by Aleksander Novitz
Translated by Jerrold Landau

1898 – 1958

He was a native of the village of Zelanshchivna near Kobrin in White Russia. Upon the completion of his studies, he dedicated himself to agriculture and ran the farm of his parents, who were landowners and farmers for generations. After the Russian revolution, during the era of Denikin and Petliura[1], when he bravely stood up and risked his life for the independent defense of the local Jewish community, he was accused by the hooligans and sentenced to death. There was a hairbreadth between him and death and it was only through a miracle that he escaped the noose. Later he did everything he could to make *aliya* to the Land, and he arrived in 1923, after the tribulations of the journey. Here he worked for several years at difficult outdoor work at a kibbutz, and then he moved to Tel Aviv, where he was one of the initiators of Hebrew labor for porting at the port of Jaffa, and a founder of the Hachof Cooperative. When the unification, he joined Shalev, and bore his load as a man of rank. He was faithful and dedicated, and always suffered with the pain of the union.

His death shook his friends and acquaintances, for everyone who came in contact with him held him in honor and esteem on account of his good temperament, his readiness to help his fellow, and his boundless dedication to the enterprise.

He was a faithful husband and a good, dedicated father to his four children. With his death, we have lost a good and dedicated friend, and an exemplary head of a family.

May his memory be a blessing.

Translator's footnote
1. See http://en.wikipedia.org/wiki/Anton_Denikin and
   http://en.wikipedia.org/wiki/Symon_Petliura

Esther Biribis of Blessed Memory
by Sara Boretsky Biribis
Prepared by Myrna Siegel

She was born in a hospital in Afula, Israel July 1, 1949 to parents Avraham Biribis and Sarah Boretsky Biribis, members of Kfar Yehoshua. There was great love between parents and daughter; especially because of the difficulties of her growth and development from an early age, in spite of the indulgence of her devoted parents.

[Page 373]

She had very unusual talents; her studies and handicraft, which were wonderfully thought out. She never refused to work in the house and the fields. She was truly a modern version of a woman of valor.

She was also blessed with a beautiful voice and excellent hearing. She filled the house with sounds of joy and happiness -- this was a pleasant reward for parents who had suffered so much in her youth.

And with everything she excelled with a good heart and gentle soul in her relationships with her parents, Rena her sister, to everyone who came to the house, and to children her age. The closets in the house were filled with toys and Purim costumes that she used from time of kindergarten through school. But she never got rid of them. She kept them for those who didn't have. She was very industrious, always offering help for everything, both in the house and outside.

On that bitter morning during the Passover vacation, Esther got up early and prepared to go out with her classmates for an outing from which she never returned. With her death her parents lost a child and their joy and happiness was destroyed. Also her sister Rena and her classmates felt a burning pain of the absence of a sister, comrade and good friend.

The pamphlet "Esther", which was published at the end of the year of her tragic death, contained her personal diary beginning in the second grade, with lists, poems and letters; reflecting a young and talented author.

Thus the years of her youth passed full of love and joy until the bitter day when the tender flower was plucked and ran it over to death.

[Page 373]

Translated by Jerrold Landau

Reb Yehoshua Aharon Lozovski and his wife of blessed memory - see articles on pages 59, 238

Reb Yisrael Zalman and his wife Zlata Shlovski of blessed memory - see article on page 98.

Reb Aryeh Shmulevicz of blessed memory - Born in 1909 in Maytchet. Made *aliya* to the Land in 1933. Died in the Land on August 30, 1946.

Reb Avraham Kaplan of blessed memory - Died in Israel on 10 Tishrei 5722 (September 20 1961). (Translator's note: Yom Kippur).

Reb Yisrael Savitzki of blessed memory - The son of Moshe and Sheina Savitzki. Made *aliya* with his wife Buna as chalutzim in 1925. Died in Israel on 29 Elul 5721 (1961).

Reb Avraham Zev Savitzki of blessed memory - The son of Moshe and Sheina Savitzki. He was born in Maytchet in 1895, made *aliya* with his wife Sara in 1934, and died in Israel in 1959.

Reb Ezriel Korn of blessed memory - See the articles on pages 61, 256.

Mrs. Sima Ben-Hur - See the article on page 221.

Mrs. Sima Ginzberg (nee Dvorjetski) of blessed memory -- She was born in 1906 in Maytchet, made *aliya* to the Land in 1946, and died on the 23 of Tammuz 5728 (1968).

Malka Chalamish (Rabinovitch) - She was the daughter of Reb Yechiel Yitzchak and Chana Gela Dvojetski. She was born in Maychet in 1880, made *aliya* to the Land in 1918, and died in Rechovot on the eve of Chanukah, 5732 (1971).

Elkanah Ben-Hur - -- See the article on page 221.

[Page 374]

Avraham Zeev Savitzki of blessed memory

Yisrael Savitzki of blessed memory

Malka Chalamish (Rabinovitch)

Sima Ginzberg, nee Dvorjetski

[Page 375]

Elkana Ben-Hur

Sima Ben-Hur (Abramovski)

Leibel Shmulevicz of blessed memory

Reb Avraham Kaplan of blessed memory

[Page 377]

Memorial Pages and Pictures

**Translated by Jerrold Landau, Esther Muller, Ron Rabinovitch,
Martin Small a/k/a Mordechai Leib Schmulewicz & Myrna Siegel**

מצבת זכרון לקדושי קהילת
מייצ'עט
והסביבה (מחוז ברנוביץ)
שנרצחו ושניספו על קדוש השם
ע"י הנאצים ימ"ש
בשנות השואה תרצ"ט-תש"ה 1942,
יום הזכרון ראש חדש אב
ת. נ. צ. ב. ה.
מנציחים יוצאי מייצ'עט והסביבה בישראל ובתפוצות

A Memorial to the Martyrs of the congregation of
MaytchetA
nd the environs (District of Baranovich)
Who were murdered and exterminated on the
sanctification of the Holy Name
By the Nazis (may their names to blotted out)
In the years of the Holocaust 5639-5705, 1942
Memorial day the first of the Month Av
May their souls be bound up in the bond of everlasting life
Perpetuating their memory, the countrymen
of Maytchet and the environs in Israel and the Diaspora

(**Translator's note:** Located in the Memorial Hall [Martef Hashoah] on Mount Zion,
Jerusalem. Photo of the unveiling of the sign (July 9, 1964) is on page 197)

[Page 379]

From the Kehilah of Maytchet

For Eternal Memory

Our Father: Reb Shlomo son of Reb Yakov Aharonovitz
Our Mother our teacher: Bracha, daughter or Reb Dovid
Our Sister: Bluma, Mina and their families

During the rising of the sun and the descent of night: during the holidays and the festivals, in the day of our happiness, their memory will accompany us for eternity.
You were murdered and you gave your souls in sanctification of the Divine Name.

Their souls should be bound in the bond to the living

> The survivors:
> Chaya Lubchick-Aharonovitz
> Devorah Mlinikovsky-Aharonovitz

In Internal Memory

With Great Pain and with deep sorrow, for eternity, I enter in the "Book of Remembrance," my loved and dearest, who perished together with all of the Jews from Maytchet, through the murderous Germans.

My Father: Rav Shlomo son of Rav Eliezer , (Shlomo the scribe) Ozerski.
My Mother: Elka (Berel Pesha (Channah's))
My Sister: Malkah
My Brothers: Berel Dove and Elchanan

Hashem should avenge their blood
I will remember you forever

> Your dearest son and brother:
> Lazar Ozerski, Canada

[Page 380]

For Eternal Memory

We memorialize in the "Memorial Book" of the Maytchet Jewish Kehila (community)
The glowing memory of our dear parents and sister:

Our Father Reb Osher Orzechovsky (Hashem avenge his blood) was killed in the slaughter in Maytchet.
Our Mother: Shayna Orzechovsky (of blessed memory) died in the year 1941 in Maytchet.
Our Sister: Chaya Sarah Ross (of blessed memory) born in Maytchet (from home (nee) Orzechovsky)
Died in Chicago- America, 17 Cheshvan 5724 – 4/1//1963

We will always remember you with the greatest awe and respect!

> In sorrow:
> Fayga Rochel – Chicago
> Chasha Freyda – Los Angeles
> *see picture in the front of the book*

In Eternal Memory

I record for eternity, in the Yizkor Book of Maytchet, my closest and dearest:

My Father: Reb Chaikel Israelvitz (of blessed memory) who died in Maytchet
My Mother: Tzivia (from the home (nee) Lubetzki) (hashem avenge her blood) was killed in Maytchet
My Sister: Dobeh with her family (Hashem avenge their blood) was killed in Vilna
My Sister: Liebkeh with her family (Hashem avenge their blood) was killed in Maytchet
My Sister Rosa (Hashem avenge her blood) Was killed in Maytchet

May their souls be bound to eternal life

> In sorrow:
> Isser Israeleitz (of blessed memory)
> Argentina

[Page 381]

An Eternal Memorial in the Yizkor Book

Of the community of Maytchet that was destroyed, to my dear parents and sisters who perished:

Father: Yona the son of Reb Asher Orzechovsky, may G-d avenge his blood
Mother: Kreina nee Volinski, may G-d avenge her blood
My sisters, Chana Mere, and Chasha, may G-d avenge their blood

Their memory is guarded forever in my hearts and in the hearts of all the members of my families

The perpetuator:
Nachum Naor (Orzechovsky)

A Candle for the souls of my dear ones

My dear father: Yosef Boretcky
My dear mother: Sheina-Yafa
My dear brother: Aryeh Dov
My dear sisters: Zelda and Shoshana

The perpetuator:
their son and brother – David Boretcky

A Candle to the memory of my dear ones
Victims of the Holocaust in Maytchet

My dear father: Tzvi Brunitzki , may G-d avenge his blood
My dear mother: Pesia, may G-d avenge her blood
My dear sister: Chaya, may G-d avenge her blood

Honor to their memory!
The son and brother – Yerachmiel Brunitzki

[Page 382]

In Eternal Memory

With deep pain I remember my family, murdered in Maytchet, by the Nazi Bandits, (eradicate their names)

My beloved father: Reb Shlomo Barda (Hashem avenge his blood) Killed in Dvoretz
My beloved Mother: Nechama (Hashem avenge her blood) Killed in Dvorets
My beloved brother: Shmeil (hashem avenge his blood) Killed in Vilyeyka
My beloved sister: Esther Rochel and her husband Beryl Rovcha, (Hashem avenge their blood) Killed in Pinsk

Honor their Memory!

In sorrow:
Yisroel Barda – America

For Eternal Memory

With sorrow and with burning pain, I raise up in the "Book of Remembrance" of our city Maytchet the memory of those precious to my soul:

My dear Father: Noach Boretcky– passed away in 1930
My dear Mother: Alteh (of the house of (nee) Dvorjetski) (hashem avenge her blood) met her end in Maytchet
My dear sister: Faygeleh (Hashem avenge her blood) met her end in Maytchet
My dear Brothers: Hertzl and Meirim (Hashem avenge their blood) met their end in Maytchet

May their souls be bound in eternal life and this page should be an everlasting memorial to their memory

The Mourners:
Channah Mechtiger (from the home (nee) Boretcky and her family

See the family pictures at the front of the book

[Page 383]

Sitting in the center: **Mother Sima, to her right Moshe, and
to her left Chaya-Dvora, may G-d avenge their blood**.
Standing from the right: **Chana may G-d avenge her
blood, on the left: Sara-Rivka may she live long**

My father: Reb Shepsl the son of Yosef Boyarski of blessed memory –
perished at the hands of the murderers in 1916 during the First World
War.
My mother: Sima, may G-d avenge her blood – perished in Maytchet during
the Holocaust
My sister: Chana may G-d avenge her blood – perished in Maytchet during
the Holocaust
My brother Moshe, his wife Chaya-Dvora and their children, may G-d
avenge their blood – perished in the Baranovich Ghetto

The mourner:
Their daughter and sister:
Sara-Rivka Blumbsein

[Page 384]

For These Do We Mourn

Our dear father: Reb Leib-Chaim Volinski of blessed memory – died in 1923
Our dear mother: Konia Rivka, may G-d avenge her blood – perished in Maytchet
Our dear brother: David, his wife Teiba Rivka and their children, may G-d avenge their blood – perished in Lubtsh
Our dear brother: Eliezer may G-d avenge his blood – perished in the Kozlikova Camp
Our dear brother: Zelig, his wife and their children, may G-d avenge their blood – perished in Maytchet
Our dear sister: Golda, her husband Leizer Polonski and their children, may G-d avenge their blood – perished in Maytchet
Our dear sister: Lea Freidel may G-d avenge her blood – perished in Maytchet

May this page in the Yizkor Book of our town Maytchet serve as an eternal monument to their memory

The mourners and perpetuators:
Shifra Losovski (Volinski)
Miriam Kleinshtov (Volinski)

[Page 385]

For Eternal Memory

I hereby perpetuate the memory of my dear parents in the Yizkor Book of our town

My mother Chasia (nee Shershovski), may G-d avenge her blood

My father Ben-Zion Boretcky may G-d avenge his blood

Who perished during the time of the Holocaust
May their memory be blessed!

The perpetuator:
Their daughter; Alta Katz
(nee Boretcky)

[Page 386]

Always to remember and never to forget

My dear father: Shmuel Boretcky of blessed memory
My dear mother: Ethel of blessed memory
My dear brothers: Nathan, Meyerim, Menachim and Fischl of blessed memory
My dear sister: Channa Leah of blessed memory

Who were killed in Maytchet during the Holocaust

May their souls be bound up in eternal life

Submitted by:
Daughter and sister:
Sarah Boretcky Birbis, (from the house of Boretcky)

[Page 387]

To always Remember

We are inscribing this in the Yizkor book from Maytchet

Our grandfather: Yitzckak, the son of Meyerim Boretcky, born in Molchad and died in Baranovich
Our grandmother: Sarah Rachel born in Molchad and died in Molchad

May their souls be bound up in eternal life

The grandchildren:
David, Leib amd Eliezer Shmuel Lubetcky – In America

For These Do I Mourn

My dear father: Yekutiel Lublinski of blessed memory
My dear father: Reb Moshe Belski, may G-d avenge his blood
My dear mother: Rivka, may G-d avenge her blood
My dear sister: Meere and her husband Hershel Tzvi Rubizewski, may G-d avenge their blood
My dear brother: Shmuel, may G-d avenge his blood
My dear sister: Nechama, may G-d avenge her blood

Perished in the Holocaust in Maytchet

In grief:
The daughter and sister: Vichna Ezrachi (nee Belski)

[Page 388]

Reb Alter Eliahu Chaim Gorski of blessed memory. Died in the forests on 21 Adar I, 5703 (1943).
Mrs. Miriam, nee Turetzki, perished in the Holocaust.

The perpetuators:
Their daughter – Mina Levin
Their sons – Tuvia Gorski, Mordechai Gorski

[Page 389]

In Eternal Memory

My dear father: Hirsch (Tzvi) Viloikhinski, may G-d avenge his blood
My dear mother: Rachel, may G-d avenge her blood
My dear brothers: Chaim-David, Theodor, and Pesach, may G-d avenge their blood.
My dear sisters, Rishel and Malka, may G-d avenge their blood

Who were murdered in Maytchet during the Holocaust by the German murderers, may their names be blotted out, and their evil assistants.

May this page serve as an eternal monument to their memory

The perpetuator:
The daughter and sister
Rashel Boimel (Viloikhinski)

[Page 390]

In Eternal Memory

On the left: **Mother Leah Hanelis.**
On the right: **Aunt Chaya Dubkovski**

My dear father: Yaakov Hanelis, may G-d avenge her blood – perished in the Horodisht Ghetto.
My dear mother: Leah (nee Dubkovski) of blessed memory – died in 1936
My dear brother: Yitzchak, may G-d avenge his blood – perished in the Horodishtch Ghetto
My dear sister: Sonia, may G-d avenge her blood – perished in the Horodishtch Ghetto
My dear sister: Chienke of blessed memory – fell in a partisan action
My aunt: Chaya Dubkovski, may G-d avenge her blood – perished in the Horodishtch Ghetto

May their memories be blessed!

The perpetuator:
Abrasha Hanelis

[Page 391]

For Eternal Memory

We are memorializing in the memorial book of Maytchet
Our dear sister: Sarah Rachel (Sylvia) Weiss (ne Lubetsky)
Born in Maytchet and died in America

May her soul be bound in eternal life

The brothers:
Dovid Leib and Eliezer Shmuel
Lubetsky-America

For Eternal Memory

The names of my beloved and dearest parents, brothers and sisters, who were killed for the holiness (sanctity) of Hashem, in Maytchet, through the Nazi murderers and their accomplices should be recalled for eternal memory in the Memorial book of our town (shtetl), Maytchet.

Honor their memories!

In sorrow, the survivor:
Nachum Yachatz - South Africa

Candle for the Soul (Memorial Light)

Our Dear Uncle: Reb Gedaliah Yotvitsky of blessed memory.
Died in Maytchet 1933, was brought for burial to Warsaw.
Our dear Aunt Nechama Yotvitski -- perished during the Holocaust in Maytchet

May their memories be blessed!

The perpetuators:
Yitzchak Binyamini (Yotvitsky)
Eliezer Yotvitsky

[Page 392]

For Eternal Memory

My dearest and nearest should be memorialized for future generations:

My father: Reb Isser Zusman , (of blessed memory) died in Maytchet
My Mother; Chayenkeh, (Hashem avenge her blood) was killed in Maytchet
My Brother: Shmuel, with his family (Hashem should avenge their blood) were killed in Pinsk
My Sister: Etl with her family, (Hashem should avenge their blood) were killed in Maytchet
My Brother: Yosef, (Hashem should avenge his blood) was killed in Maytchet

I will forever remember them and never forget

In sorrow:
Faygle Zinger nee Zusman
America

Memorial For My Unforgettable Relatives

by Isaac Lublinski

My dear father: Yekutiel Lublinski of blessed memory
My dear mother: Henya Lea of blessed memory
My dear brother: Moshe and his wife Rosa and daughter Henya (murdered)
My dear sister: Sara, her husband Israel Chaim Shinevski and children: Yekutiel, Asher, Michal, Alke, and Hilel (murdered)
My dear sister: Rivka, her husband Zelig Ravatz and their children Yekutiel, Devora and Isaac (murdered)
My dear sister: Freidke, her husband David Shviranski and their son Yekutiel (murdered)

Let This Memorial Page in the Molchad Community Book be for their Holy Sign

Their son & brother: Isaac Lublinski

[Page 393]

For Eternal Memory

I will forever mourn and remember my beloved brother
Shimeon Lakhovitski, his wife Sorah Rochel, with their son
Yitzchak Hashem should avenge their blood, who were murdered in
Maytchet through the German murders with their accomplices.

Honor their memories!

In Sorrow:
Hertzel Lakhovitski - America

[Page 394]

For Eternal Memory

My dearest and nearest should be memorialized for future generations:

Our Father: Yitzchak Akiva son of Reb Meirim Lubetsky of blessed memory.
Our Mother: Yachneh Rivkah of blessed memory.
Born in Maytchet and died in America

May their souls be bound to eternal life

The children:
Dovid Leib and Eliezer Shmuel Lubetsky – America

See picture in front of the book

For Eternal Memory

We memorialize in "the Memorial Book" of the Kehilah of Maytchet
The memory of our grandfather Reb Meirim Lubetsky
and our Grandmother, Dobeh of blessed memory, lived in Maytchet
and passed away in Maytchet

May their souls be bound to eternal life

The grandchildren:
Dovid Leib and Eliezer Shmuel
Lubetsky – America

A Candle for the Soul (Memorial Candle)

My Husband and our father dear and venerated, Reb Yehoshuah Melishansky of blessed memory.
Passed away during the time of the wandering in the forest and bunkers (in hiding)

His soul should be bound to eternal life

The survivors:
The wife: Devorah Melishansky
The daughter: Esther Lubetsky
The son: Meir Melishansky

[Page 395]

An Eternal Memorial to Those Not Forgotten

My dear brother: Mordechai-Izak Lisagorski
My dear sister-in-law: Alta, and their dear children:
Gavriel, Michael, Ezriel, Rafael, and Grona

May G-d avenge their blood!

The perpetuator:
Their brother: Chaim-David Zeler – United States

[Page 396]

In Memory of Those Dear to our Souls

My dear father: Yekutiel Lublinski of blessed memory
Our dear mother: Batya of blessed memory – died in 1936
Our dear father: Zeev. Our dear brother: Chaim, and our dear sisters: Pesia and Chaya, may G-d avenge their blood

**Who were murdered during the period of the Holocaust
by the destroyers of the Jewish people in Poland and Europe**

The perpetuators:
The son and brother: Yitzchak Movshovitz – Israel
The daughter and sister: Miriam Eizenwasser – Israel
The daughter and sister: Roza Sobalf – Canada

For Eternal Memory

Our father: Reb Yaakov Nachum Mlinikovski of blessed memory
Our mother: Sara of blessed memory
Our sister: Bracha of blessed memory
Our brother: Moshe of blessed memory
Our brother: Meir and hs wife Sara, may G-d avenge their blood, perished in the Holocaust in Zhetl
Our sister: Chaya-Musha and her husband Yaakov, may G-d avenge their blood, perished in the Holocaust in Horodishtch

May this memorial page serve as a memorial and monument to their holy memory

Those who sanctify and perpetuate their memory:
YudelMlinikovski -- Argentina
Moshe Zelner (Mlinikovski) – Israel
Pesach Mlinikovski – Israel

[Page 397]

"For these do I weep, my eyes, my eyes, my eyes drop water, for the comforter is far from me"*

Perpetuating our not to be forgotten dear ones who perished in the Holocaust

Standing from the right: **Moshe Margolin, may they live, Nachum and Freidel Margolin, Yaakov Margolin**
Sitting: **The parents Aryeh-Leib and Bodna, and their young son Mordechai**
At the bottom: **Chasha and Abba Margolin**

May this page serve as a memorial and marker to the holy memory of our dear parents, sisters and brothers, and an eternal monument for their unknown graves

---

*

Translator's footnote: Lamentations 1:16.

[Page 398]

For Eternal Memory

To my dear parents, sisters and brothers who perished, were murdered, and died:
My father: Reb Mordechai Margolin of holy blessed memory – He was the prayer leader and *shochet* in the town of Starobin (Russia). Died in Warsaw, 17 Av 5681 (1921).
My mother: Sheina Margolin nee Kadoshin, may G-d avenge her blood – perished in the Holocaust in Maytchet
My sister; Dvosha, her husband and children, may G-d avenge their blood – perished in the Holocaust in Maytchet
My sister Sara, her husband and children, may G-d avenge their blood – perished in the Holocaust in Maytchet
My brother Avraham, his wife and children, may G-d avenge their blood – perished in the Holocaust in Maytchet
My brother Yaakov of blessed memory – Died during an air raid in Baranovich at the beginning of the Second World War – his wife and children perished in the Baranovich Ghetto.
My father's brother of blessed memory – died in Maytchet in 1938

May their souls be bound in the bonds of eternal life

The perpetuator:
Chemda Lubrani (nee Margolin) Negba

See the family picture earlier in the book

For Eternal Memory

Our dear mother: Nechama-Dvora of blessed memory – died in Maytchet in 1918
Our dear, not to be forgotten father: Reb David Tzvi Novomishiski may G-d avenge his blood – perished in the Holocaust in Maytchet at the hands of the troops of the German murderers, may their names be blotted out, and died in sanctification of the Divine Name. A refined soul, an observer of Torah and the commandments.
Brother: Nathan Feitel and sister Chana
Our dear sister: Pua (Paya), her husband and son, may G-d avenge their blood – perished in Maytchet during the era of the Holocaust

The grief will never depart from our midst forever

The perpetuators:
The daughter and sister: Sara Ahronovski and family, Israel
The sons and brothers: Avraham Yosef, Meirim, Yehoshua Moshe, Meir and their families, Argentina

See family photos earlier in the book

[Page 399]

In grief and agony, I mention the memory of my family who perished
in the Holocaust in the Yizkor Book of our town Maytchet:

My dear father: Reb Zimel, may G-d avenge his blood
My dear mother: Chaya-Charna, may G-d avenge her blood
My dear brothers: Leibel and Moshe, may G-d avenge their blood, and my dear sister Sheina, May G-d avenge her blood.
My uncle: Reb Michel Stolovitzki, his wife Eshke, and their children Nachum and Chasha, may G-d avenge their blood
My aunts: Miriam, Rachel, and Esther, and their families
My uncle: Reb Nisel Shlovski, his wife Itka, and their children Kunia and Binyamim, may G-d avenge their blood
My uncle: Reb Yakkov Okun, my aunt Chasha, and their son Binyamin, may G-d avenge their bood
My uncle: Reb Zeev Shlovski, his wife and children, may G-d avenge their blood

May their memory be blessed!

The perpetuator:
Binyamin Stolovitzki, Petach Tikva

See the family photograph earlier in the book

In memory of my dear family who died and perished in the Holocaust

My dear father: Reb Avraham Abba Polonski, of blessed memory
My dear mother: Mrs. Musha Polonski, the son of Reb David Eidlin
My sisters: Freidel, her husband Yisrael Moshe Izralvitz, and their children: Reizele, Asnale, and Iserke – who perished in Baranovich
My dear brother: Moshe Chaim of blessed memory – who died in Argentina in 1970
My brother: Yechezkel, his wife Menucha, and their children Estherke, Sarale, and Asnale, who perished in the Dvorets Ghetto
My sister Pesha and her husband, whose blood was spilled in the garden next to our house in Maytchet
My brother Davidke, may G-d avenge his blood – who was murdered while wandering along the paths
My paternal grandmother: Liba Polonski
My grandparents: Reb David Eidlin and his wife Hinda

The grief will never depart from our midst forever

The perpetuator:
Tova Shomroni, nee Polonski

See the family photo earlier in the book

[Page 400]

An Eternal Memorial to Those Not Forgotten

My father: Reb Shalom Peltzok, may G-d avenge his blood
My mother: Ita, may G-d avenge her blood
My brother: Moshe and his wife Mara, may G-d avenge their blood
My sister: Reizel, may G-d avenge his blood
My brother: Moshe, may G-d avenge his blood

**The blood of all of them was spilled like water, with nobody to save them,
and for this the heart is agonized, and is unable to be comforted.**

The perpetuator:
The survivor of the annihilated Peltzok family:
Chanan Peleg (Peltzok)

For my dear brothers and sisters,
who were tragically killed in Maytchet during the Holocaust

My brother: Yaakov Kosterovitzki, his wife Chana and their children
My brother: Noach Kosterovitzki, hs wife Gudtil
and their children
My sister: Chasha, her husband Nota Lozovski and their children
My sister Malka and her children
My sister: Beila

Let these lines in the Maytchet Yizkor Book serve as a symbolic monument

The perpetuator:
 Berl Kosterovitzki
Argentina

[Page 401]

I will always weep and remember my beloved and dear ones who died
and were murdered at the hands of the murderers in Maytchet

My father: Moshe Kravtzik of blessed memory
My mother: Sara, may G-d avenge her blood
My sisters: Malka, Esther, and Sheina Feiga, may G-d avenge their blood
My brother: Mordechai of blessed memory

May these lines in the Maytchet Yizkor Book serve as an eternal monument

In sorrow:
Their daughter and sister, Mina Rasales, nee Kravtzik, Canada

[Page 402]

Eternal Memorial Not To Forget Our Family

Our dear father: Rabbi Israel Rabinovitch
Our dear mother: Gania
Our dear sisters: Miriam and Fani
Our dear brothers: Shimon and Nechemia
Our dear grandfather: Rabbi Hazel Tsvi Mochkovski
Our dear grandmother: Razel Mochkovski

This Memorial Page is for their Holy Rememberance

Reuven Rabinovitch - Israel
Nachum Rabinowicz – USA

[Page 403]

I will always weep for and remember my beloved dear ones who died
and were murdered in sanctification of the Divine Name in Maytchet

My father: Reb Izik Ravitz of blessed memory
My mother: Sara Ravitz, nee Dikshtejn, may G-d avenge her blood
My sister: Beilka Epshtejn and her family
My sister: Sheinke Pintzinski and her family
My sister: Chana Ravitz and her family
My sister: Itka Shlovski and her family
My brother: Zelig Ravitz and his family
My late husband: Zeev Kaplan and our dear children: Izik, Leibl and Fayele,
and his parents Yitzchak-Tzvi and Relke Kaplan, may G-d avenge their blood.

Their holy memory will be guarded in my heart forever.
May their souls be bound in the bonds of eternal life.

Let these lines serve as a symbolic monument:
Tzirel Royak – United States

[Page 404]

Glory Memorial for our unforgettable relatives

by Dov and Chaikel Shlomovitch

Our dear father: Rabbi Shlomo Tzvi Shlomovitch
Our dear mother: Hanna
Our dear brother: Eliezer
Our dear sisters: Chaya Sara, Shaina, Miriam and Sola

They were all murdered in the Holocaust at Molchad by the Nazis

Dov Shlomovitch, Israel
Chaikel Shlomovitch, Canada

For Eternal Memory

We perpetuate our near and dear ones in the Yizkor Book of our town Maytchet

Our father: Michel Shmulevicz
Our mother: Leah
Our sister: Dvosha

Who were murdered in Maytchet by the Nazi murderers and their assistants, may their names and memories be blotted out

In sorrow:
Chanan and Moshe Shmulevicz, America

[Page 405]

A Candle to the Memory of my Dear Ones

Natives of Maytchet who died in the United States

My dear father: Reb Shlomo Chaim the son of Reb Yitzchak Krolvitzki of blessed memory
My dear mother: Rachel of blessed memory
My uncle: Reb Alexander-Zisel the son of Reb Yitzchak Krolvitzki of blessed memory
My uncle: Reb Eliezer the son of Reb Yitzchak Krolvitzki of blessed memory

**May this page in the Yizkor Book of Maytchet serve
as a monument to their memories and a candle to their souls
May their souls be bound in the bonds of eternal life**

The perpetuator:
Rabbi Mordechai the son of
Reb Shlomo Chaim Kaplan (Krolvitzki) – Israel

For These Do We Mourn

Our dear father: Reb Moshe Aharon Shevchik of blessed memory, died in Maytchet in 1933
Our dear mother: Elka – perished in Maytchet during the Holocaust
Our dear brother: Aharon, his wife Sonia, and their dear son Moshe – perished in the Holocaust in Maytchet
Our dear brother: Velvel – perished in the Holocaust in Maytchet
Our dear sister: Rivka – perished in Maytchet during the Holocaust with her husband and children
Our dear sister: Alta – died in the United States
Our dear sister: Merke, her husband and children – perished in the Holocaust in Slonim

The perpetuators:
Yehuda the son of Moshe – Israel
Yechiel Shef – United States

[Page 406]

A Candle to the Memory of my Dear Ones

My uncle: Reb Avraham Yitzchak Novomishiski and his entire family
My aunt: Chaya Vilkormirski and her entire family

Perished in Maytchet during the Holocaust – may their memories be blessed

The perpetuator:
their niece Sara Ahronovski (nee Novomishshki)

For Eternal Memory

Of my dear parents and brothers who perished during the era of the Holocaust:
My dear father: Reb Avraham-Dov, may G-d avenge his blood, perished in the first group of martyrs in Maytchet
My dear mother: Liba, may G-d avenge her blood – perished in the Dvorets Ghetto
My dear brothers: Ezriel, Shepsl, Mordechai, Feivel and Leib, may G-d avenge their blood

The perpetuator: Moshe Korn

In Eternal Memory

Of the destruction of my entire family, who perished at the hands of the enemy:
My father: Shalom
My moher: Rivka
My sisters: Sara, Sheina, Reizel

My soul mourns and cannot be comforted
Your bodies were annihilated, but your sublime images will always be before my eyes

The perpetuator:
Eliezer Rom (Romanovski)

[Page 407]

Memorial of Shlomo Chaim, Esther, Pesha and Elka Schmulewicz

I will always remember my beloved ones who perished in Molchad during the Shoah

My father Shlomo Chaim Shmulewicz
My mother Esther
My two sisters Pesha and Elka

These words in this Yizkor book for my town Molchad shall be a memorial forever

Tearfully,
Mordechai Leib Schmulewicz, America

[Page 408]

In Eternal memory

I uphold my holy duty to perpetuate the memory of my beloved uncles in the Yizkor Book of the destroyed community of Maytchet:

Kasriel Likter, may G-d avenge his blood, and his family, who were murdered in Maychet by the German murderers, may their names and memories be blotted out.
Moshe Lis (Lisagorski), born in Maytchet, died in America in 1967

Their niece:
Zelda Rozovski of Kfar Saba

See the photo earlier in this book

[Page 409]

Memorial Pages
to the Martyrs of Communities Close to Maytchet

In Eternal Memory

We perpetuate the names of our beloved ones in the Yizkor Book of the Jews of Maytchet and its region

Our father: Reb David-Heshel Katz, may G-d avenge his blood – perished in the Treblinka Death Camp
Our mother: Hinda of blessed memory – died in Israel
Our brother: Yitzchak of blessed memory – fell in the partisan actions in the forests of Goshorda in the area of Kovno
Our sister: Bluma, my G-d avenge her blood – perished in the Kovno Ghett

May G-d avenge their blood!

Mourning in grief and sorrow, the daughters:
Sonia Korn (nee Katz)
Genia Barnak (nee Katz)

[Page 410]

A Monument

With great pain and deep sorrow, I perpetuate in the Yizkor Book of my wife's native town of Maytchet my dear loved ones who died and were murdered by the Nazi murderers:

My beloved father: Reb Aharon Katz, may G-d avenge his blood
My beloved mother: Chaya Sara, may G-d avenge her blood
My dear sister: Esther Schveitzer, with her husband and children, may G-d avenge their blood
My dear sister: Freida Mehal, with her husband and children, may G-d avenge their blood
My beloved brother: Berl Katz, with his wife and children, may G-d avenge their blood
They were all murdered in our former town of Okuniev
My dear brother: Avraham Hirsch and his wife Bluma of blessed memory – died in Brazil

May their souls be bound in the bonds of eternal life

Reb Aharon and his wife Sara-Chaya Katz
of blessed memory. May he live long, Shmuel Katz

Perpetuated by their son and brother:
Shmuel Katz and his wife Alta

[Page 411]

For Eternal Memory

I recall the memory of my dear parents in the Book of Maytchet

My revered father: Reb Chaim the son of Yaakov-Leib and Chana, may G-d avenge his blood

My revered mother: Gittel the daughter of Yaakov and Feiga, may G-d avenge his blood.

My brother: Yaakov, and my sisters: Chana, Pesia, Rachel, Sima, and Sara, may G-d avenge their blood

Who perished in the Holocaust in my native town of Kowal

If there is anything good in me – I inherited it from you.

May their souls be bound in the bonds of eternal life

The perpetuator:
Tzipora Margolin (Ber) and her husband Nachum

[Page 412]

For Eternal Mmemory

To our family members in Haradzieja

Our father: Reb Leibel Perlman of blessed memory – died in Haradzieja
Our mother: Chaya, may G-d avenge her blood – perished in the Haradzieja Ghetto
Our sister: Golda of blessed memory – perished in Haradzieja
Our sister: Chasha and her husband, may G-d avenge their blood – perished in the Haradzieja Ghetto

May their souls be bound in the bonds of eternal life

The mourners:
The daughters and sisters: Batya Sadovsky nee Perlman – Israel, Gitel Stat, nee Perlman – United States

[Page 413]

A Candle for the Souls

I recall the memory of my dear ones in the Yizkor Book of the community of Maytchet:

My dear father: Reb Yechiel of blessed memory – died in 1925 in Baranovich
My dear mother: Mrs. Beila, may G-d avenge her blood – perished in the Baranovich Ghetto
My dear brother: Avraham Yitzchak of blessed memory – died in 1933 in Baranovich

May their souls be bound in the bonds of eternal life

The perpetuator: The son and brother – Lazer Rabinovitch

A Candle for the Souls

For eternal memory in the Yizkor Book of Maytchet of my dear family members from Zhetl

My dear father: Reb Yosef Rozovski of blessed memory – died during the German occupation
My dear mother: Chana of blessed memory – died in Zhetl in 1936
My dear brothers and sisters: Berl, Moshe, David, Keila, and Itka –perished in the Holocaust at the hands of the murderers, may their names be blotted out.

May their memories be a blessing!

The perpetuator:
The son and brother: Shlomo Rozovski of Kfar Saba

For Eternal Memory

I hereby perpetuate in the Yizkor Book of Maytchet the memory of my dear mother
Mereh Yarmelovski, nee Lubetzki, may G-d avenge her blood, who lived in Slonim and perished during the time of the Holocaust in Maytchet

May her memory be blessed!

The perpetuator:
Doba Leterman nee Yarmelovski – Israel

[Page 414]

A Candle to the Souls of my Dear Ones

My revered mother: Chana Lubchik of blessed memory – died in 1916 in Haradzieja
My revered father: Reb Moshe-Yosef Lubchik of blessed memory – died in 1939 in Haradzieja
My sister: Menucha and her husband Yaakov Sabin and their children – perished in Stowbtsy
My sister: Sara Batya, her husband Berl Kroshinski and their children, may G-d avenge their blod – perished in Haradzieja
My brother: Avraham, his wife and children, may G-d avenge their blood – perished in the Holocaust
My brothers: Shmuel and Shlomo of blessed memory – perished in exile behind the iron curtain

May this page in the Yizkor Book of the community of Maytchet serve as an eternal flame to their souls and a perpetual monument to their memories

The perpetuators:
Their son and brother: Shimon Lubtzik and his wife Chaya

For Eternal Memory

We recall the memory of our dear ones in the Yizkor Book of the community of Maytchet

Our dear father: Reb Moshe Aharon Lebovitz of blessed memory – died in 1929 in Zhetl
Our dear mother: Leah, may G-d avenge her blood – perished in the Holocaust in 1942
Our dear sister: Michla of blessed memory – died in Zhetl in 1929
Our dear sister: Risha, her husband David Yarmovski and their children, may G-d avenge their blood – perished in the Holocaust
Our dear sister: Batya, may G-d avenge her blood – perished in the Holocaust

May their souls be bound in the bonds of eternal life

The perpetuators:
The daughters and sisters:
Yafa Harpaz nee Lebovitz – Raanana
Chasha Alter nee Lebovitz – Petach Tikva

[Page 415]

For Eternal Memory

I hereby perpetuate the memory of my dear ones in the Yizkor Book of the community of Maytchet:

My dear father: Yaakov Sochaczewski of blessed memory – died in Łodz in 1940
My dear mother: Sheindel. May G-d avenge her blood – perished in the Treblinka Death Camp
My dear brother: Shimon and his wife, may G-d avenge their blood – perished in the Holocaust
My dear brother Yeshayahu of blessed memory – fell in the Second World War in Poland-Germany
My dear sister: Chana and her family, may G-d avenge their blood – perished in the Holocaust
My dear sister: Tzipora, may G-d avenge her blood, perished in the Holocaust

May their souls be bound in the bonds of eternal life

The perpetuator:
Bella Gorski nee Sochaczewski

For Eternal Memory

Our dear father: Reb Binyamin Yatvitzki, may G-d avenge his blood
Our dear mother: Tova, may G-d avenge her blood
Our dear brother: Chaim, may G-d avenge his blood
Our dear sister: Beila, her husband Leizer Fiksztejn, and their children Aharon and Chana, may G-d avenge their blood
Our dear sister: Leah, her husband Yitzchak Menker, and their children, may G-d avenge their blood

All perished in the Dvorets Ghetto at the hands of the Nazi murderers and their assistants

May their memory be blessed!

The perpetuators:
the sons: Yitzchak Binyamini (Yatvitzki), Eliezer Yatvitzki

[Page 416]

In Memory of Those Dear to our Souls

Our dear father: Reb Shlomo Mechtiger, may G-d avenge his blood – perished in the Holocaust in his native town of Zawiercie
Our dear mother –Hodel of blessed memory – died in Zawiercie

**Shlomo Machtiger,
may G-d avenge his blood**

Hodel of blessed memory

**Let this page in the Yizkor Book of the community of Maytchet serve
as an eternal flame to their souls and a perpetual monument to their memories**

The perpetuators
The son Yechiel Mechtiger, the daughters – Hela, Rachel, and Shoshana

[Page 417]

A Candle to the Memory

My dear father: Reb Yaakov the son of Reb Tzvi Makarensky, may G-d avenge his blood

My dear mother: Beila the daughter of Avigdor Ratanski, may G-d avenge her blood – perished in the Pruzhany Ghetto

My dear sister: Rivka and her husband Yosef Shifman, may G-d avenge their blood – perished in Szereszów

My dear sisters: Liba and Esther, may G-d avenge their blood – perished in Auschwitz

Yaakov and Beila Makarensky

Liba Makarensky   Esther Makarensky

May this page in the Yizkor Book of the community of Maytchet serve as an eternal monument to their memory

The perpetuators:
Their son and brother Moshe Makarensky and his wife Freidel

[Page 418]

In Memory of Those Dear to our Souls

Our dear father: Reb Mordechai Leib Likter of blessed memory – died in Zhetl during the Russian occupation
Our dear mother: Rivka, may G-d avenge her blood
Our dear brothers: Isser, Zalman Our dear sister: Beila, may G-d avenge her blood

Murdered in Zhetl by the murderers, may their names be blotted out, during the era of the Holocaust

Our brother: David, killed on the front near Bialystok in the Red Army

May this page in the Yizkor Book of the community of Maytchet serve as an eternal monument to their souls

Sitting: Father Mordechai Leib Likter and mother Rivka nee Lisagorski.
Standing from left to right: David, Zalman, may she live long Zelda, may she live long Liba, Beila, Isser, and Yerachmiel

The perpetuators:
The daughters and sister: Zelda Rozovski nee Likter – Israel, Liba Solkin nee Likter – United States

[Page 419]

A Monument

In eternal sorrow for my beloved parents

My beloved father: Meir Cerulnik
My beloved mother: Zlata

Murdered in the Baranovich Ghetto

Honor to their memory!

In sorrow:
Mere Barda-Cerunlik, United States

In Eternal Memory

My revered father: Reb Yehoshua Kozol, may G-d avenge his blood – perished in Baranovich during the Holocaust
My revered mother: Mrs. Golda of blessed memory the daughter of Reb Yisrael Zalman and Zlata Shlovski - died in Baranovich in 1939
My brother Moshe and his family, may G-d avenge their blood – perished in Baranovich during the Holocaust
My brother: Avraham and his family, may G-d avenge their blood – perished in Baranovich during the Holocaust
My sister: Gitel and her family, may G-d avenge their blood – perished in Baranovich during the Holocaust
My sister: Esther may G-d avenge her blood – perished in Baranovich during the Holocaust
My brother: Mordechai, may G-d avenge his blood – perished in exile in Russia
My brother: Leibel of blessed memory – fell in a partisan action

May their souls be bound in the bonds of eternal life

The perpetuator:
Their son and brother – Eliahu Tenenhoiz

[Page 420]

Eternal Remembrance in the Memorial Book

Our dear sister Badna, her husband Moshe Chaim Nibsky and their dear children: Avraham Shmuel, Yoseph, Eliyahu, Zalman Yitzchak, Sarah Leah, and Shulamit

-----that met their end Kiddush Hashem (sanctifying G-d's name) in the Holocaust in the ghetto if Baranovichi

Their soul should be remembered among the living

Our pain is great and there is no consolation for us

Commemorators:
Sister: Henya Piklani Rosenbloom
Brother: Yoseph Eliyahu Pinual-Piklani

These Are the People We Mourn

We are commemorating the memory of our loved ones, members of our family that died and were destroyed by the Nazi's (may their names be erased) in Baranovichi

The ones who are standing left to right:
Our brother Aba Sduvitsky – he was killed in a German bombing raid.
Will be blessed for a long life Mordechai Sduvitsky (Israel) Will be blessed for a long life Kalman Sduvitsky (Israel)
Seated left to right: Our sister Kheina, our mother Rivke, their end came in Baranovichi,
Our father Yakov Sduvitsky (may his memory be for a blessing) who died in the year 1940.
Our brother-in law Moshe Pikus, his end also came in Baranovichi Bottom row left to right: The children of our sister Kheina: Chasha, (and may they live long) Mordechai, Avraham and Aharon.
Their end was also in Baranovichi

Our pain is great and there is no consolation for us

The commemorators:
Mordechai and Kalman Slduvitsky

[Page 422]

Yizkor – List of Holy Ones

SURNAME	FIRST NAME	ADDITIONAL FAMILY
Abramovitz	Alter	and family
Abramovitz	Zlata	and family
Abramovski	Zln	and family
Abramovski	Mordechai	and family
Afrin	Hertzen	and family
Ahronovitz	Hirshl	and family
Ahronovitz	Chana	and family
Alpert	David	and family
Bar	Chaim "Shub"	and family from Ustrulnik
Bas	Yakob	and family
Belski	Abraham	and family
Belski	Mendl	and family
Belski	David	and family
Belski	Israel	and family
Belski	Moshe Yehuda	and family
Belski	Tvi	and family
Belski	Koniah Rivka	and family
Belski	Freidl	and family
Belski	Shmuel Noach	and family
Berman	Gershon	and family
Berman	Israel	and family
Gutman	Leibl	and family
Bilitzki	Leizer	and family
Bilus	Iser	and family
Bilus	Zeidl	and family
Binyamin	Hertzen	and family
Bisl	Alter	and family
Bitenski	Chaia Cherna	and family
Bitenski	Mereh	and Reuben and the "haorim"
Bitenski	Sonia	and family

Bodovla	Yoel	and family
Bodovla	Israel	and family
Bortzka	Ariah	and family
Bortzka	Yosef	and family
Bortzka	Feigl	and family (from Klshniki)
Boruk	Hakurk	and family
Breski	Reuben	and family
Brishinski	Leibl	and family
Brishinski	Moshe	and family
Drbinski	Yakob	and family
Dubkovski	Efrim	and Yosef
Dubkovski	Yakob	and family
Dubkovski	Itzak	and family
Duzitzki		and family
Dvortzki	Gneshe	and family
Dvortzki	Yosef	and family
Dvorz'tzki	Yakob	and family
Ehetz	Aizik	and family
Epshtein	Iser	and family
Feder	Moshe	and family
Garbarz	Abraham (Kosher butcher)	and wife Chana (SZELUBSKI)
Garbarz	Golda	husband and 2 sons
Garbarz	Dobe	
Garbarz	Peszja	
Garbarz	Judith	
Garbarz	Tauba (daughter)	
Garbarz	(son)	
Garbarz	Josel	
Girshovitz	Elkhanon	and family
Girshovitz	Yosef Shimon haLevi	and wife
Gildshtein	Rabbi Elkhanon	and family
Gildstein	Noach	and family
Gilrovitz	Abraham	and family

Gilrovitz	Dinke	and family
Gilrovitz	Keikl	and family
Gilrovitz	Yakob	and family
Gilrovitz	Itzak	and family
Gilrovitz	Leibl	and family
Gilrovitz	Nachum	and family
Gilrovitz	Shimon	and family
Ginburg	Rabbi Yakob	and family
Ginchinski	Alter	and family
Ginchinski	Yakob	and family
Ginzburg	Yakob	and family
Girski	Bashke	and family
Gordon	Leizer	and family
Gorski	Hinda	and family
Gorski	Chaim Meir	and family
Gorski	Ekhial	and family
Gorski	Elke	and Aidela
Gorski	Kopl	and family
Gorski	Krushe	and family
Itvitzki	Nechama	
Kaplan	"Der"	
Kaplan	Dvora	and children
Kaplan	Zev	and children
Kaplan	Itzak Tzvi	and family
Kharlap	Alter	and Sarah Reikl
Khasid	Zishke	and family
Khasid	Yosef	and family
Khenls	Aharon	and family
Khrvrovitzki	Idl	and family
Khrvrovitzki	Mordechai	and family
Khrvrovitzki	Shmuel	and family
Khrvrovitzki	Shimon	and family
Kobinski	Nachum	and family

Korn	Yosef	and family
Korn	Itzak	and Kreina
Korostovski	Deikeh	and Kreina
Korostovski	Moshe	and Kreina
Kostlinski	Khenon	and family
Kostrovitzki	Beila	and family
Kostrovitzki	Yakob	and family
Kostrovitzki	Yakob	and family
Kostrovitzki	Noach	and family
Kotin	Itzak	and Kreina
Kozlovitzki	Abraham Ekhial	and family
Kravchik	Eliahu	and family
Kravchik	Sima	and family
Kravchik	Shmuel	and family
Krulvitzki	Tzira	and family
Krulvitzki	Hertzl	and family
Krushinski	Shmerl	and family
Kushnrovski	Shimcha David	and family
Leib	Hngr	and family
Levin	David	and family
Libman	Zev	and family
Libman	Itzak	and family
Libman	Moshe	and family
Lipshitz	Tzvi	and Feigl
Lisker	Abraham	and family
Lkhovitzki	Shimon	and family
Lmshovski	Ben-Zion	and family
Lmshovski	Yehuda Leib	and family
Lmshovski	Mordechai	and family
Lmshovski	Reuben	and family
Lozovski	Zeidke	and family
Lozovski	Israel	and family
Lozovski	Note	and family

Lozovski	Rakhel Leah	and family
Lozovski	Shaul	and family
Lozrovitz	Zelig	and family
Luski	Yosef	and family
Mendelvitz	Chaim	and family
Mirski	David	and family
Mirski	Shimon	and family
Mishkin	Grune	and family
Miskin		and family
Mlvovski	Aharon	and family
Moleh	Mariashe	and Chana and family
Mordkovski	Yona	and family
Mordkovski	Yosef	and family
Mordkovski	Mordechai	and family
Mordkovski	Tzira	and family
Movshovitz	Asher	and family
Movshovitz	Shlum	and family
Nesviz'iski	Heniah Bashe	and family
Nesviz'iski	Hirsh	and family
no surname	HaRav Abel Dov	and family
no surname	Moshe (Chaia Rakhel's)	and family
no surname	Sulke (Chana)	and family
Novogrodski	Idl	and family
Novogrodski	Shlomo	and family
Novogrodski	Shimon	and family
Novomishiski	Itzak	and family
Okun	Yakob	and family
Polonski	Eliezer	and family
Rabitz	Iser	and family
Rabitz	David	and family
Rabitz	Yehoshe	and family
Rabitz	Mina	and family
Rabitz	Nachum	and family

Rabitz	Shlomo Leizer	and family
Rabitz	Shmeia	and family
Rozik	Eliezer	and family
Rozinski	Ekhial Leib the Shamos	and family
Rozinski	HaKhnoni	and family
Rubinovitz	Ester	and family
Rubinovitz	David (Duziah)	and family
Rubinovitz	Yehoshe	and family
Rubinovitz	Yudl	and family
Rubinovitz	Monia	and family
Rubinovitz	Mikl	and family
Rubinovitz	Moshe Tzvi	and family
Rubinovitz	Pinchas	and family
Rubinovitz	Tzira	and family
Rubinovitz	Tzvi	and family
Rubinovitz	Shlum	and family
Rubizovski	Yakob Israel	and family
Rubizovski	Hirshl-Tzvi	and family
Rubizovski	Berl	and family
Rubizovski	Yakob	and family
Rubizovski	Leibl	and family
Rubizewski	Reizl	and family
Rukovitzki	Gershon	and family
Safir	Shmariah	and Alte
Shimshelvitz	Yona	and family
Shimshelvitz	Itzak	and family
Shinovski	Zev	and family
Shinovski	Yosef	and family
Shinovski	Pinchas	and family
Shinovski	Ester	and family
Shinovski	Zev	and family
Shinovski	Chaim	and family
Shinovski	Israel	and family

Shinovski	Moshe	and family
Shinovski	Nisl	and family
Shkolnikovitz	Aba	and family
Shkolnikovitz	Efrim	and family
Shkolnikovitz	Boruk	and family
Shkolnikovitz	Yosef	and family
Shkolnikovitz	Meirim	and family
Shkolnikovitz	Moshe	and family
Shkolnikovitz	Ezrial	and family
Shkolnikovitz	Pesach	and family
Shkolnikovitz	Rafael	and family
Shkolnikovitz	Shlomo Henok	and family
Shkolnikovitz	Shlomo	and family
Shlomovitz	Abraham Moshe	and family
Shlomovitz	Itzak Heikl	and family
Shlovski	Tzvi	and family
Shlovski	Sheina Malka	and family
Shmulvitz	Aba	and family
Shmulvitz	Abraham	and family
Shmulvitz	Berl	and family
Shmulvitz	Ziml	and family
Shmulvitz	Yosef	and family
Shmulvitz	Yakob	and family
Shmulvitz	Mikal	and family
Shmulvitz	Moshe ben Abraham	and family
Shmulvitz	Moshe ben Shaul	and family
Shnitzki	Shlomo	and family
Shtein	David	and family
Shushen	Asher	and family
Shvirnski	David	and family
Shvtz'ik	Abraham Gitl	and family
Shvtz'ik	Berl	and family
Shvtz'ik	Zavl	and family

Shvtz'ik	Itzak Yakob	and family
Shvtz'ik	Moshe Aharon	and family
Shvtz'ik	Moshe	and family
Singlovski	Israel Yehuda	and family
Sinvski	Israel Chaim	and family
Slutziak	Dvora	and family
Srverovski	Abraham	and family
Srverovski	Dinka	
Srverovski	Ziml	and family
Srverovski	Chaia	and Golda
Stulovitzki	Leizer Kadish	and family
Stulovitzki	Mikl	and family
Stulovitzki	Tzvi	and family
Stulovitzki	Shimon	and family
Stulovitzki	Abraham	and family
Syitzki	Yehuda Leib	and family
Syitzki	Moshe	and family
Syitzki	Nekeh	and family
Talor	Meir	and family
Tzimerman	Chaim Leib	and family
Tzirinski	Yehoshe	and family
Tzirulnik	Efrim	and family
Tzirulnik	Berl	and family
Tzirulnik	Velvel	and family
Vankadlu	Yehoshe	and family
Vilkomirski	Zvi	and family
Vinograd	Leibl	and family
Vlfovitz	Chaim	and family
Yoselvitz	Abraham	and family
Zbortzki	Zavl	and family
Zilberman	Yakob	and family
Zimrinski		and family
Zlotnik	Yakob	and family

Zlotnik	Shmel	and family
Zmuchik	Abraham	and family
Zpolinski	Henfa	and family
Zpolinski	Feivl	and family
Zukovitzki	Abraham David	and family
Zukovitzki	Lipa	and family
Zusman	Iser	and family
Zusman	Yosef	and family

[Page 427]

Epilogue
Translated by Jerrold Landau

Thirty years have passed since the destruction of our town Maytchet, ten years have passed since our organization in Israel decided to publish this memorial book, and nearly four years have passed since the introduction to this book was written. These dates prove that our path was not paved in roses. We needed powerful energy and a deep will in order to not despair of the task that we took upon ourselves. During those years, we were forced to overcome deep difficulties in various areas, in the gathering of material, the gathering of photographs for the plates, and especially in the collecting of the financial means to fund the publication of the book. Finally, all these difficulties are behind us, and at the time that these words are being written, the book is already under the printing press, and the day that the book will appear in publication is approaching. In the wake of the many efforts that we imbued in the publication of the book, it is appropriate to clarify our aims for ourselves in full detail.

Three goals stood before us in the publication of this book.

1. To fulfill the Divine decree: Remember... and do not forget.
2. To perpetuate the memory of the martyrs of Maytchet and the region.
3. To unite the Holocaust survivors of Maytchet in Israel and the Diaspora.

The survivors of Maytchet and their descendants who come after them, as all the nation of Israel, will recall that which the modern day Amalek, the descendents of the most cultured people in the world, perpetrated against us in our day. We will never forget this. We will remember them for eternal disgrace and disparagement. This book will remind every generation that follows us not to forget.

As in all holy communities, we have also established an eternal light and permanent monument as an appropriate memorial to the martyrs of Maytchet for the children of the People of the Book.

Throughout the years that we worked toward the publication of this book, we have felt ourselves as a united tribe. All of the meetings contributed greatly to bringing the hearts together, and we hope that in the future, the connections amongst us will strengthen, the brotherhood and friendship amongst us will increase, we will rejoice with the achievements of each person, we will come to the assistance of our fellow at a time of need, and perhaps we will succeed in planting the best of our aspirations in the hearts of our descendents - the young generation growing up before our eyes.

[Page 428]

However, we must not avoid the truth, and we must not hide a specific point that in our opinion represents a partial lack. Today, the book is not open to everybody. We have not succeeded in including all of the Maytchet natives in the Diaspora in the publication of the book, despite our many approaches to them to help us in our holy task. Throughout all these years, we have never stopped turning to and requesting our fellow natives to become partners with us in actualizing our objective; however, to our dismay, not all of them responded to our call. Even as this book is already under the printing presses, they still refused to believe that we were achieving our objective. Due to the lack of appreciation on the part of a portion of the Maytchet natives in the Diaspora, it will not be possible for us to bestow this book to their descendants in their language.

Aside from a few isolated articles, the content of this book is published in the language in which it was written. The majority of the Jews of Maytchet to whom this book will reach know both languages, Hebrew and Yiddish. The number who know only one is small. We planned at the outset to present a translation of a summary of the articles in additional foreign languages, so that they descendants of the Maytchet natives who are located primarily in the United States and Argentina will also be able to read the book. However, unfortunately, due to a dearth of financial means, we were forced to forgo this. We can only hope that the natives of our town overseas will enlist everything that remains in their memory from their childhood learning, from the Hebrew that they studied in *cheder*, in the Talmud Torah and in school, so that they can also understand that which was written in Hebrew, and that they will volunteer to read, tell and explain the content to their descendants.

Our thanks and gratitude are hereby extended to all those who helped us with the publication of the book. We also express our gratitude to the owner of the zincograph, Mr. Gershon Caspi and his staff, for preparing the plates to our satisfaction, and to the owner of the Mofet Printing Press, Mr. Yitzchak Reisman, and his workers, for producing such a fine work in the form of this book.

[Page 429]

Memorial Prayers for the Deceased and Communion
Compiled into English by Amir Shomroni
Sequence of the Memorial Service

a. Evening prayer in public, full Kaddish (*Kaddish Titkabal*)

b. Kindling of 6 candle Menorah in memory of the six million Jews who were murdered in the Shoah.

c. The Head of the Congregation opens the memorial ceremony with awakening speech and eulogy.

d. The participants pray Yizkor in the order set forth.

e. The Cantor recites two chapters of Psalms – 69 and 83, followed by the recitation of the Mourners Kaddish with the entire congregation.

f. Studying two Mishnayoth from the daily Mishnah, and then Kaddish DeRabbanan by the entire participants.

g. Prayer of Aleynu LeShabeach and singing of Any Maamin

h. Studying two *Mishnayoth* from the daily Mishnah, and then *Kaddish DeRabbanan* by the entire participants.

i. Prayer of *Aleynu LeShabeach* and singing of *Any Maamin*.

For the martyrs of the Maytchet Communuty

May God remember the thousands holy and dear victims of the magnificent and extolled Community of Maytchet. Fathers and sons, mothers and babies, old and young, descendants of honorable and righteous, the innocent and the pious, Torah scholars and traditionally observant, merciful, charitable, and public servants. With their pure blood being spilled on the mass graves in the soil of the *Chabonik*, and breathed their last breath in holiness and purity. For their yearning to our holy land may their souls be bound in the Bond of its children, builders and defenders.

For the martyrs of the Shoah of the People of Israel

May God remember the pure and innocent souls of the millions of the children of Israel who were tortured furiously and cruelly murdered in all kinds of unusual deaths: who by water and who by fire, who by sword, who by beast, who by famine, who by thirst, who by storm, who by plague, who by strangulation, and who by stoning. Holy and pure were they all, among them scholars and saints, righteous and pious, authors and poets, leaders and public servants, innocent and charitable. For their sacrifice on the sanctification of God's name and being Jews, may their souls be bound in the Bond of the heroes and saints of the People of Israel for eternal memory.

[Page 430]

For the family martyrs

May God remember the souls of my father and mother, my grandfathers and grandmothers, my brothers and sisters, my uncles and aunts, my relatives, my friends who were killed, slaughtered, burned, drowned, strangled and buried alive, for the sanctification of God's name and the People of Israel who passed away. Because of that I vow charity in their behalf, memorializing their souls, and on account of that may their souls be bound in the Bond of Life, together with the souls of Abraham, Isaac and Jacob; Sarah, Rebecca, Rachel, and Leah; and together with the other righteous men and women in the Garden of Eden. And let us say Amen.

El Male Rachamim - God full of mercy

God full of mercy, protector of widows and fathers of the fatherless, please be not silent, and show no restraint on their behalf for the Jewish blood that has been spilled like water. Grant perfect rest on the wings of Your Divine Presence in the lofty abode of the holy, pure and valiant, who shine as the brightness of the heavens to the souls of millions of children of Israel, among them three thousands children of the holy community of Maytchet, and its environs; men, women and children who were put to death, slaughtered, burned, drowned, strangled, and buried alive for the sanctification of God's name and the People of Israel.

Because all the children of Maytchet in Israel and elsewhere pray for the elevation of their souls, therefore, shall the Master of mercy care for them under the protection of his wings for all time, and bind their souls in the Bond of everlasting life. Their resting place shall be in the Garden of Eden. God is their heritage, may God remember their sacrifice, and may their righteousness stand for us and for all the People of Israel.

O Earth! Do not conceal their blood and let there not be a resting place for their cries. In their merit shall the remnant of Israel return to its rightful place and as for the holy ones, their righteousness shall be a presence before God as an everlasting memory. They will come in peace and will rest in peace, and they will meet their rightful destiny at the end of days. And let us say Amen.

Name Index

People, places, events, concepts

[**Note:** the following three names were not in the original index, and were added by the coordinator]

Disin	Mina	269
Disin	Rabbi Peretz	269, 270
Disin	Yona	269
Dombrovitz		246
Drivinski	Yakob	283
Drutz'in		26, 43, 214, 215, 352, 360, 361
Drutitzin		26, 232
Druzdin		67
Dubkovski	Chaya	188, 191, 286, 321, 351, 388
Dubkovski	Efraim	188, 191, 286, 321, 351, 388
Dubkovski	Noach	188, 191, 286, 321, 351, 388
Dubkovski	see Chaneles, Leah	
Dukrova		41, 297, 330, 352-353
Dvina		27
Dvinsk		27
Dvorets		33, 35-36, 40, 42-43, 48, 67, 71, 224, 236, 257, 259, 295-297, 308, 330, 346, 348, 350-351, 358-359, 360
Dvorjetski [Boretsky]	Alta	184, 226, 282 ,382
Dvorjetski	Naftali-Hertz	275
Dvorjetski	Sima	275
Dvorjetski	see Abramovski, Nachum	
Dvorjetski	see Ginzburg, Sima	
Dvorjetski	see Lipshitz, Liza	
Dvorjetski	see Luria, Sima	
Dvorjetski	see Rabinovitch, Hadasah	
Dvorjetski	see Rabinovitch, Malka	
Dvorjetski	see: Liberman, Sonia	
Divrei Menachem	B Rabbi Menachem Rizikof	119
Edlin	David	252, 280, 397

Kobinski	Eliahu	359
Kobinski	Nachum, R'	51, 123
Kobrin		31, 110-116, 125, 192, 372
Kadelichova		97, 233, 294, 329, 334, 346, 348
Koidanow		125
Kochav MiYaakov	By Rabbi Yaakov-Sender Grynberg	107
Kolodni	Khesha	209, 219
Kolodni	Yoel	209, 219
Kolokovski-Gozinitzki	Masha	360, 363
Korman	Dr.	255
Mizrachi fund		61
Korn	Abraham-Dov	256-257, 285, 293-294, 101
Korn	Aharon ("the doctor")	255-256, 291
Korn	Ezrial	257, 348, 354, 404
Korn	Ezrial, R'	61-63, 256-257, 291, 294, 373, 404
Korn	Feivel-Leib	257, 348, 354, 404
Keren HaYesood		61, 141, 167
Korn	Yitzchak	61, 255-256
Keren Kayemet		61, 123, 141, 146-157, 163, 167, 175, 178, 191, 260, 273
Korn	Kreina	61, 255-256
Korn	Leba	256-257, 285, 293-294, 101
Korn	Mordechai	257, 348, 354, 404
Korn	Moshe	61, 196-198, 237, 257, 293, 352, 404
Korn	see Stolovitzki, Sara-Rivka	
Korn	Shepsel	257, 348, 354, 404
Korn	Sonia (Katz)	407
Korn	Yosef	257, 348, 354, 404

Lemshovski	Ruben	145, 146
Lemshovski	Yehuda-Leib	145, 146
Leterman	Tzira (Yarselovski)	411
Lev	Mordechai	323
Levin	Boruk	299, 337, 352
Levin	Mina (Gorski)	198, 237, 323, 353, 385
Levinvik	"Der" Z	353, 362
Lexicon Hagevurah		348, 352, 354, 357, 358, 359-362
Lexicon of Geography-History		30
Liberman	Saul	114
Liberman	see Eker, Aryeh	
Libman	Shaul, Rabbi Prague	114, 217
Lida		31, 40, 88, 309, 313, 334, 339, 346, 348, 355, 358, 370
Lida Yeshiva		88, 89
Lidowski	Leizer	358, 363
Likter	Beila	265, 416
Likter	Chaya-Sara	132, 141, 154, 169-170, 264-265, 283-284, 292, 406
Likter	David	265, 416
Likter	Erekhmial	265, 416
Likter	Iser	265, 416
Likter	Kutrial	132, 141, 154, 169-170, 264-265, 283-284, 292, 406
Likter	Liba	265, 416
Likter	Mordechai-Leib	264-265, 416
Likter	Rivka	264-265, 416
Likter	see Sulkin, Liber	
Likter	Yakob	265, 416
Likter	Zalman	265, 416
Likter	see Roski, Vlada	
Lichtenstein	Kalman	43

The Tzukunft	[The Future – newspaper]	250
Amateur theater		54, 145, 176,
Tiktinski	R' Chaim-Leib	118
Flourmill		49, 52, 54, 64, 75-6, 148
Vilna Technion		153
Jerusalem Talmud		110, 114
Topoli	Itzak-Meir	233, 386
Topoli	Rosa (Wolinski)	233, 386
Torah and Scholarship		30, 40, 89, 90, 100-105, 121-124, 134, 139, 145, 149, 151-153, 160, 236
Torah Scribes		94
Treblinka		413
Trink	Yesheya	348, 354-355, 362
Truba	Leib	358, 363
Truki		31
Tatars		27, 34, 47
Turetzki	see Gorski, Miriam	
Tzeiri Zion		159
Tzeshele		209
Tzeshler	see Mordukovski, Nachum	
Tzig	see Shvartzik, Elke	
Chiganov Partisan Unit [Otriad]		358
Tzinovitz	Moshe	113, 159, 251
Tzirbanski	Sonia	257
Tzirulnik	see Barda, Mereh	
Band		260
General Zionists		141, 163, 165
Tzorboim	Chaim-Zelig	44,45
Tzrulnik	Ester	257
Tzrulnik	Meir	417
Tzrulnik	Zlata	417
Czeczak	Rabbi Moshe	96

Tzukerkof	Malek	330, 335
Charny Partisan Group [Otriad]		46
Okun	Binyamin	397
Okun	Chasha	397
Okun	Yakob	397
Ukrainians		35
Ulasik	Valia	301, 332, 354
Irgun Yotzei Maytchet	Organization of Maytchet Natives	195-200, 369
Urul	Ester	215, 255
Urul	Moshe (Feldsher)	215, 255
Urul	Zilpa	215, 255
Orzechovaky	(Neiten) Nachum	218-220, 269
Orzechovaky	Asher	129-130, 155, 107-208, 218-219, 243, 269-270, 272, 276
Orzechovaky	Chana	269
Orzechovaky	Chana	304, 379
Orzechovaky	Chana-Leah (Ginzburg)	218-220, 269
Orzechovaky	Chasha	304, 379
Orzechovaky	Kreina (Olinski)	107, 218, 269, 335, 379
Orzechovaky	Mereh	304, 379
Orzechovaky	Nachum-Eli (Rozanski)	269
Orzechovaky	Sheina (Chertak)	129-130, 155, 107-208, 218-219, 243, 269-270, 272, 276
Orzechovaky	Yona	107, 218, 269, 335, 379
Ushrovski	Iziah	358
Utbotzk		93
Ovadya	Hachshara Kibbutz of Hapoel Hamizrachi	192
Warsaw		118, 147, 185, 187, 193, 203, 236, 261, 361
Wasserman	Rabbi Elchonon	219
Council of Russian Zionists		38

List of Pictures

Note: Page number listed on the right are page numbers in the Original Yizkor Book, not this translation.

List of Pictures (cont.)

[See the enlarged pictures by clicking on the thumbnails]

APPENDIX

This material was not in the original Yizkor Book.

It is deemed worthwhile so it is included in this appendix.

Article about Yizkor Book from Yiddish Paper

Translation of a review article written for a U.S. Yiddish Newspaper after the Molchad Yizkor Book was published in 1973. Given to Myrna Siegel 1990 by Maytchet survivor Tsira Rabets Kaplan Royak who was living in Peoria, Illinois, U.S.A.

Molchad was a small Jewish shtetl far away in White Russia by the Polish/Soviet Union border. Yiddish life in the broader world seldom heard about Molchad and the surrounding towns.

But the Jews of Molchad had an active Jewish life for several centuries. It is all told in the Yizkor book, which was published in Israel by the people of Molchad, with the assistance of "Maitcheters" from different countries. It has 450 pages and the book was written in Hebrew and Yiddish and has many pictures. The publisher of this valuable book is Ben Zion Haim Ayalon.

Reading the book you get to know how Jews lived in Molchad since the middle of the 17th century. For many years the people there had a good life. Parents worked hard to have their children educated so it should be the Youth in the Darkness looking for the Highway of Tomorrow. Many generations continued a Goldenah Yiddishkiet. Today it is still and dead in Molchad. Life has been emptied out from Molchad. Death is our beloved home. But in our hearts live the memories of the dead Jews of Molchad. At all our celebrations you are with us. With your names we call our children. There is an honorable rememberance of you. In that book which includes six different chapters, they describe in detail what was the life of Jews in Molchad. Organizations, personalities, education, daily life, everybody alike without discrimination.

At first Molchad was under the Russian occupation. Later in June, 1941, when Hitler invaded the Soviet Union, the little town of Molchad experienced the same destiny as the other little towns of the area. They fell into the hands of the murderers of Hitler. About the sufferings and annihilation and heroism of the Jews of Molchad.

In the book they tell of how the majority of the Jews there were murdered on the spot by Hitler and his collaborators. Many Jews from Molchad also fought heroically as partisans. More and more I would like to write. My little town. How beautiful, natural, modest and good heart and good characteristics.

But I open my eyes and see the big grave near the Green Bridge where the train went. The earth is moving still fresh because they were buried alive------the holy ones that were not totally killed.

The book has 48 pages of memorials with names and photos from the annihilated holy ones.

History of Molchad from USHM

The United States Holocaust Memorial Museum Encyclopedia of Camps and Ghettos 1933-1945, vol. 2 Ghettos in German-Occupied Eastern Europe, vol. ed. Martin Dean, series ed., Geoffrey Megargee (Bloomington: Indiana University Press in association with the United States Holocaust Memorial Museum, 2012), pp. 1241-1243.

Mołczadż

Pre-1939: Mołczadż (Yiddish: Meytshet), town, Nowogródek województwo, Poland; 1939-41: Molchad', Baranovichi oblast', Belorussian SSR; 1941-44: Molczadz, Rayon Goroditsche (Horodyszcze), Gebiet Baranowitsche, Generalkommissariat Weissruthenien; 1944: Molchad', Baranovichi oblast', Belorussian SSR; 1954: Baranovichi raion, Brest oblast'; 1991: Republic of Belarus

Mołczadż is located 139 kilometers (87 miles) southwest of Minsk. Jewish settlement here dates back at least to the sixteenth century. The first synagogue was built in 1648. In the mid-eighteenth century, the town's owners invited Jews to open two flour mills; others were then invited to open shops, a tavern, and workshops. In 1765, the Jewish population was 369. The town also attracted several Hasidic leaders and their followers. After the Third Partition of Poland in 1795, Mołczadż came under Russian rule. In the nineteenth century, Jews also worked as fur merchants, horse traders, shopkeepers, peddlers, and artisans. In 1897, the Jewish population was 1,188, out of a total population of 1,733 (68.5 percent). At this time Mołczadż developed as a popular resort, and Jews provided services for vacationers. In World War I, the German army occupied the town between 1915 and 1918. There were severe shortages of food, but the Jews enjoyed some increased freedom in their personal and communal affairs.i

After World War I, the Jews of Mołczadż received financial support from the American Jewish Joint Distribution Committee (AJDC) and other organizations. Subsequently a Jewish cooperative bank and a mutual aid society were established to assist small merchants and craftsmen. In 1922, the synagogue was refurbished and there were six Bet Midrash study centers. In the 1920s, most of the streets in Mołczadż were unpaved and unlit and most houses were built of wood. In the interwar years, the Jews were negatively impacted by Polish economic policies. Heavy taxes and unemployment led to increases in the numbers receiving communal assistance and in emigration. The Zionists ran a summer training camp for young Jews preparing to make aliyah.

On September 17, 1939, the Red Army entered Mołczadż and imposed a Soviet regime. The town was flooded with Jewish refugees from Nazi-occupied western

Poland, some of whom subsequently fled to Wilno, in the hopes of escaping to Palestine and the West. The Soviets closed down or nationalized most private businesses. Several Jewish owners were arrested and exiled to punishment camps in the interior of the USSR. Craftsmen were organized into an artisanal cooperative. The two Hebrew-language schools were closed and replaced by a Yiddish-language school with a Soviet curriculum.ii

After the German invasion on June 22, 1941, Soviet forces withdrew and some Jews fled with them into the Soviet Union. The Germans captured Mołczadż on June 29. On that day, they caught several Jewish youths that didn't make it across the former Polish-Soviet border. The Germans murdered them on the road to Slonim. Some sources indicate that soon after the occupation, Jews living with non-Jews were forced to move to separate houses together only with Jews (perhaps creating a de facto open ghetto). However, most surviving Jews recall that no formal ghetto was established in Mołczadż.iii Among other anti-Jewish restrictions imposed by the new German authorities, Jews were ordered to wear yellow patches, they were prohibited from having contacts with non-Jews, they were forbidden to use the sidewalks, and they were forced to surrender their horses.

The Germans set up a local auxiliary police under the command of a rabid anti-Semite. They ordered the Jews to select a five-man Judenrat headed by Ehrlich, a refugee from Częstochowa. They compelled the Judenrat to collect and pay special taxes. The Germans demanded money, gold, and jewelry, and subsequently clothing, shoes, furniture, and other items. Whenever a fine was levied, the Germans threatened to kill some Jews, if their demand was not met promptly. The Judenrat members did everything they could to meet these demands. The Judenrat also had to supply people for forced labor. Every day groups of men and women were sent on work assignments around the town, guarded by local overseers. On their way to and from work the guards beat and humiliated the laborers. Groups of Jews were sent to various labor camps. From one group of more than 20 people sent to the camp in Koldyczewo, several Jews managed to escape to join the partisans in the Naliboki Forest. iv

On February 14, 1942, members of the local police, on their own initiative removed 20 Jewish men and women from their houses. They took them to a tar pit outside of town and murdered them. The Jews protested this Aktion to the German authorities in Baranowicze, which resulted in a death sentence being passed on the local police chief. However, his colleagues helped him to escape into the surrounding forests.

In January 1942, several members of prewar Jewish youth groups made contact with Soviet partisans operating in the area and also fled into the forests. In March they and their families then slipped into the Horodyszcze ghetto. In April 1942, several youths from Mołczadż working at a farm in Dobrowszczyzna rose up and killed the anti-semitic farm manager and his helpers. In early summer, a group of younger Jews, some of whom had experience in the Polish Army, formed an underground resistance group. They even approached the Judenrat to try to get some money to buy arms. From various sources, they obtained three rifles and several revolvers and began to train. There was also spiritual resistance in Mołczadż, guided by the Stolowicze rabbi. Jews met in secret to teach the children and pray for deliverance.v

As news spread about the liquidation of other ghettos, many in Mołczadż hoped that they would not share the same fate. In late May or early June 1942, the police ordered the Judenrat to mobilize 200 Jews to dig pits, allegedly for fuel storage tanks, in Burdykowszczyzna, next to the Russian Orthodox cemetery of Horodyszcze. On June 3, 1942, after they finished digging, the Germans shot the 200 Jews at the pits. Around this time, sensing an impending Aktion, the Jews of Mołczadż began to dig bunkers and seek hiding places. Young members of the underground set up a guard to warn of the approach of hostile forces.vi

Before dawn on July 15, 1942, truckloads of German Gendarmes and local police from various posts in Gebiet Baranowitsche surrounded the town. At daybreak the Jews were ordered to assemble in the market square. Local police then combed the houses for stragglers. When the Stolowicze rabbi emerged in his prayer shawl, he was shot to death. The Jewish underground group sought to disrupt the encirclement by firing their weapons, hoping to create enough confusion for a mass escape. The Germans opened fire with machine guns and killed 20 Jewish fighters. Only nine made it to the forest. Another 60 Jews fled into the Horky Forest where, under the protection of partisans, they set up a family camp.

About 3,300 people assembled in the market square. They were lined up facing the wall, hands up, and searched for valuables. Then the Germans and local police took them in groups of 100 to the pits outside of Mołczadż. After ordering the victims to line up next to the pits and undress, they shot them. Over several days, from July 15-18, approximately 3,300 Jews were murdered. The operation was probably organized by the Security Police outpost in Baranowicze, assisted by German Gendarmes and police auxiliaries from the Baltic States as well as Belorussia, including some local police from Rayon Neswish (Nieśwież).vii

A number of Jewish specialist workers and their families were initially spared during the Aktion and put into a remnant ghetto. In August 1942, the Germans urged everyone still hiding in the forest or elsewhere to come back to Mołczadż, guaranteeing their safety in the "new ghetto for the workers." About 200 people were gathered in Mołczadż altogether. After twenty days, on the pretext that they were heading for a new work site to dig peat they were taken to the pits and murdered.viii

Young men in the forest joined various Soviet partisan brigades. Jewish partisans from Mołczadż settled accounts with several collaborators from their town and participated in other acts of sabotage along the railway lines. Some were caught, turned in by informants, or killed in action. A few sought refuge in the nearby Dworzec ghetto/forced labor camp. A number of Jews from Mołczadż survived until the return of the Red Army in summer 1944. They included partisan fighters, people still in hiding, and refugees who had escaped into the Soviet Union in summer 1941.ix

Sources:

Information about the Jewish community of Mołczadż can be found in the following publications: "Molczadz," in Shmuel Spector and Bracha Freundlich, eds., *Pinkas Hakehillot. Encyclopaedia of Jewish Communities: Poland, Vol. 8 Vilna, Bialystok, Nowogrodek* (Jerusalem: Yad Vashem, 2005), pp. 404-408; Benzion H. Ayalon, ed., *Sefer-zikaron le-kehilat Meytshet* (Tel Aviv: Meytscher Societies in Israel and Abroad, 1973); and Leonid Smilovitskii, *Katastrofa evreev v Belorussii 1941-1944 gg.* (Tel Aviv: Biblioteka Matveia Chernogo, 2000), p. 187.

Documents regarding the destruction of the Jews of Mołczadż can be found in the following archives: AUKGBRBMO (Arch. No. 3617, Case No. 35694); GARF (7021-81-102); NARB (845-1-6, p. 31); and YVA.

Samuel Fishman and Martin Dean

---

i "Molczadz," in Shmuel Spector and Bracha Freundlich, eds., *Pinkas Hakehillot. Encyclopaedia of Jewish Communities: Poland, Vol. 8 Vilna, Bialystok, Nowogrodek* (Jerusalem: Yad Vashem, 2005), pp. 404-405.

ii Ibid., pp. 405-406.

iii Ibid., p. 406; Benzion H. Ayalon, ed., *Sefer-zikaron le-kehilat Meytshet* (Tel Aviv: Meytscher Societies in Israel and Abroad, 1973), e.g., p. 304, "there was no ghetto in Mołczadż." See also the comments of survivors posted (as of April 8, 2009) at http://www.jewishgen.org/Yizkor/belarus/bel178.html. Martin Gilbert, *The Holocaust: The Jewish Tragedy* (London: William Collins, 1986), p. 380 and *Rossiiskaia Evreiskaia Entsiklopediia* (Moscow: Russian Academy of Natural Sciences, Jewish Encyclopedia Research Center, "Epos," 2004), vol. 5, p. 442, however, both refer specifically to a ghetto in Mołczadż.

iv *Pinkas Hakehillot: Poland, Vol. 8 Vilna, Bialystok, Nowogrodek*, pp. 406-407.

v Ibid., p. 407; and Shalom Cholawsky, *The Jews of Bielorussia during World War II* (Amsterdam: Harwood, 1998), p. 127.

vi *Pinkas Hakehillot: Poland, Vol. 8 Vilna, Bialystok, Nowogrodek*, p. 407.

vii Ibid., p. 407; and NARB, 845-1-6, p. 31. On the participation of police from Nieśwież (now Nesvizh), see AUKGBRBMO, Arch. No. 3617, Case No. 35694, against Petr Sergeevich Korolev, born 1915, 2 vols. On the nationalities of the perpetrators, see also http://www.jewishgen.org/Yizkor/belarus/bel178.html.

viii *Pinkas Hakehillot: Poland, Vol. 8 Vilna, Bialystok, Nowogrodek*, p. 407. According to Marat Botvinnik, *Pamyatniki Genotsida Evreev Belarusi* (Minsk: Belaruskaia Navuka, 2000), p. 100, the 200 Jewish specialist workers and their families had been assigned to dig peat and were moved into an enclosed ghetto in August.

ix *Pinkas Hakehillot: Poland, Vol. 8 Vilna, Bialystok, Nowogrodek*, p. 408.

Zelda and Litman in Naples, Italy 1948 after receiving visas to go to U.S.

Biography of Zelda (Gilerovitz) and Litman (Litowarski) Litow

Submitted by Dena L. Hirsh and Leon Litow

Our mother, Zelda Gilerovitz, lived in Molchadz with her family, including her mother Dena; her brothers Label, Yankel and Moshe; and her sister Yache. Her father Yisrael died before she was born, and Dena managed the family business until Label took over as head of the family. He was very involved in various Zionist organizations in Molchadz, and served as head of the Jewish Council there. Yankel attended university and became a grain exporter. Moshe studied medicine at the University of Wilno. All three were excellent orators and commanders in a semi-military organization. Yache was involved in the Revisionist Party's youth group, Betar. Zelda, the baby of the family, also attended gymnasium in Baranowicze.

Litman Litowarski, our father, and his family lived in a village called Zverovshchina. He and his older sister Shifra, lived in Molchadz for a few years while they worked as tutors in order to earn money to attend school there themselves. Litman knew the Gilerovitz family through the school they attended and his involvement with the various Zionist organizations.

When the Germans came to the area in 1941, they began the wholesale slaughter of the Jews in what is now western Belarus. Litman, Shifra, older sister Grunia, younger brother Pinchus, cousin Gershon (Jerry) Siegel, and Shifra's eventual husband Zigmund (Saul) Mintz fled to the nearby forest with other family members, determined to become partisans. Such were Litman's successes as an underground leader that the Nazis put a price equivalent to $2,600 on his head, a tremendous bounty for that time. After Zelda's entire family was killed, she made her way to Litman's group and remained with him thereafter. For a while they were a part of the Bielski group, made famous by the 2009 movie *Defiance*. Although he was only about 22 years old at the time, Litman was put in charge of a squad of 200 men by Tuvia Bielski.

Litman and Zelda were married by Litman's Uncle Shepsel Shushan on the day that Berlin fell in 1945. They returned to Baranowicze, and Litman worked on the railroad militia for the Soviets and Zelda worked as a typist for a Soviet Jewish major. After a while they decided to try to make it to Palestine and set out through various DP camps for Austria and then to Italy, where they were reunited with Shifra and Saul.

Sponsored by Zelda's cousin, Isidore Rabinowitz, they immigrated to the United States in 1948 due to Zelda's health. They first settled in Rehobeth Beach, Delaware, and ultimately in Salisbury, Maryland. Shifra and Zigmund immigrated to Worcester, Massachusetts. Grunya and Pinchus made it to Palestine, and Gershon to Canada. Litman returned to his agrarian roots, working for Rabinowitz's Paramount Poultry in Harbeson, Delaware, and establishing his own successful poultry business, Litow, Inc.

Litman and Zelda had two children, Leon (Yisrael Yitzhak) and Dena. Litman was very involved with Beth Israel Synagogue in Salisbury, serving as its ex-officio cantor, occasional fill-in rabbi, president, school principal, founder of their adult education program and leader of the local Jewish War Veterans. He was a frequent contributor to letters to the editors of various newspapers. He spoke at schools and churches, primarily about his experiences in, and lessons of, the Holocaust.

Zelda died in 1969, and in 1973 Litman married Jean Mandel Hayes, who had two children, Alan Hayes and Susan Hayes Westenburger. Together they had four children, ten grandchildren, and six grandchildren. Litman died in June 2012, followed by Jean in July 2012. He was the last of the family group that survived the Shoah.

Family meant everything to Litman not only because he was a devoted and loving husband, father, grandfather, and great-grandfather, but also because Litman's family represented his personal victory over the many forces who sought to kill him and his family. A favorite statement of his, uttered when he looked at a picture taken at the US Holocaust Museum with his children, grandchildren and nephew Harry Mintz (Shifra and Saul's son) and his family was, "Hitler, you bastard, you lost and I won."

Printed with the permission of Mr. Stacy Karten, a retired free-lance writer in Owings Mills, Maryland. A version of this article entitled, "Daring to Survive," was published as a special to the *Baltimore Jewish Times* in October 2003.

Photo not published with article.

Littman Litow 1st row left kneeling – Bielski Partisans

Miracles and Wits Aided Survival
By Stacy Karten

Don't tell Litman Litow miracles are events that only happened in Biblical times. Through incredible perseverance and miracles, the 81-year-old Salisbury, MD, resident survived World War II and the Holocaust by being a resistance fighter and hiding in the forest for four years in Poland. From 1941 until Berlin fell in 1945, Mr. Litow banded together with 1,500 other partisans to combat the Germans, bad weather and every other conceivable obstacle associated with trying to survive day to day.

"To survive you need a lot of miracles and to use your wits," states the very well spoken Mr. Litow. Those ingredients played a major part in his being alive today.

Born Litman Litowarski in 1922 in Molczdaz, he grew up on his family's farm. "When the Germans came into Poland, they forgot us at first. They were too busy and we were off the beaten track," recalls Mr. Litow. Then the wit and miracles started coming into play.

"I owe my life to a German major in charge of agriculture," Mr. Litow claims. Their only cow wandered off to a German controlled farm and was "arrested." Mr. Litow decided he would go talk to the officer to get the cow back. "When I left, my family was crying because many people did not come back from such visits," explains Mr. Litow.

The protocol called for speaking to the Underfuhrer through a translator. To his good fortune, Mr. Litow also spoke German so he could hear the translator saying that Mr. Litow stole wood (which he did to keep his family warm in the blizzard conditions) and not mentioning the cow. "I could see where this was headed so I asked the German major if I could speak to him directly. The translator looked at me and if looks could kill, ..." remembers Mr. Litow. The major listened to Mr. Litow's explanation and allowed him to take the cow back under the conditions he would work the German farm for a few days.

"I was a good farmer and miller and was put in charge of eight Russians. The Germans came to watch how a Jew works. The propaganda was we were lazy," says Litow. "The Russians told me to 'slow down, you're going to kill us,'" adds Mr. Litow. The special German officer praised Mr. Litow's farming.

Mr. Litow's family consisted of his father, five sisters and a brother. His mother died of natural causes about the time the Nazis marched into Poland. He attended a Hebrew day school and celebrated his bar mitzvah. "My bar mitzvah wasn't like they are today. I went to shul on a Monday morning, read the torah, had an old piece of cake and vodka," he remarks.

Jews in the overlooked rural areas started to be rounded up by the Germans. The village elder came to the Litowarski family and announced they had two hours to get their belongings together as they were going to be relocated. About half way on their journey, they stopped in Polanka and lodged with a Jewish settler. "The Germans said if we leave the house, we'll be shot," Mr. Litow says.

While in the house, they heard gunshots. A naked woman was seen running. "The Germans shot her several times," remembers Mr. Litow. "I saw bloody tracks in the white snow."

Call it a coincidence or call it a miracle, but another stroke of luck came Mr. Litow's way. "I heard sleigh bells, which meant a big shot was coming through," said Mr. Litow. He went outside and recognized the German officer who befriended him during the cow problem. "The officer said, 'My son, what can I do for you?' I had such a warm feeling when I heard this," says Mr. Litow. To the officer, Mr. Litow replied, "We didn't commit any crime against the Third Reich. We haven't done anything." Several days later the major had the Litowarski family taken to Nova Mesh. They did not register as Jews living there as required but hid in the attic of a house.

Once again, Mr. Litow was aggressive and went to the German major to seek work as a farmer. Not only did he get a job, Mr. Litow bargained for the lives of two of his sisters, his brother and a couple of friends to get hired, too. "We were desperate and would drown our despair in hard work," Mr. Litow says.

The reality of what was happening to Jews in the towns started hitting harder. People began discussing escape plans but there was a big problem. "If we escaped, our family members left in the town would be treated like hostages and killed," explains Mr. Litow. According to Mr. Litow, one plan they kept in mind was to carry kerosene and torch the whole town. "This way the Germans wouldn't know whether to save their families or catch Jews," he remarks.

Mr. Litow cites another miracle in the course of these events. "We were producing food for the German army, so they needed us alive to do the harvest quickly," he states. Working gave them more time to plan.

Stories about mass murders and graves in the area were becoming more common. "One time I saw my father, and he looked like he returned from the dead," remembers Mr. Litow. It seems they marched people to a mass grave but were told they had the right day but the wrong month, so they marched the people back. "That was the last day I saw my father and three of my sisters," Mr. Litow comments.

With the town now surrounded by the German army and no family hostages left, it was time to get out. "I acquired a rifle, 50 rounds of ammunition and two grenades from my best friend. He was the son of a Catholic priest," says Mr. Litow.

While discussing escape plans, Mr. Litow was speaking with his Hebrew school principal, who wondered what would happen to them. "Through our history we were down but never out," Mr. Litow responded.

The small Jewish group decided they would escape into the forest. "We put our ears to the ground, it's like a telegraph, and we heard explosions. We knew the Germans were killing the people in town," comments Mr. Litow. They split into three groups and escaped into the woods, meeting up with other partisans, including Russians. "We said to a Russian commander, if you try to betray us, the first bullet in this gun is for you," Mr. Litow remembers.

The resistance groups, totaling as many as 1,500 people, remained in the forest for four years. They started acquiring more weapons from retreating and dead soldiers and would barter with farmers for food. Some tactics they employed to fight the army included cutting phone wires and loosening nuts and bolts on the ties to derail trains. They were successful, and at one point Mr. Litow says, "There was a $2,600 bounty on my head." Hiding in the forest also gave the resistance a strategic advantage. "We would ambush any Germans who came into the forest so they wouldn't come in," remarks Mr. Litow.

The Jews living in the forest tried to maintain their religious observances during these difficult times. "Before Yom Kippur in 1942, the forest was surrounded by 1,400 Germans," Mr. Litow recalls. They heard the army truck engines and soon came upon a mass grave. The partisans tried to give some of the dead proper burial. When they returned from dealing with this horror, it was sunset. "A school teacher and I knew enough by heart to say Kol Nidre," Mr. Litow says.

Mr. Litow's two sisters and brother survived through the war with him, and on the day Berlin fell Mr. Litow married his first wife, Zelda. She was the remaining survivor of an extended family of 74 people. After the war, Mr. Litow gained employment for the railroad militia in the Soviet Union, but his dream was to reach Palestine. A Russian leader legally helped him embark on travels which took him to Poland, Czechoslovakia, Hungary, Austria and finally to Italy. While in Rome, his wife suffered two nervous breakdowns.

Doctors advised him that his wife would recover better in a Jewish environment. Her breakdown was somewhat related to verbal conflicts with some non-Jews in Rome. "I decided I would sacrifice my dream of going to Palestine and not my wife," states Mr. Litow. They came to America on April 13, 1948, through the help of a cousin in Philadelphia who provided them the certificates and money they needed to immigrate.

A bright new world and life was on the horizon for Mr. Litow. The family in Philadelphia owned a poultry business in Georgetown, Delaware, and Mr. Litow started working there. "I had to learn English fast and became supervisor of plant operations after a year," he says. He moved on to head the chicken-growing operation and eventually bought some of his own chicken farms.

In 1949, Mr. Litow moved to Salisbury to be closer to his workplace. He has been a stalwart in the Jewish community there for over 50 years. Mr. Litow has served as cantor of Beth Israel Congregation since 1950, was a board member and president. He also initiated the popular Breakfast Club, a Sunday morning adult education program which features a mix of religious and professional speakers. The Breakfast Club runs weekly except in the summer.

"Litman is an inspiration to people," remarks Rabbi H. Richard White of Beth Israel. "It isn't that he just survived. He didn't watch what happened. He took survival into his own hands," adds Rabbi White. Mr. Litow also frequently visits schools to talk about the Holocaust, which Rabbi White says is of "great value."

Mr. Litow's wife, Zelda, died in 1969 and he remarried his current wife, Jean, in 1972. "I have been very lucky to have had two beautiful women in my life," he boasts. He has two children from his first marriage, and he and his second wife have a total of 10 grandchildren.

Litman Litow survived the worst ordeal and went on to make immense contributions to the Jewish community. Thinking back, he cannot believe he made it. States Mr. Litow, "I never even dared to dream to survive. I dreamed to get weapons to fight."

Photo taken at 10th anniversary of the U.S. Holocaust Museum in Washington, D.C.

Litman considered himself a very lucky man to have had two beautiful wives. With his first wife Zelda he had a daughter Dena 2nd row 2nd from right and son Leon last row, third from right, Litman's wife Jean sitting to his right.

He was very proud of his Combined family, 4 children and their spouses, 10 grandchildren and 4 great-grandchildren.

He would look at this photo and say, "Hitler, you S.O.B.-------you lost and I won!"

A Tribute to Martin Small
By Pedro Antonio Rubio, MD, PhD

Mordechai 'Motel' Leib Schmulewicz was born in Molchad, Russia (now Belarus) in 1916.He graduated from Hebrew school, attending Yeshiva as well as other Russian and Polish schools. During the Holocaust, their Polish neighbors hideously murdered 86 members of his family when the Nazis invaded Molchad. These included his father Shlomo, his mother Esther, and his two sisters Pesha and Elke. Martin believes that they were buried in Molchad on July 1942 in the mass grave that contains 3,600 bodies.

Mordechai Leib was forced to live in various ghettos, labor and concentration camps finally ending at Mauthausen. The camps of Mauthausen-Gusen were the last to be liberated during World War II. On May 5, 1945, the camp at Mauthausen was approached by soldiers of the 41st Recon Squad of the US 11th Armored Division, 3rd US Army.

After the war, Mordechai Leib was relocated from a hospital in Linz, Austria to a convalescent home in Salzburg, Austria and then boarded a train for Italy with Italian POWs returning home from the Russian front. In Italy he joined the 'Bricha Aliya'. He worked with the Jewish Brigade to acquire ammunition that was sent illegally to Palestine. During this time he also participated in the 'Aliya Bet' and helped send countless illegal immigrants to Palestine. In 1948 Mordechai Leib traveled to Israel and fought in the war of Independence.

In 1950 Mordechai Leib immigrated to the United States and took the name Martin Small. It was a few weeks later that he met Doris, also a Holocaust survivor, whom he married in 1951. They settled in Manhattan and had two children, Miriam Esther and Stuart Michael. Unfortunately their son died at the tender age of eleven.

After a successful career in business, at age sixty-five Martin retired and moved permanently to the family's summer home in Huntington, New York. After his retirement Martin, a self-taught artist, began creating art inspired by poetry and Hebrew liturgy. Although he uses a variety of media, he works primarily in wood sculpture, carving and relief. He enhances his surfaces and images using a variety of stained and painted materials. Martin also writes vivid poetry based on his life tragic experiences.

The subject matter that Martin portrays is deeply personal. He has often said, "I am the Holocaust!" and with that personal statement the images that emerge from his creative energies are from the depths of his soul and from personal experiences. His 'Holocaust' pieces are deeply moving and have to be looked at carefully to extract their full meaning and intent. The images of folk-life are wonderfully charming recollections of his youth in Molchad, the little town in which he was raised. The works based upon Hebrew liturgy are gracefully created and express Martin's deep personal faith, despite the horrors and tragedy that he has lived through.

Martin's work is part of the permanent collections of the Holocaust Art Museum and Remembrance of Martyrs and Heroes at Yad Vashem, in Jerusalem, Israel; the Holocaust Memorial & Tolerance Center of Nassau County, Glen Cove, New York: and the Faith Bible Chapel in Arvada, Colorado. Reflecting on his ability to speak many languages his work is international and can be found in private collections throughout the world (Israel, England, Russia, Poland, Italy, Argentina, Colombia, and United States among them).

The Office of the Town Council of the Town of Huntington, New York issued a Proclamation on May 2, 2000 recognizing Martin "as an important artist and a tremendous resource in our community". Martin and Doris left Huntington in April 2003 and moved permanently to Broomfield, Colorado, to be close to their family. Their daughter Miriam and her husband William Saunders have two children, Jennifer and Jacob, who are married and have blessed Martin and Doris with six great grandchildren.

Martin was diagnosed with advanced pancreatic cancer in March 2008 and decided not to have treatment. His dying wish to see his life story in print became a reality in May 2008 when his book 'Remember Us: From My Shtetl Through the Holocaust' was released. 1986 Nobel Peace Prize recipient Elie Wiesel wrote: "Like all Holocaust survivors' memoirs, Martin Small's poignant recollections of his experiences in German concentration camps, as told to Vic Shayne, constitute an important contribution to the literature of the most tragic chapter of contemporary history."

He donated his portion of the proceeds from his book towards the purchase of a Torah scroll for Congregation Bonai Shalom in Boulder. A Torah that survived the Holocaust (Shoah) was located by Rabbi Marc Soloway. On July 31, 2008, Martin in his weakened condition proudly carried the Torah into the sanctuary and read a portion of that week's chapter fulfilling his dream.

After a heroic battle with his illness Martin passed away in his sleep at his home in Broomfield, Colorado on Saturday, November 29, 2008 (Hebrew date 2nd Kislev 5769). He dedicated his life to share his Holocaust experiences with groups of all ages. An accomplished educator, artist, poet, lecturer, and author, whose sweetness and compassion touched the hearts of everyone he had contact with; Martin will be sorely missed by all.

החיים ורבצר צרורה נשמתו תהי

May his soul be bound in the "Bond of Life"

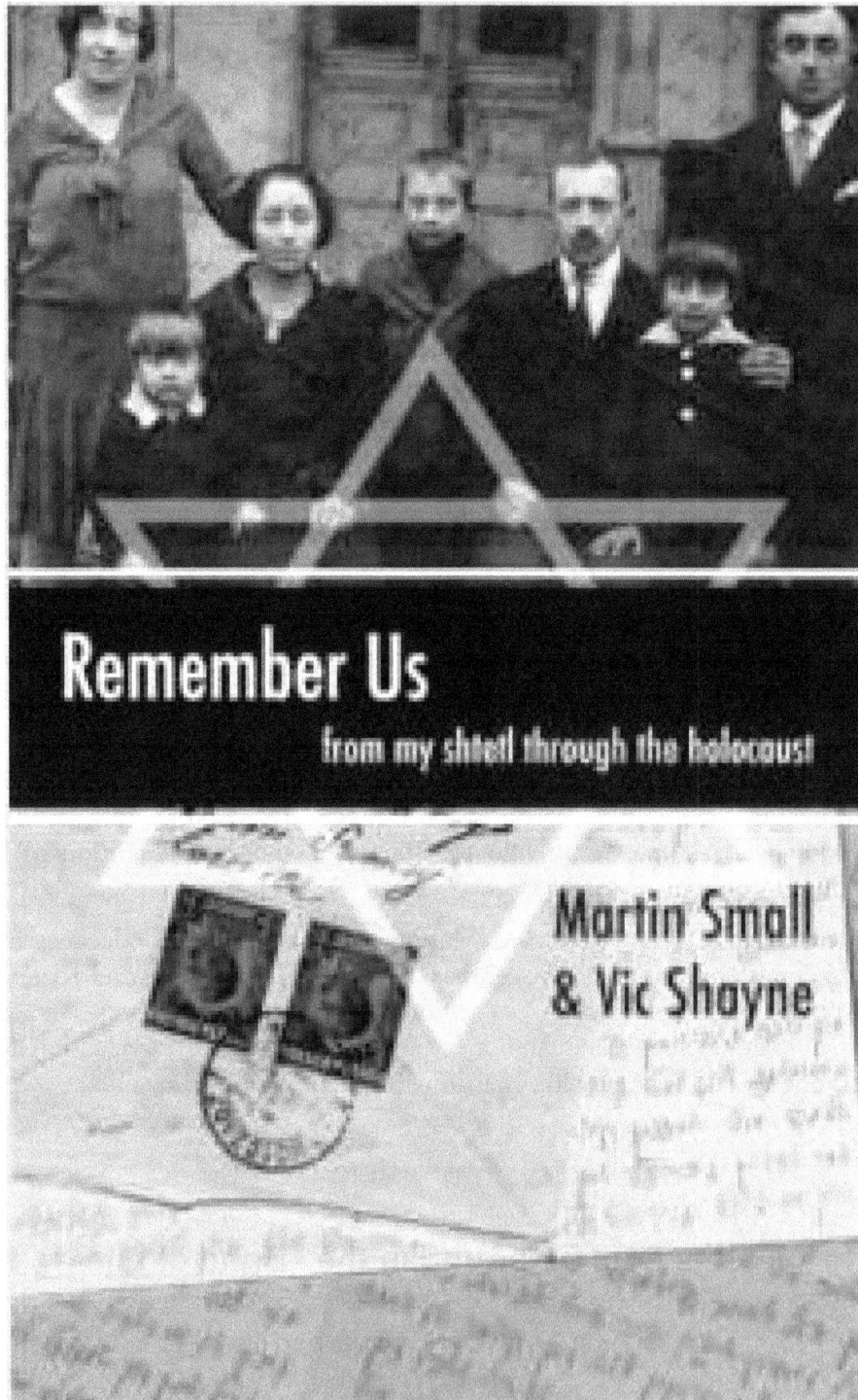

Remember Us

from my shtetl through the holocaust

Martin Small
& Vic Shayne

Photo on book cover is Martin (center between parents) with his two sisters

Far left Elka and far right Pesha   Aunt and Uncle standing in back

Following article appeared in local Boulder Paper
Martin Small's First Book Signing Sold-Out

Martin Small, the subject of the new book, **Remember Us: From my shtetl through the Holocaust**, appeared at his synagogue in Boulder Thursday night, June 19, 2008 for a book signing along with writer Vic Shayne. This event was scheduled to be a little gathering for a book signing, but with the great organization of Rabbi Marc Soloway and his staff at synagogue Bonai Shalom, there was not one book left unsold within a couple of hours.

Vic Shayne spoke about the process of writing this book as it was told to him by Holocaust survivor, 91-year-old Martin Small, resident of Broomfield, CO. Shayne said that although Martin Small's life is filled with painful memories, it would be even more painful not to remember, and he referred to Mr. Small as a hero whose book is no less than the story of a hero's journey.

Shayne also elaborated on Mr. Small's unusual ability to remember details, names, places and events that live in his memory from more than seven decades in the past. Some of these memories, said the writer, came to Mr. Small in the middle of the night, embedded in dreams and nightmares, adding to the pain and tears that went into this book.

Speaking from the audience, Shael Siegel, who, with his wife Myrna, traveled twice to Mr. Small's hometown of Maitchet, Poland, agreed with Vic Shayne's assessment of Mr. Small's uncanny memory. Mr. Siegel relayed how Mr. Small remembered every street and landmark in his hometown of Maitchet well enough to draw a detailed map for the Siegels that turned out to be not only accurate and useful, but also more detailed than the city officials were able to provide.

Myrna and Shael Siegel's trip to Maitchet was a bittersweet journey. Mrs. Siegel was able to visit the site of her (Boretsky) family's flour mills and neighborhood as well as the burial site of more than 3,600 Jews (including members of her and Martin Small's family) who were murdered by their Polish neighbors in July 1942 when the Nazis invaded the Belarus shtetl.

Martin with Torah

Torah Presentation at Congregation Bonai Shalom

One of Martin Small's deepest dreams was to have a Torah scroll at Congregation Bonai Shalom, the Boulder community in which he has played such a significant role in his years in Colorado. To help accomplish his dream Martin donated his portion of the proceeds from the sales of his recently published book "Remember Us from my shtetl through the holocaust".

Martin and his Rabbi Marc Soloway, chose a Torah that is 65-70 years old and was originally from Poland or Southern Germany. It is believed that before the war the Torah escaped to Israel and eventually came to the United States. Martin is proud of the fact that both him and the Torah are holocaust survivors.

On July 31, 2008 the memorable evening's celebration took place at the shul (synagogue) at Bonai Shalom. Martin looked reasonably well despite his condition and marched the Torah into the sanctuary just as he had dreamed. He then walked under the chuppah (traditional canopy) and told the capacity crowd that he was giving the proceeds from his book to help pay for the Torah. Martin walked the room embracing the Torah to connect with all of those in attendance. He then read from the Torah and mentioned that he had gone through the 'gates of hell' but was ready to go through the 'gates of heaven'. As the Torah was placed in the ark both Martin and Doris were chanting "the Torah is coming home."

Rabbi Marc Soloway commented: "It was a highly charged and very emotional ceremony that deeply honored our beautiful new Sefer Torah, as well as our friends Martin and Doris Small. Martin was so joyful, spoke about achieving this final dream and prayed that his grandfather would open the sha'are Tzedek (Gates of Righteousness) for him to return home. It was a deeply moving, powerful and significant ritual.

Martin Small with wife Doris at Torah presentation

Mordechai Leib's parents wedding Circa 1914

Eliyahu and Sheyna Bielous (Bride's parents); Esther and Shlomo Chaim Schmulewicz (Martin's parents); and Shifra and Avraham Schmulewicz (Grooms parents)

"Cries In The Fire"

This Hand-carved wood sculpture is in vivid colors and can be appreciated more by going to the web site:

http://www.martinsmallholocaustsurvivor.com.

Piece recounts Martin's initial impression soon after arriving at Mauthausen. Included are scenes of a small girl watching her mother being told that the grandmother is in the gas chamber, groups of Jews herded to the chambers, people carrying the bodies of their dead friends, and piles of bodies. (Holocaust Art Museum and Remembrance of Martyrs and Heroes at Yad Vashem, in Jerusalem).

This black and white sketch is how Martin envisioned the tragedy of the
mass killings in Maytchet July, 1942. He specifically blamed their
neighbors, who had once been their friends, as the Nazi collabortors

The Rubizewski Family

By Pedro Antonio Rubio, MD, PhD

The Rubizewski family was Chassidic Orthodox Jews that moved from Rubez to Koidenova after Rabbi Shlomo Chaim Perlow founded the Koidenov Chassidic Dynasty in 1833. The Koidenover Rebbe was a Lithuanian Chassidic Rebbe. After WWI the dynasty was moved to Baranovichi, Poland. Many of our family moved to Maytchet after Yankef Yisroel married and established himself in Maytchet.

The Jewish population of Maytchet in 1900 was 1,188. The name came from the Molchad River, which passes through the region and flows into the Molchadaka River. Maytchet was a miasteczko (small city) that was the seat of the council office of Molczadz. The Justice of the Peace was in Horodyszcze and the justice court in Nowogrodek. The 1928 population was 483. The railway was 4 km away on the line Baranowicze-Lida. The post office and telephone were in Molczadz and the telegraph was in Nowojelnia. Molczadz had the council office, one Catholic Church, one Orthodox Church, the Cooperative Office, and the Association Polish Primary School Personnel. Markets were on Wednesdays and the fairs were held on 29 June, 20 July, and 14 September every year. Maytchet had an electric power station, a tannery, a pitch factory, and sawmills.

Shloime Zalman Rubizewski was a Chassid from the Koidenover Rebbe who married Feige and had at least five living children: Yankef Yisroel, Leibl, Leah, Berl and Reizl. Yankef Yisroel married Ameleh Belouse, whose family lived for many generations in Maytchet, an ultra orthodox Jewish community where they established and prospered. The rest of his siblings also moved to Maytchet were Leibl and his family, Leah (married to Michel Schmulevicz) and her daughter Dwoshe, Berl and his family, and Raizl were murdered in the 15-17 July 1942 Aktion perpetrated by the Nazi's and their local sympathizers

Michel Schmulevicz and two of his sons, Moishe and Chonye, survived and immigrated to New York in the 1950s. When they arrived to the US, Moishe became Morris Samuels who never married and lived in Queens, NY. Chonye became Charles Samuels who married Genny Jean in New York.

My great grandfather Yankef Yisroel Rubizewski was born in 1871 in Koidenova and was a Chassid from the Koidenover Rebbe. After marrying Ameleh Belouse and establishing himself in Maytchet he became a very successful and wealthy merchant of forests. He bought forests, cut down the trees, processed them in his sawmills, and sold the lumber to the Russian government. Also, he sent ready-made wood to Germany, to private parties to build houses. He also sold logs to heat the houses in the *shtetlach* (small villages) around the forest. A Chassid and Talmudic scholar, he was also an arbitrator and a benefactor, who gave much to charity. He was the head of a *yeshiva* (religious school) for orthodox boys. This was a volunteer position in which he took great pride. Physically he was over six feet tall, with a handsome blood-red beard. In the *shul* (synagogue) he had two *mizrach* (honor) places for himself and his children, where he *davened* (prayed) three times daily.

There were only two brick houses in Maytchet, both owned by Yankef Yisroel. One was his home (surrounded by a wooden fence) and the other one a house that he converted into a tavern for his wife Ameleh to run. The Rubizewski's large brick home in Maytchet was located about 50 meters from the Rad Kromen on the same street. It was one of the few houses with a wooden fence around it. The crossroads were Baselum Gas (to the cemetery) and Mitkovichecy Gas (to Mitkovich, a small town).

Rad Kromen is Yiddish for the 'market place' or 'row of shops'. The Rad Kromen was located just across from the High Synagogue. The 1929 Ksiega Adresowa Polski (Polish Business Directory) was published on 07 November 1928 and it shows Rubiezewski J. in the Drzewo (bois) lumber business. A prosperous Jew, Yankef Yisroel had his place at the front of the synagogue.

Ameleh and Yankef Yisroel had six living children in order of birth: My grandfather Yudel Leib, Grunia, Benzion 'Ahlter', Meishl, Etel, and Yirshl Tzvi. In between there were five male children who were either stillborn or died in infancy. Ameleh owned and ran the family tavern (inn and restaurant where light fare, liquor and homemade wine was served).

During the Great War of 1914, the German army took over the Rubizewski house as headquarters and occupied the *shtetl*. The family was now crowded in a small house across the road from their own home. In 1917, the *Commandature* vacated Yankef Yisroel's house and departed from Maytchet so the Rubizewski family reclaimed their home. Later, a new *Commandature* arrived and took over the shtetl. The benevolent occupation of Maytchet was now ended. The new regime changed everything. The harsh, unforgiving life in Maytchet became harsher, more unforgiving. In 1918 the war was finally over and the occupation of Maytchet ended. Russia ceded the Grodno Gubernye to Poland and now the people of Maytchet had to adjust to a new language and a new government.

Yankef Yisroel died in 1935 and Ameleh died in 1936 both in Maytchet. During the Great Holocaust in the tragic years 1941-3, in which the beastly Nazis annihilated 6 million Jewish martyrs, the Jews of Maytchet met their bitter end, on the first to third days of Av 5702 (1942) during the German Aktion. It is during this Aktion that all the living members of the Rubizewski and the Belouse families in Maytchet perished on 15-17 July 1942.

Grunia was born in 1901 and became the great beauty of the family and perhaps in all of Grodno Gubernye. She was very much like her father, demanding, impatient, imperious, self-centered and self-absorbed. In 1917, her brother Ahlter brought Dr. Leon Rubinfeld, a dentist from Przemysl, Prussia, to his home. Leon was stationed as a Captain in the Austrian army in Molchad during WW I. Grunia fell in love with him and Yankef Yisroel arranged the marriage directly with Leon's parents. They married and settled in Przemysl around 1918, shortly after the end of the war. In Przemysl Leon opened a thriving dental practice but died prematurely in 1936. They had two sons, Lotek and Tzeshik. Grunia and the children were killed during the holocaust in Przemysl.

Grunia Rubizewski, David Zirinsky, Etel Rubizewski Zirinsky

All Three murdered in Shoah

Etel was born after 1904 (date unknown). During a day trip to Baranowicz, Etel met a local youth, Pesach Tsirinsky. At first she did not like him but he pursued her in Maytchet until she agreed to marry him. Yankef Yisroel arranged the marriage with the Pesach's parents who due to their land ownership, manufacturing and selling hardware, were quite wealthy. Pesach and Etel lived in Baranowicz but returned to Maytchet every summer to stay in a bungalow that they bought just outside of town. Etel was the fun-loving, mischievous one, the vamp, and the flirt in the family. On July 15, 1942 during the Holocaust, Etel and her two sons, Yaakov and David, hid in a neighbor's barn in Maytchet, The neighbor, a Pole, entered the barn to feed his animals and heard one of the children cry out. He found Etel and her two young sons and forced the children to watch as he raped and murdered their mother. Then he slaughtered both children. Everyone in Maytchet knew that the farmer had a crush on Etel when they were young and that she had rejected him. Pesach owned a hardware store in Baranowicz, was religious, and because he did not travel on Shabbos stayed in Baranowicz where he was murdered during the Holocaust.

Yirshl Tzvi was also born after 1904 and was the youngest brother. A maid accidentally dropped him when he was a baby, damaging his spine. He developed a hump that grew as he aged. He never forgave the world for his affliction. He lived in Maytchet and married Miriam Mera Bielski who was an accountant. It is unclear if the marriage was for love or was arranged by his father. Yirshl Tzvi was a merchant and was murdered along with his family in the Aktion of 15-17 July 1942.

1936 Miriam Bielski Rubizewski and Hershl Rubizewski

Both born in Maytchet---- both murdered in Maytchet

A great deal of gratitude is due to my great uncle Benzion 'Ahlter' Rubizewski who was born on July 16, 1902, the third living child and second son. If it had not been for him leaving Maytchet and later bringing his brothers Yudel Leib to Mexico and Meishl to Guatemala, my family would no longer exist. He was originally referred to as 'Benchele' but after his birth he was taken to a rabbi who gave him the nickname 'Ahlter' (old one) to wish him a long life. He attended the Cheder (traditional elementary school teaching the basics of Judaism and the Hebrew language) in Minsk but after years of pain and suffering at the hands of his father, he stole his brother Yudel Leib's passport and left Maytchet permanently at age 15 (1917) to avoid any more abuse and beatings. Because of the facial similarities between the two brothers he was able to use the passport for many years.

Yudel Leib RUBIZEWSKI 1927

After the Russian army, the Polish army, Berlin, and Paris he finally set up residence in Havana for a couple of years. Ahlter set sail to Mexico and became an itinerant hardware salesman. He built a small house in Pachuca and a small store next door. He arranged to buy a Mexican birth certificate and changed his name to Alfredo Rubio. Once Alfredo obtained his Mexican passport he burned Yudel Leib's passport stolen so many years before.

At the time, my grandfather Yudel Leib Rubizewski was married and lived in Kletsk with Elke and their three sons who agreed to come to Mexico. Alfredo sent Yudel Leib a one-way ticket to sail to Mexico. He arrived on April 26, 1927 by ship from Rotterdam and gave him a room in his house in Pachuca.

In February of 1929 Alfredo left Mexico for Guatemala after the two brothers quarreled and he settled in Antigua, Guatemala (the capital) and soon thereafter opened a hardware store in the business district. When his brother Meishl wrote to Alfredo that Jews could not find work in Poland, Alfredo sent him a one-way ticket to Antigua. His wife Esther and daughter Lize stayed in their apartment located behind the Rubizewski house in Maytchet.

Because of Zionist activities illegal in Guatemala, Alfredo and Meishl fled to Costa Rica, El Salvador and Panama. From there Meishl headed for Mexico to live and work in Toluca with Yudel Leib.

As a reward for his Zionist fund-raising activities in Central America, Alfredo received a certificate of entry to Eretz Yisrael as a legal immigrant. He decided to first go home to Maytchet to visit his family and find a bride. He took the train to Maytchet for his first home visit in more than 15 years.

ALFRED RUBIO 1920

When Alfredo returned to Maytchet he lived in an apartment on the second floor of the Rad Kromen [market place or row of shops] located across from the High Synagogue. Rivke Novogrudsky was 22 and Alfredo planned to settle in Tel Aviv and open an import business. He travelled through Europe looking for products to sell. He then returned to Maytchet for a second time and asked Rivke Novogrudsky to marry him. They had a small engagement party in the Rubizewski's house.

Six days after their engagement a neighbor alerted them that the police was asking questions about Ahlter. He did not hesitate and left Maytchet that night by train to Warsaw where he married Rivke. Later they embarked on the SS Martha Washington to Jaffa in third class. In Tel Aviv, Ahlter spent most of his time with the Ze'ev Jabotinsky's Revisionist Zionists. One day in Jaffa, Ahlter saw a shipload of *olim (*new immigrants) disembarking from Germany. He began to plan selling trips to Jaffa to coincide with the docking of ships from Germany and other European countries. Ahlter found a brand-new apartment located at

Nachmani 41 corner with Yehuda HaLevi. Rivke became pregnant and on October 3, 1933 she delivered Besodia.

Ahlter helped them out of the rowboats and escorted them onto the beach where others took over. Sometimes Ahlter, Abraham Stavsky, Abraham Stern and others stood for hours in the cold sea, silently waiting for the ships, helping the escaping Jews, usually women and children, enter the country illegally, right under the noses of the British.

To protect themselves from the British, they used code names. Avraham Stern was "Yair" and Ahlter's was "Nachmani." The Betar organization had learned that the British had alerted the Polish Government of Ahlter's activities and that the Polish police had a price on his head. They agreed that if they found him they would turn him over to the British Mandate immediately.

It was in February 1936 around nine o'clock at night when a Jewish policeman came looking for "Nachmani". The Jewish policeman told Ahlter that he must escape that night. He went to Haifa and then swam to a particular ship he knew was docked there. The Captain knew Alfredo and ordered his men to provide him with a change of clothes and then take him to the Captain's cabin. Alfredo explained to the Captain that he must leave Palestine immediately because there was a price on his head and the police came to arrest him that night. Henceforth, to everyone but Rivke, he will again be known only as Alfredo.

From Marseille Alfredo went to Paris but because of the German occupation of France, on January 6, 1941, Alfredo and family boarded the train for Spain. On March 15, 1941, they boarded the SS Serpa Pinto and on March 31, 1941 docked at New York Harbor, carrying 640 frightened Holocaust Escapers to safety and freedom. They were detained at Ellis Island along with hundreds of other passengers. They held them captive for three or four days. At night, the men and women were separated.

Alfredo had planned on finding some way for them to return to America as immigrants from Mexico and if that did not materialize then he would attempt to get them into Canada. They did not leave for Mexico but rather stayed in New York illegally. Some weeks later, an immigration lawyer arranged for them to go to Windsor, Ontario, Canada. They stayed overnight and the next morning returned to America from Canada crossing the border in Detroit, Michigan. as legal immigrants with the names Alfred, Ruth and Caren Besodia.

Amelia 'Amy' Rubio was born on September 21, 1943 in New York City. She was named after her paternal grandmother Ameleh.

Caren, Amy and Alfred Rubio

Alfred Rubio became ill with leukemia January 5, 1980 and died on January 25, 1980 at the Roosevelt Hospital in Manhattan aged 83. He is buried at Mount Lebanon Cemetery on the grounds of the Maitcheter Fraternal Aid Society. Ruth died on December 12, 2007 and was interred at Mount Lebanon Cemetery next to Alfred. Caren died on September 27, 2012 from a stroke. She was buried in Beth Moses Jewish Cemetery in Farmingdale, Long Island.

My grandfather Yudel Leib Rubizewski, the oldest child was born on December 25, 1894 in Maytchet. At age 13 in 1907 he went to the Baranovichi Yeshiva. On March 7, 1919 Yudel Leib married Elke Lotvin who was born on September 25, 1894 in Kletsk. After their marriage they moved to Maytchet where their sons Yitzjak (19 April 1921), Moishe (14 April 1923) and Berl (25 March 1927) were born.

Thanks to Alfredo's efforts on April 26, 1927 Yudel Leib arrived to Veracruz, Mexico by ship from Rotterdam via Cuba aboard the S/S Edam, was admitted as a legal immigrant and went to Pachuca were Alfredo made him his partner in the hardware business and gave him a room in his house.

February 1929 after the two brothers quarreled, Alfredo left Mexico to establish himself in Guatemala. Soon thereafter Yudel Leib moved to Toluca, Mexico and opened Rubizewski

Hermanos, a hardware store. Yudel Leib obtained the necessary permits to bring his wife and children to Mexico. Elke and the children (Yitzhak, Moishe and Berl) sailed from Danzig and on July 1, 1929 arrived in Veracruz and were admitted as legal immigrants and joined Yudel Leib in Toluca.

Yudel Leib obtained a permit for his brother Meishl to be allowed to remain in Mexico. On March 17, 1933 Leon visited Alfredo in Palestine and then sailed from Haifa and visited Maytchet. On December 2, 1977, Leon died in Mexico City.

Moishe, the middle of three sons, was born on April 14, 1923 in Maytchet. On July 1, 1929 he arrived in Veracruz with his mother and two brothers from Gdansk. His name was changed to Moises Rubio. In 1957 after Leon retired and the hardware store was closed Isaac and Moises opened a doll factory called Industrias Rubio, SA. They manufactured dolls branded Muñecas IRSA. Among others they produced the Flintstones characters from 1957 to 1967.

The doll factory was closed in 1967 and Isaac and Moises obtained the Shakey's Pizza franchise for the country of Mexico. On May 7, 1968 Shakey's opened its first restaurant in Mexico City located in San Angel. The business grew and there were many other restaurants opened in many cities. On November 5, 1976 Moises died at the American British Cowdray Hospital in Mexico City from complications of a gunshot wound. Moises was an engineer, businessman, industrialist, restaurateur and most of all, my best friend.

Berl, the youngest son was born on March 26, 1927 in Maytchet. On July 1, 1929 he arrived in Veracruz with his mother and two brothers from Gdansk. His name changed to Boris Rubio.

He became a physician specializing in Obstetrics and Gynecology. He married Paulina Freidberg. On August 21, 1997 Boris died.

Yitzhak, my father, was born in Maytchet on April 19, 1921, the eldest of three sons to Yehuda Leib Rubizewski and Elke Lotvin. On July 1, 1929 he arrived in Veracruz with his mother and two brothers from Gkdansk. His name changed to Isaac Rubio. He married Esther Schwartzman on March 12, 1944. He died on September 17, 1998. Isaac and Esther had four daughters, Mirna Linda, Ana Griselda, Yolanda Beatriz and Norma Leticia and one son Pedro Antonio.

30 Mar 1934 Erev Pesach Boris Moises Isacc Elena Leon Meizsl Esther Leah Sara
(Vainer) - Rubio Home Toluca, Mexico

Meishl was the fourth living child born in Maytchet on October 10, 1904. As a toddler he had taken a hammer and attempted to hit a nail with it, as he had seen his father's laborers do many times. Instead of hitting the nail he smashed his left hand and lost its use for the rest of his life. He married Esther Kamenomovski in Maytchet where they lived. They had a daughter named Lize that was born on May 31, 1930. They lived in a private three-room apartment behind the Rubizewski house. Meishl left for Guatemala and left Esther and Lizele behind in the little house in the back yard. Meishl told them that he would send for them when he got settled. In 1936 Meishl won $3,000 pesos in the lottery and was able to bring his wife Esther and daughter Lize to Mexico. All of them arrived by ship to Veracruz and settled in Toluca.

Esther Kamenomovski died on May 29, 1980 aged 75. Meishl died on December 2, 1989 aged 85. Jacobo died on October 6, 1990 aged 52.

The Belouse Family

Seated: Ameleh Nehome Belouse Leah between and Yankel Israel Rubiewski
Second row: Esther, Hershl, Meizel (Hershl murdered in Maytchet)

The Belouse family had lived in Maytchet for generations. Moshe Yeckel Belouse was married to Soreh (1871) and had four daughters, Chaya Lifsche, Ameleh, Alte and Faiga

Chana. In addition they had three sons, Isser, Eliyahu and a third one is unknown to me. The Belouse brother (unknown name) found work in Tykocin and eventually moved his sisters Chaya Lifsche, Faiga Chana and Alte there. The sisters married into the Charlap family famous for its long line of rabbis and cantors.

Chaya Lifsche married Yitzhak Yaakov Charlap who was a rabbi, chazzan and composer. Later they moved to Tel Aviv, Toronto and Brooklyn. They had a son Boris who became a famous chazzan in. She died of the Spanish Flu in Brooklyn. Alte married Yitzhak Yaakov Charlap's brother (first name unknown) and had a son Leibl. They immigrated to New York City. Faiga Chana, who previously owned a bakery in Maytchet, married cousin Yaakov Harlaff and immigrated to Haifa. Isser stayed in Maytchet with his sister Ameleh. He manufactured clothing and had a store where he sold dry goods, linens and materials to make clothes. He was murdered during the 15-17 July 1942 Aktion (Holocaust) in Maytchet along with his family including his wife and son Zeidel.

Eliyahu married Sheyna and had four children Frieda, Sarah, Yossel and Esther. Frieda and Sarah immigrated to New York City and changed their last name to Berman. Yossel stayed in Maytchet and was murdered in the July 1942 Aktion. Esther married Shlomo Schmulevicz and had three children, Mordechai Leib, Peshia and Elka. Esther, Shlomo, Peshia and Elka were murdered in the July 1942 Aktion in Maytchet. Mordechai Leib survived the Holocaust and immigrated to New York City and changed his name to Martin Small. Martin died in Broomfield, Colorado on November 29, 2008. Eliyahu and Sheyna later moved to Morozovichi where Shayna's family lived and owned a flourmill.

My great grandmother, Ameleh was the youngest child of Soreh and Moshe Yeckel Belouse. She was about five feet tall with dark hair, indeed a very pretty woman. She was a very good mother and person. At the table there were always strangers, including a *yeshiva bocher* (young male yeshiva student) who ate with them every week. Ameleh was very smart and a good businesswoman who devoted little of her time to cooking or other household chores because she disliked housework. Ameleh always had a cook and a maid for housecleaning. Because she was bored and needed something to do they opened the tavern.

Ameleh operated the family tavern and inn, where light fare, liquor and homemade wine and liquor were served to travelers. During the First World War, after both the Russians and the Germans confiscated his forests, the tavern became the family's sole means of support. At the inn she had a special room where traveling Jews were accommodated when they could not afford to pay for a regular room.

Grunia Rubizewski Rubinfeld & Lotek Rubinfield

Born in Maytchet & Murdered in Przemysl

Rivka Novogrudsky, Alte Boretsky, Etel Rubizewski

Etel murdered in Maytchet

Pesach Zirinsky, Etel Rubizewski Zirinsky, with son David

All three born in Maytchet and murdered in Maytchet

Grunia Rubizewski Rubinfeld, Lotek Rubinfield. Esther Rubizewski Kamenomotsky,

Lize and Hershl Rubizewski Grunia born in Maytchet and murdered in Przmysl,

Lotek born and murdered in Przmysl, Hershl born and murdered in Maytchet

17 Dec 1962 Rubio Family, Mexico – left to right: Sisters Ana and Yolanda, Mother Esther, sister Norma, Father Isaac (born in Maytchet), - Pedro (author of this article)

ABARASHA CHANALAS – SURVIVOR FROM MAYTCHET
BY LEAH CHANALAS

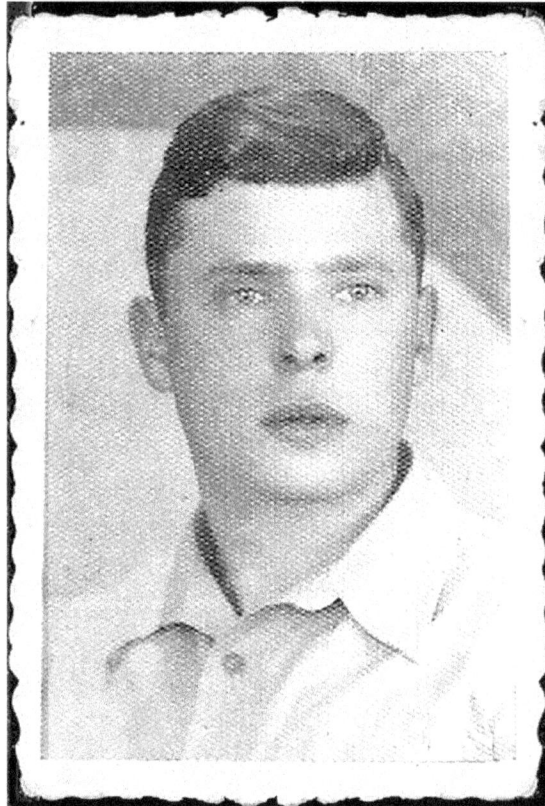

Abrasha in Israel 1946

My father Abrasha Chanalas was born in Molchad, close to Baranovichi in Poland in 1924. His parents were Yakov and Leah, his older brother Yitzchak was born 1922, sisters Sonia born 1929 and youngest sister Channa was born 1932. His mother, Leah died when Abrasha was 12 years old.

He lived on a large farm and his family had a successful dairy farm; they also grew and sold vegetables and grains. His father ran the business with his uncle Boris and the two families lived together in the same house and made a good living.

When the Germans invaded Poland his family was forced to leave the farm and had to relocate to the Horodishtch Ghetto as were all the other Jews of the area. Their possessions were stolen from their houses and divided up between the non-Jewish neighbors of the area.

In the Ghetto (December 1941-July 1942) they lived with two other families in an incredibly small apartment with little food or supplies. The Nazi Aktion was in July and here in the neighboring forest, Jews were shot and thrown into an enormous grave that had been prepared ahead of time.

Abrasha and his cousin Meir were taken from the Ghetto (the same day of the Nazi Aktion) and sent, along with two Polish bodyguards, to bring alcohol spirits back to the farm they were forced to work at. Far away they could hear the sound of the loudspeaker from the Ghetto, "All Jews must leave their homes and gather in the center of town." The boys understood what was going on and with the sticks they had hidden, just in case needed, Abrasha and Meir were able to knock out the bodyguards, free themselves, and escape to the nearby forest.

On the very same day, all of the Jews of the town were murdered, including the families of Meir and Abrasha. Rumors were heard of groups of Partisans in the forest, and since the boys knew the area well, they were able to locate their hiding spots. Finally, after careful interviews and probing questions, they joined a group led by Kovalyov. Because of Abrasha's bravery the captain favored him and gave him more difficult missions such as blowing up trains that brought supplies to the German soldiers on the front, and the placement of land mines; he also rounded up Nazi conspirators, and confiscated their food supplies.

Abrasha's father, brother Yitzchak and sister Sonia were all murdered in the Horodishtch ghetto and buried in the mass grave. His youngest sister Channa managed to run away from the ghetto. She joined a group of gentile girls who gathered wild flowers to decorate the rooms of the German soldiers. Eventually she was successful and reached the camp of Jewish Partisans. Abrasha met up with his sister and he brought her food and clothes. He was sent out on a mission one day and when he came back Channa was no longer in the camp. Several days later he was in the house of a non-Jewish farmer and he saw his sister's shirt with a bullet hole. The gentile bragged that he and his friends killed Jews. Abrasha killed the man.

His cousin Meir was killed in an attack between Russian and Polish partisans. He discovered this when he found Meir's rifle by the Polish Partisans.

During one of his particularly courageous missions, Abrasha broke into the Ghetto and released some young men that were hidden and brought them to the Partisan's forest hideout. One of the young men was Mordechai Leib Shmulewicz, with whom Abrasha kept in touch with after the war.

Abrasha was formally honored by the Partisans because of his bravery in action during this period. While he was with the Partisans he carried out many actions against the Nazis blowing up train rails, ambush individual soldiers along the road, attacks on German camps. In 1944 the area was freed and Abrasha dealt, within the framework of the Soviet Government, in the uncovering of Nazi conspirators and had many brought to trial.

Abrasha's Soviet Partisan and Israeli medals and awards

In 1945 he joined the Repatriation movement and helped the return of the citizens of the USSR to Poland. In this way he learned of the organization called Bricha and gradually crossed border after border finally reaching Italy and from there he was able to board a ship to Eretz Yisrael.

The Cyprus ship (called antsho-sireni, Ma'apilim) was stopped by the British and all the passengers were sent to a prison camp in Atlit, in British Mandated Palestine.

After some time they were released because of the number of Jews that were allowed to come into Israel according to the rules of the 1939 White Paper.

During Israel's War of Independence he joined Givati and was active in many important battles. By the end of the war, he settled in Rishon le Zion and there discovered friends from his hometown Maytchet who had also survived. In 1955 he married Miriam Troibee, the daughter of Rachel and Tzvi, and they lived in Moshav Kfar Yechezkel. Together they took over the family farm raising chickens, cows for milk, turkeys and other livestock and growing various crops and vegetables.

Their devoted daughter Leah was born July 31, 1956.

Abrasha Chanalas was a courageous and brave man who was instrumental in saving a lot of Jewish lives during the Holocaust as well as killing a lot of Nazis. Abrasha passed away Oct. 18, 2007 from complications of Parkinson's disease.

Note: Memorial to Abrasha's family murdered in Shoah page 390.

There are several stories by and about Abrasha in the original Yizkor book.

Bat Mitzvah 1968: Leah Chanalas (center) with parents

MY GORSKY AND BORETCKY FAMILY FROM MAYTCHET
Myrna Brodsky Siegel

MY GORSKY FAMILY

My father Shmaya Gorsky was born in Maytchet during Chanukah 1898; the same shtetl that both his parents were born in. He later took the name of Samuel Brodsky when he immigrated to the United States in 1913. When he arrived in Chicago he lived with his maternal grandfather Yakov Yosef (Boretcky) and other family members who had Americanized their name to Brodsky. Only one uncle (Yudel) retained the original name and spelled it Baretzky.

My paternal grandfather was Menachim Mendel Gorsky son of Noach, born about 1870. Shortly after my father was born he and his parents moved to nearby Baranovichi, which was a relatively new town. Founded in 1883 it was situated at the hub of newly built railroad lines, north south from Vilna to Lvov and west east from Warsaw to Moscow. There were others from Maytchet who also moved to Baranovichi, probably looking for new opportunities in a larger town.

My grandmother Peshe (name in U.S. Bessie) was born about 1875. Six months after she was born her mother was killed when a bull gored her. Pesha married Menachim Mendel Gorsky; they had 2 sons who lived to adulthood: my father and his brother Max. A few babies died at birth and/or shortly after and my father spoke of walking to the cemetery to help bury them.

My grandfather Menachim Mendel was described as being short in stature; he had red hair and a red beard. He fasted from sunrise to sun set on Mondays and Thursdays when the torah was read. This was a minhag (custom) among the very righteous. He was a follower of the Hasidic sect. He had 3 jobs in addition to being a shammes; he was a glazer, fixed umbrellas and worked in a factory where they made raincoats. He died in Baranovichi 1909 when my father was 10 years old.

As a widow Pesha was a hard worker and did not have an easy life. In Baranovichi, she sold bakery goods going from house to house in the morning and after that would go to work in the mikvah. She would give half of her meager wages to charity. Peshe struggled to support herself and her son Max until they came to the U.S. 1922. Once here she continued working, but had the security of knowing that my father would always see that her needs would be taken care of.

In 1930 my grandmother married a Maytchet and Baranovichi landsman Eliezer Savitsky. He passed away 1932 and six months later she married Ben Kriesman. Bessie would grind and sell horseradish at a nearby fish store and again give half of what she earned to charity. She was a good cook and a hard worker. She passed away in Chicago 1961.

My father had two brothers, Noach and Meyerim. Noach died at the age of six and Meyerim was born 1905 in Baranovichi, emigrating to the U.S. with my grandmother in 1922. In the 1970's he and his wife Channa moved to Israel where two of their three children were living.

Koppel Gorsky is the only brother of my grandfather that I know of. My mother and Maytchet survivors all gave the same description of him, a teacher with a long grey beard, and orthodox. He taught his students Talmudic studies. His wife Elke Perel had a small grocery store that sold herring and beans. In the Slonim Yeshiva book of Baranovichi there are the Gorsky names of two Yeshiva Bochers (students) from Maytchet, R'Yechhiel Gorski and R' Kopel Gorski. I know the names of three of his children, two sons Yichael and Avramke and a daughter Alte a/k/a Krusha.

One survivor related the following story: "Rabbi Koppel Gorsky was my teacher. He had a rubber-covered belt from a sewing machine. I was "a rascal" and Rabbi Koppel would try to hit me with the belt. When that thing landed on you, it left its mark and really hurt. My only advantage was that he had a long table and he was an old man who had difficulty bending down. I would get under the table and watch his feet move so I could always figure out how to stay out of his reach. He used to swing the belt blindly under the table hoping that it would catch me."

Rabbi Koppel Gorsky, his wife and the rest of immediate family were all murdered in Maytchet.

Everyone who knew him admired my father Sam Brodsky. In addition to his keen sense of humor he was motivated by strong principles. When my grandmother Peshe married her second husband Eliezer Savitsky, they bought cemetery plots together. When she passed away her last name was that of her third husband, Kriesman. Pondering what name to have on her headstone my father with his Solomon wisdom decided to have it read Bessie Brodsky, the Americanized version of her maiden name Boretcky. My father passed away February 1974, five weeks after my parents celebrated their 50th wedding anniversary.

MY BORETCKY FAMILY

Some members of Yakov Yosef and Tamara Brodsky (Boretcky) Family circa 1908

Left to right: Nathan, Lena, her husband Sam Kantor, David, Tamara, her sister Libby, Yakov Yosef, Louie, Sam

My keen interest in family history unfortunately came after my father passed away. So most of my paternal grandmother's Boretcky family information is from my father's two uncles Nathan and Sam who were respectively just six months and 2 years older then him.

My paternal great-grandfather was Yakov Yosef Boretcky, son of Meyerim Arieh, son of Leib Ha Kohane. He had a sister Nechama Dvorah and two brothers, Itsele and Moshe Arieh. There is a wide discrepancy when Yakov Yosef was born, ranging from 1830 to 1850. I was told that Yakov Yosef fathered 20 children with his two wives; I have information about 14 of his children. After his first wife Rasha Yenta passed away he married Tamara Bogatien from Novogrudok. Yakov Yosef supposedly had smicha (graduated as a Rabbi), as did several other members of the Boretcky family. Family members told of his personal siddur or chumash that had the names, birth and death dates of all his children as well as other family members born several generations back. Unfortunately this book was lost, never to be found.

In the middle of the 19th century the Prince of Russia said that flourmills should be built in Maytchet to benefit the people. Various stories are told: 1.Meir Arieh built three flourmills for each of his sons. 2. That there were only two flour mills built, 3.Two were built in Maytchet and two were built elsewhere. Survivor's say they knew of two mills; one on each end of town. We saw the remnants of the flourmill that my great-uncles Nate and Sam told me about with the 1866 date and symbol of being insured for fire. Another story they told me that was verified is that it was the only building in town to be insured.

Yakov Yosef (Jacob) by profession was a mechanical engineer and learned this trade from his father who was a builder of bridges and mills. A story is told that he was the first man in Europe to move a house from one place to another intact. He was also given a government job to rebuild a bridge. He had a passport that allowed him to travel all over Europe because of his knowledge of mechanical engineering. He even went to Germany to purchase special kinds of stones for grinding flour. He was also an excellent mathematician and used an abacus proficiently. He performed the mitzvah of circumcising all his sons.

When he was 40 years old he contracted typhus and became critically ill. They put leeches all over his body and the name Yisrael was added to his name of Yakov Yoseph to extend his life. Superstitious as it may be, he survived and lived a very long life.

Yakov Yoseph's first wife Rashi Yenta died after a bull gored her. My grandmother Peshe was only 6 months old at the time of her mother's death. Yakov Yoseph's second wife was Tamara Bogatien from Navaradok. She was only 16 years old when they were married and assumed the responsibility of instant motherhood to six children.

Names of the six children with his first wife Rashi Yenta and approximate year of birth: Baila Haskel 1859, Hershel Nachum 1860, Aaron David 1862, Yudel 1873,Dvorah 1874, my grandmother Peshe 1875.

Names of eight children with his second wife Tamara: Ben 1878, Rose 1882, Louis 1886, Max 1889, Lena 1890, David 1892, Sam, 1896, Nathan Noah 1897.

The story family members told me is that Yakov Yoseph had an argument with his brother Moshe Aaron regarding the inheritance and ownership of the flourmills after their father Meyerim Arieh passed away. (I was told that he died on Yom Kippur, year unknown). In 1906 a Rabbi asked Jacob to go to Tiblisi, which is the capital of Georgia in the Caucasus, to teach Judaism to a wealthy "Mountain Jew" and his family. Jacob, his wife Tamara and their three youngest children, Lena, Sam and Nathan walked to the train station and took the long train ride to Tiblisi. They spent the next six months living in "oriental" luxury. While there they went to an area where they were able to see Mount Ararat; locals claim this is the site where Noah's ark came to rest and survive the flood.

1916 Photo of the train station in Molchad

April 1907 Yakov Yoseph, his wife Tamara and children Lena, Sam and Nathan emigrated to the U.S. They were delayed at Ellis Island because they did not believe Tamara was his wife because of the age difference. Yakov's nephew Yekusiel Hurwitz was hoping they would live in New York near him but the pull of Yakov's two sons Ben and Yudel already in Chicago won out. Others followed and my grandmother Pesha was the last one to emigrate in 1922.

Only one son, Aaron David, remained in Navaradok with his family. Two of his sons, Harry and Morris, emigrated to the U.S. and changed their name to Boretz. A survivor from Novogrudok (nephew of Yakov Yoseph's 2nd wife) reported that the Poles and not the Nazis murdered 39 members of Aaron David's family.

Jacob's knowledge of mechanical devices led him to an invention in the U.S. He, together with his son Max who was a baker, received a patent on a dough- making machine. The patent did not succeed and the only one who made money was the patent attorney. Nontheless, the entire family always credited him with an outstanding mechanical mind.

Tamara died Feb. 1923 and Jacob married his housekeeper who was hired to help him after he became a widower. According to Jewish law an observant man could not live under the same roof with a woman to whom he was not married. Although much younger she also preceded him in death.

The afternoon before Yakov Yoseph's death a Rabbi visited him and the two of them had a lengthy discussion regarding the Torah portion of the week. Thanks to my computer savvy cousin, the torah portion that shabbos was Parashas Bamidbar in Sefer Bamidbar (which is the fourth book of the Five Books of Moses). His mind was very sharp until the end. But the question of when he was born will always be a puzzle. Some family members say he was 103 when he died and others say he was 85. Nevertheless he did pass away June 4, 1932 in Chicago, Illinois at a ripe old age.

CONNECTING DESCENDANTS OF MEYERIM ARIEH BORETCKY

Myrna Brodsky Siegel

Thanks to the Maytchet Yizkor book I have been able to connect the descendants of my great-great-grandfather Meyerim Arieh Boretcky's four children: 1) Nechama Devorah 2) Yitzchak (Itsele) 3) Yakov Yoseph 4) Moshe Aaron. They all lived in Maytchet.

Left to right: 1) Rueben Rudman, 2) Meir Novomiski and 3) Myrna Siegel-----photo taken in Jerusalem 2000.

1) Rueben Rudman was the great-grandson of Nechama Devorah Boretcky Hurwitz. She was born in Maytchet about 1853 and died in Maytchet 1874. Rueben was a chemistry professor and died suddenly and prematurely 2006 shortly after retiring and making aliyah with his wife Idelle. The story of Rueben's Hurwitz family, which was written by Rueben's cousin Sheryl Prenzlau, is in this section of the book.

2) Meir Novomiski was born in Maytchet and is the grandson of Yitzchak (Itsele) Boretcky. Meir's mother, the daughter of Itsele, was Nechama Devorah Boretsky, born in Maytchet and his father was David Zvi Novomiski. Meir read Mein Kampf in the 1930's and convinced his father to sell his business and house and get out of Maytchet. They went to Argentina and lived in Buenos Aires, Berisso and La Plata. Meir was a journalist in Argentina.

Meir's sister Sarah, also born in Maytchet, came to Eretz Yisrael in 1935 after marrying Aryeh Aharonovsky. They were pioneers and farmed the land in Kfar Azor, Israel. Sarah wrote a story about her family page 248 of this book. Also page 398 is a memorial to the Novomishiski family that was murdered in the Shoah. Meir visited Sarah in 1966 and eventually made aliyah with his daughter Gracella Novomisky and her family.

3) Myrna Siegel – I am the great granddaughter of Yakov Yoseph Boretcky and his story is in this section along with my Gorsky and Plofsky families from Maytchet.

4) Sara Boretcky Biribis and daughter Rina Biribis 1987, Kfar Yehoshua, Israel

Thanks to the Molchad Yizkor book I discovered Sarah Boretcky Biribis in 1985 from a story she wrote about Maytchet and her grandfather Moshe Aaron Boretcky, along with a photo of him with his grandchildren. I had been told that my great-Grandfather Yakov Yoseph Boretcky had a brother Moshe Aaron who remained in Maytchet. I was able to contact Sarah, with the help of the publisher of the Yizkor book, and in 1986 I traveled to Israel to meet with her. Even though we did not share a common language we formed a close bond and connected our mutual families. Finding Sarah was the key to my discovering the 4 branches of the extended Boretcky family.

From the age of 10 Sarah belonged to HaShomer Hatzair, which prepared young people to make Aliyah. Sara came to Eretz Yisrael 1935 with her friend Hende Margolin, also from Maytchet, and they lived in Kibbutz Helon. Sara is the only member of her immediate family to have survived the Shoah and a memorial with a photo of her family is on page 386 in this Yizkor book.

Two other grandchildren of Moshe Aaron also survived the Shoah and came to Eretz Yisrael after the war, Channa Boretcky Mechtiger and Miriam (Alte) Boretcky Katz. Channa had two daughters born in Israel Hayuta Sagi and Edna Psuk; Miriam had one daugher Hassida also born in Israel. Channa was on the Yizkor book committee and wrote a story about her family on pages 224-229 and a memorial page 382. Miriam a/k/a Alte wrote a memorial for her family, which is on page 385.

1947 Sara married Avraham Biribis in Kfar Yeahoshua Moshav where they lived until their deaths, Avraham in 2003 and Sara in 2011. They had two daughters: Esther born 1949 tragically died 1965 from injuries sustained when she was run over by a car the last day of Pesach 1965. A photo of her is on page 371 of this book. A second daughter Rena was born 1950; she was very devoted to her parents. Today she is living Kfar Yeahoshua, Israel.

MY MATERNAL PLOFSKY FAMILY FROM MAYTCHET
BY MYRNA BRODSKY SIEGEL

Dora, Sam and Madeline Brodsky abt. 1926

Both of my parents were born in Maytchet. My mother Doba (Dora) Plofsky was born April 1905 and my father Shamaya Gorsky (a/k/a Sam Brodsky) was born Chanukah 1898. Maytchet was a word used very frequently in our house.

So much so that my sister Madeline, my parents first born child (in Chicago) did not learn to speak English until she started grade school. When people would hear her speaking Yiddish they would ask her where she was born; she would reply "MAYTCHET'.

My grandfather, Yoseph Eliyahu (Joseph) Plofsky was born 1863. His parents were Itzchak and Mariasha Ginsburg Plofsky; she is my namesake. Yoseph's first wife was Leah and they had two daughters, Becky and Blanche. Leah passed away and Joseph married my grandmother Frieda Leah Kovensky who was born 1870 in Slonim. Her parents were Shlomo and Shaina Rachel Kovensky. Joseph and Frieda had 6 children that lived to adulthood, 3 boys and 3 girls all born in Maytchet. Abe, Ida, Morris, Dora (my mother), Minnie and Irving.

My grandfather was very strict both in his demeanor and religious practices. In particular I remember Passover sedars in their house. Every year he would come to our house and in the garage we had a large barrel, which he would fill with grapes. He then would climb into the barrel and smash the grapes with his bare feet. I was told he made wine for the sedarim the same manner when he lived in Maytchet. At the sedar, in their home, he would sit at the head of the table wearing his white kittel. The only time any of his grandchildren were allowed to get up from the table was when we would look for the afikomen. I also remember that he would "shmeck"tobacco from his beautiful tortoise shell snuffbox.

Plofsky Family Sedar in Chicago, Illinois

My grandmother Frieda's personality was the opposite of my grandfather's. She was sweet, loving, a fabulous cook, baked the best pastries and always had a smile on her face. The priest from the Greek Orthodox church across from their house would order my grandmother's pastries when he had guests. I could still sense the smell of the delicious Zemerlach which were her specialty.

As a side note, when we returned from our first trip to Maytchet in 1995, my mother was 90 years old and suffering with dementia. When we showed her the video of our trip she jumped up with excitement when she saw the church and immediately said, "that is the church in Maytchet that I lived across the street of". She had left Maytchet 75 years before!

My grandfather used to travel to Slonim from Maytchet twice a week with his horse and wagon and bring merchandise back and forth for their store as well as for others. A childhood friend of my mother's from Maytchet told me that they would call my grandfather "halbe taches". He would sit on the edge of his seat in the horse and wagon so he could take passengers with him. When I read the translation of the story Trade and Labor on page 153 of the Yizkor book, I was very surprised that on page 155 my grandfather Joseph Eliyahu Plavski is listed under transportation. This book was written in 1973 and my grandfather left Maytchet in 1920, 53 years earlier.

My mother lived in nearby Slonim for a few years where she went to school and helped take care of her blind grandfather Shlomo Kovensky who she adored. My brother Sidney was named after him. Shlomo was a shammes in a synagogue and every morning she would walk him to shul and help him set up for the morning minyan. From there she would go to school. 1915 when the Germans marched into Slonim my grandfather came to take my mother back to Maytchet. As they were fleeing the city she saw bridges burning and cannons firing.

Back in Maytchet she attended school that had been set up in the cloister of the church. A Polish teacher wanted to show the strength of the Poles and arranged for a poetry contest. Not wanting to take part of this my mother never returned to that school. The wounded soldiers would be brought to the church and my mother helped take care of them. This is where she learned to speak several different languages. The German soldiers were customers in the store and there were never any problems. My mother spoke about having a lot of girl friends in Maytchet; they would have parties, dance and have good times together.

Left to right: Dora, Frieda, Irving, Joseph, Minnie Plofsky, circa 1914 in Maytchet

After World War I the immediate family which already had been in the U.S. for over 25 years, sent money for my grandparents and their family to leave Poland and come to the U.S. They rented an apartment in Warsaw where they went to live for six months. Every day my grandfather would go to the U.S. Embassy, spending hours waiting in line with hopes that this would be the day that their exit visas would be granted. My mother and her siblings took turns keeping their father company. After six months they finally got their visas. My grandfather had written on his application that he was coming to the States to be a farmer, apparently filling a need for that occupation to benefit the U.S.

Each one of them had a money belt hidden and sewn under their clothes. From Warsaw they took a train to Danzig, Germany where they boarded the ship "New Rochelle" landing in Ellis Island, New York. September, 1920. From there they took a train to Chicago where they were reunited with the rest of their family, just in time to be together to celebrate Rosh HaShonna.

PLOFSKY FAMILY REUNITED IN CHICAGO, IL.   1920

Left to right: Ida, Morris, Frieda, Minnie, (Irving between his parents) Joseph,
Abe and Dora

The Romanovski Family from Maytchet

written by Tzivia Malka (nee Romanovski) Fishbane

Left to right: Yoseph Ehrlich, Mirel, Malka (holding baby), Sara and Berel Romanovski

My father Sholem Yehudah Romanovski a"h was born in his mother's hometown of Slutzk, where she traveled to give birth from Maytchet, on May 7, 1910. His grandparents were Sholem and Hinda Romanovski from Maytchet, who started the family wholesale and retail grocery and supplies business. This business gave the Romanovski family a nice livelihood until the Nazis came. Both the local Jewish and non-Jewish people were their customers. They extended credit to all and were well liked and admired members of the community. Later on, before the Nazis invaded, my father tried to warn his father of the evils of the goyim. His father Berel answered "I always was nice to them and helped them, they wouldn't hurt us". Unfortunately, we know how his words were proven wrong, since these very neighbors and supposed "friends" collaborated with the Nazis and became their murderers.

My father's parents were Yechiel Dov known as Berel and Malka Faiga Chaya (nee Schiff from Slutzk). Rose nee Sinofsky Lifshutz was my grandmother's first cousin. The Sinofskys were also from Maytchet. Rose and her brother Meyer Sinofsky came to the USA probably in the 1920s. Among Rose's children was her son, Rabbi Oscar Michael Lifshutz who was a chaplain in the American army after WW 2 and lived in Chicago afterwards. He and my father met after the war in the DP camp. There is an interesting story about how they met. Chaplain Oscar Michael Lifshutz was called to the DP camp of Bindermichel to mediate between different groups in the camp. My father who was head of Agudath Israel in Bindermichel was advocating for the religious rights of the survivors, while there were others who were more interested in the material rights. Chaplain Lifshutz did not know who my father was but after hearing him speak said "you are so stubborn and the people I know who are like that came from a town called Maytchet." They then discovered that they were cousins and my father told him about everything that happened in Maytchet. Rabbi Lifshutz wrote a letter to his parents describing what he had heard from my father.

My father was one of 5 children. His brother was Zev or Velvel who was single. He had three sisters Devorah, Mirel (Miriam) and Sara who were known as Sarake, Sara also was single. Devorah was older and was married but we don't have details about where she lived. Mirel was married to Yoseph Ehrlich from Lodz. They had a child and lived in Maytchet. In the picture of Beryl and Malka Romanovski, Malka is holding the baby and Mirel, her husband and Sara are also in the picture.

Yoseph Ehrlich's cousin was Avraham Werdyger from Lodz. Avraham's family was sheltered in Maytchet by the Romanovski family when they escaped from Lodz. They were taken to Samarkand in Siberia and survived the war. Avraham Werdyger lived in Jerusalem, Israel and was a Chaver Haknesset representing Poalei Agudath Israel. I interviewed Avraham in July, 1966. He passed away in 2012.Avraham had in his possession the picture of my grandparents(we never had a picture until then of Berel) and the postcard written by Yoseph Shmulevitz on Sept. 29, 1944 ,in answer to Avraham's postcard, asking who had survived from Maytchet. This is the translation of the postcard.

"Dear Mr. Werdyger,

I, Yoseph Shmulevitz, am answering your letter inquiring about the survivors from Maytchet. From all the ones you inquired about, the only survivor is Sholem Romanovski, who was in the partisans and is presently in the army. I am also the only survivor of my family. There is so much to discuss about this problem and subject matter. I think you must be aware of everything that happened.

Be well, Yoseph Shmulevitz"

Unfortunately Yoseph Shmulevitz was killed at the end of the war.

My father Sholem Yehudah was married to Miriam Bitensky from Horodets that was near Maytchet. They had a son named Zvi. They first lived in Baranovitch and then Maytchet.

My father and his brother were Yeshiva students in Radin by the famous Torah scholar, Rabbi Yisroel Meir Kagan, known as the Chofetz Chaim. In 1929 my father got a draft notice to go into the army. He assumed Rabbi Kagan would encourage him not to serve. Instead he told my father "that hard times were coming and he should learn how to shoot." My father joined the army and learned this skill. Later on he joined the Bielski Partisans and saved many Jewish lives including Tziri Royack from Maytchet, who later lived in Peoria, Illinois.

I interviewed Morris Samuels (Shmulewitz) from Maytchet in 2000. I will always be grateful to Myrna Siegel for connecting me to Morris, since he and my father were hidden together during the war and he told me many details about my father I never knew.

He described life in Maytchet before the war. Three women would gather together every Thursday morning to discuss the tzedakah (charity) needs of the town. They were called "drei (3) Bar Mitzvahniks." One was my grandmother Malka Romanovski, one was Morris Samuels's grandmother Shifra Shmulevitz and one was Berel Shlomovitz's mother. Berel Shlomovitz managed to go to Israel before WW 2. He lived in Chaifa in Shikun Vishnitz with his wife and 4 children. When I studied in Israel, in 1966-67, they were very hospitable and helpful to me. I was once in Israel at the Yahrzeit gathering in Av of the Maytchet survivors and the Shlomovitz men, who live in Bnei Brak and are Slonimer Chassidim, were also there.

Malka Romanovski would give food and goods from her store. Shifra Shmulevitz, who owned an inn, would provide meat and challohs to distribute for Shabbos. Mrs. Shlomovitz would go collecting from storeowners the shoes and clothing they would give to the poor. Ephraim Silverman(who was killed at the end of the war) would collect wood and distribute it according to their instructions.

Malka Romanovski had two other beautiful customs. She would make charoses for the entire towns' Pesach Seder. On the way home from shul people would pick it up from her home. She also provided the towns' boys with tzitzis (fringed garments). The Romanovskis gave jobs to orphan girls. In fact one of them was Esther Baskowitz also from Maytchet who came to Chicago in the 1920s.We still keep in touch with her daughter Diane Baskowitz.

When the Nazis invaded Maytchet my father hid his wife and baby in one bunker but since there was no room for him, he ran and hid somewhere else. My father unfortunately became the sole survivor of his entire family. My father together with another Maytcheter survivor Avraham Osheranski ran to the Dvoretz ghetto. They escaped from the ghetto the night before it was liquidated. They joined Morris Samuels who was being hidden by a Gentile farmer named Yan Alaky. This righteous Gentile saved the lives of 10 Jews including Elchanan and Moshe Shmulevitz, Martin Small, Chatzkel Ravitz and Tziri Royak. They lived there for almost a year until it became too dangerous. After the war these Jews who were saved would send the farmer money and packages in appreciation for everything he did for them.

My father then joined the Russian Partisans (where there was a lot of anti-Semitism) but soon switched to the Jewish Partisans called the Bielskis and stayed with them until mid 1944. He enlisted in the Russian Army and hoped to take revenge on the Germans. He was sent straight to the front and was wounded in the chest and cheek. He begged the Jewish Doctor in the Moscow hospital not to release him until the war ended.

When the war ended, my father who was still dressed in his army uniform, saw non Jewish Russian soldiers taking a group of Jewish women. My father knew the soldiers did not have good intentions, so he convinced them that he would take responsibility for these girls. He saved them from a terrible situation. That is the picture of my father surrounded by these women.

Afterwards my father moved to Linz, Austria to the DP Camp called Bindermichel. He was head of Agudath Israel and was instrumental in rescuing Jewish children who had been hidden in Gentile homes and convents. He helped establish whatever was necessary to rebuild the Torah life that had been torn away from them. He established the synagogue, kosher kitchen and Talmud Torah for the children to learn in. There is a picture of my father surrounded by these beautiful children.

In April, 1948 he married my mother, Yehudis nee Hirsh, from Fekete Ardo, Hungary who was a survivor of Auschwitz. My mother lost her entire family except for two sisters. My parents' backgrounds were different. My mother came from a Munkatcher Chassidishe home and my father was Litvish. After the war, you were happy to find an Orthodox person who was kind and nice to marry, even if your backgrounds were different. I, Tzivia Malka Fishbane was born in January, 1949 in the Bindermichel DP camp, and we arrived in New York in January, 1950. We lived in Brooklyn and my twin sisters Fagie Padawer and Leah Katz were born in Feb, 1953. In New York my father was reunited with his cousin Gershon Romanoff (shortened from Romanovski) from Maychet. He had arrived before the war and was a Rabbi in the Bronx. We have stayed in touch with his family. In 1957 due to difficulties in livelihood, we moved to Dubuque, Iowa, where my father worked as a Rabbi and Kosher Supervisor at the Dubuque Packing Company. I remember Nachum Rabinowitz, another Maytcheter, visiting us in Dubuque and afterwards we stayed in touch with him when we moved to Chicago. We moved to Chicago in 1962 so we could continue our Jewish education and be part of the Orthodox Jewish community. My father once again undertook a leadership role and helped establish Chicago's Bnos Agudas Israel, an all girls youth group. My niece, his granddaughter, is head of Bnos in Chicago more than 50 years later.

In December, 1968 my father died of a sudden massive stroke. He unfortunately did not live to see one grandchild. I gave birth two weeks later to my oldest child named Sholem Yehudah after him. My mother died in September, 2011 and lived to see much Yiddishe nachas.

We thank G-d have all established beautiful Jewish families who continue in their parents, grandparents and great grandparents path. There are dozens of descendents from our parents, these two precious souls, who survived the terrible war years and picked themselves up and rebuilt their lives. Every birth is revenge on Hitler and his evil forces. We, the Jewish people, are eternal and we thank G-d that we are part of his glorious nation.

Sholom Yehuda and Yehudis Romanovski and Family 1967

Center photo is Tzivia, bottom Fagie and Leah

Chaplain Aaron Kahan
Capt. U.S.Army

Linz,March 7th,1946.

Mr.

Shulem Romanofsky

Linz/Austria.

Dear Mr. Romanofsky;

      Our division is leaving this theatre toward
the end of this week. I hope to go with them.Before
leaving I should like to express to you my sincere
appreciation for the tireless efforts you have exhibited in behalf of the Jews in the camps of Upper-
Austria.Since I arrived,about three months ago,hardly
a day has passed without your coming to me for assistance
of one kind or another,for some needy person.

      In a spiritual vein it was through your efforts
that much progress has been made in the establishment
of Synagogues,schools,kosher kitchens and other religious institutions for our people.

      It is extremely commendable when I remember
that your personal status economically,physically and
socially is no more secure than that of the people for
whom you work.May God bless you for your efforts. I trust
that you will carry on with this selfless work after I
leave and that you will receive the full cooperation
of all military and civilian agencies,to whom you may
turn.

      With every good wish for your speedy rehabi-
litation in the Holy Land and looking forward with
you to the restauration of Zion and Israel

                 yours sincerely

                 Ch. Capt. Aaron Kahan.

Letter sent from Austria
by U.S. Army Chaplain Rabbi Oscar Lifshutz
To his mother in Chicago, IL,
1946

Rabbi Oscar M. Lifshutz was a U.S. Army colonel and his chaplaincy included much direct involvement with freed concentration camp inmates after W.W. II. His mother was born in Maytchet and this letter was written to his parents when Oscar was stationed in Vienna, Austria 1946 and had a chance meeting with a member of his mother's family, Sholom Romanofsky, survivor from Maytchet. It was at this time he wrote the following letter to his mother.

Coincidentally when my husband Shael Siegel was stationed in Salzburg, Austria 1954, he met Rabbi Lifshutz and worked closely with him helping Jews who were living in a nearby D.P. camp. At that time my husband had no idea he would marry someone with Maytchet roots and have still another bond with Rabbi Lifshutz!
Sholom Romanofsky married his wife Yehudis in1948 in the D.P. camp in Austria where this letter was written. Sholom passed away in 1968—as of the year 2000 there are 55 direct descendants from the one Maytchet Jewish life that was fortunately saved during the Holocaust.

Myrna Brodsky Siegel
This is the letter as written:

June 9, 1946

My Dear Father and Mother,

I am writing this letter to tell you the story that Sholom Romanofsky gave me when I saw him in Salzburg and Linz.

On July 15, 1942 (Rosh Chodesh Av) the people of Maytchet ran away into the woods. Terror had already broken loose. On the 16th of July the Romanofsky family was murdered. Malke and Judel Chorobrowicki and the children were also murdered. That included Bashka as well. This continued from the 16th until the 18th of July. The Romanofsky family on the 16th and the Chorobrowicki on the 18th. Nechamya alone was left alive.

Things were in a turmoil until December 18, 1942. The people still hid in the woods. Then the tragic blow fell again. Workers were needed in the village of Dvoritz. Israel Chaim believed the Germans. Romanofsky pleaded with him not to go. But he decided to go and he and the family were wiped out. (Nechamya too.) They were buried two kilometers outside of Dvoritz on the road to the cloister. Two thousand Jews were murdered there, and buried in one large grave.

Judel and the family were buried near the Bahnhof (train station) of Maytchet in a large grave where 3,500 other Jews were placed.

Of the 500 people that ran away, only 15 were left. The first were murdered by the quislings and the later ones by the Germans.

The only ones he knows to alive today are:

Shmuel Schiff family

Yoseph Yudel and his wife

Rosa, her husband and child

Meyer's two children

He also located-------of the family Moshe, Channa and Mottel. They claim to have an aunt in America and are looking for her.

This is all he told me. Sholom was wounded a couple of times and joined the partisans. He caught several of the murderers and finished them off. Today he is waiting in Bindermichel (D.P. Camp) near Linz to go to America. He has a relative☐ Epstein in New York ☐ who is helping him out. He is also the representative of Agudah of Linz.

That is the complete report he gave me. It reads like an unbelievable novel. That people could be so cruel is hard to imagine. But the stories are true. I saw a grave of 1,000 Jews. Houses with chains where they burned Jews. Only a couple of years ago they did all this.

What is gone is lost. The souls of these people will not be unavenged. Innocent blood must be paid for before a world forgets. I can reach Sholom at all times. Please write.

With love, your son,

Osher Michel

OUR RAVITZ AND EPSTEIN FAMILY FROM MAYTCHET

Information compiled from Julio and Jaime Epstein and
Sergio Kowensky and Bella Kowensky Cantor

Eliezer, a/k/a Leizer Epstein was born in Maytchet around 1903. He went to Buenos Aires, Argentina with his sister Esther Epstein in 1927. They attempted to go to an uncle, Abraham Epstein, who had a restaurant in New York but were unable to get into the States. They sailed instead to Argentina where their uncle Sheleizer Ravitz had emigrated from Maytchet with his family; his three sons were Oscar, Isaac, and Julio. The ship from Cherbourg, France to Buenos Aires, Argentina was named Arlanza and Leizer made lifelong friends with other immigrants while on the ship.

1926 Maytchet

Bottom left to right Leizer and Tsira. Behind them Esther and Miriam

Both Eliezer (Leizer) and Esther married in Argentina and raised their families there. Esther and her husband Jaime Ojman were married six months after her arriving in Argentina. Their children are Perla Luisa and Isidoro. Leizer Epstein married Flora Scharager and they had two sons, Jaime and Julio.

Iser Epstein was born 1879 and Beile Ravitz Epstein was born 1885 in Maytchet. Their nine children were also born there. The Nazis and the collaborators murdered Iser and Belle and six of their children in the Shoah. Chaim together with his wife and two children Nechamale and Moshele, Abraham, Moshe, Mordechai, Yechiel, Zelda and her husband Shmuel and two daughters. Esther and Leizer left Maytchet 1927 making Leah the only child of Iser and Beile living in Maytchet at the time of the Shoah to survive. In this section of the book you can read the story of her harrowing experiences and the will to survive in her Yad Vashem testimony.

Chaim Epstein – murdered in the forests of Poland together with his wife and children Nechamale and Moshele

Iser Epstein lost one leg in World War I and several years later had his other leg amputated. He was a grain merchant and managed to get around in a cart he sat in and turned the wheels with his hands.

Iser Epstein and sons

After the war Leah married Ben Zion Kowensky, also from Maytchet. Their daughter Bella was born in Lyakhavichy, not far from Maytchet. In the DP camp in Austria a son was born named Shimon. Unfortunately he passed away at the age of one while they were still in the camp. Their son Sergio was born in Argentina.

Leah and Ben Zion Kowensky in DP Camp Austria

with Son Shimon who died age 1 year and daughter Bella

Also in the DP camp with them was a cousin from Maytchet, Chaskell Ravitz. He made his way to Argentina also.

A sister of their mother Beile also survived. Tsira Ravitz Kaplan was married to Victor Kaplan and they had three children. Victor and the children were all murdered in Maytchet. After the war Tsira married Eli Royak and they had a daughter. The two families made their way to Argentina at different times.

Ben Zion Kowensky was the only member of his immediate family to survive the Shoah. The following were all murdered: Father Shimon, Mother Zlate, Sisters Chaia and Miriam, Brothers Aharon and Jacob.

Leah in Maytchet with two brothers who were murdered, Abe and Moshe

The doors to Argentina and the U.S. were closed to the survivors who were now free but they had no place to go.

Leah and Ben Zion made their way to Argentina with their daughter Bella who was born in Lyakhavichy, not far from Maytchet. Their son Sergio was born in Argentina. Tsira and her husband Eli Royak also went to Argentina.

Leizer made arrangements to meet Leah and Ben Zion in Paraguay. The Kowenskis took a ship to Brazil and then went to Paraguay to meet Leizer who took a train there from Buenos Aires. When he got to the prearranged meeting place in Paraguay he was unable to find them. After several frustrating days they managed to connect. They brought with them many personal possessions, including a feather blanket (called a "perana"), which they carried in large baskets. Leizer managed to get them and their belongings on a small boat and crossed the Parana River from Encarnacion, Paraguay to Posadas, Argentina where there were not any border guards. From there they got on a train and went to Buenos Aires.

Leah and her husband Ben Zion Kowensky moved to Israel in 1981. Sergio moved to Israel in 1969 and left for South Africa in 1973 where he married Allison Kaplan; they have 3 children. Bella, husband Angel and her 2 children went to Israel in 1971 and a third was born in Israel. Their cousin Chaskel Ravits moved to Brooklyn, New York.

Julio and Jaime Epstein were born in Argentina. Julio is a retired physician and currently lives in the U.S. Jaime remained in Argentina; his wife is Ana Maria Lucia Ciani. He also has a daughter Alicia Epstein.

After living a few years in Argentina Tsira, together with her husband Eli Royak and daughter Mania, moved to Peoria, Illinois, U.S.A.

In the Maytchet Yizkor book the family name is Ravitz, in Argentina the name was Rabec. Aunt Tsira Royak told the following anecdotal story: Iser Epstein's father's name was Benjamin Alper and not Epstein. He gave each of his male children a different last name to keep them out of the army. At that time in Russia an only child was not obligated to serve in the army.

Keren Kayemet group in Maytchet – Esther Epstein top row center

Others Not idedntified

Purim in Maytchet - Leizer Epstein seated front row left Others not identified

Rod Kromen (row of shops) Left to right: Yakov Margolin, Yoseph Lasovxky, little boy and man next to him unidentified, Mordechai Ravitz, unidentified.

Israel 2011--- family of Leah and Ben Zion Kowensky

as a result of their surviving the Shoah

Lea and Benzion Kowenski with son Shimon and daughter Bella in DP camp, Austria

YAD VASHEM TESTIMONIES OF LEA EPSZTEIN KOWENSKY AND BEN ZION KOWENSKI FROM MAYTCHET

Number of Testimony in Yad Vashem museum: 5261/03
Name of person giving the testimony: Kowenski

Lea, from the Epsztein family Daughter of Bejla and Iser born 1920 in Molczadz, Baranowicz district.

Document origin: Yad Vashem archives - Jerusalem
Date and place of events: Molchad – 1939-1945, Puszcza Lipiczanska
Language: Translated from Yiddish to Hebrew by Moshe Gal.
          Translated from Hebrew to English by Tamar Lionarons.
Length: 25 pages.

Recorded testimony – Lea Kowenski

I was raised and educated in a traditional Jewish home. My father traded in grains and crops. He had recently lost both his legs and my mother was a housewife.
On September 17th 1939 the Russians invaded our town, and I left to study in Moscow for a year. I was trained as a bookkeeper for the train company. Then the Germans arrived.

Q: What changes occurred in the lives of the Jews of the town?
A: When the Soviets arrived they began to harass the Jews who belonged to Zionist movements. They wrote down all their names. In my passport they wrote that I am the daughter of a Jewish Merchant and that made it difficult for me to find work.
I suffered a lot and had to work hard because of that. They exiled the rich Jews to Siberia. My father wasn't taken because he didn't have any legs. I could not be taken either and so it happened that we both stayed in the town.

Q: If you were the daughter of a Merchant, how did the Russians send you to study in Moscow?
A: I took some courses as well and because I learned in a trade school, they sent me. I studied in Moscow for one year and I finished my studies as a bookkeeper. I worked in Baranovichi, at the main bookkeeping offices of the train route between Brest and Litovsk. I worked there until the war broke out. When the war started, everyone went

with the Russians. But I know that I had a father with no legs. I couldn't leave him and the family so I returned to my little town; there I was taken to work.

Q: Where did the Germans take you to work?

A: They took me to Maytchet to work at different jobs. A *Judenrat* (= Jewish council, T.L.) was established. One of the men was called Ehrlich and he was appointed as the head of the Judenrat. He was a refugee and he knew German well; he handled all the affairs. I wasn't in Maytchet for long. My father was a grain Merchant and he was well known. In fact, I was accepted to the job because of my fathers' acquaintances; I was taken to work at an estate in Bloshniwa. The manager there knew my father well. He had done him many favors and so I got my job there.

Q: What sort of job did you do there?

A: I dug up potatoes and planted tomatoes. We did all the hard agricultural jobs; we received 300 grams of bread and we had to live on that. We also got a little soup. My father's brother also worked with me; he got into an argument with one of the Germans and was told to leave. He indeed left. He went to work at a different place and there he was killed.

Q: How many Jews worked on the estate?

A: There were about 80 workers.

Q: Were you guarded when you were taken to work?

A: We worked during the morning hours. We indeed were guarded while going to work but we could move freely on the estate. Once a week we were allowed to go home. Once a week there would be a wagon going into town. It was 10 kilometers away from Maytchet. I asked to go with the wagon. I don't know why but I knew in my heart that I had to travel and see my parents. That was the last time that I saw my family.

I arrived in town. My father took a gold watch, took it apart and put in it a piece of *Affikoman* and told me: "here you go, this will lead you to a straight path". And I asked: "mother, where shall I run to?" and she says: "I don't know my child, run wherever you can, just run from the slaughter. Then you might save yourself"

This gave me a lot of courage and helped me.

I separated from my parents for the last time. The following morning we were going to work and we heard the sound of cannons firing on Maytchet; the town was burning in the fire of hell.

And the Jews were being killed; the youth tried to resist and my brother Moshele was there and he was tragically killed there, with a rifle in his hand. He died in the battle for freedom.

After that, my brother Motel came running to me in Sieniawa. He wasn't allowed to be with us, he was already sentenced to death. He hid in the village and came in the night to beg for bread. And I gave him some bread, and after he left us he was caught by a *Goy* (a non Jew) who killed him and took his boots. He buried him on the way. After the slaughtering we spent another month in Sieniawa.

Q: Maybe you can tell me some more details about the slaughtering, that you have been told by others?

A: We heard the shooting; we saw the burnings, the fire of hell. A friend of mine called Wichne was brought to us. A German caught her in a field of rye. We asked her to wait a few days. We started to prepare to leave Sieniawa. But she couldn't wait any longer. It was very hot then and we couldn't sit in the heat and suffocate in the rye field. She went alone, was caught and killed. One day we awoke at 4 am and we felt that we were surrounded. We were only wearing nightgowns and we were scared and confused. We were put on trucks and taken to Polomka.

Q: When did that happen?

A: It happened on the 10th of August, 1941. That's when we were surrounded and taken to Polomka. We made a vow that none of us will try to escape on her own; only if we can we will try to escape together.

Q: Actually it was only a couple of months after the Germans invaded, wasn't it?

A: Yes. Each one of us had a certificate around her neck, and a razor as well, because we thought that if someone would try to kill us we would cut our veins. That was what we decided and perhaps one of us will be able to save herself.

The way was sandy. There were no roads; when the trucks started to move we decided to cut the canvas and jump off.

I was the first to jump. Because I had no brother or sister to say goodbye to, I was pushed first and they all followed.

Q: How did you jump off the truck if it was going fast?

A: On the sandy routes the car doesn't go fast, rather it's dragged along. We were on the last truck; the others had left earlier and were ahead. They started shooting at us but there were fields of rye which grew high.

Q: Did everyone escape from the truck?

A: No. Nine of us escaped and ran in different directions, for a kilometer or two. The Germans saw us running and started shooting at us but we knew the tactics to escape. We had to crawl on our stomachs in a zigzag way so that they wouldn't catch us. We ran and fell; we understood that someone will remain alive and we thought that we'd meet in the forest and there each one of us will shout: "cockadoodledoo". At nights the echo is good and if we will meet we will decide what we should do next. When we met in the forest we were only six and each one said: "I'll go and look for my brother". There were rumors that my brother, who was a man of the field, was there, and they suggested that I'd go and search for him. I wanted to go but at the same time I didn't want to go, but I knew that if we would save ourselves we would go to a Christian called Reginowitz, who was in a village near Maytchet. I finally decided that I would go and search for my brother. I knew the routes well because my father, who traded in grains, would send me sometimes on my bicycle to inform the estates that grains had arrived from the trains. And I had ridden on my bicycle to those *Goyim*.

Since I knew the roads, I went to a *Goy* whom my brother was on his field... That *Goy* told me: "yes I heard that your brother Chaim lives with his family, with his wife and children. One is called Nechamale and the boy is called Moshele".

I didn't know how to get there and I was afraid to walk alone on the roads because if I would be caught I would be immediately killed. I knew that my brother Motel was killed there. I was walking and walking in the fields and instead of going farther away from Sieniawa, I was getting closer. I got back to my starting point; I saw that I was in trouble and so I began to go back. I started running with all my might in the middle of the night. I ran with my remaining strengths and I was wearing a nightdress. I returned to that same *Goy*. I didn't ask him what direction I should take, because I knew that if I'd ask him it would raise his suspicion and I didn't want that to happen. I didn't ask him and I continued.

Q: Where did you get to?

A: I walked without knowing the direction. I met another *Goy* and he asked me: "where are you going at night? It isn't allowed" A lot of things aren't allowed but if you must... and so I went on until I met a *Goy* who pitied me and gave me food and drink. But he immediately said: "I am afraid to keep you here. I will give you food but you must leave my home immediately".

I continued from there and I reached a large estate, with which my father had business connections. When the landlord saw me he burst out crying. It was upsetting to see the man react like this. He said: "I want to help you but I cannot because I know that sooner or later it will be known that I am keeping a Jewish girl in my home. They will kill me together with you. If you'd like, stay in the fields and when you come at night I'll give you food." And I answered him: "fine, I agree." Did I have any other choice?

I went to the forest and stayed there until midday, at 12 pm.

Life had grown tedious; I had nothing to live for and no one to live for. I want to walk, to go to and be slaughtered. Go to the grave, where my dear family members are.

I remained there disappointed without knowing what to do. I met a *Gentile* woman and she wanted to help me, because my father had helped her before the war. She told me: "go between the flowers, sit there until nightfall and when everyone leaves, go with them!" Fine, I went into her house and she gave me food and drink. I sat between the flowers until I saw that everyone was leaving the field. She gave me simple dress from local material which the *Goyot* wore.

And again she says: "go, you must cross the train tracks, sit and be careful of the Germans." I left and the *Goya* followed me to see where I was going.

I arrived at a village where everyone knew my parents. My father was a well known merchant and everyone knew him. I was afraid that I would be taken to be slaughtered, because whenever a Jew would be caught he'd be taken to be slaughtered.

I encountered a Christian family and I told them: "did you know that I can bring you good things tomorrow? You only need to tell me how to get there and how to get to some other place, and tomorrow I'll bring you some good things." I promised this to them just so that I wouldn't be caught. They showed me where to go. I needed to get past the Molchadka river behind the town of Maytchet, and there were deep swamps. I managed to get through the swamps. I met another *Goy* and I asked again: "how do I get here and how do I get to there?" He gave me food and comforted me. My cousin Hezkel Rabets was there. He was sleeping at the *Goy*'s house but the *Goy* didn't want to tell me that there was a Jew staying with him. He was afraid of me so he told me: "go and take look, I heard that your brother is alive, go look for him."

And so again I left. I met a peasant and I asked her for directions and she said: "where are you going? Come with me I will take you to the Germans." It was nighttime by then, again I began to run. I ran until I wasn't seen. I went on and got lost. On the way I met Reginowitz in the night. It was dark, there was no light and I ask: "is this where Reginowitz lives?" but no one answered and so I shouted in a louder voice: "is this where Reginowitz lives?" and they said "yes" and so I asked: "where is your daddy?" and the little boy answered: "he is there, behind the granary." I went there and who did I see? My cousin was there and also more people from Maytchet who were my friends. So I said to myself: it's good that I am not alone! It was my destiny not to be completely lonely. And then the landlord says to me: "you know that your brother is alive but he is not with me and I cannot tell you where he is. You can stay here for a couple of days or go somewhere else. In the forest you will be with his family and then you'll know where to find your brother, and if not then stay with me and I will give you food." And I said: "no, I want to go to the forest and be free."

I went to the forest and found my family: my aunt Rivka and Hezkel Rabets. I met Zelig, Hirshel and the other Riva. I had an aunt Rivka and an aunt Riva. I spent two days with them and the children. After two days, Ruwitz led me to the edge of the forest, in the corner, and there my brother was waiting for me. When my brother saw me he burst out crying. It was such an unexpected meeting.

Q: Which brother was it?

A: My brother Chaim. He was older than me. He told me that his family was alive and that I shouldn't worry about him. He will be like a father to me and look after me. He will see that I lack nothing and he will take me in to his family. His family was staying with a *Goy* family but this *Goy* wasn't to be trusted because he had told on him.

Brother Haim Epstein

He took me there. We were supposed to go into a place which was a granary but we had to crawl so that dogs wouldn't notice us and when we approached the door we had to crawl so that no one would hear.

We entered. The children were waiting for me and greeted me with joy. They had been sent to search for me after they heard that I had escaped, but they didn't find me. I was with them for 6 weeks. On Rosh Ha'Shana of 1942, the *Goy* came and told us: "today is your festival of RoshHa'Shana" and he brought us better food. We stayed in the attic of the barn, together with cows and horses.

Q: What was the name of that village?
A: The name of the village was Snoznitz.

Q: How long did you live in that village?
A: Only for a few weeks. The *Goy* came to milk his cows and brought better food. He said: "now is your new year." After a few weeks a man by the name of Monya Shmuelwitz came with some *Goyim* and wanted to take from our *Goy* his last cow. And then our *Goy* came out and said: "because I hide Jews, we must help him so that they don't take the cow."

Q: Who was this Monya Shmuelwitz?
A: He was from Maytchet

Q: But why did he come to that *Goy* and try to take his cow?
A: He was a Partisan and he told his friends to take me to Partiznka and not to leave me here. But they had something else in mind and a different reason to take me. They thought that if they take women she would be theirs.
After we all got to the forest, my brother gave me a rifle. At night I saw that the situation was not good and so I left and ran away from them.
I ran into the forest, I was left without my brother and my sister in law, without the children and without anybody.

Q: Where were you taken to?
A: I was taken once more into a different forest but I escaped to a different place.
Morning came, the partisans went and I heard people speaking in Yiddish. I approached them and I told them the truth and I asked them to take me away from here, since I'd be killed if I stay. They wanted to shoot me, they claimed that I must escape; they cannot take me with them because they were going to blow up a train. During that time a Soviet offence was beginning and it included the explosions of

trains. They said that today they cannot take me with them, but when they get back from their operation they will take me with.

In the meanwhile I hid between the bushes, day and night. Towards evening they arrived and brought a wounded man with them. I looked after him and asked them to take me with them and indeed they did.

Q: Were these Jewish Partisans?

A: Yes, they were Jewish Partisans.

Q: Which unit were they from?

A: They were from the unit of Bolkov. They called themselves "Bolkovski". I walked with them a couple of hundred kilometers. We walked in the direction of the caves of Puszcza Lipiczanska The place is in the area between Slonim and Zhetl. I was brought to the commander and he wanted to check whether I knew how to shoot. I was given a machine gun that weighed 16 kilos and another machine gun that shot 63 bullets in a second. I was told to shoot far distances. I was taught to shoot and I shot well the first time and even better the second. I had a good vision for long distances and I shot so well they appointed me number one on the shooting machine. I had two helpers who carried the disks of the ammunition and also parts of the machine. And so I joined in the shooting practices of the unit.

Q: Which unit was this?

A: It was the unit of Bol Bolkov, he was a Belarusian. The commander's name was Bolk and so the unit was named after him. He organized all the Partisans of the area. He later belonged to a unit named after Lenin.

Q: How many Jews were in this unit?

A: We were very few Jews in the unit; perhaps 5 in total. The Jews were not well accepted there. I was known to be a Jew but I spoke excellent Russian and I had a good Russian accent; my Russian was that of a learned person so they didn't know that I was Jewish. No one asked me and of course I didn't tell. I was called "the girl fighter". Every patrol that a good shooter was needed, I was sent. Whenever they needed to place an explosion on a train, I was included in the mission.

Wherever we had to go, I was first.

It was on March the 3rd 1943. It was the Woman's Day in Russia. And so women were ordered to go and explode a train. We were under the command of a woman called Lydia. I do not know her surname; she was a small woman. We were 6 women in total. We blew up a train and then went back. It was known that if you didn't take part in exploding the train, you had better not return, and whoever forgot his weapon should also not return. We performed the mission and when we returned the commander praised us.

One night we went to look for food. Where would we go? We needed to get within half a kilometer or a kilometer away from the Germans. We surrounded the village. It had to continue for a couple of minutes, until we got the food provisions out. We took whatever food we could take with us; meat, bread, salt, and potatoes. We were not allowed to take eggs or clothes. We had some of our people guarding us; we would go in and take what we needed and then we immediately had to return and clear out. But how many times did we need to clear out? We had horses. We would sit on the wagons and when we'd finish with one village we'd travel to the next one. We would take different horses in every village. We'd do that so that we wouldn't leave traces and so no one would know that we had been there.

Q: You said that you went to blow up a train with women. Were these Russian women?
A: Yes, they were Russian women. I was the only Jew. All the time I was around *Goyim*. I once had a Jewish cousin and he was executed for no reason. Once a Partisan came and told us that he fell asleep while he was on guard duty. He was shot dead in front of me. A week later I saw the scum who killed him, sleeping while guarding. I was going to replace him and I saw it. I brought the commander of the guards and I showed him and they told me: "you did the right thing, telling that the man was sleeping. This is a serious crime and we shall give him a warning. We shall explain it thoroughly to him and this must not happen again. " I asked: "and what would you have done to me if you would have found me sleeping?" and the man answered: "we would have shot you right on the spot." -"Why?" -"Because you are a Jew." They were very honest. They would kill a Jew for doing nothing. They once shot a Jewish partisan in the presence of the entire unit, because he stole a pair of boots from a *Goy*.

We once went to blow up Broda Yivorska. There were Germans, Russians and Ukrainians there. There was a big camp and we went to blow it up. The Byelorussians were bribed and the rest we had to do on our own. We surrounded the camp. We spread out over a distance of 100 meters from each other. We had to shoot at them from all directions and then attack. When we got near their bunkers we started to throw hand grenades but the Germans managed to throw them back. We had 6 people killed. We had never yet lost more than one person in battle and 6 is a tragedy. It happened at the biggest battle we had at Partizanske all the time.

Once we had to attack; I cannot remember in what year or month it was. We had to blow up all the train tracks in White Russia because the Russians were planning to attack the Germans, and we had to blow up all the train tracks at precisely the same hour and minute. That's why we left earlier. We were sent near the swamps in the area of Finsk.

Q: Who do you mean by "we"?

A: We were an entire unit, 30 partisans. I was the only female Jewish partisan. We made our way towards the target and we approached the tracks. We walked for 24 hours. We would rest during the day. When we got close to the tracks and the Germans noticed us, we would have to retreat. But we couldn't go back without completing the mission. We would all be killed. So we returned and kept watch in the forest the whole day.

We moved nearer and blew up the tracks and the train came off the tracks and all the dishes that were on board broke. We heard someone shouting: "break the dishes" and we shouted to the train "break the dishes". On the way back we were exhausted and very tired. We sat down to rest and took off our boots. We didn't think of food, even though not eating for two whole days wasn't a simple thing.

When we sat down to rest we felt that we were surrounded. They were shooting at us from all directions; we started to run and I was alone. We had a code for 24 hours but the hours went by and there was no more code. The partisans could catch me and shoot me. I ran and I was alone in the forest. I didn't know where I was because it wasn't a partisan area, it was a German area. I didn't know where to turn. I didn't have the code and I didn't know anything. How did I walk despite this? I walked there facing the moon and back from there with my back to the moon. I knew I had to see the moon in my face on my way back and that's how I reached the place where we picked carrots. At night we would pick them and that's what we would eat. I reached a fork of paths. I looked up and saw that they were selling wood and that there was a water trough for horses. I drank there but I had to go on. I couldn't stay because I didn't know where I was. I walked on and on until the sun came up and it was morning. I hid behind some bushes. I lay there and thought how I would pass the day.

I saw a shepherd who seemed to have noticed me. I asked him: "are there partisans here?" and he answered: "no, they aren't but there are Germans." I asked: "where are they?" and he answered: "they went to eat lunch. They will be back soon." That was by the rivers of Nieman and Shtashra, in a place where the two rivers combine. I knew how to swim well but I couldn't leave the gun. I thought that I must disappear immediately. I started swimming and I crossed the river. When I started to get out of the water it was very shallow. I began pulling out the weeds and they indeed came out easily but the next time when I grabbed some weeds I was stopped. The Germans started shooting at me and they injured my arm. But I did not know it because I didn't feel anything.

I crawled up and laid down on the weeds. They were very high because nobody would come there. I lay down there until nightfall and I saw that my clothes had dried off but one place was still wet. I put my hand in and I saw that I was covered in blood. I lay there till night time and it was dark. And then I got up and started walking, because staying there would have meant certain death. Only death, it's better to walk. I saw a house on fire and I asked: "are there any partisans here?" someone answered: "yes." I asked him: "can you take me to them?" and he said: "no." I raised my rifle and I told him: "either you take me to them or I will kill you on the spot" and so he said: "okay, I'll take you."

He took me to the partisans and they ordered: "put your hands up and place the rifle on the ground." They started to question me who I was. Then I was in the Lenin unit in the Bolkov division. The commander was Volentine. I went with them and they questioned me. They were paratroopers who had parachuted in from Moscow. They interrogated me for a long time and when they saw that everything fit they told me that just yesterday all of my friends had passed through this spot. They said that one woman had died, and they were talking about me.

They bandaged my wounds and I went with them. They gave me cigarettes and food and promised they would transfer me to my unit. I was with them for 2 days and they took me to my friends. When everyone saw me and they cried and they were very happy that I came back to them.

We needed to cross the Shtashra River, which was very deep. Only a horse could get through because he could swim and indeed he got me through and when I got there I met all the partisans.

We once went to strike an explosion in the city of Zhetl. We had our own technicians, engineers and even a tank. But instead of the tank going where it was supposed to, it blew up near mine and we had to retreat. We had to have a combined attack so we joined all the units of White Russia. We had to attack the Zhetl forest together. All of us together... and then split up, and that's how I fought in 18 battles.

I always went first. Once, before the Germans decided to retreat, they decided to eliminate the forest of partisans. They took an entire battalion and began combing the forests looking for partisans. We divided up into two groups to ambush from both sides and we struck them with fire from hell until the Germans started running.

When the Germans started with their elimination attack they would walk very closely to each other. There was a German solider for each meter, because when you shoot in the forest sometimes the trees get the bullets. And so we also decided to walk closely to each other with a meter between each of us. We walked before them and we walked after them for about a kilometer and we saw many dead people from the Family Camps which were lying there.

Q: In what area was this?

A: In the forests of Labiszyn. From there we went to Voltunari. We couldn't be in that forest any longer because the Germans were looking for us. We were situated on the main road to Bialystock. We had c o n t r o l o f the River Shteshra. They needed a strategic point and we had to retreat but they followed us and aimed to destroy us. We walked to Volto Naro and when we felt that they were retreating we returned, because we were not allowed to fight in the area of other partisans. We had to protect our place and our place was Drohitchin, Zhetl and Kozlovoshchina.

I was in a unit with a man named Siyuma Shlovski. He was a cousin of Dr. Dvorjetski There was Siyuma and there were Vitia, Sima and Faygele.

Q: All from the Dvorjetski family?

A: Yes. Faygele was killed because she forgot her rifle in the tank. All those who were killed had been searched. There was another cousin of Dr. Dvorjetskii, she was called Vitia Dvorjetski. Dr. Dvorjetski writes that she was killed but that isn't true because she died of hunger in our forest. We had more battles in Kozlovoshchina. We conquered the forest and we camped there for a fortnight. We didn't let any Germans enter but one time when they arrived they surrounded us.

We surrounded them and stopped them and killed many of them.

We killed a lot of Germans also during the release and we caught a lot of prisoners. We weren't allowed to kill them.

Q: Were there few Jews during all the time that you were in the Bolkov unit?

A: Very few, almost none. There was one Jewish cook. I cannot remember her surname. Other than that there was one small fighter, I have mentioned her already, Goya. There was a compassionate Jewish nurse but she didn't consider herself Jewish. She used to say every once in a while that she was a *Goya*. She was as small as a dwarf and she always repeated what the commander Volentin said. She told everyone that she was a *Goya* but we knew that she was Jewish.

I never said that I wasn't Jewish. No one ever asked me but they thought I was a *Goya*.

Comment: And you indeed don't look Jewish.

A: I once wrote to a hospital where an injured man named Viteh stayed. I wrote the letter in Yiddish and my commander came up to me and asked cynically: "what, are you Jewish?" and I said: "yes commander-friend, I am Jewish." And he said in Russian:

"what a shame that you are Jewish." And ever since then I was provoked. That was very bad. My membership was canceled and I had to join a Family unit.

Q: Where was the "Family unit"?
A: The Family Unit was in the forest where Yurkeh Kobanski was, who today lives in Ramat Gan. The Family Unit didn't have a commander. Each one lived the way he wanted to. In the camp of the Family Unit, each one had his own shovel and cared only for himself. We once dug a trench for ourselves and we were busy. One bright morning we were surrounded and we had to leave.

Q: How many Jews were at the Family Camp?
A: We were all Jewish but I cannot remember the number.

Q: It's odd, weren't there any commanders at the Family Camp?
A: We all were Jewish, each one searched for food for himself. The truth is that I wasn't at the Family Camp for long. I was there for a day or two and then I returned to the unit named after Lenin. The Family Camp didn't suit me because I was always part of a fighting unit.

Q: And were you accepted back at the unit named after Lenin?
A: Yes, I was accepted back. We once had to take Germans; not Germans but White Russians who had killed partisans. We entered the village and we surrounded it but the women had to ask for food. We all had weapons on us, so we chose 5 women who were sent to ask for food. We knocked on the door because they hid so we wouldn't catch them. We asked in Russian: "give us some bread," but behind us the partisans stood. When they opened the door, we surrounded them and caught 8 men and lead them out. When we lead them on the way back it was snowing and there was frost outside. We traveled on sleighs and on the journey we met a man from my town who was a cousin Moshele Ravitz. I asked him: "Moshele, do you know whether my brother Chaim is still alive? I haven't seen him for a long time." And he was silent. I asked him: "why are you silent? Answer me, is he alive?" and he said: "no, he is not alive. He was killed." And I asked him: "who killed him?" and he answered: "the partisans killed him, because he had a golden watch and they found the watch on him."

Q: Did the Russian partisans kill him?
A: Yes, the Russian partisans killed him. I didn't want to go and catch the White Russians any more and the commander told me: "listen, you must avenge your brother's death". Just imagine how I felt, having been told that my last brother was killed and that I should avenge his death. But it really was avenge. We caught 8 men.

When they brought them and questioned them, they told me that I tohether with another woman must guard them. They all were tied up. One needed to go and relieve himself but I didn't let him go; I shot in the air and then everybody came and led them back tied up and we all went up to them and kicked them. "Do you see? This is what the partisans do, you see? You deserve this and that's why we are kicking you."

I took part in 18 open battles. Telling about them all will take a long time and I cannot tell all the details. I have gone through a lot in my life.

Q: When were you freed?

A: We were freed on June 13th, 1944. The Russians freed us. We then took 178 German captives. They wanted to hide in the forest and we weren't allowed to kill them. One of the German captives asked me for some water. I was guarding him and I told him: "do you know, I am a *'Juda'*, a Jew", and he remained dazed. He was very young.

After the war I remained only with my aunt, Tzira Ravitz Kaplan (now Royak) from Maytchet and also my cousin Moshele Ravitz. He passed away here in Israel, and so did Hezkel Ravitz. When we were freed, everyone from our unit was sent to the military front, without any preparations or training.

Q: Did they take the men immediately?

A: Not only the men. They also took the women and 'wiped' out everyone in one moment. No one stayed alive, there was no memory. They couldn't take me because I had worked at the general headquarters of the trains. So they told me that I must go to work immediately within 12 hours, and so I did. When they saw this, they gave me a conformation that I had participated in 18 open battles and that I had excelled in them. Also that I had been injured. I was immediately given a flat and they ordered a policeman to clean out a flat for me which had belonged to Germans. When I got the flat I met my aunt; I hadn't known that she was still alive. I was together with my aunt. We went to our town, to Regineyvitz. He gave me something to eat and something to wear. But we didn't have a bed and so we slept on the floor. We met an acquaintance who gave us a bed made of planks of wood. But the flat was ours. In those days, whoever had a flat in his possession was happy. I was given a flat because I worked in a very responsible position. I was a deputy-technician and we started to build our life again. I was the family and my aunt was the landlord. That's how we began to manage our lives.

Later on I met my husband who is from the same town Maytchet. His name is Ben-Zion Kowenski. His real name is Zaydel. He was a little religious. He began coming to our flat because he also had been given an important position and he started bringing us food. We and our two cousins started to manage a family life together with us. This happened slowly until we got married and that's how we began to succeed.

Q: How long did you stay in Maytchet for after the release?
A: We didn't stay in Maytchet for a long time; we found pits that were shaped like the Hebrew letter "Lamed" (ל). The pits were dug by the Jews themselves. The Germans had their tactics; they cheated their victims. They would build in a strict manner, according to centimeter and meter and they would tell them that the pits was made for storing gasoline, and when the pits would be ready they'd bring all the Jews and shoot them inside the pits.
When we came to the pits we found many scattered bones. We collected them all and buried them and we swore never to return to this place.
I want to tell you a little about the town: when we lived there the Germans would come every once in a while and take something. Once they came and asked for gold; 4 kilos of gold. We began to collect rings and everything we had. But how do you collect 4 kilos of gold? In the end everything was collected. The next time they came and asked for fabrics and the time after they asked for 20 workers and a cook. They chose 20 healthy and strong looking workers; they thought they were going to work and that they would be saved. They were diligent. The Germans picked the very best and they also picked a good cook, a good looking lady. They lead them 2 kilometers away from the town and they shot them in cold blood.
Every once in a while the Germans would ask for people to work, or they'd ask for people to push their "motorbikes", broken motorbikes. They collected 40 men to push the broken motorbikes; they lead them outside the town and they shot them all.
They had all sorts of tactics and plans of deceit just in order to kill Jews.

Q: All of this was done during the extermination?
A: Indeed it was during the extermination.

Q: How many were left in Maytchet?
A: I went into Maytchet but I didn't stay there. I went from there to Baranovichi and I worked at the general headquarters of the train routes.

Q: How long did you stay in Baranovichi?
A: I stayed in Baranovichi for a few months, or perhaps for one month. I was given a months' salary and I was also given clothes. Since I was dressed in uniform, I was given a highly respectable job. One day they had to harvest the field. They used to take people from the offices to do that job. They told me that I must go there. I answered

them in Russian: "I will fulfill the order but I will also file a complaint." The officer asked me: "why?" I answered him that I am an important partisan, and that I had fought in 18 open battles. There is a German sitting and working here, send him instead! And then he told me: "but he is barefoot" and so I answered him: "and I fought barefoot."

Q: How did a German get to the general headquarters?
A: He was a German from the Polkes Deutch group, and the manager saw that indeed I could file a complaint against him because he didn't fight in the military front and I did, and also that I had made many accomplishments for Russia. When he saw that there was nothing he could do with me, he said: "you shall stay here and I'll send somebody else." He didn't send anyone but one day, as I was sitting and working, I was called to the telephone. There was a telephone on my desk. And I was told these exact words: "do not repeat these words I'll tell you, just answer what I ask you". And he added: "take your papers and all you certificates and go to the N.K.V.D." I took my papers and went to the N.K.V.D. They started asking questions: "what did your father do? And what did your grandfather do? And what did your great grandfather and grandmother do? Do you have relatives in Israel?" I was asked these sort of questions; questions that I myself didn't know the answers to. And then I was told in a clear voice: "from today onwards you will be our deliverer; from today onwards you will be given a different name and I must tell them everything I see at my work place (there were many people there, all account managers); everything I see and hear there I must tell them."
I couldn't say no, because that would imply that I was against the government. But I didn't have many options; I said yes but I went to my husband and I told him: "we must leave today, we must escape." We immediately went and signed up and escaped Russia.

Q: From where did you leave to Poland?
A: I went to Zhetl.

Q: Why did you go to Zhetl?
A: I had family there. I didn't want them to know that I had run away and so I went to my cousin and I signed up to her family. I was there for roughly a month and then we left to Poland.

Q: When was that?
A: It was in September 1954. My daughter was then 2 months old. We left because I didn't want to be an informer. I was forced to run, I was with the Kobanskis for a month

or two and I reached Lodz. But it was all done illegally. Like the Jews from Turkey. We were given handkerchiefs to put on our heads and the men were give berets so that people would think that we were from Turkey. We had to talk only in Hebrew; when Russian was spoken we had to act as if we didn't understand what was being said. And what we had to say we had to do the opposite.

There was one man with us who was a little confused. When he was asked: "are you Russian?" he would answer: "'*happy are those who dwell in your home.*' "(This is a quotation from Jewish prayers: *'Ashrey Yoshvey Beytecha'*, T.L.)."Are you from Tatar?" and again he would reply with a *pasuk* (=quotation from the Bible, T.L.). They would tell him: "the devil knows who you are. Had you been Jews from Turkey you wouldn't have known the difference between Greek and Hebrew."

Q: Where in Poland were you?
A: When we got to Poland we went to Lodz. My aunt had left before us and she left us her flat. During the week that we were in Lodz we did everything we could in order to leave Poland fast and reach Czechoslovakia. And indeed that is what happened. We reached Czechoslovakia and we moved as fast as we could to Austria. In Austria we were in Braunau, the place where Hitler was born. From there we drove to Linz; we were there for a year. From there we continued to Adelsburg. Salzburg where I lost my son; he was in Salzburg and the next day I found him dead.

When we were in Salzburg my husband got a position as a teacher and he was very successful there. There was a shortage of teachers. He was given a job and I also wanted to work in the kitchen so that I could work in my free time in the offices of UNRWA.

Later I read in the newspaper that they were looking for family members from Maytchet. It was Robinzshwsky and I thought that perhaps I should send him a letter and he will help me to look for my brother and sister who are living in Argentina. I wrote him that I am the youngest daughter of Iser Epstein; my father was a grain merchant. I added in the letter that he was a friend of my older brother and that I am looking for family members. I would highly appreciate if he could help me look for my family, other than my brother and sister who are in Argentina.

Apparently he received my letter and he was moved by it; he replied warmly. He immediately sent me chocolate and packages with food which were very useful. I received 9 letters from America. They arrived from my father's sister and from my mother's family. He writes that my letter will be passed on to Argentina and that I must wait for their answer; they'll probably reply upon receiving the letter.

Q: Did Alter Robinzshwsky help you a lot during that time?

A: Alter Robinzshwsky indeed helped me a lot and was very attentive. That was real help. He even helped me leave France. They didn't want to give us a visa for Argentina. In those times, Jews weren't permitted to go there.

My brother wanted us to show up as non-Jews, as *Goyim*. I answered my brother: "I was Jewish until now and I shall stay a Jew. I have suffered long for being a Jew, under the Nazi Occupation. Now, after the war, I am proud to be a Jew." And so my brother suggested that I collect the papers in order to go to Paraguay and when we get there he will meet us and try to get us through to Argentina.

Q: How long were you in Austria for?

A: We were in Salzburg for 4 years and in the D.P. camps.

My brother paid a lot of money and he got us from Paraguay to Argentina. We waited 10 days at the border and they wouldn't allow us in. My brother thought that we were in prison.

We finally arrived in Argentina. I worked as a teacher in a Jewish school. I taught Literature, Yiddish and Hebrew at a high school.

I taught Hebrew, Torah and Tanach (= Bible, T.L.) at the school for beginners, but the children there don't learn a lot because they usually learn Spanish and Yiddish for them is a foreign language.

I worked at the school until I retired. The school was in Moisesville, I worked there for 11 years at the seminar which my husband managed. I also worked at the "Shalom Aleichem" school in Florida.

Q: When did you get to Israel?

A: We reached Israel on the 5th of February, 1981.

Interviewer: Yitzchak Alperovitz.
Date: February 1983.

i

Number of Testimony in Yad Vashem museum:
5262/03 **Name of deliverer of the testimony:**
Kowenski Benzion **Born** in 1912, Molczadz,
Baranowicz district.
Document origin: Yad Vashem archives - Jerusalem
Date and place of events: Turets, Novy Svyerzhan, 1939-1945
Language: Translated from Yiddish to Hebrew by Moshe Gal.
                Translated from Hebrew to English by Tamar Lionarons.
Length: 10 pages.

Recorded testimony – Benzion Kowenski

In Molchad I learned at the "Tarbut" school; after which I moved to Krozac, Krinki, which
is a village between Novogrudok, Torz and Kreliz. My father was a tenant there. He ran
a flour mill which ran on steam. I continued my elementary studies at Novogrudok and I
finished my elementary classes there in "Tarbut" school. Then I moved to Vilna, I
studied there in the seminar for Hebrew teachers.

I didn't complete my studies at the seminar because my father needed me to help him
at work. Our family was quite large by then and so I had to go and help my father. And
so it happened that I stayed in the village until I was called up for the military service.

Q: In the Polish army?
A: Yes indeed, in the Polish army.

Q: Where exactly did you serve?
A: I served in the city of Pruzhany, in the artillery corps.

Q: What was your profession after finishing the military service?
A: When I finished my military service I was at home for a while and then, when the
war broke out between Germany and Poland in 1939, I was called up to serve. I left to
the military front, to the city of Malba. I was a sniper in the artillery corps. We held up
for 3 days until we were forced to retreat, and then the artillery fighters had to carry the
horse we continued in this way for 10 kilometers and then we got into position, only
that's when the German planes "got rid" of us. We sat on the horses and we left our
cannons. Each soldier mounted a horse until we reached Warsaw.

When we got to Warsaw, the city was already surrounded, until it gave in to the Germans. The Germans held us captive for a month. We were released with the rest of the war prisoners who were on the other side of the river Bog, and that's how we got home. At that time the Germans didn't yet ask who was Jewish but the soldiers knew more or less who was Jewish, and so they gave us the worst and most difficult jobs. During that month we didn't get any food.

Q: Where was the prisoners' camp?
A: In Warsaw, and as I said- we didn't get any food. And then the soldiers searched for a horse and when they found one, they lay him down, cut out chunks and ate them. When we reached the River Bog the Germans handed us over to the Russians.
We arrived in the evening and we were given food there.

Q: The Germans simply put you through the river and handed you over to the Russians?
A: Yes, they transferred us to the other side of the Bog and gave us to the Russians. From there I got home.

Q: Home meaning Krinki?
A: Indeed, to Krinki.

Q: What did you do during the Soviet period?
A: We were in Krynki for a short while and then the Soviets sent us away from the village. They nationalized the flour mill and all of the belongings, and so we went to Novogrudok empty handed. My father was a butcher. We had left everything in the village and arrived to Novogrudok empty handed. During those times, the Russians prohibited the butchering of young cattle. Then Father teamed up and became a partner with 3 or 4 other families. They bought cattle at the market, butchered it and divided the meat between them.

Q: I asked you, what you did before the Russians?
A: I worked at the station for the Russians until the Germans came. When they came, we had no acquaintances in Novogrudok. We believed that we would be safer in Krynki; until an order came from the Germans that all the Jews that live in the area must go to the city of Turets. We reached Turets and we joined a family that owned a large flat. They gave us a room and we lived there for a few months. We were sent to work at places that the Germans ordered us.

Q: Was there a unit of the White Russian police in Turets?

A: Indeed a unit was established there; it gave us orders and sent us to work. But there wasn't much work there.

Q: What sort of jobs did the Jews do?
A: They beat and tread on the crops of the estate owners, until one day the Germans shot 20 young Jews who had been caught.

Q: When did the murder of the 20 Jews occur?
A: It happened after a couple of months. In the meanwhile they sent Jews to dig pits. The Germans said that the pits were made to store gasoline and other things. We had no idea what purpose they meant. One clear morning the Germans issued an order that all the Jews of Turets must gather in the market square; everyone- young and old, and whoever who would be found at home would be shot on the spot. Everybody took a package as heavy as he could carry and they gathered at the market square. There were a couple of hundred people gathered and they chose 80 young people from them. I was between those 80 men. We were separated and taken by special cars to Shverzna, by Stowbtsy. The rest of the Jews were lead to the pits and shot dead.

Q: When did this occur? Perhaps you can recall the date?
A: It was around the High Holidays. We were sent to work at a saw mill. Some worked at the saw mill and some at a mine that grinded stones into gravel. After that the mine was closed and they were send to work at the saw mill. I worked until the beginning of the winter of 1943.

Q: At the Shverzna camp there was an underground organization. Do you know of this? What can you tell me about the underground organization?
A: At the beginning we didn't know how much longer we had in Shverzna. We were given little food. I forgot to tell you beforehand that during the murder of the Jews of Turets they also murdered the Jews of Shverzna, but a few of them were kept alive. There were around 200 people who formed a Ghetto in the courtyard of the synagogue. In a few small houses they put the Jews of Turets together with the Jews of Shverzna. I lived in the house of the Herkebi family. There were father, son and grandson. The Jews of Shverzna could work for their living; they had good acquaintances who were Christians. But we, who had just arrived there, were penniless and suffered from hunger. At that time I found a man who acted as a middleman between me and one of the supervisors, so that I would get permission to go to Krinki and I will get him a suit of clothes. Indeed, he gave me permission and I traveled to the mill in Krinki with a Christian I had hired. I bought a sack of flour from there and we had to live on it until the

butchering took place. The head of the camp was a German Jew. The Rabbi was killed together with his daughter, and only the Rabbi's wife and son were left.

Q: Do you mean the Rabbi from Shverzna?
A: Yes, the Rabbi from Shverzna. We felt that it was becoming rather threstening and so we organized ourselves. They started killing Jews from neighboring towns. We understood that our turn would be coming soon. We started to get organized for an escape from the camp. I was part of that group.

Q: Who were the people that were at the head of the underground organization? Who were the leaders?
A: There was a father and son, a tailor that was at the camp. Tailors worked at their profession. The camp was surrounded by a large quantity of wooden planks with sand at the top. On one side there was a river which froze completely in the winter. There was no block from there. The Germans assumed that we wouldn't escape via the river. There were White Russian policemen guarding us. We felt that time was running out and that things were getting bad and so we started preparing. We got hold of a rifle and we hid it between the planks. One man, a tailor, wasn't careful. While working for them, they once asked him: "what do we need to pay you?" and he, in his stupidity answered: "pay me in bullets, enough for a rifle." There was one thin man, who hated Jews (*"Soneh Israel"*), and he immediately informed the Germans about the incident. They took the man and called for the head of the Judenrat for investigation. When we knew of this we moved the rifle to a different place. We were scared that the man would be tortured and that he would tell about the hiding place and so we moved it.

Q: What happened to the tailor and the head of the Judenrat?
A: They didn't come back. They were both murdered. Before arresting the head of the Judenrat he called us and asked: "tell me the truth, do you have a rifle or not?" We obviously denied the entire story and he was convinced that we didn't have a rifle. That was our luck. Had he said that we have a rifle, we would all be murdered immediately. When he asked us we answered him: "and what do you think? That if we'd had a rifle we wouldn't have told you?" he accepted our words but the Germans didn't believe him and shot him and they also shot the father and son.
At that time the Germans began burning down the Ghettos in the area. They burned down Stolpce and another town in our area. We decided to escape no matter what happens. We were in a tough situation because during the time that passed, many of us had perished. I was one of the leaders of the underground organization and the wife of the Rabbi who had a son aged 16 told me: "come to my home, and when you escape

take us with you too." I stayed at the Rabbi's wife's home for a while and then Hershel Poserski came. How did he reach us? He had a sister at the Shverzna camp. When we would go to work at the saw mill we would walk as a group, and when we returned we also walked in a line. It was possible to enter the mill; the Christians would come there to buy wood. And that's how Poserski entered one morning, wearing a fur coat.

Under the coat he had a gun and on the way back he walked in line with us and nobody noticed him. We were about 300 people. We entered the camp and we began preparing an escape.

It was winter. The river was frozen. When it became known that we were going to escape, some of the Jews of Shverzna said- where will we go? It's freezing cold outside and there's snow as well. But we didn't listen to them and we got out of there.

A great noise started at the camp and a movement began.

Q: When did this happen?
A: It was on the 29th of January, 1943. The date is engraved in my memory.

Q: How many people were you when you escaped?
A: We were 150 people when we left.

Q: Were you in Herkevi's group?
A: Herkevi was with me in one room. He left with us. When we left we were 150 Jews from the town of Turets and they knew the area well. They said: why should we go to an unknown place? We'd best go home. I cannot remember the surnames of their leaders, but they went separately from us. We walked for about 5-6 kilometers, I can't remember because it was snowing when we left and it was very cold. Our legs were literally frozen and for a moment I thought that I will not be able to move on but there was a great pressure and after a few moments I continued walking. We entered the village. We had only one rifle and Poserski had his gun. We entered the village and we organized the Christians there to leave the village on winter wagon. We got divided into 2 or 3 on a wagon and we left to the forest, to the partisans.

Q: Which unit was this?
A: The commander was Giltshok and I think that the unit was called after Ponemrnko.

Q: Who was that Giltshok?
A: He was an officer in the Russian army. He was originally from the city of Kapoliya. He was a Jew and being so, he accepted us with open arms.

Q: In fact, was it the same Giltshok who had sent Poserski to the Shverzna camp to get you out of there?

A: We had a problem. We were three classes and it wasn't accepted to have mixed classes. I would like to point out that before we reached Giltshok's unit, he had a few people from Stolpce, from Neshviz. There was one named Halvski and there were some other young men. And whatcould he do with us? We were around 90 people who'd joined his unit and then they formed a special battalion whose commander was a Christian. I cannot remember his name. I remember that we were divided; the adults between us went with Herkevi, as well as the women and girls and then they created the Family Camp and we were the Fighting Battalion. We barely had any guns but we started fighting and we became partisans. We received guns when we had to go on military missions. Sometimes we had to go on purchase missions, in order to get guns ourselves; that was until they started chasing us. There was once a chase but you need luck for everything. I was positioned with 6 men. We knew the Germans were nearing and we positioned the shooting machine and the heavy weapons so that the Germans won't be able to come through to us. 6 partisans stood in the narrow passageway, like sacks, so that the Germans wouldn't be able to pass. In the early hours of the morning the shooting began. That was an unusual attack; after an hour we heard that the shooting was coming from behind us. We stood and it became quiet. We decided not to stand and wait but to go and see what was going on there.

Q: And what did you find?

A: Apparently the Germans had gone ahead and we were behind them. The members split up in groups and we continued with them. There were days when we entered a village in the evening hours and the *Goyim* would tell us: "children, the Germans passed through here only a while ago." Some of them belonged to a unit but they suffered from hunger. They would eat leaves of plants and some of them died from that. But we had food. When we entered the village we would get a lot of food from the *Goyim*.

Q: All this happened during the time that you were in Giltshok's unit?

A: Yes, it all occurred then.

Q: How many Jews were you in that unit?

A: The Jews were in the Family Camp. I believe there were around 110 Jews.

Q: In which area did the transfer from the unit take place?

A: We were in the area of Ciepielow, in the "Mashok" forests; that's how they're called. When we would blow up a train line we would walk in group to the military mission.

When the mission was fulfilled we notify the headquarters about the location of the line which we'd exploded and the length of it. There were times when all the partisan units would take part in an attack of the Red Army against the Germans. In situations like these, we would get an order to blow up the tracks of so and so train, and then all the units would go. Each unit had its own area and place where it would operate. Sometimes we would also attack them; we would hide near the road where the Germans were supposed to travel on and we would attack them without them expecting it. We would shoot at them only when a small German group would pass, but when a large group came we would refrain from attacking them. I must point out that our partisans didn't demonstrate a lot of courage, like the original Russian units who were trained, but our unit fought according to its strength, as much as we could. The reason was that this was a Jewish headquarters that the Politrok was an anti-Semite *Goy*, a hater of Jews. In the last few months before the release, the

Russian policemen came to us, from the police of White Russia. They had escaped the Germans and had reached us. We had many troubles with them; they brought an air of anti-Semitism to the unit.

On the last day before the release, we had to blow up a bridge. The German army had left the military front and we were sitting in an area of light forests. Apparently the Germans smelled that we were there and they began shooting at us. To our great happiness, no one was hurt. The Germans ran away and the following day we were released.

Q: When was the release?
A: It was apparently in June. We were brought to the city of Lyakhavichy. We were there for about a week and during that time we were given positions. Some of the partisans were given the most important positions. The Soviet government was renewed and civil life was starting up again.

They were drafted to the police or to work at the banks; to all the financial and social institutes. Partisans were placed at the head of the Artels, the Combinats. I was positioned as a director of a peat factory. I was given note and I was appointed the director. The rest were sent to a Russian church, they were held there for a few days and then they were drafted into the Red Army. Imagine that the new recruits were sent immediately to the military front! Many of them died in battle. I was lucky to have been left in a position of responsibility because many didn't return from the front. When shooting, a partisan would respond with 5 minutes of shooting. He didn't have a lot of experience. The soldiers who passed Stalingrad and got to Berlin- they had a lot of experience. The partisans didn't have such training. In addition to that, their commanders didn't have much faith in them. They were sent straight to battle and almost nobody returned.

Q: How long did you work as the director of the peat factory?

A: I worked as the director for the time from the release in June 1944 until we left there in August, 1945. The work was interesting. I didn't know anything about peat, especially I had to work a lot and show a lot of devotion with the Russians. But a Jew manages to find himself a solution. There was one man who was born in a village and he was the manager of the work in practice. The *Goyim* know a lot about peat. He was a "brigadier" and he managed everything there. Don't think that he didn't have any problems. Each area had a peat factory. The end came when I had to leave. My wife told you that. We signed up as Polish citizens and that's how they allowed us to leave Russia.

Q: Do you mean that you left as a returning citizen to Poland?

A: That's right. We left as returning citizens. We arrived to Poland and there we were taken care of by the "Bricha". We joined a group and we had to introduce ourselves as Greek citizens returning to Greece. We had a little baby by then and we arrived with the baby to Austria. We "stole" the border from Poland. In Austria we were in camps and I worked there as a teacher.

From there we reached Argentina; all this in an illegal way. We wanted to go Eretz Israel but we were taking care of a baby who was only a few months old. We also had to "steal" the border to Austria and climb over the Alps. And so it happened that we weren't taken and we had to wait. When the state of Israel was established we were still in the "Dama" camp and so we contacted my wife's brother and we reached Argentina. Jews weren't allowed in at that time. We had to

"steal" the border once more because we traveled via Uruguay. In the end we arrived safely to Argentina.

Q: What did you do in Argentina?

A: I was a teacher there.

Q: In which area?

A: We arrived between Rosh Ha'Shana and Yom Kippur; it was a time when there was a holiday. I went to teach the Hebrew language. I brought a certificate saying that I used to be a teacher and they said: alright, we'll allow you to teach a few courses. I started teaching courses during the holidays. The holiday lasted there for 3 months;

December, January and February. So I worked with these courses for 5 months. We lived then in "Moisesville"; a city that was called "Yerushalaim de Argentina" (=the Jerusalem of Argentina, T.L.). There was a seminar where they taught Hebrew and Yiddish. This seminar trained teachers for the field cities. During that time there were very few teachers and the field cities didn't have enough teachers, even though there were many Jews living there. There was a big demand because the teachers who had completed their training in Buenos Aires didn't want to go and work in the smaller cities. That's why they decided to establish a seminar for teachers in Moisesville.

There was a woman there named Freeda Gutman and she was the head of the seminar. The principle was Derznin. He was a highly devoted man. There was no recognition in Moisesville that a teacher needs to have an income. It was new to them, because prior to that, teachers in Argentina were in serious trouble. They had students who only studied during the summer.

During the immigration from Europe, the immigrants wanted to assimilate completely. I am referring to the first immigration. The J.C.A. was an important institution which directed the immigrants to the village. That was a healthy immigration, but those who came to the cities suffered from anti-Semitism and wanted to leave Judaism. They didn't want to establish a Jewish school but rather to live as the *Goyim*.

At the time went by, something was created. Schools were established here and there and in another place people left their jobs and committed themselves to education. They took children during the long summer holidays and the parents realized that there was no point in their children hanging around outside and so they sent them to learn; but there were very few teachers. After a while, when there were more students, they brought a family from Buenos Aires and they brought a headmaster who's name was Baruch Tennenbaum. He was a talented man but he didn't get on with the management and so they searched for a different headmaster.

Since our son was ill and needed fresh air, we were advised to go there, and have our rent covered and receive a high salary; even though Moisesville was 600 kilometers away. Friends asked me: "Kobanski, where are you going? Moisesville is a small town and what if you don't succeed?" It was good for me there. In Abizshnada they didn't want me to leave under any circumstances, but in Moisesville they were looking for a headmaster and as I said, the doctor had advised us to move, and so we went there.

We had good conditions: a good flat and a high salary. At the beginning the budget was low. I had to work 40 hours with only one other teacher. The demand for more teachers was high and as the time went by we received more teachers.

The general community, which provides all the school with a certain support budget, saw that the situation of the Jews in the field cities was dire and so they decided to form a seminar for teachers with a boarding school; meaning that the children who came to study from the provinces would receive accommodation and support. When we established the seminar, children started coming from all over the Republic. We had approximately 150 families and we began working properly. We taught there for 5 years and we trained teachers who finished with graduation reports. As the time went by, the number of teachers grew and we started opening seminars and high school also in the field cities.

Q: How long did you work there for?

A: 11 years. After which we returned to Buenos Aires and I went to work as a headmaster at the school named after Weitzman; until I came to Israel in February 1981.

Interviewer: Yitzchak Alperovitz.

Date: February 1983

End of the testimony.

MY GRANDFATHER RABBI YEKUSIEL RAPHAEL HURWITZ

BY SHERYL WACHSMAN PRENZLAU

R' Yekusiel Raphael Hurwitz

1872- 1945

Rabbi Yekusiel Raphael Hurwitz, was born in 1872 in Maitchat, to parents (Rabbi Shmuel Meir Hurwitz and Nechama Devorah Boretcky, the daughter of Meir Arieh Boretcky Hakohane) who had both lived in Maitchet before their marriage. Rabbi Hurwitz descended from a long line of famous Rabbis (he was the 17th generation of sons to become Rabbis) and Rashi was his ancestor. After his mother died when he was quite young, his father remarried, and had several children with his new wife.

Grave of Nechama Devorah (Boretcky) Hurwitz
Died, November 6, 1874, Maitchat, Woman standing: Unknown

When Yekusiel Raphael was ten years old, the family moved to Novogrodek (Novardok). Rabbi Hurwitz was known for his photographic memory, and at a young age (16), was offered a full scholarship to study medicine in London, but he declined, preferring to study Torah. Rabbi Hurwitz learned in the Volozhin Yeshiva under Rav Chaim Brisker until it closed in 1893, and then received his smicha (Rabbinical ordination) from the son of Rabbi Yitzchak Elchanan Spektor (after whom Yeshiva University's RIETS Rabbinical School is named).

Rabbi Hurwitz was a cousin and close friend of Rabbi Shlomo Polachek, known as the Maichater Illui (one of the early Roshei Yeshiva at RIETS- Yeshiva University's Rabbinical School), and knew the Soloveitchik family from Volozhin. Like many students in Volozhin, Rabbi Hurwitz was an Ohaiv Zion, a lover of the land of Israel. He was a co-founder of Chovevei Zion, one of the first Zionist organizations in America. Later on, he taught his American-born children to speak Hebrew and even purchased land in Ranaana through the Achuza Aleph Society. Evidently, the Zionist feelings ran in his family, because his grandfather had traveled to Palestine and was buried on the Mount of Olives in 1899, and his brother, Rabbi Shimon Hurwitz, was one of the founders of the city of Petach Tikvah).

In 1903 Rabbi Hurwitz moved to the United States, settling in N.Y. He was involved in Jewish education, and tried to start a Hebrew school in Hartford, Connecticut, where his uncle, Rabbi Yitzchok Simcha Hurwitz, was the chief Rabbi, but the idea was before its time. He became a businessman, establishing a large textile dyeing and finishing mill in Greenpoint, Brooklyn, which he ran until his retirement in 1936. In 1908, He married Esther Gavrin, daughter of Rabbi Moshe Eliezer Gavrin, who was one of the founders of Rabbi Jacob Joseph School. They had three children, a son and two daughters.

A story is told in the family that one day Rabbi Hurwitz found himself seated next to a priest on a long train ride. In the course of their conversation, the Priest quoted many verses from Scripture. Rabbi Hurwitz wondered if his own children also knew any verses by heart, and upon returning home, he questioned them, discovering that they did not. He made a decision and began the practice of reciting the Ten Commandments in a sing-song chant every Friday night with his family, following the Shalom Aleichem, and before Kiddush. Before long, his children could recite the Ten Commandments by heart. Many of his grandchildren continue this practice even until today, and some grandchildren have even reported getting extra credit in school for knowing this!

When the Hurwitz's son, Benjamin, (a popular student, and president of his school's student organization) finished Talmudical Academy (later known as Yeshiva University High School), he wanted to continue his Torah learning. Rabbi Hurwitz decided to send his wife and three children to live near their cousins in Petach Tikvah, Palestine, during the years of 1927-1929, so that his son could learn in the Holy Land. He planned to join them later on, after he could arrange his business holdings.

Rabbi Hurwitz never made it to Israel to join his family, and they began making plans to return to the states in the summer of 1929, but Benjamin had requested to stay for at least another year, in his yeshiva, Slobodka of Hebron.

Benjamin Hurwitz learned in Hebron until the fateful day of 18 Av 5789 (Tarpat) (August 24, 1929) when the Arabs of Hebron rioted and killed 67 people, including many yeshiva students who were learning there during their bain hazemanim (summer intersession break). At the tender age of 19 years and 3 months, Benjamin HaLevi Hurwitz was among those brutally murdered on that holy Shabbat in the month of Av, who are known as the "Martyrs of Hebron".

בנימן הלוי הורביץ ז"ל

Benjamin (Binyamin) Halevi Hurwitz   1910 - 1929

The Arab rioting was front page news throughout the world, as it seemed that it would lead to a full blown Arab rebellion against the British. The New York Times carried Benjamin Hurwitz's name and some family details every day from August 26 to August 30, 1929.

The family was told that he tried to protect some of the women and children before he was killed. The Kedoshim (holy martyrs) were buried in a Kever Achim (mass grave) - due to the severe mutilations, which made individual burials impossible, however individual stones were also constructed with names of the martyrs. Later on, the neighboring Arabs turned all of this into a tomato patch, and the memorial was destroyed, broken into little pieces. It was rebuilt after 1967, when Jews returned to Hebron.

Memorial stone from 1929 (with Benjamin's name) destroyed by Arabs

New Memorial Stone (with Benjamin's name) put up after Jews returned to Hebron 1967

Needless to say, the Hurwitz family was devastated by the loss of their son, Benjamin. Following his death, one of the most significant actions Rabbi Hurwitz took, in spite of the fact that he had lost his only son, was opening his home to the Yeshiva community. In 1920, he had bought a spacious home in the Wavecrest section of Far Rockaway, Queens. It was a 15-room house standing on nearly an acre of ground, with many guest rooms, open lawns, shaded sections and formal gardens.

Rabbi Hurwitz had previously welcomed guests there for many years. For example, when the Rosh yeshiva of Mir, Rabbi Eliezer Yehuda Finkel, (son of Rabbi Nathan Tzvi Finkel, the famed Alter of Slabodka), and his brother-in-law, Rabbi Avraham Tzvi Hirsch Kamai, Rav of the town of Mir, had been on a fundraising tour of the United States in the mid-1920s, they stayed at this house and wrote a wonderful thank you letter upon their return to Mir. The Maichater Illui, a cousin, had also visited often, before 1928. Rabbi Moshe Soloveichik, Rosh yeshiva at RIETS after the Maichater, spent his first Pesach in the United States as personal guests of the Hurwitz family. (Many years later, their great grandchildren would marry each other!)

After 1929, The Hurwitz's hospitality took on a different dimension. During the summer breaks between 1930 and 1933, they invited groups of senior RIETS (Yeshiva University's

Rabbinical school) students to spend 10-14 days with them near the seashore, thereby allowing them to get away from the hot tenements in the city. Thus, their late son's classmates and contemporaries surrounded Rabbi and Mrs. Hurwitz for weeks at a time. The boys grew to love and admire them. One can only empathetically visualize how the Hurwitz's must have felt inwardly while talking to these young men.

The family went on, mourning Benny's loss. His parents established a memorial scholarship award for Excellence in Talmud, which is given to a deserving student of the Isaac Breuer College of Hebraic Studies (formerly Teachers Institute for Men) of Yeshiva University even to this day. Rabbi Hurwitz's second means of response to Benjamin's loss was the founding support of one of Yeshiva University's first serial publication. Starting with Volume 1, Number 1 in Nissan 5694 (1934), the Beit Midrash LeMorim (Teachers Institute) published a semi-annual Hebrew journal, Chorev, edited by Dr. Pinkhas Churgin. Until at least 1943, the cover of each issue carried the notice: Published by the Benjamin Hurwitz Foundation. In addition to supporting Chorev, Rabbi Hurwitz also helped raise funds for charity from people he knew in the textile business

The loss of their only son weighed heavily upon the Hurwitz's, and even though grandsons were born in their lifetime, neither one could bear the pain of having the name Benjamin being used. It was not until both of them had passed, that the name was given out again to family members.

Wedding of Leah Hurwitz Wachsman, New York, Dec. 24, 1939

Standing: (L to R) Dora (Hurwitz) Rudman, Mrs. Esther (Gavrin) Hurwitz, Leah (Hurwitz) Wachsman
Sitting: Rabbi Yekusiel Raphael Hurwitz, child-Reuben Rudman

The Hurwitz's two daughters, Leah (Wachsman) and Dora (Rudman) both married and had families, and all of their grandchildren have remained true to Torah traditions. Many of the grandsons and great- grandsons have continued the family tradition of becoming Rabbis, and several of the grandchildren have made Aliyah and live in Jerusalem, Israel.

Rabbi Shmuel Meir Hurwitz and his family (majority of his children missing from picture)

Standing (from left): Rabbi Shimon, Moshe Reuven,
Seated (from left): Anna, Rabbi Shmuel Meir, Rabbi Yekusiel Raphael

Maitcheter Ilui and his family in 1928 (Story of Ilu on page 73 in this book)

Standing (fom left): Harry, the Rabbanit Haya Rivka, R' Shlomo, Rose
Seated (from left): Sarah, Abraham, Libby

My parents, Meir and Esther Lozovsky
By Shoshana Lazovsky Ginzbursky

My father Meir was born in Maytchet, 1908, the youngest of 10 children. He studied for 5 years at elementary school and then attended a Yeshiva until he was 17 years old. Meir and his brother Yosef were the sole survivors of the Shoah from his immediate family; both made aliyah to Israel. Yosef together with his wife Shifra and baby daughter Sara came in 1933, and Meir in 1946.

My paternal grandfather, Yehoshua-Aaron Lazovsky, was a construction contractor, and Meir and two of his brothers worked with him. In 1930 my father Meir married and had 2 children. His wife and children were murdered in the Shoah.

Before the war, Meir was sent by the local council to build an airfield near Volkavisk. He worked there for a few months until the war began. The airfield was bombed and Meir fled returning to Maytchet to his family. On that same day (it was a Shabbat) the Germans came to Maytchet and gathered the learned people, carters and porters and killed them. There was not a ghetto in Maytchet but the remaining Jews were scattered between the gentiles. All the Jews were forced to wear the Yellow badge in the shape of a Jewish star on the back of their garments.

After a few weeks the Nazis established the Judenrat,

(Jewish council) who were a group of Jews who were forced to implement the laws for the Jews only. The officers of the Judenrat wore a black uniform, they were not given any weapons but did carry cudgels (short black stick used as a weapon).

After a few months the Judenrat gathered the young and healthy men and sent them to dig pits. They were told that those pits will be used for storing crude oil, but in fact they were mass graves where the people of Maytchet were murdered and buried.

Months later the Judenrat gathered the professional Jews to work in Koldichevo (concentration camp). This camp was located 18 km. from Baranovichi. Meir was forced to leave his wife and his children and go to Koldichevo together with his brother Notee (Natan).

They arrived in Koldichevo at the end of 1942. They lived in a shed that they built along with all the other workers of the prison, totaling approximately 400 internees. While Koldichevo concentration camp was in operation from 1942 to 1944, 22,000 people, mostly Jews, were murdered there.

Meir worked as a builder and was put in charge of several laborers. One day two people from his group escaped. Protocol demanded that the internees immediately report any such happenings to the Commander of the camp. Meir did not report this escape because he thought that should one of them succeed and make their way to join a Partisan group, they would report that all the weak and sick persons in the camp were being killed. (Just like his brother Notee (Natan) who became sick and could not work. He died of injuries inflicted upon him by his commander who crushed his skull with a board).

When they came back to the camp the commander counted the prisoners and found that two people were missing.

At midnight four policemen and the commander came to the shed and ordered Meir to come down from his bench and lie down on the floor. Each of them then beat him twenty-five lashes with a rubber stick. Then they beat-up the others in the group and then once again returned to beat Meir. They forced him to count out loud each blow until he fainted on the fiftieth .One of the policemen asked the commander if he could take Meir for further interrogation because he was certain that he could "break" him and get him to tell where the two escapees were. He got a needle from a tailor, and stabbed Meir's tongue 10 times. (Dr. Levinbuk relates this story in the book on Baranowicze).

After the beating the prisoners covered Meir with a wet sack cloth, and put him on a bench. The next morning the commander came with Dr Levinbuk, and asked how many days it would be until he recovered. The doctor said 12 days, gave Meir some medicine and quietly advised him to go back to work or he will be killed.

Just before Passover 1944, all the Jewish prisoners broke the wall of the shed and escaped. The night before the escape, a Polish policeman brought them 10 pistols, 10 grenades and 2 pliers to cut the fence, and told them that the next night would be a good time to attempt an escape. They escaped in groups of 10. One group unfortunately was caught by the Nazis and killed. My father and his group succeeded in escaping to the forest, and joined the Bielski Otriad. He met my mother Esther there.

After the war my father Meir went back to Maytchet and discovered that his entire family was murdered. He went to work in Baranowicze for a few months where he was reunited with my mother Esther and other people from Maytchet. In 1946 they made their way through Austria and Italy and finally arrived to Israel where they were married. They had two children, myself Shoshana am named after my maternal great grandmother, and my brother Yehoshua named after my maternal grandfather.

My mother was on the Maytchet Yizkor book committee and her family's story is on page 70. Meir's brother Yosef left Maytchet for Eretz Israel in 1933 and his story of the Lasovsky family is on page 238 as well as a family photo on page 171 (these page numbers are page number of the original Yizkor book, not the translation page numbers).

Left to right: Meir Lazovsky, Abrasha Channales, Yoseff Lazovsky
Between Meir and Abrasha, Yoeff's wife Shiffra & daughter Sara

MY GRANDMOTHER ELKA KORZON
a/k/a HELEN GOLDMAN

My maternal great grandparents and my grandmother and her sisters were all born in Maytchet. Great-grandfather Morris Korzon born 1872 and great-grandmother Sara Rabetz was born in 1873. My grandmother Helen (Elka) was born in Maytchet in 1905 and died in 1991. Her sisters also were born in Maytchet, Anna 1900, Dora 1904, Celia 1910, and Molly 1912.

My grandmother's Yiddish name was Elka and when she immigrated to the United States in 1920, her name was changed to Helen Korzon. After marrying my grandfather, she assumed my grandfather's surname, and became Helen Goldman.

My grandmother was a very kind and loving woman. I will always treasure the times we spent together when I was growing up. When I was a child, my grandmother would always tell me stories about Maychet. It wasn't until later in life that I was able to locate Maychet on a map, as the town had gone through so many name changes and the Internet was in it's infancy. I finally was able to find Maychet on a map, when my grandmother told me it was near Slonim and Baranavichi. On a WW I era map, there I found Maytchet, under it's Polish name of Molchad.

One of the most interesting stories that my grandmother had told me was about the years during WW I, when she was a young girl of 7-11 years old. During the war, she told me about the German occupation of Maytchet, and how the German soldiers had occupied her home along with her family. During the war years my Great grandmother Sara, was alone in her house with her five daughters including my grandmother. My Great grandfather Morris Korzon had emigrated to New York in 1914 to find a job and a home, hoping his wife and children would soon follow him. The family became separated by the war.

When the German army first came to Maytchet, my grandmother, who at the time, was an innocent and naïve young girl, told me that she thought the Germans were fellow Jews, as they were speaking in German, a language similar to Yiddish and intelligible to the Jews of the town. She said that when the German army arrived in Maytchet, that the townspeople were very happy to see them, as the governing Russians had not treated the Jews well at all.

The Russian Empire restricted where they could live, the professions they could hold, where they could travel, and their access to higher education. While the German army occupied her home, she informed me that they were treated well by the invading army. Luckily, my grandmother, along with her mother and sisters, would leave Maytchet and come to America, where they were told, "the streets were paved in gold".

My great-Grandmother along with her five daughters emigrated to the U.S. in 1920 joining their husband and father. They were all members of the Meicheter Landsleit Society in New York. My great-Grandparents and maternal grandparents are interred in the "Meicheter" section of Mount Lebanon Cemetery in Glendale (Queens County), N.Y.

I thought how ironic it was that the Germans in WWI, would treat the Jews so well, while nearly thirty years later, they would horrifically murder the Jews of Maytchet in a systematic decimation of the Jewish population, along with the rest of Germany occupied Europe, in what came to be called the Holocaust.

Alan Gregg Cohen

November 19, 2014

Dunetz Family visits Maitshet, August 2000
By Ronnie Dunetz

In the year 2000, my family made a visit that is what we might also call a "once in a lifetime". My two brothers and I and my mother accompanied my father for the first time to the place of his birth, youth and upbringing in what is today Belarus, and was once Poland. Not only was it once Poland but it was once a type of Jewish existence that for most intents and purposes, outside perhaps of some Hasidic Jewish enclaves, has become extinct from the world. The shtetl does no longer exist.

My father was born and raised in Zhetel and that was the focus of our visit, the town and the cemetery where his parents and younger brother were killed on August 2, 1942 in the second massacre in Zhetel. His older sister was taken away and killed a year before, my father, Mordechai (Mot'l) and his sister Fanya, survived the massacres, labor camp and life as partisans. We are fortunate to have had both my father and Fanya live to a ripe old age, Fanya is 94 and my father is 92, may they be blessed with continued health and a good life.

Maitshet, however, always had a special place in their hearts! Their mother, Basya Belsky (later Dunetz) was born and raised in Maitshet and it was Maitshet where the children visited every summer in their younger days, to be with their grandmother, Rachel Dvosha, and the many aunts, uncles and cousins. It was their "second home" and since Maitshet was a smaller and poorer village, closer and much more integrated with the surrounding forests, Maitshet was the subject of many memories of nature, simple life and free-floating childhood play.

We visited Maitshet on the third day of the 5-day visit to the area and for my father it was a huge rush of emotion and recollection. During all the years that had passed, my father had consistent reinforcement of his life in Zhetel, frequent interaction and communication with "Zhetlers" around the world and he visited Zhetel in 1991 right when the iron curtain was lifted and travel to the area was allowed. In Israel he was a prime leader of the Hazkarot every year but as for the connection to Maitshet---there was next to none! Part of the reason was that no one living in Maitshet at that time from his immediate family survived the Nazi killing machine, other than having the Maitshet Yizkor Book in the family bookcase, there was nothing to grab hold of, nothing to generate memories from.

Mordechai (Max) Dunetz – grandson of Rachel Dvosha Belsky

This all changed in a flash as we entered the town of Maitshet. To be sure, it was hard to remember that we were in the year 2000 as all the village homes seemed to have remained unchanged from World War II days, the only thing that was from the "after war period" was a huge Soviet-looking military statue. Mordechai's memory was quickly jabbed as he looked around the town trying to get his bearings. We were quite a scene for this laid-back summer-time resort of sorts, a bunch of "Westerners" moving around with cameras, speaking Hebrew, English, Russian and Yiddish amongst us (we had relatives with us). Mordechai approached the house of his uncle Shmuel and aunt Freidl, that is the place, which was once there home. There was a very elderly couple in the garden with whom we engaged in conversation, they had come there just after the war. No, they did not know anything about who lived there before, they knew nothing of the family who had lived there and were no longer among the living. It was a sad story, in a place where there were only sad stories to tell, it seemed. Uncle Shmuel had left Zhetel some time in the 1930's for Argentina, leaving behind his wife Freidl, the well-regarded seamstress of the town and their three little children. The idea was for Shmuel to get settled in Argentina and then send for the family. Just before the war broke out Shmuel had sent a visa for his eldest son Alter who was about to embark on the journey at age 15. He never did. The gates closed and the end was on the way.

While in the Town Square we were approached by an older gentleman who came with a photo of himself and an Israeli man. The Maitshet person explained that he was now responsible for looking after the cemetery gravestone marking the massacre of the Jews of Maitshet on 15 July 1942- a man by name of Rachmiel Bar in Tel-Aviv would send him money every year to look after the site. He accompanied us there, we questioned him (cautiously) as to the events of the war and he explained to us that he was only 15 but he remembers it well. They were asked to drag the bodies of those who were killed in their homes to the cemetery pit. To his knowledge, informed by Rachmiel Bar, only 7 Jews miraculously survived the massacre.

Some of Maitshet's Jews were killed in their homes; others were killed at the pits in the graveyard. For some reason my great- grandmother, Rochel Dvosha, who was killed in Maitshet was not listed in the Yizkor Book. Perhaps now she will be remembered as well…

A typical House in Maytchet (2000)

Tracing our Belsky family (the family of Basya, Mordechai and Fanya's mother, who came from the town of Maychet)

**(Unfortunately we know relatively little about the details of the Maychet family as none of the immediate family survived, only uncle Shmuel who left well before WW II on his own, never to be seen again- he died in 1960 in Buenos Aires).

Mordechai and Fanya's grandmother, Rachel Dvosha married Anzel Belsky around 1880-1885. Anzel and Rachel Dvosha had the following children:

Shmuel (circa 1886)- married Freidel who was a successful seamstress who lived by herself in Maychet along with their children after Shmuel left for Argentina. Freidel and children perished in the Holocaust. Shmuel died in 1960 and is buried in Buenos Aires.

Abraham(circa 1892)- married a woman by family name of Ravitz- they and their children-perished.

Zvi (Hirshel)- (Circa 1888)- was said to have suffered from mental disabilities after falling from a horse as a child- he perished.

Basya- (Circa 1899). Basya married Yoel David in Zhetl about 1914, which led to our part of the Dunetz family. As we know, she was killed along with the others in Zhetl on 6 August 1942.

Rochel Dvosha was one of 11 children (from 2 different mothers)- all 10 of her brothers and sisters immigrated to the US in and around 1910, she was the only one left behind. This family, called Makovsky or Maskovsky or otherwise (each of the children took a different name upon reaching the US), quickly spread out to various parts of the US: most of the siblings stayed in the NY area, two brothers, Max Moskovitz and Hyman Levine went to Nashville, Tennessee, one nephew, Harry Moss eventually made his home in the Detroit, Michigan area.

We are told that Great-grandfather Anzel Belsky left Maitshet by himself somewhere around the turn of the century but details about his trip are not clear. Apparently he had a brother living there (in the U.S.) already, definitely nephews, but the interesting and unusual thing about this trip is that it ENDED when Anzel decided to return to Maitshet for the reason that he felt that life in America was "too secular" for him, he feared for his Jewish identity in that country. Anzel died around 1930.

One cousin from the Maitshet family did survive and made her home in Haifa, Israel-Vichna Belsky Ezrachi, the daughter of Rivka and Moshe Belsky, the latter being a brother to Anzel Belsky, my great-grandfather.

My father Mordechai Dunetz, born in Zhetl, was with the partisans and also in a labor camp in Novogrudok.

His sister Fanya Dunetz (Brodsky) was also in a labor camp in Novogudok and the Bielski partisans.

Yoel David Dunetz, my father's father, was killed in the Zhetl massacre August 6, 1942.

Rachel Sara Dunetz, my father's grandmother, died in 1939 of natural causes.

Anzel Dunetz, my father's younger brother, was killed in the Zhetl massacre, August 6, 1942.

Basya Dunetz, my father's mother, was killed in the Zhetl massacre August 6. 1942

My father's cousin Rosalie, who was living in another city, Volkovysk, was killed with her mother (Yoel), David's sister Minnoeta, father and brothers in 1943 in Treblinka.

My father's uncle Shmuel Dunetz was my paternal grandfather, Yoel David's youngest brother. Shmuel was a halutz and made Aliyah to Eretz YIsrael in 1921 and came back to Zhetl in 1934 to get married to Bracha (probably a shiduch). Bracha lived in Israel, remarried and died in Israel many years later of natural causes. Shmuel was tragically killed in a work accident in 1938 and he is buried in Tel Aviv.

Shifra Dunetz was my father's oldest sister. She was a nurse working in Lita, came back to Zhetl when she heard of the occupation and German invasion. She was taken away right at the onset of the German occupation when they took 120 of the town's leaders in all fields to some unknown destination. We are told that she found out that her father Yoel David was rounded up in the village square for deportation, as one of the 120. She pleaded with the SS to let her father go, and was then taken instead. (The story goes that a gentile informant told the SS that Shifra was a "communist", which was not true but enough for the SS). The 120 were later reported as taken to a nearby forest and shot to death. This was only known some years later.

After the war, my father returned to Zhetl and later made his way with his sister Fanya to Berlin where refugees were gathered in a former German air force base. Soon afterward he made his way to the Eschewege D.P. camp which was in the area of Kassel, Germany; he was there for nearly three years, 1947-1949. He was the editor of "Our Hope", which was the first Yiddish newspaper in that area after the war. He was quite a "rising star", doing all this at the age of 25 with no education in journalism, no experience, no guides or mentors; just a drive to write, create, report and document life as it came about after the Holocaust. In 1949, he immigrated to the US where he would make his life for the next 29 years before making Aliyah in 1978. He married my mother, Tziona Cohen Dunetz, an 8th generation Jerusalemite; together they had three children: David, born 1957, myself (Ronnie), born 1959 and Arnon (Arnie) born 1964.

OUR RETURN TRIP TO MAYTCHET 2004
Myrna and Shael Siegel

In 2004 when we told our friends and family we were going to make a return trip to our ancestral towns in Lithuania and Belarus, their reaction was almost unanimous, "You were there 9 years ago, why do you want to return; what more can you learn? They obviously do not share the feeling of intrigue and mystique that my ancestral shtetl Maytchet holds for me.

Maytchet, Belarus is the ancestral town of both my parents. Throughout the years I was told endearing stories of a town so far away from my home in Chicago. Part of my dream to do a return trip, was with a survivor of Maytchet who would be able to point out the homes and places of Jewish interest. I so much wanted to walk the streets in hopes of recapturing what had once been there. Imagination can only take you so far and I needed someone to share their own personal first hand experiences of this once, living Jewish community (80% of the population of Maytchet before 1941 was Jewish).

In the ensuing nine years I had spoken to and met with several survivors and gathered much more information. Many of the survivors carry bitter memories of the Nazi's marching into their beloved shtetl and the mass killings. They also have horrendous animosity against their non-Jewish neighbors who collaborated with the Nazis. When these survivors saw the video we took after our first trip, they told me that the only satisfaction they had is that the town, and its now inhabitants, had not moved into the 21st century and continued to live the life of a typical pale peasant.

For a moment let us turn the clock back 9 years to our first trip in 1995.

My husband Shael and I frequently spoke of our desire to visit our ancestral towns. In the summer of 1995, after visiting a friend who was near death, we realized that waiting for the perfect time to travel was not an option. We hurriedly made our plans and left six weeks later.

A message on Jewishgen supplied us with logistical help, including guides, who we fortunately were able to contact and confirm quickly.

In 1995 we heard about the serious difficulties regarding border crossings between Lithuania and Belarus. We flew from Vilnius to Warsaw and took another plane to Minsk; an expensive and lengthy method of traveling a short distance. In 2004 we were informed that things have eased and that the border crossings were less threatening. We decided that we would take a four-hour train from Vilnius to Minsk.

At the border crossing several Lithuanian and then Belarus police got on the train and after looking at our passports they left with our passports in hand. We were a little nervous at this point but when they returned with our passports we were more at ease. As we traveled through the heavily forested areas and a vast open farmland, I shuttered thinking what stories these trees would tell if they could talk. I tried to imagine how many Jews ran, hid, were often discovered by Nazis and their local collaborators.

At the Minsk train station we were met by our guide Galina, and her husband Frank Swarz. As we traveled the short distance to our hotel, we were amazed to see the bright streetlights and new modern buildings as well as older ones that had been updated. In 1995 only every third or fourth street light was illuminated with a low wattage bulb. This certainly was not the same drab, depressing city we remembered. We also had vivid memories of our depressing hotel room. We had to sleep with all our clothes on because heat was not turned on until November. This trip our hotel was up to Western standards.

The next morning our drive to Maytchet took 2 hours. On this trip there were no visible police or frequent roadblocks where we had to stop and show our transit papers as we had done in 1995.

Myrna and Shael Siegel standing next to sign entering Maytchet 2004

I am going to turn the clock back once more.

My paternal great-uncles Sam and Nathan Brodsky gave me so much family information about Maytchet. They told me time and time again about the flourmill that their grandfather Meir Arieh Boretcky had built and that there was an engraved symbol on the corner stone indicating that it was insured for fire-------the only building in Maytchet to have fire insurance. In 1995 when we saw the flour mill there was in fact a corner stone with a date of 1866 on it and an unusual symbol under the date. The next day in Minsk I asked an architect, Galina Levina, what the symbol meant, not telling her what my great-uncles had told me. She immediately confirmed that it meant the building was insured!

Corner stone Meir Arieh Boretcky's Flour Mill 1866

I asked our guide Oleg to send a message to the mayor in Maytchet and tell him that if the building was ever demolished I would be interested in getting the cornerstone. A year later I received a letter saying that the mill was being turned into a bathhouse and the stone was removed and in the mayor's safe keeping for me to come and reclaim. A U.S. embassy representative in Minsk told me that it was unlikely that I would be able to take the stone out of the country. So, as much as I wanted the cornerstone, I decided that I should put the idea out of my mind. Although I had reconciled myself to the fact that I would not be able to get it, I still fantasized that the stone would one day be in my possession.

Our first stop was the flour mill. When we got out of the car we immediately noticed that there was a gaping hole where the corner stone had resided. I said that I suspected that the mayor had it. This was the one known object remaining that connected a physical presence of my family to this shtetl.

Flour Mill of Moshe Aaron Boretcky

Our next stop was the center of town. Several women were sitting on a bench that was situated at the end of a triangle street where shops had once stood. One of the seated women offered to take us to the home of a resident who had lived in Maytchet before the war. She ended up escorting us all over the town; pointing out the cemetery, the mass grave, the former synagogue, spending over two hours with us. A typical peasant woman, Ludmila Golonsko, said she was born 1924 in the Ukraine and spent the war in a labor camp in Austria. After the war she married a man from Maytchet and moved there.

As we walked a man riding a bicycle approached us and lo and behold he was the same man we met in 1995, Lev Tolkatch. After a few minutes he rode off. Our local guide walked with us to the Jewish cemetery. The few headstones that remain are badly weathered and the only one that was perfectly legible was that of Mayta Chaya, daughter of Itsele Boretcky, the brother of my great-grandfather Yakov Yoseph Boretcky.

Gravestone in Maytchet Jewish cemetery of Mayta Chaya, daughter of Itsele Boretcky

Unattended and Overgrown cemetery in Maytchet

I took some small stones from the cemetery and we walked down a sandy lane to the main road. This must have been the path the Jews took as they marched to the mass grave where they were murdered. As we walked we could see the spires of the church and realized this was probably the last view of Maytchet the poor souls saw as they marched to their death.

Russian Orthodox Church

On the main road, across from the gentile cemetery and near the train tracks was one lone house; we were told that this is where people from Maytchet bought their train tickets. Lev now lives in this house and he came out and joined us. We walked together for a short distance into the woods, stopping in front of the mass grave containing 3,600 murdered Jewish souls. I placed 2 stones on the Hebrew memorial and Shael recited El Moleh Rachamim. The gravestone reads July 15, 1942, the date of the mass killings, which was just 3 weeks after my 6th birthday. Had both my maternal and paternal families not left Maytchet in the early 1900's I very likely would have been in that grave.

Funds donated by the Maytchet survivor group had a second stone in Hebrew made and placed alongside the original Russian stone saying that in this place are buried the Jewish citizens of Maytchet and its surroundings who were killed and destroyed by the Nazis and their collaborators July 15, 1942. The Russian stone made no mention of Jewish people buried here. A Maytchet survivor Rachmiel Bar, together with his son Paz, put up the Hebrew stone in September, 1993.

Mass grave outside of Maytchet where 3,600 Jews were murdered July, 1942

Lev described, much too vividly for our comfort, how the Nazis stood on a bluff a short distance away and kept shooting at the people as they approached the open pit. Our "local resident guide" said she was told that the women walked quietly and told the children that this was G-d's will. When the Nazis came to Maytchet they first killed the young men because they were afraid they would rebel and fight back. Then they killed the woman, children and elderly men.

We walked back to the town going from one house to another looking for people who possibly remembered the Jewish residents. Most people said they came there after the war possibly not wanting to admit that they remembered anyone or anything. One lady told us that Jews sold things on credit and would open up their stores at any hour if someone needed something. We stopped at a house and an elderly woman came out. She told us her father owned the house and rented it out as a Tarbot school. Of course we did not believe her but the building has a strong resemblance to the photo in the Yizkor Original book, page 144.

Former Tarbut School Building

The former "Kalte Shul" is now a collective farm office and the only building of the former three synagogues that is still standing. On our 1995 trip people were leaving the building and they refused to let us in. According to what we saw on Rachmiel Bar's video of his visit 1993, he also was refused entrance to the synagogue. On our return trip we found the main door was open, and we just walked in and up the stairs. It appeared that the rooms on the upper floor were offices and we did see a few people working. We did not see any thing that indicated that this building had been a synagogue. There was a door on the first floor that was locked. When I returned home Martin Small told me that the synagogue was actually below ground so the locked door may have led to it. Another survivor described the beautiful biblical paintings on the ceiling of the synagogue. Our lady friend said that the top part of the building was blown off during the war and rebuilt. When she moved to Maytchet after the war she remembered children playing near this building with chips that were painted different colors.

"Kalte Shul" now collective farm office

We were invited into our new found friend Ludmila's house for tea and something to eat.

She insisted we come in but we convinced her that we did not have enough time. Her front porch was filled with apples and she gleefully filled a large bag saying that we should take these apples from my ancestral town.

We thanked her, said our good-byes and continued on to the town hall hoping to find the mayor. The offices were empty except for one lady sitting at a desk. She told us that the current mayor and the rest of the staff were on their farms gathering crops since it was harvesting time. We explained to her that we were looking for the corner stone from the mill. She informed us that the former mayor, Ivan Nikolayevich Shileyko, who was the mayor at the time of our first visit, was most likely the person we were looking for. She called his house as well as his secretary; there was no answer at either home. Coincidentally two men entered the building and she introducd us to them. One man was the Assistant Deputy chairman from Baranavichi and he invited us to come to his office the next day. Our guide Galina gave the secretary her cell phone number to call us in Baranovichi that night or tomorrow during the day if she is able to find the former mayor.

A short distance out of town we passed the new train station in Muskevtch. I had been told stories that when someone would emigrate from Maytchet the townspeople would walk them to the train station to say good-bye and wish them well. The musicians who were from the all-Jewish volunteer fire department accompanied them. They were the only orchestra in town and would have concerts and show silent films to raise money to buy equipment for the fire department.

The next morning in Baranovichi we met Phillip, a current representative of the Jewish Community.   He took us to the two sites of mass killing fields, which were adjacent to rail tracks. Jews from Czechoslovakia were brought by train here and then killed and their bodies were thrown into the mass graves. He took us to the area of the former ghetto, and pointed out a building that had once was a branch of the highly regarded Slonim Yeshiva. It is now been converted to a sport complex. Throughout much of Europe former synagogues and buildings of Jewish institutions have been converted to museums, theaters and local community centers. We went to the current Jewish cemetery to view typical East European headstones with lengthy bios and ornate metal work on each gravesite. Our last stop was the mayor's office. He gave us a book that detailed the impact of the war on the communities of that area. I have since given that book to the Yad Vashem library in Jerusalem.   He also related a story that his mother lived in a small village near Maytchet and frequently spoke of her Jewish childhood friend Mina Gorsky (Levin) who I had the pleasure of meeting on a visit to Israel.

We drove on to Slonim and went to the museum, which was built on the site where the weekly open market had once been. I told the curator that I had my mother's Slonim school pin hoping she would tell me something about the school. She did not have any information for me but did ask if I would give the pin to her museum.

From there we walked the streets and saw the former Jewish Hospital, which is now a medical school.   Across the street is a former synagogue that the medical school now uses as a sport's facility. Nearby is what had once been a magnificent 17th century synagogue; there has been talk of this synagogue being restored. My husband Shael managed to get into building that was filled with rubbish and could see that it once had been the center of Jewish life. It is located next to a large market on the grounds of where a Jewish cemetery once stood. Across the street is a furniture store that was another former synagogue. Architectural designs on the front of the nearby houses indicated they had been Jewish homes.

Later that afternoon we received a call from the Mayor's secretary telling us that the stone had been found. We quickly left Slonim and the 20 min. ride back to Maytchet was filled with excited anticipation.

The current mayor's secretary, also named Galina, was waiting for us on the corner and excitedly took us to the ex-mayor's home that was unfortunately ill and in the hospital. His wife led us on a path behind her house. There alongside the barn she pointed to a huge boulder covered with underbrush. We estimated the boulder to be well over 500 pounds.

Shael immediately said this was not the corner stone that we had seen in 1995, which was just a little larger then a few bricks. Also there was no date or insurance symbol to be seen. She insisted that it was in fact the corner stone and said the markings were on the under side of the boulder. How were we to turn this huge thing over? The secretary said her husband would be able to do that and ran home to get him. A short while later they came carrying two large steel bars. He handed one to our driver and motioned for Shael to push. After much strenuous effort the three managed to flip the boulder over. No markings could be seen. The former mayor's wife ran back to the house and returned with a bucket of water and a stiff brush. In just a minute or two, after pouring the water and scraping the mud off the boulder the date of 1866 and the insurance symbol were clearly visible. Shael acknowledged he was wrong and after Galina translated what he said the others had a hearty laugh claiming that this was the first time they ever heard a man admit he was wrong.   I did not know if I should laugh or cry.

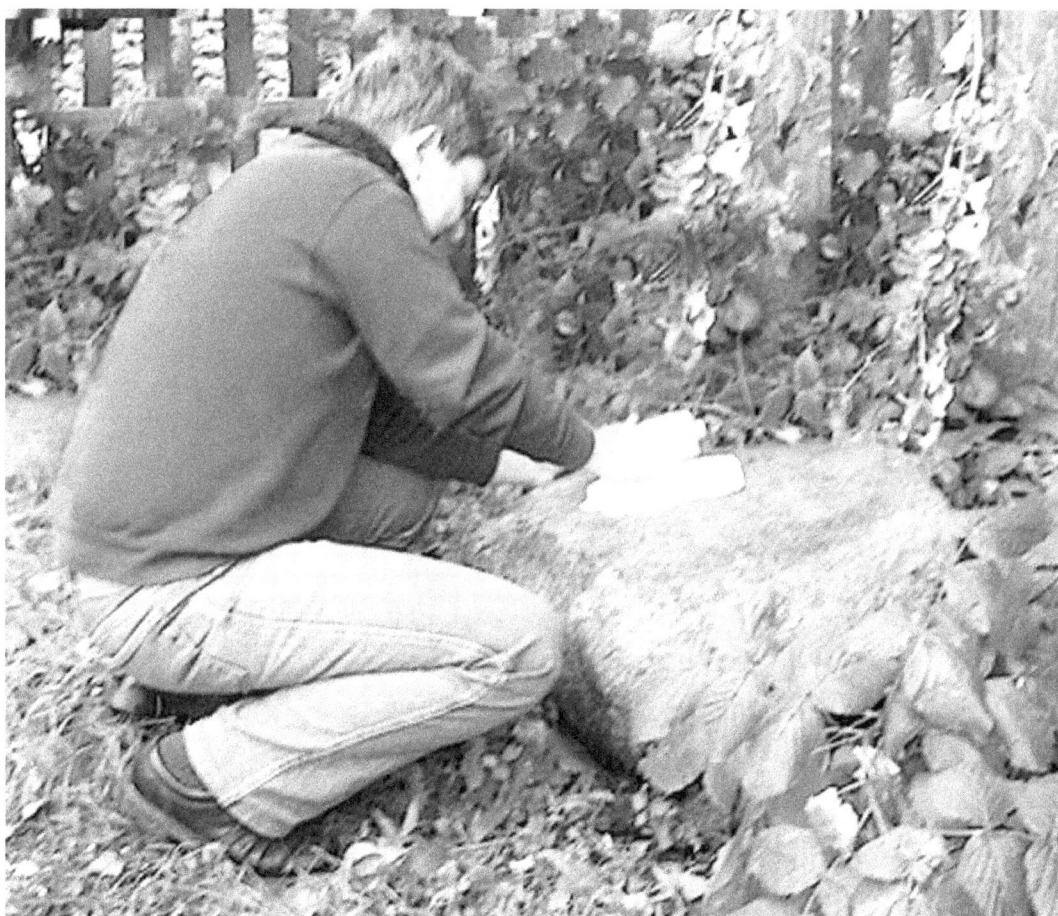

Making a clay mold of flour mill corner stone with the year 1866 and a symbol that the building had insurance, the only one in town.

We had molding clay and tried to get an imprint of the date and insurance symbol that was on the face of the large corner stone. We were informed that even if the stone had been smaller we would never have been able to take it out of the country. We carefully carried the mold through security, through customs and onto our next part of the trip.   Unfortunately within a few days it began to disintegrate; we were now left with only memories and photos.

I suggested they place the boulder in front of the town hall with a memorial plaque saying that it was from the flourmill built by Meier Arieh Boretcky in 1866. It should also acknowledge that the murdered Jews once comprised 80% of the population of Maytchet. We returned to Minsk that evening excited about our two days experience.

Although I did not return home with the corner stone, I learned that even with the passage of time there are discoveries that sometimes take repeat visits to unlock. And if I am ever given the opportunity to return to Maytchet with a survivor or a member of my family, it would not take me long to pack!

I admit that I did not come home empty handed. If you remember I took small stones from the Jewish cemetery and placed two of them on the mass grave. I brought the additional stones I took back home with me. Together with my brother Sidney and sister Madeline we buried a few stones at the graves of my grandparents and parents in Chicago, Illinois thus bringing back a piece of their birthplace to them.

Left to right: Myrna Siegel, Madeline Shiffman, Sidney Brodsky

Bielski Partisans

Victims, including several from Maytchet, took active part in anti-fascist Resistance. The underground activists made weapons in the ghettos and joined the partisan guerrilla fighting. The Bielski partisans camped out in the Naliboki forest N.E. of Novogrudok on the northern back of the Nieman River. Between 1942 and 1944 the Bielski group was one of the most significant Jewish resistance efforts against Nazi Germany during World War II. While its members did fight against the Nazis and their collaborators, the Bielski group leaders main concern was providing a safe haven for Jews; in particular women, children and the elderly. They defied the Nazis and built a village in the forest. Under the protection of the Bielski group more then 1,200 Jews survived the war. Tuvia Bielski used to say, "I'd rather save one old Jewish woman then kill 10 Nazis"

BIELSKI PARTISANS FROM MAYTCHET & NEARBY
Most of following Names were copied from a list and may not be complete.

Bronicki Rachmil 1928   Molchad
Boretcky Fischel 1923 Molchad
Chlasnovich Meyer Born 1911 Molchad
Dunetz, Fanya (Belsky family) Born 1920 Zhetl
Falda Chaim   Born1910   Molchad
Gilerovich Zelda Born 1920 Molchad
Govlyach Yudel Born 1890 Molchad
Govlyach Pesach Born 1922 Molchad
Gutman Movsha 1902 Molchad
Kaplan Chaya Esther Born 1909 Molchad
Kaplan Matus 1927 Molchad and father
Kaplan Tzira (Rabets) Born 1909 Molchad
Kushnerovski Shmaya 1929 Molchad
Lazovski Meyer Born1912 Molchad
Malishanski Esther Born 1923 Molchad
Margolin Friedl Born 1904 Molchad
Mordkovski Noach 1911   Molchad
Pilshchik Chonon 1922 Molchad
Ravitz, Tzira (Kaplan – Royak) Born 1909 Molchad
Romanovsky, Sholom born 1910 in Slutzk-lived in Molchad
Rozhanski Meyer Born 1924 Molchad
Shmuilovich Yosef Born 1907 Molchad
Snyadovski Solomon Born 1912   Molchad
Tilshchik Chonon Born1922 Molchad

Zegerman Vanya Born 1925 Molchad
Zhukhovicki Solomon   Born 1909 Molchad
Litavorski Grunia Born   Born 1917 Zverovshchina
Litavorski Litman Born   Born 1925 Zverovshchina
Litavorski Pinchus   Born 1922   Zverovshchina
Litavorski Shifra Born 1921 Zverovshchina

War Crimes Trial Records from U.S. Holocaust Museum
THE BRUTALITY OF THE BYELORUSSIANS

John Loftus in his book *"Secret War Against The Jews"*, Chapter 21, *"The Victors and the Victims"*, writes of the brutality of the Byelorussians against the local Jewish population of Maytchet and Baranovichi. If you can handle the descriptive brutality you will understand the extent of these heinous crimes against the unsuspecting local Jewish population.

THE FOLLOWING INFORMATION IS COURTESY OF DR. MARTIN DEAN, U.S. HOLOCAUST MUSEUM

Regarding the trial of war criminals in connection to Molchad, I have the following information about War Crimes trials in Poland:

Wladyslaw Filipowicz born October 8, 1920 and who served in the Belorussian Police in Molchad was sentenced to 5 years six months by a Polish court on February 27, 1974 for participation in "killing." He was released on June 7, 1974. The court case is held by the Polish Institute of National Remembrance (IPN), ref. SWZG sygn. 41-52.

At the same trial Jan Woroniec born October 2, 1922, was sentenced to 7 years on February 27, 1974, for taking part in killings of the Jewish population as an official of the Belorussian Police in Molchad. He was released conditionally on June 24, 1975. Both these men were of "Polish nationality" although they served in the Belorussian local police under the Nazis.

The entry in the USHMM *Encyclopedia of Camps and Ghettos* Vol. 2, pp. 1243-1244 (electronic version attached) mentions also a case from the Belorussian KGB archives, but this concerns the involvement of local policemen from Nieswisz in the murder of the Jews in Molczadz. There were almost certainly other trials of local Belorussiaan policemen from Molchad in Belorussia, but it is difficult to uncover these, unless they are also mentioned in the Polish trial record. The issue of whether there was actually a ghetto in Molczadz is debatable, as a formal ghettoization process did not take place there, although some Jews were forced to move in with other Jews.

The events in Molcahd are also mentioned in passing in German postwar investigations, for example into Gendarmerie chief Max Eibner in Baranowicze, conducted in Oldenburg, but a specific trial on the events in Molczadz did not take place.

Soviet Extraordinary Records

Article and Names

THE SOVIET EXTRAORDINARY COMMISSION DATABASE

This database includes over 60,000 records from the Soviet Extraordinary Commission. Created by the Soviet Union at the end of World War II to document German fascist crimes during the occupation in Soviet territories. The Soviet Extraordinary Commission compiled testimonial information gathered from the evidence of neighbors, eyewitnesses, and survivors.

Not all lists have the same information and this report was for all victims, Jewish and non-Jewish. Information collected was not based on documents but rather on individual local testimony, which had some variables.

These records are from Fond 7021 of the State Archive of the Russian Federation (GARF), formerly known as the Central State Archive of the October Revolution (TsGAOR), in Moscow. Microfilmed copies are located in the Archives of the U.S. Holocaust Museum and Yad Vashem.

Yad Vashem's database of Shoah Victims Names is an ongoing project. They do take names from the Soviet Extraordinary Commission, as this is often the only source they have if a page of testimony was not filled out. If you see an error please notify them. And if you have information about someone not on the list, fill out a Page of Testimony and register that name.

The information sent to me contains five lists from Molczadz, in the Baranovichi district and Novogrudok region. List includes itemization of property damage of Jews from Molchadz who perished between 1941-1944 which was prepared by the Soviet Extraordinary State Commission collected on the following dates: 15/02/1945, 15/03/1945, 27/03/1945, 31/03/1945, 02/04/1945

Record Group M33 – Records of the Extraordinary State Commission to Investigate German-Facist Crimes Committed on Soviet Territory

File Number: JM/23630

Type of material: List of murdered/persecuted persons

Language: Russian

Below are the names translated phonetically from the Russian and when indicated number of people in household.

List #12 February 4, 1945

Lozovski Noman 6
Shleimovitch Shloma 8
Lotvitski Aron 5
Zlotnick Yankel 3
Zlotnick Shmuel 4
Shevchuck Aron 5
Volfovitch Chaim 4
ShiniavskyIsrael 6
Girshovich Shimon
Romanovski Abram 5
Yatvitskaya Nechama 1
Urinovitch Girsh 5
Belsky Israel 8
Belsky Moishe 5
Ramanovski Berko 6
Rabets Girsh 4
Gilerovich Itsko 6
Shmulovich Miche 3
Zegerman Efraim 6
Schkolnikovitch Abe 6
Okun Yankel 5
Biniunsky Shleime 8
Zamoshick Yudel 5
Mirski Shimon 5
Shkolnikovitch Meer 5
Shmuukivich Michoel 4
Shmuilovich Shleima 4
Dvorzhetski Yankel 4
Shmuilovitch Zimel 5
Lozovskya Momaya 3

List #13   Feb. 15, 1945

Nesvizhsky Abram 5
Grinberg Yankel 3
Bronitsky Gersh 2
Ribizhevsky Gersh 2
Tsirinsky Peisach 2
Sheeimovitch Moishe 6
Rabets Chaim 6
Shubsky Chaim 5
Zhuchovitsky Abram 2
Kostrovitsky Yankel 4
Koton Itsko 6
Abramovits Abram 3
Kovensky Yankel 4
Scholnikovitch Chaim 5
Shmulevitch Moishe 5
Scholnikovitch Abram 3
Lyachovitsky Rocha 2
Israelevitch Mina 6
Zapolsky Tirtsa 4
Abol Berna 5
Goldstair Chaya 6
Sinyavsky Tinya 6
Kravchuck Mila 4
Chomts Meir 5
Lazovsky Mueya 4
Belsky Freida 3
Chorocrovitsky Itzko 2
Kozlovsky 4
Zamoschek Lea 3
Abramovitch Zalman 3
Dubnovsky Abram 4
Novomushensky Itzko 4
Butyansky Sonia 4
Schoenikovitch Ioksha 5
Schoenikovitch Rafael 5
Schoenikovitch   Moishe 4
Sapir Yankel 2
Lomachevsky Mordechai 5
Schoenikovitel David 4

List #11 March 15, 1945

Pilnick Sholom 3
Gilerovitch Abram   15
Shirinskya Etka 3
Kriskevitch 3
Polonsky, Chaskel 2
Stolovitsky Zimel 4
Garbach Abram 2
Belsky Abram 4
Pesis Shaina 9
Penchanskaya Zlata 3
Mordkovsky Moishe
Rabinovich Pinya 6
Savitsky Moishe   1
Mordkovsky Moishe   4
Mirtrovsky Eina   6
Mordkovsky Eisat 4
Gordon Leiser 4
Rabinovich Mitel 5
Rabinovich Abram 2
Rabinovich Moishe 5
Pilscheick Moshe 3
Gariska Shaina 1
Kovensky Leibe 3
Gutman Mordechai
Chasid Ziska 5
Abromovsky Mordechai 4
Gertsel 3
Charlaf Alter 2
Epstein Moishe 4
Urinovich Abram 6
Vinograd Leiba 4

March 27, 1945

Epshtein Chaim Iserov
Shelubovsky Nisel
Lichter, Kasriel
Krivetsky Leibl
Kriveetskyt Yudel
Zapolonsky Leiba
Pekelnik Voulf
Shkoelnikovitch Girsh
Rabets Sarah
Rabets Zelick
Shevtshick Fruma
Kushnerovsky Peisach
Rabets Itsick
Braverman Berko
Falevitch Frieda
Shenyavsky Josel
Kaplan Itsick
Feder Moishe
Zhukhovitsky Lipa
Nevizhsky Girsh
Kaplan Boruch
Shoimovitch Manya
Karolitsky Moishe
Rozhaiskov Malka
Ioselevitch Reishke
Miskin Girsh
Kyshnerovskaya Sara
Tsirulnick Tsilia
Gilerovich Leiba
Gilerovich Danka
Yazas Itzick
Zapolonsky Elina
Braverman Volf
Kaplan Iechiel
Tsirulnick, Volf
Kroshinovsky Shmerka

List #14 March 31

Serebrovski Abram 6
Gorski, Meir 3
Pinchuck Zevel 4
Chorobrovitz Judel 9
Epstein Iser 5
Shimshelevitch Itsko 4
Derevenski Yankel 3
Shevcheck Yankel
And Itsko   5
Shevcheck Zavel 2
Rabinovich Mesha 6
Borushanski Moisha 5
Shimshelevitch Euna 6
Orzhachovski Euna 5
Novomyshenski Girsh 5
Zhuchovitski Dovid 3
Shmuilovich Berko 8
Shmuilovitch Abram 7
Rabets Shimon 5
Leizerovich Zelik 4
Slizack Afroim 2
Novogrutski Yudel 2
Krovtchuck Elya 6
Nesvizhskya Basya Lea 7
Bushel Almy & Rabetz Iser 8
Chorobrovski Yudel 2
Ozerovski Yankel 5
Zusman Chaika 5
Berkner Moisha 6
Reznick Shleima 5
Gershovitch Yona 7
Shevchuck Abram 6
Shevchuck Shmuel 4
Kostulyanski Chaim 6
Kotolovskya Rosa 5
Korostovski Moishe 5
Rabinovich Sholom 2

Plus 12 families from different places (no names listed)

Appendix to the Molchad Yizkor Book
Not in the original Yizkor Book

Microfilm of records

Record Feb. 4, 1945-1

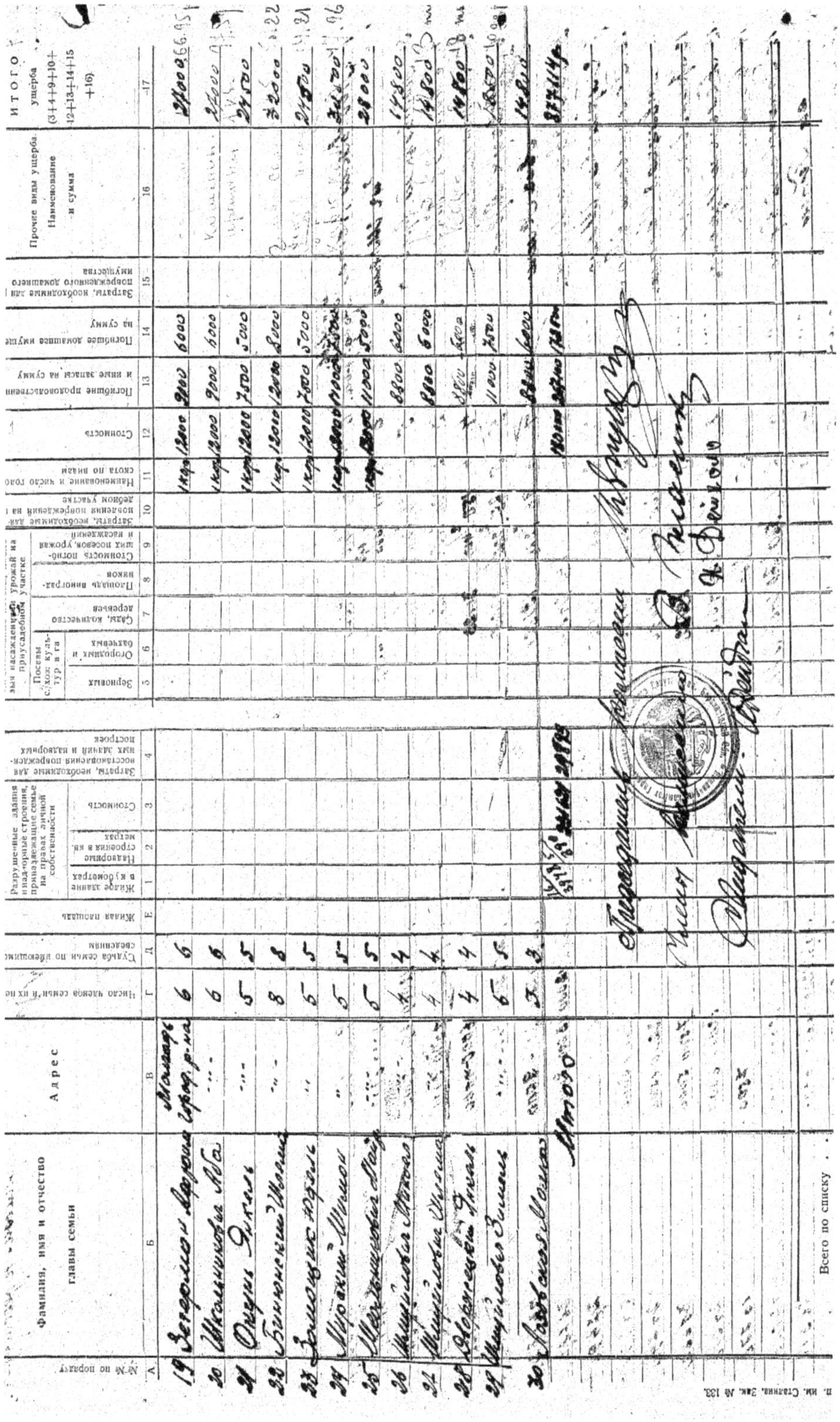

Record Feb. 4, 1945-2

Appendix to the Molchad Yizkor Book
Not in the original Yizkor Book

АКТ- СПИСОК №13

Record Feb. 15, 1945-1

№	Фамилия, имя и отчество главы семьи	Адрес																ИТОГО
19	Заполянин Аврам	Молчад	4	4	60	1/30	134		3892	1								17198
20	Лебо Берко	— " —	5	6	58	1/68	1		2264	1					Мар.	14000	18000	30364
21	Голдштейн Хая	— " —	6	6	56	1/68	1		2664	1					Янв.	14000	24000	4996
22	Синявски Янк	— " —	6	4	40	1/20	1/30		9312	1					Мар.	14000	21600	56912
23	Абравух Мина	— " —	4	4	35	1/05	1		6000	1					Мар.	15000	6600	17520
24	Лазовски Мунь	— " —	5	6	35	1/05	1		6000	1					2/Кв	3000	7500	24520
25	Холм Мазер	— " —	4	4	20	1/60	1		4017	1					Апр	1800	3800	19817
26	Берская Фрейда	— " —	3	3	220	1/60	1		44127	1					—		6000	5413
27	Хербровский Иуда	— " —	3	2	220	1/60	1/90		44187	1					Нов	7000	3000	96187
28	Лозловский	— " —	4	4	90	1/30	1		19400	1					Кор	1400	14400	55390
29	Заполянин Лея	— " —	3	3	16	1/13	1		3213	1					2/Кв	3000	4500	13713
30	Абрамович Золмон	— " —	4	3	35	1/05	1/30		4039	1					Нов	1500	4500	16039
31	Дубивски Абрам	— " —	4	4	108	1/88	1/98		30297	1					Нов	35000	14400	85797
32	Новочужснси Ицко	— " —	4	4	113	1/89	1/36		25913	1					Мар	16000	14400	60913
33	Бишменская Сонь	— " —	4	4	140	1/20	1/63		25423	1					Нов	1200	14400	25723
34	Школниковиль Ивин	— " —	5	5	63	1/89	2/74		15634	1					Нов	1500	7500	25434
35	Школниковиль Рефуел	— " —	5	5	108	1/44	1		46536	1					Мар	30000	10000	84635
36	— Мовша	— " —	4	4	21	1/63	1/54		4400	1					—		8000	26806
37	Сотир Янкел	— " —	3	3	54	1/04	1/04		13099							7500	7500	
38	Лонель Элиез Моррис	— " —	3	3	52	1/03	1/08		2054							7500		
39	Школниковиль Давид	— " —	4	4	50	1/00	1		1174							6000	6000	
	Всего по списку																	1.901.566

Appendix to the Molchad Yizkor Book
Not in the original Yizkor Book

АКТ - СПИСОК

195... г. Мы, нижеподписавшиеся, Председатель комиссии ... и члены комиссии: 1) ... составили настоящий акт-список о том, что Вторжением см и разбойничьими действиями немецко-фашистских оккупантов причинен ущерб поименованным ниже в списке семьям граждан СССР: ...

№ № по порядку	Фамилия, имя и отчество главы семьи	Адрес		ИТОГО
1	Пилвский Иосиф	Дильский		122260
2	Лимбович Абрам			77000
3	Ширинская Двойра			16800
4	Юрицкий			16800
5	Полонский Хоскиль			23530
6	Столовицкий Зиндель			34400
7	Гарбат Абрам			24000
8	Глуский Абрам			24000
9	Геле Шейно			26500
10	Пехтангская Итно			18500
11	Мордковский Мовша			19831
12	Рабинович Лина			72773
13	Савицкий Мовша			232200
14	Мордковский Мойсей			20061
15	Мартиновский Бино			35400
16	Мордковский Бизар			43961
17	Гордон Лейзар			29800

№ по порядку	Фамилия, имя и отчество главы семьи	АДРЕС																ИТОГО ущерба
18	Рабинович Михел	Полгард			49	149	9842								3200	7500	3200 2000	5000 руб
19	„ Абрам	Майина													7500	10000	247342
20	Майина				49	149	9842								7500	10000	247342
21	Гинзбург Любчо														4100	10000	21000
22	Эфрон Шейна														1500	2000	3500
23	Ковенские Либа														7500	8000	15500
24	Кушман Мордух				48	144	9641								7500	10000	27199
25	Лейбиц Зисель				36	108	7231								10000	10000	27231
26	Абрамовский Иосиф														4600	9000	12600
27	Абрусия														10000	9000	19000
28	Хорилер Эдлир				36	108	7231								5000	4000	9000
29	Глинштин Любша				47	144	9641								6600	6000	19831
30	Эрлинских Абрам				76	384	682								13300	13000	39841
31	Ринограф Либа				76	48									11600	2000	47807
	Итого					454									83000		822 792
	Всего по списку																

Appendix to the Molchad Yizkor Book
Not in the original Yizkor Book

АКТ СПИСОК

Record March 27, 1945-1

Appendix to the Molchad Yizkor Book
Not in the original Yizkor Book

АКТ- СПИСОК № 14.

281

31 Марта 195 г. Мы, нижеподписавшиеся, Председатель

комиссии: 1) ...
2) ...

составили настоящий акт-список о ... что ... сожжен ... и разбоем ... действиями
немецко-фашистских оккупантов причинен ущерб поименованным ниже ...
семьям граждан СССР:

№	Фамилия, имя и отчество главы семьи	Адрес															ИТОГО
1	Серебровек Абрам	местечк															48.300.00
2	Гурвич Мер	"															42.058.00
3	Гинзук Довид	"															28.874.00
4	Хорафейн Юдель	"															42.232.00
5	Эпштейн Шер	"															38.029.00
6	Мишишин Лука	"															33.474.00
7	Кербелевин Бутек	"															40.483.00
8	Шеарин Шкейлик	"															21.73
9	Шиевин Довид	"															27.362.00
10	Ребельман Менч-Ар	"															47.791.00
11	Брокельмен Мовша	"															25.200.00
12	Дешинтевич Зина	"															75.222.00
13	Фошелевен Эина Лия	"															50.284.00
14	Новинович Гутма	"															32.283.00
15	Жирофигин Лейба	"															19.542.00
16	Минчукин Берко	"															28.7.00
17	Шицукин Абрам	"															89.965.00
18	Райбу Мина	"															24.896.00

Record March 31, 1945-1

СТРАНИЦА ОРИГИНАЛА ПОВРЕЖДЕНА
MUTILATED PAGE

Record March 31, 1945-2

MAYTCHET MEMORIAL MONUMENTS

These two memorial stones are located at the site of the mass grave of 3600 murdered Jews from Maytchet and surrounding shtetls July 7, 1942.

Translation of original stone in Byelorussian: In this place on June 15, 1942 the fascist invaders murdered 3600 peaceful (innocent) civilians of the village of Molchad and other surrounding settlements.

In September 1993, survivor Rachmiel Bar and his son Paz, representing the Maytchet Survivor group, went to Maytchet to set up the Hebrew stone.

Translation of Hebrew stone: In this place were buried the Jewish citizens of Maytchet and its surroundings who were killed and [their memory] destroyed by the Nazis and their collaborators... On the first day of MenachemAv 5702 - 15 July 1942...May their memory be blessed.

1977 a monument for Soviet Citizens executed by the fascists was constructed (in the center of town at the end of a square where the shops used to be. Large Russian soldiers and four panels with names and date of birth of Gentile citizens who were killed in World War II. Bottom line of 4th panel reads 3600 other Soviet civilians, not specifying they were Jews.

Appendix to the Molchad Yizkor Book
Not in the original Yizkor Book

НЕДВЕДСКАЯ ОЛЬГА МИРОНОВНА   1929
НЕДВЕДСКАЯ МАРИЯ МИРОНОВНА   1931
                    д. МОЛЧАДЬ
ДАНИЛЕВИЧ ВЛАДИМИР МИХАЙЛОВИЧ 1908
ВИННИЧЕК ВЛАДИМИР ОЛИМПИЕВИЧ 1910
БОГУШ ИОСИФ ИОСИФОВИЧ   1906
               д. САВЦЕВИЧИ
ГОВОР ЮСТИН ЯКОВЛЕВИЧ   1894
ГОВОР АНДРЕЙ ЯКОВЛЕВИЧ   1910
ГОВОР СЕМЕН ЯКОВЛЕВИЧ   1885
ГОВОР МАРИЯ ИГНАТЬЕВНА   1902
ГОВОР НИНА   СЕМЕНОВНА   1921

ГОВОР ЕФИМ АДАМОВИЧ   1884
ГОВОР НИКОЛАЙ ЯКОВЛЕВИЧ   1995
ГОВОР ЮЛИЯ АНДРЕЕВНА   1899
ГОЛЧЕНОВИЧ МАРИЯ СЕЛЬВЕСТРОВНА 1908
ВОРОНЕЦ ВИКТОР ТИМОФЕЕВИЧ   1921
СЕМЕНЯКО НИКИФОР ВАСИЛЬЕВИЧ 1900
СЕМЕНЯКО ЛЕВ НИКИФОРОВИЧ   1927
СЕМЕНЯКО АДАМ АНДРЕЕВИЧ   1901
СЕМЕНЯКО АНАСТАСИЯ ЯКОВЛЕВНА 1906
               д. КРУТОВЦЫ
БЕРНАТ СПИРИДОН СТЕПАНОВИЧ 1886
БЕРНАТ МАРИЯ АНТОНОВНА   1894
БЕРНАТ КОНСТАНТИН   1905

ГРИС МЕФОДИЙ НИКОЛАЕВИЧ   1835
КУХТА ФОМА ИВАНОВИЧ   1831
КУХТА КОНСТАНТИН ВАСИЛЬЕВИЧ 1903
               д. КАТМИНОВЦЫ
ПИШКЕВИЧ ФИЛИПП ФИЛИППОВИЧ 1907
СИПЮТА СЕРГЕЙ МИХАЙЛОВИЧ 1924
БУРШКО СТЕПАН ГРИГОРЬЕВИЧ 1888

И 3600 ДРУГИХ СОВЕТСКИХ
            ГРАЖДАН

This is the fourth panel of the monument shown on the previous page. The bottom line indicates **"3600 other Soviet civilians,"** however it does not specify that these were Jews, which was common practice by the Communist governments.

מצבת זכרון לקדושי קהילת

מ י י צ ׳ ע ט

והסביבה (מחוז ברנוביץ)
שנרצחו ושנספו על קדוש השם
ע״י הנאצים ימ״ש
בשנות השואה תרצ״ט-תש״ה. 1942
יום הזכרון ראש חדש אב
ת׳ נ׳ צ׳ ב׳ ה׳
אנציהים יוצאי מייצ׳עט והסביבה בישראל ובתפוצות

Translation:

A Memorial to the Martyrs of the congregation of Maytchet
And the environs (District of Baranovich)
Who were murdered and exterminated on the sanctification of the Holy Name
By the Nazis (may their names to blotted out)
In the years of the Holocaust 5639-5705, 1942
Memorial day the first of the Month Av
May their souls be bound up in the bond of everlasting life
Perpetuating their memory, the countrymen
Of Maytchet and the environs in Israel and the diaspora

Located in the Memorial Hall [Martef Hashoah] on Mount Zion, Jerusalem.
Photo of the unveiling of the sign (July 9, 1964) Maytchet survivors and family members
shown in above photo.

לזכר קדושי
קהילת

מייטשעט
ודווארעץ

והסביבה

שהושמדו ע״י
הנאצים ועוזריהם
הי״ד
ת נ צ ב ה

יום הזיכרון ר״ח מנ-אב
יום הזיכרון כ טבת

Maytchet - Dvorets memorial at the Holon Cemetery, Holon, Israel,

erected by the survivors in the 1970's.

Translation:

In Memory of the Martyrs of the congregation of
MAYTCHET And DVORETS and environs,
Who were destroyed by the Nazis and their collaborators,
May the Lord revenge their blood, May their souls be bound up in the bond of everlasting life.
Memorial day the first of the Month of MenachemAv
Memorial day the twentieth of the Month Teveth

Maytchet - Dvorets memorial in Forest of the Martyrs

outskirts Jerusalem on the western edge of the Eshtaol Forest.

Translation:

Monument In Memory of the Martyrs Of the congregation of MAYTCHET And DVORETS and environs Who were killed and destroyed by The German Nazis and their collaborators. May the Lord revenge their blood. May their souls be bound up in the bond of everlasting life.

Memorial day the first of the Month MenachemAv

Memorial day the twentieth of the Month Tebeth.

Maytchet (Molchad) is among the 5,000 names of communities that are
engraved on stonewalls of the Valley of the Communities at Yad Vashem

This memorial commemorates the Jewish communities that were destroyed by the Nazis
and their collaborators.

Fleeing Baranovich to Shanghai – The Aronowitz/Nayman Family
Esther Nayman Muller

My mother Chaya Aronowitz Nayman was born in Baranovich, Poland before Chanukah in 1914. She was the eldest daughter of Pesach and Rachel Aronowitz. Her grandparents were Reb Zvi Hirsch and Shaina Chieshe Aronowitz who lived in Maychet. (I only learned of this through working on this Yizkor book).

There were survivors who spoke in great detail about their experiences during the Shoah, and there were others, such as my mother, who never spoke about it. In our family we were always careful not to discuss specifics of her family and her life during the war because it was too painful and my father was extremely protective. My mother always maintained a misguided hope that somehow her younger siblings survived, and were perhaps spared, although she understood that this wasn't possible. Not knowing how or when her mother and siblings were murdered, or what their fate was left her with no peace – she had no closure. Only recently did I discover through a family tree that a distant cousin provided, the names of my mother's siblings and the year in which they were murdered.

This Yizkor book will be the first time their names and their existence will be recorded.

Moshe Aronowitz born 1922 died 1942, 20 years old

Sarah Rivah Aronowitz born 1926, died 1942, 16 years old

Dvorsha Aronowitz born 1930 died 1942, 12 years old

Malke Aronowitz born 1933 died 1942, 9 years old

Nechemya Aronowitz born 1936, died 1942 6 years old

Rachel Aronowitz, my grandmother, died with her children in 1942. Unfortunately I do not know my grandmother's maiden name, where or when she was born. I also do not know how she and her children were murdered or their actual date of death.

To provide context I will try to recount what I have heard about life in Baranovich before the war. I have included the few pictures that survived of my mother's life during that period. Lest one assume that Baranovich was a one-horse shtetl, the pictures reveal a relatively sophisticated small European city.

Before the war Jewish life thrived and my grandparents lived very well. I don't know much about their circumstances but I do know that they were prominent in Jewish life religiously and culturally. My mother was extremely well educated--- she went to gymnasia, played the piano, wrote poetry and studied literature (Dostoyevsky, Tolstoy, Chaim Nachman Bialik, etc.). She spoke at least four languages and was a "melumedes." She studied Chumash, Navi and spoke Hebrew fluently. When she first came to Chicago she taught Tanach (Hebrew Bible) for a short period of time.

When we sat shiva (official week of mourning) for my mother in Israel, the most prominent Roshei Yeshiva came to be menachem avel (comfort the mourners). They told us stories about how they were childhood friends with my mother and one even described how they played ball together as children. Life was different in the Yeshiva world when she was a young woman.

She spoke of life before the war and how she and her friends would wait for the train from Warsaw to arrive with the latest fashion magazines, such as L'Officielle from Paris, and copy the latest designs. Anyone who knew my mother in Chicago would remember her finely tuned sense of esthetics and style. I recount this to give you a sense of the diversity and richness of life in Baranovich.

Mother (wearing hat) with friends, the Gerrer Rebbe's grand-daughters.

My Grandmother Rachel was a descendant of Reb Levi Yitzchak Berditchover and related by marriage to the Chofetz Chaim (late 19th c. Torah scholar)I know virtually nothing about my maternal grandmother's family other than she came from great Yichus (famous antecedents, yichus can be inherited but must be deserved and earned as well) and traced her family back to the Metzudat David (Biblical commentary of the 18th century). My mother described her as a great beauty and said she looked like Grace Kelly.

My grandparents hosted the scions of the Jewish World and when it was time to marry; my mother was presented to the greatest eligible Torah scholars. My father was one of the few talmidim of the Brisker Rav and when this shiddach (arranged marriage) was proposed, she (accompanied by my grandmother), went to meet my father at a small hotel located somewhere between Brisk and Baranovich. When the prospective suitor (eventually to be my father) met them at the train, my father offered to carry the basket containing the linen, china, silver, food and cakes they were to share over tea at the hotel. My mother famously told him, at the ripe age of 17 that, "in this life we each must carry our own burdens."

After they married, my parents lived in their own home in Baranovich, which was adjacent to her parent's home. My father learned B' Chavrutah with Rav Elchonan Wasserman for a period of six years and was a close friend of the Slonimer Rebbe. When the war came to Baranovich they fled across the Polish border into Lithuania in the middle of Rosh Hashanah, 1939. The Slonimer Rebetzin in Baranovich pleaded with my father to convince her son (the Rebbe) to join them and flee but the Rebbe refused to leave even one of his students behind; resulting in his death and all the students.

My parents were "Sugihara" survivors and spent most of the war in Vilna, Japan and Shanghai. When they were in Vilna they were busy with the refugee life of survival. There was an incredible group of some of the most prominent leaders and students of the Torah world seeking refuge in Vilna. My mother's sister Sarah Rivah would have possibly survived with them, but she returned to Baranovich to get a passport photo and wasn't able to cross the border back into Vilna.

When the Brisker Rav left Vilna he was able to arrange for visas for my parents to the United States. My father went to the American consulate daily but the visas never showed up. In 1970, when my parents visited Montreal after my wedding, Rabbi Kramer told them how the visas were ultimately discovered in the US consulate. They were there the entire time. In the Cyrillic alphabet the letter N looks like a K and the visas for Nayman were misfiled. As a result they spent the next 6 years in Japan and China.

When it became known that the Japanese Consul to Lithuania was issuing transit visas with end visas to Dutch Curacao, they stood in lines for days while Consul Sugihara signed off on thousands of transit visas through Japan. For this act of bravery and compassion he was ultimately recalled to Japan and stripped of his diplomatic status and reduced to selling light bulbs on the street to support his family until he died. He was honored posthumously and is among the righteous gentiles at Yad Vashem.

Baranovich – left to right: Sister Sarah Rivah who was murdered in Shoah, parents

Chaya and Rav Yakov Nayman, 2 unidentified men

In late 1940 my parents and two older sisters Fayge and Sarah traveled by the trans-Siberian railway across Russia to Vladivostok, where they boarded a cattle boat with 300 other passengers, to Japan. The trip from Vladivostok to their destination port, Suruga took six days.

When they arrived, the officials wanted to send them back, but through the intervention of the Jev-Com (Jewish committee in Japan) they were given permission to remain and were moved to Kobe, where they settled for the next ten months.

In October 1941 the Germans insisted that the Japanese "get rid" of their Jews. They were sent to Shanghai where they lived in the Hongkew Ghetto until the end of the war. Life was challenging but the Jews who lived in this group took over the Khaduri Shul and established the "Asian branch "of the Mir Yeshiva. They established a network of schools including a Bais Yaakov, published a newsletter, learned and wrote seforim, married, had children and made a life of sorts for themselves.

BAIS YAKOV SHANGHAI

Fayge Nayman seated 4th from left 1st row, Sarah Nayman far right 1st row center the teacher was Esther Rogow-Bakst

After two months in Shanghai my parents received visas to go to Israel through Burma and India but the Saturday night before they were supposed to leave, they were advised that Pearl Harbor was bombed and as a result they were stranded in Asia for six years. My father was one of three "representatives of the Polish Government in Exile". There were two attorneys and my father who adjudicated disputes between Polish Nationals in China. Shanghai, was an international port city divided into international 'concessions." My father had a special pass, which allowed him to move between the various concessions. Despite the impossible living conditions, the fear, the hunger the loneliness and worry about their families left behind, they managed to make a life. In addition to my sisters Fayge and Sarah who were born in Europe, my siblings Shoshanna, Miriam and Shlome were born in Shanghai. I was born in Chicago, Illinois.

Leaders in the Shanghai Jewish community who organized life of the refugees.

Left to right first row: Rav Shmuel Dovid Warshavchik my father Rav Yakov Nayman seated 2nd from left. Mr. Sasoon, middle seat white suit, Rabbi Ashkenazi, chief rabbi of Shanghai before the war lived in the French concession (wearing sun glasses, long white beard) seated next to Mr. Sasoon) Also in the picture were, Rav Shlomo Shapira and Rav Brielovsky (I don't know which they were but their names are on the back of the original picture).

Conditions in Shanghai were terrible. One of my sisters developed rickets from malnutrition (it affected her health throughout her life), and my father almost died of malaria. My parents lived in one room with 5 children. Guests were put up when necessary under the dining table. The mats they slept on were rolled up during the day and served as couches. They cooked on a coal burner and one of my sisters was severely burned when the coals were knocked over. They shared a public bathroom down the hall with all the other tenants on their floor. My mother was always meticulous; it must have been quite a challenge to keep 5 children clean and fed. Life was hard and food was very scarce. My mother would stay up nights polishing shoes, washing shoelaces, and ironing the few clothes they had so they didn't look poor.

Most of the Mir bochrim were single and the few married women tried their best to be "mothers" to the single men, who didn't cook, etc. My father told a story about when my mother had given birth and he went to one of the other married women to pick up soup she cooked for the family. He stumbled on the way back and spilled the soup and literally cried with such grief over the spilled soup. The married families with children sometimes fared a little better because they had multiple food allowances from The Joint - Vaad Hatzalah and Jev-Com and a local organization in Shanghai, the Jewish committee, which gave some assistance to the refugees. My mother described the high inflation that was prevalent; one could barely buy a bag of rice with a bushel full of Yen. She said she used to make a gefilte fish for Shabbos with no fish, but used one beet and made it work to feed the entire family and guests. She was always an amazing cook.

Dinner reception in parent's one room apartment for American soldier (Seated 4th from right) visiting Shanghai, sister Sarah first row left with bow in her hair, 3rd person left, Mr. Sasoon, 4th person Rabbi Warshavchik, 5th person my father

Despite poor living conditions note beautifully set table

This story brings to mind the Shanghai version of the Chanukah miracle. When they lived in Japan my mother heard there was a place to buy a chicken so she went on her own to find it. After hours of being gone my father was frantic. Eventually my mother turned up with a chicken and a few Japanese soldiers in tow; they escorted her home and stayed for tea.

After the capitulation of Japan on August 10, 1945 an international relief organization became involved with the Jewish refugees. By 1946 the Joint and the NY Vaad Hatzalah sent delegations to Shanghai and the Jews were dispersed to many destinations around the world. My sisters Fayge and Sarah remember, as young children when the first transport departed Shanghai, they went to the port to say good-bye to the departing. At the port, the remaining Jews sang Aney Maamin (I believe) while the sailors stood to attention and saluted them as the ship left port with its cargo of passengers. My parents were supposed to be on that ship, but gave their place to a family whose child was desperately ill; they left a few months later on the USS General Meigs. They arrived in San Francisco and traveled by train across the US to their destination in Chicago where my father was guaranteed a job as Rabbi of Congregation Adas Bnei Yisroel.

My Fathers parents Rav Matisyahu Nayman, his wife Esther Malkah Nayman and their 19 year-old son Shmuel Dov Nayman remained in Brisk (Brest Litovsk). They were murdered by the Nazis in an infamous round up of Jews in Brisk and were buried alive in the forest near Brisk. My father was told that the ground moved for three days at that site. The sole survivors of this family were my father and two brothers, Aryeh Leib emigrated to Chicago and Yitzchak, who emigrated to Israel and became the chief rabbi of Kiryat Chaim. They were all married at the time the war broke out and were not in Brisk.

My parents came to Chicago and built a life. My mother brought with her to America the heritage and beauty of the family she lost. She was determined not to bow to the status that was conferred to the new immigrants of "Greener" and refused to accept the pity and lack of understanding that came with that designation. In their darkest days she was unique in her ability to maintain hope and optimism.

My father recounted, until he passed away at 100, how she would encourage him to go on; she would say, "today is so dark, but tomorrow it will be light." She confirmed this in her own actions daily. Instead of conforming to the roles that were expected of her as "rebetzin" (wife of Rabbi) she created controversy in a social structure that was universal in those days and was truly a trailblazer of women's rights. Despite the dismay of many of my father's congregants, my mother had a vision, which she pursued. In her broken English, she marched into the office of the President of American National Bank and convinced him to loan her the money to purchase the mansion of the Checker Cab family on Sheridan Road, in Chicago, in order to start a business. The best revenge is success and she brought the intellect and talent to encourage my father to continue to evolve and succeed as a great Torah scholar. They were both the last living link to a generation of Lithuanian "gedolim" (refers to great revered Rabbis) that our children studied about in school. They were intimately connected to a segment of Jewish Torah aristocracy that my mother encouraged my father to perpetuate and transplant to "the new world."

During the war years, my parents didn't know the fate of their families who were left behind. The rumors that made it to Shanghai were too fantastic to be believed. My grandfather Pesach was in London when the war broke out and was not able to get back into Poland to be with his wife and children. He eventually went to South Africa. My Mother and Father never saw either of their parents from the time they fled Baranovich to Vilna. The remnants of both their families perished.

My parents didn't know the fate of their families who were left behind. The rumors that made it to Shanghai were too fantastic to be believed. My maternal grandfather Pesach Aronowitz was in London when the war broke out and was not able to get back into Poland to be with his wife and children. He eventually went to South Africa. My mother and father never saw either of their parents from the time they fled Baranovich to Vilna.

My maternal grandfather Pesach Aronowitz

This Yizkor book serves to memorialize the existence of my maternal grandmother Rachel and her children and my Paternal Grandparents Matisyahu and Esther Malkah and their son Shmuel Dov, whose memories would have been forever lost. Now they will not disappear into the abyss of history unacknowledged.

The following article appeared in the Chicago Daily News on January 28, 1947, with this picture. The text of the article is reproduced below for clarity of reading.

Fled Nazis in '39 –In Chicago with a group of rabbinical scholars are (1) Rabbi B.L. Sassoon (2) Jacob Nayman (3) Abraham Kalmanowitz, (4) Ezekiel Levinstein, (5) Mendel Kaplan, and (6) Lazar Horedsky

JEWISH EXILES NEAR END OF 8-YEAR TREK

"At last we are home"

The words were spoken fervently by a little old man with a beard who had never been in Chicago or any part of this country until last week.

"Now we can settle down again and live like human beings, and open our seminary and not worry who comes knocking at the door at night."

Rabbi Moshe Wernick, the speaker, was one of a group of 25 rabbinical scholars and students to arrive at the North Western Station today on their way to New York.

It is the first segment of the traveling "Yeshivah of Mir," the Jewish seminary which fled before the Nazis in 1939. After eight years they are almost at their goal,-----a new college in New York.

There were 30 seminaries in Poland before the Germans came," said Wernick quietly. "Only one escaped----Mir"

Their 20th century exodus included a year in Lithuania, a year in Kobe, Japan, and 5 1/2   years in Shanghai.

"In Japan, in 1940, the government became suspicious," Wernick said. "They never saw or heard of us before. So they sent a royal commission member, a professor.

"He reported back that we were only a religious group and the Japanese government sent us paper for our books.

The group was welcomed to Chicago by Rabbi Abraham Kalmanowitz, head of the New York Theological seminary, and representatives of orthodox Chicago congregations.

NACHUM RABINOWICZ
A portrait compiled from interviews
Merle Kharasch Gross

I was privileged to facilitate the Survivors of the Shoah Visual History Foundation's interview of Nachum Rabinowicz on November 10, 1997. A deep friendship developed during the many hours we spent together before the taping and after. In this essay, what appears in "standard quotes" are Nachum's <u>actual</u> words. Should you listen to his video testimony, you will hear him saying much of what is written here, you'll get to know his voice and the unique manner in which he spoke. This *Yizkor* project, gave me the opportunity to add more of Nachum's own words that were "recorded" in pages and pages of furiously scribbled notes that I made during many of our rich conversations. As best I could, I've transcribed those notes with loyalty to his actual words and I believe they, too, transmit his unique "voice." Nachum was a scholar of Talmud and history and life...a natural, almost compulsive, teacher, a profound thinker and compelling storyteller. Every anecdote carried a message and, if not a judgment, at least a strong opinion that reflected his personal ethic.

Nachum introduced himself, saying, "In Maytchet, where I was born, we had four seasons. It was a resort town, the air was good and people came to heal." He said, "Maytchet is a symbol for all the communities." I believe, too, that the basic values and goals that were common to Jews throughout Poland are exemplified by Nachum's life, his actions, the choices he made and the work that he did.

Yisroel Rabinowicz was a grain dealer and Genia Mochkovsky, "a typical Yiddishe Mama and a *'tzaddeket'* ". They had a typically big family: Miriam was born in 1917, Reuven in 1921, Fania in 1923. Nachum was born on March 8, 1924, then came two more boys, Shimon in 1925 and Nehemiah in 1927.

The family lived in a *"dacha"* in the forest, "It was a beautiful new, big house, modern but no indoor plumbing, no electricity. We cut logs in the forest to keep it warm. We rented it in summer to the 'health tourists.' "Twice a year, for *Rosh Hashanah* and *Pesach*, we went for new custom-made clothes and shoes."

According to Nachum, there were maybe 2,000 Jews, about 300 families in Maytchet. He said that 25% were *Hasidim*, and 75% were *Mishnagdim*, focused on Talmud and traditional study, more academic and intellectual, Zionistic, opposed to *Hasidism*.

"Maytchet was an agricultural area, we were the basket of bread" Nachum's mother, Genia, helped Yisroel manage the family business including the export of wholesale grain. Often, Yisroel loaned money to local farmers, literally "seed money" for them to plant and later he bought their harvest.

"Most Jews were in business...like leather goods, like my grandfather Muchkovsky, or in fabrics or hardware. At home we spoke Yiddish but on the street we spoke White Russian. We always knew what was going on because we got news from the radio and three Jewish newspapers: *Haynt, Tageblatt* and *der Moment* which was the Jabotinsky paper. In Maytchet, there was very well established Jewish life and very Zionistic. A challenge, an aim, in life was to leave Poland and emigrate to Palestine. The *Hasidim* were not interested to go to Palestine, they wanted to have their Jewish life and stay where they were."

Left to Right: Nachum, Sister Fania Tzipora, grandmother Reisel Tevelevicz Mochkovsky, Brother Shimon

The countries in Europe were becoming more nationalistic and there was increasing anti-Semitism. "About a thousand Jewish refugees fled to Maytchet in the 30's and stayed mostly because life was pretty good and there was no place to go."

Bicycling, horseback riding, ping-pong, volley ball, soccer, ice skating and cross country skiing were common activities. Slonim was "one hour by bike" from Maytchet. From the time he was twelve, every Wednesday Nachum would go to the weekly market in Slonim to sell alfalfa to farmers for animal feed.

"Each little town had a different character and Maytchet was considered 'intelligent.' The mayor ran the town. There wasn't any violence....maybe a few drunks."

"The big s*hul, Ezras Noshim,* was very old; it was tall and domed and the women sat in the balcony." Nachum sang in the choir. Nachum insisted that it was "the most beautiful synagogue in the world--but only in summer, because it had no heat!" (It is referred to as the "*Kalte Shul*") Nachum said the *Beis Midrash* was a heated brick building in the center of town; "in back, was a place like a soup kitchen, where poor people from big towns would come and they were supported by the charity of the community". The pharmacy was nearby and there was "a line of stores". There was a *shtibele* built of wood for the *Hasidic* Jews. Shared by all was the Jewish cemetery and a *mikveh* for women and men.

"The Jewish Holidays were all good, every holiday had special foods. Between *Purim* and *Pesach* our family baked 100 kilos of flour for Passover Matzos. There was a special place where everybody baked matzoh. Even the children were involved, I went with a special little wheel and cut the holes in the dough."

"My grandfather taught me my Torah portion, *Nitzavim in Devarim*."

In town there was a Hebrew School where families paid tuition and children attended from the time they were five until 6th grade. Nachum, went to the *Tarbut* School and, later, he was the only Jew in the "*Szkola Powszechna*," the free Polish school, until September, 1939.

"Here's what my generation knew: First, was Your People because we were in *Galut* for a thousand years. Second, we had to fight and keep fighting by preparing young generations for the future. Zionism, *Eretz Yisroel*...the Dream." Nachum joined the youth Zionist organizations, *Betar* and Hashomer Hatzair. The motto of *Hashomer Hatzair* was "We'll do and we'll listen." They were very active "young guardians", the intelligentsia, the better educated, more elite students joined. There was physical and mental and spiritual preparation to go to *Eretz Yisroel.* "Our main aim in *Hashomer Hatzair* was to grow up, learn, move away. Our grandfathers wanted us to be more religious but we knew we had to also learn how to defend ourselves."

"*Hechalutz* was an organization anyone could join. The *Bund* was another Jewish organization, anti-Zionist. They fought for their rights but always wanted to live where they were. For my family and most others in Maytchet, going to *Eretz Yisroel* was the goal."

Nachum's sister, Fania, joined *kibbutz Bat Telem* in Slonim with the expectation of emigrating to Palestine when she graduated but when the time came, she could not get papers to do so. Brother, Reuven, joined a *Hashomer Hatzair kibbutz* in Rovno, western Ukraine.

When Germany invaded Poland, on September 1, 1939, the government fled. "With no central government, there was anarchy. We'd always had good relations with the police--we paid them off. But at that time, a policeman came to our house and wanted the bicycle...he threatened my father with a gun. I had to save my father. I knocked the gun out of his hand. I shot him. I was fifteen, I did what I had to do. He was buried in the forest."

"After *Rosh Hashanah,* on September 17th, we were in the big *shul.* The Red Army came to Maytchet and we greeted them with bread and water. In the beginning we were happy to be rid of the Poles. Then the Russians nationalized businesses and introduced their philosophy: anti-religion, anti-Zionist, anti-business. We knew what's going to happen, no more Hebrew, no more Talmud. Everything changed, we had to go to Russian School and listen to their ideology and propaganda.   Communist civilians were appointed to run the city and there was a militia made up of townspeople and outsiders."

"The atmosphere was different. Me and my two friends talked about getting away. Everything had to be top secret, we told only our families. The winter was very cold, maybe 40 below Zero.   One of my grandfathers made me a top coat and my other grandfather made me boots, I should stay warm.   They gave me their blessing.   Binyamin Stolovitsky and Moshe Kroshinski and I decided to go underground, to disappear--and we did--we just evaporated. I was fifteen, they were older, maybe sixteen and seventeen.   We left Maytchet on a Sunday, I think, we walked south for 7 kilometers to the railway station in Mickiewicz then took the train to Lida. We knew to go to a synagogue in Lida to make contact with the underground of *Hashomer Hatzair*. They gave us a place to stay."

In late 1939 Hitler gave control of the Baltic states to the Soviet Union. Formerly controlled by Germany, Vilnius was given to Lithuania and President Smetana declared it as the capital. Smetana was admired. Vilnius was referred to as the Jerusalem of Lithuania and it became a destination for thousands of Jews fleeing oppressive regimes. Vilno is where Nachum and his friends were headed, to.

"Just before Christmas, I was with a small group crossing the border into Lithuania and they shot at us. They caught us that time. They separated me from the others, maybe because I was the youngest. I was in jail for a week; they kept interrogating me. I had no papers, I said I was from Lodz. I carried a bible and told them I was a *Yeshiva bocher*. Finally, they let me go. The others were sent to Siberia."

"We knew about the British 'White Paper,' it limited immigration to Palestine so that made us determined to help people get to *Eretz Yisroel*. The underground resistance groups were all separate and independent. In 1939 and 1940, when I was in Vilnius, the *Hashomer Hatzair* leaders were Adam Rand, Shaike Weiner and Yosef Kaplan.   They worked getting Jews to Palestine from Bialystok, Malkinia, Grodno and Slonim. We were a counter revolutionary movement."

"Tuvia from Mir was my contact in Vilno, I was called "Janek". I worked as a "runner" to see if it's okay to cross the border from Poland to Russia and from Russian into Lithuania. Thousands were coming to Vilnius.   Everyone was trying to get there and it was in disarray.   We slept in synagogues. I did different odd jobs, I'd work for factories. I cut wood...I would do anything to earn money to eat."

"Mordechai Anielewicz was helping Jews get out of Russia and into Lithuania. One night I spent with him in Grodno, and we talked about the underground and how to get people out of German occupied territories. Vilno was like one-way, no return---people got there but got stuck. I decided to devote myself to save Jewish people, help them get out of the whirlpool.   Sometimes I was shot at and caught and jailed... but I always got out."

"In Vilno, I read German papers and Russian papers, I met Ilya Ehrenburg there.   My sister wrote in Yiddish, saying simply 'Nachum...not good here.' I was the youngest one, but I knew what was going on. Lithuania was annexed by the Soviet Union. The Russians came in June, 1940, people tried to adjust to the regime, to go along with it.   But people lost their property and their businesses and thousands were sent away.   We couldn't have arms, if anyone was caught with a weapon that would be the end of them. We had to defend ourselves with our bare hands. After a while, the groups had to dismantle again. There was no more, like before; there was no organized central committee for our group. We had to disappear, to spread out."

"In 1940, Reuven's kibbutz group, *'Hakshara Ba Minhara'* (meaning, 'in the tunnel') moved from Rovno (Ukraine) to Ukmerge (Lithuania,)   Romek was my brother's name in the underground, he could write to our family, he knew where I was.   My sister Fania came to Vilno to visit me in 1941.   She went back to Maytchet." Reuven escaped to Russia and eventually got to Palestine.   He was part of *Habricha* a movement that brought Jews to Palestine illegally,

Fania and Nachum in Vilna 1941

"My friends and I were lucky enough to get out of Europe before the Germans came in June. We lived in fear, help didn't come. We mostly got work cutting wood, waiting for a miracle--for someone to take us in---nothing. The Movement gave us *'leydemas'*, false papers; my papers say I was born in Kleck. The Organization paid our way to Palestine. It took two years to get there. We got to Odessa and, by boat, we went to Varna (Bulgaria), to Constantinople (now Istanbul, Turkey), to Aleppo (Syria), to Beirut (Lebanon) and, finally, one night we got to Palestine. The Organization knew we were coming and they met us in the dark."

"I went to a *kibbutz* near Haifa, *Mishmar Ha Emek*, and worked clearing the fields. The Italians were bombing the refineries in Haifa. *Kibbutz* life was nice. I looked after the animals, feeding the cows and horses and raising alfalfa and harvesting it.   On one hand we were all happy to be in Palestine but also concerned about families left behind.   Reuven's group moved to Tashkent,

Uzbekistan in Russia and he knew about me and let our family know that I was in Palestine."

Palmach was established in 1941. "I joined. I went to *Gan Shmuel* for military training. It was illegal; the British did not allow weapons so we trained with 'cold arms, sticks, not rifles. There was no Jewish Brigade yet. I joined the British Royal Navy in 1943. The point was to fight the common enemy, the Nazis. I wanted to be a pilot but I was not allowed to because I was not a British subject, I was not a citizen of any country. I joined the Navy as an ordinary seaman but I was promoted to 'leading seaman'. There were some Jews in the Navy, even some officers. We were in the Mediterranean...North Africa and I was in Italy when the war ended."

NACHUM IN BRITISH NAVY   1943

I asked Nachum about his reaction to the news of Hitler's suicide. He laughed, he scoffed at the idea and said, "Hitler didn't commit suicide, we all knew Rommel killed him."

"My brother in Russia told me about what happened to my family. There were no Germans--just one who came with the collaborators, natives, Latvians, neighbors...they did the dirty work. They surrounded the town and they dug pits. Some of the Jews ran away and got to partisans in the forest and many were killed but some did survive. It was *Rosh Hodesh, Tamuz*, July. The executions were in the forest, south of the Jewish cemetery.   I was told that my father put up resistance to protect the family, so they killed him right away. In a short period of time they tore down 800 years of Jewish history."

In June,1946, Nachum was in Cairo, Egypt when he was released from service in the Royal Navy. "They told me I could go anywhere in the UK, like Australia. I said I wanted to go to Palestine. I was 22, I had to start life."   He joined the *Haganah* immediately.

The British were not allowing immigration, they were sending ships with refugees to Cyprus. "Funny, first I fought **with** them and **for** them. We'd had a common enemy, the Nazis.   But now, the British were enemies and I fought **against** them."

The U.N. declared the Partition of Palestine on November 29, 1947.   The Arabs rejected the proposal outright and the fighting began.

Nachum parked his truck in an alley behind his apartment in Tel Aviv. One day in 1948 a beautiful young woman called down to him complaining that his diesel truck made so much noise it wakened her at all hours whenever he'd park it. Beatriz Rosner and her mother had survived the war in Berlin. She had a beautiful little baby girl and no husband. That winter, Nachum and Beatriz were married. Beatriz' daughter, Miriam was just a year old...they were a ready-made family. They lived in Yad Eliyahu, a suburb of Tel Aviv, in a house that was built for ex-servicemen.

Golda Meyerson went to the United States in 1947 to raise money to buy arms. She raised fifty million dollars as a result of a single impassioned speech in Chicago. The money was used to buy arms in Europe.   "We had to unload off shore, secretly. But now we had real weapons."

"When the fighting started, we (the defense forces) had to protect the land, we had to sustain *kibbutz* life and provide food and medicine, supplies and water to Jerusalem. The settlements in the Negev, Halutza and Revivim were under siege. Kibbutz Negba---we tried to conquer.   I was in 'transportation,' Regiment 54 of the *Givati* Brigade.

In the beginning, they were just throwing stones but then they started firing at us. I was driving, I was shooting. The truck convoys had to get through.   We started to put armor on the trucks---everything was made by hand. We'd put steel plates on to wood and attach it to the trucks. It was like a 'sandwich' and that's what the armor was called.   In those days, I was almost never home. *Haganah* escorted the trucks but we had many losses. The convoys were ambushed all the time. The Mufti of Jerusalem said he'd cut off Jerusalem. The most important thing to us was to keep the land whole, keep the desolated points together and we needed to have communication and transportation."

"We'd gone to Hulda for reinforcements, it was a supply base for the convoys to Jerusalem. It was March, a beautiful night, the moon was shining, we were stopped by some British paratroopers. One asked, 'What will you do on May 15th when we leave Palestine?' I said, 'With God's help, we'll manage.' He asked if we had arms and suggested we take up positions there. He said, 'Don't go on, there are land mines.' Thirty trucks were destroyed and the highway was blocked. I was in the armored truck and that night we were shot at for seven hours. We returned to Hulda. The roads were blocked, no convoys got through to Jerusalem for the next two weeks."

"In March of 1948, during Campaign Nachson, I was part of 'The Convoy That Never Arrived.' That was during the 'Small Siege of Jerusalem', 6 of us were stuck for two weeks at the Latrun intersection, no convoys could get to Jerusalem."

"When Trans-Jordan's army came in--it was a good army, well-trained by the British and strong and they conquered the Old City just before *Pesach*, 1948. That started the 'Big Siege.' The road was blocked but on April 17th, more than 200 trucks carrying a thousand tons of food supplies got through. The trucks and drivers were stranded in Jerusalem for the next two months but they were successful in delivering medicines and arms and tons of food including matzo. It was in time for the First Seder on April 23rd."

The State of Israel was established on May 14th, 1948. The seat of government was Tel Aviv. *Tsahal*, the combined Israeli Defense Forces was established soon after. "We liberated villages near Jerusalem and opened the highway to the South. In Israel, I expected to build a country, to defend a country. Your dream come to realization. We were home. You went out in the street erectly. You shaped your own destiny...not the FINAL, that you can't change, but you can guide it, otherwise it will be blind. Everything has a point, every bullet has a direction--if you're supposed to survive, you survive. Our house was the memorial for *Maytcheters*. We had many friends and a good life."

"Beatriz's mother and brother were in Chicago. We got a call one day saying that her mother was very sick and she should come soon. Beatriz went to Chicago and her mother was operated on but she had very advanced liver cancer and surgery would not help. She died soon after."

"I came to Chicago because my wife wanted to. Her brother was here. We came in August,1957, before we left Israel I served 92 days in the Sinai Campaign. I didn't really expect much, I didn't think I'd stay long here. I was selling laundry equipment, machinery, I invested in real estate and bought some buildings and I made some investments. Miriam learned English fast and she was happy and we had friends and we travelled and Miriam got married in 1969.

Nachum and Beatriz at Daughter Miriam's wedding

Our life was good and then, in 1973, we were on vacation and my wife got killed on the Wisconsin River Bridge. I was driving and the fog was very thick, nobody could see and there was a car-crash of a chain of maybe twenty cars."

"Everything is a chain of events. The Almighty knows about everything. He writes it all down. When you have your health everything comes alright. I became ill a few years ago. The doctor had no wisdom, didn't diagnose what was wrong. Now I'm on dialysis three times a week. I've had open heart surgery and cancer. I have diabetes. My eyes are not good. I wish I would have my vision, if I had my eyesight I would have everything."

"I keep up with world events. Saddam Hussein, I think will win, temporarily. History always repeats itself....I hope history won't repeat itself. The president is not doing what needs to be done. Hussein is like a cancer, needs to be cut out or it will spread. I'd say to the president 'Act! Do it!' If you want to have peace in the world you have to get rid of the cancers."

Nachum's wisdom is reflected in his own words: "The foundation doesn't change...the sky, the moon, the air is the same always. Some of the details change but not the foundation."

"Don't deny what you are, be like that and stay like that. Believe in your values, know your identity. Don't get lost in an ocean of enemies. Know yourself. Sometimes there's a whirlpool but you've got to know how to get out of it."

"We are all interwoven and we are responsible to everybody. Hope must remain. Always look forward, there is always a spark of hope. As long as you have hope...."

"You are judged by your deeds. All that I want for me is a mighty and a strong Israel. It's the dream of our forefathers. We must cherish it, defend it, nourish it. Israel is our last hope. A generation comes, a generation goes, but the land is forever. The foundation doesn't change."

"I still have faith in God, I talk to Him every day--but I don't understand Him sometimes."

"I had a purpose in this life. I saved people and I made a place for Our People." That is the message of his Torah portion, *Nitzavim*. Those goals were set in Nachum's foundation and he fulfilled them. Nachum followed the teaching of his Torah portion: his faith in God remained strong, he fought enemies and saved lives. He went to *Eretz Yisroel* and helped establish a country for his people, Israel. A life well lived, indeed.

When I met Nachum in 1996, he had myriad ailments, what doctors refer to as "multiple morbidities." I often accompanied him to doctor's appointments before our lunch "dates". He was a favorite of every one of his physicians because he was a well-informed, compliant and uncomplaining patient who criticized only those things which could be improved and changed. His doctors listened.

After years of dialysis, a weakening heart and undergoing countless surgeries and treatments intended to extend his life, Nachum decided to go in to a hospice where he could be in charge of his own case. "Genug," (enough) he told his daughter and his doctors. From now on, he would do the prescribing.

The last Sunday in April, 2001 Nachum's loving daughter and son-in-law and admiring adult grandchildren were visiting, too. The conversation was animated, everybody always had something to say. Nachum asked for some ice cream. The nurse brought three little servings in which he took much delight. After a few spoons full, he fell asleep. We all stayed silent. After a bit, I waved and mouthed a goodbye to the family members, kissed my friend's forehead ever so gently and whispered that I'd see him in the morning. I tiptoed almost all the way out of the room when he called out, "Miriam," he always called me by my Hebrew name. I turned back, "Yes, I'm still here." "Buy Home Depot," he said. Those were his last words to me.

The next morning, when I came into his room I knew at once there'd be no more lively discussions, no more stock tips. His daughter, Miriam, was there already. It seemed like minutes between breaths. Suddenly, eyes open, he sat up, as if to get out of bed. The hospice nurse and I held him tight to us, our arms around him and each other, during the long drawn out final breaths. A man I'd know for only five years. Holocaust survivor, freedom fighter in Palestine, Talmudic scholar, savvy investor, he'd been a trusted and dear friend.

In Maytchet in 1942, from July 15th to July 17th, all members of the Rabinowicz family were murdered. Only Reuven and Nachum survived. Their memories will live on through their grandchildren and others.

MY FATHER REUVEN RABINOVITCH
Roni Rabinovitch

Wedding Reuven and Yael Rabinovitch 1953 Tel Aviv, Israel

Reuven, like his brother Nachum, also was part of the Hashomer Hatsair movement. In 1939 when the war began he was 18 years old; he left Maytchet and made his way to Vilnius. Reuven tried but unfortunately he was not able to convince his family to leave with him.

In 1941 when the Nazis entered Lithuania, Reuven managed to escape and make his way to Uzbekistan where he remained until the end of the war. Reuven and Nachum were in touch with each other by mail during the war years.

In 1945, after he found out that all of his family members except Nachum were murdered in Maytchet, he joined the Habricha movement. This group actively helped survivors of the Holocaust flee across the borders in Europe and make their way to the coasts where ships were waiting to take them Illegally to Eretz Israel. In 1950 Reuven arrived in Israel after the aliyah bet work was completed. He went into the army. He met Yael Kossover, who was a Sabra, and they were married in 1953. They had 3 children: Israel, Ahuva and Ron and 8 grandchildren.

Nachum and Reuven and their families lived near each other, Nachum in Tel Aviv and Reuven in Givataim.

Being the only two survivors from their family, they maintained a close relationship.

This photo and memorial to family by Reuven and Nachum page 406 in this book

Photo taken when Genia's sister Esther Krushinski (nee Mochkovski) left for Argentina abt. 1928

Second row (right to left):
Esther Krushinski
Israel Rabinovith (father) 1895 - 1942
Genia Rabinovitch (mother) 1897 - 1942
MiriamRabinovitch (sister)1915 - 1942
Fania Rabinovitch (sister) 1922 - 1942

First row (right to left)
Reuven Rabinovitch - survived
Hazel Tsvi Mochkovski (grandfather)1884 - 1942
Shimon Rabinovitch (brother)1927-1942
Raizel Mochkovski (grandmother) 1886 - 1942
Nachum Rabinovitch - survived
not in photo - Nechemia Rabinovitch 1929 – 1942

Other family members that were murdered in the Shoah

Israel's parents - David & Rachel Rabinovitch

Israel's siblings - Noach, Shalom, Baruch, Zlata (with her husband Raphael Lahawicki,) Elka (with her husband Michael Stolowscki and children - Nachum & Chasia)

Genia's sister - Nechamka (and her husband Betzalel Koren and daughter Rachel)

At Nachum's funeral, his granddaughter Yvette spoke the following words:

"It was in Israel where Pappa spent time with his eldest brother Reuven and they made a life for themselves there knowing the fate of the rest of their family. I know he would want us to take his life lessons to heart and never forget his story or our collective story. My great uncle Reuven passed away two years ago. It was one of the only times to see Pappa shed a tear. He loved his brother and he was his last surviving link to his past. It is now up to all of us to carry on the legacy which these two brothers have left us."

Appendix to the Molchad Yizkor Book
Not in the original Yizkor Book

ɪNDEX

Please note that this index applies only to the original Yizkor Book material that appears above and does not include material in the appendices..

www.ingramcontent.com/pod-product-compliance
Lightning Source LLC
Chambersburg PA
CBHW082009150426
42814CB00005BA/270